KU-602-856

Costa Rica
Nicaragua
& Panama
Handbook

Richard Arghiris & Peter Hutchison

The land is one great wild, untidy luxuriant
hothouse, made by nature for herself.

Charles Darwin

Footprint story

It was 1921

Ireland had just been partitioned, the British miners were striking for more pay and the federation of British industry had an idea. Exports were booming in South America – how about a handbook for businessmen trading in that far away continent? The Anglo-South American Handbook was born that year, written by W Koebel, the most prolific writer on Latin America of his day.

1924

Two editions later the book was 'privatized' and in 1924, in the hands of Royal Mail, the steamship company for South America, it became The South American Handbook, subtitled 'South America in a nutshell'. This annual publication became the 'bible' for generations of travellers to South America and remains so to this day. In the early days travel was by sea and the Handbook gave all the details needed for the long voyage from Europe. What to wear for dinner; how to arrange a cricket match with the Cable & Wireless staff on the Cape Verde Islands and a full account of the journey from Liverpool up the Amazon to Manaus: 5898 miles without changing cabin!

1939

As the continent opened up, The South American Handbook reported the new Pan Am flying boat services, and the fortnightly airship service from Rio to Europe on the Graf Zeppelin. For reasons still unclear but with extraordinary determination, the annual editions continued through the Second World War.

1970s

Many more people discovered South America and the backpacking trail started to develop. All the while the Handbook was gathering fans, including literary vagabonds such as Paul Theroux and Graham Greene (who once sent some updates addressed to "The publishers of the best travel guide in the world, Bath, England").

1990s

During the 1990s the company set about developing a new travel guide series using this legendary title as the flagship. By 1997 there were over a dozen guides in the series and the Footprint imprint was launched.

2000s

The series grew quickly and there were soon Footprint travel guides covering more than 150 countries. In 2004, Footprint launched its first thematic guide: *Surfing Europe*, packed with colour photographs, maps and charts. This was followed by further thematic guides such as *Diving the World*, *Snowboarding the World*, *Body and Soul escapes*, *Travel with Kids* and *European City Breaks*.

2008

Today we continue the traditions of the last 87 years that has served legions of travellers so well. We believe that these help to make Footprint guides different. Our policy is to use authors who are genuine experts who write for independent travellers; people possessing a spirit of adventure, looking to get off the beaten track.

SASHA DAVAS/SHUTTERSTOCK

Title page: Costa Rica's Caribbean coast is sparsely populated. **Above**: Hammocks for sale in Nicaragua.

The shifting landscapes of Central America's three southern-most countries reflect the New World's passion for diversity and divergence. Each nation, each people is distinct. A long-time bastion of wealth and stability, Costa Rica is the most eco-conscious and economically developed of the trio, a staunch defender of the environment with an exceptional national park system. Nicaragua is a nation steeped in poetry and revolutionary fervour. After years of civil war, it's now emerging as an adventure destination, with rickety buses, ramshackle street life and crumbling infrastructure adding to the excitement. Panama is a place of staggering promise and only just awakening to its potential. Diverse ethnic communities, abundant wildlife and vast tracts of wilderness punctuate this narrow land-bridge where two worlds meets. These three countries have disparate and contrasting characters, but they stand united in their intense natural beauty, vibrancy and irrepressible hospitality. The challenge is preserving all this in the face of booming popularity.

Caribbean Sea

NICARAGUA

Pacific Ocean

COSTA RICA

PANAMA

Contents

LUIS M. SECO/SHUTTERSTOCK

ULTRAORTO S.A./SHUTTERSTOCK

Devil mask in Panama.

Planning your trip

Where to go

Costa Rica

For tropical paradise, beach life and a sense of adventure Costa Rica is hard to beat. For a country so small, it's incredibly diverse. Erupting volcanoes, spluttering mudpots and dry tropical rainforest in the north, untouched primary rainforest in the south and beautiful beaches on all sides.

If beaches are your focus then head for the Nicoya Peninsula. For parties, dancing and facilities, head to the north around Tamarindo; for solitude and surf, the more bohemian beaches are in the south around Montezuma, Malpaís and Santa Teresa. On the Caribbean side, the best beaches are Cahuita and Puerto Viejo.

Further south along the Pacific coast, the beaches are fringed by rainforest ensuring memorable experiences of sun, sea and surf combined with full-on wilderness treks.

If you want to spend time in the hills and mountains, there's a high ridge running the length of the country. In the volcanic north is the fuming Rincón de la Vieja, close to Liberia, and the oozing, lava flows of Volcán Arenal just north of Fortuna. A little further south, but ecologically a world away, Monteverde is spectacular cloudforest. Poás and Irazú volcanoes make for dramatic day trips,

while the country's highest peak, Cerro Chirripó, provides some challenging trekking.

On this colourful landscape, apply your own, personal version of fun and you can bike, raft, trek, hike, surf, zip and fly your way to a very memorable holiday.

Nicaragua

Although memories of the 1979 Sandinista Revolution still evoke images of work crews, *comandantes* and communist sympathies, 30 years on the Nicaragua of today is a very different and rapidly changing place. The country is embracing a deluge of tourist dollars that is set to increase as word gets around: Nicaragua is cool. There is a freshness about a country where the smiles are still warm, the questions still honest and the eyes undimmed by the attitudes of thoughtless travellers. But it is the contrasts that make Nicaragua so truly fascinating. The twin colonial cities Granada and León are historic sparring partners, home to handsome plazas and a wealth of regal Spanish houses. The slender isthmus of Rivas is the most visited part of the country, where the burgeoning beach town of San Juan del Sur is attracting crowds of surfers, party-goers and real estate developers. Then there's Central America's

CHARLES TAYLOR/SHUTTERSTOCK

Above: Bus on the shore of Lake Nicaragua. **Opposite left**: The church in Grecia, Costa Rica, is made entirely of metal. **Opposite right**: Isla Bastimentos makes a good base for exploring Bocas del Toro Archipelago.

largest lake, Lago Nicaragua, where dozens of rustic islands await exploration, including Isla Ometepe, a bastion of peace, tranquillity and numinous volcanic beauty. More volcanoes lie in the rugged Northern Highlands where *campesino* culture predominates. The Caribbean coast is isolated from the rest of the country by tracts of dense rainforest. Here, Miskito villages and Afro-Caribbean communities make an intriguing divergence from Nicaragua's Hispanic mainstream.

Panama
Panama is the crossroads of the world and whilst the Panama Canal may not be natural, it is spectacular, and pure Panamanian since the country took control of it in 1999. Since then, the country has entered a new era of confidence and dynamism, evidenced by the unfettered influx of foreign investment

and 'for sale' signs across the land. The world has awakened to Panama. Its rapidly growing capital, Panama City, is unlike anywhere else in Central America, rising skyward with glimmering towers and powerful financial institutions. And beyond the big city, visitors are opening their eyes to a wealth of national parks that flank the banks of the Panama Canal, vibrant folkloric traditions on the Azuero Peninsula, and the lesser visited – but no less spectacular – natural wonders of the interior. The highlands of Chiriquí play host to misty cloud forests whilst Bocas del Toro on the Caribbean coast is developing into a hip destination with glassy waters and wondrous coral reefs. The autonomous Kuna Yala archipelago is precious haven of calm and tranquillity and, for the true adventurer, the wilderness of Darién still offers one of the great challenges this side of space travel.

Itineraries

One week

One week is just enough time to sample the essentials of one country. In Costa Rica, start by heading north to **Fortuna**, for a spot of volcano watching, with a day trek out to the waterfall. Travel by boat and jeep up to **Monterverde** to explore the cloudforest, then hot foot it to Liberia from where you can spend a couple of days trekking the upper slopes of **Rincón de la Vieja**, or relaxing on the beach at **Playa del Coco** or **Tamarindo**.

Nicaragua's key destinations can easily be reached from the Costa Rican border. The bars and beaches of **San Juan del Sur** are great for surfing or turtle-watching, followed by a day or two relaxing on **Isla Ometepe** in one of its *fincas*. Back on the mainland, colonial **Granada** is a good base for exploring Lake Nicaragua's islets, including the folkloric town of **Masaya** or the cloudforests of **Mombacho**. Alternatively, chill out in the city's bars, swapping traveller tales and enjoying the best food in the country.

Panama's principle attraction is the **Bocas del Toro archipelago**, where you'll need two to three days to relax into the Caribbean pace. Visit a few different islands looking for poison-dart frogs, snorkelling the coral reefs and sampling the local nightlife. Then head south to **Boquete** in the Chriquí Highlands,

allowing at least two days to explore the hiking trails and coffee plantations. Finally, head east on the Interamericana Highway to **Panama City** where a plethora of attractions await, including beaches, national parks and the **Panama Canal**.

Two weeks

A fortnight is enough time to explore two countries at a breathless rate, or a single one in a more measured way. In Costa Rica, you can enjoy the best of the country by getting smart with plane travel. Two days **white-water rafting** from San José will get you straight into holiday mode. Fly down to Puerto Jiménez for a short trek through **Corcovado National Park**, and then to **Tortuguero** at the other end of the country to explore the coastal canals and turtle beaches. Finish off with a few days chilling on the Caribbean beaches.

To see the best of Nicaragua, follow the one-week itinerary, but from Managua take a flight to the **Corn Islands** (or travel overland allowing an extra couple of days). After a few days languishing on Caribbean beaches, head back to Managua and make your way northwest to the buzzing colonial city of **León**, surrounded by active volcanoes and good for climbing, hiking and sandboarding.

With two weeks in Panama, start with the **Bocas del Toro** archipelago and the **Chiriquí highlands**, as described above. Head east along the Interamericana Highway and divert south into the **Azuero Peninsula**. Base yourself in **Chitré** and spend a few days exploring the villages and beaches. Continue east to **Panama City**, sampling the bars and restaurants of **Bella Vista**, as well as surrounding natural attractions, the **Pipeline road** and **Isla Barro Colorado** included. Finish your trip in the **Kuna Yala archipelago**, enjoying the stunning beaches, coral reefs and excellent seafood.

Chesnut-mandibled toucan (*Ramphastos swainsonii*), Tortuguero National Park, Costa Rica.

AGE FOTOSTOCK / SUPERSTOCK

CREATISTA/SHUTTERSTOCK

Stairs leading up from the street in Granada Nicaragua.

One month or more

A month gives you enough time to sample all three countries, mix and match different itineraries or get off the beaten track. Starting in **San José**, spend a couple of days doing day trips to **Poás**, **Irazú** or the **Orosí Valley**, before making your way to **Fortuna** and on to **Monteverde**. Head north, with a brief stop in Liberia, to explore the **Santa Rosa National Park**, including a hike down to the beach and a night at the lodging. From here a bumpy route heads east to **Los Chiles**, which you'll probably have all to yourself, before making the short trip over the border to Nicaragua. From the transport hub of San Carlos, spend a few days exploring the jungle-shrouded **Río San Juan** and the secluded **Solentiname archipelago**. Take the overnight ferry across Lake Nicaragua to **Isla Ometepe**, and beyond to **Granada**, back on the mainland. Spend a day or two exploring **Masaya** and the surrounding villages, as well as **Managua**, a much underrated if somewhat ugly city. From Managua, head north into the highlands, sampling **Matagalpa**'s coffee and hiking the rolling hills of nearby **Jinotega**. Conclude your journey in **Estelí**, where you can experience the community tourism project

of UCA Miraflor, smoke locally made cigars and learn about the Revolution.

Another suggested route combines Costa Rica and Panama. Starting in **San José**, take a couple of day trips or try some whitewater rafting. Trekking up Barva Volcano in **Braulio Carrillo National Park** is challenging but rewarding; if you've got a guide, take one of the rarely used trails down to **Sarapiquí**. Head east to **Limón**, for a few days in **Tortuguero** to the north, and then south down the Caribbean coast. Nudging right up to the coastal road, you can explore rainforest that fringes the beach at **Cahuita**, the **Hitoy Cerere Biological Reserve**, or try the many activities on offer. Cross into Panama at **Bocas del Toro**, taking time to explore the mainland as much as the islands. Head south into **Chiriquí** province, then east along the highway into Veraguas. Hit the surf at **Santa Catalina**, hike the mountains in the **Parque Nacional Cerro Hoya** and swim with sharks at **Isla Coiba**. Continue your journey east to **Panama City**, catching the train to the Caribbean coast, where the ruined fortress of **Portobelo** and the party town of **Isla Grande** await. End your trip by island-hopping on the **Kuna Yala archipelago**, or striking into the frontier land of **Darién**.

Costa Rica, Nicaragua & Panama highlights & itineraries

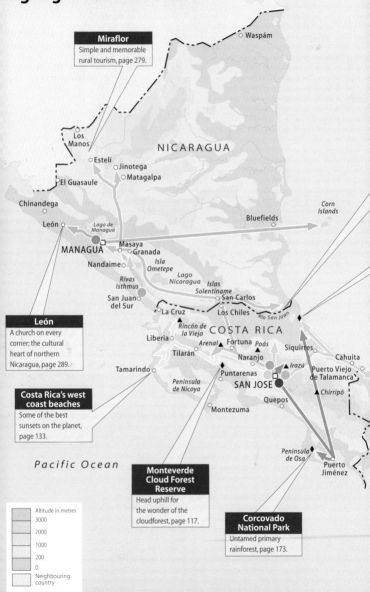

Miraflor
Simple and memorable rural tourism, page 279.

o Waspám

NICARAGUA

o Los Manos

o Estelí
o Jinotega
o Matagalpa

o El Guasaule

Chinandega o

León o

Lago de Managua

Corn Islands

Bluefields o

MANAGUA
Masaya
o Granada
Nandaime o

Isla Ometepe

Lago Nicaragua

Rivas Isthmus

Islas Solentiname

San Juan del Sur o

San Carlos o
Los Chiles

La Cruz

Río San Juan

León
A church on every corner; the cultural heart of northern Nicaragua, page 289.

Rincón de la Vieja

COSTA RICA

Liberia o

Siquirres o

Cahuita

Arenal
Fortuna
Poás

Tilarán o

Naranjo

▲ *Irazú*

Puerto Viejo de Talamanca

Tamarindo o

Puntarenas

SAN JOSE

▲ *Chirripó*

Península de Nicoya

Quepos o

Costa Rica's west coast beaches
Some of the best sunsets on the planet, page 133.

Montezuma o

Pacific Ocean

Península de Osa

Puerto Jiménez

Monteverde Cloud Forest Reserve
Head uphill for the wonder of the cloudforest, page 117.

Corcovado National Park
Untamed primary rainforest, page 173.

Altitude in metres
3000
2000
1000
200
0
Neighbouring country

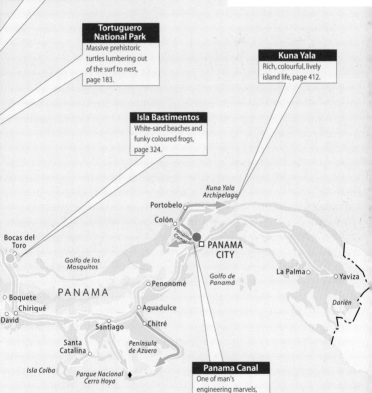

One week
Costa Rica
Nicaragua
Panama
Two-week extensions
Costa Rica
Nicaragua
Panama
One month or more
Costa Rica & Nicaragua
Costa Rica & Panama

Caribbean Sea

Río San Juan
A fine river trip with excellent wildlife spotting, page 229.

Tortuguero National Park
Massive prehistoric turtles lumbering out of the surf to nest, page 183.

Kuna Yala
Rich, colourful, lively island life, page 412.

Isla Bastimentos
White-sand beaches and funky coloured frogs, page 324.

Kuna Yala Archipelago

Portobelo
Colón
Panama Canal
□ PANAMA CITY

Bocas del Toro

Golfo de los Mosquitos

La Palma ○   ○ Yaviza

○ Penonomé   *Golfo de Panamá*

PANAMA   *Darién*

○ Boquete
Chiriqué
David

○ Aguadulce

Santiago   ○ Chitré

Santa Catalina ○   *Península de Azuero*

Isla Coiba   *Parque Nacional Cerro Hoya* ◆

Panama Canal
One of man's engineering marvels, page 383.

Volcano adventures

Volcán Arenal, Costa Rica

A silent plume of smoke puffs from the peak of Arenal's perfectly symmetrical cone. The powerful landscape seems underplayed by the absence of drama, noise and fire. Treks in the national park are filled with natural surprises. But as night falls and the light and noise of the day fade brilliant orange lines of crashing lava drizzle down the mountainside, and the eerie, crashing noise is mildly chilling. This is nature for real. Of course, nature is no TV show; it may be cloudy or Arenal may be resting for few days, but since the 1960s, she's been pushing out lava, adding layer upon layer around the summit. If you like the idea of a volcano, you have to see Arenal.

Volcáa Irazú, Costa Rica

In 1963 Irazú Volcano welcomed President John F Kennedy's visit to San José with a shower of volcanic ash across the capital. The appeal of Irazú (meaning 'mountain of quakes and thunder') is in its dormant, latent mischievous power. While earthquake swarms show magma is still active, it's a peaceful meander to the 3432 m summit along a seemingly endless road. At the top, the steep sides of the lagoon-filled craters are an impressive sight. And with an early-morning trip, the summit is often above the clouds, creating a distinctly heavenly feel.

Isla Ometepe, Nicaragua

Home to a twin volcano complex, Ometepe is the largest and most enchanting of Lake Nicarauga's rustic islands. The cones of Maderas and Concepción rise from the waters in perfect symmetry, and are steeped in legend. Their forest-swathed slopes conceal mysterious stone carvings that hint at the island's pre-Columbian past. Maderas is extinct and believed to have last erupted 800 years ago; today it's wrapped in thick cloudforest, great for hiking and wildlife observation. Concepción is dryer, harsher and very much active, periodically spewing ash over the island and its inhabitants.

Laguna de Apoyo, Nicaragua

Laguna de Apoyo, the most stunning of Nicaragua's 15 crater lakes, changes through azure, turquoise and navy blue as the sun

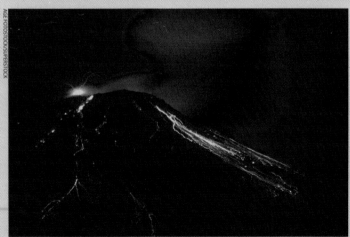

AGE FOTOSTOCK/SUPERSTOCK

BRENT WINEBRENNER/PHOTOLIBRARY

Opposite page: Volcán Arenal at night.
Above: Horses graze by Volcán Concepción.
Right: Golden frog, Panama.

DAVID M DENNIS /PHOTOLIBRARY

proceeds across the sky. Heated by thermal vents, the lake's soothing waters never grow cold, meaning they're good for a dip under a starry evening sky. Around the shore, the tropical dry forest is home to countless birds, howler monkeys, agoutis, armadillos and jaguarundis. Several endemic fish species populate the 200-m-deep lake, currently under scientific research.

Volcán Barú, Panama
On a clear day, it's possible to see both the Caribbean Sea and the Pacific Ocean from the top of Volcán Barú, Panama's highest peak at 3474 m. Imbued with rich volcanic soil and visited by endless swathes of rolling mist, the cool lush slopes of this sleeping giant are covered by a patchwork of sleepy coffee *fincas*, strawberry plantations and diminutive farming communities. Luxuriant cloudforests flourish at this elevation, accommodating dazzling birds, delicate orchids and a host of ethereal plant life. Protected as a national park, hikers and wildlife-lovers are drawn into extended explorations. But the mountains promise adrenalin-charged thrills too, with some of Central America's best whitewater rapids waiting to be tamed.

El Valle, Panama
Beset with brightly coloured humming birds, the cool mountain retreat of El Valle is renowned for its square trees, its golden frogs and its lush, brooding scenery. Nestled in an extinct crater 600 m above sea level, this amiable and modest town makes a refreshing break from the heat. Verdant forests, rushing waterfalls and mysterious stone petroglyphs await exploration in the surrounding hills, all dominated by a dark mountain peak known as 'The Sleeping Indian Girl'. The town's Sunday market showcases the best of Panama's crafts, while lodging includes several luxury spas and eco-lodges.

Island escapes

Isla del Coco, Costa Rica

Around 550 km southwest of Costa Rica, Isla del Coco is one of the best dive locations in the world. A volcanic island rising abruptly from the western tip of the Coco Plate, the waters are homes to schools of hammerhead sharks and white-tipped sharks, whale sharks, and manta rays. If diving is your thing, it's barely an island escape as the only way of staying in the area is on live-aboard boats. Visitors to the islands include legendary pirates who are believed to have buried significant quantities of treasure.

Isla del Caño, Costa Rica

Accessible from Bahia Drake on the north of the Osa Peninsula, Isla del Caño provides a little something for everyone. Divers and snorkellers can enjoy the coral beds and marine life that includes manta rays, dolphins, sea turtles and whales. The 200-ha island (just 3 km by 1.5 km) lacks the diversity of the mainland but offers good trekking. It is uninhabited, apart from a permanent ranger station that protects the biological reserve, but the island has evidence of pre-Columbian human activity including the large and mysterious stone spheres that are found throughout the Diquis Delta.

Solentiname Archipelago, Nicaragua

On the southeastern quarter of Lake Nicaragua, the Solentiname archipelago is a chain of pretty, sleepy islands that were once the focus of a famous social experiment. In 1965, the poet-priest Ernesto Cardenal came here to preach liberation theology and instruct the locals in artistic methods. His dream was a kind of radical Christian-Communist utopia that combined religion and revolution, spiritual love and community conscience. The result was a school of Primitivist art whose output is internationally renowned with paintings reaching galleries in New York, Paris and London. Life on these creative islands remains wonderfully simple – there are no roads, telephones, electricity or running water: this is Nicaragua as it was two centuries ago, with only the outboard motor as a reminder of the modern world.

Above: Corrugated-metal house, Big Corn Island, Nicaragua.
Opposite page: Houses on one of the Kuna Yala.

RICHARD ARGHRIS

Corn Islands, Nicaragua

Flanked by languid palms and white-sand beaches, Nicaragua's Corn Islands are a picture of tropical indolence, comprising two Caribbean retreats with incurably eccentric populations. The smaller of the pair, Little Corn Island, is a dive centre in the earliest stages of tourist development: sites include scintillating coral reefs and underwater caverns populated by hammerhead sharks. The larger, Big Corn Island, is home to several sizeable fishing communities and is the place to enjoy authentic Caribbean life – while it lasts. Easy-going, rum-soaked and lightly dilapidated, Nicaragua's remote Caribbean coast is a world away from its Pacific cousin, separated by language, history and miles of dense rainforest. Half the fun is getting there, but of course, once you've arrived, you won't want to leave.

Kuna Yala Archipelago, Panama

The semi-autonomous province of Kuna Yala in eastern Panama is a place of unprecedented purity, home to an archipelago of some 400 precious islands. Arcing over the Caribbean waters like a scattering of jewels, these idyllic isles are the fabled homeland of the Kuna people – one of Latin America's most vibrant and successful indigenous groups. Fascinating villages filled with cane-and-thatch houses, fishermen in dug-out canoes and women in traditional attire await intrepid travellers, ensuring a truly vivid and unforgettable cultural encounter. Many of the archipelago's islands are entirely uninhabited, home only to verdant palm trees, resplendent coral reefs, gorgeous white-sand beaches and warm, gentle waters. If you've ever wondered how it feels to kick back on your own private desert island, then this is the place to come.

Bocas del Toro Archipelago, Panama

The formerly isolated province of Bocas del Toro in northwest Panama, is home to an exceptionally striking and highly diverse Caribbean archipelago. From remote, peaceful beaches to dense, luxuriant rainforests; from schools of psychedelic fish to multi-coloured frogs; from bustling party towns to ramshackle villages on the verge of collapsing under their own easiness; these islands never fails to impress or surprise. Teeming coral reefs, underwater caves and eerie swim-throughs provide exceptional diving opportunities, whilst legendary, Hawaiian-style waves offer astonishing surfing prospects. And for those who simply want to pamper themselves, there's plenty of luxury spas and eco-lodges. It's no wonder that Bocas is booming.

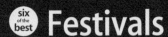

Festivals

six of the best

Día de la Raza, Carnival

Celebrating the day that Columbus 'discovered' Costa Rica, carnival in Limón has a Caribbean flavour with processions, music, dancing and partying for about a week. It's a colourful occasion, with drumming providing a rhythmic beat, and Calypso music. The greatest celebration is the main procession, held on the Saturday before 12 October. It's a friendly, family affair, with formal and informal activities throughout the city. Buses are booked well in advance, and hotels fill up as the country briefly looks east for the liveliest national celebration in the country.

Annexation of Guanacaste

In a country with more regional than national celebrations, Guanacaste's main celebration is one of the liveliest. The day celebrates the region's decision in 1824 to stay as part of Costa Rica, rather than part of Nicaragua to the north. Celebrations and festivities take place in towns throughout the region, with a particular focus on Santa Cruz.

La Purísima

In honour of the Immaculate Virgin, La Purísima is one of Nicaragua's most important national festivals. Celebrated each year in December, the festivities last for most of the month and are punctuated by evocative processions and boisterous bouts of fireworks. Private altars dedicated to the Virgin Mary are assembled in Nicaraguan homes, visited by friends and relatives who lavish her with songs and prayers. This is a time of community, family and generosity, when food and drink are freely shared among all the participants. Some families serve up as many as 5000 *nacatamales* in a night. A particularly rousing moment in the festivities occurs on 7 December, when firecrackers are ignited en masse throughout the country. La Purísima is a striking affirmation of Nicaragua's deeply felt devotion to the Catholic faith – an assuredly moving experience.

Fiesta de San Jerónimo, Masaya, Nicaragua

This is one of the longest parties in Latin America, commencing on 30 September and concluding some 80 days later in early December. Masaya's patron saint, San Jerónimo, is honoured with flower-festooned processions, fireworks and feasts. The driving music of the marimba provides the backdrop for many fascinating traditional dances, including El Baile de las Inditas and El Baile de

Above: Pile of Costa Rican maracas. Opposite page: Carnival Queen at Panama City Carnival.

MICHAEL ZYSMAN/SHUTTERSTOCK

os Diablitos, performed by the town's many competing dance troops. El Toro Venado, performed on the last Sunday in October and the third Sunday in November, is a brutally humorous mocking of Nicaragua's public figures that highlights two aspects of the national character: a robust sense of humour and an utter disdain for the powers that be.

Carnaval, Las Tablas, Panama

Carnaval is celebrated with great gusto across Latin America, but the festivities in Las Tablas are some of the most spirited and memorable of all. Commencing the Saturday before Ash Wednesday, four days and five nights of unfettered revelry blaze the streets and plazas of this normally unassuming town on the Azuero Peninsula – Panama's cradle of folklore and tradition. Drinking, dancing and spirited water fights are enjoyed by crowds of Panamanians who come from all over the country to participate in what is the nation's most raucous party. The festivities are overseen by a carnival beauty queen who is selected after the town's two principle streets – Calle Arriba and Calle Abajo – famously compete with a procession of wondrous and colourful floats.

Fiesta de Corpus Christi, Los Santos, Panama

The Fiesta de Corpus Christi (40 days after Easter) is a four-day feast and one of Panama's most famous and popular festivals. It's a glorious distillation of the Azuero Peninsula's strong Spanish roots and well worth attending. Troops of 'dirty devil' dancers dominate the proceedings, clad in wildly colourful (if deeply grotesque) masks and charging through the streets like imps unleashed from hell. Several other intriguing ceremonies form part of these must-see festivities, including a host of musical processions, dances and a bull hunt led by crowds of enthusiastic children (the 'bull' is actually man inside a costume).

When to go

If your trip is about clear skies, with a bit of beach life, then December to April are broadly the best times to visit. Temperatures vary across the region, but in general it's around 30°-32°C (85°-90°F) in the day dropping to 21°-22°C (70°-72°F) at night. Temperatures drop by a few degrees every 500-m, and by the time you've risen to the Central Highlands in Costa Rica day time temperatures are in the mid-20°s. In Nicaragua and northwestern Costa Rica temperatures rise to unbearable in late April/May, before the cool rains arrive.

The tourist-savvy Costa Ricans have rebranded the wet season as the Green Season, and why not? Visiting the tropics and rainforest, there's a huge benefit in seeing the full force of nature. The rainy season starts in May, rising to its peak between July and October. In most areas, the rains, when they fall, are intense and fairly brief. Several activities are better in the rainy season – birdwatching, whitewater rafting and some surf breaks – but others will be impossible with cloud cover, so plan your trip carefully. September and October are frequently used as times to renovate. And some places actually become inaccessible so check your hotel is open.

On balance, November is a good time to visit with the rains dropping off, or stopping, but before large number of tourists come in and change the place.

Public holidays can be a cause for celebration. Easter week is celebrated across all three countries. Independence Day is celebrated in Nicaragua and Costa Rica on 15 September. Panama celebrates Independence on 3 November. Almost everything stops on public holidays , including planes, buses and banks. Make sure you've got plenty of cash and can get to where you want to go before everything shuts.

Glass and steel towers of Panama City.

YANIK CHAUVIN /SHUTTERSTOCK

Costa Rica, Nicaragua & Panama

Activity	J	F	M	A	M	J	J	A	S	O	N	D
Climbing Volcán Concepción (Nicaragua)	★	★	★	★	★						★	★
Line handling the Panama Canal	★	★	★	★	★							★
Surfing (Nicaragua, Costa Rica and Panama)					★	★	★	★	★	★	★	
Scuba diving off mainland Costa Rica	★	★	★	★								
Turtle watching (Costa Rica)			★	★	★	★	★	★				
Whitewater rafting (Costa Rica and Panama)	★	★	★	★	★	★	★	★	★	★	★	★

Rainfall and climate charts

San José

Month	Average temperature in °C max-min	Average rainfall in mm
Jan	24 - 14	15
Feb	24 - 14	05
Mar	26 - 15	20
Apr	26 - 17	46
May	26 - 17	229
Jun	26 - 17	241
Jul	25 - 17	211
Aug	26 - 16	241
Sep	26 - 16	305
Oct	25 - 16	300
Nov	25 - 16	145
Dec	24 - 14	41

Limón

Month	Average temperature in °C max-min	Average rainfall in mm
Jan	31 - 20	317
Feb	31 - 20	211
Mar	31 - 21	234
Apr	31 - 22	276
May	31 - 22	282
Jun	31 - 22	296
Jul	31 - 22	427
Aug	31 - 22	312
Sep	31 - 22	145
Oct	31 - 22	206
Nov	29 - 21	391
Dec	31 - 21	445

Nicoya

Month	Average temperature in °C max-min	Average rainfall in mm
Jan	33 - 21	05
Feb	34 - 22	11
Mar	36 - 22	24
Apr	36 - 23	69
May	33 - 23	274
Jun	33 - 22	325
Jul	33 - 22	244
Aug	32 - 22	305
Sep	31 - 22	399
Oct	31 - 22	407
Nov	31 - 22	316
Dec	32 - 21	25

Granada

Month	Average temperature in °C max-min	Average rainfall in mm
Jan	26 - 15	04
Feb	28 - 15	02
Mar	29 - 16	05
Apr	31 - 18	21
May	30 - 19	74
Jun	29 - 19	79
Jul	28 - 18	42
Aug	28 - 18	52
Sep	28 - 18	82
Oct	27 - 18	79
Nov	26 - 17	21
Dec	26 - 16	03

Matagalpa

Month	Average temperature in °C max-min	Average rainfall in mm
Jan	26 - 15	04
Feb	28 - 15	02
Mar	29 - 16	05
Apr	31 - 18	21
May	30 - 19	74
Jun	29 - 19	79
Jul	28 - 18	42
Aug	28 - 18	52
Sep	28 - 18	82
Oct	27 - 18	79
Nov	26 - 17	21
Dec	26 - 16	03

León

Month	Average temperature in °C max-min	Average rainfall in mm
Jan	26 - 15	04
Feb	28 - 15	02
Mar	29 - 16	05
Apr	31 - 18	21
May	30 - 19	74
Jun	29 - 19	79
Jul	28 - 18	42
Aug	28 - 18	52
Sep	28 - 18	82
Oct	27 - 18	79
Nov	26 - 17	21
Dec	26 - 16	03

Panama City

Month	Average temperature in °C max-min	Average rainfall in mm
Jan	17 - 04	00
Feb	18 - 05	00
Mar	21 - 08	01
Apr	24 - 11	07
May	28 - 16	60
Jun	31 - 20	67
Jul	32 - 22	77
Aug	32 - 22	66
Sep	31 - 19	102
Oct	27 - 13	131
Nov	22 - 08	91
Dec	18 - 04	31

Bocas del Toro

Month	Average temperature in °C max-min	Average rainfall in mm
Jan	30 - 20	123
Feb	30 - 20	266
Mar	31 - 20	83
Apr	31 - 21	369
May	31 - 22	178
Jun	32 - 22	259
Jul	31 - 21	420
Aug	31 - 21	440
Sep	31 - 22	311
Oct	31 - 22	150
Nov	31 - 21	291
Dec	31 - 20	563

Santiago

Month	Average temperature in °C max-min	Average rainfall in mm
Jan	34 - 17	22
Feb	35 - 17	16
Mar	36 - 18	20
Apr	36 - 19	96
May	35 - 21	313
Jun	33 - 20	300
Jul	33 - 20	243
Aug	33 - 20	317
Sep	33 - 20	342
Oct	32 - 20	395
Nov	32 - 20	259
Dec	33 - 18	82

LUIS DA SECO/SHUTTERSTOCK

Sport and activities

Archaeology

Although not as inspiring as the Mayan temples further north, Nicaragua's pre-Columbian archaeology is fascinating. Museums display artefacts that have been discovered in each region; the best are at the Palacio Nacional de la Cultura in Managua, the Museo Antiguo Convento de San Francisco in Granada and the Museo Arqueológico in Juigalpa. In Lake Nicaragua, there are some remains on the islands of Zapatera and Ometepe, where you can see some large basalt statues. Petroglyphs are also present on many of Lake Nicaragua's islands as well as sites around the mainland.

Baseball

Baseball is the national sport in Nicaragua. The first league games were organized more than 100 years ago and there is a very hard-fought national championship for the first division. Nicaraguans follow the major leagues in the US with more fervour than many Americans and the country has put several players into the North American professional league and usually finishes in the top five in the world championships. The season runs from November until February. It's well worth going to see a match at a stadium, held on Sunday afternoons.

GUALBERTO BECERRA/SHUTTERSTOCK

Bronze plumeleteer hummingbird, Panama.

Birdwatching

With more bird species than the whole of North America or Europe – 875 at the last count – Costa Rica is a birdwatcher's paradise. Thousands visit every year to see some of the most magnificent birds in the neotropics; the resplendent quetzal (considered by many to be the most beautiful in the world), three- wattled bellbird, bare-necked umbrellabird, violaceous trogon, scarlet macaw, chestnut- bellied heron, turquoise cotinga, sun bittern and countless more. Two of the best known birding spots are La Selva Biological Station, and the world famous Monteverde Cloud Forest Reserve, while quetzals can be seen within two hours of San José in the Cerro de la Muerte highlands. Birdwatching is good all year round, but for the raptor migrations between North and South America you should come in March/April or September/October.

Nicaragua is home to over 700 bird species, including boat-billed flycatcher, collared aracari, black-headed trogon, wood stork, roseate spoonbill, long-tailed manikin and osprey. The national bird is the turquoise- browed mot mot, beautiful and common in the highlands of Managua. Reserva Biológica Indio-Maíz has primary rainforest home to the scarlet macaw. The Refugio de Vida Silvestre Los Guatuzos has gallery forest and ample wetlands teeming with birds. Islands in the the Archipiélago Solentiname are massive nesting sites. In the northern mountains of Jinotega and Matagalpa the cloudforests are home to many prize bird species. The Montibelli Private Nature Reserve, Laguna de Apoyo and the Reserva Natural El Chocoyero, just outside the capital, offers the chance to see thousands of nesting parakeets.

In Panama, more than 950 species have been recorded to date including the harpy eagle, the macaw and the rare resplendent quetzal. There are also abundant toucans, raptors, pelicans, frigates and humming- birds. The Pipeline road in the Parque

A juvenile black hawk in Costa Rica.

Nacional Soberanía, easily accessible from Panama City, is renowned as a world-class spot (with more than 500 species spotted in one day). In western Panama, the highlands around Volcán Baru and the cloudforests of the Parque Internacional Amistad are also popular locales. Both coastlines are home to abundant species of sea birds, particularly on Isla de los Pájaros in Bocas del Toro. The rainforest wilderness of Darién is also a world-class spot, albeit hard to reach.

Bullfighting

Bullfighting in Nicaragua is a strange hybrid of bullfighting and bull rodeo. The bull is not killed or injured, just intensely annoyed. The beast is brought inside the ring roped by a few mounted cowboys and tied to a bare tree in the centre. Someone mounts its back using a leather strap to hold on and the angry bull is released from the tree. The rider tries to stay on top and a few others show the animal some red capes for as long as they dare, before running off just before (in most cases) being impaled. When the bull gets too tired, a fresh one is brought in, mounted and shown more capes. Every patron saint festival has a

MOSTOVYI SERGII IGOREVICH/SHUTTERSTOCK

Try trekking in the Talamancas, either in Costa Rica or Panama.

bullfight. One of the most famous takes place at the Santa Ana festival in La Orilla.

Bungee jumping

Probably the biggest buzz in Costa Rica, Tropical Bungee on the Pan-American Highway close to Grecia, will attach you to a big elastic band and let you freefall to the Río Colorado some 80 m below. Since beginning in 1991, they have had more than 26,000 jumps to their name.

Canopy tours

The rainforest canopy is where most of Costa Rica's wildlife action takes places and there are now a multitude of ways of getting you up there. The calmest is probably exploring on a suspension bridge, strung out along the trees where you are free to walk at leisure. The main suspension tours are in Santa Elena, Fortuna and Rainmaker near Quepos. An equally calm way through the canopy

is on an aerial tour, using adapted ski lifts to carry you through the canopy. The most well known (and expensive) is Aerial Tram on the eastern fringes of Braulio Carrillo National Park and near Jacó, with another less impressive option in Monteverde. The best high-adrenalin option is the zip wire, which has hundreds of people whizzing down high-tension steel cables strung out between forest giants. You won't see much as you fly through the air, but it is good fun and you do get close to the forest canopy. Finally there is the good old-fashioned option of climbing a tree – almost. Hacienda Barú, near Dominical , and Selva Bananito Lodge, near Puerto Limón, let you use tree climbing grappling and ropes.

Climbing

Non-technical guided climbing is becoming a popular activity in Nicaragua. There is potential for technical climbing, but routes are undeveloped and you need your own gear. The most popular location is the Maribios volcanic range, set on a broad plain 40 km inland from the Pacific Ocean and made up of more than 20 volcanoes, five of which are active. Another key spot is the island of Ometepe which has two cones affording sparkling lake views. While the Pacific volcanoes are no higher than 1700 m, the climbs are not as easy as they might seem. Most routes start just above sea level and are steep with difficult conditions including sharp rocks, sand and loose terrain, combined with serious heat.

Community tourism

There are several fascinating community tourism projects, which offer the chance to participate in the life and culture of rural Nicaragua. In Granada, UCA (Unión de Cooperativas Agropecuarias) 'Tierra y Agua', www.ucatierrayagua.org, organizes visits to agricultural settlements where you can learn

Trekking and hiking

There are some excellent hiking opportunities in Costa Rica but with so many competing activities it often takes a back seat. The most popular hike is up Cerro Chirripó, the country's highest peak at 3820 m. Second on the list is hiking through the tropical wet forest of Corcovado National Park on the Osa Peninsula; it's hot, sweaty, hard work and very rewarding. Less common walks head from the cloudforests of Monteverde down the Caribbean slope to Arenal, and further north trails lead through the Rincón de la Vieja National Park. You can also complete a trip from Santa María, south of San José, down the Pacific slope to near Quepos. The ultimate trek has to be crossing the continental divide following ancient indigenous trails from Puerto Viejo de Talamanca west to the Pacific: ten tough days, carrying all your own gear; it's scenic, arduous and satisfying.

Nicaragua's Pacific Basin is great walking country. You will need to speak some Spanish to get by, but once outside the city a whole world of beautiful landscapes and friendly people awaits you. Fences in Nicaragua are for animals, not people, and if you respect the privacy and rights of the local residents, trespassing is not a problem. It is possible to trek the Maribios volcano range in northwestern Nicaragua, starting at the extinct lake-filled crater of Volcán Cosigüina, which is the most westerly point of the country, and taking in all 21 cones, five of which are active. Another great place for trekking is the island of Ometepe with its breathtaking beauty, friendly people and many dirt trails; it is essential to use local guides here.

Volcán Barú, Panama's highest peak at 3475 m, and nearby Cerro Punta are the two best climbs in the country but there are several excellent long walks. The hike from Cañita on the Darién road over the continental divide to Cartí is an alternative to flying to Yala. The Caminos de Cruces and Real are jungle walks that follow in the steps of the Conquistadors crossing the continental divide and, if combined into an ocean-to-ocean hike, take eight days. A good range for hiking is the Serranía de Majé east of Panama City, visiting Embera villages and its howler monkey population. Closer is the Parque Nacional Chagres and a three-day walk from Cerro Azul to the coast.

Hikers on a hanging bridge at the Arenal Rainforest Reserve, near La Fortuna, Costa Rica.

about farming, explore the countryside or just spend time with a local family. The most developed community tourism project is UCA Miraflor, www.miraflor.org, with horse riding, guided hikes and coffee tasting across a network of friendly highland villages. Participating in this growing tourism sector can be as rewarding as it is eye-opening; tour costs go directly to the families you meet.

Community tourism in Panama is not as well developed, but the many different cultures are fascinating and visiting an indigenous settlement can be enlightening. The Kuna are the most famous and easily encountered of Panama's cultures, populating the idyllic Kuna Yala archipelago skirting its eastern shores. Emberá-Wounaan tribal groups occupy the lands east of Panama City, particularly in Darién province, and are best visited through a good tour agency. The Ngobé-Buglé occupy their own comarca in western Panama. They can be visited independently and are reportedly very happy to receive tourists. The Naso people occupy parts of mainland Bocas del Toro and can also be visited independently, although their ancestral lands are currently under threat and they society is in the throes of a political schism. Non-indigenous, but equally fascinating are the thriving Afro-Caribbean and Congo communities on the Caribbean coast, and the strong Spanish heritage of the Azuero Peninsula.

Diving and snorkelling

The best time for diving in Costa Rica is in the dry season (November to June) when visibility is at its best. The northern Pacific coast around Playa del Coco is a local hot-spot with trips out to nearby islands. Further south, Drake, on the northern coast of the peninsula, is a popular base to visit Isla del Caño where you're almost guaranteed sightings of sharks, ray and other pelagics. On the Caribbean side, the dive action is in the coral waters off the coast of Cahuita National Park and further south around Gandoca-Manzanillo National Wildlife Refuge. The very best diving happens in the clear waters of the Cocos Islands, over 500 km southwest of Costa Rica in the Pacific. Undisturbed corals and hammerhead and white-tipped sharks await visitors on the live-aboard dive boats sailing from Puntarenas.

In Nicaragua there are professional dive operators on both of the Corn Islands. To find any depth a boat trip is needed, but the reefs lining both islands are beautiful and the marine life is rich. Snorkelling is also good around the Pearl Cays, but access is by expensive charter boat. The Pacific Coast, beaten by waves, is usually too rough for diving or snorkelling. Laguna de Apoyo offers diving opportunities for those interested in taking part in scientific research.

In Panama, diving is the best locally developed sport. The Caribbean coral reefs are similar to those of Belize and Honduras. The waters around Bocas del Toro are calm and sheltered, making them good places for casual snorkelling or diving. A handful of sites also lie off the coast of Portobelo, best accessed with local operators. The Kuna Yala archipelago is home to wondrous and pristine corals but diving is outlawed in the *comarca*. The Pacific has quite different ecosystems owing to the much greater tidal ranges, differing water temperature and density. Places to go include Taboga, the Pearl Islands and Isla Iguana. The Parque

Diving with a ray, Costa Rica.

PRISMA/SUPERSTOCK

Nacional Coiba is a very special site that's home to large sea creatures that include sharks, whales and dolphins, among the usual array of Pacific fish. Snorkelling here is also excellent. For a truly unique experience, consider diving in the lakes of the Panama Canal, mainly to visit wrecks, submerged villages and the odd train left behind by the filling of the canal.

Fishing

Sport fishing just doesn't get any better than Costa Rica, with tarpon and snook on the Caribbean; marlin, sailfish, dorado, tuna and other species on the Pacific and trout, rainbow bass (*guapote*), bobo, machaca and more in inland lakes and rivers. Peak fishing varies but hotels and boats are often hard to find when fishing is at its best, so book ahead.

Nicaragua is a fisherman's paradise, with its wide selection of rivers, lakes and seas. Deep-sea fishing can be arranged in San Juan del Sur or Marina Puesta del Sol in the Pacific and bonefishing is possible on the Corn Islands. Lake Nicaragua is great for bass fishing. The island of Zapatera and its archipelago are home to Central America's biggest annual freshwater tournament. In Pearl Lagoon on the Caribbean side and on the Río San Juan tarpon and snook fishing is very good.

Panama means 'abundance of fish' in the native tongue, so perhaps unsurprisingly, the fishing is excellent. Big game fish – marlin, tuna and swordfish – can be snagged at world-class sites off the Pacific shore. The bay of Punta Patiña near to Jaqué in Darién has broken over 170 world records for game fishing. Other prolific waters lie off the Pearl Islands and in the gulf of Chiriquí; charters can be arranged from Panama City. There is also good fishing in the Caribbean, but it does not cater as well for tourists – local boatmen, rather than tour guides, will take you out to sea. Meanwhile, if you've got a hunger for peacock bass, then head over

Fishing in Panama.

to Lake Gatún on the Panama Canal. These fish were artificially introduced to the area and have now taken over in vast numbers.

Mountain biking

Pedal power has taken over in parts of Costa Rica. You can rent a bike for a couple of hours, a day or even a couple of weeks. If you're really into biking, consider joining a tour. It's the best way to get to some of the off-road sites without leaving the whole thing down to chance. Guanacaste is ideal for hugging the coastline, getting fantastic views and a challenging ride. Several two-day trips out of San José give you the chance to get seriously muddy, ending up in places like Manuel Antonio, or mixing the biking with paddling down whitewater. The ultimate adventure is the two-week coast-to-coast trip, taking lots of muscle and determination – there are some serious uphill sections – but it's ultimately rewarded with views from the continental divide and down the Orosí Valley.

Nature tourism

With so many national parks and protected areas, much of Costa Rica's appeal lies in its natural attractions, including turtle watching

Leatherback turtle, Costa Rica.

in Tortuguero and Las Baulas National Park or dolphin/whale spotting around the Osa Peninsula. The 26 national parks and many more biological reserves, wildlife refuges and other protected areas protect 25.4% of the national territory. Entrance to all parks costs US$8-10.

Some 43% of Panama remains forested and a quarter of the land has protected status. Transport to the parks can be difficult and facilities non-existent, but some parks now have accommodation in huts for US$5 a bed. There is officially a US$3 entry fee but it is rarely charged. The Parque Natural Metropolitano is within the capital's city limits and makes a refreshing break from the hectic urban pace. Beyond, flanking the canal's eastern banks, are three excellent parks with abundant rainforest flora and fauna – Parque Nacional Camino de Cruces, Parque Nacional Soberanía, Parque Nacional Chagres. On an island inside the canal, the Barro Colorado National Monument is a haven for wildlife, lauded by biologists as much as tourists. Parque Nacional Cerro Hoya on the southwest tip of the Azuero Peninsula was formerly very isolated and home to several endemic species as well as a colony of macaws. Nature tourism is increasingly well developed in the Chiriquí highlands, where Parque Nacional Volcán Barú and the Parque Internacional Amistad play host to cloudforests. For a taste of real wilderness, Parque Nacional Darién is one of the wildest and most dangerous in Central America – don't set foot in it without a guide.

Surfing

Costa Rica offers the surfer world-class waves in beautiful surroundings with air and water temperatures averaging in the high 20°s. You can rent a board or take classes at many of the more popular destinations, and get water taxis to some of the more secluded spots. Most breaks work better at the end of the wet season, when the rivers have had time to form the sand bars properly. The tidal range for the Pacific coast is quite large, up to 12 ft, and this affects the size of the waves. On the Caribbean coast the variation is not so much of a problem with daily fluctuations of around 1½ ft. A 4WD may be necessary as access to many of the best waves is along dirt tracks and even these can be inaccessible during the wet season. Beginners should head for Dominical or Malpaís which both have good surf schools.

Nicaragua's Pacific Coast is home to countless beautiful breaks, many of which are only just starting to become popular. Most surfing is done along the coast of Rivas, using San Juan del Sur as a jumping-off point. It is possible to rent boards in San Juan, but elsewhere even wax can be hard to find. The country's biggest and most famous break is at Popoyo in northern Rivas. Surfers used to rave about the tube rides and point breaks that lie empty year round, but there have been recent complaints about surf operators converging on breaks with a boat full of clients.

In Panama, surfing is best at Isla Grande, Playa Venado on the Azuero Peninsula, Santa Catalina on the Pacific coast of Veraguas, and Bocas del Toro.

Whitewater rafting

Rafting in Costa Rica takes you through some of the most spectacular scenery in the country. One moment you're drifting through verdant valleys, the next you're fighting for dear life as your adrenalin-pumped body is forced head-first through a wall of water. It isn't everyone's cup of tea, but it is mighty refreshing. Most trips start from San José. The Reventazón, Pacuare and Sarapiquí rivers on the Caribbean slope, and the General and Corobicí on the Pacific, create a fantastic array of aquadventure. The Savegre, close to Quepos, is also a popular river.

Western Panama, where the Chiriquí river system finds its source, has some of Central America's best rafting. Grade III to IV rapids can be found on the Río Chiriquí (year round), and the Chiriquí Viejo Palón section (December-April) when the river is not in full height. There's a few tamer rides for the faint of heart, as well as some Grade V monsters, strictly for the experienced. In the Parque Nacional Chagres area, north of Panama City, you'll find Grade II and III rapids which some consider better for tubing – floating downriver on an inflated inner tube (best August-December).

Windsurfing and kitesurfing

Westerly trade winds blow across northern Costa Rica between December and April. Reluctantly the air is pushed up and over obstacles eventually being forced through the corridor that is Lake Arenal. The most reliable winds in the northern hemisphere provide the western end of the lake, and Bahía Salinas on the Pacific with world-class windsurfing destinations. Beginner courses are provided by a couple of lodges in the area, with boards, wetsuits and even money-back guarantees provided. For the experts, if you fancy a change you can try out the latest developments, including kitesurfing.

IAN WOOLCOCK/ALAMY

Surfing at dusk, Dominical, Costa Rica.

How big is your footprint?

Stilted house on Big Corn Island, Nicaragua.

The travel industry is growing rapidly and the environmental impact is becoming increasingly apparent, although the impact can seem remote and unrelated to an individual trip or holiday. Air travel is clearly implicated in global warming and resort construction can destroy natural habitats and restrict traditional rights and activities. With this in mind, individual choice and awareness can make a difference in many instances (see box, opposite); collectively, travellers can have a significant effect in shaping a more responsible and sustainable industry. Organizations such as **Green Globe 21**, Suite 8, Southern Cross House, 9 McKay Street, Turner, ACT, 2612, Australia, T+61-2-6257-

9102, www.greenglobe21.com, offer advice on destinations and sites that aim to achieve certain commitments to conservation and sustainable development. Of course travel can have beneficial impacts too, and this is something to which every traveller can contribute; many national parks are part funded by receipts from visitors. Similarly, travellers can support small-scale enterprises by staying in locally run hotels and hostels, eating in local restaurants and by buying local goods, supplies and crafts. There has been a phenomenal growth in tourism that promotes and supports the conservation of natural environments and is also fair and equitable to local communities.

Traveling light

▸ Where possible choose a destination, tour operator or hotel with a proven ethical and environmental commitment; if in doubt, ask.

▸ Spend money on locally produced (rather than imported) goods and services, buy directly from the producer or from a 'fair trade' shop, and use common sense when bargaining; the few dollars you save may be a week's salary to others.

▸ Use water and electricity carefully; travellers may receive preferential supply while the needs of local communities are overlooked.

▸ Learn about local etiquette and culture; consider local norms and behaviour and dress appropriately for local cultures and situations.

▸ Protect wildlife and other natural resources; don't buy souvenirs or goods unless they are sustainably produced and are not protected under CITES legislation.

▸ Always ask before taking photographs or videos of people.

▸ Consider staying in local accommodation rather than foreign-owned hotels; the economic benefits for host communities are far greater and there are more opportunities to learn about local culture.

▸ Make a voluntary contribution to Climate Care, www.co2.org, to counteract the pollution caused by tax-free fuel on your flight.

LUIS CÉSAR TEJO/SHUTTERSTOCK

Playa Hermosa, Guanacaste, Costa Rica.

Costa Rica, Nicaragua and Panama on screen and page

Books to read

Costa Rica's Carlos Fallas wrote *Mamá Yunita* in 1941 about the appalling conditions and poverty on the banana plantations of the United Fruit Company. Carmen Lyra – whose image appears on the 10,000 colones bill – was also critical of the industry in the 1920s and 30s, and more recently Ana Istarú has taken on the feminist literary role. Nicaragua's home-grown poetry has a very rich tradition. Rubén Darío (1867-1916) and Ernesto Cardenal (1925-) are just two internationally famous Nica poets. Salmon Rushdie's *The Jaguar Smile* provides an international perspective on the country in the mid-1980s, and Stephen Kinzer's *Blood of Brothers* provides a dramatic story of the struggle that led to the overthrow of the Somoza dictatorship in 1979.

Panama's history is the canal, and David McCullough's *The Path Between the Seas* tells the story of the creation of the Panama Canal – the why, where, how and more. And for fiction there's Graham Greene (*Getting to Know the General*), John Le Carré (*The Tailor of Panama*) and Iain Banks (*Canal Dreams*).

Films to watch

Costa Rica has no film industry to speak of although it has provided more than a reasonable list of 'green paradise' locations (*1492: Conquest of Paradise*, *Congo*, *Spy Kids 2* and *Apocalypto*).

Ken Loach's *Carla's Song* is pro-Sandanista and brutally realistic, while still managing to tell a story of personal relationships and pain in post-Revolution Nicaragua.

Panama's big-screen highlight is *The Tailor of Panama*, starring Pierce Brosnan, and more recently as a location for *Quantum of Solace*, the latest Bond movie starring Craig Daniel.

Contents

Footprint features

Essentials

Getting there

Arriving in the region, visitors can choose from any of the capital cities – Managua, San José or Panama City – depending on your plans and where you're intending to travel. Some international flights stop at both San José and Panama City either on the way out or returning so check with your airline if this is likely to cause a problem beyond length of journey. Land transport between each country is similar and there is no established route.

Air

Costa Rica

The main international airport is at San José (see page 64). There are direct charter flights in season from several European cities including Frankfurt. From most European cities flights connect in the US at Miami, Houston, Dallas and many others. Flights take around 15 hours and cost anything from around £500 upwards.

Flights from North America are many and varied (more than 20 each week), again some stop in Miami so check if a direct flight is important. **Daniel Oduber International Airport**, near Liberia, is increasingly popular, conveniently located just 30 minutes from some of Guanacaste's finest beaches. Charter specials available from time to time.

Flights from South American cities include Bogotá (**Copa, Grupo Taca**), Cali (**SAM, Grupo Taca**), Caracas (**Grupo Taca**), Cartagena (**SAM**), Guayaquil (**Grupo Taca**), Lima (**Grupo Taca**), Quito (**Grupo Taca**) and Santiago (**Grupo Taca**).

Airport information Juan Santamaría International Airport is 16 km northwest of San José on the southern outskirts of Alajuela, information T2441-0744 or T2443-2622. For arrivals the airport is simply laid out with immigration, baggage reclaim and customs following naturally one after the other. After customs, but before leaving the customs hall, there is a tourist desk which can provide maps and information, as well as book hotel accommodation and transport to San José and other areas. In the same area is a branch of Banco Nacional, which opens to meet international flights, and a line of car rental desks where you can pick up or arrange vehicle hire. Outside, the swarms of greeting taxis will compete for your business. US$15 is the standard fare to downtown San José. If you're looking for something a little cheaper it's a short walk to the bus stop where buses leave every 10 minutes for the 40-minute, 200 *colónes* (US$0.70) trip. Head out to the main road following the short airport access road, and join the queue opposite the petrol station.

Daniel Oduber Quirós International Airport, in the northwest 13 km from Liberia along Highway 21, is a much smaller airport. The modern terminal has customs and immigration, a café and a Bancredito. A good spot if you want to head straight for the beach. Transport from the airport is limited to readily available taxis – ask around to get the best price.

Departure tax The flat rate is US$26 per person when leaving by air.

Nicaragua

From **Europe** take any trans-Atlantic flight to Miami or Houston and connect to **American, Continental** or **Grupo Taca**. From **North America** there are regular daily flights to Managua from Miami, Atlanta and Houston with either **American, Continental, Delta, Iberia** or **Taca**.

There are also connections from several US cities through El Salvador. From **Latin America** there are good connections from Barranquilla, Bogotá, Buenos Aires, Cali, Cancún, Caracas, Cartagena, Guatemala City, Guayaquil, Havana, La Paz, Lima, Medellín, Mexico City, Panama City, Quito, San José, San Salvador, Santiago, Santo Domingo and São Paulo.

Airport information Managua International Airport is small and manageable and is located on the eastern outskirts of the city. Upon landing you will need to pay US$5 at the immigration counter, before retrieving your bags and passing through customs. If you want to rent a car, there are counters through the sliding glass doors on your left after the customs point. Taxis to Metrocentro, Bolonia or Martha Quezada should cost US$15 (less if you speak Spanish and know exactly where you are going). If you can lug your bags to the highway, the taxis that wait along the Carretera Norte just 100 m from the building will normally charge half the price. Be sure to have precise directions in Spanish to your desired destination. When returning to the airport from the capital, a taxi hailed on the street will charge US$5-6. If leaving early, a radio-taxi costing US$10 is safer and will not make stops along the way.

Departure tax US$32, payable when leaving the country.

Panama
There are no direct services from Europe. Connecting flights go via US cities. They take around 15 hours and cost anything from around £500 upwards. From the US there are direct flights from Atlanta, Baltimore, Houston, Los Angeles, Miami, New York (some change planes in San José), Orlando and Portland. For other US cities, connections are made in Miami or Houston.

From Central America, there are direct flights to Cancún and Mexico City, Guatemala City, Managua, San José and San Salvador. There are no direct flights to Tegucigalpa, but connections with **Lacsa** through San José or **Taca** in San Salvador.

From South America, there are lots of flights from Colombia with **Copa** (Barranquilla, Bogotá, Cartagena, Cali, Medellín) and **SAM** (Bogotá). One-way tickets are not available from Colombia to Panama on **SAM** or **Copa**, but a refund on an unused return portion is possible, less 17% taxes, on **SAM**. **LAB** fly from Santa Cruz (Bolivia). From Guayaquil and Quito, **Continental**, **Ecuatoriana** and **Copa**. **Copa** from Santiago de Chile and Lima. From Caracas, **Mexicana**, **Copa** and Aeropostal.

Airport information Tocumen International Airport is 27 km east of the city centre. Taxis (US$25) and buses run to Panama City. For a lower price, take a shared cab (*compartivo*), and while you may wait a little longer the price becomes US$10-15 for two or three people respectively. There is a US$4 tax on air tickets over US$100 purchased in Panama.

Departure tax Airport departure tax is US$20 (payable only in cash) which has to be paid by all passengers.

Road

At the top of the region, in Nicaragua, the main road links to the north are at El Guasaule (see page 294) and further inland on the Interamericana at Las Manos (see page 280), with a third option at the border north of Somoto at El Espino in Honduras (see page 280).

Crossing the border to Costa Rica in the south, the most commonly used crossing is at Peñas Blancas (see page 118), although it is also possible to leave from San Carlos for Los Chiles (see page 103), connecting with Fortuna and Lake Arenal. Crossing the border on the North Pacific is possible but immigration services are non-existent and transportation is irregular.

The main crossing on the Costa Rica–Panama border is at Paso Canoas, which is straightforward and problem free. The Río Sereno crossing is also recommended; but only passengers on public transport can pass through. A less popular but more entertaining crossing point is Sixaola/Guabito on the Caribbean Coast. Passengers and vehicles (car or motorcycle) are given 30 days at the border. There are immigration services on both sides but they are only during normal office hours. See page 337 for further details.

Overland routes to Colombia are possible through the **Darién Gap** where the purist has a difficult, but not impossible challenge. Alternatively it is possible to hop, skip and jump your way along the Caribbean coast taking canoes. For details see page 424.

Sea and river

Costa Rica
The main ports for international cargo vessels are **Puerto Limón**, with regular sailings to and from Europe, and **Caldera**, on the central Pacific Coast. Contact shipping agents, of which there are many, in Puerto Limón and San José for details.

Nicaragua
In San Carlos there is an immigration post linking with the boat journey on the Río Frío connecting to Los Chiles in Costa Rica. There is no official border crossing between San Juan del Norte and Costa Rica.

Panama
The Panama Canal is on the itineraries of many shipping services from Europe and the US which take passengers, but charges are high. There are several boats that make the journey from Isla Grande on the Caribbean across to **Cartagena**, charging US$150-200 for the journey. It is also possible to travel by sea to/from **Colombia**. A couple of boats travel weekly from Colón to **San Andrés Island**, Colombia, from where there are connections to Cartagena; the *Johnny Walker* takes 30 hours, but the service is very irregular and travellers have sometimes had to wait over a week in vain. There are (contraband) boats from Coco Solo, Colón, to the Guajira Peninsula, Colombia. The uncomfortable three-day journey is undertaken entirely at your own risk and you may have to wait days for a sailing. You have to bargain for your fare on these boats and accommodation is a little primitive.

Staying closer to the coastline it is possible to cross the border to Colombia on the Caribbean side close to **Puerto Obaldía**, and on Pacific Coast via Jaqué and possibly La Palma, see page 424. These routes are not cheap and can take several days.

Getting around

Travel within the region is simple and straightforward. There is a very good network of bus and minibus transport between towns and villages throughout the region. For popular routes, the service can be very frequent. Air travel is also reasonably affordable and very convenient with flights within each country, and international connections with domestic service providers between Nicaragua and Costa Rica, and Costa Rica and Panama. Logistically, international bus travel is very easy with international service stopping at borders to facilitate the necessary paperwork. The main concern is breaking down the journeys into manageable distances to limit discomfort, but there are few very long journeys.

Air

Costa Rica
Getting around the country by plane is straightforward. Two companies provide a scheduled service from San José to 16 destinations throughout the country: SANSA, T2221-9414, www.flysansa.com, and **NatureAir**, T2220-3054, and www.natureair.com. SANSA have also developed a mini-hub around Liberia with flights to Tamarindo, Arenal and Tambor. Scheduled services leave from Barra Colorado, Carate, Carrillo-Sámara, Coto 47, Drake Bay, Golfito, Liberia, La Fortuna, Limón, Nosara Beach, Palmar Sur, Puerto Jiménez, Punta Islita, Quepos, Tamarindo, Tambor and Tortuguero. Several charter companies also operate out of San José. Weight allowances are minimal at 12 kg (25 pounds) with a US$0.45 surcharge for every pound.

Nicaragua
La Costeña, T263-1228, operate internal air services to Bluefields, Corn Island, Minas (Bonanza/Siuna/Rosita), Puerto Cabeza, San Carlos and Waspám. **Atlantic Airlines**, T270-5355, www.atlanticairlinesint.com, provide similar coverage and connect to Tegucigalpa and other cities in Honduras. Domestic flights should be reconfirmed as soon as possible. Luggage limits are: 9 kg hand luggage; stowed luggage 13.5 kg free, maximum 45 kg. Domestic departure tax is 30 córdobas in Managua and usually 15 córdobas in outlying airports.

Panama
There are local flights to most parts of Panama by several airlines. The most reliable is **Aeroperlas**, T315-7500, www.aeroperlas.com, the **Grupo Taca** subsidiary, with destinations throughout the country. Other services include: **Mapiex**, T315-0344, www.mapiex.com, offering charter flights between Bocas del Toro, David and Panama City. **Air Panama**, T316-9000, www.flyairpanama.com, offers a wide range of domestic services. **Ansa**, T226-7891, which flies to San Blas; **Parsa**, T226-3883, provides a charter service; **Transpasa**, T236-0842, has charter flights to San Blas; **Chitreana**, T226-4116, flies to Chitré, Los Santos, Las Tablas and Guararé, and **Aerotaxi**, T226-7891, operates a service to San Blas and charter flights.

On internal flights passengers must present their identity documents and have their luggage weighed. As excess baggage charges are frequent, ask if it is cheaper to ship excess as air freight (*carga*) on the same flight.

Rail

Costa Rica

All commercial lines are closed. For the truly devoted there is talk of reintroducing a tourist 'banana' train from Siquirres to Matina on the Caribbean side. Ask locally for details. A tourist train (weekends) from San José to the Pacific, departing from Estación del Pacífico, 600 m south of Parque Central, at 0600, travelling to Caldera with a stop in Orotina; returns at 1500. Tickets (US$25 return) must be purchased Monday-Wednesday for following weekend. The tours are in refurbished 1940s German wagons. Contact **America Travel**, T2233-3300, www.ticotraintour.com.

Road

Costa Rica

Costa Rica has a total of 35,700 km of roads of which 7500 km are paved. The Interamericana (Pan-American Highway) runs the length of the country. A bridge built over the Tempisque River in the last ten years has drastically reduced travel time to the beaches of the Nicoya Peninsula. A highway has been built from Orotina to Caldera, a port on the Gulf of Nicoya, which has replaced Puntarenas as the principal Pacific port, and a highway is being built from Orotina to Ciudad Colón. Another road from Orotina to Quepos has improved access to the Pacific beaches. This is yet to be extended as far as Dominical, but continuing further south from Dominical to Ciudad Cortés, the road is generally good. All four-lane roads into San José are toll roads. It is illegal to ride in a car or taxi without wearing seatbelts.

Bus The good road network supports a regular bus service that covers most parts of the country. Frequency declines with popularity but you can get to most places with road access eventually. San José is the main hub for buses, although you can skip down the Pacific Coast by making connections at Puntarenas. Coming from Nicaragua, direct to Arenal, requires cutting in and travelling through Tilaran.

Two shuttle bus companies, **Interbus**, T2283-5573, www.interbusonline.com, and **Fantasy Tours/GrayLine**, T2220-2126, www.graylinecostarica.com, offer transport from the capital to dozens of beach and tourism destinations in comfortable a/c minibuses, bilingual drivers, hotel pick-up, tickets US$17-38 one way.

Car and motorcycle Driving in Costa Rica allows for greater flexibility when travelling. Many of the nature parks are in remote areas; 4WD and high-clearance is recommended and sometimes essential; in the wet season some roads will be impassable. Always ask locals or bus drivers what the state of the road is before embarking on a journey. Do not assume that if the buses are running, a car can get through too.

Tourists who enter by car or motorcycle pay US$10 road tax, including mandatory insurance, and can keep their cars for an initial period of 90 days. This can be extended for a total period of six months, for about US$10 per extra month, at the **Instituto Costarricense de Turismo**, or at the **Customs office**, Avenida 3, Calle 14, if you take your passport, car entry permit and a piece of stamped paper (*papel sellado*) obtainable at any bookshop. Cars are fumigated on entry: exterior US$8. If you have an accident while in the country do not move the vehicle and immediately contact **Policía de Tránsito**, San José, T2222-9330/9245.

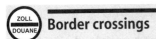

Border crossings

Nicaragua–Costa Rica
Peñas Blancas, pages 118 and 207; Los Chiles/Río Frío, pages 103 and 223; Barra del Colorado 182.

Nicaragua–Honduras
Guasaule, page 294; El Espino, page 280; Ocotal/Las Manos, page 280.

Panama–Costa Rica
Paso Canoas, pages 161 and 337; Río Sereno, page 337 (no Panamanian tourist cards available); Sixoala, page 187.

Renting a car can be a surprisingly economical way to travel if you can form a group and split the costs. As with all rentals, check your vehicle carefully as the company will try to claim for the smallest of 'damages'. Most leases do not allow the use of a normal car off paved roads. Always make sure the spare tyre is in good order, as potholes are frequent. You can have tyres fixed at any garage for about US$2 in 30 minutes. Guideline prices: smallest economy car US$34-46 per day includes unlimited mileage or US$204-276 per week; 4WD vehicle costs US$58-150 per day, US$300-900 per week, including unlimited mileage. Driver's licence from home and credit card generally required. Collision damage waiver (CDW) insurance is mandatory and costs an extra US$10-17 per day; excess is between US$750 and US$1500. Cash deposits or credit card charges range from US$800 to US$1800, so check you have sufficient credit. Discounts for car hire are available during the 'Green Season' (May-November). If you plan to drop off a hired car somewhere other than where you picked it up, check with several firms for their charges: **Elegante**, **Ada** and **National** appear to have the lowest drop-off fees. Insurance will not cover broken windscreens, driving on unsurfaced roads or damaged tyres.

Never leave anything in a hired car and never leave your car on the street, even in daylight. Secure parking lots are available in most cities. Regular reports of break-ins at national parks and other popular tourism areas. Driving at night is not recommended.

Main fuel stations have regular (unleaded) US$1.25 and diesel US$1.21 per litre; super gasoline (unleaded) is available throughout the country, US$1.27 per litre. Prices are regulated by the government. For passenger cars are between US$0.20 and US$0.40.

Cycling Cycling is easier in Costa Rica than elsewhere in Central America; there is less heavy traffic and it is generally more 'cyclist friendly'. However, paving is thin and soon deteriorates; look out for cracks and potholes, which bring traffic to a crawl. The prevailing wind is from the northeast so, if making an extensive tour, travelling in the direction of Panama is slightly more favourable.

Hitchhiking Generally easy and safe by day, but take the usual precautions.

Nicaragua

The road network has been greatly extended and improved in recent years. The Interamericana from Honduras to Costa Rica is paved the whole way (384 km), as is the shorter international road to the Honduran frontier via Chinandega. The road between

Managua and Rama (for Bluefields) is also paved. Road directions are given according to landmarks, even where there are street names or numbers.

If arriving overland, there is an US$8 charge. Exit tax for foreigners is US$2 (US$5 at weekends). Always insist on a receipt and if in doubt, go to the Immigration Department in Managua to verify the charge. Officials in Las Manos may try to overcharge – be firm.

Bus Local buses are the cheapest in Central America and often the most crowded. This is how most Nicaraguans get around and, outside Managua, the bus drivers are usually friendly and helpful. Route schedules are pretty reliable except on Sundays. It is best to arrive early for all long-distance buses, especially if it is an express bus or for a route that only runs once or twice a day. On routes that leave every hour or half-hour you only need to check the destination above the front window of the bus and grab a seat. You can flag down most buses that are not marked 'Express'. Fares are collected as you board city buses or en route in the case of intercity buses. For express buses, you need to purchase your ticket in advance at the terminal or from the driver; some buses have reserved seating. Baggage loaded on to the roof or in the luggage compartment may be charged for, usually at half the passenger rate or a flat fee of US$0.50.

Car and motorcycle Since road signage is weak at best, it is important to have a map and some basic Spanish to get even a little way off the main highway. Around 80% of Nicaragua's roads are unpaved with lots of mud bogs in the wet season and dusty washboard and stone-filled paths in the dry season so be flexible with your schedules. 4WD drive for cities or travel within the Pacific Basin is not necessary, although it does give you dramatically more flexibility across the country and is standard equipment in mountain and jungle territory. It is obligatory to wear a seatbelt. If you are involved in a car accident where someone is injured, you may be held for up to two days, guilty or not, while blame is assessed. Hiring a driver covers this potentially disastrous liability. Be careful when driving at night, few roads are lit and there are many people, animals and holes in the road.

Motorists and motorcyclists pay US$20 in cash on arrival at the border (cyclists pay US$2, up to US$9 at weekends) in addition to the entry tax for other overland arrivals. Do not lose the receipts, or you will have to pay again when you leave. Make sure you get the correct entry stamps, or you will encounter all sorts of problems once inside the country. Vehicles not cleared by 1630 are held at customs overnight. Formalities can take up to four hours. On leaving, motorists pay five córdobas, as well as the usual exit tax. For procedures at each border, see the relevant sections of text.

Petrol stations are very rare in the countryside; it's best to fill up the tank (unleaded, premium grade fuel and diesel are available everywhere) if going into the interior. There are 24-hour petrol stations in the major cities, elsewhere they close at 1800. Petrol is sold by the gallon. Regular petrol costs US$2.60 per gallon, US$2.90 for super, diesel US$2.30 super – all are unleaded. Be careful when driving at night, few roads are lit and there are many people, animals and holes in the road. Crash helmets for motocyclists are compulsory.

Car hire costs around US$30 a day for a basic car, rising to US$85 for a jeep. Weekly discount rates are significant and if you want to cover a lot of sites quickly it can work out to be worthwhile. A minimum deposit of US$500 is required along with an international driving licence or a licence from your country of origin. Insurance costs US$10-23. Before signing up check insurance and what it covers and also ask about mileage allowance. Most agents have an office at the international airport and offices in other parts of Managua.

Cycling Cycling around Nicaragua is certainly a challenge. For information on the state of the roads, see Car and motorcyclists above. Several cyclists have said that you should take a 'proof of purchase' of your cycle or suggest typing out a phoney 'cycle ownership' document to help at border crossings.

Hitchhiking Hitching is widely accepted, but not easy because so many people do it and there is little traffic – offer to pay a small contribution.

Panama

There are now about 9700 km of roads, of which 3100 km are paved. The highway running from Colón to Panama City, widened to four lanes in 1999, is the only fully paved road crossing the isthmus. A well-maintained scenic road traverses the isthmus from Gualaca in Chiriquí to the town of Chiriquí Grande in Bocas del Toro, crossing the Swedish-built Fortuna hydroelectric dam. In 1999 construction was completed to extend the road from Chiriquí Grande to Almirante and the regional centre of Changuinola, opening up a beautiful new route along the Caribbean. The Interamericana runs east from Panama City to Chepo and into the province of Darién, and west to the Costa Rican border. It is paved throughout (as far east as the Panama/Darién provincial border) and is being improved. There is a modern toll road between Panama City and La Chorrera, and the section between David and La Concepción is a modern, four-lane highway. Expressways were built in 1999 to ease traffic congestion in and around Panama City.

Bus The bus network covers the entire country, generally with efficient, timely services. Some of the long-distance buses are small 'mini' buses, normally modern and comfortable, but large, modern air-conditioned buses are being introduced. They are more expensive than elsewhere in Central America. Slower 'regular' buses run in country areas. 'Express' buses with air conditioning operate between Panama City and Colón and to David and the border with Costa Rica.

Car and motorcyle Minor roads are often poorly signed in Panama and you will require a good map for all but the most basic excursions. If you're travelling to remote locales, you'll need to hire a 4WD with high clearance (book well in advance). Such roads will be particularly difficult in the wet season. Drive aggressively in Panama City if you want to survive.

On average car hire rates range from US$24 per day for a small saloon to US$65 for 4WD-jeep with free mileage. Insurance is around US$8 per day, 5% tax is payable and around US$500 deposit must be paid. The minimum age is 23 years and home driver's licence is acceptable. If you require a 4WD it is better to book a few days in advance. If planning to rent from an international company, consult them before leaving home. Sometimes very good deals are available that cannot be made at the Panama office. Rental cars are not allowed out of the country; they are marked by special licence plates.

Super grade gasoline (called *super*) costs about US$3.40 per US gallon (3.78 litres); unleaded is available in larger towns. Low octane (*regular* or *normal*) costs about US$3.20; diesel is about US$3. For motorcyclists, note that a crash helmet must be worn.

Taking a car with Panamanian plates to Costa Rica requires a permit from the Traffic Police (*Tránsito*) obtainable on presentation of the ownership certificate and a document from the Judicial Police (*PTJ*) indicating that the vehicle has not been reported stolen. A travel agency, for example **Chadwick**'s in Balboa, will arrange this for you for US$30. Exit calls for four papers which cost US$4.20 (obtainable from customs in Paitilla Airport).

Taking a vehicle to Colombia, Venezuela or Ecuador is not easy or cheap. The best advice is to shop around the agencies in Panama City or Colón to see what is available when you want to go. Both local and international lines take vehicles, and sometimes passengers, but schedules and prices are very variable.

Sea

Costa Rica
Ferries serve the southern section of the Nicoya Peninsula from Puntarenas. The Osa Peninsula has a regular ferry service linking Golfito and Puerto Jiménez, and Bahía Drake is reached on boats from Sierpe. Boats travel to Tortuguero from Moín, close to Puerto Limón, and from Cariari, north of Guápiles.

Nicaragua
The main Pacific ports are Corinto, San Juan del Sur and Puerto Sandino. The two main Atlantic ports are Puerto Cabezas and Bluefields.

Panama
Boats and comfortable yachts provide tours all or part way through the canal. Contact tour operators in Panama City or Colón for details. It is also possible to travel through as a linehandler if you have sailing experience and turn up at the right time.

A regular ferry makes the journey to the island of Bocas del Toro from Almirante and Chiriquí Grande on the western Caribbean coast. To the east, canoes serves the archipelago of San Blas.

Access to and from Colombia is possible by sea, along the Caribbean or Pacific coasts, although the journey takes several days and can be costly, see page 414.

Maps

Costa Rica
The **Instituto Geográfico Nacional**, Calle 9, Avenida 20-22, at the Ministry of Public Works and Transport in San José, supplies good topographical maps for walkers, 0730-1600. ITM has a 1:500,000 travel map of Costa Rica, available at bookstores throughout the country. Maps are also available in San José at **7th Street Books**, Calle 7, Avenida 1 and Central, T2256-8251, **Universal**, Avenida Central, Calle 1 and Central, T2222-2222, and **Lehmann**, Avenida Central, Calle 1-3, T2223-1212.

Nicaragua
The only decent map made internationally is *Nicaragua – An International Travel Map*, published by International Travel Maps in Vancouver, or else stop by INTUR's main office in Managua, one block south and one block west from the Crowne Plaza Hotel, to get a country map. Detailed maps (1:50,000) can be bought at the government geological survey office, **INETER**, across from the Nicaraguan Immigration main office in Managua, T249-3590. Good regional maps are available for around US$6 each.

Panama
Topographic maps and aerial photos are sold by the **Instituto Geográfico Nacional Tommy Guardia (IGNTG)**, Vía Simón Bolívar, opposite the National University (footbridge

Accommodation price codes

LL (over US$150), **L** (US$100-150), **AL** (US$66-99) and **A** (US$46-65) Hotels in these categories can be found in most of the large cities but especially where there is a strong concentration of tourists or business travellers. They should offer pool, sauna, gym, jacuzzi, all business facilities (including email), several restaurants and bars. A safe box is usually provided in each room. Credit cards are usually accepted and dollars cash changed typically at poor rates.

B (US$31-45) Hotels in this category should provide more than the standard facilities and a fair degree of comfort. Many include a good breakfast and offer extras such as a colour TV, minibar, air conditioning and a swimming pool. They may also provide tourist information and their own transport for airport pickups. Service is generally good and most accept credit cards although a lower rate is often offered for cash.

C (US$21-30) and **D** (US$12-20) Hotels in these categories range from very comfortable to functional and there are some real bargains to be had. You should expect your own bathroom, constant hot water, a towel, soap and toilet paper. There is sometimes a restaurant and a communal area. In tropical regions, rooms are usually equipped with air conditioning although this may be old. Hotels used to catering for foreign tourists and backpackers often have luggage storage, money exchange and kitchen facilities.

E (US$7-11) and **F** (under US$7) Hotels in these categories are often extremely simple with bedside or ceiling fans, shared bathrooms and little in the way of furniture. Standards of cleanliness may not be high and rooms may also be rented to couples by the hour. A room with a window can often make the difference between OK and intolerable. Balance that with possible noise and security issues.

nearby, fortunately), T236-2444, www.ignpanama.gob.pa, take Transístmica or Tumba Muerto bus, Mon-Fri 0800-1530. Maps from 1:500,000 to 1:50,000 available. ITM (www.itmb.com) have a 1:800,000 travel map of Panama.

Sleeping

Accommodation in the region covers all price and service options. At the top, in Panama City, international chains provide all necessary comforts for Hollywood movie stars, presidents and international bankers, while in Nicaragua there's only a handful of top notch hotels outside the capital. Between those extremes, it's a question of matching costs and style to your budget, from boutique hotels, through to lively meeting spots.

Costa Rica

Accommodation in Costa Rica favours couples and groups – the price of a single room is often the same as a double, and the price of a room for four is often less than double the price for two. Accommodation prices during the 'green' season (May to November) are generally much lower. A 13% sales tax plus 3.39% tourism tax (total 16.39%) are added to the basic price of hotel rooms. A deposit is advised at the more expensive hotels in San José, especially in the high season (December to April), to guarantee reservations. If you arrive late at night in the high season, even a guaranteed reservation may not be kept.

Camping opportunities in Costa Rica are limited with few offical campsites. It is possible to camp in some national parks. Contact the **Fundación de Parques Nacionales** in San José for details (see page 66).

Nicaragua

Most hotels are run by independent operators with a few upmarket international chains beginning to arrive, mainly in Managua. There are motels along the Interamericana, guest houses troughout the country, campsites dotted around and resort type hotels in more touristic spots. Standards vary greatly but there is plenty of competition in the mid- to low-budget range in most towns.

Panama

The very best in five-star luxury is available in Panama City and several comfortable lodges are found in the larger towns and mountain and jungle hideaways. If travelling further afield, accommodation in our **C** category and below is available in most towns of interest. Camping is generally tolerated.

Eating and drinking

In general, eating out in Costa Rica is more expensive than elsewhere in Central America. There are some similarities throughout the region: the huge selection of fruit drinks making the most of the abundance of tropical fruits growing throughout the region; and the staples of rice, beans and tortillas. However, each country also has distinct flavours and cooking techniques. Whereas few people return from Costa Rica raving about the national dish, Nicaragua's strongest cultural marker may be its cuisine, and its most successful export is its food.

Costa Rica

The food is simple, relying heavily on the staples of rice and beans. Mixed with shredded beef, chicken or sometimes fish, served with a couple of warmed tortillas and you have the dish of **casado** that fuels the majority of the country's workers. Only you will know how long you can enjoy the pleasures of rice and beans day after day. One way of spicing up the food is with liberal helpings of *Salsa Lizano* which is always somewhere near the dinner table.

Sodas (small restaurants) serve local food, which is worth trying. Very common is *casado*, a cheap lunch which includes rice, beans, stewed beef or fish, fried plantain and cabbage. *Olla de carne* is a soup of beef, plantain, corn, yucca, ñampi and *chayote* (local vegetables). *Sopa negra* is made with black beans, and comes with a poached egg in it; *picadillo* is another meat and vegetable stew. Snacks are popular: *gallos* (filled tortillas), *tortas* (containing meat and vegetables), *arreglados* (bread filled with the same) and *empanadas. Pan de yuca* is a speciality, available from stalls in San José centre. For breakfast, try *gallo pinto* (rice and beans) with *natilla* (a slightly sour cream). The best ice cream can be found in Pops shops.

There are many types of cold drink made either from fresh fruit or milk drinks with fruit (*batidos*) or cereal flour whisked with ice cubes. Drinks are often sugared well beyond North American or European tastes (ask for *poco azúcar*). The fruits range from the familiar to the exotic; others include *cebada* (barley flour), *pinolillo* (roasted corn), *horchata* (rice

Eating price codes

¶¶¶ over US$15	¶¶ US$8-15	¶ under US$8

Prices refer to the cost of a meal with a drink for one person.

flour with cinnamon) and *chan*, which according to Michael Brisco is 'perhaps the most unusual, looking like mouldy frogspawn and tasting of penicillin'. The coffee is excellent.

Nicaragua

Nicaragua has a great selection of traditional dishes that are usually prepared with fresh ingredients and in generous portions. The midday heat dictates that you get out and tour early with a light breakfast, head for shelter and enjoy a long lunch and rest, then finish with an early dinner.

A typical Nicaraguan breakfast is coffee with *gallo pinto* or *nacatamales*. *Gallo pinto*, the dish that keeps most of Nicaragua alive, is a mixture of fried white rice and kidney beans, which are boiled apart and then fried together with onions and sweet pepper, served with handmade corn tortillas. This can be breakfast, lunch and dinner for much of the population at home and for this reason is not found in most restaurants. *Nacatamales* consist of cornmeal, pork or chicken, rice, *achote* (similar to paprika), peppers, peppermint leaves, potatoes, onions and cooking oil, all wrapped in a big green banana leaf and boiled. A normal lunch includes a cabbage and tomato salad, white rice, beans, tortilla, onions, fried or boiled plantain and a meat or fish serving. *Asado* or *a la plancha* are key words for most foreigners. *Asado* is grilled meat or fish, which often comes with a chilli sauce. In the countryside *cuajada* is a must. It is a soft feta cheese made daily in people's homes, lightly salted and excellent in a hot tortilla. If there is any room left, there are three traditional desserts that are well worth trying: *tres leches*, which is a very sweet cake made with three different kinds of milk; *Pío V*, named after Pope Pius (though no one seems to know why), is a corn cake topped with light cream and bathed in rum sauce; and if these are too heavy, there is the ubiquitous *cajeta*, which is milk mixed with cane sugar or endless varieties of blended or candied fruit. Look out, too, for *piñonate*, thinly sliced strips of candied green papaya.

Since Nicaragua is the land of a thousand fruits, the best drink is the *refresco* or *fresco*, fruit juices or grains and spices mixed with water and sugar. Two favourites are *cacao* and *pithaya*. *Cacao*, the raw cocoa bean, is ground and mixed with milk, rice, cinnamon, vanilla, ice and sugar and is refreshingly cold and filling. *Pithaya* is a cactus fruit, which is blended with lime and sugar and has a lovely, sensual deep purple colour and seedy pulp.

Panama

In Panama City the range of food available is very broad with a profusion of restaurants and well-stocked supermarkets. In the interior tastes are simpler and available ingredients less varied. The staple of Panamanian food is white rice, grown not in paddies but on dry land, and usually served at every meal. Most food is boiled or fried in vegetable oil (usually soybean oil). Virtually every restaurant will have a *comida corriente* (meal of the day) which will include a serving of meat, chicken or fish, white rice and a salad, a dish of boiled beans garnished with a *tajada* (slice) of fried ripe plantain. It will cost about US$2 in towns, perhaps more in the city, less in villages. Beef is common; pork, chicken and the excellent fish are usually a better choice. A bowl of *sopa de carne* (beef broth with vegetables) or *de pescado* (fish chowder) is usually available as a first course for US$0.50. Breakfast normally consists of eggs, a small beefsteak or a slice of liver fried with onions and tomatoes, bread and butter and some combination of *frituras*.

The national dish is *sancocho de gallina*, a stew of chicken, yuca, ñame (dasheen), plantain, cut-up pieces of corn on the cob, potatoes and onions and strongly flavoured with *culantro*, an aromatic leaf similar in flavour to coriander (*cilantro*). *Ropa vieja* ('old clothes') is beef boiled or steamed until it can be shredded, then sautéed with onions, garlic, tomatoes and green or red peppers, often served with yellow rice (coloured with *achiote*). Piquant *ceviche*, eaten as a first course or a snack with cold beer, is usually raw corvina or shellfish seasoned with tiny red and yellow peppers, thin slices of onion and marinated in lime juice; it is served very cold with crackers (beware of the bite). A speciality of the Caribbean coast is *sao*, pigs' feet pickled with lime and hot peppers. Also try *arroz con coco*, coconut rice, or the same with *tití*, tiny shrimp; also *fufú*, a fish chowder with coconut milk. *Mondongo* is the stewed tripe dish.

Among the items sold at the roadside you may see bottles stopped with a corncob, filled with *nance*, a strong-flavoured, yellow-green fruit packed with water and allowed to ripen and ferment slightly; *pifá/pixbae*, a bright orange fruit which, when boiled, tastes much like sweet potato; *níspero*, the tasty, acidic yellow fruit of the chicle tree.

There are dozens of sweetened fruit drinks: *naranja* (orange), *maracuyá* (passion fruit), *guayaba*, *zarzamora* (blackberry), *guanábana*, etc. The generic term is *chicha dulce* which also includes drinks made with rice or corn. Panamanian beer tends to be low in alcohol. *Chicha fuerte* is the alcoholic form of corn or rice drink fermented with sugar, brewed mostly in the countryside. The local rum is not bad. *Seco*, a harsh brand of 'white lightning' made from the juice of sugar cane, brand name *Herrerano*, deserves considerable respect.

Festivals and events

If the time and mood is right, there is little to beat a Latin festival. Fine costumes, loud music, the sounds of firecrackers tipped off with the gentle wafting of specially prepared foods all (normally) with a drink or two. Whether you seek out the carnival or happen to stumble across a celebration, the events – big or small – are likely to be memorable.

If you want to hit the carnivals there are a few broad dates generally significant throughout the region. Carnival is normally the week before the start of Lent. *Semana Santa* (Easter Week) is an understandably more spiritual affair. On 2 November is *Día de los Muertos* (Day of the Dead), significant throughout the region, when families visit cemeteries to honour the dead. Christmas and New Year result in celebrations of some kind, but not always public. Public holidays throughout the region lead to a complete shut-down in services. No banks, government offices, usually no shops and often far fewer restaurants and bars. Avoid changing money or trying to make travel arrangements on public holidays. The school holidays are December to March; at these times tourists spots are busy so make reservations in advance.

Costa Rica
1 Jan New Year's Day.
19 Mar St Joseph.
Mar/Apr Nearly everyone is on holiday at **Easter**; everywhere is shut on Thu, Fri and Sun, and many shops close on Sat and most of the previous week as well.
11 Apr Battle of Rivas.
1 May Labour Day.
Jun Corpus Christi.
29 Jun St Peter and St Paul.
25 Jul Guanacaste Day.
2 Aug Virgin of Los Angeles.
15 Aug Mothers' Day.
15 Sep Independence Day.
12 Oct Día de la Raza (Columbus Day). The main festival is **Carnival in Puerto Limón** where there's music, dance, street processions and general festivities. It's definitely worth making the effort to go.
8 Dec Immaculate Conception.
25 Dec Christmas Day.
28-31 Dec San José only.

Nicaragua
1 Jan New Year's Day.
Mar/Apr Holy Week 1200 Wed to Easter Sun.

1 May Labour Day.
19 Jul Revolution of 1979.
14 Sep Battle of San Jacinto.
15 Sep Independence Day.
2 Nov Día de los Muertos (All Souls' Day).
7-8 Dec La Purísima (Immaculate Conception).
25 Dec Christmas Day.

Panama
1 Jan New Year's Day.
9 Jan Martyrs' Day.
12 Feb **(around)** The Ngöbe-Bugle (Guaymí) of Chiriquí province meet to transact tribal business, hold feasts and compete for brides by tossing balsa logs at one another.
Feb/Mar Shrove Tuesday Carnival.
Mar/Apr Good Friday.
1 May Labour Day.
15 Aug Panama City only.
1 Nov National Anthem Day.
2 Nov All Souls' Day.
3 Nov Independence Day.
4 Nov Flag Day.
10 Nov First Call of Independence.
28 Nov Independence from Spain.
8 Dec Mothers' Day.
25 Dec Christmas Day.

Shopping

The best buys are wooden items, ceramics and leather handicrafts. Many wooden handicrafts are made of rainforest hardwoods and deforestation is a critical problem. Coffee should have 'puro' on the packet or it may contain sugar or other additives.

Masaya in Nicaragua is the centre for *artesanía*, selling excellent crafts, high-quality cotton hammocks, leather goods and colourful woven rugs often used as wall hangings and wicker furniture. More traditional Panamanian crafts include the colourful *molas* ('reverse appliqué' blouse). Masks, costumes and woven hats can be found in several small villages dotted around the Azuero Peninsula. And, of course, don't forget the quintessential Panama hat. Good ones are pricey. Duty-free imported goods including stereos, photographic equipment, perfume and clothes are cheap in the Colón Free Zone on the Caribbean coast.

Essentials A-Z

Accident and emergency

Costa Rica Medical (Red Cross) T128, Fire T118, Police T117/127. For Police, Fire, Red Cross emergencies/bilingual operators T911.
Nicaragua Ambulance T128; Fire T115; Police T118.
Panama Ambulance T229-1133 (Seguro Social); Fire T103; Police T104.

Children

Travel with children can bring you into closer contact with Latin American families and generally presents no special problems – in fact the path is often smoother for family groups. Officials tend to be more amenable where children are concerned. Always carry a copy of your child's birth certificate and passport photos. For an overview of travelling with children, visit www.babygoes2.com.

Customs and duty free

Costa Rica
Duty-free allowances are ½ kg of tobacco products, 2 kg of chocolate and 5 litres of liquor. Any amount of foreign or local currency may be taken in or out, but amounts over US$10,000 must be declared. Cameras, binoculars, laptop computers and other items of personal/professional use are free of duty.

Nicaragua
Duty-free import of 500 g of tobacco products, 3 litres of alcoholic drinks and 1 large bottle (or 3 small bottles) of perfume is permitted.

Panama
Customs are strict; drugs without a doctor's prescription may be confiscated. Cameras, binoculars, etc, 500 cigarettes or 500 g of tobacco and 3 bottles of alcoholic drinks for personal use can be taken in free of duty. However, passengers leaving Panama by land are not entitled to any duty-free goods.

Disabled travellers

In most Latin American countries, facilities for disabled travellers are severely lacking. Most airports, hotels and restaurants in major resorts have wheelchair ramps and adapted toilets. In general pavements are often in such a poor state of repair that walking is precarious.

Some travel companies specialize in exciting holidays, tailor-made for individuals depending on their level of disability. The Global Access-Disabled Travel Network Site, www.globalaccessnews.com, provide travel information for disabled adventurers and includes a number of reviews and tips from members of the public. You might also want to read *Nothing Ventured*, edited by Alison Walsh (Harper Collins), which gives personal accounts of worldwide journeys by disabled travellers, plus advice and listings.

Drugs

Users of drugs, even of soft ones, without medical prescription should be particularly careful, as some countries impose heavy penalties – up to 10 years' imprisonment – for even the simple possession of such substances. The planting of drugs on travellers, by traffickers or the police, is not unknown. If offered drugs on the street, make no response at all and keep walking.

If you are taking illegal drugs – even ones that are widely and publically used – be aware that authorities do set traps from time to time. Should you get into trouble, your embassy is unlikely to be very sympathetic.

Electricity

Costa Rica, **Nicaragua** and **Panama** have voltage 110, 60 Hz and US-style plugs.

Embassies and consulates

Costa Rican embassies abroad
Australia, De la Sala House, 11th floor, 30 Clarence St, Sydney NSW: 2000, T9-261-1177.
Belize, Room 3, 2nd floor, Capital Garden Plaza, Belmopan, T822-1582.
Canada, 325 Dalhouise St, Suite 407, Ottawa, ON, K1N 7G2, T613-562-2855.
El Salvador, 85 Av Sur y Calle Cuscatlán, 4415 Col Escalón, SS, T2264-3865.
France, 78 Ave Emile Zola, 75015 Paris, T4-578-9696.
Germany, Dessauerstrasse 28-29 D-10963 Berlin, T30-2639-8990.
Guatemala, 15 Calle 7-59, Zona 10, Guatemala City, T2366-9918.
Honduras, Residencial El Triángulo Lomas del Guijamo, Calle 3451, Tegucigalpa, T232-1768.
Israel, Abba Hillel Silver St, 14 Mail Box, 38 Beit Oz, 15th floor, Ramat Gan, 52506, T3-613-5061.
Italy, Viale Liegi 2, Int 8, Roma, T4425-1046.
Japan, Kowa Building, No 38, 9th floor, 901 4-12-24 Nishi Azabu Minato, Ku Tokio, 106-0031, T3-486-1812.
Mexico, Calle Río Poo 113, Col Cuauhtémoc between Río Pánuco and Lerma, México DF, T5525-7765.
Netherlands, Laan Copes van Cattenburch 46, 2585 GB, Den Haag, T70-354-0780.
Nicaragua, de la Estatua de Montoya, 2 c al lago y ½ c arriba (Callejón Zelaya), Managua, T266-2404.
Norway (covers **Sweden** and **Denmark**), Skippergat 33, 8th floor, 0154 Oslo, Noruega, T2233-0408.
Panama, Calle Samuel Lewis Edificio Plaza Omega, 3rd floor, Contiguo Santuario Nacional Panamá, T264-2980.
Spain, Paseo de la Castellana 164, 17-A, 28046 Madrid, T91-345-9622.

Switzerland, Schwarztorstrasse 11, 3007 Berna, T031-372-7887.
UK (covers **Portugal**), Flat 1, 14 Lancaster Gate, London W2 3LH, T020-7706-8844.
USA, 2114-S St, North West Washington DC 20008, T202-234-2945.
More embassy addresses are listed at www.rree.go.cr.

Nicaraguan embassies abroad
Canada, contact embassy in USA.
Costa Rica, Av Central 2540, Barrio La California, San José, T221-2924.
El Salvador, Calle El Mirador y 93 Av Norte, No 4814, Col Escalón, San Salvador, T263-2292.
France, 34 Av Bugeaud, 75116 Paris, T4405-9042.
Germany, Joachim-Karnatz-Allee 45 (Ecke Paulstr) 10557 Berlin, T206-4380.
Honduras, Col Tepeyac, Bloque M-1, No 1130, DC T239-5225.
Italy, Via Brescia 16, 00198 Roma, T841-4693.
Mexico, Prado Norte 470, Col Lomas de Chapultepec, esq Explanada, T540-5625.
Spain, Paseo de la Castellana 127, 1°-B, 28046 Madrid, T555-5510.
UK, Vicarage House, 58-60 Kensington Church St, London W8 4DB, T020-7938-2373.
USA, 1627 New Hampshire Av NW Washington, DC 20009, T202-939-6570.

Panamanian embassies abroad
Embassies/consulates in these and other countries can be checked at www.mire.gob.pa.
Australia, 39 Wardell Rd, Earlwood, Sydney NSW 2206, T9558-2500.
Austria, Elisabethstr 4/5/4/10, A-1010 Vienna, T587-2347.
Belgium, Av Louise 390-392, 1050 Brussels, T649-0729.
Canada, 130 Albert St, Suite 300 Ottawa, ON, Kip 564, T236-7177.
Costa Rica, Calle 38, Av 7 y 9, San José, T257-3241.
France, 145 Av de Suffren, 75015 Paris, T4566-4244.

Germany, Joachim-Karnatz-Allee 45, 3 OG, 10557 Berlín, T30-226-05811.
Israel, Rehov Hei Be´iyar 10/3, Tel Aviv 62998, T696-0849.
Italy, Viale Regina Margherta No 239, Cuarto Piso, Interno 11, 00198 Roma, T1156-60707.
New Zealand, Shortland St, Auckland, T379-8550.
Nicaragua, del Cuartel de Bomberos 1 cuadra abajo, Managua, T266-2224.
South Africa, 832 Duncan St, Brooklyn, Pretoria, 0181, T/F1236-22629.
Spain, Claudio Coello 86, 1° 28006, Madrid T576-7668.
Sweden, Ostermalmsgatan 59, 114 50, 102 04 Stockholm, T662-6535.
UK, 40 Hertford St, London W1Y 7TG, T020-7493-4646.
USA, 2862 McGill Terrace NW, Washington DC 20008, T202-483-1407, www.embassy ofpanama.org.

Gay and lesbian

Most of Latin America is not particularly liberal in its attitudes to gays and lesbians. Even in the cities people are fairly conservative, and more so in provincial towns and rural areas. Having said that, things are changing and you'll find there is a gay scene with bars and clubs at least in most of the bigger cities and resorts.

Health

Costa Rica
Drinking water is safe in all major towns; elsewhere it should be boiled, but bottled water is widely available.

Intestinal disorders are prevalent in the lowlands although **Chagas disease** is now rare. **Malaria** is on the increase; malaria prophylaxis is advised for visitors to the lowlands, especially near the Nicaraguan and Panama border. If visiting jungle areas be prepared for insect bites with repellent

and appropriate clothing. **Dengue** fever has been recorded throughout the country, mostly in coastal cities. Uncooked foods should not be eaten. Having said all that, the standards of health and hygiene are among the best in Latin America.

Nicaragua
Take the usual tropical precautions with food and drink. Tap water is not recommended for drinking outside Managua, León and Granada and avoid uncooked vegetables and peeled fruit; intestinal parasites abound. **Malaria** is prevalent, especially in the wet season; high risk areas are east of the great lakes, take regular prophylaxis. **Dengue** fever is increasingly present, including in Managua; avoid being bitten by mosquitoes.

Panama
Water in Panama City and Colón is safe to drink. Drink bottled water outside the cities. Yellow fever vaccination is recommended before visiting Darién. Travellers to Darién Province and San Blas Province in Panama should treat these as **malarial areas** in which there is resistance to chloroquine. Treatment is expensive; insurance underwritten by a US company would be of great help.

Insurance

Insurance is strongly recommended and policies are very reasonable. If you have financial restraints the most important aspect of any insurance policy is medical care and repatriation. Ideally you want to make sure you are covered for personal items too.

Internet

In **Costa Rica**, internet cafés are popular and connections in the towns tend to be good. Prices vary from US$1-2 per hr. The internet is widely available in main cities and in some smaller towns in **Nicaragua**. The internet has spread extensively throughout **Panama**. Charges are about US$1-2 per hr. Details of cybercafés are given in the Directory text.

Language

Spanish is the first language of all three countries. In Costa Rica you will find someone who can speak some English in most places. In the Caribbean the Afro-Caribbean population speak a regional creole dialect with elements of English. In Nicaragua, a basic knowledge of Spanish is essential for independent travel. On the Caribbean coast English is widely spoken, but in the rest of the country it's Spanish only. In Panama English is widely understood but again a knowledge of Spanish is very helpful. The older generation of West Indian immigrants speak Wari-Wari, a dialect of English incomprehensible to most other English speakers. In rural areas indigenous people use their own languages and many are bilingual.

Media

Costa Rica
The best San José morning papers are *La Nación* (www.nacion.co.cr) and business-orientated *La República* (www.larepublica.net); there is also *Al Día, El Heraldo, Diario Extra* (the largest circulating daily) and *La Prensa Libre* (www.prensalibre. co.cr). *La Gaceta* is the official government daily paper. The *Tico Times* (www.ticotimes.net) is out on Fridays, and there is the *San José*, which is great for news in English with classifieds.

There are 6 local TV stations, many MW/FM radio stations throughout the country. Local **Voz de América** (VOA) station. **Radio Dos** (95.5 FM) and **Rock Radio** (107.5 FM) have English-language DJs and music. Many hotels and private homes receive 1 of the 4 TV stations offering direct, live, 24-hr satellite TV from the USA. All US cable TV can be received in San José.

Nicaragua
All newspapers are published in Managua, but many are available throughout the country. Dailies include *La Prensa*, centre, the country's best, especially for coverage of events outside Managua; *El Nuevo Diario*, centre-left and sensationalist; *La Noticia*, right, government paper. *El Seminario* is a left-leaning, well-written weekly with in-depth analysis. The monthy *El País*, pro-government, has good features.

Panama
La Prensa is the major local daily newspaper. Others are *La Estrella de Panamá, El Universal de Panamá, El Panamá América* and 2 tabloids, *Crítica Libre* and *El Siglo*. *Colón News* is a weekly publication in Spanish and English. In English is the bi-weekly *Panama News*.

Money

Costa Rica
→ *US$1=552.5 colones (Nov 2008)*.
The unit is the colón which devalues annually at a rate of about 10%. The small, golden-coloured coins are minted for 5, 10, 25, 50, 100 and 500 colones. Notes in use are for 1000, 2000, 5000 and 10,000 colones. US dollars are widely accepted but don't depend on being able to use them.

ATMs and exchange
US dollars can be exchanged in most banks. Most tourist and 1st-class hotels will change dollars and traveller's cheques for guests only; the same applies in restaurants and shops if you buy something. Hardly anyone will change damaged US dollar notes. All state-run banks and some private banks will change euro, but it is almost impossible to exchange any other major currency in Costa Rica. For bank drafts and transfers commission may be charged.

Banks are starting to stay open later and several open on Sat. Most banks will process cash advances on Visa/MasterCard. ATMs which accept international Visa and/or MasterCard are widely available at most banks, and in shopping malls and at San José airport. Credomatic handles all credit card billings; they will not accept a credit card charge that does not have the imprint of the borrower's card plus an original signature. This is the result of fraud, but it makes it difficult to book tours or accommodation over the phone. If your card is lost or stolen, ring T0800-011-0184 (MasterCard/Visa) or T0800-012-3211 (AMEX).

Cost of living and travelling

Costa Rica is more expensive than countries to the north. While transport is reasonably cheap, you get less for your money in the hotels. You will be able to survive on US$30 a day, but that does not allow for much in the way of activities.

Nicaragua

→ *US$1=19.98 córdobas (Nov 2008).*
The unit of currency is the córdoba, divided into 100 centavos. Any bank in Nicaragua will change US dollars to córdobas and vice-versa. US dollars are accepted as payment almost everywhere but change is given in córdobas. It is best to carry US$ notes and sufficient local currency away from the bigger towns. Take all the cash you need when visiting the Caribbean coast or Río San Juan. Carry small bills when travelling outside cities or using public buses.

ATMs and exchange

Bank queues can be very long so allow plenty of time, especially on Monday mornings and the 15th and 31st of every month. When changing money take some ID or a copy. It is not possible to change currencies other than US dollars and euro (**BanCentro** only). Money changers on the street (*coyotes*) during business hours are legitimate and their rates differ little from banks.

Visa and MasterCard are accepted in many restaurants, shops and hotels in Managua, Granada and León. This applies to a lesser extent to Amex, Credomatic and Diners Club.

But don't rely exclusively on credit cards. For cash advances the most useful bank is **Banco de América Central (BAC)**. BAC offers credit card advances, uses the Cirrus debit system and changes all traveller's cheques (TCs). TCs often carry a commission of 5% so use your credit/debit card or cash if you can. TCs can only be changed in Managua at *Multicambios* in Plaza España and around the country at branches of **BAC** and **Banco de Finanzas** (Amex cheques only). Purchase receipts may be required when changing TCs in banks.

In Managua ATM machines are found in the airport, at the Metrocentro and Plaza Inter shopping malls and in many gas station convenience stores. Outside the capital ATMs are hard to find, but becoming increasingly common in the main towns and at 24-hr gas stations.

Cost of living and travelling

Nicaragua is not an expensive country as far as hotel accommodation is concerned, and public transport is also fairly cheap. For food, a *comida corriente* costs about US$1.75 (meals in restaurants US$4-13, breakfasts US$2.50-3.50). However, on the islands or in out of the way places where supplies have to be brought in by boat or air, you should expect to pay more. A tight daily budget would be around US$20-25 a day.

Panama

→ *US$1=1 balboa (Nov 2008).*
The unit of currency in Panama is the balboa, but Panama is one of the few countries in the world which issues no paper money; US banknotes are used exclusively, and US notes and coins are legal tender. There are 'silver' coins of 50c (called a *peso*), 25c (called *cinco reales* or *cuara*, from US 'quarter'), 10c, nickel of 5c (called a *real*) and copper of 1c. All coins are used interchangeably with US equivalents, which are the same in size and composition. There is great reluctance in Panama to accept US$50 and US$100 dollar notes because of counterfeiting. Do not be offended if asked to produce ID and sign a

register when spending them. You can take n or out any amount of currency. If travelling north remember that US dollar notes, especially smaller denominations, are useful in all Central American countries and may be difficult to obtain in other republics. Stocking up on a supply of US$5 and US$1 notes greatly facilitates border crossings and traffic problems in Central America where 'fees' and 'instant fines' can become exorbitant if you only have a US$20 note.

ATMs and exchange

Visa ATMs are available at branches of Telered, call T001-800-111-0016, if card is lost or stolen. MasterCard/Cirrus ATMs are available at Caja de Ahorros offices and others in the Pronto system. MasterCard emergency number i s T001-800-307-7309; Western Union is T269-1055. See Panama City Directory, page 380, for other ATMs and for credit card phone numbers.

Cost of living and travelling

Prices are somewhat higher than in the rest of Central America, although food costs much the same as in Costa Rica. The annual average increase in consumer prices fluctuates in line with US trends.

Opening hours

In **Costa Rica** business hours are Mon-Fri 0900-1200, 1400-1730 (1600 government offices), Sat 0800-1200. Shops are open Mon-Sat 0800-1200, 1300-1800 (most stay open during lunch hour), and banks are open Mon-Fri 0900-1500.

Nicaraguan businesses are open Mon-Fri 0800-1200, 1430-1730. Banks open Mon-Fri 0830-1200, 1400-1600, Sat 0830-1200/1300.

In **Panama**, government departments are open Mon-Fri 0800-1200, 1230-1630. Banks open at different times, but are usually open all morning, and often on Sat. Shop opening hours are Mon-Sat 0700/0800-1200, 1400-1800/1900.

Police and the law

Probably the best advice with regards the police in Central America is to have as little to do with them as possible. An exception to this rule are the Tourist Police, who operate in some of the big cities and resorts, and provide assistance. In general, law enforcement in Latin America is achieved by periodic campaigns, not systematically.

You may well be asked for identification at any time and should have some form of identification with you at all times. If you cannot produce it, you may be jailed. If a visitor is jailed his or her friends should provide food every day. If you are jailed, you should contact your embassy or consulate and take advice. In the event of a vehicle accident in which anyone is injured, all drivers involved are automatically detained until blame has been established, and this does not usually take less than 2 weeks.

The giving and receiving of bribes is not recommended. However, the following advice may prove useful for people travelling in Central America. Never offer a bribe unless you are fully conversant with the customs of the country. Wait until the official makes the suggestion, or offer money in some form which is apparently not bribery, for example 'In our country we have a system of on-the-spot fines (*multas de inmediato*). Is there a similar system here?' Do not assume that officials who accept a bribe are prepared to do anything else that is illegal. You bribe them to persuade them to do their job, or to persuade them not to do it, or to do it more quickly, or more slowly. You do not bribe them to do something which is against the law. The mere suggestion would make them very upset. If an official suggests that a bribe must be paid before you can proceed on your way, be patient (assuming you have the time) and he may relent.

Post

Costa Rica

Airmail letters to Europe cost 180 c, post-cards 165 c; to USA, letters 155 c, 135 c for postcards; to Australia, letters 240 c, postcards 195 c. All parcels sent out of the country by foreigners must be taken open to the post office for clearance.

Nicaragua

Airmail to Europe takes 7-10 days, US$0.80; to USA, 18 days, US$0.55; to Australia, US$1.

Panama

Airmail takes up to 10 days, sea mail 3 to 5 weeks from Europe. Example rates for airmail (up to 15 g) are as follows: Central, North and South America and Caribbean, 35c; Europe, 45c up to 10 g, 5c for every extra 5 g; Africa, Asia, Oceania, 60c. Post offices, marked with blue and yellow signs, are the only places permitted to sell stamps.

Safety

Costa Rica

Generally speaking, Costa Rica is very safe but, as ever, there are some problem areas. Look after your belongings in hotels – use the safe. If hiring a car do not leave valuables in the vehicle and leave nothing unattended on beaches or buses. Theft (pickpockets, grab-and-run thieves and muggings) is on the increase in San José, especially in the centre, in the market, at the Coca Cola bus station, in the barrios of Cuba, Cristo Rey, México, 15 de Setiembre and León XIII. Keep away from these areas at night and on Sun, when few people are around. Street gangs, known as *chapulines*, are mostly kids. The police do seem to be trying to tackle the problem but help yourself by avoiding potentially dangerous situations.

You must carry your passport (or a photocopy) with you at all times.

Nicaragua

Visitors must carry their passports with them at all times. A photocopy is acceptable, but make sure you have a copy of your visa or entrance stamp as well. Pick-pocketing and bag slashing occur in Managua in crowded places, and on buses throughout the country. Apart from Managua at night, most places are generally safe. Reports of robberies and assaults in northern Nicaragua indicate that care should be taken in this area; ask about conditions before going, especially if proposing to leave the beaten track.

Panama

Panama is generally safe and the greatest threats to the average traveller are pick-pocketing and other thefts. Carry a photocopy of your passport at all times and take the usual sensible precautions. Certain areas of Panama City should be avoided, including Curundú, El Chorrillo and Holly-wood. Santa Ana and Calidonia can also be sketchy at night. Tourists attract thieves, so watch your belongings on the beaches of Bocas del Toro. Colón is certainly dangerous and you should avoid setting foot outside the train station – use taxis to get around, watch yourself at the bus station and do not go wandering around under any circumstances. Darién should not be visited without appropriate jungle experience or the help of a qualified guide. People have been disappearing in these rainforests for centuries and the whole region also poses risks for kidnapping or worse.

Student travellers

An **International Student Identity Card (ISIC)** is very useful. You get discounts on entry to some museums, cinemas, events and even at some hotels. It'll normally only be a couple of dollars off, but it all adds up over a few weeks. You can obtain an ISIC from your college or university at home. Student status also entitles you to very good discounts on flights. The best student travel agent is **OTEC**, C 3, Av 1-3, T2256-0633, www.otec.co.cr, with stupendous discounts (up to 50%) off flights for students, teachers and others who can convince staff that they are in education. Almost enough to make you change career!

Telephone

Costa Rica
→ *Country code T+506.*
There are no area codes in Costa Rica, the **international direct dialling** code (to call out of Costa Rica) is T00. Dial T116 for the operator. In Mar 2008, Costa Rica changed telephone numbers from 7 to 8 digits. All landlines now have a 2 in front of the old 7-digit number and all mobile phones now have an 8 in front of the old 8-digit number. Nationwide phone changes are taken up by organizations and people at different rates. It'll take a year or so for the whole country to get used to the new system, so be prepared when using phones and taking down numbers.

Standard rates to US, Canada, Mexico and South America are US$0.45 a min; Panama is US$0.40 and Europe and the rest of the world (except Central America and Belize) US$0.60 a min if you dial direct; operator-assisted calls cost up to US$3.12 a min. Only variable rates are to Central America: standard rates between 0700 and 1900 (US$0.40 a min), reduced between 1900 and 2200 (US$0.35) and reduced again between 2200 and 0700 and during the weekend (US$0.28). Add 13% sales tax.

Public phones are maddening to use, various kinds are available: some use 10 and 20 colón silver coins, others use 50 colón gold coins, and still others employ at least 2 types of calling cards, but not interchangeably. The 199 cards are recommended, but it's often easiest to call collect inside (T110) and outside (T116) the country. Assistance for hearing impaired (Spanish only) is T137.

Phone cards with 'Personal Identification Numbers' are available for between US$0.80 and US$10. These can be used for national and international direct dialling from a private phone. Calls abroad can be made from phone booths; collect calls abroad may be made from special booths in the RACSA office, or from any booth nationwide if you dial T116 for connection with the international operator (T175 for collect calls to the USA). Phone cards can be used. Dial T124 for international information. Country Direct Dialling Codes to the USA are: **MCI/World Phone** 0800-012-2222, **AT&T** 0800-0114-114, **Sprint/GlobalOne** 0800-013-0123, **Worldcom** 0800-014-4444.

Nicaragua
→ *Country code T+505.*
Phone numbers in Nicaragua have 7 digits. If you are phoning from inside the prefix zone you need to dial the 7 digits, but if you are dialling a different zone you put '0' in front. For example, to call Managua from Masaya it would be T0266-8689. Phone cards are available from gas stations, supermarkets and shops. International or national calls can be made at any **Entel** office, 0700-2200. All calls paid for in córdobas. To the USA, US$3 for the 1st minute, US$1 for each following minute. Collect calls (*por cobrar*) to the USA and Europe are possible. For SPRINT, dial 171; AT&T 174 and MCI 166. To connect to phone services in Germany dial 169, Belgium 172, Canada 168, Spain 162, Netherlands 177, UK 175.

Panama
→ *Country code T+507.*
The **international direct dialling** code (to call out of Panama) is T00; **Telecarrier** T088+00; **Clarocom** T055+00. Dial T102 for the local operator and T106 for an international operator. Collect calls are permitted, 3 mins minimum, rates are higher than direct, especially to USA. Cost of direct dialled calls, per min, are between US$1-3.20. Calls are roughly 20-30% cheaper for most, but not all destinations from 1700-2200. Lowest rates

apply Sun all day. Many cheap international call centres in Panama City, check the the internet cafés on Vía Veneto for best offers. Public payphones take 5, 10 and sometimes 25 cent coins. Phone cards are available in denominations of US$3, 5, 10, 20 and 50, for local, national and international calls. There are prepaid Aló Panamá cards – dial 165 for connection in US$10, US$20, US$30 and US$50 denominations, but they are 50% more expensive than payphone cards. For **AT&T** dial T109. For *SPRINT* (collect calls only) T115 and for **MCI** T108. BT Chargecard calls to the UK can be made through the local operator.

Time

Costa Rica and **Nicaragua** are 6 hrs behind GMT. **Panama** is 5 hrs behind GMT.

Tipping

In **Costa Rica** a 10% service charge is automatically added to restaurant and hotel bills, as well as a 13% sales tax. **Nicaraguan** porters will expect US$0.50 per bag for; no tip necessary for taxi drivers. Restaurant bills include a 15% tax and 10% service is added or expected as a tip. In **Panama**, tip 10% of the bill in restuarant (though this is often added automatically in Panama City). Porters would expect US$1 for assistance at the airport. Taxi drivers don't expect tips.

Tourist information

Costa Rica

Instituto Costarricense de Turismo (ICT), underneath the Plaza de la Cultura, Calle 5, A Central-2, 0900-1700, daily, T2223-1733, www.visitcostarica.com. All tourist information is given here along with a good free map of San José and the country. See page 64, for more details. Student cards give reducations in most museums.

Useful websites

www.centralamerica.com Costa Rica's Travelnet, contains general information on tourist-related subjects.
www.infocostarica.com A Yahoo-style search engine with information, links and maps for all things Costa Rican.

Nicaragua

INTUR, the **Instituto Nicaragüense de Turismo**, Hotel Crowne Plaza, 1c sur, 1c oeste, Managua, T254 5191, www.intur.gob.ni (see page 259) has a wide range of very general brochures and information packs, www.vistanicaragua.com, Spanish only. In the USA, contact PO Box 140357, Miami, FL 33114-0357, T1-800-737-7253.

Otherwise, tourist offices in Nicaragua are often useless for travellers, as they're more concerned with internal development than public service. Tour operators and foreign-owned hotels are often better sources of information.

Gobierno de Reconciliación y Unidad Nacional
El Pueblo, Presidente!

NICARAGUA TOURISM BOARD

Nicaragua
Única... Original !

OMETEPE ISLAND
One of the seven best options around the world.
COME TO VISIT !

www.intur.gob.ni • www.visitanicaragua.com
Hotel Crowne Plaza 1 c. al Sur 1 c. al Oeste • Tel.: (505) 254-5191 • Fax: (505) 222-6610

Useful websites
www.centramerica.com Has a search engine with news links and information.
www.nicanet.org For activist issues.
www.nicaragua.com Has an e-community.
www.toursnicaragua.com Has a good selection of photographs and images.
www.vianica.com Good on hotels, transport and itineraries.

Panama
Instituto Panameño de Turismo (IPAT) toll-free T011-800-SIPANAMA from the US or Canada, www.visitpanama.com, or contact your nearest embassy. Once in country, IPAT have an office in Panama City (see page 352).

Useful websites
www.businesspanama.com Economic, political and business information.

www.panamainfo.com An excellent site in English with good general information on Panama and links to several other national sites including newspapers, government organizations and tourist services.
www.panamatours.com A pure tourism site with a good overview of the country.

Tour operators

In the UK
Condor Journeys and Adventures, 2 Ferry Bank, Colintraive, Argyll, PA22 3AR, T01700-841-318, www.condorjourneys-adventures.com, also offices in France.
Dragoman, T01728-861133, www.dragoman.co.uk.
Exodus Travels, T020-8675-5550, www.exodus.co.uk.

COSTA RICA & PANAMA
Wildlife Specialists
Tailor-Made & Group Tours Tel: **01803 866965**
mail@reefandrainforest.co.uk
www.reefandrainforest.co.uk

Reef & Rainforest

steppestravel
travel beyond the ordinary

Specialists in private tailor-made holidays and small group tours. We are passionate about travel and hand-pick destinations for their rich histories, spectacular settings and vivid cultures.

Call us to create your perfect journey.
T +44 (0) 1285 885333 latinamerica@steppestravel.co.uk www.steppestravel.co.uk

Guatemala • Belize • Honduras • El Salvador • Mexico

Explore Worldwide, 55 Victoria Rd, Farnborough, Hants, GU14 7PA, T0870-333-4001, www.explore.co.uk.
Galapagos Classic Cruises, 6 Keyes Rd, London, NW2 3XA, T020-8933-0613, www.galapagoscruises.co.uk.
Journey Latin America, 12-13 Heathfield Terr, Chiswick, London, W4 4JE, T020-8622-8464, and 12 St Ann's Square, Manchester M2 7HW, T0161-832-1441 www.journeylatin america.co.uk. Leading specialist for tailor-made holidays and escorted tours in Latin America.
Last Frontiers, Fleet Marston Farm, Aylesbury, Buckinghamshire, HP18 0QT, T01296-653-000, www.lastfrontiers.com.
LATA, www.lata.org. Useful country information and listing of UK tour operators, specializing in Latin America.
Reef & Rainforest Tours, A7 Dart Marine Park, Steamer Quay, Totnes, Devon, TQ9 5AL, T01803-866965, www.reefandrainforest.co.uk. Specialists in tailor-made and group wildlife tours.
Select Latin America, CC3.51, Canterbury Court, 1-3 Brixton Rd, Kennington Park, London, SW9 6DE, T020-7407-1478, www.selectlatinamerica.com.
South American Experience, Welby House, 96 Wilton Rd, London, SW1V 1DW, T0845-277-3366, www.southamericanexperience.co.uk.
Steppes Travel, 51 Castle St, Cirencester, Gloucestershire, GL7 1QD, T01285-885333, www.steppestravel.co.uk. Tailor-made and group itineraries throughout Costa Rica and the rest of Latin America.
Trips Worldwide, 14 Frederick Place, Clifton, Bristol, BS8 1AS, T0117-311-4404, www.tripsworldwide.co.uk.
Tucan Travel, 316 Uxbridge Rd, London W3 9QP, T020-8896-1600, www.tucantravel.com.
Veloso Tours, 34 Warple Way, London W3 0RG, T020-8762-0616, www.veloso.com.

In North America
Exito Travel, 108 Rutgers St, Fort Collins, CO 80525, T970-482-3019, www.exito-travel.com.

GAP Adventures, 19 Charlotte St, Toronto, Ontario, M5V 2H5, T1-800-708-7761, www.gapadventures.com.
LADATCO tours, 2200 S Dixie Highway, Suite 704, Coconut Grove, FL 33133, T1-800-327-6162, www.ladatco.com.
Mila Tours, 100 S Greenleaf Av, Gurnee, Il 60031, T1-800-367-7378, www.milatours.com.
S and S Tours, 4250 S Hohokam Dr, Sierra Vista, AZ 85650, T800-499-5685, www.ss-tours.com.

Visas and immigration

Costa Rica
Nationals of most EU nations, the US, Canada, Israel and Japan do not need visas for visits of up to 90 days. Nationals of Ireland, Australia and New Zealand do not need a visa, but visits are limited to 30 days. For more information check www.migracion.go.cr.

If you overstay the 30- or 90-day permitted period, you must report to immigration before leaving the country. For longer stays ask for a Prórroga de Turismo at Immigration in San José. For this you need 4 passport photos, an airline or bus ticket out of the country and proof of funds (for example TCs); you can apply for an extension of 1 or 2 months, at 300 colones per month. The paperwork takes 3 days. If you leave the country, you must wait 72 hrs before returning, but it may be cheaper and easier to do this to get a new 30-day entry. Travel agents can arrange all extension and exit formalities for a small fee.

Monetary fines for overstaying your visa or entry permit have been eliminated; tourists who overstay their welcome more than once may be denied entry into the country on subsequent occasions – part of government efforts to crack down on 'perpetual tourists'. Tourists may have to show at least US$300 in cash or TCs before being granted entry (especially if you have no onward ticket).

Nicaragua

Visa rules change frequently, so check before you travel, www.cancilleria.gob.ni. Visitors need a passport with a minimum validity of 6 months and may have to show an onward ticket and proof of funds in cash or TCs for a stay of more than a week. No visa is required by nationals of EU countries, the USA, Canada, Australia or New Zealand.

If you need a visa it can be bought before arriving at the border, it costs US$25, is valid for arrival within 30 days and for a stay of up to 30 days; 2 passport photographs are required. A full 30-day visa can be bought at the border, but it is best to get it in advance. Visas take less than 2 hrs to process in the embassies in Guatemala City and Tegucigalpa, but may take 48 hrs elsewhere. Extensions can be obtained at the **Dirección de Migración y Extranjería**, Semáforo Tenderí, 2 1½ c al norte, Managua, T244-3989 (Spanish only), www.migracion.gob.ni. Arrive at the office before 0830. From the small office on the right-hand side you must obtain the *formulario* (3 córdobas). Then queue at the *caja* in the large hall to pay US$18 for your 30-day extension or US$37 for 90 days. This can take hours. In the meantime you can complete the forms. With the receipt of payment you queue at the window on the right. With luck you will receive the extension stamp by midday. There is a small *Migración* office in Metrocentro shopping mall where you can obtain a visa extension. Another possibility is to leave the country for 72 hrs and re-enter on a new visa.

Panama

Visitors must have a passport, and in most cases a tourist card (issued for 90 days and renewable for another 90 at the Immigration Office in Panama City, David or other provincial offices, eg Changuinola) or a visa (issued for 90 days, extendable for a further 90 days). Tourist cards are available at borders, from Panamanian consulates, *Ticabus* or airlines. To enter Panama officially you must have an onward flight ticket, travel agent confirmation of the same, or be able to demonstrate that you have sufficient funds (in cash, credit card or valid traveller's cheques) to cover your stay and departure. Recent travellers report these are asked for on the land frontier with Costa Rica and at Puerto Obaldía (Darién); generally officers are not very strict unless they fear you may be destitute.

Citizens from most European (including the UK) and Central American countries do not need a tourist card or a visa. Citizens from the US, Canada, most Caribbean, South American and some Asian countries need a tourist card (US$5) available at airlines and travel agencies. Citizens of the following countries require a visa: Egypt, Peru, Dominican Republic, many African, Eastern European and Asian countries – check before travelling with your nearest Consulate office. Visa requirements can also be checked online at www.panaconsul.com.

Nationals not requiring visas can renew their 90-day tourist cards once for a total of 180 days, after which you must leave the country for 3 days. The necessary documents must all be obtained in advance: a photo-ID card (*carnet*), to be surrendered when you return for an exit visa, will be issued; allow 1 to 2 hrs for this. Requirements are 2 passport photos, a ticket out of the country or proof of sufficient funds, a brief letter explaining why you wish to extend your stay, a letter from a permanent resident accepting legal and financial responsibility for you during your extra days, and 2 photocopies of the name page and the entry stamp page of your passport. All papers must be presented at *Prórrogas* in the immigration office and a fee of US$11 paid for each 90-day extension before the photo ID card is issued. Requirements for renewing a visa are similar, but include 2 photocopies of the original visa.

Weights and measures

The metric system is official in all 3 countries, but in practice a mixture is used of metric, imperial and old Spanish measurements.

Working and volunteering

Costa Rica

Working in Costa Rica is not a problem – getting paid for it could well be. The skills that are most in demand are for qualified English teachers. You may be able to get work in the tourism industry but don't expect to get paid much.

Technically you should get a work permit from immigration. If the job is above board, you will receive support from your employer in tackling the process (which is long and drawn out, taking as much as 4 months). In reality, most people cross the border every 3 months to refresh their visa, or just pay the fine when leaving. However, government authorities have let it be known they intend to crack down on so-called permanent tourists.

Volunteering to help with environmental and conservation work is very popular, well developed and organized. Normally you have to pay for food and sometimes lodgings. (Charges usually vary from US$75-150 a week.) The workload and type varies enormously. Most volunteers organize a placement before arriving. Once working you will normally work a shift pattern with 2- to 4-day breaks for travel.

Volunteering at national parks can be organized through **ASVO**, www.asvocr.org. You can also contact organizations direct: for **Hacienda Barú** near Dominical (page 156), **Caño Palma Biological Station** in Tortuguero (page 190), **Aviarios del Caribe** (page 190), **ANAI** (page 187) and the **Talamanca Dolphin Foundation** on the south Caribbean coast close to Puerto Viejo de Talamanca, the **Children's Eternal Rainforest** in Monteverde (page 116) and **Campanario Biological Reserve** in Bahía

Drake, and **Rara Avis** near Puerto Viejo de Sarapiquí (page 180).

Nicaragua

Volunteer work in Nicaragua is not as common as it was during the Sandinista years. Foreigners now work in environmental brigades supporting the **FSLN** (Frente Sandinista de Liberación Nacional), construction projects, agricultural cooperatives and environmental organizations. Certain skills are in demand, as elsewhere in the developing world.

To find out about the current situation, try contacting non-governmental organizations in your home country, such as **Nicaraguan Network**, www.nica net.org, and Nicaraguan Solidarity Campaigns, such as **NSC/ENN Brigades**, www.nicaraguasc.org.uk, or **Dutch Nicaragua Komitee**, in Managua.

Casa Danesa, T267-8126 (Managua), may be able to help find volunteer work, usually for 3 months, but shorter times are sometimes acceptable. An excellent short-term non-profit volunteer experience can be had with **El Porvenir**, www.elporvenir.org, an outgrowth of **Habitats for Humanity**. Work is on drinking water, latrine and re-forestation projects.

Panama

Panama has plenty of volunteer opportunities in the fields of teaching, conservation and organic farming. Contact NGOs in your own country to find out about the latest schemes. **Summit Garden and Zoo**, www.summitpan ama.org, have an interesting environmental education programme where you'll contribute to the zoo's maintenance and learn about local fauna. **Global Vision International**, www.earthwatch.org, run a programme in the conservation of sea turtles in Bocas del Toro. You'll be required to tag and monitor turtles and pay a fee in addition to your work contribution. **Habitat for Humanity International**, www.habitat.org, are working in the area to provide housing.

Contents

Footprint features

Border crossings

At a glance

⊖ **Getting around** Mostly by bus, boats to Tortuguero and Bahía Drake.

◉ **Time required** Ideally 4-5 weeks.

☀ **Weather** Dec-Apr is best.

✖ **When not to go** Wet season.

Costa Rica

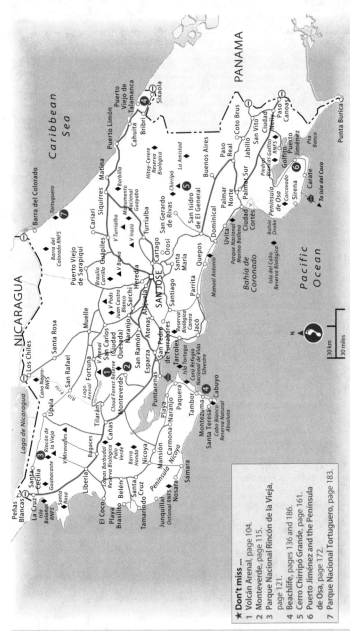

★ **Don't miss ...**
1 Volcán Arenal, page 104.
2 Monteverde, page 115.
3 Parque Nacional Rincón de la Vieja, page 121.
4 Beachlife, pages 136 and 186.
5 Cerro Chirripó Grande, page 161.
6 Puerto Jiménez and the Península de Osa, page 172.
7 Parque Nacional Tortuguero, page 183.

A beacon of neutral democratic ideals, Costa Rica stands out in a turbulent region; as far back as the 1930s one commentator called it the "Switzerland of Central America". Whatever its political credentials and claims to neutrality, this country is undeniably a nature-lovers' paradise: you'll find moss-draped cloudforest on the slopes of Monteverde, where the red and green, sacred quetzal bird hides in the treetops and humming-birds congregate to drink nectar; there's rainforest wilderness on the Osa Peninsula and remote turtle-nesting beaches on the north Atlantic and Pacific coasts. The country's volcanic peaks range from the gentle steaming lagoons of Irazú and Poás to the explosive Arenal, just outside Fortuna, where red-hot lava lights up the night sky.

Travellers looking to combine nature and comfort should head to the endless sand and surf beaches of the Nicoya Peninsula, Quepos and Parque Nacional Manuel Antonio, or to the off-beat strands of the Caribbean. For adrenalin junkies there's white-water rafting, trekking, coast-to-coast mountain biking, and the chance to climb the barren *páramo* savannahs to the peak of Cerro Chirripó.

Historically Costa Rica has avoided the extremes of external influences. The Spanish found no mineral wealth here or compliant indigenous labour to work the land. Hard conditions and poverty forced both conquerors and conquered to work and live side by side. It was only with the arrival of wealth from the magic coffee bean in the Central Highlands that a landed gentry arose to conflict with the interests of a liberal merchant class. As a result, Costa Rica's architectural highlights are somewhat limited compared to much of the region, concentrated in the churches that dot the Central Highlands.

San José

Nestled in a broad, fertile valley producing coffee and sugar-cane, San José was founded in 1737 and became capital in 1823 after struggles for regional ascendency between competing towns of the Central Valley. Frequent earthquakes have destroyed most of the colonial buildings and the modern replacements do little to inspire. But, like any city, if you can get under the skin, the mix of museums and general attractions make it worth a couple of days' stay. ▶▶ *For listings, see pages 70-83.*

Ins and outs → *Altitude: 1150 m.*

Getting there

Aeropuerto Internacional Juan Santamaría is 16 km from the centre along a good *autopista*. A taxi from the pre-payment booth costs US$15 and efficient buses running every 10 minutes leave from outside the terminal building for San José city centre. Long-distance buses have their terminals scattered round town (see map, page 68) but the majority are close to the Coca Cola Terminal, in the central west of the city. Bus connections in Costa Rica and with other Central American countries are very good.

Getting around

For the most part the city conforms to a grid systems – avenidas run east-west; calles north-south. Avenidas to the north of Avenida Central are given odd numbers; those to the south even numbers. Calles to the west of Calle Central are even-numbered; those to the east are odd-numbered. The three main streets, Avenida Central, Avenida 2 and the intersecting Calle Central, encompass the business centre. The main shops are along Avenida Central, a pleasant downtown stroll in the section closed to traffic.

Some people find the narrow streets too heavily polluted with exhaust fumes preferring to stay in the suburbs of Escazú, Alajuela or Heredia using regular bus services to make the journey to town. It's probably a good choice if you've already visited San José, but if it's your first time in the capital you should give it a try for a couple of days at least. A circular bus route travels along Avenida 3 out to La Sabana and back making a useful circuit and an impromptu city tour. Taxis can be ordered by phone or hailed in the street; they are red and are legally required to have meters and to use them. Traffic is congested especially between 0700 and 2000, so driving in the city centre is best avoided. If you do drive, watch out for no-parking zones. Seven blocks of the Avenida Central, from Banco Central running east to Plaza de la Cultura, are closed to traffic and most of the streets downtown are one-way streets.

Tourist information

Instituto Costarricense de Turismo ① *under Plaza de la Cultura, Calle 5, Av Central-2, T2223-1733, Mon-Fri 0900-1700.* Can also be found at Juan Santamaría airport (very helpful, will check hotels for you), the main post office and at borders. Free road maps of Costa Rica, San José and the metropolitan area and public transport timetables available. **OTEC** ① *Calle 3, Av 1-3, Edif Ferenz, T2256-0633, www.otec.co.cr, Apdo 323-1002 San José,* the youth and student travel office, is extremely helpful, and offers good special discounts for ISTC and FIYTO members.

Best time to visit

The climate is comfortable, with temperatures between 15° and 26°C, though the evenings can be chilly. The rainy season lasts roughly from May to November; the rest of the year it's mainly dry.

Sights

Many of the most interesting public buildings are near the intersection of Avenida Central and Calle Central. The **Teatro Nacional** ① *just off Av 2, on Calle 3, T2221-1329 (tours), T2221-5341 (event and ticket information), Mon-Sat 0900-1600, www.teatronacional.go.cr, US$5*, built in 1897, has marble staircases, statues, frescoes and foyer decorated in gold with Venetian plate mirrors. It has a coffee bar run by **Café Britt** and guided tours. Nearby is **Plaza de la Cultura** ① *Av Central, Calle 3-5*, which, in addition to being a great place for people-watching, hosts public concerts. The **Museo de Oro Procolombino** ① *entrance is off Calle 5, T2243-4202, www.museosdelbancocentral.org, daily 0930-1700, US$7, children US$1*, has a booty of golden treasure buried beneath the Plaza de la Cultura. Fine golden figures of frogs, spiders, raptors and other creatures glisten in this spectacular pre-Columbian gold museum sponsored by the Banco Central. Also here is the **Museo Numismático** with an exhibition on the history of Costa Rican money.

The **Museo Nacional** ① *Calle 17, Av Central-2, T2257-1433, Tue-Sat 0830-1600, Sun 0900-1600, US$4, children and students with ID free*, east from the Plaza de la Cultura, has interesting displays on archaeology, anthropology, national history, some gold and ex-President Arias' Nobel Peace Prize. Information is in Spanish and English. Facing it is the **Plaza de la Democracia**, a concrete cascade built to mark the November 1989 centenary of Costa Rican democracy. The **Palacio Nacional** ① *Av Central, Calle 15*, is home of the Legislative Assembly; any visitor can attend debates, sessions start at 1600.

Two blocks north of the Museo Nacional is the **Parque Nacional**, with a grandiloquent bronze monument representing the five Central American republics ousting the filibuster William Walker (see the Nicaragua History section) and the abolition of slavery in Central America. There is also a statue donated by the Sandinista Government of Nicaragua to the people of Costa Rica. To the north of the park is the **Biblioteca Nacional**. East of the library is the **Museo de Formas, Espacio y Sonidos** ① *Calle 17, Av 3-7, T2222-9462, Tue-Fri 0930-1600, US$1, students and children free, wheelchair accessible, signs in Braille*, housed in the old Atlantic Railway Station. In the old liquor factory west of the Biblioteca Nacional, now the Centro Nacional de la Cultura, is the **Museo de Arte y Diseño Contemporáneo** ① *Av 3, Calle 15-17, T2257-7202, Tue-Sat 1000-1700, US$3, students with ID US$0.50*.

One of the best museums in the city is the **Museo del Jade Fidel Tristan** ① *INS building 11th floor, Av 7, Calle 9-13, T2287-6034, Mon-Fri 0830-1530, Sat 0900-1300, US$3*, with the largest collection of jade carvings in Central America, pottery and sculpture. With explanations in Spanish and English, and topped off with a beautiful view over the city, it's a fascinating museum and shouldn't be missed.

Along Calle Central, west of the Teatro Nacional, is **Parque Central**, with a band-stand in the middle among trees, again with occasional performances. East of the park is the monumental architecture of the **Catedral Metropolitana**; to the north is the **Teatro Melico Salazar** ① *see press for details or call T2221-4952*, which has a good mix of performances throughout the year.

Further west, in **Parque Braulio Carrillo**, opposite the eclectic neo-Gothic design of **La Merced** church, is a huge carved granite ball brought from the Diquís archaeological site near Palmar Norte. There are other such designs at the entrance to the Museo de Ciencias Naturales.

At the end of Paseo Colón, at Calle 42, **Parque La Sabana** was converted from the former city airport in the 1950s; the old airport building on the east side is now the **Museo de Arte Costarricense** ① *T2222-7155, Tue-Sat 1000-1600, US$5, US$1 for students, Sun 1000-1400, free*, with a small but interesting display of paintings and sculptures. At the west end of the park is the **Estadio Nacional**, with seating for 20,000 spectators at (mainly) football matches, basketball, volleyball and tennis courts, a running track, lake and swimming pool.

Opposite the southwest corner of Parque Sabana are the impressive natural displays of the **Museo de Ciencias Naturales** ① *Colegio La Salle, T2232-1306, Mon-Sat 0730-1600, Sun 0900-1700, US$1.50, children US$1*, next to the Ministry of Agriculture; take 'Sabana Estadio' bus from Avenida 2, Calle 1 to the gate.

North of Avenida Central, on Calle 2, is the **Unión Club**, the principal social centre of the country. Opposite is the **Correo Central**, general post and telegraph office which also houses an internet café, pastry shop and the **Museo Postal, Telgráfico y Filatélico** ① *upstairs, Mon-Fri 0800-1700, free*.

A couple of blocks to the west is the hustle and bustle of the **Mercado Central**, dating back to 1881, rich with the shouts, cries, smells and chaos of a fresh produce market. Good

1 San José

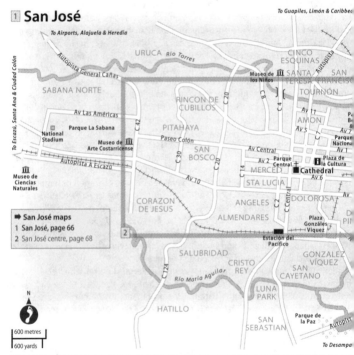

To Guápiles, Limón & Caribbean

To Airports, Alajuela & Heredia

➡ **San José maps**
1 San José, page 66
2 San José centre, page 68

600 metres
600 yards

cheap meals for sale as well as some interesting nick-nacks for the passing tourist. Often crowded; watch for thieves.

The Disneyesque building on the horizon to the north of the city is the **Centro Costarricense de Ciencias y Cultura** (Scientific and Cultural Centre) in the old city penitentiary with the **Galería Nacional**, **Biblioteca Carlos Luis Sáenz**, the **Auditorio Nacional** and **Museo de Los Niños** ① *Calle 4, Av 9, T2258-4929, Tue-Fri 0800-1530, Sat-Sun 0930-1630, US$1.60, children US$1*. Interesting as much for the well-restored building as for the exhibits using former prison cells and spaces to good effect.

Along Avenida 3, north of the Plaza de la Cultura, are the four gardens of the remodelled **Parque Morazán**, with another bandstand at the centre. A little to the northeast, **Parque España**, cool, quiet, and intimate, has for neighbours the **Casa Amarilla** (Yellow House), seat of the Ministry of Foreign Affairs, and the **Edificio Metálico**, imported from Europe to become one of the country's first schools.

To the north of Parque Morazán is **Parque Simón Bolívar**, now a recreation area, with **Simón Bolívar National Zoo and Botanical Gardens** ① *Av 11, just east of Calle 7 (go down Calle 7 about 3 blocks from Av 7), T2233-6701, Mon-Sun 0900-1630, US$3*. It's been remodelled and much improved, with all native plants numbered and listed in a brochure; animals' cages are small. There's also a restaurant and souvenir shop.

To the north of town, a reasonable walk or a short taxi ride, is **Spirogyra** ① *100 m east, 150 m south of Centro Comercial El Pueblo (near Hotel Villa Tournón), T2222-2937, daily 0800-1700, guided tours for more than 10 people (reservations required), US$6, US$5 students, US$3 children*, a fascinating butterfly farm close to the city but filled with life. To get there, take 'Calle Blancos' bus from Calle 3 and Avenida 5 to El Pueblo.

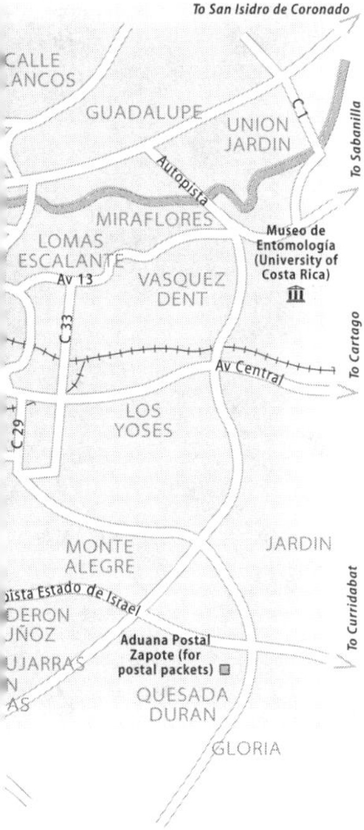

Around San José
🛏️🍴🏪🎁☕🚶‍♂️ »pp70-83.

San José is a good base for excursions into the beautiful Meseta Central. Excursions to the spectacular **Orosí Valley** and **Irazú Volcano** are given under Cártago (see page 95). **Volcán Poás** gently simmers and steams from its elevated position at the northern limit of the Central Highlands and can be visited from San José (TUASA bus departs from Avenida 2, Calle 12-14 at 0830, returns 1430, US$4.75 round trip, T442-6900), Heredia or Alajuela (see page 85). To reach **Volcán Barva** in Parque Nacional Braulio Carrillo, take a bus to San José de la Montaña (see page 88). Enquire first about the likely weather when planning a visit to Poás, Irazú or Barva as cloud will limit the views; early-morning visits recommended.

Map labels: To San Isidro de Coronado, CALLE BLANCOS, GUADALUPE, UNION JARDIN, To Sabanilla, Autopista, MIRAFLORES, Museo de Entomología (University of Costa Rica), LOMAS ESCALANTE, Av 13, VASQUEZ DENT, C 33, To Cartago, Av Central, C 29, LOS YOSES, MONTE ALEGRE, JARDIN, Pista Estado de Israel, To Curridabat, DERON, JÑOZ, Aduana Postal Zapote (for postal packets), UJARRAS, N, AS, QUESADA DURAN, GLORIA

San Antonio de Escazú, a western suburb of San José popular with expats, hosts the Día del Boyero (National Oxcart Drivers' Day) on the second weekend in March. Festivities culminate on the Sunday in a colourful oxcart parade from the school to the centre, accompanied by typical *payasos* (clowns). In the evening there's dancing to marimba music.

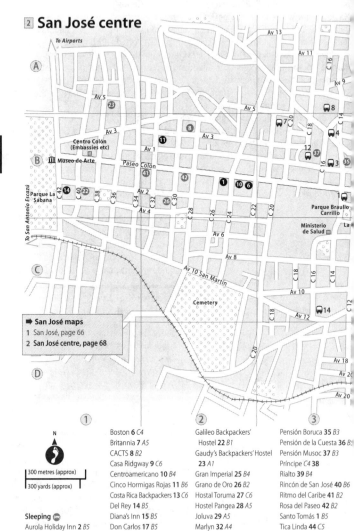

② San José centre

→ San José maps
1 San José, page 66
2 San José centre, page 68

N
300 metres (approx)
300 yards (approx)

Sleeping
Aurola Holiday Inn **2** *B5*
Avenida Segunda **3** *C5*
Bienvenido **5** *B3*

Boston **6** *C4*
Britannia **7** *A5*
CACTS **8** *B2*
Casa Ridgway **9** *C6*
Centroamericano **10** *B4*
Cinco Hormigas Rojas **11** *B6*
Costa Rica Backpackers **13** *C6*
Del Rey **14** *B5*
Diana's Inn **15** *B5*
Don Carlos **17** *B5*
Fleur de Lys **20** *C5*
Fortuna **21** *C4*

Galileo Backpackers'
  Hostel **22** *B1*
Gaudy's Backpackers' Hostel
  23 *A1*
Gran Imperial **25** *B4*
Grano de Oro **26** *B2*
Hostal Toruma **27** *C6*
Hostel Pangea **28** *A5*
Joluva **29** *A5*
Marlyn **32** *A4*
Otoya **33** *B4*
Pensión América **34** *B4*

Pensión Boruca **35** *B3*
Pensión de la Cuesta **36** *B5*
Pensión Musoc **37** *B3*
Príncipe *C4* **38**
Rialto **39** *B4*
Rincón de San José **40** *B6*
Ritmo del Caribe **41** *B2*
Rosa del Paseo **42** *B2*
Santo Tomás **1** *B5*
Tica Linda **44** *C5*
Tranquilo Backpackers **45** *A*

In La **Guácima,** 35 minutes west of San José, 20 minutes south of Alajuela, is a **Butterfly Farm** ① *daily 0830-1700, US$15 adults, US$10 students, US$7.50 children under 12, includes guided tour every 2 hrs, last one at 1500,* dedicated to rearing and exporting over 120 species of butterflies. The first such farm in Latin America, now with over 100 associated farmers

Eating 🍴
Ana Italiana **1** *B2*
Café Mundo **2** *B6*
Café Parisienne **3** *B5*
Churrería Manolo **4** *B4*
El Cuartel de la Boca
del Monte **19** *B6*
Gran Diamante **5** *B4*
La Bastille **6** *B2*
La Esquina del Café **7** *A5*
La Puriscaleña **8** *B4*
La Vasconia **9** *B5*

Lubnan **10** *B2*
Machu Picchu **11** *B2*
Pollo a la Leña **13** *B5*
Soda Tapia **14** *B1*
Tin Jo **15** *C5*
Vishnu **16** *B5*

Bars & clubs 🍸
Chelle's **17** *B5*
Disco Salsa 54 **18** *B5*
Nashville South **20** *B5*
Risas **21** *B4*

Buses 🚌
Alajuela & Airport
Buses **1** *B3*
Heredia Buses **2** *B3/B4*
Liberia Buses **3** *B3*
Panaline Bus **4** *B3*
San Isidro Buses **5** *D4*
Ticabus **6** *C5*
Transnica Bus **7** *B3*
Terminal Alfaro **8** *A3*
Terminal Atlántico
Norte **9** *A3*

Terminal Caribe
(Sixaola) **10** *A4*
Terminal Cartago **11** *D5*
Terminal Coca Cola **12** *B3*
Terminal Los Santos **13** *D6*
Terminal Puntarenas **14** *C3*
Terminal Turrialba **15** *C5*

throughout Costa Rica, it is believed to be one of the second largest exporters of farm-bred butterflies in the world (the largest is in Taiwan). Created by Joris Brinckerhoff, a former Peace Corp volunteer and his wife in 1984, the farm opened to the public in 1990. All visitors receive a two-hour guided tour. Visit in the morning as butterflies require heat from the sun for the energy to fly so when it is cool or cloudy, there may be less activity. The Butterfly Farm offers round trip minibus transportation from San José hotels (US$15, US$10 students, US$8 children, reservations required, T2438-0400). The public bus for La Guácima, leaves from Calle 10, Avenida 2-4, behind La Merced Church in San José (0800, 1100 and 1400, returns at 1230, 1530 and 1730, 1 hour, US$0.55); at the last stop walk 300 m from the school south to the butterfly sign. From Alajuela take a bus marked 'La Guácima abajo' which departs 100 m south, 100 m west of **Tikal Supermarket** (40 minutes, at 0620, 0900, 1100 and 1300; returning at 0945, 1145, 1345, 1545 and 1745).

From San José you can take a tour of **Café Britt's coffee farm** ① *near Barva de Heredia, T2260-2748, www.coffeetour.com, 1100, 1½ hrs, US$30*, where you can see the processing factory, tasting room and a multimedia presentation using professional actors of the story of coffee. You can arrange to be picked up at various points and hotels in San José. **Teatro Dionisio Chaverría** at Café Britt hosts weekend theatre and a children's show on Sundays.

⊙ San José listings

Hotel and guesthouse prices
LL over US$150	**L** US$100-150	**AL** US$66-99
A US$46-65	**B** US$31-45	**C** US$21-30
D US$12-20	**E** US$7-11	**F** under US$7

Restaurant prices
₸₸₸ over US$15	₸₸ US$8-15	₸ under US$8

See pages 43-46 for further information.

◐ Sleeping

San José *p64, maps p66 and p68*

There are cheap hotels between the Mercado Central, Mercado Borbón and the Coca Cola terminal. Cheaper hotels usually have only wooden partitions for walls, making them noisy. Hotels in the red light district, Calle 6, Av 1-5, near Mercado Central, charge on average US$10 with toilet and shower for a night.

LL-AL Grano de Oro, Calle 30, Av 2, T2255-3322, www.hotelgranodeoro.com. Exquisite converted 19th-century mansion, 35 rooms and suites, beautiful terrace gardens, renowned restaurant. Friendly, good value.

L Aurola Holiday Inn, Av 5 between Calle 5-7, pool, T2222-2424, www.aurola-holiday inn.com. Mainly business clientele, casino, good view of city from casino.

L-AL Britannia, Calle 3, Av 11, T2223-6667, www.hotelbritanniacostarica.com. 1910 Spanish-style beautifully restored mansion, high standard, antique furniture, very good service, excellent restaurant, worth the money.

L-AL Del Rey, Av 1, Calle 9, Apdo 6241-1000, T2257-7800, www.hoteldelrey.com. Nice single, double, triple rooms, standard or deluxe, suites. Landmark hotel, centre of casino and upmarket red-light district, not recommended for families, walls a bit thin. Has a restaurant.

L-AL Fleur de Lys, Calle 13, Av 2-6, T2223-1206, www.hotelfleurdelys.com. Restored Victorian mansion house, good restaurant, bar. Stylishly elegant. Recommended.

AL Don Carlos, Calle 9, Av 7-9, T2221-6707, www.doncarloshotel.com. 36 rooms, interesting traditional building, much artwork and statuary, sun deck, free coffee, Annemarie's giftshop with good selection, credit cards accepted, airport shuttle.

AL Rosa del Paseo, Paseo Colón, Calle 28-30, T2257-3225, www.rosadelpaseo.com. Beautifully restored mansion, breakfast included. Good location for access to the city centre but not in the heart of town.

AL Santo Tomás, Av 7, Calle 3-5, T2255-3950, www.hotelsantotomas.com. French Victorian mansion, 20 rooms, pool, garden, internet access, secure parking, **Restaurant El Oasis** next door, tours arranged.

A Rincón de San José, formerly **Edelweiss**, Av 9, Calle 13-15, 100 m east of **Condovac** offices, T2221-9702, www.hotelrinconde sanjose.com. English, Dutch and Spanish spoken, clean, comfortable, native hard-wood furniture and carved doors. Pleasant courtyard bar, helpful, friendly.

A-B CACTS, Av 3 bis, Calle 28-30, 3 blocks north of **Pizza Hut**, Paseo Colón, T2221-2928, www.hotelcacts.com. Safe, good service, breakfast and taxes included, TV, friendly, pets allowed. Recommended.

A-C Joluva, Calle 3b, Av 9-11, T2223-7961. With breakfast, old house, friendly, safe, good laundry service, good value. A relaxing and gay-friendly hotel.

B Aventuras Backpackers (formerly **Ritmo del Caribe**), Paseo Colón and Calle 32, diagonal from **KFC** restaurant, T2256-1636. Simple, good rooms and friendly atmosphere, free airport shuttle, good value, breakfast and taxes included. German owner Olaf and wife Patricia run the hotel. Thorsten Klier runs **Wild Rider Motorcycles** next door and rents 4WD vehicles at 'backpacker rates' (see Motorcycle rental, page 80).

B Cinco Hormigas Rojas, Calle 15, Av 9-11, T2255-3412, www.cincohormigasrojas.com. Nice decor, small house. Prices includes taxes.

B Diana's Inn, Calle 5, Av 3, Parque Morazán, near **Holiday Inn**, T2223-6542, dianas@rac sa.co.cr. An old building formerly used by the president, now restored, includes breakfast and taxes, discounts available, a/c, TV, hot water, noisy, free luggage storage, safe box.

C Centroamericano, Av 2, Calle 6-8, T2221-3362, ghcmejer@racsa.co.cr. Includes taxes, private bath, clean small rooms, very helpful, will arrange accommodation in other towns, free shuttle (Mon-Fri) to airport, laundry facilities.

C Fortuna, Av 6, Calle 2 y 4, T2223-5344, hfortuna@infoweb.co.cr. Quiet, helpful.

C Pensión de la Cuesta, Av 1, Calle 11-15, T2256-7946, www.pensiondelacuesta.com. A little off the wall in style, with artwork all over this old colonial home. Shared bath, use of the kitchen and internet, includes breakfast.

C-D Green House Hotel, Plaza González Viques, Calle 11, Av 16 y 18, T2258-0102, www.greenhousehostel.altervista.org. New hostel, very clean, both private and shared rooms come with hot water bath, free break-fast, communal kitchen, Wi-Fi, cable TV, not close to the centre, but great spot otherwise.

C-D Hostel Pangea, Av 11, Calle 3 bis, T2221-1992, www.hostelpangea.com. Friendly, clean, use of kitchen. Good local information, with free coffee, internet, breakfast and reportedly the only hostel in Central America with heated pool, jacuzzi, licensed bar and wet bar. Good spot.

C-D Tranquilo Backpackers, Calle 7, Av 9-11, T2223-3189, www.tranquiloback packers.com. Dormitory and private rooms with great, relaxed atmosphere, but not very helpful.

C-E Casa Ridgway, Calle 15, Av 6-8, T2233-6168, www.amigosparalapaz.org. 1-4 beds in room, shared bath, use of kitchen, very helpful, friendly, laundry possible, group rates and facilities.

D Avenida Segunda, Av 2 No 913, Calle 9-11, T2222-0260, acebrisa@racsa.co.cr. Includes taxes, shared or private bath, friendly, stores luggage.

D Bienvenido, Calle 10, Av 1-3, T2233-2161. Clean, hot shower, near centre and airport bus, best hotel near Coca Cola bus terminal.

D Boston, Av 8, Calle Central-2, T2221-0563. With or without bath, good, very friendly, but noisy, will store luggage.

D JC Friends Hostel, Calle 34 y Av 3, Casa Esquinera, Paseo Colon. Recently established, JC is owned by an extremely well-travelled Tico who has bucketfuls of local information to impart. Communal kitchen, lockers, a/c and internet access. Tuasa bus stops opposite. Also have a *hostal* in Tamarindo.

D Marlyn, Av 7-9, Calle 4, T2233-3212. More with bath, hot showers, good security, will store luggage, parking for motorcycles (just).

D Otoya, Calle 1, Av 3-5, T2221-3925, erickpensionotoya@24horas.com. Close to the centre, cleanish, friendly and quite popular, you're allowed to use the telephone which can be a bonus (free local calls). Hot water throughout and some rooms with private bath, includes taxes. Luggage store, laundry service and English spoken.

D Pensión Musoc, Calle 16, Av 1-3, T2222-9437. With or without private bath, very clean, hot water, luggage stored, will do laundry. Friendly, near bus stations so somewhat noisy, but recommended.

D Príncipe, Av 6, Calle Central-2, T2222-7983, with bath, hot water, TV, top rooms best, quiet, friendly, includes taxes.

D-E Casa Yoses, 8th Av 41 Street, 25 mins west from **Spoon** in Los Yoses, T2234-5486, www.casayoses.com. Popular hostel in restored mansion, located near the trendy San Pedro Mall, breakfast and internet are gratis, relaxing gardens, quiet area.

D-E Costa Rica Backpackers, Av 6, Calle 21-23, T2221-6191, www.costaricaback packers.com. Top billing at these prices with a pool, good dormitory and private rooms, kitchen and laundry services, free coffee and internet. Parking possible.

D-E Gaudy's Backpackers' Hostel, Av 5, Calle 36-38, T2258-2937, www.back packer.co.cr. Good backpacker choice, with dormitory accommodation, kitchen, communal areas and internet access. Good location and quieter than the other cheap options.

D-E Gran Imperial, on the western side of the Central Market, Calle 8, Av 1-Central, T2222-8463, www.hostelgranimperial.com. Mixed reports, small rooms, thin walls, clean, sometimes noisy, with or without private bath, limited hot showers, includes taxes, restaurant with good prices, best to reserve. Good for meeting other travellers, with balcony overlooking Central Market. A great spot for relaxing, locked luggage store, TV.

D-E Hostal Toruma, Av Central, Calle 29-31, T2234-9186. 93 beds, clean, hot water, crowded but safe, lockable storage in each room, includes breakfast. Free use of internet and kitchen for guests. A good place for meeting other travellers to arrange group travel.

E Galileo Backpackers' Hostel, 100 m east of **SodaTapia**, T2248-2094, www.galileo hostel.com. Friendly place, charming property with dorm beds and free internet.

E Pensión Boruca, Calle 14, Av 1-3, near Coca Cola terminal, T2223-0016. Shared bath, hot water, laundry service, rooms a bit dark but friendly owner.

E Rialto, Av 5, Calle 2, 1 block north of Correos, T2221-7456. Shared or private bath, hot water, safe, friendly but can be very noisy.

F Pensión América, Av 7, Calle 4. Clean, large rooms, good value.

F Tica Linda, Av 10, Calle 7-9. Dormitory accommodation, use of kitchen, hot water and laundry, TV in communal area. Will store luggage, popular with travellers. No sign, just a notice on the front. Moves often which makes finding the place a problem, but popular. Ask locally.

Near the airport
See Alajuela, page 89.

Around San José *p67*

A Pico Blanco Inn, San Antonio de Escazú, T2228-1908. All rooms with balconies and views of Central Valley, several cottages. English owner, restaurant with English pub, airport pick-up can be requested. It's recommended.

A-B Costa Verde Inn, 300 m south of the 2nd San Antonio de Escazú cemetery, T2228-4080, www.costaverdeinn.com. A secluded and charming country home with 14 imaginatively decorated rooms – a popular choice away from the centre of town.

Camping

Belén, San Antonio de Belén, 2 km west of intersection at Cariari and San Antonio, 5 km from airport, turn off Highway 1 on to Route 111, turn right at soccer field then 1st left for 1 km, T2239-0421. US$10 per day, American-owned trailer park, shade, hot showers, laundry, friendly, recommended, good bus service to San José.

🍴 Eating

San José p64, maps p66 and p68
Traditional dishes, feasting on a steady supply of rice and beans, tend to be a little on the heavy side but are definitely worth trying.

At lunchtime cheaper restaurants offer a set meal called a *casado*, US$1.50-2.50, which is good value. There are several cheap Chinese places along Av 5. For reliable and seriously cheap places, try the **Mercado Central**, around the **Coca Cola** bus terminal and the area to the southwest of **Parque Central**. *Autoservicios* do not charge tax and service and represent the best value. There are plenty of fast-food outlets dotted throughout the city.

♦♦♦ Ana Italiana, T2222-6153, Paseo Colón, Calle 24 y 26. Closed Mon. Good Italian food and friendly.

♦♦♦ Café Mundo, Av 9, Calle 13-15, opposite **Hotel Rincón de San José**, T2222-6190. Old mansion tastefully restored, good salads, great pasta, wonderful bread, a stylish joint.

♦♦♦ El Chicote, on north side of Parque Sabana, T2232-0936. Reliable favourite, country style, good grills.

♦♦♦ El Cuartel de la Boca del Monte, Av 1, Calle 21-23, T2221-0327. Live music at night but a good and popular restaurant by day.

♦♦♦ Jurgen's, Calle 41 and Paseo Rubén Darío, Barrio Dent in Los Yoses, T2224-2455, closed Sun. 1st-class service, excellent international menu, sophisticated atmosphere.

♦♦♦ La Bastille, Paseo Colón, Calle 22, T2255-4994. Closed Sun. Stylish French food in elegant surrounds.

♦♦♦ La Cocina de Leña, north of the centre in El Pueblo, Barrio Tournón, T2255-1360. Excellent menu of the very best in Tico cuisine, upmarket, pricey, but warm, friendly ambience.

♦♦♦ La Esquina del Café, Av 9, Calle 3b, daily 0900-2200. Speciality coffee roasters with good restaurant, souvenir shop, live music twice a month.

♦♦♦ La Masia de Triquell, Edif Casa España, Sabana Norte, T2296-3528. Closed Sun. Catalan, warmly recommended.

♦♦♦ Le Chandelier, 50 m west and 100 m south of the main entrance of the ICE building in Los Yoses, T2225-3980, closed Sun. One of the best French restaurants in town, reservations required.

♦♦♦ Los Ranchos Steak House, Sabana Norte near **Hotel TRYP Meliá**. Reliable, good food.

♦♦♦ Lubnan, Paseo Colón, Calle 22-24, T2257-6071. Authentic Lebanese menu, vegetarian selections, great service.

♦♦♦ Marbella, out beyond San Pedro mall, T2224-9452. Fish, paella specialities, packed on Sun, very good.

♦♦♦ Tin Jo, Calle 11, Av 6-8, T2221-7605. Probably the best Asian cuisine in town.

♦♦ Café La Bohemia, Calle Central, Av 2, next to Teatro Melico Salazar. Pastas and meats as well as light lunches such as quiches and crêpes.

♦♦ Gran Diamante, Av 5, Calle 4-6. With a 'lively kitchen' where you can watch the food being prepared.

♦♦ La Vasconia, corner of Av 1, Calle 5, great little restaurant combining a passion for football and food. Basic in style, good traditional dishes.

♦♦ Los Antojitos, on Paseo Colón, on Pavas Highway west of Sabana, in Tibás, San Antonio de Escazú and in Centro Comercial Cocorí (road to suburb of San Pedro), T2232-2411. Serves excellent Mexican food at fair prices.

♦♦ Machu Picchu, Calle 32, Av 1-3, T2222-7384. Open from 1700. Closed Sun. Great Peruvian food, good service in homely atmosphere.

♦♦ México Bar, north of the Coca Cola district in Paso de la Vaca, T2221-8461. Dead by day, comes alive at night with a flurry of music and good Mexican food.

♥ **Vishnu**, Av 1, Calle 1-3, also on Calle 14, Av 2. Daily 0800-2000. Best-known vegetarian place in town, good quality, cheap and good *plato del día*. Try their soya cheese sandwiches and ice cream, sells good wholemeal bread.

♥ **Chicharronera Nacional**, Av 1, Calle 10-12. *Autoservicio* and very popular.

♥ **China Bonita** at Av 5, Calle 2-4. One of the cheapest Chinese options in town.

♥ **Comedor**, Calle 8, Av 4-6, beneath 'Dorado' sign. Very cheap.

♥ **Corona de Oro**, Av 3, Calle 2-4 (next to Nini). An excellent *autoservicio*.

♥ **Don Sol**, Av 7b No 1347. Excellent 3-course vegetarian lunch, run by integral yoga society (only open for lunch).

♥ **El Merendero**, Av 6, Calle Central-2. *Autoservicio* serving cheap local food, popular with Ticos.

♥ **La Puriscaleña**, on the corner of Calle Central and Av 5, is a good, local *comedor*. The *menú del día* is a tasty bargain.

♥ **Pollo a la Leña**, Calle 1, Av 3-5, which has seriously cheap chicken, popular with locals.

♥ **Popular**, Av 3, Calle 6-8. Good *casado*.

♥ **Whapin**, Calle 35, Av 13, Excellent Caribbean restaurant with extensive menu, authentic rice and beans and fried plantains, live music occasionally.

Cafés sodas and ice cream parlours
Bagelman, Paseo Rubén Darío (Av Central), Calle 33, just east of **Hostal Toruma** in Barrio Escalante, T2224-2432. Smart and tasty fast- food bagel heaven, delivers to area hotels. Also in San Antonio de Escazú, T2228-4460.

Café del Teatro, Av 2, Calle 3, in foyer of National Theatre, open Mon-Sat. Pricey but worth it for the sheer style and sophistication of the belle époque interior.

Café Parisienne on the Plaza de la Cultura, the street café of the **Gran Hotel Costa Rica**. Food a little overpriced, but have a coffee and watch the world go by.

Churrería Manolo, Av Central, Calle Central-2 (restaurant upstairs), open 24 hrs. Simple, quick food with takeaway options on the street, good sandwiches and hot chocolate.

Helados Boni, Calle Central, Av 6-8. Home-made ice cream.

Helados Rena, Calle 8, Av Central. Excellent.

La Esquina del Café, Av 9, Calle 3b, Barrio Amón, T2257-9868. Daily 0900-2200. Specialty coffee roasters with beans from 6 different regions to taste, also a good restaurant with a souvenir shop. Live music twice a month.

La Nutrisoda, Edif Las Arcadas. Daily 1100-1800. Home-made natural ice cream.

Macrobiótica, Calle 11, Av 6-8. Health shop selling good bread.

Musmanni, has several outlets throughout the country, varying quality, best in the large cities and in the morning.

Pops, with several branches throughout town and the country, has excellent ice cream too.

Ruiseñor, Paseo Rubén Darío and Calle 41-43, Los Yoses, T2225-2562. The smart place to take coffee and snacks in east San José.

Soda El Parque, Calle 2, Av 4-6. Open 24 hrs. A popular spot for business people by day and relaxing entertainers by night.

Soda La Luz, Av Central, Calle 33, east towards Los Yoses. Good filling and cheap meals.

Soda Nini at Av 3, Calle 2-4. Cheap and cheerful.

Soda Tapia, Calle 42, Av 2-4, east side of Parque Sabana. Classic stopping place for Josefinos, with good food, served quickly.

Soda Vegetariana, next to **Librería Italiana**. Vegetarian with good juices and food.

Spoon has a central bakery at Av Central, Calle 5-7. Good coffee and pastries to take-out or eat in, also light lunches.

Around San José *p67*
♥ **Taj Mahal**, San Antonio de Escazú, from Centro Comercial Paco, 1 km west on the old highway, T2228-0980. Indian food for a change.

Entertainment

San José *p64, maps p66 and p68*
Bars and clubs
The *Tico Times* has a good listings section.
Beatles, Calle 9, Av Central. Good music, popular with expats.
Calle de la Armagua, San Pedro. Happening street for young Ticos from 2230 onwards.
Centro Comercial El Pueblo, north of town in Barrio Tournón, with a cluster of fine restaurants, bars and discos. This is where Ticos party the night away until dawn. **Cocoloco** is the liveliest of the discos, **Infinito** gets a slightly older crowd and **La Plaza** outside the centre, is often not as busy.
Chelle's, Av Central, Calle 9, T2221-1369. Excellent 24-hr bar and restaurant which changes its mood and clientele through the day. Great snacks and people watching.
Disco Salsa 54, Calle 3, Av 1-3. The place to go for salsa.
El Cuartel de la Boca del Monte, Av 1, Calle 21-23, T2221-0327. Live music at weekends, popular with students, hip young things but without the flashy dress. Recommended.
Key Largo, Parque Morazan. Live music, very popular with the **Hotel del Rey** crowd and all the stuff they get up to!
La Avispa, Calle 1, Av 8-10, and **Déjà vu**, Calle 2, Av 14-16. Both are gay-friendly discos, but not exclusively so.
Nashville South, Calle 5, Av 1-3. A popular Country-and-Western-style gringo bar.
Risas, Calle 1, Av Central, T2223-2803. Bars on 3 floors, good, popular with locals.
Terrau, out in San Pedro on Calle de la Armagua. The most popular of many clubs along this street. The area gets going around 2300 and keeps going till dawn. You'll need photo ID to get into the clubs.

Cinemas
Excellent modern cinemas showing latest releases are located throughout the metropolitan area, see *La Nación* for listings.

Cine Universitario at the UCR's Abelardo Bonilla law school auditorium in San Pedro, T2207-4717, shows good films at 1700 and 1900 daily, US$3-4.
El Semáforo in San Pedro shows films made in Latin America and Spain.
Sala Garbo, Av 2, Calle 28, T2222-1034, shows independent art house movies.
Variedades, Calle 5, Av Central-1, T2222-6108 is in the centre. Others can be found in Los Yoses, T2223-0085, San Pedro, T2283-5716, Rohrmoser, T2232-3271 and Heredia, T2293-3300.

Theatre
More than 20 theatres offer live productions in the San José area; check the *Tiempo Libre* entertainment supplement every Thu in *La Nación* for show times, mostly weekends.
Teatro del Angel, Av Central, Calle 13-15, T2222-8258. Has 3 modern dance companies.
Teatro Nacional, Av 2, Calle 3-5 T2221-5341 (recommended for the productions, the architecture and the bar/café), US$5 for guided tour, T2221-1329, behind it is La Plaza de la Cultura, a large complex.
Teatro Melico Salazar, Parque Central, T2221-4952, www.teatromelico.go.cr, for popular, folkloric shows.

Festivals and events

San José *p64, maps p66 and p68*
Dec-Jan Christmas/New Year: festivities last from mid-Dec to the first week of Jan, with dances, horse shows and much confetti throwing in the crowded streets. The annual **El Tope** horse parade starts at noon on 26 Dec and travels along the principal avenues of San José. A **carnival** starts next day at about 1700 in the same area. Fairs, firework displays, food and music at **El Zapote**, frequent buses from the centre.
Mar The **International Festival of Culture** assembles musicians from throughout Central America in a week of performances

in the Plaza de Cultura around the 2nd week of Mar, although concern over the future of the event exists due to lack of funding.
2nd Sun in Mar **Día del Boyero** (Day of the Oxcart Driver) is celebrated in San Antonio de Escazú. Parades of ox-drawn carts, with music, dancing and blessings from the priesthood.
Mar/Apr Street parades during **Easter week**.
Sep 15 **Independence Day**: bands and dance troupes move through the streets, although activities start to kick-off the night before with the traditional nationwide singing of the National Anthem at 1800.

O Shopping

San José *p64, maps p66 and p68*
Crafts and markets
Market on Av Central, Calle 6-8, 0630-1800 (Sun 0630-1200), good leather suitcases and wood. **Mercado Borbón**, Av 3-5, 8-10, fruit and vegetables. More and more *artesanía* shops are opening: **Canapi**, Calle 11, Av 1 (a co-operative, cheaper than most), **Mercado Nacional de Artesanía**, Calle 11, Av 4, T2221-5012, Mon-Fri 0900-1800, Sat 0900-1700, is a good one-stop shop with a wide variety of goods on sale. **La Casona**, Calle Central, Av Central-1, daily 0900-1900, a market of small *artesanía* shops, is full of interesting little stalls. **Galería Namu**, opposite the Alianza Francesa building on Av 7 and Calle 5-7, Mon-Sat 0900-1630, T2256-3412, www.galerianamu.com, is the best one-stop shop for home-grown and indigenous art, with the distinctly bright coloured ceramics of Cecilia Figueres. Items can be shipped if required and online shopping is possible. At the **Plaza de la Democracia** in front of the National Museum, tented stalls run the length of a city block, great place to buy hammocks, arts and crafts at competitive prices. Don't be afraid to negotiate. **Centro Comercial El Pueblo**, near the **Villa Tournón Hotel**, also has a number of stalls but mainly for upmarket

products and prices, built in a traditional 'pueblo' style.
In **Moravia** (8 km northeast of San José with stops often included on city tours) the block-long **Calle de la Artesanía** includes various souvenir stores, including well-known **La Rueda**, T2297-2736, good for leatherworks.

Bookshops
Casa de la Revista, Calle 5, Av 1-3, T2256-5092. Mon-Fri 0900-1800, Sat 0800-1700. Good selection of maps, newspapers, magazines and some books (mostly paperbacks) in English. Other locations include Escazú, San Pedro, Rohrmoser, Curridabat, Moravia, Alajuela, Cártago and Heredia, for information call main office of Agencia de Publicaciones de Costa Rica, T2283-9383. **Librería Lehmann**, Av Central, Calle 1-3, T2223-1212, has a large and varied selection of Spanish and English books and magazines. They also stock several maps including the 1:50,000 topographical maps produced by the Instituto Geográfico Nacional de Costa Rica (IGN). **Mora Books**, Av 1, Calle 3-5, T2255-4136, in Omni building above Pizza Hut, Mon-Sat 1100-1900. Large selection of used books, reasonable prices.
7th Street Books, Calle 7, Av Central, T2256-8251, marroca@racsa.co.cr. A wide range of new and used books covering all topics of interest to visitors to Costa Rica, including *Footprint*. Mon-Sat 0900-1800, Sun 1000-1700.

Photography
Taller de Equipos Fotográficos, 120 m east of kiosk Parque Morazán, Av 3, Calle 3-5, T2223-1146, Canon repairs – authorized workshop. **Tecfot**, Av 7, Calle Central, T2221-1438, repairs all cameras, authorized Minolta dealer, offers good service and reasonable rates.

Shopping malls
Shopping malls are popping up in different parts of town including San Pedro, on the

eastern ring rd, complete with cinema. Newly expanded **Multiplaza Mall**, near **Camino Real**, Escazú, has great shops and lots of cinemas. Across the highway toward San José is **Plaza Itskatzú**, a colonial-style shopping centre with restaurants and shops. Another is the **Terra Mall** in Curridabat.

⚤ Activities and tours

San José *p64, maps p66 and p68*
If you're planning on staying in or around San José for a while, look in the calendar pages of the *The Tico Times* for clubs and associations.

Bungee jumping
After Rafael Iglesias Bridge (Río Colorado), continue on Pan-American Hwy 1.5 km, turn right at Salón Los Alfaro, down track to Puente Colorado. **Tropical Bungee** operates 0900-1600 daily in the high season, US$65 1st jump, US$30 for the 2nd (same day only) includes transportation from San José, reservations required, T2248-2212, www.bungee.co.cr. Exhilarating.

Cycling
Coast to Coast Adventures, T2280-8054, www.ctocadventures.com, run trips in the local area.

Swimming
The best public pool is at **Ojo de Agua**, 5 mins from the airport in Alajuela, 15 mins from San José. Daily 0800-1600, US$1.55, T2441-2808. Direct bus from Calle 10, Av 2-4 (behind La Merced Church) in San José or take bus to Alajuela and then another to San Antonio de Belén. There is also an open-air pool at **Plaza González Víquez**, in the southeast section of San José, crowded, Weekends only, US$1, T2256-6517.

Tour operators
For independent travel to Tortuguero, see pages 183 and 199.

Aventuras Naturales, Av Central, Calle 33-35, T2225-3939, www.adventure costarica.com. Specialists in whitewater rafting with their own lodge on the Pacuare which has a canopy adventure tour. Also several other trips. **COOPRENA (Simbiosis Tours)**, Apdo 6939-1000, San José, T2290-8646, www.turismoruralcr.com. A group supporting small farmers, broadly working to the principle of sustainable tourism. Offers tours and has accommodation available around the country. **LA Tours**, PO Box 492-1007, Centro Colón, T2221-4501. Kathia Vargas is extremely helpful in rearranging flights and reservations. **Swiss Travel Service**, is one of the biggest tour operators with branches in many of the smarter hotels, T2282-4898, www.swiss travelcr.com. Can provide any standard tour, plus several specialist tours for birdwatchers. Good guides and warmly recommended. **Super Viajes**, American Express representative, Oficentro Ejecutivo La Sabana, Edif 1 Sabana, PO Box 3985, T2220-0400.

Those specializing in naturalist tours include **Aguas Bravas**, T2292-2072, www. aguas-bravas.co.cr. Whitewater rafting on rivers around the Central Valley, also horse riding, biking, hiking and camping. **Costa Rica Expeditions**, Av 3, Calle Central 3, T2257-0766, www.costaricaexpeditions. Com. Upmarket wildlife adventures include whitewater rafting (US$95 for 1-day trip on Río Pacuare, includes lunch and transport, good; other rivers from US$69-95) and other options. They own **Tortuga Lodge**, **Corcovado Lodge Tent Camp** and **Monteverde Lodge**. Daily trips, highly recommended. **Ecole Travel**, lobby of Gran Hotel, T2223-2240, www.ecoletravel.com. Chilean-Dutch, highly recommended for budget tours to Tortuguero, Corcovado and tailor-made excursions off the beaten track. **Green Tropical Tours**, Calle 1, Av 5-7, T2229-4192, www.greentropical.com, with options outside the norm including tours to Guayabo National Monument, Los Juncos and cloudforest. **Horizontes**, Calle 28,

Av 1-3, T2222-2022, www.horizontes.com. One of the big operators in Costa Rica, high standards, educational and special interest, advice given and arrangements made for groups and individuals. **Mitur**, T2296-7378, www.mitour.com. A range of tours throughout the country, including Ilan Ilan in Tortuguero US$199, 3-days, 2-nights. **Real Places, Real People**, T8810-4444, www.realplaces.net. 1- and 3-day tours visiting rural Costa Rica for baking, ceramics, mask making and other traditional activities. **ACTUAR**, T2248-9470, www.actuarcostarica. com, is an association of 26 community-based rural tourism groups spread across the country. **Ríos Tropicales**, Calle 38, between Paseo Colón and Av 2, 50 m south of Subway, T2233-6455, www.riostropicales. com. Specialists in whitewater rafting and kayaking, good selection and careful to assess your abilities, good food, excellent guides, US$250 for 2-day trip on Río Pacuare, waterfalls, rapids, including camping and food. Many other options throughout the country. **Typical Tours**, Las Arcadas, next to the **Gran Hotel Costa Rica**, T2233-8486. City tours, volcano tours, nature reserves, rafting, cruising.

Several companies focus on trips to **Tortuga Island** off the southern tip of Nicoya Peninsula. Try **Bay Island Cruises**, T2258-3536, bayislan@racsa.co.cr. Daily tours to Tortuga Island, US$79 includes lunch and transport from San José area.

⊖ Transport

San José *p64, maps p66 and p68*
Air
The much-improved Aeropuerto Internacional Juan Santamaría (SJO) is at El Coco, 16 km from San José along the Autopista General Cañas (5 km from Alajuela). Airport information, T2443-2622 (24 hrs). The **Sansa** terminal for domestic flights is next to the main terminal. **Sansa** runs a free bus service to the airport for its

passengers. There is another terminal, about 1 km west of the main terminal, used by charter flights and private planes. Buses to city centre from main street outside ground-floor terminal. Buses to airport, continuing on to Alajuela from Av Central-2, Calle 10, every 10 mins from 0500-2100; 45 mins, US$0.50 (good service, plenty of luggage space). Taxi to and from airport, US$12. Taxis run all night from the main square. For early flights you can reserve a taxi from any San José hotel the night before. All taxi companies run a 24-hr service. Bank at the airport 0800-1600, with ATM available as well. ICT, open in the day time, has a helpful tourist office in the main terminal for maps, information and hotel reservations.
Internal flights Sansa and Nature Air (from Tobias Bolaños, 8 km west of San José, in Pavas) operate internal flights throughout the country. **Sansa**, T2223-4179, www.fly sansa.com, check-in is at office on Av Las Americas and Calle 42, free bus to and from airport. Check schedules on **Nature Air**, T2299-6000, www.natureair.com. If you made reservations before arriving in Costa Rica, confirm and collect tickets as soon as possible after arrival. Book ahead, especially for the beaches. In Feb and Mar, planes can be fully booked 3 weeks ahead. On all internal scheduled and charter flights there is a baggage allowance of 12 kg. Oversized items such as surfboards or bicycles are charged at US$15 if there is room in the cargo hold.

From San José you can fly to **Barra del Colorado**, **Coto 47**, **Drake Bay**, **Golfito**, **Liberia**, **Limón**, **Nosara**, **Palmar Sur**, **Puerto Jiménez** (with a connecting flight to **Carate**, on the border of Corcovado National Park), **Punta Islita**, **Quepos**, **Carrillo-Sámara**, **Tamarindo**, **Tambor**, **Tortuguero** and **Granada** in Nicaragua and **Bocas del Toro** in Panama.

Airline offices
International carriers **Air France**, Condominio Vista Real, 1st floor, 100 m east of POPs,

Curridabat, T2280-0069; **Alitalia**, Calle 24, Paseo Colón, T2295-6820; **American**, Sabana Este, opposite Hotel TRYP Meliá, T2257-1266; **Avianca**, Edif Centro, p 2, Colón, Paseo Colón, Calle 38-40, T2233-3066; **British Airways**, Calle 13, Av 13, T2257-8087; **Condor Airlines**, Calle 5, Av 7-9, T2256-6161; **Continental**, Oficentro La Virgen No 2, 200 m south, 300 m east and 50 m north of American Embassy, Pavas, T2296-4911; **Copa**, Av 5, Calle 1, T2223-2672; **Delta**, 100 m east of Toyota and 50 m south, T2257-2992; **Grupo Taca**, see **Sansa** above; **Iberia**, Paseo Colón, Calle 40, T2257-8266; **KLM**, Sabana Sur, behind Controlaría General Building, T2220-4111; **Lloyd Aéreo Boliviano**, Av 2, Calle 2-4, upstairs, T2255-1530; **LTU International Airways** (German charter airline), Condominio da Vinci, Oficina No 6, Barrio Dent, T2234-9292; **Lufthansa**, Calle 5, Av 7-9, T2243-1818; **Martinair**, Dutch charter airline – subsidiary of KLM, see above; **Mexicana**, Paseo Colón Torres Mercedes, T2295-6969, Mexican Tourist Card available here; **SAM**, Paseo Colón, Calle 38-40, Edif Centro Colón, 2nd floor, T2233-3066; **Singapore Airlines**, Edificio Isabella San Pedro, T2234-2223; **Servivensa**, Edif Centro Colón, 2nd floor, Paseo Colón, Calle 38-40, T2257-1441; **Swissair**, Calle Central, Av 1-3, T2221-6613; **United Airlines**, Sabana Sur, behind Controlaría General Building, T2220-2027; **Varig**, Sabana West 150 m south of Canal 7, T2290-5222.

National and charter airlines Nature Air (see above); **Sansa** (see above); **Aerobell**, T2290-0000, www.aerobell.com, at Pavas; **Alfa Romeo Aéreo Taxi**, in Puerto Jiménez, T2735-5112 ; **Paradise Air**, T2296-3600, www.flywithparadise.com, based in Pavas; **Helicópteros del Norte**, helicopter charters and sightseeing tours out of San José, US$350 per hr, T2232-7534.

Bus

Local Urban routes in San José cost US$0.50 or less. Hand baggage in reasonable quantities is not charged. A cheap tour of San José can be made on the bus marked

periférico from Paseo Colón in front of the Cine Colón, or at La Sabana bus stop, a 45-min circuit of the city. A smaller circuit is made by the 'Sabana/ Cementerio' bus, pick it up at Av 2, Calle 8-10.

Long distance In the majority of cases, buses start or finish their journey at San José so there are services to most towns; see under relevant destination for details of times and prices. Check where the bus stops at your destination, some routes do not go to the centre of towns, leaving passengers some distance away. Up-to-date timetables are in a free leaflet *Hop on the Bus*, giving times but no prices, distributed by **Ecole Travel**.

Bus stations are scattered around town: **Alajuela** (including airport) from Av 2, Calle 12-14; **Cahuita**, **Limón**, **Manzanillo**, **Puerto Viejo de Talamanca**, **Sixaola** all served from Gran Terminal del Caribe (**Guapileños**, **Caribeños**, **Sixaola**); **Jacó**, **Carará**, **Quepos**, **Manuel Antonio**, **Uvita** all depart from Terminal Coca Cola; **Santa Cruz** (½ block west), **Peñas Blancas** (100 m north) from outside Terminal Coca Cola; **Cártago** from Terminal Cártago during the day, after 2030 from Gran Hotel Costa Rica, Av 2, Calle 3-5; **Cd Quesada (San Carlos)**, **Fortuna**, **Guápiles (Braulio Carrillo)**, **Los Chiles**, **Caño Negro**, **Monteverde** (outside terminal), **Puerto Jiménez** (outside terminal), **Puerto Viejo Sarapiquí**, **Tilarán** (½ block north) from Terminal Atlántico Norte at Av 9, Calle 12; **Playa del Coco**, **Liberia** from Calle 14, Av 1-3; **Golfito**, **Nicoya**, **Nosara**, **Palmar Norte**, **Paso Canoas**, **Sámara**, **San Vito**, **Tamarindo** from Terminal Alfaro; **San Isidro de El General** (2 companies, **Musoc** and **Tuasur**), terminal down on Av 22-24, Calle Central, **Heredia** from Terminal Heredia or a minibus from Av 2, Calle 10-12; **Volcán Irazú** from Av 2, Calle 1-3, opposite Gran Hotel Costa Rica; **Volcán Poás** from Av 2, Calle 12-14; **Puntarenas** from Terminal Puntarenas, Calle 16, Av 10-12; **Santa María de Dota** from Terminal Los Santos; **Turrialba** from Terminal Turrialba.

2 shuttle bus companies offer transport from the capital to dozens of beach and tourism destinations, see Getting around, page 64.

International buses If the timing of your journey is important book tickets; in Dec-Jan, buses are often booked 2 weeks ahead, while at other times of the year outside holiday seasons there are plenty of spaces.

Ticabus terminal at Calle 9-11, Av 4, T2221-8954, www.ticabus.com, office open Mon-Sun 0600-2200. **Ticabus** to **Guatemala City**, 3 daily, 60 hrs, US$56, with overnight stay in Managua and San Salvador. To **Tegucigalpa**, 3 daily, 48 hrs, US$35, overnight stay in Managua. To Managua 3 daily, US$14, 10 hrs including 1 hr at Costa Rican side of border and another 2 hrs on Nicaraguan side while they search bags. To **Panama City** leaves at 1200 daily, US$26 one-way, 18 hrs (book in advance). To get a Panamanian tourist card you must buy a return ticket – you can get a refund in Panama but with a discount of 15%. **Transnica**, Calle 22, Av 3-5, T2223-4242, runs new buses with TV, video, a/c, snacks, toilet, to **Managua** 4 daily, US$20 return. Before departure have your ticket confirmed on arrival at the terminal; when buying and confirming your ticket, you must show your passport. When boarding the bus you are given an immigration form.

Panaline goes to **Panama City** daily at 1300 from Calle 16, Av 3, T2256-8721, www.panalinecr.com, US$22 one way, US$41 return, reduction for students, arrives 0500; a/c, payment by Visa/MasterCard accepted. To **David**, from Terminal Alfaro, 2 daily, 9 hrs, US$18; book in advance. They are modern, comfortable buses, although there is not much room for long legs, but they have the advantage of covering a scenic journey in daylight. A bus to **Changuinola** via the Sixaola–Guabito border post leaves San José at 1000 daily, 8 hrs, US$8, from opposite Terminal Alfaro, T2556-1432 for information, best to arrive

1 hr before departure; the bus goes via Siquirres and is the quickest route to **Limón**.

Car
Car hire Most local agencies are on or close to Paseo Colón, with a branch or drop-off site at or close to the airport and other locations around the country.

International companies with services include **Adobe**, **Alamo**, **Avis**, **Budget**, **Dollar**, **Economy**, **Hertz**, **Hola**, **National**, **Payless** (formerly **Elegante**), **Thrifty**, **Toyota** and **Tricolor**.

Solid, T2442-6000, www.rentacarcosta rica.com, are a local company with several offices around town including **Hostal Toruma**, most competively priced in town; **Wild Rider Motorcycles**, also rents cheap 4WD vehicles (see below).

Motorcycle and bike
Rental **Wild Rider Motorcycles**, Paseo Colón, Calle 32 diagonal Kentucky, next to Aventuras Backpackers, T2258-4604, www.wild-rider.com, Honda XR250s, Yamaha XT600s and Kawasaki KLR650s available for rent from US$45-90 a day, US$700-1300 deposit required. 4WD vehicles also available, US$260-320 per week, monthly discounts.

Cycle repairs **Cyclo Quiros**, Apartado 1366, Pavas, 300 m west of US Embassy. The brothers Quiros have been repairing bikes for 20 years, good place for general information and repairs, highly recommended.

Taxis
Minimum fare US$0.57 for 1st km, US$0.31 additional km. Taxis used to charge more after 2200, but that rule has been rescinded. Taxis are red and have electronic meters called *marías*, if not, get out and take another cab. For journeys over 12 km price should be negotiated between driver and passenger. Radio cabs can be booked in advance. To order a taxi, call **Coopeguaria**, T2226-1366, **Coopeirazu**, T2254-3211, **Coopemoravia**, T2229-8882, **Coopetaxi**, T2235-9966, **Taxi**

San Jorge, T2221-3434, **Taxis Guaria**, T2226-1366, **Taxis Unidos SA**, which are the official taxis of the Juan Santamaría International Airport and are orange instead of red, T2222-6865, or look in the classified adverts of *The Tico Times* for car and driver hire.

❶ Directory

San José *p64, maps p66 and p68*
Banks
Queues in state-run banks tend to be long; using privately run banks is recommended. The 15th and end of the month (pay day for government employees) are especially bad. Visa and MasterCard ATMs are widespread and the best option in the capital. Queues tend to be shorter outside San José. Money can be sent through **Banco de San José** or **Banco de Costa Rica** at 4%. Credit card holders can obtain cash advances from **Banco de San José** (Visa, MasterCard) and **Credomatic Los Yoses** in colones (MasterCard ATM) and **Banco Popular** (Visa ATM) minimum cash advance: US$50 equivalent. ATMs which will accept international Visa/MasterCard are available at most banks, shopping malls and San José airport. **Banco Crédito Agrícola de Cártago**, state-run, 9 branches, also makes advances on Visa, no commission, no limits. **Banco de Costa Rica**, Av 2, Calle 4, state-run, changes TCs, open 0830-1500, long queues, 1% commission. **Banco de San José**, Calle Central, Av 3-5, private, commission 2.5%. **Banco Nacional**, head office, Av 1-3, Calle 2-4, state-run, will change TCs into dollars but you pay a commission, accepts Visa credit cards as do most of the bigger banks in San José and other major towns. Many private banks are open late and Sat, including **Banco Cuscatlán**, with 12 branches around the country, Mon-Fri 0800-1800, Sat 0800-1200, T2299-0299.

An alternative to the banks for getting money is the money transfer services: **Western Union**, T2283-6336, www.western union.com, which operates out of many pharmacies and other locations and **Moneygram**, T2295-9055, www.money gram.com. Quicker than banks but you pay a price premium. **Interbank**, transfers are cheaper and you don't need an account, but take several days or more. Ask at a bank's information desk for details.

Cultural centres
Alianza Francesa, Av 7, Calle 5, French newspapers, French films every Wed evening, friendly; **Centro Cultural Costarricense Norteamericano**, Calle 37, Av 1-5, Los Yoses, T2207-7500, www.cccncr.com, open daily till 1930, free, shows good films, plays, art exhibitions and English-language library.

Embassies and consulates
Belgium, Barrio Dent, T2280-4435, 0800-1330; **Canada**, Building 5 (3rd floor) of Oficentro Ejecutivo La Sabana, Sabana Sur, T2242-4400, Mon-Thu 0800-1630, Fri 0800-1330; **El Salvador**, Paseo Colón, from Toyota 500 m north and 25 m west, T2257-7855; **France**, Curridabat, 200 m south, 25 m west of Indoor Club, T2234-4167, 0830-1200; **Germany**, Rohrmoser, 200 m north and 75 m east of Oscar Arias' house, T2232-5533, 0900-1200; **Guatemala**, 500 m south, 30 m east of POPs, Curridabat, T2283-2557, 0900-1300; **Honduras**, Rohrmoser, T2291-5143, 0900-1230; **Israel**, Edificio Colón, 11th floor, Paseo Colón, Calle 38-40, T2221-6444, 0900-1200; **Italy**, Los Yoses, Av 10, Calle 33-35, T2234-2326, 0900-1200; **Japan**, Oficentro building No 7, La Sabana, T2296-1650; **Mexico**, Consulate, Av 7, Calle 13-15, T2225-7284, 0830-1230; **Netherlands**, Oficentro Ejecutivo La Sabana, Sabana Sur, T2296-1490, Mon-Fri 0900-1200; **Nicaragua**, Av Central, Calle 25-27, opposite Pizza Hut, T2222-2373, 0830-1130 and 1330-1500, 24-hr wait for visa, US$25, dollars only, passport photo; **Norway**, Centro Colón, 10th floor, T2283-8222. Mon-Thu 1400-1700; **Panama**, San Pedro, T2281-2442, strict about

onward ticket, 0900-1400, you need a photograph and photocopy of your passport, visa costs US$10 cash and takes up to 24 hrs; **Spain**, Paseo Colón, Calle 32, T2222-1933; **Sweden**, honorary consul at Almacén Font, 100 m east of La Pozuelo, La Uruca, T2232-8549; **Switzerland**, Centro Colón, p 10, Paseo Colón, Calle 38, T2221-4829, 0900-1200; **UK**, Centro Colón, p 11, end of Paseo Colón with Calle 38 (Apdo 815-1007), T2258-2025, 0900-1200; **USA**, in the western suburb of Pavas, opposite Centro Comercial, catch a ruta 14 bus to Pavas, Zona 1 from Av 1 and Calle 16-18, T2220-3939, 0800-1630; **Venezuela**, Los Yoses, de la 5a entrada, 100 m south, 50 m west, T2225-8810, 0830-1230, visa issued same day, US$30, helpful.

Immigration
The immigration office is on the airport highway, opposite Hospital México. You need to go here for visas extensions, etc. Queues can take all day. To get there, take bus 10 or 10A Uruca, marked 'México', then cross over highway at the bridge and walk 200 m along highway – just look for the queue or ask the driver. Better to find a travel agent who can obtain what you need for a fee, say US$5. Make sure you get a receipt if you give up your passport.

Internet
Cybercafé, in the basement of Edificio Las Arcadas, next to the Gran Hotel Costa Rica, daily 0700-2300, has a few machines. **Internet Café**, 4th floor, Av C, Calle 4, 0900-2200. A better way to spend less money as it is just c400 for full or part hr, but not a café. Several branches around town including at the western end of Paseo Colón in Edifico Colón, Calle 38-40, and if you want to type all night there is a 24-hr café in San Pedro, close to Banco Popular.

Language schools
The number of schools has increased rapidly. Listed below are just a selection recommended by readers. Generally, schools offer tuition in groups of 2-5 for 2-4 weeks. Lectures, films, outings and social occasions are usually included and accommodation with families is encouraged. Many schools are linked to the university and can offer credits towards a US course. Rates, including lodging, are around US$1,100 a month. **Academica Tica de Español**, in San Rafael de Coronado, 10 km north of San José, T2229-0013, www.academiatica.com; **AmeriSpan**, 117 South 17th St, Ste 1401, Philadelphia, PA 19103, www.amerispan. com, has affiliated schools in Alajuela, Heredia, San José and 6 others locations; **Costa Rican Language Academy**, Barrio California, T2280-5834, www.spanishand more.com, run by Aída Chávez, offers language study and accommodation with local families, and instruction in Latin American music and dancing as well; **Costa Rica Spanish Institute**, Zapote in San Pedro district, T2234- 1001, www.cosi. co.cr, US$320 per week, US$400 with home-stay in San José, also branch in Manuel Antonio; **Instituto Británico** in Los Yoses, Apdo 8184, 1000 San José, T2225-0256, www.instituto britanico.co.cr, teaches English and Spanish; **Instituto de Español Costa Rica**, A 1, Calle Central – Calle 1, Apartado 1405-2100, Guadalupe, T2283-4733, www.professionalspanish.com. Close to the centre of San José, and complete with its own B&B. English, French and German spoken; **Universal de Idiomas**, in Moravia, T2223-9662, www.universal-edu.com, stresses conversational Spanish; **Intercultura**, Apdo 1952-3000, Heredia, T2260-8480, www.interculturacostarica. com. Intensive courses with excursions to beaches, volcanoes, rainforest. Volunteer programmes.

Laundry
Washing and dry cleaning at Centro Comercial San José 2000, daily 0730-2000, US$3.75 for large load; **Lavandería Costa Rica**, Av 3, Calle 19-21, US$5 for a large

load; **Lavandería Lavamex**, below Hotel Gran Imperial at Calle 7, Av 1-Central, US$4 to wash, US$4 to dry, quick service and very friendly. Book swap, very popular with travellers, much more than a laundry thanks to the helpful owners Karl and Patricia.

Libraries

Biblioteca Nacional, opposite Parque Nacional, Mon-Fri 0830-1630, also has art and photography exhibitions; **Centro Cultural Costarricense Norteamericano**, C 37, Av 1-5, www.cccncr.com, T2207-7500, has a good English-language library.

Medical services

Dentists Clínica Dental Dr Francisco **Cordero Guilarte**, Rohrmoser 300 m east of Plaza Mayor, T2223-8890; **Dra Fresia Hidalgo**, Uned Building, San Pedro, 1400-1800, English spoken, reasonable prices, recommended, T2234-2840; **Fernando Baldioceda** and **Silvia Oreamuno**, 225 m north of Paseo Colón on the street which intersects at the Toyota dealership: both speak English; **Alfonso Villalobos Aguilar**, Edif Herdocía, p 2, Av 3, Calle 2-4, T2222-5709.

Doctors **Dr Jorge Quesada Vargas**, Clínica Internacional, Av 14, Calle 3-5, speaks German.

Hospitals and clinics Social Security hospitals have a good reputation (free to social security members, few members of staff speak English), free ambulance service run by volunteers: **Dr Calderón Guardia**, T2257-7922, **San Juan de Dios**, T2257-6282, **México**, T2232-6122; **Clínica Bíblica** Calle 1, Av 14, 24-hr pharmacy, T2257-5252, frequently recommended and the one most used by the local expatriate community and offers 24-hr emergency service at reasonable charges with staff who speak English, better than the large hospitals, where queues are long; **Clínica Católica**, northeast of San José, another private hospital with 24-hr pharmacy, T2246-3000; **Hospital CIMA**, T2208-1000, on the highway toward Escazú, country's newest and most modern private hospital, bilingual staff, expensive rates, 24-hr pharmacy, T2208-1080.

Police

Thefts should be reported in San José to **Recepción de Denuncias**, Organismo de Investigación Judicial (OIJ), Calle 19, Av 6-8, T2295-3643. Call for nearest OIJ office in outlying areas.

Post office

Calle 2, Av 1-3, open for sale of stamps Mon-Fri, 0700-1700, Sat-Sun 0700-1800. Stamp vending machine in main post office. Lista de Correos, Mon-Fri 0800-1700, quick service. **Couriers** DHL, Pavas, Calle 34, T2209-0000, www.dhl.com; **Fed Ex**, main office is in Barreal de Heredia, T2293-3157, www.fedex.com; **UPS**, 50 m east of Pizza Hut central office, Pavas, San José, T2290-2828, www.ups.com.

Telephone

Faxes and internal telegrams from main post office. Fax abroad, internet access and email from **RACSA**, Av 5, Calle 1, 0730-2200 (see also Essentials, page 75). **ICE (Instituto Costarricense de Electricidad)**, Av 2, Calle 1, for phone calls (phone card only), and fax service, 0700-2200, 3-min call to UK US$10, friendly service (cheaper than **Radiográfica**, but check). Collect/reverse charge telephone calls can be made from any public telephone. English-speaking operators are available. See also page 55.

Meseta Central West

Hilly and fertile with a temperate climate, the Central Highlands is a major coffee-growing area. Fairly heavily populated, picturesque and prosperous towns sit in the shadows of active volcanoes. Exploring the towns and villages of the region – each with its own character and style – gives good insight into the very heart of Costa Rica.

From San José, the Pan-American Highway heads east through the Meseta Central for 332 km along good roads to the Nicaraguan border. While CA1 will take you north, by sticking to it you'll miss visiting the remnants of colonial architecture found in Alajuela, Heredia and the countless smaller towns that enjoy the spring-like temperatures of the highlands. Although it's easier to explore the region in a private vehicle, frequent public buses and short journeys make hopping between towns fairly straightforward; if stepping out from San José it's probably worth dumping most of your luggage in the city and travelling light.
▶ For listings, see pages 89-94.

Northwest of San José ☺️🚶❄️🚕🏠🌀 ▶▶pp89-94.

Alajuela → *Altitude: 952 m.*
The provincial capital of Alajuela has a very slightly milder climate than San José making it a popular weekend excursion for Josefinos. Famous for its flowers and market days (Saturday market is good value for food), regular buses from San José make it an easy

Meseta Central - West

day trip. Alternatively, stay in Alajuela, and use the regular buses to visit the capital. It is 5 km from the international airport, and is handy for early flights and late arrivals.

The town centres on the Parque Central with the 19th-century domed church on the eastern side. The unusual church of **La Agonía**, five blocks further east, is an interesting mix of styles. One block to the south, Juan Santamaría, the national hero who torched the building in Rivas (Nicaragua) in which William Walker's filibusters were entrenched in 1856, is commemorated by a monument. One block north of the Parque Central, the **Museo Histórico Juan Santamaría** ① *Av 3, Calle 2, Tue-Sun 1000-1800*, tells the story of this war.

Parque Nacional Volcán Poás

① *Daily 0800-1530, 1 hr later Fri-Sun, Dec-Apr, US$10, good café next door, and toilets further along the road to the crater. If you wish to get in earlier you can leave your car/taxi at the gates, walk the 3 km up the hill and pay on your way out. The volcano is very crowded on Sun so go in the week if possible. Arrive early as clouds often hang low over the crater after 1000, obstructing the view. Wear good shoes, a hat and suncream.*

Volcán Poás (2708 m) sits in the centre of the Parque Nacional Volcán Poás (6506 ha), where the still-smoking volcano and bubbling turquoise sulphur pool are set within a beautiful forest. The crater is almost 1.5 km across – the second largest in the world. The park is rich with abundant birdlife given the altitude and barren nature of the terrain and home to the only true dwarf cloudforest in Costa Rica.

From Alajuela two paved roads head north for 37 km to the volcano. The first through San Pedro de Poás and Fraijanes, the second follows the road to San Miguel, branching left just before the town of Vara Blanca. In the park, trails are well marked to help guide you from the visitor centre to the geysers, lake and other places of interest. The main crater is 1 km along a road from the car park. There is a visitor centre by the car park with explanations of the recent changes in the volcano. There is also a good café run by **Café Britt**; alternatively, bring your own food and water.

From **Vara Blanca** the road runs north past the popular La Paz waterfall, round the east side of the volcano through Cinchona and Cariblanco. **La Paz Waterfall Gardens** ① *5 km north of Vara Blanca, T2225-0643, www.waterfallgardens.com, US$32*, has forest trails past five huge falls and one of the world's largest butterfly and hummingbird gardens, a restaurant, US$12 buffet lunch and the **Peace Lodge Hotel (LL)**. The road is twisty, winding through lush forest, with several waterfalls down to the lowlands at **San Miguel**. Here the road leads either northeast heading to La Virgen and eventually Puerto Viejo de Sarapiquí (see page 180), or northwest to Venecia (see below).

La Virgen

Ten kilometres northeast of San Miguel is La Virgen, near the Río Sarapiquí, a good spot for Grade I, II and III rafting which is organized by the hotel **Rancho Leona**. From San José, take the Río Frío bus which passes through San Miguel, or a bus from San Carlos, and ask to get off at **Rancho Leona**. Juan Carlos in La Virgen has been recommended as a guide for rafting, T2761-1148, from US$25 per person.

Venecia and around

Heading west from San Miguel, Venecia (two buses daily from San José, 4½ hours, US$3) has an interesting church. Near Venecia are the pre-Columbian tumuli of **Ciudad Cutris**. A good road goes to within 2 km of Cutris, from where you can walk or take a 4WD vehicle; get a permit to visit from the local finca owner.

West of Venecia is Aguas Zarcas where the road splits. Heading directly north, the roads descends into the jungle lowlands, following the Río San Carlos towards the Nicaraguan border, passing through several small towns. After about 40 km, in Boca Tapada, is **La Laguna del Lagarto Lodge** (see page 90).

Grecia

The road from Alajuela to San Carlos (see page 101) passes through Grecia and several towns of the Meseta Central, with good paved roads leading to others. With coffee as the mainstay of the region, the hills are covered with green coffee bushes, interspersed with other plants for shade. Grecia is also a major pineapple producer, and has an interesting church made entirely of metal. A short distance along the road to Alajuela is **El Mundo de los Serpientes** ① *T2494-3700, snakes@racsa.co.cr, 0800-1600, US$11, children US$6, reductions for biology students*, a snake farm with more than 50 species. On the old road about 10 km towards Tacares is **Los Chorros Recreational Park** ① *US$4*, with two massive waterfalls and picnic spots.

Sarchí and Naranjo

Heading west is the town of Sarchí, the country's artisan centre, where you can visit the *fábricas* that produce the intricately geometric and floral designs painted on ox-carts, which are almost a national emblem. The town is divided in two, Sarchí Norte and Sarchí Sur, separated by some 4 km. The green church (until they paint it again) in Sarchí is especially attractive at sunset. Travel agents in San José charge around US$55 for a day trip to Sarchí usually combined with a trip to Volcán Poás.

The road continues north to Naranjo, a quiet agricultural town with an exquisite bright white church, and a shocking post-modern pyramidal structure in the main square.

Zarcero

Frequent bus services from San José/Alajuela pass through Zarcero, on the lip of the continental divide, en route to San Carlos (Ciudad Quesada). The town is famous for vegetable farming, dairy products and notable for the topiary creations of Evangelista Blanco Breves that fill the main plaza. Bushes are clipped, trimmed and shaped into arches leading up to the white church with twin towers, with shapes of animals, dancing couples, a helicopter, many designs of Henry Moore-like sculptures and a small grotto. The interior of the quaint church, overshadowed somewhat by the plaza, is made entirely of wood, even the pillars, painted cream and pale grey with patterns in blue, brown, green and pink; cartouches, emblems and paintings.

San Ramón and Los Angeles Cloud Forest Reserve

West of Naranjo along the Pan-American Highway is the town of San Ramón, 76 km from San José. A clean town, known locally as the City of Poets, with an attractive Parque Central, and a street market on Saturday mornings. The **Museo de San Ramón** ① *opposite the park, Tue-Fri 1300-1700, T2437-9851*, records the history and culture of the local community. There's good walking in the surrounding area. You can visit the coffee processing plant (in season) at the **Cooperativa de Café** ① *US$15-39*, in San Ramón.

Twenty kilometres north of San Ramón is the private 800-ha Los Angeles Cloud Forest Reserve (see **Hotel Villablanca**, page 90) which offers hiking, guided tours, horse riding and canopy ascents. The local *fiesta* is around the day of San Ramón, 30 August, when local saints are carried on litters to the town's church.

Palmares and Atenas

Palmares, 7 km southeast of San Ramón, has a pretty central park with lovely tall trees, where sloths are occasionally spotted. The quiet town comes alive in January for the annual Fiestas de Palmares, with food, carnival rides, concerts and parades.

After Palmares you can pick up the Pan-American Highway and head to the coast or return to San José, or continue south to Atenas. The church and main plaza in Atenas lie on an earthquake fault. The local speciality, *toronja rellena*, is a sweet-filled grapefruit. Atenas is reputed to have the best climate in the world, with stable temperatures of between 17 and 32°C year round (plus rain, of course).

North of San José ◉❼❸⓿ ▸▸*pp89-94*.

Heredia → *Altitude: 1200 m.*

Ten kilometres north of San José, Heredia is capital of the province of the same name and an important coffee centre. It is a convenient and pleasant place to stay, away from the pollution of San José but close to the capital and the airport, and with good public transport. The town is mostly new with only the main square maintaining a colonial atmosphere in its architecture. The short squat **Basílica de la Inmaculada Concepción**, built in 1797, has survived countless earthquakes. To the north of the central plaza, with a statue to the poet Aquileo Echeverría (1866-1909), is the solitary defensive structure of **El Fortín**. Across the street the **Casa de la Cultura** is a fine colonial home that now hosts concerts and exhibitions. The School of Marine Biology at the Universidad Nacional campus has a **Museo Zoológico Marino**.

Around Heredia

One of the largest coffee *beneficios* is **La Meseta**. The bus from Heredia to Santa Bárbara will drop you at the gate and you can ask for a guided tour. A more popular tour is of **Café Britt's** ① *US$35, tours 1100, 1½ hrs, includes lunch and show, 1500 tour, US$20, T2260- 2748, www.coffeetour.com*, a coffee farm near Barva de Heredia where you can see the processing factory, tasting room and multimedia presentation of the story of coffee. You can be picked up from Heredia or at various points in San José. The **Teatro Dionisio Chaverría** at Café Britt hosts weekend theatre and a children's show on Sunday afternoons.

North of Heredia is the historic town of **Barva**, on the slopes of Volcán Barva; frequent buses to/from Heredia. At Barva, the **Huetar Gallery** is recommended for arts, crafts and delicious food. There is also a **Museo de Cultura Popular** ① *Mon-Fri 0900-1600, US$1.50*, 500 m east of the Salón Comunal de Santa Lucía de Barva. North of Heredia through San Rafael, above Los Angeles, **Galería Octágono** ① *T2267-6325 www.galeriaoctagono.com*, an arts gallery with handmade textiles by a women's community cooperative, also a B&B, including breakfast, meals available at additional cost, as is transportation, wonderful cypress cabin, hikes, friendly and informative owners. Beyond Barva, to the west, is **Santa Bárbara**, good seafood at the Banco de los Mariscos, T2269-9090, 500 m west from the central plaza. Five kilometres west of Heredia is **San Joaquín de Flores**, a small rural town with views of Barva and Poás volcanoes.

A short distance south of Heredia on the road to **Santo Domingo** is **INBio Parque** ① *T2507-8107, www.inbio.ac.cr, Tue-Sun 0800-1800, US$23, under-12s US$13*, an educational and recreational centre which explains and gives insight into Costa Rica's biological diversity. In a small area you can visit the ecosystems of central highland forest, dry forest and humid forest, with trails set out for bromelias and *guaramo*.

Volcán Barva

Parque Nacional Braulio Carrillo ① *park entry US$8, no permit needed* (see page 178), to the north of Heredia, includes Volcán Barva, at 2906 m. This section of the park is ideal for hiking with a good trail leading up to the summit with three lagoons nearby, and excellent views and wildlife encounters for the few that make the effort. The really enthusiastic can hike all the way down to the lowlands arriving close to La Selva Biological Station near Puerto Viejo de Sarapaqui, but careful planning is required. There is a ranger station and camp site near the entrance, 4 km north of Sacramento, from where it's a 3-km easy climb to the top – still a treasure and, amazingly, a well-kept secret from the hordes.

San José de la Montaña to Sacramento

From San José de la Montaña it is four hours' walk to Sacramento but some buses continue towards Sacramento halving the walk time (otherwise walk, hitchhike, or arrange a ride with the park director). Taxi Heredia–Sacramento, US$10.

South of San José

Aserrí to San Pablo de Turrubares

Ten kilometres south of San José is Aserrí, a village with a beautiful white church. On Friday and Saturday evenings, street bands begin the fiesta with music from 2000, followed by marimbas. Extremely popular among locals, the dancing is fabulous, with *chicharrones*, tortillas and plenty of other things to eat and drink. Further along the same road is **Mirador Ram Luna**, a restaurant with a fine panoramic view. At the end of the road is **San Ignacio de Acosta**, again with a good church containing life-size Nativity figures. Buses from San José (Calle 8, Av 12-14 in front of the Baptist church) via Aserrí hourly from 0500 to 2230, return 0430 to 2100, one hour. The unpaved road continues to **Santiago de Puriscal**, which was the epicentre for many earthquakes in 1990. Although the church is now closed as a result, there are excellent views from the town and the road. From here it is possible to take a dirt road to the Pacific coast, joining the coastal road near Parrita (see page 149). Alternatively, take the road to **San Pablo de Turrubares**, from where you can either head west for Orotina, via an unpaved road through San Pedro and San Juan de Mata, or for Atenas via Quebradas, then east to Escobal, next stop on railway, then 4WD necessary to Atenas.

Meseta Central West listings

For Sleeping and Eating price codes, and other relevant information, see pages 43-46.

Sleeping

Alajuela *p84*

LL Xandari, T2443-2020, www.xandari.com. Once an old coffee finca overlooking the Central Valley, now, this architectural treasure has 21 private villas, health restaurant, organic gardens, trails and waterfalls, spa treatments and many facilities. One of the best hotels in Costa Rica.

L Garden Court Hotel, T2443-0043, www.gardencourtairporthotel.com. Good comforts, including pool, but you're here for the proximity to the airport.

L Hampton Inn Airport, T2436-0000, www.hamptoninn.com. 100 rooms, double glazing, a/c, free form outdoor pool, bar, fast food places nearby, children free and discounts for 3 or 4 adults sharing.

L Hampton Inn and Suites, T2442-3320, www.grupomarta.com. Luxury suites, conference rooms and facilities for business travellers.

The 2 **Hampton Inns** and the Garden Court are the closest place to stay near the airport, 2 km east of Juan Santamaría on the main highway. **A Viña Romántica**, up in the hills near Alajuela on road to Poás volcano, 15 mins from airport, T2430-7621 www.vina romantica.com. Great spot, gourmet meals.

AL-B Hotel 1915, Calle 2, Av 5-7, 300 m north of park central, T2440-7163, www.1915 hotel.com. Old family home smartly refurbished with stylish garden patio café. Very good service. Rooms have cable TV, mini fridge, telephone, some with a/c, price includes breakfast. Best in town for the price.

A-B Islands B&B, Av 1, Calle 7-9, 50 m west of La Agonía church, T2442-0573, islandsbb@ hotmail.com. A small family-run Tico-owned B&B with 8 comfortable rooms. Some rooms have cable TV, free local calls. Airport pick-up available, very secure and 24-hr parking.

B Hotel Mi Tierra, Av2, Calle3-5 T2441-1974, www.hotelmitierra.net. New name (formerly **Villa Real**), new location, same people. Offers pool, adventure tours and parking. Popular with travellers.

B-C Charly's Place, a couple of blocks north of the central park on Av 5, Calle Central-1, T2440-6853, lilyhotel@latinmail. com. Popular place, with 14 rooms most with private bathrooms, cheaper without, some with TV. Also cheap backpackers' area. Credit cards accepted.

B-C Hotel Alajuela, on corner across from central park at Av Central and Calle 2, T2441-1241, alajuela@racsa.co.cr. 28 generally good rooms and apartments all with private bathrooms. Helpful staff, garden patio for relaxing.

C Mango Verde Hostel, Av 3, Calle 2-4, T2441-6330, mirafloresbb@hotmail.com. 6 clean rooms with private bath and hot water, close to the centre of town. Courtyard, kitchen and communal area create a relaxing atmosphere. Parking.

C Pensión Alajuela, Av 9, Calle Central-2, opposite the court house, T2443-1717, www.pensionalajuela.com. Mixed bag of 12 simple rooms, some with private bath, some without. Small bar downstairs, laundry and fax service. 24-hr parking next door.

D-F Central Alajuela, Av Central, Calle 8, close to the bus terminal, T2443-8437. Basic rooms, shared bathrooms have cold water but it is reasonably clean. Popular with Ticos arriving from out of town.

D-E Cortez Azul, Av 3, Calle 2-4, 100 m west of Museo Juan Santamaría, T2443-6145, hotelcortezazul@gmail.com. Popular spot with a handful of good, clean rooms.

Parque Nacional Volcán Poás *p85*

Camping in the park is not permitted but there are several places advertising cabins on the road up to Poás and nearby.

L-A Poás Volcano Lodge, west of Poasito, 500 m from Vara Blanca junction on road to Poasito, at El Cortijo farm, sign on gate, 1 km to house, T2482-2194, www.poas

volcanolodge.com. English-owned, includes breakfast, dinner, wholesome food, rooms in converted buildings with bath, or in farmhouse with shared bath, jungle trail, good walking, horseback riding 25 mins to volcano by car, 1½ hrs from San José.
C Alberque Ecológica La Providencia, near Poás NP (2 km from green entrance gate to volcano), T2232-2498. Private reserve, beautiful horse riding tour US$25-30 including lunch.

La Virgen p85
AL-A La Quinta de Sarapiquí Lodge, Bajos de Chilamate on the Río Sardinal, T2761-1052, www.laquintasarapiqui.com. Costa Rican-owned, family-run lodge, 23 rooms with bath and fan, bar and restaurant overlooking the rainforest, tubing down rivers, very popular with birdwatchers with bird list available. Also a frog and butterfly garden.
B Albergue Ecológico Islas del Río, T2292-2072 in San José, T2766-6524, in Chilamate, www.aguas-bravas.co.cr. Price per person. The operational centre of Aguas Bravas close to Puerto Viejo de Sarapiquí, includes meals, rooms with private and shared bathroom, ideal for groups, canopy tour, hiking. Río Sarapiquí trips arranged. If continuing to Puerto Viejo de Sarapiquí, see page 180.
C-E Finca Pedro y el Lobo, T2761-1406, www.fincapedro.com. Beautiful rustic accommodation, also options for camping, kayaking, rafting and exploring waterfalls.
E-F Rancho Leona, T2761-1019, www.rancholeona.com. Private rooms, kayaking, meals available also jungle tours.

Venecia and around p85
AL La Laguna del Lagarto Lodge, Boca Tapada, T2289-8163, www.lagarto-lodge-costa-rica.com. 12 rooms with bath, 6 with shared bath, friendly, 500 ha of forest, good for watching animals, boat trips down Río San Carlos to Río San Juan.
C Recreo Verde, Marsella, near Venecia, T2472-1020. A good choice in a recreational and ecological conservation park. There are

hot springs, primary forest, a few trails going to nearby caves and helpful, friendly staff.

Grecia p86
L-A Posada Mimosa, Apdo 135-4100, Costa Rica, T2494-5868, www.mimosa.co.cr. B&B, rooms, suites and cabins set in beautiful tropical gardens, pool. Uses solar energy.

Sarchí and Naranjo p86
A Rancho Mirador, on the Panamericana, 1 km west of the turn-off for Naranjo, T2451-1302. Good-value cabañas, restaurant with local food, a spectacular view of coffee fincas and San José in the distance. Owner Rick Vargas was formerly a stunt pilot in the US.
B Cabinas Daniel Zamora, Sarchí, T2454-4596. With bath, fan, hot water, very clean and extra blankets if cold at night.
B Hotel Villa Sarchí Lodge, 800 m north of Sarchí, T2454-5000. Has 11 rooms with private bath, hot water, cable TV and pool.
F La Bamba, Naranjo, down the hill by the football pitch. May muster up enough energy to let you stay in 1 of their simple rooms.

Zarcero p86
B-C Don Beto, by the church, T2463-3137. With bath, very friendly, clean.

San Ramón and Los Angeles Cloud Forest Reserve p86
LL Hotel Villablanca, north of town set in the 800-ha Los Angeles Cloud Forest Reserve, T2461-0300, www.villablanca-costarica.com. Naturalist hikes, some up to 8 hrs, canopy tour, horse riding, night walks, birdwatching, coffee plantation tour and the famous La Mariana Chapel with hand-painted ceiling tiles – you don't have to stay to visit.
A-B La Posada, T2445-7359, www.posadahotel.net. 400 m north of the cathedral. 35 good rooms, with private bath, hot water, use of kitchen, laundry. Parking and small patio for relaxing.
C San Ramón, 100 m east, 25m south of Banco de Costa Rica, T2447-2042. Has 35 spotless rooms (but pretty garish decor),

with private bathroom, hot water and
cable TV. Parking.
D Gran Hotel, 150 m west of post office,
T2445-6363. Big rooms, private bathrooms,
hot water, friendly, communal TV area.
D Hotel Nuevo Jardín, 5 blocks north of
the central park, T2445-5620. Simple,
clean and friendly.

Palmares and Atenas *p87*
AL El Cafetal Inn, out of Atenas, in St
Eulalia, 4.7 km towards Grecia, T2446-5785,
www.cafetal.com. Nice setting on a coffee
plantation, private house, large pool,
10 rooms, airport transport, recommended.

Heredia *p87*
AL Valladolid, Calle 7, Av 7, T2260-2905,
valladol@racsa.co.cr. 11 spacious rooms and
suites, all with a/c, private bath, telephone
and cable TV. 5th fl has sauna, jacuzzi
and **Bonavista Bar** with fine views
overlooking the Central Valley.
AL-B Apartotel Vargas, 800 m north of
Colegio Santa Cecilia and San Francisco Church,
T2237-8526, apartotelvargas@ yahoo.com.
8 large, well-furnished apartments with
cooking facilities, hot water, laundry facilities,
TV, internet, enclosed patio with garage and
nightwatchman, English-speaking staff. Sr
Vargas will collect you from airport. Excellent
choice if taking language classes and in a
group. Best option in town.
B-C Hotel Heredia, Calle 6, Av 3-5, T2238-
0880. Has 12 rooms, some quite dark, but all
have private bath and hot water, parking.
C Las Flores, Av 12, Calle 12-14, T2261-8147.
With bath, clean, quiet, parking. Recommended.
F Colonial, Calle 4-6, Av 4, T2237-5258.
Clean, friendly and family-run, will park
motorcycles in restaurant.
F El Verane, Calle 4, Av 6-8, next to central
market, T2237-1616. Rooms on street side
are slightly better, close to bus terminal.

Around Heredia *p87*
LL Finca Rosa Blanca, 1.6 km from Santa
Bárbara de Heredia, T2269-9392, www.finca
rosablanca.com. Deluxe suites in an architectural explosion of style and eloquence,
romance and exclusivity at the extremes
of imagination and fantasy. Spa facilities
for comfort. Quality restaurant and bar.
LL-AL Bougainvillea de Santo Domingo,
just west of Santo Domingo, T2244-1414,
www.hb.co.cr. Excellent service, pool, sauna,
spectacular mountain setting, free shuttle
bus to San José. Highly recommended.

✪ Eating

Alajuela *p84*
Most restaurants, cafés and sodas are within
1 or 2 blocks of the Parque Central and down
Calle Central.
♥♥ La Mansarda, central plaza. Good,
wholesome Tico dishes.
♥ Café Almibar, Av Central, Calle 1-3.
Another snacking stop popular with locals.
♥ Jalapeño's, Central T2430-4027 great
Mexican food, friendly, 50 m south of the
post office.
♥ La Cocina de Abuelita, Av Central, Calle
1-3. Simple lunchtime, buffet menu.
♥ Trigo Miel, Av 2, Calle Central-2. One of a
couple of patisserie cafés in Alajuela serving
divine snacks and good coffee.

Venecia and around *p85*
♥ El Parque, near church. Good local food.

Zarcero *p86*
Zarcero is known for cheese and fruit preserves.
♥ Soda/Restaurant El Jardín, 1st fl,
overlooking the plaza. Local lunches
and breakfasts. Good view of topiary.

San Ramón and Los Angeles Cloud
Forest Reserve *p86*
♥ Tropical, near northwest corner of the
Parque. Excellent ice cream parlour.

Heredia p87

♟-♟ La Rambla, Calle 7, Av 7. Services a good mix of *comida típica* and international dishes.

♟ Cowboy Restaurant, T2237-8719 Calle 9, Av 5. Grill option where the Mid-West meets Costa Rica. Lively bar in the evenings. Credit cards accepted.

♟ El Gran Papa, Calle 9, Av 3. Dinner only, with a good range of *bocas*, pastas and cocktails.

♟ La Luna de Valencia, a few km north of Barva, T2269-6665. Authentic paella restaurant, vegetarian options, friendly service, recommended.

♟ Le Petit Paris, Calle 5 and Av Central-2, T2262-2564. Closed Sun. A little piece of France in the heart of Heredia. The ambience shifts between the bar, restaurant and patio café. The food is divine and there is live music on Thu.

♟♟-♟ Baalbek Bar & Grill, on the road to Monte de la Cruz, T2267-6482. Good Mediterranean food, live music Fri and Sat.

♟♟-♟ Bulevar Bar, Av Central, Calle 5-7. One of the happening places with a lively balcony bar upstairs and fast food and *bocas* available.

♟♟-♟ Fresas, Calle 7, Av 1, T2262-5555. Diner-style restaurant serving everything you could possibly want including snacks, sandwiches, breakfast, full meals, fresh fruit juices and strawberries; bar upstairs.

♟♟-♟ Las Espigas, southwest corner of Parque Central. Good for coffee, pastries and lunch.

♟ Entrepanes, fine coffee and pastries, upstairs from **Pop's** diagonal to the central park.

♟ Vishnu Mango Verde, Calle 7, Av Central-1, T2237-2526. Good wholesome vegetarian served fast-food style out front or a little more leisurely out back.

❀ Festivals and events

Alajuela p84

11 Apr **Juan Santamaría Day**, a week of bands, concerts and dancing in celebration of the life of the town's most famous son.
Mid-Jul The fruitful heritage comes to the fore with a **Mango Festival** of parades, concerts and an arts and crafts fair.

○ Shopping

Alajuela p84

Bookshop Goodlight Books, Calle 1-3, T2430-4083, quality used book, mostly English, espresso and pastries. Internet.

Sarchí and Naranjo p86

One of the largest *artesanías* is **Fábrica de Chaverri** in Sarchí Sur. **Taller Lalo Alfaro**, the oldest workshop, is in Sarchí Norte and worth a visit to see more traditional production methods. Both sell hand-made furniture, cowhide rocking chairs and wooden products as well as the ox-carts, which come in all sizes.

▲ Activities and tours

Tour operators

Armo Tours, Calle 9 y Av 6, Centro Plaza, piso 2, T2257-0202, www.armotours.com. Highly recommended for national tours, good service, German, English, French and Italian spoken and an office in Germany. Offer the flexible and independent Naturepass that allows you to travel freely, with the support of a tour operator.

Calypso Cruises, Centro Colón, Paseo Colón, T2256-2727, www.calypsocruises.com. Originators of the Pacific Island Cruise with an all-inclusive day trip from US$119 – a popular trip – and several other sailing options.

Costa Rica Expeditions, Calle Central and Av 3 (1 block east of the central Post Office) T2257-0766, www.costaricaexpeditions.com. Upmarket wildlife adventures taking you to popular but out of the way places in comfort and style. Very good and knowledgeable guides. Options include whitewater rafting (US$99 for 1-day trip, including lunch and transport). Highly recommended.

Expediciones Tropicales, www.costaricainfo. com. The full range of 1- and 2-day tours. Staff are friendly, helpful and happy to talk through the options without pushing the hard sell. They operate the Four-in-One tour that everyone now tries to copy. Rent-a-car, a-van and a-bus – handy for groups.

Green Tropical Tours, T2229-4192, www.greentropical. com. Specializing in tailor-made tours with many of the normal tours and some to less widely visited areas such as Guayabo National Monument and Los Juncos Cloudforest.

The Original Canopy Tour, T2291-4465, www.canopytour.com. The pioneers in Costa Rica, with 3 canopy tours around the country. Rates from US$45 per person.

Simbiosis Tours, 200 m north, 50 m west of ICE (Instituto Costarricense de Electricidad), Sabana Norte, T/F2290-8646, www.turismo ruralcr.com. The booking arm of the Cooprena network of 8 community-based accommo- dation and camping options. Good options around the country, including horse riding and experiencing typical food, dances and music from the region. Probably the best shot at organized ecotourism in Costa Rica.

Swiss Travel Service, one of the biggest operators with several branches around town, T2282-4898, www.swisstravelcr.com. In addition to standard tours, they arrange almost anything you can imagine from birdwatching to horse riding. Good guides, with a lot of cruise experience – warmly recommended.

⦿ Transport

Alajuela p84
Bus Service to **San José** leaves from main bus terminal Calle 8, Av Central-1, or Av 4, Calle 2-4 every 10 mins, 30 mins, US$0.75, with both services arriving on Av 2 in the capital. To **Heredia** from 0400 until 2200, 30 mins, US$0.50. Buses to the Butterfly Farm at **La Guácima** marked 'La Guácima abajo' leave from Av 2 between Calle 8-10, US$0.30. 1 block south of the terminal buses depart for several small villages in the area including **Laguna de Fraijanes** and **Volcán Poás**.

Parque Nacional Volcán Poás p85
The volcano can be reached by car from **San José**. A taxi for 6 hrs with a side trip will cost about US$50-60. There is a daily excursion bus from the main square of Alajuela right up to the crater, leaving at 0915 (or before if full), connecting with 0830 bus from San José (from Av 2, Calle 12-14); be there early for a seat; extra buses run if necessary, US$5.75 return, 2. The bus waits at the top with ample time to see every- thing (clouds permitting), returning at 1430. Daily bus **Alajuela-Poasito** 1200 (US$1) will take you part way to the summit. From **Poasito** hitch a lift as it is a 10-km walk. Other options include taking the 0600 or 1600 bus from Alajuela to **San Pedro de Poás**, hitch/taxi to Poasito and stay overnight, hiking or hitching up the mountain next morning. Taking a 0500 bus from Alajuela to Poasito arrives 2 hrs before the park gates open.

Sarchí and Naranjo p86
Bus Express bus from **San José** to Sarchí, Calle 16, Av 1-3, 1215, 1730 and 1755, Mon-Fri, returning 0530, 0615, 1345, Sat 1200, 1½ hrs, US$1.45. **Tuan T2441-3781** buses every 30 mins, 0500-2200 from Alajuela bus station, 1½ hrs, US$0.50.

Transportes Naranjo, T2451-3655, have buses to and from **San José**'s Coca Cola terminal every 40 mins. US$1.25 Buses connect other towns and villages in the area.

San Ramón and Los Angeles Cloud Forest Reserve p86
Heading north the road forks, left to **Zarcero** (20 km) and finally to **Cd Quesada**. The right fork heads north to **La Tigra** and **Fortuna** passing the Los Angeles Cloud Forest Reserve. **Bus** San Ramón is a transport hub. A regular service from **San José Empresarios Unidos**, T2222-0064, at Calle 16, Av 10-12, go to **Puntarenas**, 10 a day, every 45 mins or so, US$1.70. There is also a regular service to **Fortuna** and **Alajuela**. Buses run to surrounding villages and towns.

Palmares and Atenas p87

The library on the plaza in Atenas also serves as the bus office, **Cooptransatenas**, T2446-5767. Many daily buses to **San José**, either direct or via **Alajuela**, US$1.90.

Heredia p87

Bus From **San José** from Av 2, Calle 12-14, buses every 10 mins daily, 0500-0015, then every 30 mins to 0400, 25-min journey, US$0.50. Return buses from Av 6, Calle 2-1. Local buses leave from Av 8, Calle 2-4, by market.

Volcán Barva p88

Accessible from **Heredia**, there is no route from the San José-Limón Highway. Buses leave from the market at 0630, 1230 and 1600, returning at 0730, 1300, 1700. Arriving at **Porrosati**. Some continue as far as Sacramento, otherwise walk 6 km to park entrance, then 4 km to lagoon. Be careful if leaving a car, there are regular reports of theft from rental car.

● Directory

Alajuela p84

Banks No shortage of banks, all within 3 blocks of each other and most with AMT, including **Banco Nacional**, Calle 2, Av Central-1, facing central park, **Scotiabank**, next door. 1 block south of central park is **Banco Crédito Agrícola de Cártago**, Calle 2, Av Central-2, and 2 blocks north is **Banco de Santa Cruz**, Calle 2, Av 3, which is also the office of **Credomatic. Emergency** T911. **Internet** Southside of main plaza, Mon-Sun 0900-2200, US$0.60 per hr. Also with pool tables. **Interplanet**, across from La Agonía church on Av Central and Calle 9, stands out largely due to the fluorescent lighting, daily 0830-2200. **Medical services** Hospital **San Rafael**, 200 m southeast of the airport autopista intersection, T2436-1000, can help in a crisis. **Post office** Corner of Av 5 and Calle 1, Mon-Fri 0730-1700, Sat mornings.

Sarchí and Naranjo p86

Banks **Banco Nacional** has branches in Sarchí Sur and Sarchí Norte, and on the north side of the plaza in Naranjo, with Visa and MasterCard ATM. **Post office** Services are found in both villages.

Heredia p87

Language schools Centro **Panamericano de Idiomas**, San Joaquín de Flores, T2265- 6306, www.cpi-edu.com. Accommodation with local families. Also have schools in Monteverde and Playa Flamingo. **Intercultura Centro de Idiomas**, Heredia, T2260-8480, www.intercultura costarica.com. Small classes, also with a campus at Playa Sámara, see page 147.

Intercultura

Costa Rica, Heredia & Playa Sámara

Study Spanish with our university credentialed professors at our beach and/or city campus
Free weekly cultural activities

Call us: 44-20-7993-0822/Intl. 506-22-60-8480

www.interculturacostarica.com
info@interculturacostarica.com

Meseta Central East

The eastern Central Highlands offer relative quiet, despite being close to San José. The former capital and pilgrimage site of Cártago sits meekly at the bottom of the fuming Irazú volcano before it falls away to the beautiful Orosí Valley. The thundering Río Reventazón leads the next step down the Atlantic slope, beginning its journey to the Caribbean, passing Turrialba, a good base for whitewater adventure. Meanwhile, the slopes of nearby Turrialba volcano hide the country's main archaeological site of Guayabo and good hiking opportunities to its summit.

➤➤ *For listings, see pages 98-100.*

Cártago and around ⬤🐟🔺⬤🅖 ➤➤ *pp98-100.*

→ *Altitude: 1439 m.*

Cártago, at the foot of the Irazú Volcano and 22.5 km from San José on a toll road (US$0.75), is encircled by mountains. Founded in 1563, it was the capital of Costa Rica for almost 300 years until San José assumed the role in 1823. Since then the town has failed to grow significantly and remains small, though densely populated. Earthquakes in 1841 and 1910 destroyed many of the buildings and ash from Irazú engulfed the town in 1963. While colonial-style remnants exist in one or two buildings, the town feels as if it is still reeling from the impact of so much natural devastation and is keeping quiet waiting for the next event.

The most important attraction in town, and the focal point for pilgrims from all over Central America, is the **Basílica de Nuestra Señora de Los Angeles**, the patroness of Costa Rica, on the eastern side of town. Rebuilt in 1926 in Byzantine style, it houses the diminutive **La Negrita**, an indigenous image of the Virgin under 15 cm high, worshipped for her miraculous healing powers. The basilica houses a collection of finely made silver and gold images, no larger than 3 cm high, of various parts of the human anatomy, presumably offered in the hope of being healed. The most important date in the pilgrims' calendar is 2 August, when the image of La Negrita is carried in procession to churches in Cártago with celebrations throughout Costa Rica.

Also worth seeing is **La Parroquia** (the old parish church), roughly 1 km west of the basilica, ruined by the 1910 earthquake and now converted into a delightful garden retreat with flowers, fish and hummingbirds.

Around Cártago

Aguas Calientes, 4 km southeast of Cártago and 90 m lower, has a warm-water *balneario* ideal for picnics. On the road to Paraíso, 8 km from Cártago, is an orchid garden, the **Jardín Lankester** ① *10 mins' walk from the main road, T2552-3247, daily 0830-1630, US$5*, run by the University of Costa Rica. The best displays are between February and April. While off the beaten track, the gardens are worth a visit. The Cártago–Paraíso bus departs every 30 minutes from the south side of central park in Cártago (15 minutes); ask the driver to let you out at Campo Ayala. Taxi from Cártago, US$5.

Volcán Irazú → *Altitude: 3432 m.*

① *US$10, 0800-1530 most of the year.*

Irazú's crater is an impressive half-mile cube dug out of the earth, surrounded by desolate grey sand, which looks like the surface of the moon. President Kennedy's visit in 1963 coincided with a major eruption and, in 1994 the north wall of the volcano was destroyed by another eruption that sent detritus down as far as the Río Sucio, within sight of the the San José–Limón Highway. The views are stupendous on a clear day and the main reason for the trip. But the clouds normally move in enveloping the lower peaks and slopes by 1300 (sometimes even by 0900 or 1000 between July and November), so get there as early as you can to have a greater chance of a clear view of the mountains and the sun shining on the clouds in the valley below. There's little wildlife other than the ubiquitous Volcano Junco bird and the few plants which survive in this desert, but ongoing colonization is attracting more birds.

It's definitely worth the trip and an early start. As one traveller wrote: "In the afternoon the mountain top is buried in fog and mist or drizzle, but the ride up in the mist can be magical, for the mountainside is half displaced in time. There are new jeeps and tractors, but the herds of cattle are small, the fields are quilt-work, handcarts and ox-carts are to be seen under the fretworked porches of well-kept frame houses. The land is fertile, the pace is slow, the air is clean. It is a very attractive mixture of old and new. Irazú is a strange mountain, well worth the ride up."

Orosí Valley
Further east from Cártago a trip round the Orosí Valley makes a beautiful circular trip, or a fine place to hang out for a while in a valley that is often overlooked as the crowds rush to the more popular spots on the coast. The centrepiece of the valley is the artificial Lake Cachí used for hydro-electric generation. Heading round the lake counter-clockwise, the road passes through Orosí, clips the edge of Parque Nacional Tapantí, continuing to the Cachí Dam and completes the circuit passing through Ujarrás. Along the way there are several miradors which offer excellent views of the Reventazón Valley. For transport see each destination. Day trips can be easily arranged from San José.

In **Orosí** there is an 18th-century **mission** ① *closed Mon*, with colonial treasures, and just outside two **balnearios** ① *US$2.50*, with restaurants serving good meals at fair prices. It's a good place to hang out, take some low-key language classes, mixed with mountain biking and trips to the national park and other sites of interest.

Parque Nacional Tapantí-Macizo de la Muerte
① *Daily 0700-1700, US$7.*
Twelve kilometres beyond Orosí is the Parque Nacional Tapantí-Macizo de la Muerte, one of the wettest parts of the country (some parts reportedly receiving as much as 8 m of rain a year). From June to November/December it rains every afternoon. Approached from Orosí, and just 30 km from Cártago, the national park is suprisingly easy to reach and packs in the interest.

Covering 58,000 ha, Tapantí-Macizo includes the former Tapantí National Park and much of the Río Macho Forest Reserve. The park protects the Río Orosí basin which feeds the Cachí Dam hydro power plant. Strategically, the southern boundary of the park joins with Chirripó National Park, extending the continuous protected area that makes up La Amistad Biosphere Reserve. The park incorporates a wide range of life zones with altitudes rising from 1220 m to over 3000 m at the border with Chirripó. The diverse altitudes and relative seclusion of the park has created an impressive variety of species – 260 bird species, 45 mammals, lizards, snakes – a list which is currently incomplete due to the relatively recent creation of the park. There are picnic areas, a nature centre with slide shows (ask to see them) and good swimming in the dry season (November-June), and trout fishing season (1 April-31 October).

Cachí

Continue around the lake to Cachí and the nearby **Casa del Soñador** (Dreamer's House) which sells wood carvings from the sculpture school of the late Macedonio Quesada. The road crosses the dam wall and follows the north shore to Ujarrás, then back to Cártago. The **Charrarra tourist complex** ⓘ *30 mins' walk from Ujarrás*, has a good campsite, restaurant, pool, boat rides on the lake and walks. It can be reached by direct bus on Sunday. Buses leave from Cártago one block north of the Cártago ruins.

Ujarrás

Ujarrás (ruins of a colonial church and village) is 6.5 km east of Paraíso, on the shores of the artificial Lago Cachí. There is a bus every 1½ hours from Paraíso that continues to Cachí. Legend has it that in 1666 English pirates, including the youthful Henry Morgan, were seen off by the citizens of Ujarrás aided by the Virgin. The event is now celebrated annually in mid-March when the saint is carried in procession from Paraíso to the ruined church.

Turrialba and around ⊜❼▲❺ ⤵ *pp98-100.*

➜ *Altitude: 646 m.*

Turrialba (62 km from San José) bridges the Central Valley highlands and the Caribbean lowlands, and was once a stopping point on the old Atlantic railway between Cártago and Puerto Limón. The railway ran down to Limón on a narrow ledge poised between mountains on the left and the river to the right, but no longer operates. The **Centro Agronómico Tropical de Investigación y Enseñanza (CATIE)** ⓘ *T2558-2000 ext 2275, www.catie.ac.cr, daily 0700-1600, T556-2700, US$5*, about 4 km southeast of Turrialba covers more than 800 ha of this ecologically diverse zone (with many fine coffee farms), has one of the largest tropical fruit collections in the world and houses an important library on tropical agriculture; visitors and students are welcome for research or birdwatching, botanical garden. Past CATIE a large sugar mill makes for a conspicuous landmark in Atirro, the centre for macadamia nuts. Nearby, the 256-ha **Lake Angostura** has now flooded some of the whitewaters of the Río Reventazón. What has been lost as world-class whitewater is believed, by some, to be a Lake Arenal in the making. A glimpse of the vegetation covered lake will convince you otherwise.

Around Turrialba

Many whitewater rafting companies operate out of Turrialba, with trips to the **Río Reventazón** and **Río Pacuare**. The rafting is excellent; the Pascua section of the Reventazón can be Grade V at rainy times. The Pacuare is absolutely perfect with divine scenery. By contacting the guides in Turrialba you can save about 30% on a trip booked in San José, provided they are not already contracted.

Volcán Turrialba (3329 m) may be visited from Cártago by a bus from Calle 4 y Avenida 6 to the village of San Gerardo. From Turrialba take a bus to Santa Cruz. From both, an unpaved road meets at **Finca La Central**, on the saddle between Irazú and Turrialba.

Monumento Nacional Guayabo

ⓘ *T2559-1220, Tue-Sun 0800-1530, US$6, local guides available, water, toilets, no food.*
About 19 km north of Turrialba, near Guayabo, is a 3000-year-old ceremonial centre excavated with paved streets and stone-lined water channels. The archaeological site, 232 ha and 4 km from the town of Guayabo, is now a national monument, and dates from the period 1000 BC-AD 1400. There are excellent walks in the park, where plenty of birds and wildlife can

be seen. Worth a trip to see Costa Rica's most developed ancient archaeological site but small in comparison to the great sites of the Maya. There is also a camping area.

⊙ Meseta Central East listings

For Sleeping and Eating price codes, and other relevant information, see pages 43-46.

● Sleeping

Cártago *p95*
A-B Los Angeles Lodge B&B, near the Basílica at Av 4, Calle 14-16, T2591-4169. Clean, nice rooms, restaurant.

D Dinastía, Calle 3, Av 6-8, near old railway station, at the Las Ruinas end of town, T2551-7057. Slightly more expensive with private bath. The rooms are small although better with a window. Safe hotel but in lively area north of the central market. Credit cards accepted.

Volcán Irazú *p95*
D Hotel Gestoria Irazú, San Juan de Chicúa, T2253-0827. Simple rooms, private bath, hot water and extra blankets to get you through the cold winter nights.

Orosí Valley *p96*
A Orosí Lodge, T2533-3578, www.orosi lodge.com. 6 rooms and a house with balcony overlooking the valley towards Volcán Irazú each with kitchenette, private bath, and hot water. Just about everything you could want: divine home-baked cookies, mountain bikes, kayaks and horses for rent, and an internet service. Credit cards accepted. Excellent value.

B Hotel Reventazón, T2533-3838. Rather stark, characterless rooms, with telephone, TV, fridge, internet. But clean and friendly service, and good local knowledge. Credit cards accepted.

C-F Montaña Linda, T2533-3640 (local), www.montanalinda.com. A classic and well-run backpackers' place, with a range of options. Dormitory rooms, camping, and B&B service if you just can't get out of bed! There is also a language school, with package deals for lodgers. Toine and Sara are friendly

and know their patch very well, organizing trips to local sights.

D Río Palomo, in Palomo, just south of Orosí, T2533-3128. Cabins, pool, laundry facilities, good restaurant.

Parque Nacional Tapantí-Macizo de la Muerte *p96*
A-B Monte Sky Mountain Retreat, near Tapantí, T2228-0010. Cabins with shared bath, cold water, includes meals, hiking trails through forest. Camping platforms also available. In addition to the price there is a US$8 per person entrance fee to the 300 ha private reserve.

B Kiri Lodge, 1.5 km from park entrance, T2533-2272, www.kirilodge. net. Excellent lodging and food, breakfast included. Peaceful, trout fishing, very friendly, good trails on 50-ha property.

Camping
No camping is allowed at the park, T2200-0090. See also **Monte Sky Mountain Retreat**, above.

Turrialba *p97*
AL Wagelia, Av 4, entrance to Turrialba, T2556-1566, www.hotelwagelia.com. 18 rooms, bath, some a/c, restaurant.

B-D Interamericano, Av 1, facing old railway station, T2556-0142, www.hotelinteramericano.com. Price per person. Friendly family-run place, popular with kayakers. Clean, private or shared bath. Safe for motorbikes. Internet, bar and communal area with TV and books.

C Alcázar, Calle 3, Av 2-4, 25 m north of **Banco Norte**. Small terrace upstairs, each room has cable TV, telephone, fan and a private bath with hot water. Small, cheap bar/restaurant downstairs with frightening colour schemes.

C-D Central, next to **Interamericano**, T2556-0170. Price per person, with bath, restaurant, basic.

D Hotel Turrialba, Av 2, Calle 2-4, T2556-6654. Clean simple rooms with private bath, hot water and TV. There are also a couple of pool tables and drinks for sale.

E Laroche, north of Parque Central on Calle 1. Simple and basic rooms but friendly with comfortable beds. Small bar downstairs.

F Whittingham, Calle 4, Av 0-2, T2550-8927. Has 7 fairly dark but OK rooms, some with private bath – an option if other places are full.

Around Turrialba p97

LL-L Casa Turire, 14 km southeast of Turrialba, follow signposts, T2531-1111, www.hotelcasaturire.com. Overlooking Lake Angostura, 12 luxury rooms with bath, 4 suites, cable TV, phone, restaurant, pool, library, games room, in the middle of a 1620-ha sugar, coffee and macadamia nut plantation. Virgin rainforest nearby, trails, horses, bike rental, excursions.

A Albergue Mirador Pochotel, Pavones, T2538-1010. 10 basic cabins, restaurant, a popular spot.

A Turrialtico, on road to Siquirres, T2538-1111, www.turrialtico.com. On top of hill with extensive views. Rooms are clean with private bath, comfortable, friendly. Going northeast from Turrialba, the main road follows the Río Reventazón down to Siquirres (see page 180).

E San Agustín, Vereh, 25 km southeast of Turrialba (bus via Jicotea). For a rural Costa Rica experience. Candlelit camping, river bathing, hiking and horse riding in surrounding area – basic, and a very pure rainforest experience.

Monumento Nacional Guayabo p97

D Albergue y Restaurant La Calzada, T2559-0023. Call in advance to make a reservation and check they're open.

🍴 Eating

Cártago p95

🍴 **Auto 88**, east of public market. Cafetería-style, with bar adjoining dining room.

🍴 **Soda Apollo**, northwest corner of parque, opposite La Parroquia. 24-hr snack option.

Volcán Irazú p95

🍴🍴 **Restaurante Linda Vista**. Spectacular views, as you'd expect from Costa Rica's highest restaurant, serving good food and drinks. But most people stop to post, stick, pin or glue a business card, or some other personal item, to the wall.

Turrialba p97

🍴🍴 **Pizzería Julián**, on the square. Popular.

🍴 **La Garza**, on main square. Cheap, local good food.

🍴 **Nuevo Hong Kong**, just east of the main square. Good, reasonable prices.

🍴 **Soda Burbuja**, south of square on C Central. Local dishes, excellent portions, good value.

▲ Activities and tours

Cártago p95
Tour operators
Mercatur, next to Fuji at Av 2, Calle 4-6, provides local tourist information.

Around Turrialba p97
Tour operators
See also the companies in San José (eg **Ríos Tropicales**, page 78).
Serendipity Adventures, T2558-1000, www.serendipityadventures.com. Canyoning rappelling, hot-air ballooning. Recommended.
Tico's River Adventures, T2556-1231, www.ticoriver.com. Recommended local guides.

🚌 Transport

Cártago p95
Bus A good bus service supplies the surrounding area. To **San José** every 10 mins from Av 4, Calle 2-4. Arrives and departs San José from Calle 5, Av 18-20 for the 45-min journey. After 2030 buses leave from Gran Hotel Costa Rica, Av 2, Calle 3-5. **Orosí/Río Macho**, for **Parque Nacional Tapantí** every 30 mins from Calle 6, Av 1-3, 35-55 mins. **Turrialba**, every hr from Av 3, Calle 8-10,

1 hr direct, 1 hr 20 mins *colectivo*. **Cachí**, via **Ujarrá** and **Paraíso** from Calle 6, Av 1-3, every 1½ hrs, 1 hr 20 mins. **Paraíso**, every 5 mins from Av 5, Calle 4-6. **Aguacalientes**, every 15 mins from Calle 1, Av 3-5. **Tierra Blancas** for **Irazú**, every 30 mins from Calle 4, Av 6-8.

Closest bus for **Irazú** rides to San Juan de Chichua, still some 12 km from the summit. The bus leaves Cártago from north of the central market, Av 6, Calle 1-3, at 1730, returning at 0500 the next day, so you have to spend at least 2 nights on the volcano or in a hotel if you can't get a ride. To visit **Volcán Turrialba** take a bus from Calle 4 y Av 6 to the village of San Gerardo.

Volcán Irazú *p95*

Bus It is possible to get a bus from Cártago to Tierra Blanca (US$0.33) or San Juan de Chicúa (which has 1 hotel) and hitch a ride in a pick-up truck. Alternatively you can take a bus from Cártago to Sanatorio. Ask the driver to drop you at the crossroads just outside Tierra Blanca. From there you walk 16 km to the summit. If you're looking for a day trip from San José a yellow 'school' express bus run by **Buses Metrópoli SA**, T2530-1064, runs from **San José**, daily 0800 from Gran Hotel Costa Rica, stops at Cártago ruins 0830 to pick up more passengers, returns 1230 with lunch stop at **Restaurant Linda Vista**, US$6.50.

Taxi From **Cártago** is US$32 return. A taxi tour from **Orosí** costs US$10 per person, minimum 3 people, and stops at various places on the return journey, eg Cachí dam and Ujarrás ruins. Since it can be difficult to find a decent hotel in Cártago, it may be easier to take a guided tour leaving from **San José**, about US$35, 5½ hrs includes lunch, transport from San José. If driving from San José, take the turn-off at the Ferretería San Nicolás in Taras, which goes directly to Irazú, avoiding Cártago.

Orosí Valley *p96*

Bus From **Cártago** to Orosí/Río Macho from Calle 6, Av 1-3, every 30 mins, journey time of 35-55 mins, US$0.50.

Parque Nacional Tapantí-Macizo de la Muerte *p96*

Bus The 0600 bus from Cártago to Orosí gets to Puricil by 0700, then walk (5 km), or take any other Cártago-Orosí bus to Río Macho and walk 9 km to the refuge. Alternatively take a taxi from **Orosí** (US$7 round trip, up to 6 passengers), or **San José**, US$50.

Turrialba *p97*

Bus From **San José** every hr 0530-2200 from Terminal Turrialba, Calle 13, Av 6-8, 1½ hrs, US$2 from **Cártago**, 1 hr, US$1.25, runs until about 2200. Service to **Siquirres**, for connections to Caribbean lowlands, hourly, 40 mins, US$1.50.

Monumento Nacional Guayabo *p97*

Bus From **Turrialba**, there are buses at 1100 (returning 1250) and 1710 (returning 1750), and on Sun at 0900 (returning 1700). Check times. US$0.45 to Guayabo. Several buses each day pass the turn-off to Guayabo; the town is a 2-hr walk uphill (taxi US$10, easy to hitch back). Tour operators in **San José** offer day trips for about US$65 per person (minimum 4 people), cheaper from Turrialba.

⊙ Directory

Cártago *p95*

Banks No shortage of banks, most with ATMs. Banco de Costa Rica, Av 4, Calle 5-7. **Banco Scotiabank**, Park Central at Av 2, Calle 2. **Banco Nacional**, Av 2, Calle 1-3. **Emergencies** Call T911. **Internet** Café Línea, Av 4, Calle 6-8, the only internet place in town, looks decidedly temporary. **Medical services** Dr Max Peralta, entrance on Calle 3, Av 7. The **pharmacy** is along Av 4 between Calle 1-6.

Orosí Valley *p96*

Language schools Montaña Linda Language School, T2533-3640, see Sleeping, above. Uses local teachers to get you *hablando español* with a homestay option if you want total submersion. Recommended.

Northern Costa Rica

The Cordillera de Tilarán and the Cordillera de Guanacaste stretch to the Nicaragua border. Tucked in the eastern foothills is the vast man-made Lago Arenal, resting calmly beneath the highly active Volcán Arenal. A number of quieter spots can be found in the area with fine opportunities for fishing and seeing the wildlife, while the more active can go rafting, windsurfing, horse riding and trekking. ▸▸ *For listings, see pages 106-111.*

San Carlos and around

Also known as **Ciudad Quesada**, San Carlos is the main town of the northern lowland cattle and farming region and is a hub of communications. True to form, the town has a frontier feel with an air of bravado and a pinch of indifference. Situated on the downside of the northern slopes of the central highlands mountain region, the temperature rises and the speed of life slows down. In a town without major sights, the huge church overlooking the main plaza stands out. The cavernous interior is matched for style by modern stained-glass windows and an equally massive sculpture of Christ above the altar. As a regional centre San Carlos is served by frequent buses from San José, and has good connections to La Fortuna and Los Chiles. The bus terminal, about 1 km north of town, is close to a shopping centre and cinema. From San Carlos a paved road runs northwest to **Florencia** (service station). At Platanar de San Carlos, are a couple of sleeping options, see page 106.

Los Chiles and Refugio Natural de Vida Silvestre Caño Negro

Heading through the northern lowlands, a good road carves through rich red laterite soils in an almost straight line for 74 km through flat land where the shiny leaves of orange and citrus fruit plantations have replaced forest. Just short of the Nicaraguan border is Los Chiles, where boat trips head through dense, tropical vegetation into the 10,171-ha Caño Negro Natural Wildlife Refuge and Caño Negro Lake, spanning about 800-ha in the rainy season. Birdwatchers flock to the northern wetlands to see the amazing variety of birdlife which feasts at the seasonal lake created by the flood waters of the Río Frío. The lake slowly shrinks in the dry season (January to April). The variety of habitats in the refuge makes a rewarding trip for anyone interested in seeing alligators, turtles and monkeys. Fishing trips for snook and tarpon are easily arranged.

Los Chiles is a small town on the banks of the Río Frío, a few hundred metres west of Highway 35. The central plaza is also a football pitch, and most places of interest are within a block or two. The days pass slowly as children chuck themselves off the dockside in the heat of the afternoon sun. Ask about guides at **Restaurant Los Petates**, **Restaurant El Parque** or **Rancho Eco-Directa**. A three-hour tour with Esteban, Oscar Rojas (T2471-1090) and Enrique, who have all been recommended, costs about US$60. Alternatively, **Aventuras Arenal in Fortuna** run trips to Caño Negro (see below) approximately US$55. It is cheaper to get a boat from **Los Chiles** to the park (US$60 for a boat, up to four people) rather than taking a tour from elsewhere (eg Fortuna) and convenient if you are going on to Nicaragua, but there are not always boats available nor sufficient numbers to fill one economically. Call the **Caño Negro park administration** ① *T2471-1309*, for information and reservations for food and lodging. US$10 entrance to the park.

Fishing trips are likely to be beyond the budgets of many, but then what price do you put on catching a 2-m-long tarpon. A full day's fishing on the Río Frío, Río San Juan or

Lago de Nicaragua (boat, rods and drinks included) can range from US$95 to US$500 with **No Frills Fishing Adventures** (see page 106), depending on the boat and destination.

Fortuna → *Altitude: 254 m.*

The small town of Fortuna is an ideal base for exploring the Arenal region with the ominous silhouette of the active Volcán Arenal looming above the town. Reached on a paved road running west from San Carlos/Ciudad Quesada or along the northern shore of Lake Arenal from Tilaran, it's worth a few days of your travels.

Once a quiet town that shuddered in the shadow of the volcano's power, Fortuna has grown rapidly to accommodate the steady increase in visitors keen to see the active volcano.

Transport between Fortuna and Santa Elena is time consuming by bus requiring travel to Tilarán for a connecting bus on the bumpy road up to Santa Elena. Alteratives are to get a jeep, boat, and jeep leaving Fortuna at 0830 and 1230, US$12, or horseriding to Monteverde (US$35). It is also becoming possible to get transfers to Tortuguero – ask locally for details.

Around Fortuna

About 6 km south of Fortuna are the impressive **Río Fortuna Waterfalls** ① *US$7, drinks available at the entrance*, plunging 70 m into the cloud of swirling mist and spray. It's a pleasant walk down the road for a couple of kilometres before turning off to head uphill through yucca and papaya plantations. From the entrance, a steep and slippery path leads to the falls, so take shoes with a good tread. Bathing is possible, so take swimming clothes, but it's safer 50 m downstream. If you don't want to walk, there are several options. You can drive, but 4WD is necessary. Bicycle hire (US$3 per hour, US$15 per day) is one option and hard work, or you can hire a horse for the day at around US$35. Two to three hours' climb above the falls is the crater lake of Cerro Chato. The top (1100 m) is reached through mixed tropical/cloudforest, with a good view (if you're lucky) but beware of snakes on the path. A guide, if you need one, will charge US$9.

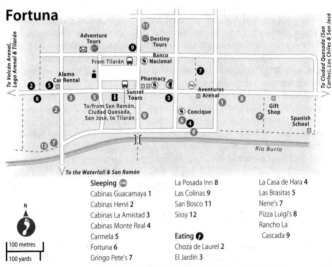

Fortuna

Sleeping
Cabinas Guacamaya 1
Cabinas Hervi 2
Cabinas La Amistad 3
Cabinas Monte Real 4
Carmela 5
Fortuna 6
Gringo Pete's 7

La Posada Inn 8
Las Colinas 9
San Bosco 11
Sissy 12

Eating
Choza de Laurel 2
El Jardín 3

La Casa de Hara 4
Las Brasitas 5
Nene's 7
Pizza Luigi's 8
Rancho La
  Cascada 9

Border essentials: Costa Rica–Nicaragua

Los Chiles → *See also page 223.*

This crossing point is now open to foreigners but the road link is a dirt track, and San Carlos on the Nicaraguan side is remote from the rest of that country.

Costa Rican immigration All formalities are in Los Chiles which is a few kilometres short of the border. The office is close to the river and leaving procedures are normally straightforward. Daily 0800-1600, usually closed for lunch. If entering Costa Rica, officials can be more difficult, mainly because they are sensitive about the many Nicaraguan immigrants wishing to enter the country. Crossing purely overland is possible. It is some 4 km to the border post, and a total of 14 km to San Carlos with no regular transport. See Nicaragua–San Carlos and San Juan del Norte/Greytown for details on the Río San Juan border, page 223.

Transport A regular launch goes down the Río Frío across the Río San Juan to San Carlos, 0800 or when full, 45 minutes, US$5. There are other launches if demand is sufficient. You can follow the track north to the Río San Juan and then find a ferry to cross, but enquire before trying this route.

Safari river floats down the Río Peñas Blancas (US$43) and whitewater rafting, best in the wet season (from US$69 for a one-day trip including all food and transport), are available through several tour operators. **Horse riding** through the forest to Monteverde costs around US$75 per person for the day trip. Luggage is taken on pack animals or by vehicles. Some operators seem to change the route once underway due to some 'unforeseen problem', so agree the route and try to arrange compensation if there are major changes. Due to competition for business, many horses are overworked on this route. Although difficult when on a budget, try not to bargain down the price, and ask to see the horses before beginning the journey. The journey is also possible by jeep-boat-jeep (US$30-35).

A small **snake farm** ① *a few kilometres west of Fortuna, US$2,* with 40 specimens is a good opportunity to get up close and personal with these rather cool creatures.

Almost 5 km north of Fortuna is the **Baldi Thermae complex** ① *T2479-9651, daily 1000-2200, US$28,* with four thermal pools ranging from 37° up to 63°C – the limits of endurance without being poached. Poolside drinks, looks good, feels great (taxi from town US$4, bus US$1).

Ten kilometres northwest of Fortuna is **Balneario Tabacón** ① *T2460-2020, daily 1000-2200, day guests welcome, entry US$60,* a kitsch complex of thermal pools, waterfalls and (for residents) beauty treatments, with three bars and a restaurant. The water is hot and stimulating; there are a pools at descending heights and temperatures as well as water-slides and a waterfall to sit under. The food is good and the fruit drinks thirst quenching. The resort (**L**) is popular with evening coach tours from San José. Taxi from Fortuna to Tabacón US$4.50. Cheaper are the hot waters about 4 km further along the road at **Quebrada Cedeña**, which are clean and safe. There is no sign but look for local parked cars.

Also near Fortuna are the limestone **Cavernas del Venado**. Tours from Fortuna with all equipment can be arranged through **Eagle Tours** ① *T2479-9091, US$40.* Buses from San Carlos en route to Tilarán daily, return transport to Fortuna at 2200.

Volcán Arenal

Skirting the slopes of the 1633-m Volcán Arenal, the road travels north around the base to the man-made **Lago Arenal** and hydroelectric dam. The highly active volcano is beautiful, a classic Stromboli-type cone shape characterized by explosions sending out hot grey clouds of sulphurous gases, which can descend the slopes at alarming speeds. The lava streams have moved from the west side to the northeast following activity in recent years. Although the side facing Fortuna is green, the side facing the lake is grey and barren, and the lava flows are clearly visible. There are three active craters and several fumaroles, with activity particularly impressive at night, as the red hot lava crashes, smashes and tumbles down the hillside accompanied by rumbles and intermittent roars (rather like someone moving furniture upstairs). Some people say there is greater volcanic activity around the full moon. The activity is fuelled by a magma chamber that vulcanologists believe is just 5 km below the surface.

Arenal has been continuously active since July 1968, when an eruption killed 78 people and more or less destroyed three villages including Tabacón which is situated above the *balneario*. The most recent continuous major activity was in May 1998, but in 2000 a small group travelled beyond the permitted area, and were engulfed by a pyroclastic avalanche and the guide later died of third degree burns. On no account walk up the volcano beyond the level of the vegetation, as it's dangerous. There is good hiking on the lower slopes from Fortuna. You can see the latest images of Arenal at www.arenal.net/arenal-volcano.htm.

If you are visiting between May and December you may not see much as the volcano is usually obscured by clouds and rain and there can be bad weather for weeks on end. Clouds and rain are common in the afternoons all year round, but the clouds do break and you may be lucky. If you can hire a taxi for a trip at about 0400-0500, and you can get up, the sky is often clearer.

To the east, the vast Lago Arenal reflects the moods of the volcano perfectly: smooth and calm from a distance, but whipped up to a waved frenzy by strong easterlies which are squeezed by the hills on either side. The surrounding area offers a multitude of opportunities for hiking, mountain biking, windsurfing and many other activities. There is also access to Santa Elena and Monteverde on foot or horseback.

Park information Much of the area surrounding the volcano is a national park which most people visit as part of a tour. The most common entrance is through **Hotel Los Lagos**, see page 108), which offers night tours at 1700 for hotel guests, if the sky is clear. **Aventuras Arenal** can provide dependable advice.

Tour operators offer trips to view the volcano at night followed by a visit to the thermal baths; a typical four-hour tour, costing US$35 per person, leaves Fortuna at about 1530 and returns by 1930. Make sure the entry fee to the baths is included.

You can also visit the park on your own. The entrance is on the western flank of the volcano, on the other side to Fortuna, 2 km down a bumpy road signposted to Arenal Observatory Lodge. Four interesting trails, taking up to 1½ hours each, lead through the national park going through a mixture of terrains, that flourish in the microclimate of heavy rainfall bought on by the volcano.

North to Upala

A quiet route north leads from Fortuna to **San Rafael de Guatuso**. There is a 'voluntary' toll of US$1 between Jicarito and San Rafael for reconstruction work on this road. You can come back to the lake either by turning off before San Rafael through **Venado** (where there are caves), or from San Rafael itself, where there are a couple of basic hotels. If you continue along the road from San Rafael northwest towards the Nicaraguan border you come to **Upala** and a poor road east to **Caño Negro**. There is a direct bus from San José to Upala, T2221-3318 (from Avenida 3-5, Calle 10 at 1000 and 1700, four hours).

Around Lago Arenal

A mostly paved road twists and winds round the northern shore of Lake Arenal, leading to Tilarán via Nuevo Arenal. Whether travelling by bus or car, you can get from Fortuna to Monteverde via Tilarán in a day, but set out early to make your connection with the 1230 bus in Tilarán or to avoid driving after dark. The lakeside road has improved greatly in recent years, but some sections are still unpaved. The main hazard is the winding road and some seriously pot-holed sections.

There is plenty of good accommodation around the lake shore, much of it in the higher price brackets. With only a couple of buses a day, and limited traffic, getting off the bus for a look will almost certainly delay you for a day.

If you do stop, an excellent café for a meal and drink with great views over the lake is **Toad Hall** ① *T2692-8020*, towards the northeastern end, which has an excellent souvenir shop with a good mix of Costa Rican crafts, some modern, some traditional, most desirable.

With a head count of just over 2500 (**Nuevo**) **Arenal** is a small town with not much to see. The town is new, because it moved from its original location which now lies deep below the surface of the lake.

Continuing west towards Tilarán, the western side of the lake is popular with **windsurfers** throughout the year, and between December and April the conditions are world class. A batch of hotels cater for windsurfers of all levels; there are many other options in the area so take your pick if you want to stop.

Tilarán

Tilarán would not appear on the list of destinations for travellers were it not for its role as a small regional transport hub for people journeying between Fortuna, Santa Elena/Monteverde and Cañas on the Pan-American Highway. In town there is pretty much nothing to do, and with luck, the connecting buses will be timed perfectly to avoid you having to wait too long. But if you do, there are several places to catch a bite to eat, and several good places to stay if you need a bed for the night.

For Sleeping and Eating price codes, and other relevant information, see pages 43-46.

💤 Sleeping

San Carlos and around *p101*

AL Hotel La Garza, Platanar de San Carlos, 8 km from Florencia, T2475-5222, www.hotel lagarza.com. 12 charming bungalows with bath and fan, overlooking river. Idyllic spot with good views of Arenal. Guided tours, boat trips, fishing, 230 ha of forest and cattle ranch.

AL Tilajari Resort Hotel, Muelle San Carlos, 13 km north of Platanar de San Carlos, T2469-9091, www.tilajari.com. Luxury rooms, and suites, a/c, private bath, tennis courts, 2 pools, sauna, bar, restaurant, horses. Excursions. Justifiably popular with luxury groups.

C Don Goyo, San Carlos, T2460-1780. A baker's dozen of clean, well-lit rooms, with private bathrooms, fans, cable TV – best value in town.

C La Central, on west side of park, San Carlos, T2460-0301, www.hotellacentral.net. Private bath, hot water, fan, TV and phone in room.

D del Valle, Av 3, Calle 0-2, San Carlos, T2460-0718. Nothing special but friendly and secure, a good deal at this price.

D-E El Retiro, on the north side of the park, San Carlos, T2460-0463. Bath, hot water, clean and comfortable, popular with local business people.

D-E Fernando, Av 1 Calle 2-4, around corner from Banco Popular, T2460-3314. Probably the best of several basic *pensiones* if you can get one of the new rooms.

E Cabinas Kimbara, on the main road 800 m north of Muelle gas station, T2469-9100. Basic rooms, private bath, fan, includes taxes, pool.

Los Chiles *p101*

A Rancho Tulipán, 1 block west of the Parque Central opposite the immigration offices, T2471-1414, cocas34@hotmail.com.

New, good restaurant, 10 clean well-appointed rooms with a/c, TV, bath and hot water, breakfast and taxes included. Can arrange a wide variety of tours in the area including river safaris and fishing trips. The manager Carlos Sequera is useful for information on travelling to Nicaragua.

C Hotel Carolina, close to main highway, T2471-1151. Clean and well maintained – the best of the budgets. Accommodation ranges from small, fairly dark rooms with shared bath to a/c cabins with TV.

D No Frills Fishing Lodge, on the main highway just before town, T2471-1410, martin nofrills@hotmail.com set on a 40-ha property, clean modern rooms, restaurant and bar, 8 boats for fishing expeditions (see page 102).

D-E Cabinas Jabirú, 100 m from the bus stop, a few blocks from the central park, T2471-1496. Cheaper price for Youth Hostel members. Good, but simple rooms, with private bathrooms, fan, some with TV and parking. Postal service, fax and laundry and a range of interesting tours. Cheapest to **Caño Negro** (US$20 per person, minimum 3) and to El Castillo de la Concepción in Nicaragua.

F Onassis, southwest corner of main plaza, T2471-1447. Your best bet of the strip facing the football pitch. Basic rooms, clean, shared bath, meals upon request.

Fortuna *p102, map p102*

Generous discounts in the green/low season are common.

L Arenal Country Inn, south of town, T2479-9670, www.arenalcountryinn.com. A former working hacienda with 20 large, fully equipped cabinas set in pleasant tropical gardens. After eating in the dining room – once a holding pen – you can rest by the pool before heading out to explore.

L-AL Las Cabañitas, 1.5 km east of town, beyond **Villa Fortuna** T2479-9400. 43 cabins with private baths, a couple of pools, observatory for viewing Arenal volcano, restaurant. Recommended.

AL Fortuna, 1 block southeast of the central park, T2479-9197.Completely new, fully accessible. Price includes breakfast.

AL Hotel Arenal Rossi, T2479-9023, www.hotelarenalrossi.com. 1 km west, towards the volcano, with breakfast, friendly owner, hot water, fan, watch the volcano from the garden, horses rented, good value.

AL San Bosco, town centre, T2479-9050, www.arenal-volcano.com. All rooms with private bath, quiet, signs on main road, clean, friendly, nice gardens with terrace, pool and view of the volcano, excellent service and attention to detail, slightly less without a/c.

AL-A Cabinas Monte Real, 1 block from the main plaza, T2479-9357. Close to the centre, quiet and friendly, big rooms with private bath and hot water, pool, internet, next to the river and also close to centre. Parking.

A Albergue Ecoturístico La Catarata, 2 km from town, rough road, T2479-9522, www.cataratalodge.com. Price per person. Reservations essential for these 8 cabins in co-operative with organic garden, home-made soaps and shampoos, good fresh food, butterfly farm, taxi US$2, hot water, laundry, all meals. Run by community association and supported by WWF Canada and CIDA Canada.

A Cabinas Guacamaya, town centre, T2479-9393, www.cabinasguacamaya.com. 8 good-sized rooms sleeping 3 or 4, all with private bath and hot water, fridge and a/c. Clean and tidy, with plenty of parking.

A Hotel Carmela, on the south side of the church, T2479-9010. Has 26 rooms with private bath, floor and ceiling fans, some with fridge. Very central, hot showers, can arrange tours. Apartment sleeping 5 available (**E** per person). Recommended.

A-B Las Colinas, southeast of the central park, T2479-9305, info@lascolinasarenal.com 20 tidy rooms, with private bathroom, some with excellent views. Friendly management, good discounts in the low season. Internet access. Recommended.

A-E Arenal Backpacker's Resort, T2479-7000, www.arenalbackpackersresort.com. Good hostel a short distance north out of town. Dorm and private rooms. Great spot

with a pool in the garden with view of Arenal for relaxing when you want to relax.

B Cabinas Las Flores, west of town, 2 km on road towards the volcano, T2479-9307. Clean, basic, but a little overpriced, restaurant.

B Hotel Villa Fortuna, 500 m south of the bridge, 1 km east from the central plaza, T2479-9139. Has 12 bright and tidy cabins, with neat bathrooms, fans or a/c, nice pool and simple gardens.

C Cabinas La Amistad, central, T2479-9364. Clean, friendly, hot water, hard beds.

D La Posada Inn, a couple of blocks east of the Parque Central, T2479-9793. Price per person. 8 simple, but spotless rooms, bath with hot water, fans but mosquitoes reported. Small communal area out front, communal kitchen and the friendly owner Thadeo is very helpful.

D Sissy, office is 100 m south and 100 m west of church, T2479-9256. Quiet spot beside the river, basic rooms with private bathroom; others have shared bath, and there's access to a kitchen and camping spaces (US$3 per person); simple but friendly. Recommended.

F Gringo Pete's, east end of town, T2479-8521, gringopetes2003@yahoo.com. Great place, dormitory and private rooms, clean and tidy. Kitchen facilities and communal area for relaxing. Good notice board and tours arranged. Recommended. Another, bigger and better **Gringo Pete**'s opening across town soon.

Volcán Arenal p104

Fortuna is the easiest place to stay if you don't have your own transport (see page 110), but the whole area from Fortuna all along the shores of the lake is littered with hotels and eating options, each taking advantage of superb views and relative seclusion. Hotels on the southern side of the lake are slightly cut off but have fantastic views. Arenal Bungee T2479-7440 in the center of La Fortuna offers, bungee, rocket launcher and big swing adventures US$39

LL-L Arenal Observatory Lodge, on the northwestern side of the volcano, 4 km after

El Tabacón, a turn towards the lake down a (signposted) gravel road, T2290-7011, www.arenalobservatorylodge.com. 4WD recommended along this 9-km stretch (taxi-jeep from Fortuna, US$25). Set up in 1973, the observatory was purely a research station but it now has 42 rooms varying from cabins with bunk beds and bath, to newer rooms with queen-size beds. There are stunning views of the volcano (frighteningly close), Lake Arenal, and across the valley of Río Agua Caliente. The lava flows on the other side of the volcano, but the trails are beautiful and the service excellent.

LL-L Montaña de Fuego, T2479-1220, www.montanadefuego.com. 66 bungalows and rooms, with the stylish (and pricey) **Acuarelas** restaurant, canopy tour.

L Los Lagos, T2479-1000, www.hotellos lagos.com. 94 comfortable cabin rooms sleeping up to 4, day visits US$20, excellent food and spectacular views of the volcano over the lake, good facilities and small café. There are 3 marked footpaths towards the lava fields and lakes through the forest.

L Volcano Lodge, 6 km from Fortuna, T2460-6080, info@volcanolodge.com. With open-air restaurant good for viewing the volcano.

L-AL Arenal Paraíso Resort & Spa, 7.5 km from Fortuna, T2479-1100, www.arenal paraiso.com. 124 rooms, good views of the volcano.

L-AL Linda Vista del Norte Lodge on the gravel road, taking the right fork (not to the Arenal Observatory Lodge), near **Arenal Vista Lodge**, T2479-1551, www.hotellinda vista.com. Nice views, several good, unspoilt trails in the area, horse riding tours, hot water. Recommended.

AL Arenal Vista Lodge, T2692-2079. Has 25 rooms with bath, arranges boat trips, riding and hiking, close to hanging bridges and canopy tour, also butterfly garden.

Camping

There is a small campsite just before the park entrance with hook-ups for vehicles, US$2.50 per person. Great views of the volcano and a good spot for walking.

Camping is also possible on the edge of the lake, no services, but good view of volcano at night.

North to Upala p105

L Magil Forest Lodge, 3 km from Col Río Celeste, near San Rafael de Guatuso, T2221-2825. Set in 240 ha on the foothills of the 1916-m **Volcán Tenorio** (now a national park of 12,871 ha with thermal waters, boiling mud and unspoilt forest). 7 rooms with private bath, price includes meals.

F Pensión Buena Vista, Upala. Basic, food available.

Around Lago Arenal p105

LL La Mansión Marina and Club, T2692-8018, www.lamansionarenal.com. On the lake, beautiful pool, very relaxing.

LL-AL Arenal Lodge, travelling round the lake from Fortuna, just north of the dam wall up 2.5-km steep road, T2460-1881, www.arenallodge.com. Stunning views to the north and south. Rooms, suites, meal extra in excellent restaurant.

L-AL Hotel Tilawa, 8 km north of Tilarán, T2695-5050, www.hotel-tilawa.com. With great rooms, restaurant, tennis and excellent opportunities for wind surfing, kayaking and birdwatching. Equipment for rent for US$55 a day. Guaranteed beginner lesson – if it's not fun it's free; try not to laugh and you've got a good deal. Good discounts off season.

L-A Hotel Los Héroes (Pequeña Helvecia), 10 km from Arenal towards Tilarán, T2692-8012, www.hotellosheroes.com. Delightful Swiss owners with inspiring energy. A superb hotel, complete with Swiss train service.

AL La Ceiba, 6 km from Arenal, T2692-8050, www.ceibatree-lodge.com. Overlooking Lake Arenal, Tico owned and run, good, helpful, great panoramic views, good breakfast.

A Chalet Nicholas, west end of lake, T2694-4041, www.chaletnicholas.com. Bed and breakfast (a speciality), run by friendly retired North Americans. Non-smokers only, children under 10 discouraged. Recommended.

A Rock River Lodge, on the road skirting the lake, T2692-1180. Rooms and bungalows, with bathroom, good restaurant. Excellent activity spot with day options for surfing (US$35) and fishing (US$55) and good mountain biking. Bikes available for hire.

B Aurora Inn B&B (Nuevo) Arenal, T2694-4590. Under new management, private bath, pool and jacuzzi, art gallery, wedding receptions overlooking Lake Arenal.

B La Alondra, west of **La Mansión Marina and Clubs**, T2692-8036. With simple, basic rooms sleeping up to 4 and great Tico restaurant from US$5.

Tilarán *p105*

C Cabiñas El Sueño, 1 block north of bus terminal/central park, T2695-5347. Clean rooms around central patio, hot water, fan, TV, friendly and free coffee. Good deal.

C Naralit, on the south side of the church, T2695-5393. Clean, new buildings and a restaurant.

D Hotel Restaurant Mary, south side of church, T2695-5479. Bath, small pleasant rooms, newly renovated, the upstairs is recommended.

D-E Central, round the back of the church, 1 block south, T2695-5363. With shared bath (more with own bath), noisy.

⊘ Eating

San Carlos and around *p101*

Variety of sodas in the central market offer *casados*, check out the great sword collection displayed at **La Ponderosa**.

ɪɪɪ Coca Loca Steak House, next to **Hotel La Central**, T2460-3208. Complete with Wild West swing door.

ɪɪ Los Geranios, Av 4 and Calle. Popular bar and restaurant serving up good *bocas* and other dishes.

ɪɪ Restaurant Crystal, on the western side of the plaza. Sells fast food, snacks, ice cream and good fruit dishes.

Los Chiles *p101*

ɪ El Parque on the main plaza. With good home cooking.

ɪ Los Petates, on road running south of the central park. Has good food, cheap with large portions but check the bill.

Fortuna *p102, map p102*

ɪɪɪ La Vaca Muca, out of the town on the way to Tabacón, T2479-9186. Typical Latino food, steak house.

ɪɪɪ Las Brasitas, at west end of town (see map), T2479-9819. Open-air restaurant serving abundant authentic Mexican fare with a laid-back European-café style.

ɪɪ Choza de Laurel, west of the church, T2479-7063. Typical food in a rustic setting, serving breakfast, lunch and dinner, US$2-US$4.50, occasionally greeted by passing hummingbirds.

ɪɪ Coco Loco, south of town, T2468-0990. Coffee, smoothies and fruit drinks, gallery and souvenirs.

ɪɪ El Jardín, on the main street opposite the gas station, T2479-9360. Good menu with a mix of local and fast food, pizza, good place to watch the world go by.

ɪɪ Nene's, 1½ blocks east of the main square, T2479-9192. Good food, pleasant service, not expensive. Recommended.

ɪɪ Pizza Luigi's, west end of town (see map), T2479-9898. Formal, open-air restaurant with distinctly Italian pretensions toward pizza and pasta. Good wine list for Fortuna.

ɪɪ Rancho La Cascada, corner of Parque with high conical thatched roof, T2479-9145. Good *bocas*, films sometimes shown in evenings.

ɪɪ Steakhouse Arenal next to **Hotel Las Flores**. Mid-priced steak house with Texan tendencies.

ɪɪ Vagabondo, west end of town, T2479-8087, www.vagabondocr.com. Reasonably priced pizza and pasta, also has rooms (**A**) with breakfast.

ɪ La Casa de Hara, round the side of **Hotel Fortuna**. Very good local food, fast service and normal prices – where the locals eat.

Around Lago Arenal *p105*

†††-† Caballo Negro, a couple of km west of (Nuevo) Arenal, T2694-4515. The best restaurant for miles, serving vegetarian, Swiss and seasonal fish dishes with organic salads. Warm family atmosphere.

††† Maverick's Bar & Restaurant (Nuevo) Arenal, T2694-4282. Grilled meat, pizza, excellent food, salad bar and very friendly.

††† Restaurante Lajas (Nuevo) Arenal, T2694-4385. Tico and vegetarian fare.

††† Típico Arenal (Nuevo) Arenal, T2694-4159. Good local dishes with seafood and vegetarian options. Large room upstairs (**C**) with private bath and hot water, the best cheap place in town.

††† Toad Hall, northeast of the lake, T2692-8020. Café, restaurant and gift shop.

Tilarán *p105*

††† Restaurant La Carreta, at the back of the church, T2695-6593. The place to go and relax if you have time to kill. Excellent breakfast and lunch only, North American food, pancakes, coffee and good local information.

† Stefanie's, out of the bus station to the left on the corner of the main plaza. Good and quick if you need a meal between buses.

▲ Activities and tours

Fortuna *p102, map p102*
Tour operators
Aventuras Arenal, on the main street, T2479-9133, www.arenaladventures.com. Provides all tours in the area, and has been around for many years. Can help with enquiries about other parts of Costa Rica.
Canopy Tour, east down the main street, T2479-9769, www.crarenalcanopy.com. Offer a short horse riding journey from Fortuna, US$50, as well as quad tours, mountain bike rental and general tours.
Desafío, just off main square by thatched restaurant, T2479-9464, www.desafio costarica.com. Full range of tours, and with office in Monteverde.

Eagle Tours, T2479-9091, www.eagle tours.net. Tours with usual tours.
Sunset Tours, T2479-9800, www.sunset tourcr.com. Reliable, long-standing company with a selection of tours. Recommended.

⊙ Transport

San Carlos and around *p101*
Bus Direct bus from Terminal Atlántico Norte, **San José**, hourly from 0645-1815, 2¼ hrs, US$2.20, return 0500-1930. From San Carlos buses go northwest to **Tilarán** via **Fortuna** and **Arenal** (0630 and 1400), other buses go to **Fortuna** through El Tanque, 6 daily, 1½ hrs, **San Rafael de Guatuso** and **Upala**, north to **Los Chiles**, hourly, 3 hrs, northeast to towns on the Río San Carlos and Río Sarapiquí, including **Puerto Viejo de Sarapiquí** (5 a day, 3 hrs), and east to the Río Frío district.

Los Chiles *p101*
Bus Going into Costa Rica, there are direct buses to **San José** daily 0500, 1500, 5 hrs, from San José Atlántico Norte Terminal, Calle 12, Av 7-9, to Los Chiles at 0530, 1530, US$4 with **Auto Transportes San Carlos**, T2255-4318. Alternatively take one of the hourly buses from the same terminal in San José to **San Carlos**, US$3.25 (**Cd Quesada**) from where there are hourly services, 2 hrs, US$2.20. From **Fortuna**, take the bus to San Carlos, get off at Muelle and wait for a connection.

Fortuna *p102, map 102*
Bus From **San José** there are daily returning buses hourly from 0500-1930 from Terminal Atlántico Norte, with **Auto Transportes San José–San Carlos**, T2255-4318, 4½ hrs, via San Carlos, US$3.25. From **San Carlos**, 6 buses daily, 1 hr, US$1. To **Tilarán** there are 2 buses daily at 0800 (connecting to 1230 bus Tilarán–Santa Elena/Monteverde and 1300 bus Tilarán–Puntarenas) and 1730, US$2.90, 4 hrs. Shuttle bus services to **Monteverde**

and **Tamarindo** (US$26 per person, min 6). Taxis in the area overcharge. Agree on price before travelling.

Leaving Fortuna, there are frequent buses to **San Ramon** with buses to San José every 30 mins, and good connections to Puntarenas. Also regular service to **Ciudad Quesada**.

Car hire Alamo, T2479-9090, has an office in town; Poás T2479-8027.

Tilarán *p105*
Bus If heading for Santa Elena and Monteverde see page 113. Direct bus from **San José**, 4 daily, 4 hrs, from Terminal Atlántico Norte. 2 daily buses to **San Carlos** via Fortuna at 0700 and 1230. To **Fortuna**, 3 hrs, US$2.00. Daily bus to **Santa Elena** (for Monteverde), 1230, 2½ hrs, US$1.65, return 0700 daily. Tilarán–Puntarenas 0600, 1300, 3 hrs, US$3. 5 daily buses to/from **Cañas** (at 0500, 0730, 1000, 1230 and 1530, 40 mins, US$1.25), where buses head north and south along the Pan-American. If you get the 1230 Tilarán–Liberia bus you can get from there to the Nicaraguan border before it closes.

❶ Directory

San Carlos and around *p101*
Banks Banco Nacional, Av Central, west of the church, T2461-9200. **Banco de Costa Rica**, east side of park and another near the market, T2461-9006, both have ATMs. Others nearby, include **Banco Popular**, T2460-0534.

Internet Ask around or try **Café Internet**, Av 5, Calle 2-4, 400c per hr, Mon-Fri 0800-2100, Sat 0800-1800. **Post office** Av 5, Calle 2-4.

Los Chiles *p101*
Banks Banco Nacional, with ATM, on central park. **Post office** Services provided by **Cabiñas Jabirú**, 25 m north of market.

Fortuna *p102, map p102*
Banks Banco Nacional de Costa Rica, T2479-9022, will change TCs, US$1 commission, ATM. **Banco Popular**, T2479-9422, Visa ATM. **Coocique**, open Sat mornings 0800-1200, Visa ATM. **Internet** Prices in Fortuna are quite expensive. Try **Eagle Tours**, T2479-9091, or **Destiny Tours**. **Laundry** Lavandería **La Fortuna**, Mon-Sat 0800-2100, US$5 wash and dry 4 kg. **Pharmacy** Farmacia Dr **Max**, east down the main street, Mon-Sat 0730-2030, Sun 0800-1200. **Post office** Down main street, shares building with the police.

Around Lago Arenal *p105*
Banks Banco Nacional (Nuevo) Arenal, beside the football pitch.

Tilarán *p105*
Banks Banco Cootilaran, a couple of blocks north of the Parque Central, has a Visa and MasterCard ATM, and there is also a **Banco de Costa Rica** in town. **Internet** Café across from bus station.

Northwest Costa Rica

The route of the Pan-American Highway heads north passing near the world-renowned Monteverde Cloud Forest in the Cordillera de Tilarán, the marshes of the Parque Nacional Palo Verde, the active Volcán Rincón and the dry tropical forest of the Parque Nacional Santa Rosa on the Pacific coast, as it crosses the great cattle haciendas of Guanacaste before reaching the Nicaraguan border. ➤➤ *For listings, see pages 122-130.*

San José to Esparza and Barranca

The Pan-American Highway from San José descends from the Meseta Central to Esparza, an attractive town with a turbulent early history, as it was repeatedly sacked by pirates in the 17th century, belying its peaceful nature today.

The stretch of the highway between San Ramón and Esparza (31 km) includes the sharp fall of 800 m from the Meseta Central, often shrouded in mist and fog making conditions treacherous for road users. Beyond Esparza is the **Bar/Restaurant Mirador Enis**, a popular stopping place for tour buses breaking the journey at a service station with fruit stalls nearby, before a left turn at Barranca for Puntarenas, 15 km.

Puntarenas and around

Puntarenas fills a 5-km spit, thrusting out into the Gulf of Nicoya, east to west, but no wider than six avenues. Although popular with locals, most visitors pass through, using it as a transport hub with links to the southern Nicoya Peninsula or to get a bus north or south to other parts of the country without returning to San José. If heading for Nicoya, see page 131. If heading to Santa Elena/Monteverde see below, and page 128. It is also the Pacific destination for the bright white, cruise palaces that float through the Central American ports, and dock at Muelle de Cruceros on the Calle Central.

Once the country's main Pacific port with rail links to the Central Highlands, it has since been superseded by Caldera a short distance to the south. The northern side of the peninsula, around Calle Central with the market, banks, a few hotels and the fishing docks, is run-down and neglected, typical of small tropical ports. The southern side is made up of the **Paseo de los Turistas**, drawing crowds to the hot, sometimes dirty beach, especially at weekends. There are several hotels along the strip, as well as restaurants, bars and a general seafront beach atmosphere. There is a public swimming pool at the western end of the point (US$1 entrance), close to the ferries, and good surfing off the headland. There is a **Museo de la Historia Marina** ① *T2661-5036, Tue-Sun 0945-1200, 1300-1715, US$1.80*, in the Cultural Centre by the main church and tourist office. Across the gulf are the hills of the Nicoya Peninsula. **Puntarenas Marine Park** ① *T2661-5272, daily 0900-1700, US$4 children US$2*, offers 28 large aquariums showing Costa Rica's marine life. In the gulf are several islands including the **Islas Negritas**, a biological reserve reached by passenger launches.

Monteverde and Santa Elena ●●●●●●● ➤➤ *pp122-130.*

Monteverde Cloud Forest Reserve is one of the most precious natural jewels in Costa Rica's crown, and an opportunity to see plants, insects, birds and mammals in grand profusion – well in theory, at least. Protected by law, this private preserve is also protected by appalling access roads on all sides (the nearest decent road is at least two hours from the town). Santa Elena and Monteverde, although separate, are often referred to as the same place; most sites of interest are between the town of Santa Elena at the bottom of the hillside and Monteverde Cloud Forest Reserve at the top.

Ins and outs

From the Pan-American Highway northwest to Km 149, turn right just before the Río Lagarto. Continue for about 40 km on mostly gravel road (allow 2½ hours) to Santa Elena. Parts of the road are quite good, but in wet weather 4WD is recommended for the rough parts. If driving, check that your car rental agreement allows you to visit Monteverde. A 33-km shorter route is to take the Pipasa/Sardinal turn-off from the Pan-American Highway shortly after the Río Aranjuez. At the park in Sardinal, turn left, then go via Guacimal to the Monteverde road.

Buses come from Puntarenas via the Km 149 route. There are also buses from Tilarán to the north, linked with Fortuna by Volcán Arenal, and Cañas on the Pan-American Highway. There are two daily buses from San José.

Alternatively you can make the journey from Tilarán by bus or private transport. It's an equally poor road – a journey that takes a couple of hours, but, if driving, you can visit the quiet and dramatic **Cataratas de Viento Fresco**, some 11 km from Tilarán, 800 m down a very steep road, followed by a 400-m walk. It's a bit hairy if it's raining but worth the effort.

Santa Elena and around

Santa Elena is a rugged and busy place, often packed with visitors exploring the options or just passing time. It is cheaper to stay in town rather than along the single, unpaved road that twists and turns for 5 km through the village of Monteverde, with hotels and places of interest situated along the road almost to the reserve itself. **Santa Elena Reserve, Sky Trek** and **Sky Walk** are to the north of Santa Elena, all other places of interest are east, heading up the hill.

Five kilometres north of Santa Elena, off the road to Tilarán, **Sky Walk** ① *T2645-5238, www.skytrek.com, daily 0700-1600, US$17, student US$13, child US$8*, uses six suspension bridges to take you through the cloudforest at canopy level, the highest being 42 m above the ground. **Sky Trek** ① *T2645-5238,www.skytrek.com, daily 0700-1500, US$44, student US$35, child US$31*, is even more popular and a breathtaking experience, as you fly through the air on a system of cables strung out from giant forest trees. On clear days the view from the highest tower is unbelievable.

Very close to Santa Elena, at the start of the climb to Monteverde, is the **Serpentarium** ① *T2645-6002, daily 0900-2000, US$8, US$6 students*, with specimens of snakes and amphibians found in the nearby cloudforest. Other natural history places of interest include the **Frog Pond** ① *TT2645-6320, daily 0900-2030, US$9*, with 25 species of frog, and **The Bat Jungle** ① *daily 0900-2000, T2645-5052, US$8*, learn about more about the nocturnal habits of over 40 bats.

One hundred metres beyond **Hotel Sapo Dorado** is the **Orchid Garden** ① *T2645-5510, daily 0800-1700, US$5, US$3 students*, with about 400 species collected by Gabriel Barboza.

A dirt road opposite the **Hotel Heliconia** leads to the **Monteverde Butterfly Garden** ① *T2645-5512 daily 0930-1600, T2645-5512, www.monteverdebutterflygarden.com, US$10, US$8 students, including guided tour, best time for a visit 1100-1300*, a beautifully presented large garden planted for breeding and researching butterflies. Near the Butterfly Garden is **Finca Ecológica**, ① *T2645-5869, 0700-1730 daily, US$10, night tours US$15, free map*, with three trails totalling around 5 km with bird lists for birdwatching and varied wildlife in this transitional zone between cloud and tropical dry forest, guides available. Good night tours. Down the same path is **Aerial Adventures** ① *daily 0800-1600, US$15, T2645-5960*, a ski-lift-style ride travelling slowly through the treetops. Ideal for birdwatching.

Santa Elena Cloud Forest Reserve

ⓘ *0700-1600, entrance US$12, students US$6, T2645-5390, www.reservasantaelena.org, for information. It is a long, steep hike from the village; alternatively hire a taxi, US$6.50 (car load).*
About 1 km along the Santa Elena–Tilarán road north, a 5-km track is signposted to the reserve, managed by the **Centro Ecológico Bosque Nuboso de Monteverde**. It is 83% primary

Monteverde & Santa Elena

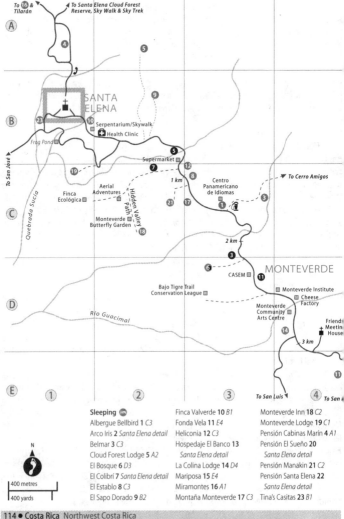

Sleeping

Albergue Bellbird **1** *C3*	Finca Valverde **10** *B1*
Arco Iris **2** *Santa Elena detail*	Fonda Vela **11** *E4*
Belmar **3** *C3*	Heliconia **12** *C3*
Cloud Forest Lodge **5** *A2*	Hospedaje El Banco **13**
El Bosque **6** *D3*	*Santa Elena detail*
El Colibrí **7** *Santa Elena detail*	La Colina Lodge **14** *D4*
El Establo **8** *C3*	Mariposa **15** *E4*
El Sapo Dorado **9** *B2*	Miramontes **16** *A1*
	Montaña Monteverde **17** *C3*

Monteverde Inn **18** *C2*
Monteverde Lodge **19** *C1*
Pensión Cabinas Marín **4** *A1*
Pensión El Sueño **20**
Santa Elena detail
Pensión Manakin **21** *C2*
Pensión Santa Elena **22**
Santa Elena detail
Tina's Casitas **23** *B1*

cloudforest and the rest is secondary forest at 1700 m, bordered by the Monteverde Cloud Forest Reserve and the Arenal Forest Reserve. There is a 12-km path network and several lookouts where, on a clear day, you can see and hear Volcán Arenal. The 'canopy tour' is recommended: you climb inside a hollow strangler fig tree then cross between two platforms along aerial runways 30 m up, good views of orchids and bromeliads, then down a 30-m hanging rope at the end. There are generally fewer visitors here than at Monteverde. The **Centro Ecológico Bosque Nuboso** is administered by the local community and profits go to five local schools. It was set up by the Costa Rican government in 1989 with collaboration from Canada. There is a small information centre where rubber boots can be hired and a small café open at weekends. Hand-painted T-shirts are for sale.

Monteverde and around

Strung out along the road to the cloudforest, the settlement at Monteverde – between Santa Elena and the reserve – was founded by American Quakers in the 1950s. Without a centre as such, it started life as a group of dairy farms providing milk for a co-operative cheese factory. Now privately owned, the factory still operates selling excellent cheeses, fresh milk, ice cream, milkshakes to die for and *cajeta* (a butterscotch spread). Shop closes 1600.

Today, Monteverde maintains an air of pastoral charm, but tourism provides more revenue for the town than dairy produce ever could. It was the vision of the dairy farmers that led to the creation of the reserve to protect the community watershed. When George Powell and his wife spent time in the region studying birds they realized the importance of protecting the area. Working with local residents they created the reserve in 1972 – foresight that has spawned the creation of many other natural attractions locally and throughout the country.

The best way of getting the full low-down on the place is at the new **Museum of Monteverde History** ① *daily 0930-1930, US$5*. A spacious museum that records the history of Monteverde, beginning with the

nta Elena detail

- ⑧
- ⑬
- ⑤ Banco Nacional
- 🛏 Sky Walk Office
- ⑫
- ② Santa Elena
- ㉒
- ⑦
- ⓪
- permarket & ATM
- ⑳
- ⑩ Canopy Tour Base Camp

Monteverde
Cloud Forest Reserve ◆

5 km

Hummingbird ▣ Gallery

4 km

㉔

Reserve Entrance & Field Station

⑤   ⑥

creation of the Central American isthmus 3 million years ago to its settlement by indigenous people – then the arrival of the Ticos, followed by the Quaker settlers, and then biologists, conservationists and ecotourism.

Reserva Sendero Tranquilo ① *daily, T2645-5010, entry restricted to 12 people at any one time,* is a private 200-ha reserve near the Monteverde cheese factory. Reservations and guides should be arranged through El Sapo Dorado hotel, which also offers night tours for US$25 per person.

Just before the entrance to Monteverde Cloud Forest is the **Hummingbird Gallery** ① *T2645-5030, daily 0700-1700,* where masses of different hummingbirds can be seen darting around a glade, visiting feeding dispensers filled with sugared water. Outside the entrance is a small shop/photo gallery which sells pictures and gifts, as well as Bromeliads Nature Bookstore and Café. There is also a slide show at **Hotel Belmar**, **The Hidden Rainforest** ① *1930 daily except Fri,* by Bobby Maxson.

Adjoining the Monteverde Cloud Forest is **El Bosque Eterno de los Niños (Children's Eternal Rainforest)** ① *T2645-5003, acmmcl@racsa.co.cr,* established in 1988 after an initiative by Swedish schoolchildren to save forests. Currently at 22,000 ha, the land has been bought and is maintained by the **Monteverde Conservation League** with children's donations from around the world. The **Bajo Tigre** trail takes 1½ hours, parking available with notice, a guide can be arranged, but no horses are allowed on the trail. Groups can arrange trips to the **San Gerardo** and **Poco Sol Field stations** ① *0800-1600, entrance US$6, students US$2, contact the Monteverde Conservation League for reservations at San Gerardo or Poco Sol, T2645-5003, www.acmcr.org,* one of Costa Rica's best kept secrets.

Guanacaste Conservation Area

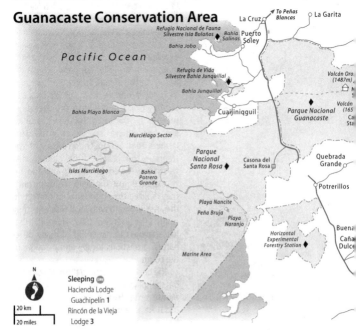

Sleeping 🛌
Hacienda Lodge
Guachipelín 1
Rincón de la Vieja
Lodge 3

Monteverde Cloud Forest Reserve

ⓘ *www.cct.or.cr. The reserve entrance is at the field station at the top of the road. Bus from Santa Elena heads up the hill leaving at 0600 and 1100 returning at 1400 and 1700. The total number of visitors to the reserve at any one time is 150, so be there before 0700 to make sure of getting in during high season (hotels will book you a place for the following day). Tour buses come in from San José daily. Entrance fee US$15 (students with ID ½-price) valid for multiple entry during the day, cannot be purchased in advance. Office open daily 0700-1630; the park opens at 0700 and closes at 1700. A small shop at the office sells various checklists, postcards and APS film, gifts and excellent T-shirts, the proceeds of which help towards the conservation project.*

Straddling the continental divide, the 10,500-ha Monteverde Cloud Forest Reserve is privately owned and administered by the Tropical Science Centre – a non-profit research and educational association. The reserve is mainly primary cloudforest and spends much of the year shrouded in mist, creating stunted trees and abundant epiphytic growth. The best months to visit are January-May, especially February, March and April. It contains more than **400 species of bird**, including the resplendent quetzal, best seen in the dry months between January and May, especially near the start of the Nuboso trail, the three-wattled bellbird with its distinctive 'bonk' call and the bare-necked umbrella bird. There are more than **100 species of mammal**, including monkeys, Baird's tapir and six endangered cats – jaguar, jaguarundi, margay, ocelot, tigrillo and puma – reptiles and amphibians. But be warned, travellers have told us there is little chance of seeing much wildlife. The reserve also includes an estimated 2500 species of plant and more than 6000 species of insect. The entrance is at 1500 m, but the maximum altitude in the reserve is over 1800 m. Mean temperature is between 16° and 18°C and average annual rainfall is 3000 mm. The weather changes quickly and wind and humidity often make the air feel cooler.

The commonly used trails are in good condition and there are easy, short and interesting walks for those who do not want to hike all day. Trail walks take from two hours but you could easily spend all day just wandering around. Trails may be restricted from time to time if they need protection. There is a trail northwards to the Arenal volcano that is increasingly used, but it is not easy. There are three refuges for people wishing to spend the night within the reserve boundaries, see Sleeping. Free maps of the reserve are available at the entrance. Follow the rules, stay on the paths, leave nothing behind, take no fauna or flora out; no radios or CD players are allowed.

Guides Natural history walks with biologist guides, every morning and afternoon, three to four hours, US$16 (children half price); advance reservations at the office or through your hotel are strongly recommended. If you

Border essentials: Costa Rica–Nicaragua

Peñas Blancas → *See also page 207.*

Immigration Office hours Monday-Saturday 0600-2200, Sunday 0600-2000, same hours on both sides. On leaving Costa Rica you have to go to Migración to surrender your passport to be stamped and to give in your immigration form. 'Helpers' may try and sell you the form before you arrive at the office – you do not have to buy it from them. Across the border, passports are inspected on the Nicaraguan side. Crossing to Nicaragua may be a slow process; if you arrive when a Tica, Sirca or other international bus is passing through this is especially true. When leaving Nicaragua you pay US$1 for the 'right to leave', another US$2 at customs and there are reports of a US$1 bus station tax on the Nicaraguan side. Visa stamps are given at the border. If you have no outward ticket for Costa Rica, and are challenged, you can buy a cheap bus ticket back to Nicaragua at the border (valid for one year).

Crossing by private vehicle Entering Costa Rica by car, first pay your entrance stamp, then go to Aduana Permiso de Vehículo for your vehicle permit (state how long you want); get insurance at the *Seguro Obligatorio* window. Your vehicle is then briefly inspected before you can depart. Fumigation cost US$3 for cars, US$4 for pick-ups. Leaving by car, hand over the printed vehicle permit you got on arrival. For documents and other requirements, see page 58.

Transport There are several express or ordinary buses a day from/to San José, 100 m north of Coca Cola terminal, five hours, US$8. Bus from the border to Liberia, US$1.50, 1½ hours. Only a few buses from La Cruz, US$0.80.

Banks There is a branch of BCR in the Customs building. Open daily 0700-1900. Money changers also available if required. Good rates if you shop around; there's no great difference between rates on either side.

use a private (non-reserve) guide you must pay his entrance fee too. An experienced and recommended guide is **Gary Diller** ① *T2645-9916*, he also does night tours. There are 25 others operating, of varying specialization and experience. Excellent night tours in the reserve are available normally with **Ricardo Guindon** or call **Monteverde Reserve** ① *T2645-5112, US$15*, at 1900 sharp. Day or night, a guide is recommended if you want to see wildlife, since the untrained eye misses a lot.

Donations and volunteer work Donations are welcomed for purchasing additional land and maintaining and improving existing reserve areas. If you are interested in volunteer work, from non-skilled trail maintenance to skilled scientific assistance work, surveying, teaching or studying on a tropical biology programme, contact the reserve (US$14 per person, board and lodging, two weeks minimum). The Conservation League works with schools in the area on education regarding conservation. Donations can be made at the **Monteverde Cloud Forest Reserve** office or **Tropical Science Centre** ① *San José, T2253-3267, www.cct.or.cr*, or the **Monteverde Conservation League** ① *Apdo Postal 124-5655, San José, Costa Rica, T2645-5003, www.acmcr.org*.

North of Barranca, the Pan-American Highway heads towards the province of Guanacaste – the cultural heartland of Costa Rica, home to the *sabanero* cowboy and the rolling plains of the northern ranches. The province also includes the Peninsula of Nicoya and the lowlands at the head of the gulf. Rainfall here is moderate, 1000-2000 mm a year. There is a long dry season which makes irrigation important, but the lowlands are deep in mud during the rainy season.

Guanacaste, with its capital Liberia, has a distinctive people, way of life, flora and fauna. The smallholdings of the highlands give way here to large haciendas and great cattle estates. The rivers teem with fish; there are all kinds of wildlife in the uplands.

The people are open, hospitable and fun-loving, and are famed for their music and dancing, and in fact, the Punto Guanacasteco has been officially declared the typical national dance. There are many fiestas in January and February in the local towns and villages, which are well worth seeing.

Heading northwest on the Pan-American Highway, turn right just after the Río Aranjuez at Rancho Grande (or just south of the Río Lagarto at Km 149) to access a dramatic and at times scenic route to Santa Elena-Monteverde (see page 113).

Forty-three kilometres north of Barranca is the turn-off for **Las Juntas**, an alternative route to Monteverde for those using the Tempisque ferry or arriving from Guanacaste; a third of it is paved. After Las Juntas, there is a mining ecomuseum at **La Sierra de Abangares** ① *daily 0600-1800, US$1.80*, with mining artefacts from a turn-of-the-20th-century gold mine.

The bridge over the Tempisque River, 4 km north, opened in 2003, ending the long waits for the car ferry. After about 6 km a road to the right at San Joaquín leads to the **Hacienda Solimar Lodge**, a 1300-ha cattle farm with dry tropical virgin forest bordering Parque Nacional Palo Verde (see below) near Porozal in the lower Tempisque River basin. The freshwater Madrigal estuary on the property is one of the most important areas for waterbirds in Costa Rica (only guests staying at the Hacienda can visit). Also surrounded by gallery forest, it is recommended for serious birdwatchers. Reservations essential, contact **Birdwatch** ① *T2228-4768, www.birdwatchcostarica.com*, see also page 124.

Sixty-seven kilometres north of Barranca, **Cañas** has little to keep the visitor for long. There are a number of interesting sights nearby and, for the traveller arriving from the north, this is the cut-through to Tilarán and connecting buses to Arenal or Fortuna. **Las Pumas** ① *behind Safaris Corobicí, Cañas, free but donations welcome and encouraged*, is a small, private, Swiss-run animal rescue centre which specializes in looking after big cats, including jaguar. It's an unmissable if rather sad experience.

Parque Nacional Palo Verde

At the south of the neck of the Nicoya Peninsula is Parque Nacional Palo Verde, currently over 18,650 ha of marshes with many water birds. Indeed, in the *laguna* more than 50,000 birds are considered resident. The views from the limestone cliffs are fantastic. **Palo Verde Biological Station** ① *T2661-4717, Reservations on T2524-0607, www.ots.ac.cr*, is a research station run by the Organization for Tropical Studies. It organizes natural history walks and basic accommodation; US$65 with three meals and a guided walk (from US$24), cheaper for researchers, make advance reservations. Turn off the Pan-American Highway at **Bagaces**, halfway between Cañas and Liberia. There is no public transport. The **Palo Verde Administration offices** ① *T2661-4717*, are in Bagaces, next to the service station. Park

entrance US$10 Camping US$5 per person and lodging US$13 in park, meals available.
There are two ranger stations, Palo Verde and Catalina. Check roads in wet season.

Liberia and around ⊜⊘⊗⊿⊖⊜⊙ ▸▸ pp122-130.

→ *Population: 40,000.*

Known as the 'White City', Liberia is a neat, clean, cattle town with a triangular, rather
unattractive modern church, and single-storey colonial houses meticulously laid out in
the streets surrounding the central plaza. The town is at the junction of the Pan-American
Highway and a well-paved branch road leads southwest to the Nicoya Peninsula.

There is a **tourist office** ① *3 blocks south of the plaza on Calle 1, Av 6, T2666-1606,* which
is helpful, English is spoken; leave a donation as the centre is not formally funded (the
information is not always accurate). In the same building is the **Museo del Sabanero**
(Cowboy Museum) ① *museum and tourist office Mon-Sat 0800-1200, 1300-1600, US$0.45,*
a poorly presented display of artefacts. You can also get some tourist information across
the plaza from the church.

Africa Mía animal park ① *T2661-8165, US$15 entry, child$10,* features animals from
Africa, including ostriches and giraffes, and has picnic areas, a restaurant and offers tours.
Further north is the turn-off northeast to **Quebrada Grande**.

Liberia

Sleeping ⊜
Anita 1
Boyeros 2
Cabinas Sagitarios 3
Daysita 4
Guanacaste 5
Hostal Ciudad Blanca 6

La Casona 7
La Posada del Tope 9
La Siesta 10
Liberia 12

Eating ⊙
El Bramadero 1

Hong Kong 2
Los Comales 3
Marisquería Paso Real 4
Panymiel 5
Pronto Pizzería 6

Parque Nacional Rincón de la Vieja

① *Park entry US$6. There are 2 ways into the park: the southern route, which has less traffic, goes from Puente La Victoria on the western side of Liberia and leads, in about 25 km, to the Santa María sector, closest to the hot springs. In this part, you can hike 8 km to the boiling mud pots (Las Pailas) and come back in the same day; the sulphur springs are on a different trail and only one hour away. The northern route turns right off the Pan-American Highway 5 km northwest of Liberia, through Curubandé (no public transport on this route). Beyond Curubandé, you cross the private property of Hacienda Lodge Guachipelin (US$2 to cross), beyond which is Rincón de la Vieja Lodge, see Sleeping. Day trips are possible to all areas, US$15 for Rincon de la Vieja, US$40 for Santa Rosa and US$50 for Palo Verde. Minimum of 4 required, prices per person. Park is closed Mon for maintenance.*

Most easily visited from Liberia, Parque Nacional Rincón de la Vieja (14,161 ha) was created to preserve the area around the Volcán Rincón de la Vieja, to the northeast of the town. It includes dry tropical forest, mud pots, hot sulphur springs and several other geothermal curiosities. The volcanic massif reaches to 1916 m and can be seen from a wide area around Liberia when not shrouded in clouds. The area is cool at night and subject to strong, gusty winds and violent rains; in the day it can be very hot, although always windy. These fluctuations mark all of the continental divide, of which the ridge is a part. From time to time the volcano erupts, the last eruption being in November 1995, when it tossed rocks and lava down its slopes.

The park is home to over **350 recorded species of bird** including toucans, parrots, three-wattled bellbirds and great curassows, along with howler monkeys, armadillos and coatis, ticks and other biting insects. It also has the largest density of Costa Rica's national flower the *guaria morada* or **purple orchid**. Horses can be rented in the park from some of the lodges. If you want to climb the volcano you will need to camp near the top, or at the warden's station, in order to ascend early in the morning before the clouds come in. Trails through the park lead to most sights of interest, including beautiful waterfalls and swimming holes. There are several accommodation options in or near the park, and shorter trips easily arranged from Liberia.

Parque Nacional Santa Rosa

About halfway to the Nicaraguan border from Liberia, is Parque Nacional Santa Rosa (38,673 ha). Together with the Murciélago Annex, the peninsula to the north of the developed park, it preserves some of the last dry tropical forests in Costa Rica, and shelters abundant and relatively easy-to-see wildlife. During the dry season, the animals depend on the water holes, and are thus easy to find until the holes dry up completely. Conservation work in the area is also trying to reforest some cattle ranches in the area – helped by the fact that cattle have not been profitable in recent years.

Close to the park headquarters and research buildings, the historically important **La Casona** was an essential visit for every Tico child as it is from here that the patriots repelled the invasion of the filibuster Walker in 1856, who had entrenched himself in the main building. Unfortunately the old hacienda building, once the Museo Histórico de Santa Rosa, was almost completely destroyed by fire in May 2001. The rebuilt La Casona was reopened in 2002. There are several good trails and lookouts in the park, the easiest of which is close to La Casona. Lasting a couple of hours, it leads through dry tropical forest with many Indio Desnudo (naked Indian) trees, which periodically shed their red flaky bark.

Deeper in the park, **Playa Naranjo** (12 km, three hours' walk or more, or use 4WD, park authorities permitting) and **Playa Nancite** (about the same distance from the entrance) are major nesting sites of **leatherback** and **Olive Ridley sea turtles**. The main nesting season is between August and October (although stragglers are regularly seen up to January) when flotillas of up to 10,000 Ridley turtles arrive at night on the 7-km long Playa Nancite. Females clumsily lurch up the beach, scoop out a deep hole, deposit and bury an average of 100 ping-pong-ball sized eggs before returning exhausted to the sea (see also Ostional). Playa Nancite is a restricted-access beach; you need a written permit to stay plus US$2 per day to camp, or US$15 in dormitories. Permits from SPN in San José, and the **Park Administration building** ① *Santa Rosa, T2666-5051, make sure you have permission before going*. Research has been done in the Playa Nancite area on howler monkeys, coatis and the complex interrelation between the fauna and the forest. Playa Naranjo is one of the most attractive beaches in the country. It is unspoilt, quiet and very good for surfing. There is good camping, drinking water (although occasionally salty) and BBQ facilities.

La Cruz and Isla Bolaños

The last town before the border, La Cruz has a bank (for cash, traveller's cheques or credit card transactions), a handful of hotels and absolutely incredible sunsets from the hilltop overlooking the Bahía de Salinas. Down in the bay the Islas Bolaños Wildlife Refuge and some of the best conditions for windsurfing in Costa Rica.

Isla Bolaños is a 25-ha National Wildlife Refuge protecting the nesting sites of the brown pelican, frigate bird and American oystercatcher. The island is covered with dry forest and you can only walk round the island at low tide. The incoming tidal surge is very dangerous, be off the island before the tide comes in. No camping is allowed.

⦿ Northwest Costa Rica listings

For Sleeping and Eating price codes, and other relevant information, see pages 43-46.

⦿ Sleeping

San José to Esparza and Barranca *p112*
L-AL Hotel Vista Golfo, 14 km off the Inter-American Hwy at Miramar, T2639-8303, www.vistagolfo.com. Wildlife, canopy tour, horse riding, waterfalls and spring-fed pool on 27 ha in what is now an adventure park.
C Hotel Castanuelas, close to the highway, T2635-5105. A/c, quiet, cooler alternative to Puntarenas.
C Hotel Río Mar, Barranca, T2663-0158. With bath and restaurant. Good.

Puntarenas and around *p112*
Accommodation is difficult to find from Dec-Apr, especially at weekends.
L-A Tioga, on the beach front with Calle 17, T2661-0271, www.hoteltioga.com. 54 rooms; those with balconies are much

better, with views. Private bath, a/c, TV and telephone. Restaurant, swimming pool, very good.
A-B La Punta, Av 1, Calle 35, T2661-0696. Good spot 1 block from car ferry, with bath, hot water, secure parking, good pool. American-owned, big rooms, friendly, clean.
A-B Las Hamacas on beach front between Calle 5-7, T2661-0398. Rooms are OK, but noisy when the bar is in full flow. Small pool. Could do with a lick of paint; for now it is overpriced.
B-C Cayuga, Calle 4, Av Central-1, T2661-0344. Has 31 rooms with private bathroom, a/c, pretty dark rooms, restaurant. There is a small garden patio but it's hardly paradise.
B-C Gran Hotel Chorotega, on the corner of Calle 1, Av 3 near the banks and market, T2661-0998. Clean rooms with private bath, cheaper with shared. Efficient and friendly service. Popular with visiting business people. A good deal.
C Gran Imperial, on the beach front, in front of the Muelle de Cruceros, T2661-0579.

leasant rooms, although a little dark, but lean with private bath and fan. Small garden atio, and a very chilled atmosphere, estaurant. Good spot and handy for buses.
Cabezas, Av 1, Calle 2-4, T2661-1045. las 23 rooms, some with private bath, heaper without. Simple rooms with no ills but bright and clean. Good deal.
-E Río, Av 3, Calle Central-2 near market, 2661-0331. Private bath, fans, good rooms. riendly Chinese owners keen to help, lively, ometimes noisy, but popular place.
Monte Mar, Av 3, Calle 1-3. Very basic, ome rooms with fan, but bearable on budget.

Around Puntarenas

A Casa San Francisco, at Roble, 10 km east f Puntarenas, on the coast, T2663-0148. lear regional hospital, run by 2 Canadian vomen, pool, clean, laundry facilities, riendly and helpful, mainly weekly or ong-term rental. Recommended.

Santa Elena *p113, map p114*

AL Arco Iris, 100 m north of **Banco Nacional**, 2645-5067, www.arcoirislodge.com. Rooms vith bath, restaurant with good healthy oreakfast, horses for rent, plenty of parking.
AL-A Finca Valverde, 300 m east of **Banco Nacional** up hill on road to the reserve, 2645-5157, www.monteverde.co.cr. Rooms vith bath, nice gardens for birdwatching, oar and restaurant.
AL-A Miramontes, leading into Santa Elena rom the north, T2645-5152, www.swisshotel niramontes.com. 8 comfortable rooms in quiet spot, Swiss-run, wonderful restaurant.
B Pensión El Sueño, T2645-5021. Very riendly, hot shower, small but nice rooms, clean, pricey meals, car park. Run by Rafa rejos who does horse-riding trips into the nountains to see quetzals, etc (US$35).
B-F Pensión Santa Elena, T2645-5051, vww.pensionsantaelena.com. Good range of ooms of varying standards and quality – all jood value for the money. Very popular, clean, good food, kitchen available.

C El Colibrí, T2645-5682, clean, friendly, timber built, with balconies.
C Hospedaje El Banco, see map. Price per person. Family-run, friendly, hot shower, clean, good information, English spoken.
D-E Tina's Casistas, T2645-5641, www.tinascasitas.de. 4 cabins with 9 rooms with private or shared bath. In a quiet part of Santa Elena and worth a look if you want a little more comfort.
F Pensión Cabinas Marín, 500 m north of the centre past the Agricultural College. Spacious rooms (room 8 has a nice view), good breakfasts, friendly.
F Sleepers Sleep Cheaper Hostel, T2645-6204, http://sleepershostel.blogspot.com. Cheap budget accommodation with dorm rooms. Kitchen and internet access too.

Monteverde *p115, map p114*

LL El Establo, next to **Heliconia**, T2645-5110, www.elestablo.com. 80 carpeted rooms with private bathroom, restaurant, 50-ha farm with 50% cloudforest, own nature guide, good birdwatching, riding stables, 35 horses, family-run, very accommodating. Recommended.
LL Monteverde Lodge, T2645-5057, www.costaricaexpeditions.com. With restaurant, jacuzzi, daily slide shows US$5 at 1800. Recommended.
L El Sapo Dorado, T2645-5010, www.sapo dorado.com. 30 suites, 10 with fireplaces, good but expensive restaurant (0700-2100).
L Fonda Vela, T2645-5125, www.fonda vela.com. 40 beautiful rooms and suites spread around 5 buildings on a 14-ha farm with forest and trail system. Private bathroom, hot water. A 25-min walk to the reserve, good birding, 2 excellent restaurants (open to public), bar, TV room, art gallery and conference room.
L Heliconia, T2645-5109, www.hotel heliconia.com. Private bathrooms, restaurant, very comfortable, excellent food, private reserve and nature rails. Highly recommended.
L-AL Belmar, 300 m behind service station, T2645-5201, www.hotelbelmar.net.

Swiss chalet-style, beautiful views of Nicoya, restaurant, good.

L-AL Hotel de Moñtana Monteverde, T2645-5046, www.monteverdemountain hotel.com Comfortable, set meals, good, wholesome food, sauna, jacuzzi, good views of Nicoya, excellent birdwatching on 15-ha reserve, transport from San José available. Recommended.

AL Cloud Forest Lodge, 300 m north of Sapo Dorado, T2645-5058, www.cloudforest lodge.com. 20 rooms with bath. Restaurant, beautiful views and tours available here with **Canopy Tours**, see Activities and tours.

AL San Luis Biological Station and Ecolodge, 40-min drive south of Monteverde, down a spur road near the top of the hill, T2645-8049 (call ahead to book), www.uha.edu/ costarica. On 65 ha of farmland and cloud-forest in the San Luis Valley, adjoining Monteverde Cloud Forest. 5 cabins, horse riding, swimming in river and other options. Price per person.

AL Trapp Family Lodge, closest to the reserve, T2645-5858, www.trappfam.com. Tidy rooms, upstairs with balconies, downstairs with terraces. Restaurant and friendly, helpful hosts.

A El Bosque, next to restaurant of same name, T2645-5158. Has 26 comfortable rooms with hot showers. Clean, fine views, beautiful gardens and short trail, safe parking.

A La Colina Lodge, between Monteverde and reserve, T2645-5009. Private bath, balconies with some rooms, cheaper in dormitory, helpful, luggage stored, small area for camping, one of the original houses of Monteverde with some nice touches. Marvin Rockwell, the former owner and one of the original Quaker settlers, pops in to give talks when requested.

A Villa Verde, 1 km from reserve, T2640-4697, www.villaverdehotel.com. Rooms with hot showers, others with shared bath, some with kitchenette, includes breakfast. Clean, nice, with restaurant and excellent views. Good package rates for students.

B Mariposa, T2645-5013. Has 3 rooms in a single block sleeping up to 3 people, with private bath. A family atmosphere with breakfast included in the price.

B Pensión Manakin, just beyond **El Establo**, along a short road on the right, T2645-5080. Offers 10 simple rooms, a few with private bath, cheaper with shared bath, also fully equipped cabins. Filling breakfast and evening meals are available, in a family atmosphere great for sharing stories with other guests. A small balcony at the back makes a calm place to sit and relax. The Villegas are very knowledgeable about the area, and will help arrange tours and transport up to the reserve if required.

C-D Albergue Bellbird, just before the gas station, T2645-5518. ½ a dozen rooms in mainly dormitory-style accommodation, with shared bathrooms, restaurant with typical food.

D Monteverde Inn, down track opposite **Heliconia**, T2645-5156. Private bathroom, quiet, breakfast included. Run-down, price per person.

Monteverde Cloud Forest Reserve *p117*
Shelter facilities throughout the reserve cost US$3.50-US$5 a night, reserve entry fee for each night spent in the park, plus key deposit of US$5. Bring sleeping bag and torch. You can make your own meals. Dormitory-style accommodation for up to 30 people at entrance, **Albergue Reserva Biológica de Monteverde**, T2645-5122, US$40 full board only, includes park entrance fee. Reservations only for all reserve accommodation (usually booked up by groups).

North to Guanacaste Province *p119*
A Capazuri B&B, 2.5 km north of Cañas, T2669-6280. Also camping US$7 per person.

A Hacienda Solimar Lodge. 8 rooms with private or shared bathroom, includes meals, minimum 2 nights, transport on request, local guide, horse riding. Recommended for serious birdwatchers, contact **Birdwatch**, T2228-4768, www.birdwatchcostarica.com, see page 119. Reservations essential.

B El Corral, Pan-American, Cañas, T2669-1467. With bath.

C Cañas, Calle 2, Av 3, Cañas, T2669-0039. With bath, clean, pleasant.

E Cabinas Corobicí, Cañas, T2669-0241. Has 11 good rooms with bath and parking available. Price per person.

Liberia and around *p120, map p120*

A Las Espuelas, 2 km south of Liberia, T2666-0144, www.bestwestern.com. Good, a/c, satellite TV, swimming pool, round trip bus service from San José.

B Boyeros, on Pan-American Hwy with Av Central, T2666-0722. Pool, bath, restaurant.

B Hostal Ciudad Blanca, Av 4, Calle 1-3, from Gobernación 200 m south, 150 m east, T2666-3962. Has 12 nice but dirty rooms, a/c, hot water, TV, restaurant/bar, parking, rooster wake up call.

B Hotel del Aserradero, Pan-American Hwy and Av 3, T2666-1939. Has 16 big rooms with bath, parking and fans.

B Santa Clara Lodge, 4 km from Quebrada Grande, T2666-4054. Has 4 rooms with shared bath, 1 room with bath, cattle farm, riding, dry forest.

C Guanacaste, Calle 12, Av 3, just round corner from bus stations, T2666-0085. Clean, bath, friendly, restaurant, safe parking, money exchange, **Ticabus** agency offers transfers and tours here. Camping area, English spoken, group discount, 15% student discount, affiliated youth hostel. Recommended.

C La Siesta, Calle 4, Av 4-6, T2666-0678. Clean, with bath, restaurant, swimming pool, helpful owner who speaks English.

C-E Hotel Daysita, Av 5, Calle 11-13, T2666-0197. Restaurant, pool, quiet, not central. Cheaper to share 6-bedded room with bath.

C-E La Posada del Tope, Rafeal Iglesias, 1½ blocks south from cathedral, T2666-3876. Clean, friendly, helpful, with shower, laundry facilities, parking, bike rentals, baggage storage. The owner Dennis has a telescope for star gazing. Price per person.

D-E La Casona, Av 6, Calle Central, T2666-2971. Rooms for up to 4 people, shared bath, washing facilities, rooms facing street get very hot; more expensive in annex with private bath.

D-E Liberia, ½ block south of main square, T2666-0161. Cheaper with shared bath, fans, clean, friendly, good information board and breakfast, laundry facilities. Recommended.

E Cabinas Sagitarios, Av 11, Calle 2, T2666-0950. With bath, run by Dutchman and Costa Rican, breakfast and dinner available on request, friendly.

F Anita, Calle 4 y Av 8, T2666-1285. Bath, clean, family-run, friendly, café, shop, parking, best of the range.

Parque Nacional Rincón de la Vieja
p121, map p116

AL Hacienda Lodge Guachipelin, accessed through the northern route, T2666-8075, www.guachipelin.com. Meals available, 50 rooms, internet, canopy tour, naturalist guides, riding, hot springs, sulphur springs, mud pools, waterfalls (transport from Liberia arranged, US$50 per person round trip).

AL Rincón de la Vieja Lodge, accessed through the northern route, T2200-0238, www.rincondelaviejalodge.net. Canopy tour, sulphur hot springs, tennis, horseback riding, internet. Also packages including transport from San José. The lodge is on the edge of the park and there are horses guides and tours. 3¼ hrs to the volcano, 30 mins to Las Pailas, 45 mins to the thermal springs, Azufrales, and 2¼ hrs to the Hidden Waterfalls.

A-B Buena Vista Mountain Lodge, accessed through the Santa María sector, T2661-8158. Rooms, waterslide, canopy tour, spa, internet, restaurant/bar.

F Miravieja Lodge, accessed through the Santa María sector, T2662-2004. Rustic lodge in citrus groves, meals, transport and tours.

Parque Nacional Santa Rosa *p121*

Camping

There is a pleasant campground at Park Administration, T2679-9692, about 7 km from the entrance with giant strangler figs that shade your tent from the stupendously hot sun, and very adequate sanitary facilities, picnic tables, and so forth for US$2.15 per person per night. There is a small *comedor* for meals (breakfast 0600-0630, lunch 1100-1200, evening 1700-1800, good) and drinks near the campground but it is advised that you bring some of your own supplies; a tent is useful and essential in the wet season. You may be able to sleep on the veranda of one of the scientists' houses. Bring a mosquito net and insect repellent. If the water is not running, ask Park Administration.

La Cruz and Isla Bolaños *p122*

L-AL Ecoplaya Beach Resort, Bahía Salinas, T2228-7146, www.ecoplaya.com. All-inclusive resort, well maintained with nice restaurant.

A-C Hotel La Mirada, on road out to the Pan-American Hwy, T/ F2679-9084. Clean, tidy rooms, ample parking.

B Amalia's Inn, 100 m south of Parque Central. Stunning views, small pool, very friendly and excellent local knowledge. Extra person US$5, and 1 room sleeps 6. Excellent value for groups and recommended.

C-D Cabinas Santa Rita, 150 m south of Parque Central, T2679-9062. Nice, clean, secure with good parking. Cheaper with fan. Would be great in any other town not competing with Amalia's.

D Hotel Bella Vista, ½ block northwest of the plaza, T2679-8060. Rooms, restaurant/ bar, great view.

Camping

Playa Morro Trailer Park y Cabinas, west of La Cruz, on Bahía Salinas looking over to Isla Bolaños. Drinking water, showers, toilets, tennis, barbecue, fishing boats and horses to rent, 1-km beach.

● Eating

Puntarenas and around *p112*

There are many bars and a couple of discos along the Paseo de los Turistas. A number of Chinese restaurants on Av Central and Calle 1 and there is good, cheap food from market stalls, eg *sopa de carne* (meat soup).

♥♥ Aloha, on the seafront on Calle 17. Worth checking out.

♥♥ Casa de Mariscos, Calle 7-9, T2661-1666, closed Wed. On the beach front, good seafood, reasonable prices.

♥♥ Jardín Cervecero Bierstube, on the seafront at Calle 23-25, T2661-5293. Good for sandwiches, hamburgers and a beer.

♥♥ Kayte Negro, north side of the peninsula on Av Badillo, Calle 17. Good local food.

♥♥ La Yunta, on the beachfront at Calle 19, T2661-3216. A popular steak house, open all night.

♥♥ Mariscos Kahite Blanco, near launch. Excellent and locally renowned seafood.

♥♥ Soda Brisas del Mar, on Calle Central, Av 2-4. Good for a snack.

♥ Soda Macarena, opposite the Muelle de Cruceros (dock). Handy while waiting for buses.

Around Puntarenas

♥♥ María Vargas, Roble, 10 km east of Puntarenas. Bar and restaurant, friendly, good food, reasonable prices.

Santa Elena *p113, map p114*

♥♥♥ Chunches, opposite **Pensión Santa Elena**, T2645-5147. Closed Sun. A very useful place with good espresso bar and snacks, used books, magazines, laundromat, fax service.

♥♥ Marisquería El Márquez (see map), T2645-5918. Closed Sun. Seafood and *casados*.

♥♥ Morphos (see map), T2645-5607. Typical and international fare, recommended, with a good atmosphere, but not cheap.

♥ Pollo Asado El Campesino (see map). Tico soda, early breakfast special.

Monterverde p115, map p114

¶¶-¶¶ Johnny's Pizza, on main road between Santa Elena and Monteverde, T2645-5066. Good wood oven-cooked pizzas in a relaxed atmosphere, café, souvenir shop. Tables outside give extra chance to see wildlife.

¶¶-¶¶ Restaurant Lucia's, down road opposite **Heliconia**, T2645-5337. Tasty lasagne, international and vegetarian fare.

¶¶ Restaurant El Bosque, on road to reserve, next to **Casem**, open from 0630. Shop, good food, clean.

¶ Stella's Bakery, opposite **Casem**, T2645-5560. Excellent wholemeal bread, cakes and good granola – there's a café if you want to eat in.

North to Guanacaste Province p119

¶¶¶ Rincón Corobicí, next to **La Pacífica**, Cañas, T2669-6191. Clean and pleasant, with a small zoo and offers rafting down Río Corobicí.

¶¶ Central, main square, Cañas. Good Chinese restaurant.

¶¶ Restaurant Panchitos, main square, Cañas. Good and inexpensive.

Liberia and around p120, map p120

¶¶¶ Marisquería Paso Real, south side of main square. Great ceviche and seafood.

¶¶ Chop Suey, Calle Central. Chinese, big helpings.

¶¶ Copa de Oro, next to **Hotel Liberia**. Chinese, huge servings, good value.

¶¶ El Bramadero, part of the **Hotel Bramadero** on the Pan-American Hwy. Popular, breakfast from 0630, lively bar in the evenings.

¶¶ Jardín de Azúcar, just off plaza, T2666-3563. Self service, good variety and tasty.

¶¶ Pronto Pizzería, Calle 1, Av 4. Good food (not just pizzas) in a charming colonial house.

¶¶-¶ Hong Kong, 1½ blocks east of church. Chinese, cheap and cheerful.

¶ Los Comales, Calle Central, Av 5-7. Daily 0630-2100. Traditional Guanacaste dishes prepared with maize, run by women's cooperative.

¶ Panymiel, Av Central, Calle 8-9, and Av 3, Calle 2. Bakery, snacks and drinks, good value.

La Cruz and Isla Bolaños p122

¶ La Orchidea, La Cruz, T2679-9316. Seafood, cheap, daily 0630-2200.

¶ Restaurant Telma, La Cruz, T2679-9150. Tico food, cheap.

¶ Soda Estadio, La Cruz. Good, cheap.

¶ Soda Marta, La Cruz, T2679-9347. Cheap Tico fare.

⊛ Festivals and events

Puntarenas and around p112

Jul Fiesta de la Virgen del Mar, on the Sat closest to the 16 Jul, with a week of festivities leading to a carnival and regatta of decorated fishing boats and yachts.

Monteverde p115, map p114

Dec-Mar Monteverde Music Festival, T2645-5053. Classical and jazz concerts at sunset, local, national and international musicians. Programme from local hotels, US$10.

Liberia and around p120, map p120

25 Jul Guanacaste Day sees dancing, parades and cattle-related festivities.

O Shopping

Monteverde p115, map p114

Casem, a co-operative gift shop, is located just outside Monteverde on the road to the reserve next to **El Bosque** restaurant, T2645-5190. It sells embroidered shirts, T-shirts, wooden and woven articles and baskets. Next door, there's a shop selling Costa Rican coffee.

Liberia and around *p120, map p120*
Mini Galería Fulvia, on the main plaza,
sells **Tico Times**, English papers and books.
English spoken and helpful.
Tiffany's, Av C-2, Calle 2, general gifts, cigars.

▲ Activities and tours

Puntarenas and around *p112*
Tour operators
See under San José Tour operators,
page 77, for Gulf of Nicoya cruises.

Monteverde *p115, map p114*
Canopy Tours, at **Cloud Forest Lodge**,
T2645-5243. Offer tours of 5 platforms,
connected by steel cables, to explore the
forest canopy, US$45 per person, US$35
for students at **Cloud Forest Lodge**.

North to Guanacaste Province *p119*
Tour operators
CATA Tours, Cañas, T2296-2133, full-day tours
to Parque Nacional Palo Verde. **Safaris
Corobicí** is 4 km past Cañas on the Pan-
American Hwy, 25 m before the entrance to
Centro Ecológico La Pacífica, T2669-6191.
Float tours down the Río Tenorio, US$37 per
person for 2 hrs' rafting, US$60, ½-day, under
14 yrs ½-price.

Liberia and around *p120, map p120*
Tour operators
Hotel Liberia can organize tours, rent
out bikes and assist with enquiries.
A recommended guide for the national
parks nearby is **Alejandro Vargas Rodríguez**,
lives in front of the Red Cross, T2666-1889.

⊙ Transport

San José to Esparza and Barranca *p112*
Bus If going from **San José** to Monteverde
it is possible to change buses in Barranca,
rather than going all the way to Puntarenas,
if you leave the capital before 1230.

Puntarenas and around *p112*
Bus Terminal for San José is at Calle 2,
Av 2-4. Buses every 40 mins, 0415-1900 to
San José, 2 hrs, US$3. Buses from San José
leave from Terminal Puntarenas Calle CB16,
Av 10-12, T2222-0064, 0600-1900. Daily bus
to **Santa Elena** for Monteverde, T2222-3854
0630 and 1430, US$4.25, 5 hrs. Buses south
to **Quepos** from main bus station, 6 daily via
Jacó, US$5.00, 4 hrs, return 0430, 1030,
1630. To **Liberia** with **Empresa Pulmitan**,
first at 0600, last 1500, 4 hrs, US$4.75. To
Tilarán via **Cañas** at 1130 and 1630. Good
café at bus terminal where you can wait
for your bus.

Ferry Check which dock your ferry leaves
from. For the **Nicoya Peninsula**, see page 131.
To southern Nicoya Peninsula from the
dock at Calle 35. To **Playa Naranjo** at 1000,
1420,and 1900, returning at 1250, 1700 and
2100, 1½ hrs. T2661-1069 for exact times.
Pedestrians US$1.60, motorbikes US$3, cars
US$12. The ferry dock is about 1 km from
Puntarenas bus station, local buses run
between the two, otherwise walk or get a
taxi. Buses meet the ferry for **Nicoya** (through
Carmona, 40 km unpaved, 30 km paved
road, crowded, noisy, frequently break
down, US$1.25, 2¼ hrs), **Sámara** (US$1.30),
Coyote, **Bejuco** and **Jicaral**.
   From the same dock a car ferry goes to
Paquera at 0830, 1330, 1830 and 2230,
returning at 0500, 1100, 1700 and 2030,
1½ hrs, T2641-0118 to check the times.
On arrival, get on the bus (which waits for
the ferry) as quickly as possible (to **Cóbano**,
2-3 hrs, US$1.25, bad road, to **Montezuma**
US$2.60, 1½ hrs at least), pay on the bus,
or get a taxi. **Hotel Playa Tambor** also runs
a car ferry to **Paquera** 7 times daily leaving
Paquera 0500, 0700, 1000,1145,1500,
1630 and 2000. A bus to **Tambor** will
be waiting at Paquera on your arrival.
T2661-2084 for information.
   Launch **Paquera–Puntarenas** leaves from
behind the central market, directly north of

the bus stop at 0600, 1100 and 1515, returning at 0730, 1230 and 1700. Pedestrians US$1.50, motorbikes US$1.80. Tickets are sold when the incoming boat has docked.

Santa Elena *p113, map p114*
Bus From **Puntarenas, Terminal Empresarios Unidos**, daily at 1415, occasionally at 1315 as well, 2½-4 hrs, returns 0600, US$2.20. This bus arrives in time to catch a bus to **Quepos** for Manuel Antonio. See Monteverde Transport, below, for buses from **San José**.

To **Tilarán** the 0700 (US$1.80, 3 hrs) connects with the 1230 bus to **Fortuna** and others to **Cañas** for the Pan-American Hwy, Liberia and Nicoya Peninsula.
Car There is a service station, Mon-Sat 0700-1800, Sun 0700-1200.
Horse Several places rent horses; look for signs between Santa Elena and Monteverde or ask at your hotel. Try not to hire horses that look overworked.

Taxi Santa Elena–Monteverde, US$6, and Monteverde–the reserve, US$5.75 (hunt around for good prices). Not so easy to find a taxi for return trip, best to arrange beforehand.

Monteverde *p115, map p114*
Bus From **San José** a direct bus runs from Av 9, Calle 12, just outside Terminal Atlántico Norte daily at 0630 and 1430, 4½ hrs, US$4. Leaves Monteverde from **Hotel Villa Verde** also at 0630 and 1430, picking up through town, stopping at Santa Elena bus stop (be early). Check times in advance, Sat bus does not always run in low season (T2645-5159 in Santa Elena, T2222-3854, in San José). This service is not 'express', it stops to pick up passengers all along the route, and is not a comfortable ride. Keep your bag with you at all times; several cases of theft reported. Alternatively, get a bus to **Puntarenas** and change there for Santa Elena, see above.

North to Guanacaste Province *p119*
Bus The Cañas bus station is 500 m north of the centre, where all buses depart from except for those to San José, which leave from the terminal 300 m west of Parque Central on the Pan-American Highway. To **San José**, Transportes La Cañera, T2669-0145, 8 daily from 0400, 3½ hrs, arriving and departing from Calle 16, Av 1-3. To **Liberia**, 10 daily from 0530. To **Puntarenas**, 8 daily from 0600. To **Upala**, for Bijagua and Volcán Tenorio, 7 daily from 0500, 13/4 hrs, US$1.50. To **Tilarán**, 7 daily from 0600. Buses to Tilarán for **Nuevo Arenal**, past the volcano and on to **Fortuna**, or for connections to **Santa Elena** and **Monteverde**. If going by road, the turn-off for Tilarán is at the filling station, no signs. For a description of this route in reverse see page 94.

Liberia and around *p120, map p120*
Air The Aeropuerto Internacional Tomás Guardia, about 13 km from Liberia (LIR) on the road to the Nicoya Peninsula was reopened in 1992, revamped in 1995 and renamed **Aeropuerto Daniel Oduber Quirós**, after the former president who came from Guanacaste. The new runway can handle large jets and charter flights, and direct daily flights to **Miami**. Lacsa, T2666-0306; **Sansa**, T2221-9414; **Nature Air**, T2220-3054. There is a direct weekly flight to **New York** arriving Sat, through **Air-Tech**, www.airtech.com, Wed, Sat and Sun. **Delta** flights from **Atlanta**. **American** flights from **Miami**, **Continental** from **Houston**.

Bus To **San José** leave from Av 5, Calle 10-12, with 14 a day, US$4.25, 4 hrs. Other buses leave from the local terminal at Calle 12, Av 7-9. Liberia to **Playa del Coco**, hourly, 0500-1800, **Playa Hermosa** and **Panama**, five daily from 0730 to 1730, 1½ hrs, **Puntarenas**, 7 a day, 0500-1530, **Bagaces/ Cañas**, 4 a day, 0545-1710, **Cañas Dulces**, 3 a day, 0600-1730, **La Cruz/**

Peñas Blanca, 8 a day 0530-1800. **Filedefia-Santa Cruz-Nicoya**, 0500-2020, 20 a day.

Car Car rental **Sol** and **Toyota** car rental agencies (see map) offer same prices and allow you to leave the vehicle at San José airport for US$50.

Parque Nacional Rincón de la Vieja *p121*
A taxi costs US$30 one-way from Liberia. Most hotels will arrange transport for US$15 per person, minimum 6 passengers. Departure at 0700, 1 hr to entrance, return at 1700; take food and drink. You can also hitch; most tourist vehicles will pick you up. If you take your own transport a 4WD is best, although during the dry season a vehicle with high clearance is adequate.

Parque Nacional Santa Rosa *p121*
Parque Nacional Santa Rosa is easy to reach as it lies west of the Pan-American Hwy, about 1 hr north of Liberia. Any bus going from Liberia to Peñas Blancas on the Nicaraguan border will drop you right at the entrance (US$0.70, 40 mins), from where it's a 7-km walk, but you may be able to hitch a ride. Last bus returns to Liberia about 1800. Coming from the border, any bus heading south will drop you off at the entrance.

La Cruz and Isla Bolaños *p122*
Bus Regular buses to **San José** from 0545 until 1630, 5½ hrs. To **Liberia**, 5 daily 0700-1730, 1½ hrs. To **Peñas Blancas**, 5 daily 0730-1730, 1 hr. To **Playa Jobo** in Bahía Solanos, at 0530, 1030 and 1500, from main plaza.

● Directory

Puntarenas and around *p112*
Banks Banco Nacional and Banco de Costa Rica, on Av 3, Calle 1-3 near the Central Market, changes TCs, and with ATM.

Internet Millennium Cyber Café, on the beach front with Calle 15, only one in town so popular, 1000-2200, 600c per hr. Free coffee if you're lucky. **Post office** Av 3, Calle Central-1, close to Central Market. **Telephone** ICE and Radiográfica, Av C, Calle 2-4.

Santa Elena *p113, map p114*
Banks Banco Nacional, daily 0900-1500, to change TCs with commission and advance cash against Visa. ATM machine for Visa in the supermarket opposite the post office. **Internet** Several places are opening up, but with poor communication links are charging exorbitant prices. Try Treehouse Cafe, T2645-5751 US$3 per hr 0700-2200 and Pura Vida.

Monteverde *p115, map p114*
Cultural centres Galería Extasis, 250 m south of La Cascada, T2645-5548, exhibits sculptures by the Costa Rican artist, Marco Tulio Brenes. **Language schools** A branch of the Centro Panamericano de Idiomas, in Heredia, has opened a school on the road up to the reserve, T2645-6306. Accommodation is with local families.

Liberia and around *p120, map p120*
Banks Banco Popular and Bancrecer both have Visa ATMs. Banco de Costa Rica is on the main plaza. Credomatic, Av Central, MasterCard ATM. For money exchange, try *casa de cambio* on Calle 2 or ask around, eg Restaurant Chun San, behind the cathedral. **Internet** Planet, ½ block south of the church, cheap, with good machines, Mon-Sat 0800-2200, Sun 0900-2100. Ciberm@nia, north side of main plaza, T2666-7240, US$1.25 per hr. **Medical services** Enrique Baltodano Hospital, T2666-0011. **Pharmacies** close to the main plaza.

Península de Nicoya

Fringed by idyllic white-sand beaches along most of the coastline, the Nicoya Peninsula is hilly and hot. There are few towns of any size and most of the roads not connecting the main communities are in poor condition. While several large hotel resorts are increasingly taking over what were once isolated coves, they are generally grouped together and there are still many remote beaches to explore. A few small areas of the peninsula are protected to preserve wildlife, marine ecosystems and the geological formations of Barra Honda. ▸▸ *For listings, see pages 136-147.*

Ins and outs

Getting there There are several ways of getting to the Nicoya Peninsula. The **Taiwan Friendship Bridge** over the Tempisque saves time and gas money getting to the peninsula, eliminating the ferry. Just across the river is **Hotel Rancho Humo** ① *T2255-2463* with boat trips on the Tempisque and Bebedero rivers, visits to Palo Verde and Barra Honda national parks.

A second route takes the **Salinero car ferry** from Puntarenas across the Gulf of Nicoya to Playa Naranjo. Buses meet the ferry for Nicoya (US$1.25, 2¼ hours), Sámara (US$1.30), Coyote, Bejuco and Jicaral. A fourth route also departs from Puntarenas to Paquera from the dock at Calle 35. On arrival, get on the bus (which waits for the ferry) as quickly as possible (to Cóbano, two to three hours, US$1.25, bad road, to Montezuma US$2.60, 1½ hours at least), pay on the bus, or get a taxi. **Hotel Playa Tambor** also runs a ferry service, **Naviera-Tambor SA**, between Puntarenas and Paquera, with a bus running between Paquera and the hotel in Tambor.

Getting around All the beaches on the Nicoya Peninsula are accessible by road in the dry season. Most places can be reached by bus from Nicoya. However, the stretch from Paquera to Montezuma and the Cabo Blanco Reserve is connected to Playa Naranjo and the north only by very poor roads. There is no bus connection between Playa Naranjo and Paquera and the road is appalling even in the dry season.

Beaches Even in high season, you will be able to find a beautiful beach which is uncrowded. There are so many of them, just walk until you find what you want. You will see plenty of wildlife along the way, monkeys, iguanas and squirrels as well as many birds. There can be dangerous undertows on exposed beaches; the safest bathing is from those beaches where there is a protective headland, such as at Playa Panamá in the north.

Santa Cruz and around

Heading from Liberia by road, the first town you reach is Santa Cruz, known as Costa Rica's National Folklore City for its colourful fiestas, dancing and regional food. January is the month for the fiesta dedicated to Santo Cristo de Esquipulas, when it can be difficult to find accommodation. There is also a rodeo fiesta in January. But for the rest of the year, it's a quiet little town, with a charming modern church, providing supplies for the beach tourism industry. If you need to buy food, Santa Cruz is a good place to stock up.

In **Guaitíl**, 9 km east of Santa Cruz and 19 km north of Nicoya, local artisans specialize in reproductions of indigenous Chorotegan pottery. They work with the same methods used by the indigenous long ago, with minimal or no use of a wheel and no artificial paints.

Ceramics are displayed at the local *pulpería*, or outside houses. At **San Vicente**, 2 km southeast of Guaitíl, local craftsmen work and sell their pottery.

West coast beaches ⊕🏄🦜⛺▲⚓⚑ ›› pp136-147.

A number of beaches are reached by unpaved roads from the Santa Cruz-Liberia road. Many can be accessed by bus from the Liberia bus station, others may require you to change buses at Santa Cruz. Each of the beaches has its appeal – Tamarindo and Playa del Coco for partying, Flamingo to the north and Junquillal for their greater seclusion, and Grande for nesting turtles and surfing.

Playa del Coco and around

After the town of **Comunidad**, a road leads east to Playa del Coco and Playa Hermosa, and the ever-pending resort development of Playa Panamá, see below.

Playa del Coco is a popular resort some 8 km from the highway, set in an attractive islet-scattered bay hemmed in by rocky headlands. It's a good place to chill out, with a

Península Nicoya

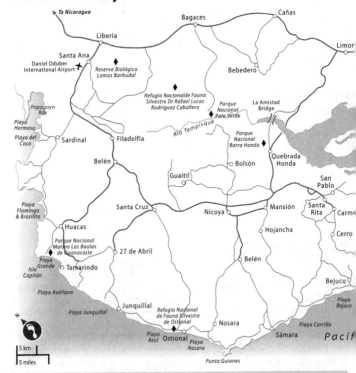

mix of good services without being too developed. The best beaches are to the south. All activities concentrate on the beach and fishing. Coco is the starting point for surf trips to Santa Rosa spots by boat, such as **Witches Rock**. Snorkelling and diving are nothing special, but for a diving expedition to the **Islas Murciélago**, see page 145. Sightings of manta rays and bull sharks are common around Islas Catalinas and Islas Murciélago.

There are bars, restaurants and a few motels along the sandy beach. It is too small to get lost. To reach it, leave the road at Comunidad (road paved). Be wary of excursions to secluded Playa Verde, accessible by boat only, as some boatmen collaborate with thieves and reap the rewards later. A 2.5-km road heads southwest from Playa del Coco to **Playa Ocotal**.

Playa Hermosa and Playa Panamá

A spur road breaks from the main road to Playa del Coco heading north to Playa Hermosa. This is one of the nicest resorts and served by a paved road. Accommodation is mixed, but it's a good quiet alternative to other beaches in the region. Walking either to the left or the right you can find isolated beaches with crystal-clear water.

The big **Papagayo** tourist complex near Playa Panamá, which once planned to provide as many as 60,000 hotel rooms, started in 1993. Objections from many quarters have delayed construction, but the project continues at a slower pace.

Playa Tamarindo and around

South of Filadefia, close to Belén, a mostly paved but poor road heads east to the beach and popular surf spot of Playa Tamarindo, www.tamarindobeach.net, and other nearby beaches. Looking directly out to the west, the sunsets are incredible and while most make their way to the beach for that magic moment, the strong beach culture makes this a popular place to hang out.

Either side of the sunset, Tamarindo is a flurry of activity, easily the liveliest beach resort on the Nicoya Peninsula and development is quickly changing the place. The beach is attractive – although not stunning – with strong tides in places so take care if swimming. Three good breaks provide a variety of options for the surf crowd. Beyond surf and sun, the most popular excursion is an evening trip to Playa Grande and the leatherback turtle nesting sights from October to March. While the town is driven by surfing, there's a good blend of hotels and bars to make it a good beach stop – not too busy, but not so quiet that it's dead.

Playa Grande

North of Playa Tamarindo is Playa Grande and the **Parque Nacional Marino Las Baulas de Guanacaste** (485 ha terrestrial, 22,000 ha marine), well known as a nesting site for **leatherback turtles** (October-February). Organized trips to the beaches are possible from Tamarindo. Also in town is **El Mundo de La Tortuga** ① *T2653-0471*, an unusual turtle museum. The road from the main highway at Belén leads directly to Playa Grande, a sleepy town with almost no transport and no way of getting around.

Playa Flamingo and beaches to the north

North of Tamarindo and Playa Grande are the beaches of **Conchal**, **Brasilito**, **Flamingo** and **Potrero**. It's a collection of beaches with subtle changes of atmostphere. Conchal is a beautiful 3-km beach full of shells, but with only luxury accommodation; most budget travellers stay at Brasilito and walk along the beach. Further north, the bay around Playa Flamingo has white sand, although the actual beach has some fairly intrusive developments with a grab-all approach to beachfront properties; in fact, the beach is now polluted and not as beautiful as it once was. But several other smaller beaches retain a relaxed atmosphere where life is governed by little more than the sunrise and beautiful sunsets. Further north is the isolated beach of Potrero with pockets of visitors largely enjoying their own company.

Playa Junquillal

South of Tamarindo, Playa Junquillal, one of the cleanest beaches in Costa Rica, is still very empty. Completely off the beaten track with almost no tourist facilities, it does have a selection of stylish hotels (most quite pricey) but there is also camping if you have a tent.

Nicoya

Nicoya, at the heart of the peninsula, is a pleasant little town distinguished by possessing the country's second oldest church, the 17th-century church of San Blas. Damaged by an earthquake in 1822 it was restored in 1831, and is currently undergoing renovations. The Parque Central, on Calle and Avenida Central, is leafy and used for occasional concerts. Buses arrive at Avenida 1, Calle 3-5. Most hotels and banks are within a couple of blocks of the central park. The area **Conservation Offices** (**ACT**) are on the northern side of central park. There is no general information for visitors, but they can assist with specific enquiries.

Parque Nacional Barra Honda

① *Entry US$6, no permit required.*

A small park in the north of the Nicoya Peninsula (2295 ha), Barra Honda National Park was created to protect a mesa with a few caves and the last remains of dry tropical forest in the region. The **park office** is near Barra Honda at **Santa Ana**, at the foot of the mesa, and there are two different trails to the top; two hours' hiking.

Sámara and Playa Carrillo

Sámara, samarabeach.com, is a smallish Tico village that has maintained some of its regular way of life alongside tourist develop- ment. The beautiful beach, 37 km from Nicoya, is probably the safest and one of the best bathing beaches in Costa Rica. Playa Carrillo is 5 km away at the south end of the beach. The litter problem is being tackled with rubbish bins, refuse collections and bottle banks. Both places have airstrips served by scheduled services from San José.

Nosara

Nosara, www.nosara.com, is a small village about 26 km north of Sámara without much to see or do in it – which makes it ideal if you like lying around on beaches. Indeed most come for the three unspoiled beaches which are not particularly close to the village.

Playa Nosara is north of the village across the Río Nosara where you may see turtles (see Ostional below); Peladas is the prettiest and smallest, south of the river, and Guiones is safe for swimming and good for surfing. Expatriates have formed the Nosara Civic Association to protect the area's wildlife and forests and prevent exploitation.

Playa Ostional

North of Nosara, at Playa Ostional, **Olive Ridley turtles** lay eggs July to November along the coastal strip of the Refugio Nacional de Vida Silvestre Ostional. The turtles arrive for nesting at high tide. The villagers are allowed to harvest the eggs in a designated area of the beach, the rest are protected and monitored. Outside the egg-laying period it is exceptionally quiet. Contact the MINAE (Ministry of Environment and Energy) ranger station for details.

Southern Península de Nicoya ☺❶❷❸❹❺ ▸▸ pp136-147.

The southern Nicoya Peninsula is almost completely cut off from the north. Roads are appalling and those that exist are frequently flooded in part. For this reason most access the region by ferry from Puntarenas. Arriving at **Playa Naranjo** there are several expensive eating places by the dock and a gas station. Beaches and stopping points are dotted along the southern shore of the peninsula passing through low key coastal centres of Tambor, Montezuma, Cabuya, Mal País and Playa Santa Teresa.

Paquera

Paquera is a small village 22 km along the coast from Playa Naranjo. There are a few shops and some simple lodgings, for example **Cabinas Rosita** on the inland side of the village. It is separated from the quay by 1 km or so; apart from a good soda, a restaurant, a public telephone and a branch of **Banco de Costa Rica**, there are no facilities.

Tambor, Curú National Wildlife Refuge and Cóbano

The small village of **Tambor**, 19 km from Paquera, has a dark sand beach, some shops and restaurants. The beach is beautiful, 6 km long with rolling surf; 1½ hours on a bone-shaking road from the ferry. However cruise ships from Puntarenas come here, and part of the beach has been absorbed by the large and controversial **Hotel Playa Tambor**. Built around a cattle farm by the Barceló group of Spain, the resort is alleged to have encroached on the public beach and drained a swamp which was a wildfowl habitat. A second stage is planned at Punta Piedra Amarilla, with a 500-boat yacht marina, villas and a total of 1100 rooms. Buses travelling from Paquera to Montezuma, pass through Tambor, connecting with the car ferry arriving from Puntarenas, US$2.60, two hours.

North of Playa Tambor is the **Curú National Wildlife Refuge** ⓘ *T2661-2392, in advance and ask for Doña Julieta*. Only 84 ha, but with five different habitats and 110 species of bird. Access is through private land.

Cóbano, near Montezuma, can be reached by bus from Paquera ferry terminal, and buses for Tambor, Cóbano and Montezuma meet the launches from Puntarenas (there is an airstrip with flights from San José). Roads north, west and south out of Cóbano, require 4WD. Cóbano has a petrol/gas station.

Montezuma

No longer a quiet sleepy hamlet, Montezuma is a very popular small village on the sea. It is a well-liked backpacking destination and at busy periods hotels fill up every day, so check in early. Although it gets crowded, there are some wonderful beaches; many are rocky, with strong waves making it difficult to swim, but it's very scenic. There are beautiful walks along the beach – sometimes sandy, sometimes rocky, always lined with trees– and impressive waterfalls. The village can be reached in four hours from Puntarenas if you get the early launch. There's a helpful tourist office at **Aventuras Montezuma**, which often knows which hotel has space; ask here first before looking around. The once-popular **Cabinas Karen** are now closed and house park guards. Prior to her death in 1994, Doña Karen donated her land to the National Parks in memory of her late husband creating what was to become Reserva Natural Absoluta Cabo Blanco (see below).

Around Montezuma

Close to the village, 20 minutes up the Río Montezuma, is a beautiful, huge **waterfall** with a big, natural swimming hole, beyond which is a smaller waterfall. Intrepid walkers can carry on up to further waterfalls but it can be dangerous and accidents have been reported. There's another waterfall, 6 km north of Montezuma, with a pool right by the beach – follow the road out to the beach at the north end of town and keep going past three coves for about half an hour until you reach the trail off to the left (you can't miss it).

You can use Montezuma as a base for exploring the **Reserva Natural Absoluta Cabo Blanco** ① *Wed-Sun 0800-1600, US$6, jeep/taxi from Montezuma US$7, first at 0700, returns 1600.* The 1172-ha reserve is 11 km from Montezuma. The marine birds include frigate birds, pelicans and brown boobies; there are also monkeys, anteaters, kinkajou and collared peccary. You can bathe in the sea or under a waterfall. At the beautiful **Playa Balsitas**, 6 km from the entrance, there are pelicans and howler monkeys.

At **Cabuya**, 2 km from Cabo Blanco Reserve, the sea can be cloudy after rough weather. Cabuya Island can be visited on foot at low tide. On the road west out of Cabuya, **Cafetería El Coyote** specializes in local and Caribbean dishes. On the west coast of the peninsula is the little village of **Mal País**. The coast here is virtually unspoilt with long white beaches, creeks and natural pools, and the facilities stretch north up the beach to blend with **Santa Teresa**. The surfing appeal of the area is growing with Mal País best suited for beginners, and the more experience crowd going up to Santa Teresa.

You can also arrange tours to **Isla Tortuga**. Many businesses rent horses; check that the horses are fit and properly cared for. Recommended for horses are **Cocozuma Traveller** and **Aventuras Montezuma**.➤ *For organized tours and expeditions, see Tour operators, page 145.*

ⓘ Peninsula de Nicoya listings

For Sleeping and Eating price codes, and other relevant information, see pages 43-46.

ⓢ Sleeping

Santa Cruz *p131*
B Diria, on the main road, T2680-0080. Bath, restaurant, pools.

B-C La Pampa, 25 m west of Plaza de los Mangos, T2680-0586. A/c, cheaper without, near parque, good, clean.
D-E Anatolia, 200 m south, 100 m west of plaza, T2680-0333. Plywood partitions, dirty bathrooms.
F Pensión Isabel, behind the church, T2680-0173. Price per person, simple box rooms.

Playa del Coco and around *p132*

Good discounts (up to 40%) in green season. At Playa Ocotal, only top end accommodation, but good diving services.

LL-AL El Ocotal Resort Hotel, Playa Ocotal, T2670-0321, www.ocotalresort.com. Rooms, suites and bungalows, PADI dive shop on beach, sport fishing, surfing, tennis, 3 pools, car hire, excursions.

AL Villa Casa Blanca, Playa Ocotal, T2670-0518. 15 idyllic rooms, with breakfast, friendly and informative, family atmosphere, small pool. Pricey but very good.

AL-A La Puerta del Sol, north of Playa del Coco, T2670-0195. Great little family-run hotel. Good food in Italian restaurant, small pool and gym, friendly atmosphere and free scuba lesson in hotel pool.

A Villa del Sol, at northern end of Playa del Coco, T2670-0085, www.villadelsol.com. Canadian-owned (from Quebec), with pool, clean, friendly, safe, big garden with parrots. Recommended.

B Coco Palms, Playa del Coco, beside football pitch, T2670-0367. German-run, large pool, gringo bar and parking.

B Pato Loco Inn, Playa del Coco, T2670-0145. Airy rooms, Italian restaurant, internet for guests.

B-D Cabinas Chale, north of Playa del Coco, T2670-0036. Double rooms and villas, with private bath. Pretty quiet, small resort-style spot, small pool, 50 m from beach. Good deal, especially villas which sleep up to 6.

C Cabinas El Coco, just north of the pier right on the beach, T2670-0110. With bath and good reasonable restaurant.

C Witch's Rock Surf Camp, Playa del Coco, T2670-1138. Simple rooms.

C-D Luna Tica, Playa del Coco, south of the plaza, T2670-0127. Also with an annex over the road (friendly, clean). Both usually full at weekends.

Playa Hermosa and Playa Panamá *p133*

The Playa Panamá area has several all-inclusive resort-style hotels (**L**), including:

El Nakuti Resort, Hotel Costa Blanca, Hotel Esmeralda and the Four Seasons.

AL El Velero, Playa Hermosa, T2672-1017, www.costaricahotel.net. With an airy villa feel, nice rooms with a/c and bathrooms, pool, clean, good restaurant.

AL Villa del Sueño, southern end of Playa Hermosa, T2672-0026, www.villadelsueno.com. Canadian-owned, with big rooms, good restaurant, pool and live music. Apartments for longer stays.

B Hotel Playa Hermosa, southern end of Playa Hermosa, T2672-0046. Italian-run, 22 clean rooms, better prices for groups, very good Italian restaurant overlooking gardens. Recommended.

B Iguana Inn, 100 m from the beach, T2672-0065. Has 9 rooms, some with kitchen. Relaxed, laid-back spot, with use of kitchen, and laundry.

Playa Tamarindo and around *p133*

Plenty of accommodation – best in each budget range listed. Book in advance at Christmas and New Year.

LL Capitán Suizo, a long way south of the centre towards Playa Langosta, T2653-0075, www.hotelcapitansuizo.com. 8 bungalows, 22 rooms with patio or balcony, a/c, pool, restaurant, kayaking, scuba-diving, surfing, sport fishing available, riding on hotel's own horses, Swiss management. One of Costa Rica's distinctive hotels.

L VOEC, on the beach, T2653-0852, www.voecretreats.com. A woman's retreat, which offers a 6-night package which includes accommodation, meals, daily surf and yoga lessons, 1 private surg lesson, 2 spa treatments at Coco Spa, a surf excursion to remote waves and the use of surfing equipment. Price per person.

L-AL Tamarindo Diria, near centre of town, T2653-0032, www.eldiria.com. Full range of services, good restaurants, beautiful pool, expensive tours offered with good guide, now with a golf course nearby.

A-B Cabinas Hotel Zullymar, at the southern end of town, T2653-0140, www.zullymar.com. Rooms with a/c and cheaper cabins, good beach bar. Recommended.

B Cabinas Marielos, near the bus stop, T2653-0141, www.cabinasmarieloscr.com. Clean basic rooms, with bath, use of kitchen, popular, book ahead.

B Pozo Azul, at the northern entrance to town, T2653-0280. Cabins, a/c, cheaper in low season, cooking facilities, clean, good, swimming pool.

C Frutas Tropicales, just south of **Tamarindo Vista Best Western**, T2653-0041. Has 3 simple, spotless and quiet rooms.

C Villas Macondo, 1 block back from the beach, T2653-0812, www.villasmacondo.com. Rooms with shared kitchen, and apartments. Swimming pool, washing machine, safety boxes, fridge and friendly people too.

D Botella de Leche, at the southern end of town, T2653-0189, www.labotelladeleche. com. Hostel rooms, very clean, use of kitchen, big communal lounge. Good choice.

E Rodamar, 50 m from **Tamarindo Vista**, T2653-0109. No a/c or fan, no mosquito nets, but clean, helpful, kitchen, shared bath. Family atmosphere and cheapest good deal.

F Tsunami, at the northern end of town. Basic, tidy rooms, private bath and use of the kitchen. Turn up and see if there's space, it's probably full of surfers more interested in water than comfort. Great value.

Playa Grande *p134*

AL-A Hotel Las Tortugas, right on the beach in the centre of town, T2653-0423, www.lastortugashotel.com. 11 rooms with bathroom, pool, restaurant, meals included, tours arranged.

A-B Playa Grande Inn, T2653-0719, www. playagrandeinn.com. Formerly **Rancho Diablo**. 10 rooms with fan, good set up for surfers.

E Cabinas/Restaurante Playa Grande, 500 m before beach at the entrance to town, T8354-7661 (mob). 8 cabins with bath and kitchen, also has camping. Price per person.

Playa Flamingo and beaches to the north *p134*

AL Mariner Inn, Playa Flamingo, T2654-4081. Has 12 rooms with bath, a/c, free camping on the beach.

A Bahía Potrero Beach Resort, Playa Potrero, T2654-4183. Bar, pool, 10 rooms with bath.

A-B Cabinas Bahía Esmeralda, Playa Potrero, T2654-4480. Garden, pool, hot water, roof ventilator, Italian restaurant.

A-B Cabinas Isolina, Playa Potrero, T2654-4333, www.isolinabeach.com. 250 m from beach, nice garden, roof ventilator.

B-C Hotel Brasilito, Playa Brasilito, close to beach on plaza, T2654-4237, www. brasilito.com. Good rooms. Horses, kayaks and bikes to rent. **Los Arcades Restaurant**, run by Charlie and Claire, mixing Thai and local dishes, closed Mon.

C Cabinas Mayra, Playa Potrero, T2654-4213. On beach, friendly, with pretty, basically equipped cabins. Camping on the beach.

C Ojos Azules, Playa Brasilito, T2654-4343. Run by Swiss couple, 18 cabins, good breakfasts with home-baked bread, nightmare decor.

F Brasilito Lodge, Playa Brasilito, right on the beach, T2654-4452, www.brasilito-conchal.com. Big rooms, good beds, bit of a bargain really. Internet service, several tours available. Also camping. Price per person.

Playa Junquillal *p134*

A-AL Iguanazul, T2658-8124, www.iguana zul.com. 24 different sizes of tiled-roof cabins on a cliff, great spot, hot water, fan or a/c, pool, restaurant, bar, sport fishing on 27-ft *Marlin Genie*, close to good surfing.

A El Lugarcito, T2658-8436, ellugarcito@ racsa.co.cr. B&B, ocean views, restaurant/bar, tours, diving, boutique.

A Tatanka, T2658-8426, tatanka@racsa.co.cr. 10 cabins with a pool. Good restaurant serving Italian, French and Tico dishes.

A-C Guacamaya Lodge, T2658-8431, www.guacamayalodge.com. Immaculate bungalows and 1 fully equipped house with pool, ocean views, Swiss cuisine.

B El Castillo Divertido, T2658-8428,
www.costarica-adventureholidays.com.
Castle rooms, restaurant, gardens, rooftop
star-gazing deck, music.
B Playa Junquillal, on the beach, T2653-0432.
Sleeps 2-4. Ideal for surfers and beach lovers.
B-C Hibiscus, close to the beach, T2658-
8437. Big rooms with big windows, seafood
restaurant with German specialities, garden,
50 m to beach, German-run.

Camping
Camping Los Malinches, after **Iguanazul**
at the northern entrance to town off main
road down a dirt track. Spectacular location,
clean bathroom provided. Worth the effort,
but bring all your own food.

Nicoya *p134*
A-AL Hotel Turístico Curime, 500 m south
of the centre on road to Sámara, T2685-5238.
Fully equipped bungalows, 3-m-deep pool.
D Jenny, or **Yenny** as the sign says, on the
corner of Calle 1, Av 4, T2685-5050. Spotless,
with bath, a/c, towels, soap and TV. Cavernous
rooms – book in with a friend and play hide
and seek. Recommended.
D Las Tinajas, opposite Liberia bus stop on
Av 1, T2685-5081. With bath, modern, clean,
good value.
D-E Pensión Venecia, opposite old church
on square, T2685-5325. Squidgy beds but
good value for the price. Recommended.
E-F Chorotega, Calle Central, Av 4-6,
T2685-5245. With bath (cheaper without),
very good value, clean, quiet. Rooms at back
have windows. Clothes-washing facilities
(good Chinese soda opposite).

Sámara *p134*
AL Hotel Fénix, on beach about 2 km east
of the village, T2656-0158, www.fenix
hotel.com. 6 slightly cramped double
units with fans, kitchenettes, hot water,
small pool, friendly. Internet for guests.
AL Mirador de Sámara Aparthotel,
rising up the hill above the village, T2656-
0044, www.miradordesamara.com. Very

friendly, German-owned. 6 large, cool and
comfortable suites with bath and kitchen.
Recommended.
A-B Belvedere, sloping up the hill, T2656-
0213. Very friendly German owners.
A cosy hotel with 10 small rooms, very
clean. Recommended.
B Marbella, inland, road going south, T2656-
0362. German-run, beautiful grounds, pool,
good service, close to beach. Recommended.
B-C Casa Valeria, on the beach near the
supermarket, T2656-0511. Friendly and
good value, especially for 3 sharing, breakfast
included, various different rooms, some with
sea view, all nicely decorated, most with bath,
hot water. Kitchen and laundry available,
small bar, tours, tickets and car rental
arranged. Recommended.
D Arenas, at the western end of town,
T2656-0320. Comfortable, cheaper for
longer stays, good restaurant opposite,
pleasant bar next door.

Camping
Camping Coco, near the beach, T2656-0496.
With toilets, electricity until 2200. The same
family own **Camping San Martín**, T2656-
0336, same deal, also offers **La Tigre Tours**
kayak, snorkel, diving, trips to see dolphins.
Camping Los Mangos, slightly further
from the beach.

Nosara *p135*
A Villaggio, Punta Guiones de Garza, close
to Nosara, 17 km north of Sámara,
T2654-4664, www.flordepacifico.com.
An upmarket yet simply furnished beach
hotel with vacation ownership plan, 30
bungalows, international restaurant, club
house, bars, pool, disco, good packages
arranged in San José, T2233-2476.
B Blew Dog's Surf Camp, near Playa
Guiones, T2682-0080, www.blewdogs.com.
Comfortable cabins, also flop house for
US$10 per person, pool table, videos, full
service reggae bar/restaurant.
B Rancho Suizo Lodge, Playa Pelada,
T2682-0057, www.nosara.ch. Swiss-

owned bungalows, restaurant, credit
cards accepted, whirlpool, hiking, riding,
bird and turtle watching.
C Casa Río Nosara, on the road to the
airstrip, T2682-0117. Rancho-style house
with cabins and nice garden, clean, friendly,
camping, canoe tours and horse riding
arranged, German owners.
D Cabinas Agnell, in the village, T2682-0142.
With bath, good value.
E Cabinas Chorotega, in the village near
the supermarket, T2682-0129. Has 8 simple,
clean rooms, shared or own bath. Bar and
restaurant downstairs, so can be noisy.

Playa Ostional *p135*
You can camp on the beach.
F Cabinas Guacamaya, T2682-0430. With
bath, clean, good food on request. Price
per person.
F Cabinas Ostional, next to the village shop.
Very basic accommodation in cabins with
bath, clean, friendly.

Southern Península de Nicoya *p135*
A-B Oasis del Pacífico, on beach, Playa
Naranjo, T2661-0209. A/c, old building,
clean, quiet, with pool, good restaurant and
free transport from ferry. Recommended.
C El Paso, north of ferry, Playa Naranjo,
T2641-8133. With bath, cheaper without,
cold water, clean, restaurant and pool.
E Cabinas Maquinay, 1.3 km towards Jicaral,
Playa Naranjo, T2661-1763. Simple rooms with
a pool and the attached **Disco Maquinay**.

**Tambor, Curú National Wildlife Refuge
and Cóbano** *p135*
LL Tango Mar, 3 km from Tambor,
T2683-0001, www.tangomar.com. All
services including golf course and its own
spectacular waterfall.
C Dos Lagartos, Tambor, T2683-0236.
Cheap, clean, good value.
C-D Cabinas Cristina, on the beach,
Tambor. With bath, T2683-0028, cheaper
without, good food.

Montezuma *p136*
Montezuma is a very small place; hotels
furthest from the centre are a 10-min walk.
L-A El Jardín, T642 0074, www.hotelel
jardin.com. 15 rooms and 2 fully equipped
villas located on the hill overlooking the
town and ocean beyond. Shower, hot
water, a/c, private terraces and hammocks.
In the grounds is a pool with a little waterfall,
very restful and great views, superb spot.
AL El Tajalín, T2642-0061, www.tajalin.com.
Very smart hotel, spotlessly clean, rooms
come with private hot water shower and a/c,
located in a quiet out of the way spot and yet
moments from the high street. Hammock
terrace for relaxing.
AL-B Los Mangos, a short walk south of the
village, T2642-0076, www.hotellosmangos.
com. Large site comprising 9 bungalows,
each accommodating 3 people, with bath,
hot water and fan. Also 10 rooms, some
with shared bath, some for 4 people. Yoga
classes run from an open-sided pagoda on
the grounds. Different and fun and lots of
free mangos (when in season).
AL-C Amor de Mar, T2642-0262, www.
amordemar.com. This well-loved hotel
has the feeling of a special place. Rooms
are pristine with private bath and hot
water. Breakfast and brunch is served on
a very pretty terrace that joins well-
manicured gardens, where visitors can
recline in hammocks and stare out to sea.
AL-E Hotel Montezuma, in the centre of
town, T2642-0058, www.playamontezuma.
netecotours/hotel.htm. Rooms on 3 sides of
the central junction. The cheapest are located
above **Chico's Bar** and **Moctezuma Bar** –
hence they can be very loud at night. Mid-
range rooms upstairs with private bath and
hot water, some have sea view and there is a
terrace overlooking the sea on 1 side, the town
on the other. Across the street to the beach
side, all rooms have private hot water showers
and sleep 1-4. On the other side of the street,
over the shops, they offer fully equipped
rooms with small kitchen, fridge, etc.

A Horizontes, on road to Cóbano, T2642-0534, www.horizontes-montezuma.com. Language school, restaurant, pool, hot water. Highly recommended.

B Cabinas Mar y Cielo, on the beach, T2642-0261. Has 6 rooms, sleeping 2-5 people, all with bath, fan and sea view. Recommended.

B Montezuma Paradise, 10 mins' walk out of town, on the road to Cabuya, past the waterfall entrance, T2642-0271. Very friendly owners have rooms with shared bath and 1 with private, overlooking the ocean and minutes from a secluded beach cove.

B Pargo Feliz, T2642-0065, elpargofeliz@costarricense.cr. Cabins with bath. Serves good food in a peaceful atmosphere – something the owners are keen on.

B-C La Cascada, 5 mins' walk out of town, on the road to Cabo Blanco, close to the entrance to the waterfalls, T2642-0057. Lovely hotel with pretty, well-kept rooms and a wide hammock terrace overlooking the ocean for relaxing. Restaurant serves local food for breakfast, lunch and dinner.

B-C Montezuma Pacific, 50 m west of the church, next to El Tajalin, T2642-0204. With private bath, hot water and a/c.

D Lucy, follow road south past **Los Mangos**, T2642-0273. One of the oldest hotels in town and one of the most popular budget options, due to its location on the sea. 10 rooms with fans, some with sea view. Shared bath, pleasant balcony. Ultra-friendly Tica owner. Restaurant next door opens during high season. Recommended.

D-F El Tucán, at the top of the road down to the beach, T2642-0284. Wooden hotel on stilts, clean, small wood-panelled rooms, shared shower and toilet, fan, mosquito net on window. Recommended.

E Hotel El Capitán, on the main street, T2642-0069. Old wooden house with an endless variety of rooms, most with shared cold water bath, but some with private. Very friendly owners and good location, can get a little noisy, good for backpackers.

E Pensión Arenas, on the beach, T2642-0308. Run by Doña Meca, rustic small rooms, with fan, shared bath, no frills but pleasant balcony and sea view. Free camping. Laundry service.

E Pensión Jenny, at the end of the track by the football field, T2642-0306. Basic lodging with shared bath, cheap and clean, nice out of the way location. Laundry service.

Around Montezuma *p136*

L Milarepa, Playa Santa Teresa, on beach, T2640-0023, www.milarepahotel.com. Nice bamboo bungalows, open-air bathroom.

AL Celaje, Cabuya, on beach, T2642-0374. Very good Italian restaurant. Pool, rooms with bath, hot water, good.

AL-A Los Caballos, 3 km north on road to Cóbano from Montezuma, T2642-0124. Has 8 rooms with bath, pool, outdoor restaurant, ocean views, gardens. 5 mins from beach, horses are a specialty.

AL-C Mal País Surf Camp, Mal País, T2640-0031, www.malpaissurfcamp.com. Restaurant, pool, also has camping.

AL-D Funky Monkey Lodge, Santa Teresa, T2640-0317, www.funky-monkey-lodge.com. The same very friendly and hospitable owners have extended their relaxed and very attractive resort. They now have one bungalow sleeping 8 people, 3 private bungalows and 2 apartments, sleeping 2/4 and a suite with a large balcony overlooking the ocean. They also have a rather upmarket dormitory with individual beds. The apartments have a/c, ocean view, access to the kitchen and face the swimming pool. They have a restaurant, bar, TV, DVD, ping-pong table, surfboard rental and organize surf lessons, local tours, car or ATV rental. Recommended.

A-C Cabinas Las Rocas, 20 mins south of Montezuma, T2642-0393, www.caboblancopark.com. Good but quite expensive meals, small, seashore setting, isolated.

A-E Frank's Place, Mal País, the road junction, T2640-0096. Set in tropical gardens. Wide variety of rooms with private or shared bath, and self-catering options available. Good range of services and local advice.

B-C Cabañas Bosque Mar, Mal País, T2640-0074. Clean, large rooms, hot water shower, attractive grounds, good restaurant on beach nearby, 3 km to Cabo Blanco Reserve.

B-C Cabañas Playa Santa Teresa, Playa Santa Teresa, T2640-0137. 150 m from beach, surfboard rental, horses, German-run.

C Cabinas Mar Azul, Mal País, T2642-0298, Run by Jeannette Stewart, camping possible, delicious fried fish, shrimp, lobster.

C Linda Vista, on the hill over Montezuma, T2642-0274. Units sleep 6, with bath (cold water) and fan, ocean views.

C Mochila Inn, 300 m outside Montezuma, T2642-0030. Cabinas from US$30, also houses and apartments for around US$350 per month.

C-E Cabinas y Restaurante El Ancla de Oro, Cabuya, T2642-0369. Some cabins with bath, others shared bathroom, seafood restaurant, lobster dinners US$10, filling breakfasts, horses US$20 per day with local guide, mountain bike rental, transport from Paquera launch available. **El Delfín** restaurant at crossroads, friendly, good-value local food.

D Casa Zen, Santa Teresa. Smart, budget accommodation with shared bath and one fully furnished apartment. Camping area also available. Close to the beach, restaurant on site.

E-F Cabañas Playa El Carmen, Playa Santa Teresa, T2683-0281. Basic cabins and camping, shared bath and kitchen. **Jungle Juice**, vegetarian restaurant, serves smoothies and meals from US$4.

Camping

Rincón de los Monos, 500 m along the beach from the centre of Montezuma, T2643-0048. Clean, well organized, lockers for rent. Lots of monkeys around.

🍴 Eating

Santa Cruz *p131*
🍴 **Coopetortilla**, 3 blocks east of the church. A local institution– a women's cooperative cooking local dishes. Cheap and enjoyable.

Playa del Coco and around *p132*
🍴🍴🍴 **Mariscos la Guajira**, on southern beach. Popular and beautiful beach-front location.

🍴🍴🍴 **Papagayo**, near the beach, T2670-0298. Good seafood, recommended.

🍴🍴 **Bananas**, on the road out of town. The place to go drinking and dancing until the early hours.

🍴🍴 **Cocos**, on the plaza, T2670-0235. Bit flashy and pricey for the area, good seafood.

🍴🍴 **El Roble**, beside the main plaza. A popular bar/disco.

🍴🍴 **Playa del Coco**, on beach. Popular, open from 0600.

🍴 **Jungle Bar**, on road into town. Another lively, slightly rougher option.

Playa Tamarindo and around *p133*
🍴🍴🍴 **Fiesta del Mar**, on the loop at the end of town. Large thatched open barn, good food, good value.

🍴🍴🍴 **Ginger**, at the northern end of town, T2672-0041. Tue-Sun. Good Thai restaurant.

🍴🍴🍴 **Iguana Surf** restaurant on road to Playa Langosta. Good atmosphere and food.

🍴🍴 **Coconut Café**, on beach near **Tamarindo Vista**. Pizzas, pastries and good fish. Check the sodas. Good breakfasts and cheap suppers.

🍴🍴 **El Arrecife**, on roundabout. Popular spot to hang out, with Tico fare, good chicken and pizzas.

🍴🍴 **The Lazy Wave**, on road leading away from the beach, T2653-0737. Menu changes daily, interesting mix of cuisine, seafood.

🍴🍴 **Portofino**, at end of road by roundabout. Italian specialties and good ice cream.

🍴🍴 **Stellas**, on road leading away from the beach. Very good seafood, try dorado with mango cream. Recommended.

🍴 **Arco Iris**, on road heading inland. Cheap vegetarian, great atmosphere.

🍴 **Frutas Tropicales**, near **Tamarindo Vista**. Snacks and breakfast.

Playa Flamingo and beaches to the north *p134*
🍴🍴 **La Casita del Pescado**, Playa Brasilito. Some reasonably priced fish dishes which

you have to eat quickly because the stools are made of concrete.

ⵌ Marie's Restaurant, Playa Flamingo, T2654-4136. Breakfast, seafood, *casados* and international dishes.

ⵌ Pizzeria Il Forno, Playa Brasilito. Serves a mean pizza.

ⵌ Restaurant La Boca de la Iguana, Playa Brasilito. Good value.

ⵌ-ⵌ Las Brisas, at the northern end of Playa Potrero. A great spot for a beer and a snack, and surprisingly popular – well, 5 people – for its cut-off location.

ⵌ Costa Azul, Playa Potrero, by the football pitch. One of several restaurants in the area, popular with locals.

ⵌ Cyber Shack, Playa Brasilito. Internet, coffee, breakfast and UPS service.

ⵌ Hillside Café, Playa Flamingo, T2654-4226. Breakfast.

Playa Junquillal *p134*

ⵌ La Puesta del Sol, T2658-8442. The only restaurant along the strip, but then nothing could compete with the dishes from this ittle piece of Italy. Spectacular setting. Very popular so reservations required.

Nicoya *p134*

ⵌ Café de Blita, 2 km outside Nicoya towards Sámara. Good.

ⵌ Soda El Triángulo, opposite **Chorotega**. Good juices and snacks, friendly owners.

ⵌ Teyet, near **Hotel Jenny**. Good, with quick service.

ⵌ Daniela, 1 block east of plaza. Breakfast, lunches, coffee, *refrescos*, good.

Sámara *p134*

There are several cheap sodas around the football pitch in the centre of town.

ⵌ Restaurant Delfín, on the beach. Very good value and French owned. They also have cabinas.

ⵌ El Ancla Restaurant, on the beach, T2656-0716. Seafood.

ⵌ Las Brasas, by the football pitch, T2656-0546. Spanish restaurant and bar:

ⵌ Restaurant Acuario, on the beach. Serves Tico and other food.

ⵌ Soda Sol y Mar, on the road to Nosara. Costa Rican and Western food.

Nosara *p135*

ⵌ Gilded Iguana, Playas Guiones. Gringo food and good company.

ⵌ La Dolce Vita, south along the road out of town. Good but pricey Italian food.

ⵌ Casa Romántica, Playas Guiones. The European restaurant.

ⵌ Corky Carroll's Surf School, T2682-0385. Surf lessons and a good Mexican/Thai restaurant (closed Sun).

ⵌ Giardino Tropicale, in the middle section. Pizza.

ⵌ Hotel Almost Paradise, Playas Guiones, T2682-0173. Good food with a great view.

ⵌ La Luna, slightly up the hill. Good food and ambience.

ⵌ Olga's, Playa Peladas. Seafood on the beach.

ⵌ Soda Vanessa, Playas Guiones. One of several sodas in the village. Good and very cheap.

Playa Ostional *p135*

ⵌ-ⵌ Mirador de los Tortugueros, 1 km south of **Cabinas Guacamaya**. Good restaurant with coffee and pancakes. Great atmosphere. Recommended.

Montezuma *p136*

ⵌ Playa de Los Artistas/Cocina Mediterránea, about 5 mins south of town on the road to Cabuya. Best restaurant in town.

ⵌ Bakery Café, north end of town. Great for breakfast, with bread, cakes and excellent vegetarian food.

ⵌ Brisas del Mar, just south of the Santa Teresa soccer ground. Great local seafood – tuna or mahi mahi straight from the boats at Mal País. Great service and atmosphere. Highly recommended.

ⵌ Chico's Playa Bar, on the beach. Popular hangout, great sushi. No food in the low season.

ⵌ Cocolores, on the beach behind **El Pargo Feliz**, T2642-0096. Closed Mon. Good for seafood and nice veggie options.

♦♦ **El Pulpo Pizzeria**, Santa Teresa. Good value pizzeria that also delivers.

♦♦ **El Sano Banano**, on the road to the beach. Health food restaurant, good vegetarian food, large helpings, daily change of menu, milkshakes, fresh fruit and yoghurt, owned by Dutch/Americans, free movies with dinner.

♦♦ **Pizza Romana**, opposite **El Capitán**. Good Italian food cooked by Italians, pizzas, pesto, fresh pastas, etc.

♦♦-♦ **Tayrona**, behind **Taganga**. Great pizza, Italian owned, attractive restaurant off the main street.

♦ **Soda El Caracol**, located by the football field. One of several sodas around town serving good Tico food, very cheap.

♦ **Soda Monte Sol**, on the road to Cabo Blanco. Recommended for good Mexican burritos, good value, big helpings.

♦ **Taganga**, at the top of the high street, opposite El Tucán hostel. Argentine grills, chicken and meat.

◉ Entertainment

Playa Tamarindo and around p133
With a long beachside strip, it's a question of exploring town until you find something that works. Call it bar surfing if you like.

Sámara p134
Bars and clubs
Bar **La Góndola** is popular and has a dart board. Opposite is **Bar Colocho**. **Dos Lagartos** disco is on the beach near **Al Manglar** and the disco at **Isla Chora** is the place to be during the season if you like resort discos.

Nosara p135
Bars and clubs
Some of the nightlife is in the village as well – **Bambú**, **Disco Tropicana** and various others line the football pitch.

Montezuma p136
Bar Moctezuma, usually open the latest, but not as loud as the others.

Chico's Bar and **Chico's Playa Bar**, a relaxing cocktail by the beach, or late night salsa dancing ad very loud reggaeton parties.
Congo Azul Bar, reggae nights Thu and Sat.

Around Montezuma p136
There are a number of new bars opening up on the beach front at Mal País each season. For a treat try a mojito on the terrace at the exclusive resort of **Flor Blanca** at the northern edge of Santa Teresa.
Bar Tabu, Santa Teresa. Probably the most popular bar in the area, great location on the beach; good music, always lively, open late.
La Llora Amarilla, Santa Teresa. Now very popular, large venue that hosts regular disco and party nights.
Mal País Surf Camp, Mal País. Bar open every night, live jam night on Wed.

◎ Shopping

Playa Tamarindo and around p133
The town is increasingly a retail outlet selling everything you need for the beach, as well as general living with a couple of general stores in the centre of town.

Sámara p134
The **supermarket**, near **Casa del Mar**, is well stocked and you can get fresh bread and croissants from **Chez Joel**. **Free Radical** super/soda on main road, 1 km east of town centre, offers fresh *ceviche*, delightful pastries, beer, wine, natural juices, local honey and unusual hand-blown glass products.

Montezuma p136
There are now a number of rather pricey, boutique-style souvenir and clothes shops in Montezuma, most sell a very similar range.
Librería Topsy, T2642-0576. Mon-Fri 0800-1400, Sat 0800-1200. Sells books and maps and will take postcards and small letters to the post office for you.

▲ Activities and tours

Playa del Coco and around p132
Tour operators
Agua Rica Charters, T2670-0473, www.agua
ricacharters.com, or contact them through
the internet café. Can arrange transport to
Witch's Rock for surfers, approx US$400 for
up to 10. **Deep Blue Diving**, beside **Hotel
Coco Verde**, T2670-1004, www.deepblue-
diving.com, has diving trips to Islas Catalinas
and Islas Murcielago, where sightings of
manta rays and bull sharks are common.
2-tank dive from US$55. Will also rent gear.
Also **Rich Coast Diving**, TT2670-0176,
www.richcoastdiving.com.

Playa Hermosa and Playa Panamá p133
Diving
Diving Safari, based at the **Sol Playa
Hermosa Resort** on Playa Hermosa,
T2453- 5044, www.billbeardcostarica.com.
One of the longest-running diving
operations in the country, offering
a wide range of options in the region.

Playa Tamarindo and around p133
Diving
Try the **Pacific Coast Dive Center**,
T2653-0267, or **Agua Rica Dive Center**,
T2653-0094.

Surfing and yoga
VOEC, on the beach, T2653-0852, www.
voecretreats.com. A woman's retreat that
offers 6-night packages, which include
surf and yoga lessons. See Sleeping,
page 137.

Tour operators
Many tours to see the turtles nesting at
night in Playa Grande. **Iguana Surf Tours**,
T2653-0148, rent surfboards, they have
one outlet near the beach, opposite the
supermarket, the other in the restaurant
of the same name. **Hightide Adventures
and Surfcamp**, T2653-0108, www.tamarindo
adventures.net, offers a full range of tours.

Sámara p134
Tour operators
Most hotels will arrange tours for you.
You can rent bikes from near the *ferretería*
on the road to Cangrejal. Recommended,
though, is the newer **Tip Top Tours**,
T2656-0650, run by a very nice French
couple, offering dolphin tours (from US$45
per person), mangrove tours (US$43 per
person) and waterfall tours (US$20 per
person). Naturalist guided tours to Barra
Honda and Isla Chora (US$70 per person),
as well as slightly more unusual trips like
Journée Cowboy where you spend a day
on the ranch roping cattle and eat with a
Tico family. **Wing Nuts Canopy Tour**,
T2656-0153 US$40, kids US$25, family-run,
friendly service, spectacular ocean views
from the treetops, newly expanded to
12 platforms, lots of wildlife close up, great
photo opportunity, 1st-class equipment.

Nosara p135
Tour operators
Casa Río Nosara for horse or river tours,
and **Gilded Iguana** for kayaking and fishing.
For turtle tours, try **Rancho Suizo**, T2682-
0057, or **Lagarta Lodge**, T2682-0035, who
are both sensitive to the turtles and don't
exploit or bother them.

Montezuma p136
Tour operators
Aventuras en Montezuma, T2642-0050,
avenzuma@racsa.co.cr. Offers a similar
range, snorkelling to Tortuga Island,
canopy, sunset and wildlife tours for
similar prices, also taxi boat to Jacó,
US$35, minimum 5 people. Ivan and
his staff are also exceptionally helpful as
a tourist office and can advise on hotels
and other matters locally and nationally.
They also book and confirm flights.
Cocozuma Traveller, T2642-0911, www.
cocozumacr.com. Tico-owned company,
now one of the best in Montezuma. Runs
all the usual tours including horse rides and
Isla Tortuga. Their boat taxi now runs to Jacó

(US$35), Sámara (US$50) and Puntarenas (US$40). They will also arrange hotels, transfers, car rental and have quadbikes for hire. Very helpful staff are happy to give information about the area.

Eco Tours Montezuma, T2642-0058, on the corner opposite **Soda Monte Sol**. Offer a wide range of tours, including shuttle to Cabo Blanco (US$3), kayaking/snorkelling at Isla Cabuya (US$25 per person), day trip to Isla Tortuga (US$40 per person), horse rental (US$25) and bike rental (US$5 per day). Also boat/road transfers to Jacó/Tamarindo for around US$150 for up to 6 people.

Montezuma Expeditions, top of the high street, T2642-0919, www.montezuma expeditions.com. Very efficient set up – organize private and group transport around the country, trips between US$35 and US$48 per person, these include, San José, Fortuna (Arenal), Monteverde and Jacó.

Zuma Tours, Cóbano, T8849-8569, www.zumatours.net. Lots of information available on their website.

⊙ Transport

Santa Cruz p131
Bus Buses leave and arrive from terminals on Plaza de los Mangos. From **San José**, 9 daily, 0700-1800, 4½ hrs, US$5, Calle 18-20, Av 3, ½ block west of Terminal Coca Cola, return 0300-1700; to **Tamarindo**, 2030, return 0645, US$1, also to **Playa Flamingo** and nearby beaches, 0630, 1500, return 0900, 1700, 64 km; to **Liberia** every hr, US$1, 0530-1930; to **Nicoya** hourly 0630-2130, US$0.35.

Taxi To **Nicoya**, US$10.50 for 2 people.

Playa del Coco and around p132
Bus From **San José** from Calle 14, Av 1-3, 0800, 1400, 5 hrs, return 0800, 1400, US$4.50. 6 buses daily from **Liberia** 0530-1815, return 0530-1800.

Playa Hermosa and Playa Panamá p133
Bus From **Liberia**, Empresa Esquivel, 0730, 1130, 1530, 1730, 1900, return 0500, 0600, 1000, 1600, 1700, US$0.80.

Playa Tamarindo and around p133
Air Several daily flights from **San José** with **Sansa** (US$78 one way) and **Nature Air** (US$90) from **San José**. Daily flight from **Fortuna** with **Sansa**.

Bus From **Santa Cruz**, 0410, 1330, 1500 daily. Tamarindo to Santa Cruz first bus at 0600, US$1. Express bus from **San José** daily from Terminal Alfaro, 1530, return 0600 Mon-Sat, 0600, Sun 1230, 5½ hrs. Bus back to San José, can be booked through Hotel Tamarindo Diria, US$5.

Playa Flamingo and beaches to the north p134
Bus From **San José** to Flamingo, Brasilito and Potrero, daily from Av 3, Calle 18-20, 0800, 1000, 6 hrs, return 0900, 1400. From **Santa Cruz** daily 0630, 1500, return 0900, 1700, 64 km to Potrero.

Playa Junquillal p134
Bus Daily from **Santa Cruz** departs 1030, returns to Santa Cruz at 1530.

Nicoya p134
Bus From **San José**, 8 daily from Terminal Alfaro, 6 hrs; from **Liberia** every 30 mins from 0430-2200; from **Santa Cruz** hourly 0630-2130. To **Playa Naranjo** at 0500 and 1300, US$1.45, 2¼ hrs. 12 buses a day to **Sámara**, 37 km by paved road, 1 to **Nosara**.

Sámara p134
Air Daily flights from **San José**, Sansa US$78, **Nature Air**, US$90.

Bus From **Nicoya**, 45 km, US$1.15, 1½ hrs, 0800, 1500, 1600, return 0530, 0630, 1130, 1330, 1630. Express bus from Terminal Alfaro, **San José** daily at 1230, return Mon-Sat 0430, Sun 1300, 5-6 hrs. School bus to **Nosara**

around 1600 – ask locally for details. It is not possible to go from Sámara along the coast to Montezuma, except in 4WD vehicle; not enough traffic for hitching.

Taxis Official and others stop outside bus station (US$20 to **Nosara**, US$10 to **Nicoya**).

Nosara *p135*
Air Sansa has daily flights to **San José**, US$78, **Nature Air**, US$90.

Bus Daily from **Nicoya** to Nosara, **Garza**, **Guiones** daily from main station, 1300, return 0600, US$2, 2 hrs, 65 km; from **San José** daily from Terminal Alfaro at 0600, 6 hrs, return 1245.

Playa Ostional *p135*
Bus There is 1 a day at 0500 to **Santa Cruz** and **Liberia**, returns at 1230 from Santa Cruz, 3 hrs, US$1.75.

Montezuma *p136*
Bus To **Paquera** daily at 0530, 0815, 1000, 1215, 1400 and 1600, connecting with the car and passenger ferry to **Puntarenas** central docks. Tickets available in advance from tourist information centre; be at bus stop outside **Hotel Moctezuma**, in good time as the bus fills up quickly, US$2.60, 1 hr (the road has been paved). To **Cabuya** US$1, buses run 4 times a day. Change at Cóbano for **Mal País** – 2 buses run daily from Cóbano, 1100 and 1400 (check as times can change).

Taxi To **Cóbano** US$5; to **Paquera** US$20.

✪ Directory

Santa Cruz *p131*
Banks Banco Nacional, with ATM, on main road. **Post office** 400 m west of Plaza de los Mangos.

Playa del Coco and around *p132*
Banks **Banco Nacional**, closed Sat. **Internet** Café Internet 2000, on road out of town, also try **E-Juice Bar**, T2670- 05563 and **Leslie Café**.

Playa Tamarindo and around *p133*
Banks Banco Nacional, opposite Hotel Diria. **Internet** Tamarindo Internet, T2653-0404.

Nicoya *p134*
Banks With ATMs on main square and Calle 3, with very welcome a/c. **Post office** On corner of main square.

Sámara *p134*
Banks There is no bank in Sámara, although hotels may change money. **Internet** Tropical Latitudes Internet Café in centre of town, and hotels may offer access. **Language** Intercultura Centro de Idiomas, 150 m from El Dorado restaurant, www.samaralanguage school.com. Also in Heredia, page 94. **Post office** Almost on the beach.

Nosara *p135*
Internet and telephone Nosara Office Centre, offering email, fax, photocopies and international calls. **Language schools** Rey de Nosara language school is in the village, T2682 0215, www.reydenosara. itgo.com. Classes from US$18 per hr. They can often advise about other things to see and do in the area and arrange tours and homestays.

Montezuma *p136*
Banks Change money at **Hotel Moctezuma**, **Aventuras en Montezuma** and **Cocozuma Traveller** (otherwise go to the **Banco Nacional** in Cóbano, T2642-0210). **Internet** There is an internet café in **Pizz@net** next to the Hotel Moctezuma, US$2 per hr. **Sano Banano** has an all-Macintosh internet, a little pricey at US$3 per hr and can be slow. Another is located behind El Parque Hotel. **Laundry** Laundrette in **Pensión Jenny** and **Hotel Arenas** (on the beach). **Medical services** If you need a pharmacy, you will have to go to Cóbano.

Central Pacific coast

West of the Central Highlands lies a slim lowland strip of African palm with just the occasional cattle ranch. But, for the visitor, it is the miles of beaches stretching from Jacó almost continuously south to Uvita that are the real attraction. Parque Nacional Manuel Antonio is a major destination with developed services. Further south, the beaches are quieter and the Parque Nacional Marino Ballena, which is harder to get to, is barely developed; but it's of interest to divers and whalewatchers. For listings, see pages 153-159.

Esparza to the Pacific coast

From Esparza on the Pan-American Highway a road runs 21 km southeast to **San Mateo** (from where a road runs northeast to Atenas and the Central Highlands – see Meseta Central section). Just before San Mateo, at Higuito de San Mateo, is **Las Candelillas** ① *T2428-9157*, a 26-ha farm and reforestation project with fruit trees and sugar cane. There is a day use recreational area with showers, pool and riding, trails and bar/restaurant.

From San Mateo a road runs south to **Orotina**, which used to be an important road/rail junction on the San José-Puntarenas route. Today the area is home to **Original Canopy Tour at Mahogany Park** ① *T2257-5149*, which charges US$45 to fly through the trees; transportation is available.

West of Orotina the road forks northwest to the port of **Caldera,** via Cascajal, and southwest to the Pacific coast at Tárcoles.

The Costanera to Quepos 🔲🕐😊🅿️⛰️💲🕐 ›› *pp153-159.*

The Costanera or coastal road passes through Jacó, Manuel Antonio and Quepos and on to Dominical before heading inland to San Isidro de El General or continuing south to Palmar Norte. If you want a popular beach, pick somewhere before Manuel Antonio. Beyond, although not deserted, you'll find things a lot quieter. If driving yourself, check the state of the roads and bridges before setting out to San Isidro. Just because buses are getting through, it doesn't mean cars can. Leave nothing of value in your vehicle; thefts, robberies and scams are regularly reported in the area. The road is paved as far as Quepos and with few potholes. Thereafter it is a good, but dusty, gravel road, paved in villages until Paquita, just before Quepos. After Quepos the road is unpaved to Dominical. From Dominical the road inland through Barú to San Isidro is paved but landslides can make this section hazardous. High clearance is needed if a bridge is down. South from Dominical, the Costanera drifts through small expat communities which are only just being explored by visitors. They cover a range of budgets, but all are for people seeking a little solitude while it lasts.

Reserva Biológica Carara

① *Daily 0700-1600, US$7.*

Between Orotina and Jacó the Carara Biological Reserve (5242 ha) is rich in wildlife. Three trails lead through the park: one lasting a couple of hours leaves from close to Tarcoles bridge; the others lasting a little over one hour from the ranger station to the south. The reserve protects a transitional zone from the dry north coast of the country to the very humid region of the southeast. Spider monkeys, scarlet macaws and coatis can all be seen in the reserve.

One of the most popular free experiences in Costa Rica is to peer over the side of the Río Tárcoles bridge to see the opaque sediment-filled waters broken by the bony backs of the somnolent crocodiles below. It's easy to find the spot to stop, as cars cram the roadside, especially at dawn and dusk when scarlet macaws can be seen returning to their roosts from Carara Biological Reserve on the southern banks of the river.

You can get a closer look by taking a boat tour with **Jungle Crocodile Safari** ① *T2292-2316*, or **Crocodile ECO Tour** ① *T2637-0426*, US$25 per person from the dock in Tárcoles, US$35 round trip from Jacó.

Next to Carara is **La Catarata** ① *T2236-4140, 0800-1500, 15 Dec-15 Apr, US$7.50*, a private reserve with an impressive waterfall with natural pools for bathing; take the gravel road up the hill beside **Hotel Villa Lapas**: it's 5 km to the entrance, and a 2.5-km hike to falls and pools, but it's worth the effort. There are signs on the main road. **Bijagual Waterfall Tours** ① *T2661-8263*, offer horse riding or 4WD to the falls.

Jacó

A short distance from Carara is Jacó, a large stretch of sandy beach, with a lively and youthful energy. It is popular with surfers and weekenders from San José, and comes with a rough'n'ready, earthy commercial appeal. If you want to learn to **surf**, this is as good a place as any, with several surf shops offering courses and boards for rent. If you want to party with crowds on their annual holiday, it's a great spot. If you're looking for peace and quiet, go elsewhere.

Jacó to Quepos

From Jacó the potholed road runs down the coastline with lovely views of the ocean. The beaches are far quieter and, if you have a car, you can take your pick. A few kilometres south is **Playa Hermosa**, which is right on the main road and has a popular surfing beach. If travelling by car, 20 km further and a few kilometres off the road is **Playa Bejuco**, **Esterillos Centro** and **Playa Palma**, near Parrita; definitely worth exploring. Beyond **Parrita** (Banco Nacional, Banco de Costa Rica, a gas station and a few stores) the road travels through a flat landscape of endless African palm plantations. Many of the plantation villages are of passing interest for their two-storey, balconied houses laid out around a central football pitch, a church of some denomination and the obligatory branch of AA. The carriageway narrows to single track on bridges along this road so take care if you're driving, especially at night.

Quepos

Developed as a banana exporting port by United Brands, Quepos was forced to recreate itself following the devastation of banana plantations in the region overwhelmed by Panama disease, in the early 1950s. Endless rows of oil-producing African Palm have replaced the bananas and Quepos has long since shrugged off the portside image, to the extent that few even bother to explore the dock at the southern end of town.

South of Quepos, a winding road, lined with hotels, bars, restaurants and stores rises and falls for 7 km before reaching the beautiful coastline of Parque Nacional Manuel Antonio (see below) and nearby beautiful beaches. The impact on what was once an attractive stretch of jungle-clad coastline is indisputable. For some it is an environmental catastrophe, for others it is a demonstration of the importance of planning to protect. Quepos plays an important role as a service town for local and foreign tourists. It is cheaper than the Manuel Antonio road, there is no shortage of restaurants, bars and shops, and regular buses make the journey to the national park. Tell the bus driver where you are going and he will drop you at your chosen hotel.

Parque Nacional Manuel Antonio
① Tue-Sun 0700-1600, closed Mon, US$7. Guides available, but not essential, at entrance. Early and late are the best times to see the wildlife. Breakfast and other meals available from stalls just before the river, where cars can be parked and minded for US$1 by the stallholders. Basic toilets, picnic tables and drinks available by the beaches, cold water showers at Manuel Antonio and Espadilla Sur beaches.

From the southeastern corner of Quepos, a road winds up, over and round the peninsula of Punta Quepos, passing the flourishing hotels, restaurants, bars and stores along the length of this rocky outcrop. Travelling the road for the first time, you can't fail to be impressed by the beauty of the views. And at night, you can't help being blinded by the neon lights that speckle the hillside – evidence of the vibrant tourist trade. At times it is difficult to believe a national park flourishes on the other side of the watershed.

With 683 ha of mangrove swamps and beaches, home to a rich variety of fauna and flora, Manuel Antonio National Park can rightly claim to be one of Costa Rica's most popular protected areas – second only to Volcán Poás. Just 7 km south of Quepos on

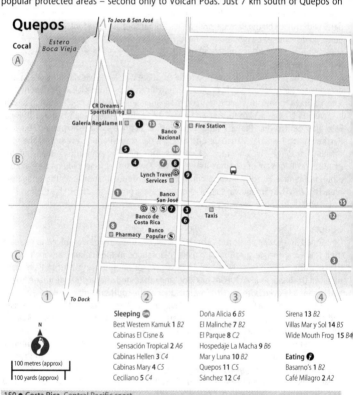

Sleeping ⓢ

Best Western Kamuk 1 *B2*
Cabinas El Cisne &
 Sensación Tropical 2 *A6*
Cabinas Hellen 3 *C4*
Cabinas Mary 4 *C5*
Ceciliano 5 *C4*

Doña Alicia 6 *B5*
El Malinche 7 *B2*
El Parque 8 *C2*
Hospedaje La Macha 9 *B6*
Mar y Luna 10 *B2*
Quepos 11 *C5*
Sánchez 12 *C4*

Sirena 13 *B2*
Villas Mar y Sol 14 *B5*
Wide Mouth Frog 15 *B4*

Eating ❶

Basarno's 1 *B2*
Café Milagro 2 *A2*

a paved road, three beautiful, forest-fringed beaches stretch along the coastline and around the headland of Punta Catedral: **Espadilla Sur**, **Manuel Antonio** and **Puerto Escondido**. Iguanas and white-faced monkeys often come down to the sand.

In addition to enjoying the beaches, hiking is also good in the park. A 45-minute trail, steep in places, runs round the Punta Catedral between Espadilla Sur and Manuel Antonio beaches. If you're early, and quiet, it is possible to see a surprising amount of wildlife. A second walk to Puerto Escondido, where there is a blow hole, takes about 50 minutes. The map sold at the entrance shows a walk up to a mirador, with good views of the coastline.

Manuel Antonio has been a victim of its own success with some of the animals becoming almost tame. But for all the criticism of recent years, it is still beautiful and highly enjoyable. Overdevelopment outside the park and overuse within has led to problems of how to manage the park with inadequate funds. In 1992 the National Park Service (SPN) threatened to close it and a number of tour operators removed it from their itineraries. You are not allowed to feed the monkeys but people do, which means that they can be a nuisance, congregating around picnic tables expecting to be fed and rummaging through bags given the chance. Leave no litter and take nothing out of the park, not even seashells.

Dos Locos **3** *C2*

The range of activities in the area outside the park is slightly bewildering. Sea kayaking is possible, as is mountain biking, hiking, canopy tours, canyoning, deep-sea fishing and even quad biking. Most hotels can assist with booking trips, and there are agencies in Quepos that can also advise. The beaches in the park are safer than those outside, but rip tides are dangerous all along the coast. Beaches slope steeply and the force of the waves can be too strong for children.

Quepos to Palmar Norte
⬤⬤⬤⬤ ⇥ *pp153-159*.

Playa Matapalo
Beaches, beaches, endless stretches of sandy beaches. Thirty kilometres southeast from the congestion of Quepos towards Dominical the unpaved coastal road drifts almost unnoticed through Playa Matapalo, where you'll find an expansive, beautiful sandy beach recommended for surfing, relaxing and playing with your ideas of paradise. Other activities, in an overwhelmingly Swiss community, include fishing, horse riding and hiking to mountain waterfalls.

Dominical

Twelve kilometres further on, at the mouth of the Río Barú, is Dominical (www.dominical.biz), a small town with a population of a few hundred. No more than 500 m from one end to the other it's popular with surfers and often busy. It's a great spot for surfing. Hotel prices soar in high season and most hotels are close to noisy bars. Treks and horse riding trips to waterfalls are possible if the beach is too much to bear. Just north of the town **Hacienda Barú** has a **national wildlife preserve**, with activities like abseiling, canopy tours and nature walks (see below). If you want to touch up your Spanish try the **Adventure Education Center** ① *T2787-0023, www.adventurespanishschool.com*, with an immersion Spanish school. They have schools in Arenal and Turrialba as well. Most people come here for the surfing; if you want to learn visit the **Green Iguana Surf Camp** ① *T8825-1381, www.greeniguanasurfcamp.com*, who provide board hire, group lessons, individual lessons and package deals.

Punta Dominical is 4 km south of town (no transport). A poor dirt road follows a steep path inland up the Escaleras (stairs) to some secluded accommodation blending beach and rainforest.

Uvita

If you get the impression the southern Pacific coast is about beaches, you'd be right. The village of Uvita, 18 km south of Dominical, has beautiful beaches all along the coastline. You can walk in the nearby forests, swim in nearby waterfalls or at the beach, take a boat trip and watch birds. Ballena National Marine Park (see below) protects over 5000 ha of Pacific coral reef, and humpback whales can be sighted at nearby Isla Ballena between December and April.

The road south from Uvita is being repaved as far as Ciudad Cortés, and access to the beaches of Playa Ballena and Playa Bahía is getting easier with consequent development of the area.

Parque Nacional Marino Ballena

The vast majority of Ballena (Whale) Marine National Park is coastal waters – 5161 ha against 116 ha of protected land – which may go some way to explaining why there isn't a lot to see at this least-developed national park. The underwater world is home to coral reefs and abundant marine life that includes common and bottle-nosed dolphins as well as occasional visits from humpback whales at times seen with their calves.

Although there is a rarely staffed **rangers station** ① *T2786-7161*, in Bahía, and signposts line the Costanera, the infrastructure in the park is non-existent. There is a nominal entrance fee of US$6 which is rarely collected. Along the beach at Bahía is a turtle-nesting project administered by the local community. As with the park itself, the organization is very ad hoc – visitors and volunteers are welcome. Beachcombing is good, as is snorkelling when the tides are favourable. Boat trips to the island can be arranged from Bahía, and diving is starting up with the most recommended local being Máximo Vásquez, or Chumi as he is known. The coastal road continues south beside **Playa Tortuga**, passing small communities of foreigners hiding and enjoying one of the quietest spots near a beach in Costa Rica, to join the Pan-American Highway at Palmar Norte (see page 163).

Central Pacific coast listings

For Sleeping and Eating price codes, and other relevant information, see pages 43-46.

Sleeping

Esparza to the Pacific coast *p148*
AL El Rancho Oropéndola, San Mateo, T2428-8600. Cabins with private bath or rooms with shared bath, rustic and peaceful, pool, nature trails.
C Cabinas Kalim, Orotina, near plaza, T2428-8082.

Reserva Biológica Carara *p148*
LL Villa Caletas, Punta Leona, to the south of the reserve, T2637-0505, www.hotelvilla caletas.com. One of the distinctive hotels of Costa Rica. French-owned, divine rooms and 14 villas atop a mountain with amazing views, spectacular sunsets, lush gardens, pool, restaurant, boat and nature tours.

Jacó *p149*
Accommodation in Jacó is overpriced; look for discounts May-Nov.
L-AL Cocal, on beach near the centre of town, T2643-3067, www.hotelcocaland casino.com. 2 pools, hammocks, German-owned, restaurant. Highly recommended.
AL-B Cabinas Las Palmas, northern end of town, T2643-3005. Neat rooms, some with kitchenette, all with bath and fan, clean. Pretty gardens.
A-B Alice, south of centre, T2643-3061. Tidy rooms, private bath, small terrace and pool.
A-B Los Ranchos, central and close to the beach, T2643-3070. 4 bungalows and 8 rooms sleeping 4-8 people, lively spot.
A-B Pochote Grande, northern end of town, T2643-3236, www.hotelpochotegrande.net. Beautiful, German-owned hotel with bar and restaurant. Good rooms, free-form pool and a superb 500-year-old *pochote* tree shading the grounds. Good value.
B Cabinas La Cometa, central, T2643-3615. With fan and hot water, very clean.

B El Jardín, at northern end of town, close to the beach, T2643-3050. Has 10 rooms in quiet spot, friendly with small pool.
B Hotel Paraíso Escondido, 150 m east of the Catholic church on Calle Los Cholos, T2643-2883, www.hoteljaco.com. All rooms with a private bath, patio and a/c, rooms cheaper with fan. Swimming pool and laundry service. The owner often meets arriving buses. Good spot and worth the price.
B-E Hotel Kangaroo, at the southern end of town, T2643-3351, www.hotel-kangaroo. com. Mix of dorms and private rooms, but it's the atmosphere that keeps people happy and recommending this new place in town.
C Bohío, central and near beach, T2643-3017. Private bath, cold water, fan, camping.
D Cabinas Gipsy Italiano, near beach at northern end, T2643-3448. With bath and hot water.
D Cabinas Wahoo, behind the restaurant of the same name not far from buses, T2643-3513. Simple rooms, with private bath and fan. Good value.
E Hotel de Haan, at the beach end of Calle Bohio, T2643-1795, www.hoteldehaan.com. Popular backpacker spot, with pool, laundry, kitchen facilities, Good choice.

Camping

Camping El Hicaco, slightly south of the centre, T2643-3226, and **Restaurant Los Hicacos** are both down same access route to the beach.
Camping Madrigal, at the southern end of the beach, T2643-3329. A quiet spot.

Jacó to Quepos *p149*
AL Hotel El Delfín, Esterillos Centro and Playa Bejuco, T/F2778-8054. Completely renovated with swimming pool, all rooms with breezy balcony, secluded, clean, good restaurant, considered by many to be one of the best beach hotels in Costa Rica. Recommended.
AL La Isla, Playa Palo Seco, T2779-9016. Bar, pool, horse and canoe trips, hot water, a/c.

A Beso del Viento, Playa Palo Seco, 5 km, T2779-9674, www.besodelviento.com. Swimming pool, French owners, stylish rooms.
A La Felicidad Country Inn, Esterillos Centro and Playa Bejuco, T2778-6824, www.lafelicidad.com. Oceanfront, pool and restaurant.
A Vista Hermosa, Playa Hermosa, T2643-3422. Pool, simple rooms with a/c, restaurant, secure parking.
A-B Auberge du Pelican, Esterillos Este, T2778-8105, www.aubergepelican.com. Café, French-Canadian owners, restaurant. Great spot, private airstrip out back, beach out front.
A-B Hotel Sandpiper Inn, T2643-7042, www.sandpipercostarica.com. Spacious cabins, pool, restaurant, sportfishing.
B-C Cabinas Maldonado, Playa Palma, T2227-5400. Rooms sleeping 4, with bath, cold water, kitchen.
D Finca Don Herbert, Playa Palma. With bath, clean, parking.
D Rooms/Restaurant Alex, Playa Palma, T2779-6667. 2.6 km south, with bath, fan. Recommended.
D-E Jungle Surf Café, Playa Hermosa. Basic cabins with a Tex-Mex burger bar.
E Rancho Grande, Playa Hermosa, T2643-3529. Large wooden house with communal kitchen, popular with surfers, great atmosphere. Small store for supplies.
F Las Brisas, Playa Palma. Simple rooms near beach.

Quepos *p149, map p150*
It's difficult to find accommodation on Sat Dec-Apr, and when schools are on holiday.
A Best Western Kamuk, central, near the bus terminal, T2777-0811, www.kamuk.co.cr. Shower, TV, a/c, some ocean views, bar and restaurant with large-screen videos.
A Cabinas Pedro Miguel, towards Manuel Antonio, T2777-0035, www.cabinaspedromiguel.com. Simple rooms, small pool and very friendly Tico owners. Next door is **Centro de Idiomas del Pacífico**.
A Hotel Sirena, near bus station, T2777-0528. Has 14 quite good rooms with private bathroom, a/c. Restaurant and pool.

B Cabinas El Cisne and Sensación Tropical, 75 m north of Catholic church and football pitch, T2777-0719. Safe, family-run, secure parking, bigger rooms on left. Recommended.
B-C El Malinche, close to bus station, T2777-0093. Has 27 clean and good rooms, simply decorated, some with a/c much cheaper without.
B-E Wide Mouth Frog, short distance from the bus terminal, T2777-2798, www.widemouthfrog.org. Private rooms and dorms.
C Villas Mar y Sol, towards the eastern side of town, T2777-0307. Has 8 rooms with private bath and hot shower. Relaxed spot, parking.
C-D Ceciliano, towards the eastern side of town, on the road leading to Manuel Antonio, T2777-0192. Family-run, quiet, small rooms, with bath, hot.
C-D Hotel Quepos, eastern side of town, T2777-0274. With bath, cheaper without, simple, recommended.
D Cabinas Hellen, eastern side of town, T2777-0504. Quite small rooms with private bath and fan, but clean and plenty of parking.
D Cabinas Mary, by football pitch close to **Iguana Tours**, T2777-0128. Clean, friendly, OK.
D-F Hospedaje La Macha, next to post office on walkway by the football pitch, T2777-0216. Includes the cheapest beds in town. Very basic but clean.
E Cabinas Kali, 200 m northeast of bus station, T2777-1491. Nice rooms, family-run, clean, friendly, safe but noisy.
E Doña Alicia, on walkway by football pitch, T2777-0419. Big cabin with bath, friendly, quiet, parking, can wash clothes.
E El Parque, on waterfront road, T2777-0063, Price per person, friendly, clean, a bit run-down but good value, private bath, fan.
E Mar y Luna, central, T2777-0394. With or without bath, quiet, clean, friendly, popular.
E Sánchez, a couple of blocks east of the bus terminal, T2777-0491. Without bath, OK.

Parque Nacional Manuel Antonio *p150*
There are hotels all along the road from
Quepos to Manuel Antonio, many of them
expensive. Many shut in the low season; in
high season, it's best to book ahead. The
area is full to bursting at weekends with
locals camping on the beach. The parked
Second World War plane – decked out as
a bar – marks the start of the downhill to
the beach.
LL El Parador, 2 km from the main road,
T2777-1414, www.hotelparador.com.
80 rooms, all facilities, stunning views of
the ocean, in style of Spanish parador,
helicopter landing pad – just in case!
(**AL** in low season).
LL Makanda by the Sea, down a dirt road
leading to Punta Quepos from opposite **Café
Milagro**, T2777-0442, www.makanda.com.
11 villas and studios with superb open
design. An idyllic and romantic paradise spot.
LL Sí Como No, T2777-0777, www.sicomo
no.com. A superb hotel with beautiful
touches of design using stunning stained
glass, all the comforts you would expect,
and service par excellence plus a cinema.
LL-L Byblos, on the main road, T2777-0411.
All-in bungalows in a resort, sleeping 1-4,
French restaurant, pizzería, pool (**AL** in
low season).
L-AL Costa Verde, at the train carriage
restaurant and reception, T2777-0584,
www.costaverde.com. Apartments for
2-4 people, with kitchenette and bath,
2-bedroom villas available, well-appointed,
pool and a couple of restaurants. Several
nature trails out the back. Recommended.
L-AL Karahé, along the main road towards
the beach, on private road, T2777-0170,
www.karahe.com. Includes breakfast,
cabins on a steep hillside with lovely view,
sleep 3-4, recommended, fridge, bath, a/c
or fan, good restaurant, swimming pool
across the road, access to beach, walk to
park along the beach.
L-A La Arboleda, T2777-1056, www.hotel-
arboleda.com. Cabins on hillside leading
down to beach sleep 2-3, bath, fan,

Uruguayan restaurant, 8-ha wood. Beware
snakes, crabs and monkeys in the yard at
night. Recommended.
AL Villa de la Selva, overlooking the bay,
T2777-0434. Has 5 simple rooms, some
with kitchenettes. Up above most of the
activity, this is a charming spot away from
the mêlée. Recommended.
A Hotel del Mar, on the main road towards
Quepos, T2777-0543, www.gohoteldelmar.
com. Rents surfboards, sells drinks and light
meals and has a collection of English novels
to read in the bar.
A Hotel Manuel Antonio, T2777-1237.
Good breakfast, camping possible nearby,
ask in the restaurant. Handy, just minutes
from the national park and the beach.
A Vela Bar, T2777-0413, www.velabar.com.
Large rooms with bath, fans, safes, very good
restaurant, fishing and other trips, also has a
fully equipped house to rent.
A-B B&B Casa Buena Vista, T2777-1002.
Offers a breathtaking view and wonderful
breakfast terrace, friendly owner.
A-B Plinio, on hillside, T2777-0055,
www.hotelplinio.com. 13 rooms, award-
winning restaurant, plus bar and pool.
7-km nature trail with an 18-m observation
tower. Recommended.
B Mono Azul, T2777-1954, monoazul@
racsa.co.cr. 20 rooms, conference rooms,
library, internet, 2 nightly movies, international
headquarters of **Kids Saving the Rainforest**
and souvenir store with profits going to save
the rainforest. Friendly place with a couple
of pools, and a good restaurant.
C Cabinas Ramírez, towards the end of the
road, T2777-5044. With bath, food and bar,
free hammocks and camping, guests can
help with cooking in exchange.
C-E Vista Serena Hostel, at the start of the
road, T2777-5132, www.vistaserena.com.
Good quality budget option on the Manuel
Antonio strip. Good rooms, private or dorms,
and balconies with hammocks looking out
to the coast.
E Costa Linda, up the side road just before the
park, T2777-0304. Double rooms or 4-bedded

room, fan, water shortage, watch out for racoons raiding the outdoor kitchen in the night, good breakfasts; dinner rather pricey.

Dominical *p152*

Booking hotels is slightly easier in the Dominical and Uvita area using regional specialists and booking service **Selva Mar**, T2771-4582, www.exploringcostarica.com.

L Villas Escaleras, Punta Dominical, T2771-4582, www.villas-escaleras.com. Beautifully equipped villas sleeping up to 10 people, spectacular views, a great spot to hide away.

AL Diuwak, back from the beach, T2787-0087, www.diuwak.com. Rooms and suites, sleeping up to 4 people, with private bath. Mini supermarket and internet service, pool.

AL Hotel/Restaurant Roca Verde, on the beachfront about 1 km south of Dominical, T2787-0036, www.rocaverde.net. Tropical rooms with a/c. Small balcony or terraces, with a pool. Big bar and restaurant. Recommended.

AL Villas Río Mar Jungle and Beach Resort, out of town, 500 m from beach, T2787-0052, www.villasriomar.com. 40 bungalows with bath, fridge and fan, pool, jacuzzi, tennis court, trails, riding, all inclusive.

AL-B Hotel Pacífico Edge, Punta Dominical, T2771-4582, www.exploringcostarica.com. **Selva Mar** service. 4 large cabins with great views of ocean and rainforest.

A Hacienda Barú, about 2 km north of Dominical, T2787-0003, www.hacienda baru.com. A 332-ha reserve that began life as a private reserve in 1972. Cabins sleeping 3 or more with private bath, hiking, riding. So much to see and do in such a small area. There is a canopy observation platform, tree climbing, night walks in the jungle and several self-guided trails and a butterfly garden.

B Bella Vista Lodge, Punta Dominical, T2388-0155 or T2771-4582 (through the **Selva Mar** reservation service). Great view, good large meals, owned by local American 'Woody Dyer', organizes trips in the area. There are also houses to rent.

B Posada del Sol, 100 m from beach, T2787-0085. Owned by local historian Mariela Badilla, 20-odd rooms, bath, fan, patio with hammocks, also 2-bedroom apartment with kitchen for US$150 per week. Rooms vary.

B-C Río Lindo, at the entrance to town, T2787-0028. Clean, tidy rooms with a balcony or terrace. Private bath with fan or a/c. Pool and bar area.

B-C Tortilla Flats, formerly **Cabinas Nayarit** right on the sea front, T2787-0033. Rooms sleeping up to 3 people, with private bath and hot water. A bit overpriced if just for 2.

B-E Cabinas San Clemente, on beach, T2787-0026. Clean, with or without a/c, friendly, US-owned, restaurant, also cheaper, basic dorm rooms, shared bath, fan; **San Clemente Bar and Grill**, under same ownership, good, big portions.

C-E Cabinas El Coco, at end of main street, T2787-0235. With or without bath, negotiate price, unfriendly, noisy, a last option. Camping possible.

Uvita *p152*

The central booking service **Selva Mar**, T2771-4582, www.exploringcostarica.com, makes booking a hotel in this area easier.

AL Canto de Ballenas, 6 km south of Uvita, close to Parque Nacional Marino Ballena, T2248-2538, www.turismoruralcr.com. Rustic, but fine, wooden cabins in a simple land-scaped garden. Great spot in a quiet location.

AL Villa María Luisa Lodge, Bahía Uvita, T2743-8094. Simple cabins sleeping up to 6.

B Cabinas El Chamán, 2 km south on the beach, T2771-2555. Nice location, 8 simple cabinas with private bathroom, camping US$4 per person.

C-D Coco Tico Ecolodge, Uvita village, T2743-8032. 6 clean cabinas, sleep 3, with private bathroom and trails outback.

D Cabinas Las Gemelas, Playa Bahía Uvita, T2743-8009. Simple rooms, with showers and bathrooms. Quiet spot with gardens for camping.

D Cabinas Los Laureles, Uvita village, 200 m turn on the left from the main road, T2771-8008. Nice location, 3 cabinas with private bathroom, simple and quite good.
D Roca Paraíso, near **Cabinas El Chamán**, T2220-4263 for information. Basic.
E Cabinas Punta Uvita, opposite **Restaurant Los Almendros** close to the beach. Simple, basic *cabinas* with private bathroom.
E-F Cascada Verde, Uvita village, up the hill, www.cascadaverde.org. *Hostal*, educational retreat and organic farm, German-run, vegetarian food, yoga and meditation workshops available. Pay for a bed, hammock or camp, or work for your lodgings. Long-term lodgings preferred, great spot if you take to the place.
F Steve's Toucan Hotel, Uvita village, just off the main road, T2743-8140, www.tucan hotel.com. Low-key and pleasant spot in Uvita. Dormitory and private rooms, kitchen available, and advice on local travel options.

Parque Nacional Marino Ballena *p152*
AL Hotel Villas Gaia, Playa Tortuga, 200 m to the beach, T2244-0316, www.villasgaia.com. 12 spacious cabins with private bathrooms (hot water), fan and terrace. Swimming pool and restaurant serving Swiss, international and vegetarian dishes. Ocean view, diving school, horses. Several other quiet secluded options opening up.
A Posada Playa Tortuga, Playa Tortuga, T2384-5489. Run by Gringo Mike, a great spot and place to stay, and Mike knows everything there is to know about the area.

⑦ Eating

Jacó *p149*
There are lots of *sodas* in Jacó.
🍴🍴🍴 **Sunrise Grill Breakfast Place**, centre of town. Breakfast from 0700, closed Wed.
🍴🍴🍴 **Wishbone**, on the main street. Big plates of Mexican food, from US$6.

🍴🍴🍴 **Chatty Cathy's**, on the main drag. A popular dining spot.
🍴🍴🍴 **La Ostra**, centre of town. Good fish in this pleasant open-air restaurant open all day.
🍴🍴🍴 **Wahoo**, just within the centre to the north. Good Tico food, mainly fish.

Jacó to Quepos *p149*
🍴 **Doña María's Soda**, small central market, Parrita, T8842-3047. Tasty *casados*.

Quepos *p149, map p150*
There are many good restaurants along the road towards Manuel Antonio.
🍴🍴🍴 **Basarno's**, near the entrance to town. Bar, restaurant, club, daily 1000-0100. Good mix of snacks and a lively spot later in the night.
🍴🍴🍴-🍴🍴🍴 **El Gran Escape**, central, T2777-0395. Lively collection of restaurants and bars offering Tex Mex, pizza and sushi. Good food and service, recommended.
🍴🍴🍴 **Dos Locos**, central, T2777-1526. Popular with Mexican and Tico fare, open to the street, occasional live music.
🍴🍴🍴 **El Banco Restaurant and Sports Bar**, near **El Gran Escape**, T2777-0478. Newly remodelled long bar with bright neon, good Tex Mex food and will cook your catch.
🍴🍴🍴 **Escalofrío**, next to **Dos Locos**. Pizza, pasta and ice cream to die for from US$4.
🍴🍴🍴 **Gardin Gourmet**, opposite **Escalofrío**. Great deli with lots of imported treats.
🍴🍴🍴 **Pizza Gabriels**, central, T2777-1085. Popular little spot with a lively undercurrent. Fine pizza and pasta from US$6.

Cafés, snacks and bakeries
The municipal market (for fruit and bread) is at the bus station.
Café Milagro, on the waterfront, T2777-0794, www.cafemilagro.com. Best expresso, cakes, pies, Cuban cigars, souvenirs, freshly roasted coffee for sale; another branch on the road to Manuel Antonio.
L'Angolo, opposite **Dos Locos**. Serves a mix of breads, olives, hams and everything you'd need for self-catering or picnicking in style.

La Buena Nota, on road near the beach in Manuel Antonio, T2777-1002. Sells English-language newspapers. A good place to seek local information, run by Anita Myketuk, who has initiated publicity on rip tides.
Pan Aldo, right in front of the soccer pitch, T2777-2697. Italian specialties, wholewheat sourdough, pastries, great bread and pastries.

Dominical *p152*

♔♔ **Jazzy's River House**, down the main street. More an open-house cum cultural centre, occassionally have meals followed by an open mike set up on Wed.
♔♔ **Restaurant El Coco**, in town. Serves good food and rents budget rooms.
♔♔ **San Clemente**, in town. A good mix of Tex Mex with big servings.
♔♔ **Thrusters**, in town. A hip spot for the surf crowd, with sushi in the front restaurant.
♔ **Soda Nanyoa**, Dominical, offers Costa Rican specialities.

⊕ Entertainment

Jacó *p149*
Bars and clubs
Discos in town include **Central**, close to the beach, T2643-3076, **Los Tucanes**, **El Zarpe Sports Bar**, T2643-3473, **Club Olé**, T2643-1576, restaurant, bar, disco and games.

▲ Activities and tours

Quepos *p149, map p150*
Tour operators
Amigos del Río, opposite the football pitch, T2777-0082, amigorio@racsa.co.cr. River rafting, kayaking, canopy and horse riding tours, good guides. **Iguana Tours**, close to the church on the football pitch, T2777-2052, www.iguana tours.com. Excellent local knowledge with many tours available. Friendly and helpful. **Lynch Travel Services**, right in the centre of town, T2777-0161, www.lynchtravel.com.

⊙ Transport

Jacó *p149*
Bus From **San José** Coca Cola bus station, 3 daily, 3½ or 4½ hrs, US$3.80 or US$4.60, arrive at Plaza Jacó-Complex terminal at north end of town, next to **Pizza Hut**. Also several buses to **Quepos**.

Quepos *p149, map p150*
Air There are several daily flights from **San José**, with **Sansa** and **Nature Air** (US$50 one way). The **Sansa** office is under Hotel Quepos, T2777-0683.

Bus There are 3 express buses a day leaving **San José** Coca Cola bus station, T2223-5567, at 0600, 1200 and 1800, returning at 0600, 0930, 1200 and 1700, 3½ hrs, US$4.50, book a day in advance, 6 regular buses, 4½ hrs, US$4. There are buses northwest along the coast to **Puntarenas**, 3½ hrs, 0430, 1030, and 1500, return 0500, 1100, 1430, US$2.10. 2 daily buses via **Dominical** to **San Isidro de El General**, T2771-4744, 0500, and 1330, 3½ hrs, US$2.00, connections can be made there to get to the Panamanian border, return 0700, 1330.

Taxi Taxis congregate opposite the bus terminal, just up from **Dos Locos** restaurant. Minibuses meet flights.

Parque Nacional Manuel Antonio *p150*
Bus There are 3 express buses a day (see Quepos, Transport, above), direct from **San José**, 4 hrs, US$4.50. At weekends buy ticket the day before; buses fill to standing room only very quickly. Roads back to San José on Sun evening are packed. A regular bus service runs roughly ½-hourly from beside **Quepos** market, starting at 0545, to Manuel Antonio, last bus back at 1700, US$0.35.

Car If driving, there is ample guarded parking in the area, US$6.

Taxi From **Quepos**, approximately US$10. Minibuses meet flights from San José to the airport at Quepos (see above), US$2.25.

Dominical *p152*
Bus to **Quepos** 0545, 0815, 1350 (Sat and Sun) and 1450. To **San Isidro**, 0645, 0705, 1450, 1530, 1 hr. To **Uvita** at 0950, 1010, 1130 (weekends) 1710 and 2000. To **Cd Cortés** and **Cd Neily** 0420 and 1000. To **San José**, 0545, 1340 (Sat and Sun), 7 hrs.

Uvita *p152*
Bus From **San José** Terminal Coca Cola, Mon-Fri 1500, Sat and Sun 0500, 1500, return Mon-Fri 0530, Sat and Sun 0530, 1300, 7 hrs. From **San Isidro** daily 0800, 1600, return 0600, 1400. From **Dominical**, last bus 1700 or 1800.

○ Directory

Jacó *p149*
Banks Banco Nacional in centre of town. **Internet** Iguana Mar, Centro de Computación and Mexican Joe's Internet Café. **Language schools** City Playa Language Institute, T2643-4023, www.ipai languageschool.com, offers Spanish classes with or without homestay, and the novel option of free surfing lessons. **Post office** Near Municipalidad offices.

Quepos *p149, map p150*
Banks Several branches in town including **Banco Nacional** which has a Visa ATM as does **Banco Popular** and **Banco San José**. The best place to exchange TCs or US$ cash is at **Distribuidora Puerto Quepos**, opposite Banco de Costa Rica, 0900-1700, no paperwork, no commission, all done in 2 mins, same rate as banks. **Immigration** On the same street as the Banco de Costa Rica. **Internet** Access available from Internet Quepos, fast machines, good service, US$1.50 per hr. Several others in town including **Arte Net**, **Quepos Diner & Internet Café**, **Internet Tropical**, **CyberLoco** and **Internet Cantina**. **Language schools** Escuela D'Amore, in a great setting overlooking the ocean, halfway between Quepos and the national park, T2777-1143, www.escueladamore.com. Believes in the immersion technique, living with local families. **Costa Rica Spanish Institute**, T2234-1001, www.cosi.co.cr. **Laundry** Lavanderías de Costa Rica, near the football pitch, good. **Medical services** The **hospital** is out of town, T2777-0922. **Red Cross**, T2777-0118. **Police** T2777-0196. **Post office** On the walkway by the football pitch, 0800-1700.

San José to Panama

Heading through the Talamanca mountains, the Pan-American Highway reaches its highest point at Cerro de la Muerte (Peak of Death) and passes El Chirripó, Costa Rica's highest peak at 3820 m, as the scenic road drops down through the valley of the Río de El General to the tropical lowlands of the Pacific coast and the border with Panama. Private reserves along the route are ideal for birdwatching – here the resplendent quetzal enjoys a quieter life than his Monteverde relations – and mountain streams are stocked with trout providing both sport and food. Lodges and hotels are usually isolated, dotted along the highway. Towards Costa Rica's most southerly point, the Península de Osa is a nature haven of beautiful pathways, palm-fringed beaches and protected rainforest – well worth the effort if you have the time.

▶▶ *For listings, see pages 165-170.*

Travelling the Pan-American Highway ●❻▲●● ▶▶ *pp165-170.*

From San José the Pan-American Highway runs for 352 km to the Panama border. It's a spectacular journey but challenging if you're driving, with potholes, frequent rockslides during the rainy season, roadworks and generally difficult conditions.

From Cártago, the route heads south over the mountains, beginning with the ascent of **Cerro Buena Vista** (3490 m), a climb of almost 2050 m to the continental divide. A little lower than the peak, the highest point of the road is 3335 m at Km 89 which travels through barren *páramo* scenery. Those unaccustomed to high altitude should beware of mountain sickness brought on by a too rapid ascent, see Health, page 50. For 16 km the road follows the crest of the Talamanca ridge, with views of the Pacific 50 km away, and on clear days of the Atlantic, 80 km to the east.

Some 4.5 km east of Km 58 (Cañón church) is **Genesis II**, a privately owned 40-ha cloudforest **National Wildlife Refuge**, at 2360 m, bordering the **Tapantí-Macizo de la Muerte National Park**. Accommodation is available here and at several other places along the way, see Sleeping, page 165. At Km 78 is **Casa Refugio de Ojo de Agua**, a historic pioneer home overlooked but for a couple of picnic tables in front of the house. At Km 80 a steep, dramatic road leads down the spectacular valley of the Río Savegre to **San Gerardo de Dota**, a birdwatchers' paradise. The highest point is at Km 89.5, where temperatures are below zero at night.

San Isidro de El General → *Altitude: 702 m.*

The drop in altitude from the highlands to the growing town of San Isidro passes through fertile valleys growing coffee and raising cattle. The huge **cathedral** on the main plaza is a bold architectural statement, with refreshing approaches to religious iconography inside. The **Museo Regional del Sur** ① *Calle 2, Av 1-0, T2771-5273, Mon-Fri 0800-1200, 1330-1630, free*, is in the old marketplace, now the Complejo Cultural. The 750-ha **Centro Biológico Las Quebradas** ① *7 km north of San Isidro, T2771-4131, Tue-Fri 0800-1400, Sat and Sun 0800-1500, closed Oct*, has trails and dormitory lodging for researchers. San Isidro de El General is also the place to stock up for a trip into Parque Nacional Chirripó and to climb Cerro Chirripó Grande (3820 m), see page 162.

Border essentials: Costa Rica–Panama

Paso Canoas → *See also page 337.*

Shops sell 'luxury' items brought from Panama at prices considerably lower than those of Costa Rica (for example sunglasses, stereo equipment, kitchen utensils, etc).

Immigration Border open 0600-2200 (Costa Rica time). Costa Rica is one hour behind Panama. For information on entering Panama, see Visas and immigration on page 58.

Customs No fruit or vegetables can be taken into Panama.

Crossing by private vehicle Those motoring north can get insurance cover at the border for US$17, this will cover public liability and property damage.

Parque Nacional Chirripó

ⓘ *US$7, crowded in season, make reservations in Oficina de los Parques Nacionales (OPN), Calle 4, Av Central-2, San Isidro de El General, T2771-3155, open 0600-1700. If you want to walk or climb in the park, get food in San Isidro and book accommodation at the OPN. Take the 0500 Pueblo Nuevo bus from northwest corner of Parque Central, or the 1400 from the bus station to San Gerardo de Rivas (US$1.05, 1½ hrs, return at 0700 and 1600), which passes the entrance to the park. Interesting trip up the Río Chirripó valley.*

San Isidro de El General is west of Costa Rica's highest mountain Cerro Chirripó Grande (3820 m) in the middle of Parque Nacional Chirripó (50,150 ha). Treks starts from San Gerardo de Rivas (see below). The views from the hilltops are splendid and the high plateau near the summit is an interesting alpine environment with lakes of glacial origin and diverse flora and fauna. The park includes a considerable portion of cloudforest and the walk is rewarding.

Parque Nacional Chirripó neighbours **Parque Internacional La Amistad** (193,929 ha), established in 1982, and together they extend along the Cordillera de Talamanca to the Panamanian border, comprising the largest area of virgin forest in the country with the greatest biological diversity.

San Gerardo de Rivas

Situated in a cool, pleasant spot, San Gerardo de Rivas is at the confluence of the Río Blanco and the Río Pacífico Chirripó. Close to Parque Nacional Chirripó entrance, it is the starting point for the climb up **Cerro Chirripó Grande**. If you haven't booked accommodation at the refugio in San Isidro you can book it at the **MINAE office** (see page 173).

As interest in this quiet area grows, new tours are appearing including horse riding up to Llano Bonito (US$50), trips to local waterfalls (US$40) and nature tours.

Handy for weary legs after the climb, there are **hot springs** ⓘ *daily 0700-1800, entrance US$1, in the area. Before crossing the new concrete bridge turn left to 'Herradura' for 10 minutes then look for the sign after Parque Las Rosas; go down to the suspension bridge, cross the river and continue for 10 minutes to the house where you pay. Information about the town on www.sangerardocostarica.com.*

Buenos Aires to Paso Real

Continuing southeast, a good road sinks slowly through the Río General valley where the Talamanca Mountains dominate the skyline. At Km 197 (from San José), the change from coffee to fruit is complete; at the junction for **Buenos Aires** is the huge Del Monte

Climbing the Chirripó peaks

The early morning climb to the summit of Cerro Chirripó, Costa Rica's highest mountain, is a refreshing slog after the relative comforts often encountered in Costa Rica. The hike takes you through magnificent cloudforest draped in mosses and ephiphytes before entering a scorched area of *páramo* grasslands with incredible views to the Pacific and Atlantic coastlines on clear days. The wildlife – birdlife in particular – is incredible and, even if you don't see it, you will certainly hear it. The trek itself is not difficult but it is tiring being almost consistently uphill on the way and a knee-crunching, blister-bursting journey down.

From the *refugio* inside the park, you can also explore the nearby Crestones, a volcanic outcrop that has been etched on to the minds of every Costa Rican, and the creatively named Sabana de los Leones and Valle de los Conejos.

If you wish to climb the 3820m Cerro Chirripó, Costa Rica's highest mountain, you must make advance reservations by calling the park service office in San Gerardo, T2771-5116, located to the east of San Isidro de El General. After phoning for reservations you are given a couple of days to pay by bank deposit to guarantee your space. Visitors are not allowed into the park without reservations at the *refugio*. During the dry season it's often full, so it's a good idea to make arrangements as soon as possible. Start in the early morning for the eight- to ten-hour hike to the *refugio*. The cost is US$7 entry for each day spent in the park, plus US$6 shelter fee per night.

The *refugio* has simple but adequate accommodation, with space for about 80 people and a large kitchen area.

The cold – often frosty in the morning – is a bit of a shock in contrast to the rest of Costa Rica, but you can rent blankets and sleeping bags from the *refugio* (US$1 each). Gas cookers are also available for hire (US$2). There are sufficient water supplies en route so you will need only to carry your food supplies. Electrical power at the *refugio* is only for a couple of hours each night, so be sure to bring a flashlight. The top of Chirripó is located another 5.1 km from the Crestones base camp.

In addition to the high camp there is a shelter about halfway up, **Refugio Llano Bonito** (2500 m), which is simple and occasionally clean, with wooden floor, two levels to sleep on, no door but wind protection, drinking water and toilet. It's about four hours' walk from San Gerardo and three hours' walk on to **Refugios Base Crestones**. Plan for at least two nights on the mountain – although you can do it with only one night if you're tight for time, rising very early to summit on the second day in time to go all the day down in one hit. While nights can be cold, daytime temperatures tend to be warm to hot, so go prepared with sunscreen and hat. In the rainy season, trails up the plateau are slippery and muddy, and fog obscures the views. Time your descent to catch the afternoon bus back to San Isidro.

cannery. The town, a few kilometres off the Pan-American Highway, has some simple accommodation.

Heading 17 km east towards the mountains is the **Reserva Biológica Durika**, a privately owned reserve of roughly 800 ha, aiming to create a self-sustained community in the Talamanca mountains. Accommodation is available in some rustic cabins.

South along the highway, the small towns of Térraba and Boruca are the most prominent remains of the nation's indigenous population. The community of **Boruca**, with a small *hostal* (**F**), has a small, poorly maintained museum, but every year the **Fiesta de los Diablitos** on the last day of December and first two days of January, and the last day of January and the first two days of February in **Rey Curre**, see the culture come alive in a festival of music, dance and costume. There is a daily bus to Boruca from Buenos Aires at 1130 (1½ hours).

At **Paso Real** the highway heads west to Palmar Norte, with a turn heading towards San Vito (see below) and the Panamanian border.

Palmar Norte and Palmar Sur

Taking a sharp turn at Paso Real (straight on for San Vito – see below), the Pan-American Highway heads west to Palmar Norte (Km 257 – with gas station) from where a paved road leads to Ciudad Cortés. A new road heads northwest to Dominical (see page 152).

Crossing the Río Grande de Terraba leads to Palmar Sur, which is 90 km from the Panamanian border. There are several stone spheres in the area. A banana plantation close to town has stone spheres – 1.5 m in diameter and accurate within 5 mm – of pre-Columbian manufacture, though their use is a matter of conjecture. Recent theories are that they were made to represent the planets of the solar system, or that they were border markers.

From Palmar Sur the Pan-American Highway heads southeast to Chacarita (33 km) where a road turns off to the Osa Peninsula, to Río Claro (another 26 km) where a road leads to Golfito, another 15 km leads to Ciudad Neily which is 16 km from the border at Paso Canoas.

Sierpe

Through a matrix of cooperative banana and African plantations, a road leads to Sierpe, on the Río Sierpe, where there are several small hotels and the departure point for boats to Bahía Drake, see page 173.

Paso Real to San Vito ⊜❶❷❸❹ ⨠ *pp165-170.*

The road from Paso Real to San Vito is now paved and has lovely views. **La Amistad International Park** has few facilities for visitors at present, but one lodge is found way up in the hills beyond Potrero Grande, just south of the Paso Real junction on the way to San Vito. Near the border is **San Vito**. Originally built by Italian immigrants among denuded hills, it is a prosperous but undistinguished town.

On the road from San Vito to Ciudad Neily at Las Cruces are the world-renowned **Wilson Botanical Gardens** ① *T2773-4004, www.ots.ac.cr*, owned by the **Organization for Tropical Studies**, 6 km from San Vito. In 360 ha of forest reserve over 5000 species of tropical plants, orchids, other epiphytes and trees with 331 resident bird species. It is possible to spend the night here if you arrange it first with the **OTS** ① *T2240-6696, in San José:* **L** *per person all inclusive, US$24 per person for day visits with lunch*. On the same road is **Finca Cántaros** ① *T2773-3760*, specializing in local arts and crafts, owned by Gail Hewson Gómez. It's one of the best craft shops in Costa Rica – worth a look even if you don't buy anything.

Border with Panama-Sabalito

The road from San Vito to Ciudad Neily is paved, in good condition and offers some of the best coastal views in the country as the road rapidly falls through the hills. From San Vito a good gravel road, paved in places, runs via Sabalito (Banco Nacional) to the Panama border at Río Sereno. There are buses from Sabalito to San José. See Panama chapter, page 337, for details of this border crossing.

Golfito and around ⊜❼▲⊜❶ ➺ *pp165-170.*

Thirty-one kilometres north of the border a road branches south at Río Claro (several pensiones and a fuel station) to the former banana port of Golfito, a 6-km long linear settlement bordering the Golfo Dulce and steep forested hills. While elements of hard sweat and dock labour remain, Golfito's prominence today comes from being Costa Rica's only free port, set up in 1990, selling goods tax free at about 60% of normal prices. Popular with shoppers from throughout the country, it can be difficult to get a hotel room at weekends. Check out www.golfito-costarica.com for information on lodging and activities in the area.

Golfito also provides boat and ferry access to Puerto Jiménez and the Osa Peninsula, and popular fishing and surfing beaches to the south of the town.

Entering the town from the south heading north there are a few hotels where the road meets the coast. In 2 km is the small town centre of painted buildings with saloon bars, open-fronted restaurants and cheap accommodation – probably the best stop for budget travellers. Nearby is the dilapidated *muellecito* used by the ferries to Puerto Jiménez and water taxis. A further kilometre north are the container port facilities and the **Standard Fruit Company**'s local HQ, though many of the banana plantations have been turned over to oil palm and other crops. Beyond the dock is the free port, airstrip and another set of hotels.

The **Refugio Nacional de Fauna Silvestre Golfito**, in the steep forested hills over-looking Golfito, was created to protect Golfito's watershed. Rich in rare and medicinal plants with abundant fauna, there are some excellent hikes in the refuge. Supervised by the University of Costa Rica, they have a field office in Golfito.

Thirty minutes by water taxi from Golfito, you can visit **Casa Orquídeas** ① *T2775-1614, tours last about 2½ hrs, US$5 per person, US$20 minimum, closed Fri*, a family-owned botanical garden with a large collection of herbs, orchids and local flowers and trees, that you can see, smell, touch and taste.

To the north of Golfito is the **Parque Nacional Piedras Blancas** tropical wet forest. The area was being exploited for wood products, but has been steadily purchased since 1991 with help from the Austrian government and private interests, notably the classical Austrian violinist Michael Schnitzler. All logging has now ceased and efforts are devoted to a research centre and ecotourism, concentrated in an area designated **Parque Nacional Esquinas**. Near the village of **La Gamba** a tourist lodge has been built (see Sleeping, below). La Gamba is 6 km along a dirt road from Golfito, or 4 km from Briceño on the Pan-American Highway between Piedras Blancas and Río Claro.

Beaches around Golfito

Playa de Cacao is about 6 km (1½-hour walk) north of Golfito round the bay, or a short trip by water taxi. Further north is the secluded beach of **Playa San Josecito** with a couple of adventure-based lodges.

About 15 km by sea south of Golfito, and reached by water taxi or a long bus journey (US$2 by *colectivo* ferry from the small dock; 0600 and 1200, return 0500, 1300), **Playa Zancudo** is a long stretch of clean golden sound, dotted with a few rustic hotels ideal for relaxing and lazing away the days. Still further south is **Pavones**, where a world record left-hand wave has elevated the rocky beach to the realm of surfing legend. South of Pavones, towards the end of the peninsular and at the mouth of the Golfo Dulce is **Punta Banco**.

Ciudad Neily, Paso Canoas and the Panama border

Ciudad Neily is an uninspiring town providing useful transport links between San Vito in the highlands and the coastal plain, and is roughly 16 km from Paso Canoas on the border with Panama. Paso Canoas is a little piece of chaos with traders buying and selling to take advantage of the difference in prices between Costa Rica and Panama. With little to hold you, there is little reason to visit unless heading to Panama. If misfortune should find you having to stay the night, there are some reasonable options.

◉ San José to Panama listings

For Sleeping and Eating price codes, and other relevant information, see pages 43-46.

● Sleeping

Travelling the Pan-American Highway *p160*

L Hotel de Montaña Savegre, San Gerardo de Dota, T2740-1028, www.savegre.co.cr. Waterfalls, trout fishing, prices include meals.

A-B Trogón Lodge, San Gerardo de Dota, T2740-1051, www.grupomawamba.com. 23 fine wooden cabins with private bathroom, set amongst beautiful gardens connected by paths used by divebombing hummingbirds.

B Finca Eddie Serano Mirador de Quetzales, Km 70, T2381-8456. A 43-ha forest property at 2650 m. Eddie Serrano has passed away, but one of his sons will show visitors quetzals (almost guaranteed, but don't tell anyone at **Monteverde Cloud Forest**) and other endemic species of the highlands. 10 cabins, sleeping 2-5, with wonderful views, private bath, price per person includes breakfast, dinner and guided hike.

D Hotel and Restaurant Georgina, Km 95, T2770-8043. At almost 3300 m, Costa Rica's highest hotel, basic, clean, friendly, good food (used by southbound **Tracopa** buses), good birdwatching; ask owners for directions for a nice walk to see quetzals.

Camping

Los Ranchos, San Gerardo de Dota, at the bottom of the hill, T2771-2376. Camping in perfect surroundings. No transport down here, but pick-ups from the highway can be arranged.

See also **Los Genesis II Lodge**, above.

San Isidro de El General *p160*

A Rancho La Botija, out of town on the road to San Gerardo, T2770-2147, www.ranchola botija.com. Restaurant, pool, hiking to nearby petroglyphs, open 0900 at weekends, great restaurant littered with fragments of *botijas*. Recommended.

B Talari Mountain Lodge, 10 mins from San Isidro on the road to San Gerardo, T2771-0341, www.talari.co.cr. 8-ha farm, with bath, riverside cabins, known for birdwatching, rustic.

C Hotel Los Crestones, in town, T2770-1200, www.hotelloscrestones.com. Big rooms, with TV and pool. Wheelchair accessible.

C-D Astoria, on north side of square, T2771-0914. Tiny but clean rooms.

D El Valle, Calle 2, Av Central-2, T2771-0246. Cleanish, one of the better cheapies.

D Hotel/Restaurant Amaneli, in town, T2771-0352. 41 quite good rooms with private bathroom, fan, some noisy.

D Hotel Iguazu, Calle Central, Av 1, T2771-2571. Hot water, cable TV, clean, safe with parking.

D-E Hotel Chirripó, south side of Parque Central, T2771-0529. Private or shared bath,

clean, very good restaurant, free covered parking, recommended.
E Lala, Calle Central, Av 1, T2771-0291. Basic and simple.

San Gerardo de Rivas p161

All accommodation is on the road up to the park.
D El Uran, at the very top, closest to the park entrance, T2742-5003, www.hoteluran.com. Simple, clean rooms, lots of blankets and a restaurant that will feed you early before setting out.
D Marín, next to MINAE office, T2742-5099. Basic but friendly and good value.
D Pelícano, T2742-5050, www.hotel pelicano.net. 11 rooms sleeping between 2 and 5 people, with great views, a bar and restaurant. Beautiful setting with countless birds. Also has a pool.
D-E Roca Dura, opposite the football pitch, T2742-5071, rocadurasangerardo@ hotmail.com. Built on a huge boulder, 7 rooms with hot showers, good *comedor*, nice view, shop next door, friendly owners.
E Cabinas Bosque, T2742-5021, elbosque@ gmail.com. With a small bar and restaurant. Looks a bit scruffy from the outside, but spotless rooms and great views over the valley from some rooms.
E Cabinas El Descanso, T2771-7962, eldescanso@ecotourism.co.cr. 7 bunks, bathroom, hearty meals available, gas stove for hire, horses for rent and guide services offered, recommended. Price per person.
E Cabinas/Restaurant Elimar, 500 m out of village. Swimming pool, simple restaurant, 4 quite good cabinas with private bathroom, hot water.

Camping

You can camp at or near the park office, in San Gerardo near the bus stop. Check in first and pay US$0.30.

Buenos Aires to Paso Real p161

B-C Cabañas, Durika Biological Reserve, T2730-0657, www.durika.org. Rustic cabins.
Includes 3 vegetarian meals a day, with a wide range of activities including walks, hikes to the summit of Cerro Durika and cultural tours. Around US$10 per person on top of the daily rate.
E Cabinas Violeta, Buenos Aires, next to the fire station, 200 m west of the plaza, T2730-0104. Clean, simple, central and OK if you're stuck for the night.
F Cabinas Mary, Buenos Aires, 800 m south of the centre close to the **Aridikes** office, T2730-0187. Quiet spot which tries to be clean.

Palmar Norte and Palmar Sur p163

C-E Hotel y Cabinas Casa Amarilla, 300 m east of bus station on the plaza, T2786-6251. With fan, cabins are more expensive than the hotel rooms, rooms at back quieter, rooms over restaurant noisy but cheaper.
D Cabinas Tico-Alemán, on the highway near the gas station, T2786-6232. 25 cabinas with private bathroom. Best in town.
F Hotel Xinia, 150 m east from bus station, T2786-6129. 26 rooms, very basic but OK, shared bathroom.

Sierpe p163

A Río Sierpe Lodge, T2384-5595. All-inclusive plan with an emphasis on fishing.
B Oleaje Sereno, T2786-7580. Good rooms, with restaurant on river bank.
E-F Margarita, T2786-7574. Has 13 good rooms. Friendly owners and good value.

Paso Real to San Vito p163

B El Ceibo, just down from main plaza, T2773-3025. With bath, hot water and TV, good restaurant.
C-D Cabinas Rino, right in the centre of town, T2773-3071. Clean and well maintained. Good deal.
D Cabinas Las Huacas, near **Cabinas Firenze**, T2773-3115. 13 OK cabinas with private bathroom, hot water, TV, which were looking very run-down when visited.
E Las Mirlas, 500 m out of town on road to Sabalito, T2773-3714. In same location as **Hotel Pitier**, but more attractive.

F Cabinas Firenze, close to the gas station, on the road from San Isidro, T2773-3741. Has 6 basic cabinas, sleep 5, with private bathroom.
F Colono, plaza area, T2773-4543. Cheap and central.
F Hotel Pitier, 500 m out of town on road to Sabalito, T2773-3027. Clean, with bath.

Golfito p164

L Esquinas Rainforest Lodge, near La Gamba, 6 km from Golfito, T2741-8001, www.esquinaslodge.com. Full board, private baths, verandas overlooking the forest, tours, all profits to the local community.
B Las Gaviotas, next to El Gran Ceibo, T2775-0062, lasgaviotas@hotmail.com. 21 cabins and rooms, with bath, a/c and with excellent restaurant looking out over the waterfront.
B Sierra, at the northernmost part of town, near the airport and free zone, T2775-0666. 72 double rooms, a/c, a couple of pools, restaurant. Rooms are better than the place looks from the outside.
C Golfo Azul, T2775-0871. Has 20 comfortable large rooms, with bath and a/c, good restaurant.
C La Purruja Lodge, 4 km south of Golfito, T2775-5054, www.purruja.com. 5 duplex cabins with bath, plus camping US$2 per tent.
D Delfina, town centre, T2775-0043. Shared bath, fan, friendly, basic. Some rooms with private bath much better. Rooms on street are noisy, parking available.
D Mar y Luna, T2775-0192. Has 8 rooms sleeping 2-4, with bath, fan, restaurant on stilts above the sea, quiet spot, good deal.
D Melissa, behind **Delfina**, T2775-0443. Has 4 simple rooms, with private bath, clean and quiet, great spot overlooking bay. Parking available. Recommended.
D-E Del Cerro, close to the docks, T2775-0006. 20 simple rooms sleeping 1-6, private bathroom, laundry services, fishing boat rentals.
D-E Golfito, central, T2775-0047. Quiet, with a couple of rooms overlooking the

bay and an apartment at US$30. A little run-down but OK.
E Costa Rica Surf, T2775-0034. Has 25 dark rooms, most with private bath. Big bar downstairs. Not the best in town but OK.
F El Uno, above Chinese restaurant of same name, T2775-0061. Very basic and mildly amusing if you fancy pretending to be a banana in a packing case, but friendly.

Beaches around Golfito p164

L Tiskita Jungle Lodge, Punta Banco, T2296-8125, www.tiskita-lodge.co.cr. A 162-ha property including a fruit farm, with excellent birdwatching, 14 cabins overlooking ocean. Overlooks beach, cool breezes, waterfall, jungle pools, trails through virgin forest – great spot.
L-A Cabinas La Ponderosa, Pavones, T8824-4145 (T954-771-9166 in USA), www.cabinaslaponderosa.com. Owned by 2 surfers, large cabins, fan or a/c, with bath (hot water), walking, horse riding, fishing, diving and surfing; also house for rent (sleeps 6), restaurant.
A-B Oasis on the Beach, Playa Zancudo, T2776-0087, www.oasisonthebeach. com. Cabins and apartments with kitchenettes, internet and tours. Great spot and atmosphere.
A Latitude 8, Playa Zancudo, T2776-0168, www.latitude8lodge.com. A couple of secluded, tranquil cabins with full kitchen and hot water.
A Los Cocos, Playa Zancudo, Apdo 88, Golfito, T2776-0012, www.loscocos.com. Beach front cabins at the ocean with private bathroom, hot water, mosquito net, fan, kitchenette, refrigerator, veranda. Also provide boat tours and taxi service. Discounts for longer stays. Heavenly.
B Pavones Surf Lodge, Pavones, T2222-2224 (San José). Includes meals, 2 cabins with bath, 6 rooms with shared bath.
B-C Coloso Del Mar, Playa Zancudo, T2776-0050, www.coloso-del-mar.com. Great little spot with 4 simple cabins

overlooking the beach and a Tico/Caribbean restaurant.

B-C Mira Olas, Pavones, T2393-7742. Cabins with kitchen and fan, low monthly rates, jungle trail.

B-C Sol y Mar, Playa Zancudo, T2776-0014, www.zancudo.com. 4 screened cabins, hot water, fan, 3-storey rental house (US$700 per month), 50 m from ocean, bar/restaurant, meals 0700-2000, home-baked bread, great fruit shakes, volleyball with lights for evening play, badminton, paddleball, boogie boards, library. Highly recommended.

D-E The Yoga Farm, Punta Banco, www.yogafarmcostarica.org. A laid-back retreat, set on a mountainside surrounded by primary rainforest and near the beach. A great place to get back to nature, it offers a range of activities (see Activities and tours, page 169). Price includes accommodation, food and yoga. Price per person.

E Pensión Fin del Mundo, Playa Zancudo, over **Restaurant Tranquilo**. 6 simple rooms with fan, mosquito net, clean, shared bathroom. English book exchange at **Tienda Buen Precio**.

E Rancho Burica, Pavones. With thatched cabins, horse riding, fishing, tours to Guaymí indigenous reserve.

Ciudad Neily, Paso Canoas and the Panama border *p165*
Ciudad Neily

C Cabinas Andrea, T2783-3784. 18 clean cabinas with private bathroom, a/c or fan, TV. Popular with Ticos coming through town, handy for main bus terminal.

D-E El Rancho, just off the highway, T2783-3060. Has 50 resort-style cabins with bath, TV (cheaper without). Restaurant open 1600.

E Cabinas Heileen, north of plaza, T2783-3080. Simple cabinas with private bathroom, fan.

E Hotel Musuco, just off the Pan-American Hwy, T2783-3048. With bath, cheaper without, fan, clean and quiet. Good deal.

F Hotel Villa, north of **Hotel Musoc**, T2783-5120. Cheapest and last option in town.

Paso Canoas

D Cabinas Interamericano, T2732-2041. With bath and fan, some with a/c, good value upstairs, restaurant.

E Cabinas Jiménez, T2732-2258. Quite good cabinas with private bathroom, fan. Very clean, good deal.

E Cabinas Jiménez Annexe, T2732-2258. OK if all else is full.

E Hilda, south of town, T2732-2873. Good rooms, very clean, restaurant over the road. Recommended.

F Cabinas El Paso, T2732-2740. OK rooms with shower.

Eating

San Isidro de El General *p160*

♔ **La Cascada**, Av 2 and Calle 2, T2771-6479. Balcony bar where the bright young things hang out.

♔ **Restaurant Crestones**, south of the main plaza, T2771-1218. Serves a good mix of snacks, drinks and lively company.

♔ **Restaurant El Tenedor**, Calle Central, Av Central-1, T2771-0881. Good food, friendly, big pizzas, recommended.

♔ **Soda Chirripó**, south side of the main plaza. Gets the vote from the current gringo crowd in town.

♔ **La Marisquería**, corner of Av 0 and Calle 4. Simple setting but great *ceviche*.

♔ **Soda J&P**, indoor market south of the main plaza. The best of many.

Paso Real to San Vito *p163*

♔ **Lilianas**, San Vito. Still showing homage to the town's Italian heritage with good pasta dishes and pizza.

♔ **Restaurant Nelly**, San Vito, near **Cabinas Las Huacas**. Good wholesome truck drivers' fair.

Golfito *p164*

Many seafood places along the seafront.

♔ **Cubana**, near post office. Good, try *batidos*.

♔ **El Uno**, near **Cubana**. Good, reasonably priced seafood.

♈♈ **La Dama del Delfín Restaurant**, downtown. Breakfast from 0700, snacks, homebaked goods, closed for dinner and Sun.
♈ **Le Eurekita**, centre. Serves a mean breakfast of *huevos rancheros*.

Beaches around Golfito *p164*
♈♈ **Bar y Restaurant Tranquilo**, Playa Zancudo. A lively spot between **Zancudo Beach Club** and **Coloso del Mar**.
♈♈ **Macondo**, Playa Zancudo. Italian restaurant which also has a couple of rooms.
♈ **Soda Katherine**, Playa Zancudo, T2776-0124. From US$4, great Tico fare; also simple cabins.

▲ Activities and tours

San Isidro de El General *p160*
Tour operators
Ciprotur, Calle 4, Av 1-3, T2771-6096, www.ecotourism.co.cr. Good information on services throughout the southern region.
Selvamar, Calle 1, Av 2-4, T2771-4582, www.exploringcostarica.com. General tours and the main contact for out of the way destinations in the southern region.

Golfito *p164*
Tour operators
Land Sea Tours, T2775-1614, landsea@racsa.co.cr. Know everything there is to know about the area. They can organize almost anything including national and international flights, and can advise on crewing on yachts heading up and down the coast.

Beaches around Golfito *p164*
Yoga
The Yoga Farm, Punta Banco, www.yoga farmcostarica.org. Yoga, horse riding and hikes through the rainforest. Also organize homestay with an indigenous family.

⊖ Transport

San Isidro de El General *p160*
Bus Terminal at Av 6, Calle Central-2 at the back of the market and adjacent streets but most arrive and depart from bus depots along the Pan-American Hwy. From **San José** (just outside Terminal Coca Cola), hourly service 0530-1730, US$3.30, 3 hrs (buses to the capital leave from the highway, Calle 2-4). To **Quepos** via **Dominical** at 0500 and 1330, 3 hrs. However, **Tracopa** buses coming from **San José**, going south go from Calle 3/Pan-American Hwy, behind church, to **Palmar Norte**, US$2.25; **Paso Canoas**, 0830-1545, 1930 (direct), 2100; **David** (Panama) direct, 1000 and 1500; **Golfito** direct at 1800; **Puerto Jiménez**, 0630, 0900 and 1500. Waiting room but no reservations or tickets sold. **Musoc** buses leave from the intersection of Calle 2-4 with the Pan-American Hwy.
Most local buses leave from bus terminal to the south of the main plaza. Buses to **San Gerardo de Rivas** and **Cerro Chirripó** leave 0500 and 1400, return0700 and 1600.

Taxi A 4WD taxi to San Gerardo costs about US$20 for up to 4 people.

Palmar Norte and Palmar Sur *p163*
Air Daily flights with **Sansa** (US$72)and **Nature Air**, San José-Palmar Sur (US$73 one way).
Bus Express bus to **Palmar Norte** from Terminal Alfaro, with **Tracopa** from **San José**, 7 daily 0600-1800, 5 hrs, via **San Isidro de El General**, 5 buses return to the capital 0445-1300. 5 buses daily to **Sierpe** for the boat to **Bahía Drake** (page 173) 45 mins. Also buses north to **Dominical**, and south to the **Golfito** and the Panamanian border.

Sierpe *p163*
Bus and Boat 5 buses daily to **Palmar Norte**, 0530-1530, 45 mins. Boats down Río Sierpe to **Bahía Drake**, 1½ hrs, US$70 per boat. Many hotels in Drake have boats, may be able to get a lift, US$15 per person.

Paso Real to San Vito *p163*
Bus Direct buses **San José** to San Vito, 4 daily, 0545, 0815, 1130 and 1445, from Terminal Alfaro, Calle 14, Av 5; direct bus San Vito-San José 0500, 0730, 1000, 1500, 6 hrs, corriente buses take 8 hrs. Alternative route, not all paved, via Cd Neily (see below); from San Vito to **Las Cruces** at 0530 and 0700; sit on the left coming up, right going down, to admire the wonderful scenery; return buses pass Las Cruces at 1510.

Golfito *p164*
Air Several daily flights to **San José**, with Sansa (US$75 one way). Runway is all weather, tight landing between trees; 2 km from town, taxi US$0.50.

Bus From **San José** 0700 (8½ hrs) and 1500 (6 hrs express) daily from Terminal Alfaro, return 0500 (express), 1300, US$6; from **San Isidro de El General**, take 0730 bus to Río Claro and wait for bus coming from Cd Neily. To **Paso Canoas**, US$1.25, hourly from outside Soda Pavo, 1½ hrs. To **Pavones** at 1000 and 1500, and return at 0430 and 1230, 3 hrs, US$2.50. A spit of land continues south to Punta Burica with no roads and only a couple of villages.

Sea Water taxis in and around Golfito, **Froylan Lopex**, T8824-6571, to Cacao Beach, Punta Zancudo, Punta Encanto or to order, US$20 per hr up to 5 persons. **Docks** Land Sea Tours (see Tour operators, above) and **Banana Bay Marina** (T2775-0838, www.bananabaymarina.com) accommodate boats up to 150 ft – either of these places might be an option if heading south on a boat, but you'll need to ask nicely and be a bit lucky.

Ciudad Neily, Paso Canoas and the Panama border *p165*
Bus The terminal in Cd Neily is at the northern end of town, beside the Mercado Central. Daily bus to **San José**, with **Tracopa**, from main square (6 daily, US$6, 7 hrs, on Sun buses from the border are full by the

time they reach Cd Neily). Buses arrive at Av 5 and Calle 14 in San José. Services to **San Vito** inland, and to **Palmar**, **Cortés** and **Dominical** (0600 and 1430, 3 hrs). Also to **Puerto Jiménez** at 0700 and 1400, 4 hrs. Bus for **Golfito** leaves from the centre of town every 30 mins. The Pan-American Highway goes south (plenty of buses, 20 mins, US$0.35) to Paso Canoas on the Panamanian border. *Colectivo* US$1.10, very quick.

San José–Paso Canoas, US$9, 8 hrs from Terminal Alfaro at 0500, 1100 (direct), 1300, 1800, return 0400, 0730, 0900, 1500 (T2223-7685). Not all buses go to the border. International buses that reach the border after closing time wait there till the following day. Hourly buses to Cd Neily, ½ hourly to Golfito.

ⒹDirectory

San Isidro de El General *p160*
Banks Banco Nacional, on north side of plaza, Mon-Fri, 0830-1545. **Internet** Bruncanet, on north side of plaza, and MS Internet Café. **Post office** 3 blocks south of the church. **Telephone** ICE office on Calle 4, Av 3-PAH.

Paso Real to San Vito *p163*
Banks There are branches of **Banco Nacional** and **Banco Popular** in San Vito. **Post office and internet** Post office at northern end of town.

Golfito *p164*
Banks Banco Nacional near dock, Mon-Fri 0830-1535, T2775-1622. **Internet** Internet café, on ground floor below Hotel Golfito.

Ciudad Neily, Paso Canoas and the Panama border *p165*
Banks In Cd Neily, there are branches of Banco Nacional and Banco de Costa Rica. At Paso Canoas, banks on either side of border close at 1600 local time. Slightly better dollar rate for colones on the Costa Rican side. **Internet** Planet Internet at the northern end of Cd Neily.

Península de Osa

Across the Golfo Dulce is the hook-shaped appendage of the Osa Peninsula. Some distance from most other places of interest in the country, the journey is worthwhile as the peninsula is world famous for the diversity of flora and fauna in Parque Nacional Corcovado, with some of the best rainforest trekking and trails in the country. ▸▸ *For listings, see pages 175-177.*

Ins and outs

Getting there Getting to the peninsula is getting easier. There is a daily ferry service from Golfito arriving at the small dock in Puerto Jiménez. There are also bus services from San José, passing through San Isidro de El General and Palmar North, and from the south at Ciudad Neily. Boats ply the coastal route from Sierpe to Bahía Drake and you can fly from San José.

Puerto Jiménez

To Dos Brazos, Rincón & San José

To Golfito

Golfo Dulce

Osa Natural
Football Pitch
Bus to Carate
Café El Sol
Tonsa Tours

MINAE National Park Office

To ⑥ & Playa Platanares

Sansa Banco Nacional

To Matapalo, Carate & Corcovado

N

100 metres
100 yards

Sleeping
Agua Luna 1
Cabinas Bosque Mar 2
Cabinas Marcelina 3
Cabinas Puerto Jiménez 4
Cabinas Thompson 5
Crocodile Bay Lodge 6

Iguana Iguana 7
La Choza del Manglares 8
Oro Verde 9
Parrot Bay Village 10
Pensión Quintero 11
Puerto Jiménez Yacht Club 12

Eating ●
Agua Luna 1
Carolina &
  Escondido Trex 2
Il Giardino 3
Juanita's Mexican
  Bar & Grille 4
Pizza Rock 5

Puerto Jiménez

Once the gold-mining centre of the Osa Peninsula, Puerto Jiménez still has the feel of a frontier town although most miners were cleared from the Parque Nacional Corcovado area in 1985.

Today, Puerto Jiménez is a popular destination with its laid-back, occasionally lively atmosphere, reasonable beaches nearby and, of course, the beautiful national park on the Pacific side of the peninsula. Look out for *El Sol de Osa*, www.soldeosa.com, an up-to-date community information service. A particular charm of Puerto Jiménez, barely five blocks square, is its relative freedom from road traffic – Scarlet macaws can be seen roosting in the trees around the football pitch. There are good local walks to the jungle, where you will see monkeys and many birds, and to beaches and mangroves. There is a seasonal migration of humpbacks between October and March.

Geological treasures can be seen at the gold mine at **Dos Brazos** about 15 km west of town; ask for the road which goes uphill beyond the town, to see the local gold mines. Several *colectivo* taxis a day to Dos Brazos, last bus back at 1530 (often late); taxi US$7.25. You can also take a long walk to **Carate** (see below) which has a gold mine. Branch to the right and in 4 km there are good views of the peninsula. A topographical map is a big help, obtainable from Instituto Geográfico in San José. At **Cabo Matapalo** on the tip of the peninsula, 18 km south of Puerto Jiménez, are several expensive sleeping options.

Southern Costa Rica & the Osa Peninsula

Bahía Drake

Arriving by boat from Sierpe, Bahía Drake provides a northern entrance point to the Osa Peninsula and Parque Nacional Corcovado. In March 1579, Sir Francis Drake careened his ship on Playa Colorada in Bahía Drake. A plaque commemorating the 400th anniversary of the famous pirate's nautical aberration was erected in Agujitas. Life in the bay is not cheap, and combined with transport, costs can quickly mount up. Bahía Drake, which continues south merging seamlessly with Agujitas, is a popular destination for **divers** with Isla Caño nearby. Open water PADI courses (US$325) are available at **Cabinas Jinetes de Osa** or through **Caño Divers** at Pirate Cove.

Parque Nacional Corcovado 🌐 ↦ *pp175-177.*

Corcovado National Park, including **Reserva Biológica Isla del Caño** (84 ha), comprises over 42,469 ha – just under half the Osa Peninsula. Consisting largely of tropical rainforest, swamps, miles of empty beaches, and some cleared areas now growing back, it is located on the Pacific Ocean at the western end of the peninsula. An ideal spot for just walking along endless beaches, the park is also filled with birds, mammals and six species of cat.

Ins and outs

If short of time and/or money, the simplest way to the park is to take the pick-up truck from outside **Tonsa Tours** in Puerto Jiménez to Playa Carate (most days at 0600 and 1400, 2½ hrs, US$7 one way, returning at 0800 and 1600, ask in advance about departure). Or call **Cirilo Espinosa** (T2735-5075), or **Ricardo González** (T2735-5068), for a 4WD jeep taxi. It is possible to book a flight from Puerto Jiménez to Carate or La Sirena in the park for US$99 per person, minimum five people. Ask at the airstrip or call T2735-5178. The **MINAE office** ① *Puerto Jiménez, near the airport, T2735-5036, daily 0830-1200, 1300-1700,* will give permits for entering the park (US$7) and will book accommodation at **La Sirena** in dormitories, maximum 20 people, **(F)** for bed (reservation essential), take sheets/sleeping bag, camping **(F)**, no reservation needed, three meals available. Bring mosquito netting. Hiking boots and sandals are useful if you are walking any distance in the park.

Around the park

At **Carate** there is a dirt airstrip and a store, run by Gilberto Morales and his wife Roxana (they rent rooms, but they are often full of

Península de Osa – rain, snakes and mosquitoes

Avoid the rainy season. Bring umbrellas (not raincoats, too hot), because it will rain, unless you are hiking, in which case you may prefer to get wet. Shelters can be found here and there, so only mosquito netting is indispensable. Bring all your food if you haven't arranged otherwise; food can only be obtained at Puerto Jiménez and Agujitas in the whole peninsula, and lodging likewise. The cleared areas (mostly outside the park, or along the beach) can be devastatingly hot. Chiggers (*coloradillas*) and horseflies infest the horse pastures and can be a nuisance, similarly sandflies on the beaches; bring spray-on insect repellent.

Another suggestion is vitamin B1 pills (called thiamine, or *tiamina*). Mosquitoes are supposed to detest the smell and leave you alone, but see Health, page 50. Get the Instituto Geográfico maps, scale 1:50,000. Remember finally that, as in any tropical forest, you may find some unfriendly wildlife like snakes (fer-de-lance and bushmaster snakes may attack without provocation), and herds of peccaries. You should find the most suitable method for keeping your feet dry and protecting your ankles; for some, rubber boots are the thing, for others light footwear that dries quickly.

gold miners; they also have a tent for hire, but take a sleeping bag). There are several luxury options here and a couple more lodges 30 minutes' walk west along the beach.

Five minutes' walk further down the beach is **La Leona** park wardens' station and entrance to the park. To go beyond here costs US$7 per day, whether you are walking along the beach to La Sirena (18 km, six hours, take sun protection), or just visiting for the day. Lodging is available (see page 177). Beyond here to the end of **Playa Madrigal** is another 2½ hours' walk, partly sandy, partly rocky, with some rock pools and rusty shipwrecks looking like modern art sculptures. The shore rises steeply into the jungle, which grows thickly with mangroves, almonds and coconut palms. Check with wardens about high tide so you don't get stuck. There are a couple of rivers along the beach, the first, Río Madrigal, is only about 15 minutes beyond La Leona (lovely and clear, deep enough for swimming about 200 m upstream, a good place for spotting wildlife). The best place for seeing wildlife, though, is La Sirena, where there are paths inland and the terrain is flatter and more isolated.

You can head inland from Sirena on a trail past three conveniently spaced shelters to **Los Patos**, after passing several rivers full of reptiles (20 km, six to nine hours depending on conditions). The wooden house is the ranger station with electricity and TV, and four beds available at US$1.75 per night; meals possible if you do not bring your own food. Its balcony is a great observation point for birds, especially the redheaded woodpecker. From Los Patos you can carry on to the park border then, crisscrossing the **Río Rincón to La Palma** (small *hostal*), a settlement on the opposite side of the peninsula (13 km, six more hours), from which there are several 'taxis' making the one-hour trip to Puerto Jiménez (see above). An offshoot of this trail will lead you to a raffia swamp that rings the **Corcovado Lagoon**. The lagoon is only accessible by boat, but there are no regular trips. Caymans and alligators survive here, sheltered from the hunters.

From Sirena you can walk north along the coast to the shelter at Llorona (plenty of waterfalls), from which there is a trail to the interior with a shelter at the end. From

Llorona you can proceed north through a forest trail and along the beach to the station at **San Pedrillo** on the edge of the park. You can stay here, camping or under roof, and eat with the rangers, who love company. From San Pedrillo you can take the park boat (not cheap) to Isla del Caño, a lovely manned park outpost. See under Quepos for Taximar boat service from Quepos and Dominical to Isla del Caño or Bahía Drake.

Isla del Coco

This has to be one of the world's most distant island destinations: the steep-sided and thickly wooded island and national park of 24 sq km lies 320 km off the Osa Peninsula, on the Cocos Ridge, which extends some 1400 km southwest to the Galápagos Islands. There is virtually nothing on the island, apart from a few endemic species, but you can visit for some of the world's best diving. The BBC/Discovery Channel shot some dramatic silhouetted images of tiger sharks here for their *Blue Planet* series. Historically, though, it was a refuge for pirates who are supposed to have buried great treasure here, though none has been found by the 500 or so expeditions looking for the 'x' that marked a spot. Travel by chartered boat can be made in Puntarenas, after a government permit has been obtained, or you can take a scuba-diving cruise on the **Okeanos Agressor** ① *T2232-0572 ext 60 (in US: PO Drawer K, Morgan City, LA 70381, T504-385-2416)*. The twice-monthly 10-day trips are understandably expensive (about US$3095 for 10 days).

◉ Península de Osa listings

For Sleeping and Eating price codes, and other relevant information, see pages 43-46.

◉ Sleeping

Puerto Jiménez *p172, map p171*
Website covering Jiménez hotels at www.jimenezhotels.com.
LL Crocodile Bay Lodge, south of town, T2735-1115, www.crocodilebay.com. All comforts including pool, swim-up bar, massage and luxury sportfishing.
L Parrot Bay Village, left from the pier, T2735-5180, www.parrotbayvillage.com. Fully equipped wooden cabins sleeping 1-5, restaurant, beautiful spot, almost private beach. Cheaper in groups.
A La Choza del Manglares, right beside the mangrove on the river, T2735-5002, www.manglares.com. Clean, well-maintained cabins with private bath. In the day regular visits from monkeys, scarlet macaws and the occasional crocodile in the grounds by the river. Completely renovated.

A-B Agua Luna, facing pier, T2735-3593, agualu@racsa.co.cr. New rooms sleeping 2-4 with bath, good, although pricey; restaurant next door.
A-B Cabinas Puerto Jiménez, on the gulf shore with good views, T2735-5090. Remodelled big rooms, many with private decks looking out to the gulf, spotless.
B-C Cabinas Marcelina, down main street, T2735-5007. With bath, big clean, friendly, nice front yard, totally renovated, small discount for youth hostelling members.
D Cabinas Bosque Mar, T2735-5681. Clean, large rooms and restaurant.
D Hotel Oro Verde, down main street, T2735-5241. Run by Silvia Duirós Rodríguez, 10 clean, comfortable rooms, with bath and fan, some overlooking the street.
D Iguana Iguana, on road leading out of town, T2735-5158. Simple rooms with private bath, restaurant, small bar, pool.
E Pizzería Cabinas Mariel, T2735-5071. Simple cabins.
F Cabinas Thompson, 50 m from the centre, T2735-5910. With bath, fan, clean but dark.

F Pensión Quintero, off main street, T2735-5087. Simple wooden building, but clean and good value, will store luggage. Fernando Quintero rents horses and has a boat for up to 6 passengers, good value; he is also a guide, recommended. Price per person.

Around Puerto Jiménez

LL Lapa Ríos Wilderness Resort, at Cabo Matapalo, T2735-5130, www.laparios.com. The cream of the crop. Includes meals. 14 luxury palm-thatched bungalows on private 2400-ha reserve (80% virgin forest, US owners Karen and John Lewis), camping trips, boats can be arranged from Golfito. Idyllic, fantastic views, recommended.

AL-A El Remanso Rainforest Beach Lodge, Cabo Matapalo, T2735-5569, www.elremanso.com. Houses and cabins for rent, all fully equipped and with ocean views, an oasis of peace.

A Iguanal Lodge, 5 km southeast of Puerto Jiménez behind the airstrip, T8829-5865, www.iguanalodge.com. 4 cabins, good swimming and surfing.

Bahía Drake p173

LL Aguila de Osa Inn, the normal landing point, T2296-2190, www.aguiladeosa.com. Includes meals; fishing, hiking, canoeing and horse riding available, comfortable cabins made with exotic hardwoods. Recommended.

LL La Paloma Jungle Lodge, T2239-0954, www.lapalomalodge.com. Price per person includes meals. 9 cabins with bath, guided tours with resident biologist. Packages.

L Drake Bay Wilderness Camp, opposite **Aguila de Osa Inn**, T2770-8012, www.drakebay.com. Price per person, with meals, cabins, tents available, pleasant family atmosphere, pool, 2 restaurants. Great views. Wide ranges of tours available.

AL Cabinas Jinete de Osa, T2236-5637, www.costaricadiving.com. Good hotel, run by 2 brothers from Colorado. Diving a speciality, PADI courses offered. Spacious and airy rooms, all with bath, hot water, fan. Recommended.

AL-A Pirate Cove, northern end of the beach, T2786-7845, www.piratecove.com. Very nice tent-like cabins emulate an outdoor experience minus the mud. US$55 per person shared bath, US$70 with bath, 3 meals included.

B Rancho Corcovado Lodge, in the middle of the beach, T2786-7059. Price per person. Simple, rustic rooms, many with view, all with bath. Friendly Tico owners, nice open-air restaurant on beach serves *comida típica*. Camping permitted.

D Bella Vista Lodge, on the beach at the southern end of town, T2770-8051. The only budget option in town and disappointing. Basic rooms, 2 with bath, 3 shared (even more basic), meals (US$3-5) not included.

Camping

Camping is allowed outside **Rancho Corcovado** (use of electricity and bathrooms included) or outside **Pirate Cove** (north end of beach), no fixed price, small charge for baths.

Parque Nacional Corcovado p173

MINAE office, facing the airstrip, Puerto Jiménez, T2735-5036. For booking dormitory accommodation and camping facilities in Corcovado National Park.

LL Casa Corcovado Jungle Lodge, along the coast from San Pedrillo, T2256-3181, www.casacorcovado.com. Outside the park in the forest, but with 500 m of beach more or less opposite Isla del Caño, 14 bungalows, many facilities, packages from 2 nights full board with boat transport (2 hrs) from Sierpe.

L-AL Corcovado Lodge, 30 mins' walk west of Carate along the beach, T2257-0766, www.costaricaexpeditions.com. 20 walk-in tents with 2 campbeds in each, in a beautiful coconut grove with hammocks overlooking the beach; walk-ins are possible but to be sure of space book through **Costa Rica Expeditions** in San José. Clean showers and toilets; good food, take a flashlight. Behind the camp is a trail into the jungle with a great view of the bay from a clearing; many birds to be seen, plus monkeys and frogs.

A La Leona Eco-Lodge, 30 mins' walk west of Carate along the beach, T2735-5705, www.laleonalodge.com. Rustic tent cabins, crocodile spotting, rappelling, yoga and night hikes. Price per person.
F La Leona park wardens' station, at entrance to the park. Maximum 12 people in basic rooms or camping, meals available. Book in high season through SINAC.

🍴 Eating

Puerto Jiménez *p172, map p171*
🍴🍴🍴 **Agua Luna**, on the seashore near the dock, T2735-5033. Stylish setting, beautifully presented but pricey.
🍴🍴🍴 **Il Giardino**, just off the main street. Quiet little Italian, intimate setting, and good food.
🍴🍴-🍴🍴 **Carolina**, down the main street, T2735-5185. Highly recommended for fish (everything actually), good prices. **Escondido Trex** office at back of restaurant.
🍴🍴 **Juanita's Mexican Bar and Grille**, central, T2735-5056. Happy hr, crab races, good Mexican fare, seafood from US$4.
🍴 **Pollo Frito Opi Opi**, north end of town, T2735-5192. Fried chicken, hamburgers, fries.
🍴 **Soda Bosquemar**, on main street, T2735-5681. Good food at good prices.

🥾 Activities and tours

Puerto Jiménez *p172, map p171*
Tour operators
Aventuras Tropicales, opposite the football pitch, T2735-5195, www.aventuras tropicales.com. Can book accommodation and has a couple of computers.
Escondido Trex, in the back of **Carolina**, T2735-5210, www.escondidotrex.com. Excellent local information, treks, kayaking and jungle trips.
MINAE office, facing the airstrip, T2735-5036, for booking dormitory lodging and camping facilities in Corcovado National Park.

Tonsa Tours, see map. Run by the quiet Jaime, provides many of the normal tours, and also jungle treks across to Carate. Not for the faint-hearted, but certain to be fascinating.

🚌 Transport

Puerto Jiménez *p172, map p171*
Air There are daily flights between Puerto Jiménez and Golfito with **Sansa** (US$78) and **Nature Air** (US$65 one way) from San José.

Bus 1 block west of the main street. A café by the bus terminal is open Sat 0430 for a cheap and reasonable breakfast. From **San José**, just outside Terminal Atlántico Norte (C 12, Av 9-11), there are 2 buses daily to Puerto Jiménez at 0600 and 1200 via San Isidro, US$7, 8 hrs, return 0500, T2735-5189. There are also buses from **San Isidro**, leaving from the Pan-American Hwy at 0930 and 1500, US$4.50, returns at 0400 and 1300, 5 hrs. To **Cd Neily** at 0500 and 1400, 3 hrs, US$3. A few *colectivos* to **Carate** depart from outside **Restaurant Carolina** daily 0530 and 0600, cost US$7. Service may be restricted in the wet season.

Car To reach Puerto Jiménez from the Pan-American Hwy (70 km), turn right about 30 km south of Palmar Sur; the road is newly paved to Rincón, thereafter it is driveable with many bridge crossings. There is a police check point 47 km from the Pan-American Hwy.

Sea Boat leaves from the dock in **Golfito** 1130, US$2.50, 1½ hrs, return 0600, or can charter a taxi boat for US$60, up to 8 passengers.

ⓘ Directory

Puerto Jiménez *p172, map p171*
Banks Branch of **Banco Nacional**, T2735-5155. **Internet** Café El Sol, on main street, 0700-1900, US$8 per hr.
Post office Opposite the football pitch.

San José to the Caribbean

Heading east from San José the Central Highlands quickly fall away to the sparsely populated flat Caribbean lowlands. The tropical rainforest national parks of Tortuguero and Barra del Colorado, leading through coastal canals and waterways, are a nature lover's paradise with easily arranged trips, normally from San José, into the rainforest. South of the distinctly Caribbean city of Puerto Limón, coastal communities have developed to provide comfortable hangouts and laid-back beach life for all budgets. ▸▸ *For listings, see pages 188-202.*

There are two routes from San José to Puerto Limón on the Atlantic coast. The newer main route goes over the Cordillera Central, through the Parque Nacional Braulio Carrillo down to Guápiles and Siquirres. This highland section is prone to fog and if driving yourself, requires extra care. The second, more scenic but considerably longer, route follows the old Atlantic railway to Cártago, south of Irazú volcano to Turrialba, joining the main highway at Siquirres.

Parque Nacional Braulio Carrillo

The third largest of Costa Rica's national parks Parque Nacional Braulio Carrillo was created to protect the high rainforest north of San José from the impact of the new San José–Guápiles–Puerto Limón highway. It extends for 47,583 ha, and encompasses five different types of forest with abundant wildlife including hundreds of species of bird, jaguar, ocelot and Baird's tapir. Various travel agencies offer naturalist tours, approximately US$65 from San José. San José to Guápiles and Puerto Limón buses go through the park.

The entrance to the **Quebrada González centre** ① *daily 0800-1530 US$7*, on the highway is 23 km beyond the Zurquí tunnel, just over the Río Sucio at the Guápiles end. It has a new administration building. To get there, take any bus to the Atlantic and ask to be dropped off. There are three trails: **Las Palmas**, 1.6 km (you need rubber boots); across the road are **El Ceibo**, 1 km, circular; and **Botarrama**, entry 2 km from Quebrada González (El Ceibo and Botarrama are to be joined). The trail has good birdwatching and the views down the Río Patria canyon are impressive. The Zurquí centre near the tunnel has been closed but may open again soon so ask at headquarters. It has services and the 250-m Los Jilqueros trail to the river.

Beyond Quebrada González (1.5 km) is **Los Heliconios** ① *entry US$7*, butterfly garden with an insect museum and amphibians. Adjoining it, **Reserva Turística El Tapir** ① *entry US$7*, has a 20-minute trail and others of one to two hours.

An ingenious **Rainforest Aerial Tram** (*teleférico*) ① *Tue-Sun 0630-1600, Mon 0900-1530, 90 mins' ride costs US$49.50, students with ID and children ½-price, children under 5 are not allowed*, lifts visitors high up into the rainforest, providing a fascinating up-close and personal view of the canopy life and vegetation. The price includes a guided nature walk. It's best to go as early as possible for birds. Tourist buses arrive 0800. There's a guarded car park for private vehicles and restaurant for meals in the park. It can be difficult to get reservations during the high season. There's a **Rainforest Aerial Tram office in San José** ① *Av 7, Calle 7, behind Aurola Holiday Inn, T2257-5961; there's an all-inclusive package from San José leaving around 0800 daily, US$78.50, students and under 11s US$53.75, with pick-ups at most major hotels.*

Further on, at the Soda Gallo Pinto is the **Bosque Lluvioso** ① *T2224-0819, daily 0700-1700, entry US$15*, a 170-ha private reserve. It is at Km 56 on the Guápiles highway (**Rancho Redondo**), with a restaurant and trails in primary and secondary forest.

The turn-off at Santa Clara to Puerto Viejo de Sarapiquí is 13 km before Guápiles. At the junction is **Rancho Robertos**, T2711-0050, a good, popular and reasonable roadside restaurant). For Guápiles see below. Nearby is a **Tropical Frog Garden**, an interesting short stop if you have the time.

Parque Nacional Braulio Carrillo & Puerto Viejo loop

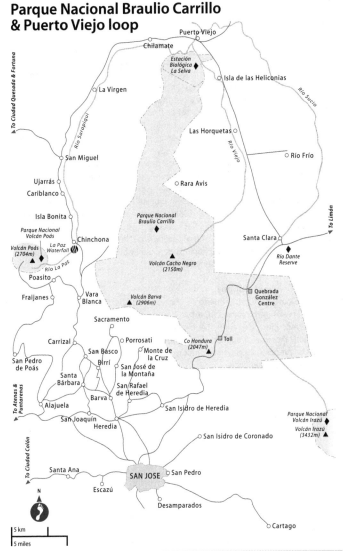

There is a private reserve bordering the Parque Nacional Braulio Carrillo called **Río Danta**, with 60 ha of primary rainforest and short limited treks (US$4) arranged with meals (US$6-9). For information contact **Mawamba Group** ① *T2223-2421; must be pre-arranged; no drop-ins.*

Puerto Viejo de Sarapiquí

Puerto Viejo de Sarapiquí is 40 km north of the San José-Limón highway and 20 km from La Virgen to the southwest. Once an important port on the Río Sarapiquí, only occasionally do launches ply the Río Colorado to the Canales de Tortuguero. There is reported to be a cargo boat once a week to Barra del Colorado (no facilities, bring your own food, hammock, sleeping bag; see box, page 174), and on to Moín, about 10 km by road from Puerto Limón. But there is little traffic, so you will need a bit of luck and a fair amount of cash. There is good fishing on the Río Sarapiquí.

In the neighbourhood is **La Selva Biological Station** ① *T2766-6565, www.ots.ac.cr, 3½-hr guided natural history walk with bilingual naturalists daily at 0800 and 1330-1600, US$36 per person,* on the Río Puerto Viejo, run by the Organization for Tropical Studies. The floral and faunal diversity is unbelievable. Several guided and self-led walks are available but to visit it is essential to book in advance. Accommodation is also available.

The Río Sarapiquí flows into the San Juan, forming the northern border of Costa Rica. The Río San Juan is wholly in Nicaragua, so you technically have to cross the border and then return to Costa Rica. This will cost US$5 and you will need a passport and visa. Trips on the **Río Sarapiquí** and on the **Río Sucio** are beautiful (US$15 for two hours); contact William Rojas in Puerto Viejo (T2766-6108) for trips on the Río Sarapiquí or to Barra del Colorado and Tortuguero. He also offers packages of three days and two nights for US$275 or ask for the Lao brothers who will advise you. The cost of a launch to Tortuguero is about US$150 (US$350 for four people), but you may be able to find a place on a boat for US$40 or less. The trip takes about five hours.

Las Horquetas de Sarapiquí

Seventeen kilometres south of Puerto Viejo, near Las Horquetas de Sarapiquí, is **Rara Avis** ① *T2764-1111, www.rara-avis.com,* rustic lodges in a 600-ha forest reserve owned by ecologist Amos Bien. This admirable experiment in educating visitors about rainforest conservation takes small groups on guided tours (rubber boots provided), led by biologists. You must be prepared for rough and muddy trails, lots of insects but great birdwatching and a memorable experience.

Guápiles, Guácimo and Siquirres

One hour from San José (bus US$1.45), Guápiles is the centre of the Río Frío banana region. It is another 25 km from Guácimo to Siquirres, a clean, friendly town and junction for roads from Turrialba with the main highway and former railways.

Matina

Twenty-eight kilometres beyond Siquirres, heading north at the 'techo rojo' junction is Matina, a small, once-busy town on the railway but off the highway. Today, it is an access point to Tortuguero and the less well-known private **Reserva Natural Pacuare**, 30 km north of Puerto Limón, which is accessible by canal from Matina. Run by Englishman John Denham, it has a 6-km stretch of **leatherback turtle nesting beach**, protected and guarded by the reserve. Volunteers patrol the beach in May and June, measuring and tagging these magnificent marine turtles (US$50 per person per week, includes good meals and accommodation). For volunteer work, contact Carlos Fernández, **Corporación de Abogados** ① *Av 8-10, Calle 19, No 837, San José, T2233-0508, fdezlaw@racsa.co.cr, organization information at www.turtleprotection.org.*

Puerto Limón and the Caribbean coast ⊖🔊🖰🕻 ›› *pp188-202.*

On a rocky outcrop on an almost featureless coastline, Puerto Limón is the country's most important port. Between Puerto Limón and the Río San Juan on the Nicaraguan border, the long stretch of Atlantic coastline and its handful of small settlements is linked by a canal system that follows the coastline. The region encompasses Parque Nacional Tortuguero, famed for its wildlife and turtle nesting beaches, and Refugio Nacional de Fauna Silvestre Barra del Colorado. The Río San Juan forms the border between Costa Rica and Nicaragua, however the border is not mid-river, but on the Costa Rican bank. English is widely spoken along the coast.

Puerto Limón

Built on the site of the ancient indigenous village of Cariari, Columbus dropped anchor at Punta Uvita, the island off the coastline, on his fourth and final voyage. The climate is very humid and it rains almost every day. With a mainly black population, and a large Chinese contingent, the town has a distinctly Caribbean feel expressed particularly during carnival each October, but in most bars every weekend.

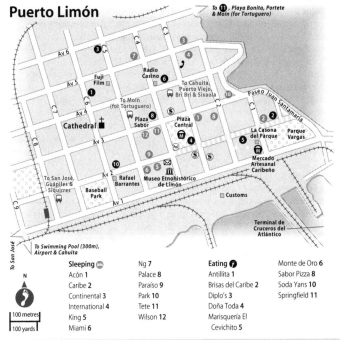

Puerto Limón

Sleeping	Ng **7**	Eating 🍴	Monte de Oro **6**
Acón **1**	Palace **8**	Antillita **1**	Sabor Pizza **8**
Caribe **2**	Paraíso **9**	Brisas del Caribe **2**	Soda Yans **10**
Continental **3**	Park **10**	Diplo's **3**	Springfield **11**
International **4**	Tete **11**	Doña Toda **4**	
King **5**	Wilson **12**	Marisquería El	
Miami **6**		Cevichito **5**	

Border essentials: Costa Rica–Nicaragua

Barra del Colorado

Costa Rican immigration This is not a regular border crossing and there are no formal facilities on the Costa Rican side. Do not leave for Nicaragua by boat or on foot without checking with the Guardia Civil in Barra del Colorado or Tortuguero, who are very helpful. Similarly, check with them if arriving from Nicaragua.

Transport Transport, mostly by boat, is costly and with current changes in fuel prices, it's difficult to provide a reliable guide. There are several fishermen who will take you up the coast on their way to fish in Nicaraguan waters, US$40. You can go by irregular boat from Barra up the Río Colorado, Río San Juan and Río Sarapiquí to Puerto Viejo, five-six hours. A small boat for four without roof costs US$200 (or US$65 per person), a larger boat with roof (recommended) costs US$185 for four; you see caimans, turtles and lots of birds. There are several border checkpoints. Foreigners travelling along Río San Juan must pay US$5 entry and exit tax at Nicaraguan checkpoint and receive stamp in passport. If you have arrived from Nicaragua, an alternative to going south along the coast to Puerto Limón is to take a bus from the river bank opposite Isla Buena Vista 25 km up the Río Colorado, daily except Sunday, leaves 0600, by dirt track to Cariari and then to Guápiles.

Parque Vargas and the seafront promenade at the rocky headland are popular places for social gatherings and killing time, making for ideal people-watching territory, especially in the evening. Parque Vargas, sadly rather run-down, is an impressive botanical display with a colourful mural depicting the history of Limón and a bandstand.

On the upside, the nightlife is good, particularly for Caribbean music and dancing, culminating in carnival every October, Costa Rica's largest festival. There is a small **Museo Etnohistórico de Limón** ① *Calle 2, Av 2, Mon-Fri 0900-1200, 1300-1600*, featuring material relating to Columbus' arrival in Limón. The cargo docks are still active with international crews making regular journeys, as well as being the landing point for pristine floating palaces cruising the Caribbean. The **carnival**, which lasts a few days leading up to 12 October, is Costa Rica's biggest; it's crowded, prices rise, but is definitely worth seeing if you can get a room.

Around Puerto Limón

Playa Bonita and **Portete** have pleasant beaches about 5 km along the coastal road from Puerto Limón. **Moín**, a further 1.5 km east along the road, is the sight of the international docks which exports some 2.8 million bunches of bananas annually. The docks are also the departure point for barges to Tortuguero and Barra del Colorado (eight hours). Boats also run from Moín to Tortuguero (see below) and may be hired at the dockside. Buses run to Moín every 40 minutes from 0600-1740, 30 minutes, US$0.10. If shipping a vehicle check which dock. Some simple accommodation options are available if you end up waiting here.

Parque Nacional Tortuguero ⊜❼▲⊖ » pp188-202.

① *Tortuguero Information Centre, T8833-0827, safari@racsa.co.cr.*

Tortuguero is a 29,068-ha national park, with a marine extension of over 50,000 ha, protecting the Atlantic nesting sites of the green and leatherback turtle and the Caribbean lowland rainforest inland. As with much of Costa Rica, getting the timing right to see this natural phenomenon is essential. The green turtles lay their eggs at night on the scrappy, rather untidy beach from June to October, with the hatchlings emerging from the depths of their sandy nests until November at the latest. Leatherbacks can be seen from March to June. Hawksbill and loggerheads also nest at Tortuguero but numbers are minimal. Trips to look for nesting turtles are carefully monitored and you must be accompanied by a licensed guide at all times. » *For transport details and tour operators, see pages 199 and 201.*

While your visit may not coincide with those of the turtles, the canals of jungle fringed waterways, teeming with bird and insect life, behind the beach are a pleasure throughout the year.

A **visitor centre**, close to the village of Tortuguero, has information on the park and the turtles. Round the back of the headquarters there is a well-marked 1.4-km nature trail, recommended. In the centre is a small gift shop. To the northern end of the village is the **Caribbean Conservation Corporation**, which has played a fundamental role in the creation and continued research of the turtle nesting grounds. There's an interesting and very informative **natural history museum** ① *T2224-9215 (San José), www.cccturtle.org, daily 1000-1200, 1400-1730, donation US$1.* Information about all this and more can be found on the village website, www.tortuguerovillage.com.

A guide is required for trips along the beach at night and recommended for trips through the waterways. Do not swim at Tortuguero as there area sharks. If travelling with a lodge, tours will be arranged for you. If organizing independently, contact the information kiosk in the village for instructions and to link up with a registered guide. To visit the turtles at night you must pay US$7 park entrance fee, and US$5 each for a guide. A guide and tour in no way guarantees you will see a turtle or hatchlings.

Tours through the water channels are the best way to see the rainforest, ideally in a boat without a motor. The canal, bordered with primary rainforest, gives way to smaller channels, and, drifting slowly through forest darkened streams, the rainforest slowly comes alive with wildlife including birds – over half of those found in Costa Rica – monkeys, sloths and, for the lucky, alligators, tapirs, jaguars, ocelots, peccaries, anteaters and even manatees. You can hire a canoe and guide for about US$6 per hour per person in a boat without motor, US$12 with a motor, minimum four. Night tours, US$15 per person per hour. Fishing tours, all equipment included are US$35 per person, minimum two. (See Directory, below, for tour operators and guides.) Take insect repellent.

Barra del Colorado ⊜⊖ » pp188-202.

The canals are part artificial, part natural; originally they were narrow lagoons running parallel to the sea separated by a small strip of land. Now the lagoons are linked, and it is possible to sail as far as Barra del Colorado, in the extreme northeast of Costa Rica, 25 km beyond Tortuguero. They pass many settlements. The town is divided by the river, the main part being on the northern bank. Secluded and difficult to get to, the Refugio Nacional de Fauna Silvestre Barra del Colorado (81,213 ha) is a national wildlife refuge. The reserve and the Parque Nacional Tortuguero share some boundaries, making for a far more effective protected zone. The fame of the region's fauna extends to the waters which are world renowned for fishing.

Once across the Río Colorado (which in fact is the south arm of the Río San Juan delta), you can walk to Nicaragua (see under Nicaragua, San Juan del Norte) along the coast, but it is a long 30-km beach walk, take food and lots of water. Most hikers overnight en route. Seek advice before setting out.

South from Puerto Limón » pp188-202.

Penshurst

South of Limón, a paved road shadows the coastline normally separated by little more than a thin line of palms. Beyond Penshurst is the **Hitoy Cerere Biological Reserve**. If you have time, camping is easy in the hills and there are plenty of rivers for swimming. Further south the road leads to Cahuita, Puerto Viejo and on towards Manzanillo – all sleepy beach towns, with lively centres, comfortable hideaways, and coastal and nature

Cahuita

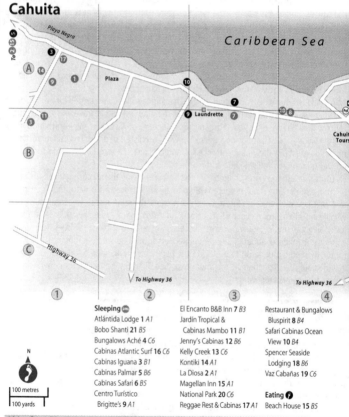

Sleeping 😴	El Encanto B&B Inn 7 *B3*	Restaurant & Bungalows
Atlántida Lodge 1 *A1*	Jardín Tropical &	Bluspirit 8 *B4*
Bobo Shanti 21 *B5*	Cabinas Mambo 11 *B1*	Safari Cabinas Ocean
Bungalows Aché 4 *C6*	Jenny's Cabinas 12 *B6*	View 10 *B4*
Cabinas Atlantic Surf 16 *C6*	Kelly Creek 13 *C6*	Spencer Seaside
Cabinas Iguana 3 *B1*	Kontiki 14 *A1*	Lodging 18 *B6*
Cabinas Palmar 5 *B6*	La Diosa 2 *A1*	Vaz Cabañas 19 *C6*
Cabinas Safari 6 *B5*	Magellan Inn 15 *A1*	
Centro Turístico	National Park 20 *C6*	Eating 🍴
Brigitte's 9 *A1*	Reggae Rest & Cabinas 17 *A1*	Beach House 15 *B5*

opportunities to explore. If heading for the border, heading inland just north of Puerto Viejo takes you through Bri Bri and on to Sixaola.

From Penshurst it is 11.5 km to **Cahuita**; this stretch of the road is paved to the edge of Cahuita.

Cahuita and Parque Nacional Cahuita

ⓘ *Entry to the park US$7. The official entrance is at Puerto Vargas, about 5 km south of Cahuita, where there are the park HQ, a nature trail, camping facilities and toilets. Take the bus to Km 5, then turn left at the sign. There is a tourist complex in the area, and the restaurant Marisquería, at Puerto Vargas park entrance, Italian, with a jovial host, who also has rooms. You can enter the park for free from the southern side of Cahuita, which is ideal for relaxing on the beach, but leave a donation. If you have the option, visit during the week when it is quieter.*

The small town of Cahuita hides 1 km back from the main road, and enjoys a sleepy feel accordingly. A laid-back community, it's a good place to hide away in one of the secluded spots or to party in the centre of town. North of the town there is a beautiful black-sand beach ideal for swimming or just lazing about in a hammock, while to the south is the national park. Most people stay in Cahuita to explore the park.

Cahuita National Park (1068 ha) is a narrow strip of beach protecting a coral reef off shore and a marine area of 22,400 ha. The length of the beach can be walked in about three hours, and passes endless coconut palms and interesting tropical forest, through which there is also a path. It is hot and humid, so take drinking water, but a wide range of fauna can be seen, as well as howler monkeys, white face monkeys, coatis, snakes, butterflies and hermit crabs. Over 500 species of fish inhabit the surrounding waters and reef tours are available. An old Spanish shipwreck can be seen and reached without a boat. Snorkellers should take care to stay away from the coral which is already badly damaged by agricultural chemicals and other pollutants. The park extends from the southern limit of Cahuita town southeast to Puerto Vargas.

Note: Cahuita and Puerto Viejo have suffered from what locals believe is a lack of support and investment from central government. An undercurrent of problems, partially based on the perception that everyone on the Caribbean coast takes drugs, does mean that you may be hassled for drugs. If you are not interested, just say no.

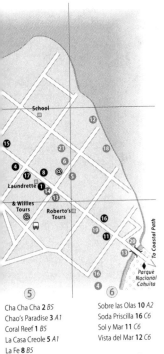

Cha Cha Cha **2** *B5*
Chao's Paradise **3** *A1*
Coral Reef **1** *B5*
La Casa Creole **5** *A1*
La Fe **8** *B5*
Mango Tango Pizzeria **17** *B5*
Miss Edith's **6** *A4*
Palenque Luisa **4** *B5*
Pastry Shop **7** *B3*
Pizzería El Cactus **9** *B2*

Sobre las Olas **10** *A2*
Soda Priscilla **16** *C6*
Sol y Mar **11** *C6*
Vista del Mar **12** *C6*

Bars & clubs 🎵
Cocos **14** *B5*
Rikki's **13** *B5*

Puerto Viejo de Talamanca

Puerto Viejo is a good base and a quietly happening party town, with a number of good beaches stretching out to the south. Activities in the area are numerous and you could spend many days exploring the options. There is reef diving nearby, or you can head south to Mandoca for lagoon diving from canoes. Surfers seek out the glorious **Salsa Brava** wave which peaks from December to February. Away from the beach nature trips range from tough treks in Gandoca-Manzanillo Wildlife Refuge (see page 187) through to gentle strolls around the self-guided botanical gardens to the north of

Puerto Viejo de Talamanca

Sleeping		Eating 🍴	Red Stripe Café 20
Bull Inn 20	Cabinas Tropical 4	Amimodo 9	Salsa Brava 12
Cabinas Casa Verde 2	Cabinas Yucca 19	Bread and Chocolate 1	Soda Miss Sam 7
Cabinas Grant 3	Cashew Hill 5	El Parquecito 3	Soda Palmer 19
Cabinas Lika 21	Coco Loco Lodge 6	Hot Rocks 14	Stanford's 10
Cabinas Los Almendros 1	Fortaleza 14	Jammin Juices &	Tamara 8
Cabinas Popular 17	Guaraná 13	Jerk Chicken 17	
Cabinas Rolando 15	Jacaranda 7	La Terraza 15	**Bars & clubs** 🍸
Cabinas Soda Mitchell 16	Las Olas Camping	Lidia's Place 5	Baba Yaga 25
	& Cabinas 18	Monchies 23	Sunset 24
	Los Sueños 8	Pan Pay 6	
	Maritza 9	Peace & Love Coffee 22	
	Puerto Viejo 10	Pizza Boruca 21	
	Pura Vida 11	Pizzeria Rusticone 13	
	Rocking J's 12	Pollo Frito 18	
	Tamandua Lodge 22		

Border essentials: Costa Rica–Panama

Sixaola

Costa Rican immigration Straightforward crossing, with formalities either side of the bridge. The border is open 0700-1700. They shut for lunch for 45 minutes on Saturday and Sunday. The immigration office is just before the railway bridge, over the river Sixaola, which marks the border with Panama. Advance watches by one hour on entering Panama.

Sleeping At the entrance to town is **Imperio (E)**, eight basic cabins with ventilator, shared bath; and **Cabinas Sánchez (E)**, T2754-2105, clean and tidy, best option.

Transport Moving on in Panama, the simplest option is to get a taxi to Changuinola Marine Terminal for the boat to Bocas del Toro. A railway runs to Almirante (Panama) from Guabito, on the Panamanian side. If crossing to Panama take the earliest bus possible to Sixaola. Direct San José–Sixaola from Terminal del Caribe, Autotransportes Mepe (T2221-0524), 0600, 1000, 1400 and 1600, return 0600, 0800, 1000 and 1500, 5½ hours, US$9.50. Also six daily from Puerto Limón (Radio Casino), four hours.

Banks There are no banks in Sixaola, but you can change money in the supermarket. Rates, especially to the US dollar, are very poor. Shops near the border in Panama will accept colones but shops in Changuinola and beyond do not. Dollars are used as national currency in Panama.

---

town. There are also several cultural trips to KeKöLdi and BriBri indigenous reserves and the newest offering takes dug-outs to the inland town of Yorkin. The **Asociación Talamanqueña de Ecoturismo y Conservación** ⓘ *ATEC, T2750-0191, www.greencoast. com/atec.htm*, provides tourist information, sells locally made crafts and T-shirts, and also offers guide services, rainforest hikes, snorkelling and fishing trips. The **South Caribbean Music Festival** takes place in the months leading up to Easter.

South Caribbean coast

Moín
Puerto Limón
COSTA RICA
Penshurst
Playa Negra
Valle de Estrella
Cahuita
Hitoy Cerere Research Centre
Bribri
Reserva Biológica Hitoy Cerere
Parque Nacional Cahuita
Puerto Vargas
Refugio Nacional de Vida Silvestre Gandoca-Manzanillo
Punta Pirikiki
Puerto Viejo
Manzanillo
Gandoca
PANAMA
Sixaola

10 km
10 miles

Around Puerto Viejo

There are a number of popular beaches southeast along the road from Puerto Viejo. Traffic is limited, buses occasional, but it is walkable. About 4 km away is **Playa Cocles** which has some of the best surfing on this coast, and 2 km further on is **Playa Chiquita** with many places to stay. Next is **Punta Uva**, beyond which, after another 5 km, you arrive in **Manzanillo**, followed by white-sand beaches and rocky headlands to **Punta Mona** and the **Gandoca-Manzanillo Wildlife Refuge** ⓘ *ANAI, T2224-6090*, a celebration of Costa Rican diversity largely left alone by prospectors and tourists alike. Among other projects, marine scientists are studying protecting the giant leatherback turtle. Volunteer work is possible.

Bribri

At **Hotel Creek**, north of Puerto Viejo, the paved road heads through the hills to the village of Bribri, at the foot of the Talamanca Range Indigenous Reserve. Halfway between is **Violeta's Pulpería**. From Limón, **Aerovías Talamaqueñas Indígenas** fly cheaply to **Amubri** in the reserve (there is a *casa de huéspedes* run by nuns in Amubri). Villages such as Bribri, Chase, Bratsi, Shiroles and San José Cabécar can be reached by bus from Cahuita. Several buses daily to Bribri from Limón. Continuing south is Sixaola, on the border with Panama (see page 187).

◉ San José to the Caribbean listings

For Sleeping and Eating price codes, and other relevant information, see pages 43-46.

◉ Sleeping

Puerto Viejo de Sarapiquí *p180*
AL Selva Verde Lodge, out of town, heading west a few km towards La Virgen, T2766-6800, www.holbrooktravel.com. On over 200 ha of virgin rainforest reserve, 40 double rooms, 5 bungalows for 4, includes meals, caters mainly for tour groups. Sensitively set in amongst the rainforest, evening lectures by biologists, excellent for birdwatchers and naturalists with extensive trail system, rafting, canoeing and riding through property; tours with biologists organized.
AL-B El Gavilán Lodge, on the southern bank of the Río Sarapiquí, reached by taxi, T2234-9507, www.gavilanlodge.com. Includes breakfast, set in 100-ha private reserve by the river pier, good restaurant, good jungle paths, riding and river tours, 12 rooms private bath, garden jacuzzi, special group and student/reseacher rates, day trips and overnight trips from San José.
A El Bambú, in centre north of park, T2766-6359, www.elbambu.com. Bath, fan, TV, pool, gym, including breakfast, very nice.
B Posada Andrea Cristina, just out of town near the main road junction, T2766-6265, www.andreacristina.com. Comfortable small cabins, set amongst tropical gardens. Good local knowledge.

C Mi Lindo Sarapiquí, overlooking park, T2766-6074. Has 6 spotless rooms with bath, fan, hot water and restaurant downstairs. Recommended.
E Cabinas Monteverde, next to **El Bambú**, T2766-6236. Bath, restaurant, but pretty dirty.
E Hospedaje Gonar, on road to the dock above hardware store without signpost, T8844-4677. Basic rooms, ones with windows slightly better. Shared bath, pretty dirty.

Las Horquetas de Sarapiquí *p180*
AL River-Edge Cabin and **Waterfall Lodge**, T2764-3131, www.rara-avis.com. Accommodation at Rara Avis, the Lodge is beautiful 8-room jungle lodge in an idyllic setting, the Cabin is deeper in the rainforest for even more seclusion. There is also treetop accommodation and rates for backpackers at the **Las Casitas**.

Guápiles, Guácimo and Siquirres *p180*
A Casa Río Blanco, Guápiles, about 6 km west of Guápiles look out for the big yellow road sign on, take first right before the Río Blanco bridge and follow signpost for 1 km, T2710-4124, www.casarioblanco.com. Accommodates 12 guests in comfortable cabins, with breakfast, run by Herbie and Annette from Amsterdam. Beautiful gardens and a great spot for people interested in the environment. Recommended.
B Río Palmas, Guácimo, 1 km past EARTH School, T2760-0330. Has 30 rooms, private bathroom, pool, restaurant. The 200-ha

property includes ornamental plant farm and rainforest.

C Cabinas Car, Guápiles, 50 m west of church, T2710-0035. Has 10 clean, tidy rooms, with private bath, hot water, fan and TV.

C Centro Turístico Pacuare, Siquirres, T2768-6482. Renovated, with large pool.

C Centro Turístico Río Blanco, Guápiles, on main road at entrance to town, T2710-7857. With bath, fan. Recommended.

D Alcema, Siquirres, 50 m east of market, T2768-6004. Some dark rooms, with fan, clean, shared bath.

D Cabinas de Oro, Guápiles, northeast of bus terminal, T2710-6663. Clean rooms, private bath with hot water, cheaper without. Restaurant nearby.

D Don Quito, 3.5 km towards Siquirres, T2768-8533. Pleasant, good restaurant.

E Hotel Alfaro (El Túnel), Guápiles, 50 m west of bus terminal, T2710-6293. Simple rooms, no frills, but clean. Open 24 hrs, with a rather funky aluminium stairway. Good value.

Puerto Limón *p181, map p181*
Beware of theft at night, and remember it is a port; there are a lot of drunks roaming the streets.

A-B Park, Av 3, Calle 1-2, T2798-0555. Neat little hotel with 34 rooms, sea facing rooms, quiet and cool, restaurant good.

B-C Acón, on corner of main square, Calle 3, Av 3, T2758-1010. Big rooms with private bath, a/c, clean, safe, good restaurant, a bit run-down, popular daily disco **Aquarius** except Mon.

B-C Caribe, facing Parque Vargas, Av 2, Calle 1-2, T2758-0138. Big, immaculate rooms with private bath, hot water and big fan. Good deal.

C-D Miami, next to **King** on Av 2, Calle 4-5, T2758-0490. Has 35 rooms, all with private bath, some with a/c, others with fans. Secure and efficient. Credit cards accepted.

C-D Tete, 1 block west of main square, Av 3, Calle 4-5, T2758-1122. Clean bright rooms, good beds. Some rooms sleeping up to 6 and some with balconies overlooking the square.

D Palace, 1 block north of bus stops, Calle 2-3, Av 2. Family-run hotel, with 33 mostly big rooms. Pretty clean, balcony overlooking street, popular with travellers and good place to make up groups for Tortuguero.

D-E International, opposite the **Continental**, Av 5, Calle 2-3, T2758-0434. Private bath, some with a/c other with fan, good deal.

E Continental, a little north of the centre, Av 5, Calle 2-3, T2798-0532. Has 25 big, good and clean rooms with ceiling fans.

E King, next to post office near main square on Av 2, T2758-1033. Simple rooms, pretty dark, but clean and secure.

F Hotel Wilson, on street west of main square, Av 3, Calle 4-5, T2758-5028. Clean, tidy and central, OK.

F Ng, Calle 4, Av 5-6, T2758-2134. Has 15 basic rooms some with bath, cheaper without. Basic and a bit untidy, but friendly. Price per person. Good for the price.

F Paraíso, Av 2, Calle 4-5. Plyboard partitions divide a once-beautiful house into tiny, dark, box rooms. Hard core roughing it and a little sad.

Parque Nacional Tortuguero *p183*
Top-end hotels normally target package deals; walk-in rates given where available. There are many cheap cabañas in town; the boatmen or villagers will help you find them. Staying in town is better for the truly local economy.

In town
B Casa Marbella, in front of the Catholic church, T2709-8011, http://casamarbella. tripod.com. B&B with 4 small rooms, with private bath. Run by local guide Daryl Loth. Good source of information and in centre of village.

B Miss Junie's, T2709-8102. Has 12 good cabins at the north end of town.

D Cabinas Tortuguero, T2709-8114, tinamon@racsa.co.cr. 5 little cabins, each sleeping 3 with private bath, pleasant little garden with hammocks. Nice spot.

D Yoruki Lodge, T2709-8068. Clean, simple rooms looking over the river.

D-E Cabinas Sabina's, T2709-8069. Winding down, the end of an era, with just 16 rooms remaining. Good views looking out over to the Caribbean.

D-E Mary Scar, T2711-0671. Basic stuff: foam mattresses, but friendly enough if things elsewhere are full.

Out of town

Places out of town, best visited as part of a package, include:

LL Jungle Lodge Hotel, north end of the lagoon, T2233-0133, www.grupopapagayo. com. 50 big, wooden panelled rooms, complete with pool, wet bar, games room and disco.

L Tortuga Lodge, T2257-0766 (San José), www.costaricaexpeditions.com. Price per person includes meals. Very comfortable accommodation, in big rooms each with veranda or balcony.

AL Mawamba Lodge, T2293-8181, www.grupomawamba.com. Comfortable cabins with fans, pool, walking distance to town. Turtle beaches are behind property.

AL Pachira Lodge, across the canal from the town, T2223-1682, www.pachiralodge. com. 3-day/2-night package includes transport, food, tours with bilingual guide, US$269.

AL Turtle Beach Lodge, T2248-0707, www.turtlebeachlodge.com. 2- to 7-day packages from US$210 in 48 ha of beautifully landscaped tropical grounds.

A Laguna Lodge, T2225-3740, www.laguna tortuguero.com. 50-odd cabins, with bath and fan, restaurant, bar, beautiful gardens, pool and conference room.

B Caribbean Paradise, 1 channel back from Tortuguero, T2223-0238 (difficult to reach, try going direct when you arrive). Run by Tico Carlos and his wife Ana, includes 3 meals. 16 simple rooms, no set itinerary, personal service, activities as you want them. A refreshing change from the general offering and very enjoyable.

B El Manati, T2534-7256. Tico family-run, simple rooms with a terrace. Relaxing spot, work with Ecole Travel in San José. Price includes breakfast, good value.

B-E Tortuguero Caribe Lodge, near **Ilan Ilan**, T2385-4676. Offers 10 simple cabins, friendly Tico-run and owned. Book direct or as package through **Ecole Travel** in San José. More expensive price includes breakfast and dinner.

D Ilan Ilan, through the **Agencia Mitur** in San José, T2296-7378, www.ilan-ilan lodge.com. All-inclusive packages, simple rooms in a line, with small terrace. Pool, jacuzzi and riverside bar. 2-day pacakage US$160. Recommended.

F Caño Palma Biological Station, 6 km north of Tortuguero, administered by the **Canadian Organization for Tropical Education and Rainforest Conservation** (in Canada T905-683-2116). Basic rooms for volunteer staff. Price per person, includes meals. A good place for serious naturalists or just for unwinding, accommodation for up to 16 in wooden cabin, freshwater well for drinking and washing. Minimum stay 2 weeks.

Camping

You can sometimes camp at the national park office for US$2.50.

Barra del Colorado p183

L Silver King Lodge, T2711-0708, www.silverkinglodge.com. Price per person. Deluxe sport-fishing hotel, 5-night packages includes flights, meals, rooms with bath, a/c, hot water, pool.

D Tarponland Lodge, T2710-2141. Cabins, run by Guillermo Cunningham, very knowledgeable and helpful. If you have a tent you may be able to camp at **Soda La Fiesta**, lots of mosquitoes.

Penshurst p184

AL Los Aviarios del Caribe, 30 km south of Limón just north of Penshurst, T2750-0775, www.ogphoto.com/aviarios. A sloth rescue sanctuary with a small nature reserve. The friendly owners offer canoe trips in the Estrella river delta and there's a volunteer programme if you have time to spare. They also have a number of comfortable rooms. Recommended.

AL Selva Bananita Lodge, 20 km from Puerto Limón at Cerro Mochila heading inland at Bananito, T2253-8118, www.selva bananito.com. 7 cabins on secluded farm, solar heating, primary rainforest tours, tree climbing, horses and bikes to rent.

Cahuita and Parque Nacional Cahuita
p185, map p184

Beware of theft on the beach, and drug pushers who may be undercover police.

L-AL El Pizote Lodge, Playa Negra, T2750-0227/0088. Rooms, bungalows and fully equipped houses in private gardens. Nice family feel, swimming pool.

L-A La Diosa, Playa Grande, past Playa Negra, T2755-0055, www.hotelladiosa.net. Colourful bungalows with luxury jacuzzi, a/c, private hot water bath, hammocks, pool, gym, massage, games room, internet, surf/kayak equipment – all this and on the beach – cheaper out of season.

AL La Casa de las Flores, Cahuita, T2755-0326, www.lacasadelasflores hotel.com. Centrally located, this Italian-run hotel is brand new, modern and very clean, however the black and white minimalism is quite harsh in the bedrooms.

AL Magellan Inn, 2 km north of Cahuita, T2755-0035, www.magellaninn.com. Includes breakfast, 6 beautifully decorated rooms with bath and fan, and 10,000-year-old pool (honestly) set in peaceful gardens and with renowned French Creole restaurant.

AL-A Bunglalows Malu, Playa Negra, T2755-0114. Extremely well-built bungalows in manicured gardens, a/c, private bath, hot water, one with kitchen. Swimming pool and jacuzzi for guests, bar and breakfast.

AL-A El Encanto Bed and Breakfast Inn, Playa Negra, T2755-0113, www.elencantobed andbreakfast.com. Attractive place built by

very stylish French owners, among shady gardens with pool. 3 bungalows with private bath, hot water, fan, mosquito net, terrace and hammocks and 1 3-bedroom apartment. Yoga and massage are available.

AL-C Kayas Place, Playa Negra, T2750-0690, www.kayasplace.com. Beautifully hand built with reclaimed wood, each room is a little different and accommodation ranges from simple to more luxurious cabinas. Opposite the beach, a nice chilled spot.

A Resort style Atlántida Lodge, Playa Negra, north of Cahuita, main road, T755- 0115. With private bath and ceiling fan. Pleasant gardens, pool, jacuzzi, massage, safe parking for cars and motorcycles. Bar and restaurant onsite.

A-B Bungalows Aché, by the entrance to the national park, T2755-0119, www.bunga lowsache.com. A little off the beaten track in a very tranquil and attractive location. Well-kept bungalows with private hot water bath, mosquito nets, coffee maker, fridge and hammocks, friendly owners.

A-B Chimuri Beach Cottages and **Jungle Lodge**, Playa Negra, T2750-0119, www.green coast.com/chimuri.htm. Rustic, painted wooden cottages in private gardens, close to the beach. Cottages sleep 1-4 and all have fully equipped kitchens. Owners can organize tour to the Kekoldi Indigenous Reserve and birdwatching tours in their own reserve.

A-C Jardín Tropical and Cabinas Mambo, Playa Negra, north of Cahuita, T2755-0033, jardintropical@racsa.co.cr. 2 decent bunga-lows sleeping 2-4, or a house with kitchen for 5. Poison dart frogs in the gardens.

B Kelly Creek, within a couple of blocks of the centre of town, by entrance to national park, T2755-0007, kellycr@racsa.co.cr. Large rooms with veranda, ceiling fan to assist fresh sea breezes, good service and great spot.

B-C Cabinas Iguana, 800 m north of Cahuita, T2755-0005, www.cabinas-iguana.com. Swiss-owned, very friendly, cabins or houses to rent, kitchen, fan, mosquito netting, balcony, clean, waterfall-fed pool, nice location. Big 2-for-1 book swap. Very good value. Recommended.

C Cabinas Palmar, down a little road from the bus stop which goes straight to the seafront, T2755-0243. Tico-run, clean, good, friendly and very helpful. Internet café.

C Cabinas Tito, Playa Negra, north of Cahuita, T2755-0286. Clean, quiet cabins sleeping 2-3, good for families, good value.

C Jenny's Cabinas, heading to the beach, T2755-0256. Balconies with view, Canadian owned, bath, fan, breakfast available, running water, close to the sea but surrounding area a bit scruffy.

C Spencer Seaside Lodging, on beach close to **Jenny's Cabinas**, T2755-0027. Beachfront basic rooms, internet, community kitchen. Price per person.

C-D Cabinas Atlantic Surf, south end of town near the beach, T2755-0116. Wooden hotel with communal balconies and hammocks and relaxed vibe. Rooms come with private hot water bath, fan and mosquito nets.

C-D Centro Turístico Brigitte's, Playa Negra, north of Cahuita, down a small track, T2755-0053, www.brigittecahuita.com. Friendly, quiet, Swiss-run, good restaurant, wildlife, 2 small cabins sleeping 2 – one with kitchen, excellent local information, internet, laundry service, bike rentals, horse riding and many different tours. Recommended.

C-D Hotel National Park, opposite **Kelly Creek**, by entrance to national park, T2755-0244. Bright rooms, fan, just about friendly but the beach front restaurant makes it a good spot.

C-D Reggae Rest and Cabinas, near **Chao's Paradise** in Play Negra, T2755-0515. Basic cabinas all with private bath in nice location by the beach.

C-D Restaurant and Bungalows Bluspirit, just out of town on the road to Playa Negra. Gorgeous split-level bungalows with private bath, hot water and hammocks, by the beach. Run by a very friendly couple who also serve fresh fish and Italian home-cooked meals in their bar and restaurant.

C-D Safari Ocean View, towards Play Negra, T2755-0393. 5 decent cabinas with private bath and hot water, also terrace and hammocks, great location a short amble to the shore and good value for the price.

D Cabinas Belo Horizonte, Playa Negra, north of Cahuita, T2755-0206. A couple of good rooms, quite simple but on the beach, rent for US$200 per month or US$20 per day.

D Cabinas Mina, main street. Very friendly owners offer very basic rooms with private bath and cold water.

D Cabinas Nirvana, towards Playa Negra, T2755-0110, nirvana99@racsa.co.cr. Wooden rooms in a very tranquil spot, hot water private bath, swimming pool in gardens.

D Cabinas Safari, opposite **Cabinas Palmar**, T2755-0405. Simple rooms with fan and shared bath and hot water, friendly owner Wayne Palmer, clean, price per person, good value.

D Cabinas Surf Side, facing the school, T2755-0246. Clean, good value. Parking.

D Coco Congo, Playa Negra, T2750-0652. Rather overpriced rooms which are dark and tatty, but pleasant owners, in front of beach, restaurant on site, 5-min walk to town.

D New Cabinas Arrecife, right on the coast close to **Miss Edith's**, T2755-0081. OK rooms, but great spot and view from restaurant.

D Sol y Mar, on the road to parque nacional, T2755-0237. Friendly owners have rooms that sleep 2-6 people, with private hot-water bath. Rooms are a little tatty, but fine and some very spacious. Their local restaurant is good for breakfast.

D Vaz Cabañas, towards the park entrance, T2755-0218. Friendly, cold shower, some fans, quite clean, good restaurant, safe parking. Recommended. Same owners have now opened more cabañas (**C**), under the same name, in front of the bus station. Clean and bright with private hot water showers.

D Villa Delmar, close to national park entrance, T2755-0392. Rooms with private shower, cold and hot water. Bicycle rental, laundry service and parking.

D-E Bobo Shanti, around the corner from **Cabinas Safari**. Colourfully painted in red, green and gold, a rasta-relax. Rooms have private bath, hot and cold water. Chilled vibes.

D-E Cabinas Margarita, Playa Negra, north of Cahuita, down a 200-m path, T2755-0205. Simple rooms, quiet spot, nice atmosphere, clean.

Camping

It's possible to camp in Cahuita National Park. **Kontiki**, near Playa Negra, T2755-0261. With laundry, showers and toilets, also a few cabins. **Colibrís Paradise**, out of village close to Playa Negra.

Puerto Viejo de Talamanca *p186, map p186* Discounts are often available May-Nov.

L-AL Samasati Lodge & Retreat Center, near Hone Creek on junction halfway between Cahuita and Puerto Viejo, T2750-0315, www.samasati.com. Beautiful mountain location with 100-ha reserve, vegetarian restaurant, meditation courses, reservation recommended.

AL-A Cabinas Los Almendros (see map), T2750-0235, flchwg@racsa.co.cr. 3 fully equipped apartments and a complex of conventional rooms with private hot water bath, a/c and cable TV in the more expensive ones. None of the Caribbean charm but good facilities, especially for families. Cash exchange, credit card advances, tour advice, good, friendly service.

A Escape Caribeño, 500 m along road to Punta Uva, T2750-0103. German-run, well-furnished cottages, fully equipped, some a/c.

A Lizard King, out of town, heading north, T2750-0614/0630. Smart cabinas located upstairs at their Mexican restaurant, not always open. Swimming pool.

A-B Bungalows Calalú, on the road to Cocles, T2750-0042, www.bungalows calalu.com. Bungalows with and without kitchen, also swimming pool and beautiful butterfly garden in the grounds.

A-B Cabinas Casa Verde, central, T2750-0015, www.cabinascasaverde.com. Comfortable rooms with hammocks, private bath, cracked tile showers in beautiful gardens. A pool and open-air jacuzzi add to the relaxation. The owner collects Central

American poison dart frogs and keeps them in tanks dotted around the grounds; ask to take a look, even if you are not a guest. Very nice owners and staff, recommended.

A-C Cashew Hill, south of town, T2750-0256, www.cashewhilllodge.co.cr. Re-developed in the last few years, although retaining rustic charm. 6 family-orientated rooms, with both private and shared bath, fans and mosquito nets. Set in 1 ha of beautiful gardens on the rolling hills above the town, mirador looks out over the jungle tops to the sea. Yoga massage retreats and classes available. Quiet, very chilled atmosphere.

A-C Coco Loco Lodge, south of town, T2750-0281, www.cocolocolodge.com. Quiet spot in expansive garden south of town, nice thatched wooden and stone cabins, some fully equipped with kitchen and cable TV. Popular. English, German and Spanish spoken.

B Guaraná, opposite **Lulu Berlu Gallery**, T2750-0244, www.hotel guarana.com. Very attractive hotel if a little pricey, well kept. All rooms with private, hot water bath, fans, mosquito nets, private balconies and hammocks. They also have a communal kitchen and parking space.

B Maritza, central, T2750-0003. In cabins, with bath, clean, clean, friendly. Affiliated to International Youth Hostel Association, English spoken. A map in the bar shows all the hotels and cabinas in the area. Highly recommended.

B-C Cabinas David, just out of town past **Lizard King**, T2750-0542, cabinas_david@ yahoo.com. Cabinas with private, hot water shower, individual terrace with hammocks.

B-C Jacaranda, a few blocks back (see map), T2750-0069, www.greencoast.com/ jacaranda.htm. A very relaxed spot away from the beach set in beautiful gardens, with coloured mosaic pathways and private areas to read and relax. Rooms are fixed with colourful throws and side lights, showers are spacious. Very attractive place, hot water throughout, fans, mosquito nets. Communal kitchen. Massages can be booked to take place in a pagoda in their flower garden.

C Cabinas Grant, on the road out of town (see map), T2752-0292. Local ownership, large clean rooms, with private bath and fan. Each with a small terrace. Restaurant upstairs is now a seafood eatery.

C Cabinas Tropical, on the coast, T2750-0283, www.cabinastropical.com. 8 spotless rooms, some with fridges, with good mattresses, private bath and hot water. Pleasant gardens with shaded garden house for relaxing, small bar/café. The German owner, Rolf Blancke, is a tropical biologist and runs tours. Recommended.

C Cabinas Yucca, north of town, T2750-0285. Has 5 cabinas with private hot water showers, good value and great spot, nice beach garden, parking, friendly, German-run.

C Hotel Fortaleza, on main street, T2750-0028. New establishment in the middle of town. Rooms with private hot water bath, not a particularly special building, but fine, clean and a very relaxed friendly atmosphere with communal terrace for watching street life.

C-D Cabinas Dolce Vida, past **Carlos Pool Bar**. Rooms with private showers.

C-D Cabinas Rolando, in the side street behind **Soda Lidia**. Well recommended cabinas, private shower, hot water.

C-D Cabinas Soda Mitchell, close to Soda Lidia. 3 sparkling new rooms sleeping 2-3 people, with private shower and (usually) hot water. Very pleasant owner and quiet out of the way location.

C-D Café Rico, north end of town. Coffee shop with a couple of rooms with private shower and hot water. Very friendly English owner and probably the best coffee in town.

C-D Pura Vida, a few blocks back from the main street (see map),T2750-0002, German-Chilean run, friendly, very clean, hammocks. Sadly lacking in character but recommended.

C-E Puerto Viejo, just off the main street (see map), T2750-0620. Great management make the place the most chilled in town. 78 beds in basic rooms sleep 1 to 5, 3 have private hot-water bath, the rest are shared hot and cold water showers. There is a communal kitchen and large areas to eat,

chat and be social. 1 fully equipped apartment for monthly rental (approx US$500). Owners are all surfers and they offer board rental, buy and sell, also wave info. Scooter rental available. Popular with surfers.

C-F Las Olas Camping and Cabinas, next to **Salsa Brava Restaurant**. Basic for the price – camping from US$6, rooms from US$25 – rooms with private bath and hot water, but great spot on the beach and friendly local owners. Showers and toilet facilities for campers.

D Bull Inn, first left after new **Harbor Supermarket**. Locally owned, very clean and bright rooms with private bath, hot water, and a communal balcony.

D Los Sueños, main steret (on map), T2750-0369, www.costaricaguide.info/lossuenos.htm. Laid-back and very relaxing, just 4 colourful and bright rooms.

D-E Cabinas Popular, opposite the back entrance of **Casa Verde**. Nicely located at the back of the town – very peaceful with rural backdrop – rather basic rooms and a little dark, but extremely good value, private shower, but cold water.

D-F Rocking J's, on the beach out of town, towards Cocles, T2750-0657, www.rocking js.com. A sprawling multi-coloured campers' paradise. Huge covered hammock hotel and area for tents – bring your own or rent one of theirs. They also have a 'tree house' room, with double bed under a retractable ceiling so you can watch the stars, also a music system and fridge (you need never come down) and the 'King Suite', an open-sided, colourful room, with private bath. Coloured mosaic murals, communal kitchen, toilets and restaurant, all done by guests. They also offer kayak, surfboard and bike rentals, and the occasional full moon party.

E Cabinas Lika, southern end of town (see map). Friendly back backers set up with private rooms, dorms and hammocks, shared kitchen and laid-back vibe.

E Cabañas Yoli, 250 m from bus stop. Clean, basic, fan, OK – one of the last Tico-owned places.

E Hotel Oro, central, T2750-0469. Budget rooms with private shower.

E Sol y Sombre, at entrance to town, with the style of the French. 5 clean rooms, with fan and mosquito nets. Small restaurant downstairs.

F Cabinas Salsa Brava, popular with surfers.

F Tamandua Lodge, behind **Cabinas Dolce Vida**. Very basic budget accommodation, with shared rooms, shared bathroom and shared kitchen.

Around Puerto Viejo p187

LL-A Aguas Claras, 4.5 km from Puerto Viejo on road to Manzanillo, T2750-0131, www.aguasclaras-cr.com. 5 beautiful cottages each painted a different colour with pretty white wooden gables and balconies. All fully equipped and very close to the beach. **Restaurant Miss Holly** serves gourmet breakfast and lunch. Recommended.

L Tree House Lodge, Punta Uva, T2750-0706, www.costaricatreehouse.com. Dutch owner Edsart has 3 apartments – 2 of which are the most unusual in Costa Rica: the treehouse and the beach suite (there is also a beach house). All are fully equipped with kitchen facilities and hot water, and all are equally luxurious.

L-AL Shawandha, Playa Chiquita, T2750-0018, www.shawandhalodge.com. Beautiful bungalows in the jungle with a calm and private feel and fantastic mosaic showers. Massages now available. Very stylish restaurant serving French Caribbean fusion, pricey.

AL Hotel Kasha, Playa Chiquita, T2750-0205, www.costarica-hotelkasha.com. 14 bungalows in lush gardens on the beach, beautiful pool, jacuzzi and restaurant.

AL Hotel Las Palmas, Playa Uva, T2759-0303, www.laspalmashotel.com. Cabins, 26 rooms, pool, snorkelling, rainforest, tours, transport from San José on Wed, Fri, Sun, US$30 return, US$20 one way.

AL-A Banana Azul Guest House, Playa Negra, T2750-2035, toll free T1-800-821-5352, www.bananaazul.com. New accommodation offering neat and comfortable rooms with private bath as well as beach houses. Breakfast included.

AL-A Cariblue Bungalows, Playa Cocles, T2750-0035, www.cariblue.com. Nice natural complex with palm roofs, set in beautiful garden. Restaurant and bar on site along with a games room and library.

A Almonds and Corals Tent Camp, Playa Uva, T2272-2024, www.almondsandcorals.com. Luxury camping with bath and hot water in tents on platforms in the forest, pool, restaurant, trips arranged to Punta Mona, snorkelling, bike hire, breakfast and dinner included. Sleeping in the wild, with some comfort thrown in.

A Playa Chiquita Lodge, Playa Chiquita, T2750-0408, www.playachiquitalodge.com. The lodge labels itself a beach jungle hotel and that's exactly what it feels like. They have 11 rooms and 3 houses (monthly rentals accepted) all with hot water, hammocks and plenty of space, easy beach access and breakfast included.

A Totem Cabinas, Playa Cocles, T2750-0758, www.totemsite.com. Surf-orientated hotel heavy on the bamboo furniture. Luxury rooms with lounge areas, private shower, hot water, cable TV and private balconies overlooking Playa Cocles. Italian bar and restaurant, internet room and swimming pool. Surf board rental and surf and Kite school.

A-B La Costa de Papito, Playa Cocles, T2750-0080, www.lacostadepapito.com. 11 beautifully designed bungalows with all the style you'd expect from Eddie Ryan (**Carlton Arms Hotel**, New York). Rooms with fan and bath. Great owners who love to make their guests happy, recommended. **Costa de Papito** now host **Pure Jungle Spa**, T2750-0536, www.purejunglespa.com, Tue-Sat, or by appointment. Treatments are organic and handmade and sound good enough to eat … They range from chocolate facials to banana body wraps.

A-B Miraflores Lodge and Restaurant, Playa Chiquita, T2750-0038, www.miraflores lodge.com. 10 rooms (2 with kitchen), a/c, breakfast included, with bath, fan, gardens, lots of wildlife. English and French spoken. Cheaper rates in low season.

B Azania, Playa Cocles, T2750-0540, www. azania-costarica.com. Beautiful thatched-roof bungalows with great facilities in garden setting, restaurant, pool and jacuzzi, parking.

B Cabinas Pangea, Manzanillo, behind **Aquamor**, T2759-9012, www.greencoast. com/aquamor.htm. 2 nice rooms with bath, also house on beach with kitchen.

C-D Cabinas Something Different, T2759-9014, Manzanillo. 10 very clean rooms, 6 with a/c, all with private bath and hot water, parking area and kitchen available, nice local people.

E Cabinas Las Veraneras, Manzanillo. Rooms with shared bath.

E Cabinas/Restaurant Maxi, Manzanillo, T2754-2266. Basic rooms, highly respected seafood restaurant.

E Selvin Cabins and restaurant, Playa Uva. With room and dormitory accommodation.

● Eating

Puerto Limón *p181, map p181*
Cheap food is available in and around the Central Market. *Casados* in market in the day, outside it at night, good, cheap food. Try *pan bon*, spicy bread from Creole recipe, sold near bus stop for San José.

†† Springfield, north of town opposite the hospital. Stylish with a mix of Tico and international dishes. Best restaurant in town.

†† Antillita, Calle 6, Av 4-5. Caribbean rice and beans, meat, open evenings only.

†† Brisas del Caribe, facing Parque Vargas, Av 2, Calle 1, T2758-0138. Cheap noodles, meat, seafood, and good service.

†† Marisquería El Cevichito, Av 2, Calle 1-2, T2758-1380. Good fish, steaks and *ceviche* and good spot for people-watching.

†† Monte de Oro, Av 4, Calle 3-4. Serves good local dishes, in a rough and ready atmosphere.

†† Park Hotel, Av 3, Calle 1-2. Does good meals overlooking the sea.

†† Sabor Pizza, corner of Av 3 and Calle 4. Good pizza.

† Soda Yans, Av 2, Calle 5-6. Popular spot.

† Diplo's, Av 6, Calle 5-6. The best, and cheapest, Caribbean food in town.

† Doña Toda, near market on main square. Good.

† Milk Bar La Negra Mendoza, at the central market. Good milk shakes and snacks.

† Samkirson, Calle 3, Av 3-4. One of several Chinese restaurants. Good value.

† Soda Mares, overlooking market square, daily 0700-1400. Good food.

Parque Nacional Tortuguero *p183*
†† Café Caoba, Tortuguero village. Cheap and has excellent pizza, sandwiches and shrimp.

†† Miss Junie's, north end of Tortuguero village. Very popular, has good local dishes, reservation necessary.

†† The Vine, Tortuguero village. Pizzas and sandwiches.

† El Dolar, Tortuguero village. Simple restaurant, small menu, good *casado*.

† Restaurant El Muellecito, Tortuguero village, T2710-6716. Also 3 simple cabins.

Cahuita and Parque Nacional Cahuita *p185, map p184*
If the catch is good restaurants have lobster.

††† La Casa Creole, Playa Negra, by the **Magellan Inn**, 2 km north of Cahuita, T2755-0104 (for reservations). Mon-Sat 0600-0900. A culinary feast of French and Creole creations, from US$8. Recommended.

†† Cha Cha Cha, Cahuita, T2755-0191. Opens at 1700, closed Mon International menu, great food and service, refreshing chic decor, very good pasta from US$4.

†† Chao's Paradise, T2755-0421, Playa Negra. Typical Caribbean food and seafood specials, good little reggae bar, with oropendula nests overlooking the beach.

†† Coral Reef, next to **Coco's Bar**, Cahuita. Very accommodating management can cook to your tastes, great local food with seafood specialties.

†† Mango Tango Pizzeria, Cahuita. Great home-made pasta with a wide variety of

Italian sauces, quite a rarity in these parts, good pizza, good restaurant.

Miss Edith's, Cahuita, T2755-0248. Open daily until 2130. Almost legendary. Delicious Caribbean and vegetarian food, nice people, good value, no alcohol licence, take your own, many recommendations for breakfast and dinner, but don't expect quick service.

Pizz n' Love, Cahuita, Excellent new restaurant run by a Dutch hippy, pizzas named after celebrities with loads of good toppings such as ricotta, parmesan and ginger prawns, served on tables painted with slogans such as 'give pizza a chance'. Recommended.

Restaurant Banana, top of Playa Negra. A good restaurant and bar away from the crowds. Recommended.

Restaurant & Marisqueria Tio Cayman, Cahuita. Serves fish and seafood.

Restaurant Palenque Luisa, Cahuita. Has the distinctly tropical feel with split-bamboo walls, sand floors and a good *menú típico*.

Restaurant Relax, Cahuita, over **Rikki's Bar**. Fantastic pizzas, pastas, some Mexican and fish, good Italian wines.

Sobre las Olas, Playa Negra, T2755-0109. Closed Tue. On the beach serving Tico and Italian, popular bar in the evening.

Sol y Mar, Cahuita. Open 0730-1200, 1630-2000, need to arrive early and wait at least 45 mins for food. Red snapper and volcano potato especially wicked, US$5; also good breakfasts, try cheese, egg and tomato sandwich, US$2. Good value.

100% Natural Coffee Shop, Cahuita. Snacks, tapas and cocktails, and of course, natural coffees. Internet.

The Beach House, Cahuita. Bar and restaurant, cocktails served, laid-back establishment on the high street. Surf lessons and information available.

Rest Le Fe, opposite **Coco's Bar**, Cahuita. Large variety of dishes all centered round rice and beans, good typical food.

Ice Cream Shop, high street, Cahuita. Ice cream and juice kiosk.

The Pastry Shop, Playa Negra, T2755-0275. Delicious breads, brownies and pies.

Soda Priscilla, opposite **Sol y Mar**, Cahuita. Good budget breakfast pinto, eggs and fresh juices.

Puerto Viejo de Talamanca *p186, map p186*

Amimodo, north end of town, overlooking the beach, beyond **Standord's**. Fine Italian restaurant with prices to match. Reputedly fantastic. Weekend Latin nights. Doesn't always come with a smile.

Stanford's, north end of town. Upstairs restaurant has a rather pricey, but good menu in arty surroundings.

Chili Rojo, is east of town, past **Stanfords**. Thai, Eastern and vegetarian food including humous and falafel platters and coconut curries and delicious home-made ice cream.

El Parquecito, facing sea in the centre. Nice breezy atmosphere, specializes in pizza and Italian dishes.

Grant Seafood, main street. New seafood restaurant located over **Cabinas Grant**.

Jammin Juices and Jerk Chicken, by the coast. Roast chicken with a variety of home-made sauces and salsas, also great vegetarian selection, open for breakfast, lunch and early dinners. Recommended.

La Terraza, main street, above **Frutería Ivone**. New Italian. Lovely owner and chef, will cook to your requirements – ravioli, lasagne, pastas and seafood and tiramisu for afters.

Pizzeria Rusticone, 1 block back from main street (see map). Best pizzas in town cooked in original ovens, excellent pastas including home-made ones, all at good prices, recommended.

Salsa Brava, north end of town (see map). Spanish food, closed Sun. Recommended.

Tamara, on main street, T2750-0148. Open 0600-2100. Good local fish dishes, popular all day and packed at weekends.

Bread and Chocolate, centre of town (see map). A breakfast café well-renowned for home baking and the morning menu is filled with good, home-made choices, ranging from eggs, bacon and fresh bread to oatmeal with apple and cinnamon. Breads and cakes, mint and nut brownies and divine chocolate truffles are home-made and the café is well recommended.

₩₩-₩ Hot Rocks, main street. American joint that serves steak, nachos and pizzas, cocktails and beers served in front of cinema-size movie screen – they show 3 films a night, free with dinner or drinks.

₩ Carlos Pool Bar, 1 block from the main street, behind **Pollo Frito**. Locally owned bar that serves cheap and large *casados*, soda included in the price. Pool tables and sometimes a movie showing.

₩ Lidia's Place, south of centre. Good typical food and to-die-for chocolate cake that does not hang round.

₩ Peace and Love Coffee, south end of town. Ex-**Bambú** owners. Italian crew making fantastic home-made breads and pizzas, lasagnas and other mouthwatering delicatessen items at surprisingly reasonable prices.

₩ Pizza Boruca, opposite the church (see map). Best pizza slices in all Costa Rica, cheap and delicious – this man is always busy.

₩ Pollo Frito, north end of town, opposite **Stanford's** (see map). Affectionately named the 'fried chicken place' – no one ever remembers its real name. A late-opening café, perfect for late-night snacking, serves mainly (as you would guess) fried chicken and yucca, but also rice and beans, *casados* and sandwiches.

₩ Red Stripe Café, south end of town, opposite the bus stop (see map). Snacks and smoothies.

₩ Soda Miss Sam, south of the centre, good local food piled high, good value.

₩ Soda Palmer, north end of town (see map). Cheap Chinese food, big plates, nice people.

Cafés and bakeries

Monchies, 2 blocks off the main street (see map). Delicious baked goods.

Pan Pay, beachfront. Good bakery. Also serve great breakfasts: eggs with avocado, fresh bread and tomato salsa, omelettes, pastries, etc. A good place to read the paper and nod at the locals – a very popular spot in the morning.

Around Puerto Viejo *p187*
₩ El Living, Playa Cocles. Pizza, drinks and music, very laid back, and good prices.
₩ La Isla Inn, Playa Cocles. Serves Japanese Caribbean fusion, including sushi, soups, salads, and stir-fry.
₩ Magic Ginger, Hotel Kasha, Playa Chiquita. Restaurant and bar serving gourmet French cooking, seafood specials and exotic salads.
₩ Rest Maxi, Manzanillo. Reggae-style restaurant serving typical Caribbean food and seafood specials.
₩ Aguas Dulce, Playa Cocles. Ice creams, pastries and sandwiches.

❸ Entertainment

Cahuita and Parque Nacional Cahuita *p185, map p184*
Bars and clubs
Coffee Bar, on the shore near **Cabinas Jenny**, is a good reggae spot.
Rikki's Bar and **Cocos Bar** in the centre of Cahuita; the latter is the livelier of the 2 and hosts reggae nights on Fri and live music.

Puerto Viejo de Talamanca *p186, map p186*
Bars and clubs
Puerto Viejo is still lamenting the loss of **Bambu Bar**, which was burnt down in 2005. Puerto probably has the most lively nightlife on Costa Rica's entire Caribbean coast and has always run on an unspoken rota – each bar having a particular night, and this is still (loosely) the case. Various bars have bid for **Bambu's** Mon and Fri reggae nights, which now run between **Sunset Bar** (by the bus stop) and **Baba Yaga** (next to **Hotel Puerto Viejo**). **Sunset** has live events and pool tables, they have also taken over **Jam Night** on Wed (that used to be held at **Tesoro** in Cocles). **Baba Yaga** is smaller and more intimate; and they run the occasional dance music event. **Jhonny's Bar** (or **Mike's Playground**, depending on how local you are – **Jhonny's** is the original) is perhaps the best night now

in town on Thu, Sat and Sun. Right on the beach, with Puerto's reggae/dancehall best. **Stanford's Disco**, tends to be the quietest, despite being one of the originals. **Dubliner Irish Bar** is past Salsa Brava, Don't get too excited, they're apparently often out of Guinness and there's nothing in the way of traditional ale, but there's a flag on the wall and lots of Irish music, so if you fancy something not very tropical. **Bar In and In**, over **Rest Tamara** in the high street is a much more laid-back reggae bar for pre-party drinks and cocktails. There is a small bar at **Café Puerto Viejo**, with olives and expensive cocktails – ambient and chilled music makes a change from the reggae everywhere else.

▲ Activities and tours

Parque Nacional Tortuguero *p183*
Tour operators
Most people visit Tortuguero as part of a 2- or 3-day package tour from San José flying into the airport, or catching an agency bus and boat from Matina. It is possible to travel to Tortuguero independently (see Transport, below). Tours from San José include transport, meals, 2 nights' lodging, guide and boat trips for US$215-330 per person (double occupancy).
Caño Blanco Marina, 2 Av, 1-3 C, San José, T2256-9444 (San José), T2710-0523 (Tortuguero). Runs a daily bus-boat service San José–Tortuguero at 0700, US$50 return, Book in advance – if you miss the boat, there is nothing else in Caño Blanco Marina.
Mawamba, T2223-2421, www.grupoma wamba.com. Minimum 2 people, 3 days/ 2 nights, daily, private launch so you can stop en route, with launch tour of national park included. Accommodation at the very comfortable **Mawamba Lodge**, 3-day/ 2-night package, Tue, Fri, Sun US$330. Other accommodations have very similar packages, with the difference being the level of comfort in the hotel. **Ilan Ilan Lodge**, T2255-3031, www.ilan-ilan

lodge.com is one of the more affordable at US$199 for 2 nights.
OTEC (see page 64) runs 3-day/2-night tours for US$180, with small student discount; a trip to see the turtles in Jul-Sep costs extra. Tours from Puerto Viejo de Sarapiquí, including boat trip to Tortuguero, meals, 2 nights' lodging, guide and transport to San José cost US$275-400 per person (double occupancy). *Riverboat Francesca*, T2226-0986, www.tortuguero canals.com, costs US$195 per person 2 day-1 night trips exploring the canals for exquisite wildlife, sportfishing. Longer packages are also available.

Organizing a package trip from **Puerto Limón** is more difficult. **Viajes Tropicales Laura**, T2795-2410, www.viajestropicales laura.net, have been highly recommended, daily service, open return US$60 if phoned direct, more through travel agencies, pick-up from hotel, will store luggage, lunch provided, excellent for pointing out wildlife on the way. An inclusive 2-day, 1-night package a from Puerto Limón with basic accommodation, turtle-watching trip and transport (no food) costs from US$99 per person.

Guides Several local guides have been recommended, including **Johnny Velázquez; Alberto**, who lives next to Hotel Mary Scar; **Rubén Bananero**, who lives in the last house before you get to the National Park office, sign on pathway, recommended for 4-hr tour at dusk and in the dark; **Chico**, who lives behind Sabina's Cabinas, US$2 per hr, and will take you anywhere in his motor boat; **Ernesto**, who was born in Tortuguero, and has 15 years' experience as a guide, contact him at Tropical Lodge or through his mother, who owns Sabina's Cabinas; **Rafael**, a biologist who speaks Spanish and English (his wife speaks French), and lives 500 m behind Park Rangers' office (ask rangers for directions); he also rents canoes. **Ross Ballard**, a Canadian biologist who can be contacted through Casa Marbella.

Daryl Loth lives locally and runs **Tortuguero Safaris**, T8833-0827, safari@racsa.co.cr. **Barbara Hartung** of **Tinamon Tours**, T2709-8004, www.tinamon tours.de, a biologist who speaks English, German, French and Spanish, is recommended for boat, hiking and turtle tours in Tortuguero (US$5 per person per hr; all-inclusive trips from Limón 3-days, 2-nights, US$135). Both Daryl and Barbara are strong supporters of using **paddle power**, or at most electric motors.

There are several **boats for rent** from Tortuguero, ask at the *pulpería*. The use of polluting 2-stroke motors is outlawed in Tortuguero, and the use of 4-stroke engines is limited to 3 of the 4 main water channels.

Cahuita and Parque Nacional
Cahuita *p185*, map *p184*
Snorkelling equipment and surfboards available for rent. **Horses** can be hired, but try to ensure they are in good shape. **Bicycles** can be hired for about US$7 per day and you can cycle to Puerto Viejo and the Panamanian border through some beautiful scenery.

Tour operators
Wide range of activities available including water sports and nature tours. **Cahuita Tours**, T2755-0232, exotica@ racsa.co.cr, excursions by jeep and glass-bottomed boat tours over the reefs, bike, diving and snorkelling equipment rental, international telephone service (ICE) and Western Union money transfer. **GrayLine** bus travel can be arranged here. **Roberto's Tours**, office located at his restaurant (**Roberto's**) on the main street. Very nice people run all the usual tours of the area including snorkelling and diving. **Willies Tours**, T2755-0267, www.willies-costarica-tours.com. Willie is most helpful and knows everything about Cahuita and surrounding areas. He runs tours to Tortuguero, Panama, Bri Bri indigenous

reserve and whitewater rafting in the Pacuare river. The office is located opposite Restaurant Palenque on the main street, where he also runs an internet café.

Puerto Viejo de Talamanca *p186*, map *p186*
Tour operators
Tours in Puerto Viejo include canopy, snorkelling, boat trips and diving in Cahuita and Manzanillo, trips to an indigenous reserve, rafting in Pacuare, kayaking, birdwatching, etc. **ATEC** is the easiest source of information (www.ateccr.org) and the original provider of information and tours combining ecotourism and conservation but you can also try **Canopy Tour** and **Terraventuras**, T2750- 0750, www.terraventuras.com, **Exploradores Outdoors**, T2750-6262, www.exploradores outdoors.com, **Atlántico Tours**, T2750-0004, offer several trips. **Reef Runner Divers**, T2750-0480, www.reefrunnerdivers.com, Yuppi & Tino, T2750-0621, **Dragon Scooter Rental**, T2750-0728, www.dragonscooter rentals.com in Puerto Viejo, and **Aguamar Adventures**, in Manzanillo, who have been operating since 1993, offer diving courses and local trips. Prices from US$35.

Transport

Puerto Viejo de Sarapiquí *p180*
Bus Buses stop on north side of park. From **San José** 7 daily from Gran Terminal del Caribe, 1½ hrs through PN Braulio Carrillo, or through Heredia, 4 daily, 3½ hrs. From **Cd Quesada**, 5 daily, 2½ hrs.

Car To get there by car from **San José**, after passing through the PN Braulio Carrillo take Route 4, a paved road which turns off near Santa Clara to Puerto Viejo; it bypasses Río Frío and goes via Las Horquetas. A more scenic but longer route leaves from Heredia via San Miguel and La Virgen, and on to Puerto Viejo.

Guápiles, Guácimo and Siquirres *p180*
Bus In Guápiles, buses leave from a central terminal a block to the north of the church. Regular buses to **San José** and **Puerto Limón**. Buses to **Puerto Viejo de Sarapiquí** ever 2½ hrs, and to **Río Frío** every 1½ hrs.

For Siquirres, at least 1 bus per hr leaves Gran Terminal del Caribe in **San José**, 2½-hr journey.

Puerto Limón *p181, map p181*
Bus Town bus service is irregular and crowded. Service from **San José** with **CoopeLimón**, T2233-3646 and **Caribeño**, T2222-0610, at least every hr, 0500-2000, daily. Arrive and depart from Calle 2, Av 1-2, US$3, 2½ hrs. Also services to **Guápiles** and **Siquirres**. From same stop buses to Siquirres/Guápiles, 13 daily, 8 direct. Near Radio Casino on Av 4, Calle 3-4, buses leave for **Sixaola**, first 0500, last 1800, US$2.50, stopping at **Cahuita**, **Puerto Viejo** and **Bri Bri** en route. To **Manzanillo**, at 0600, 1430, returning 1130, 1900, 1½ hrs, US$1.50. To **Moín** from Calle 5, Av 3-4, every 30 mins between 0600-2200.

Parque Nacional Tortuguero *p183*
Air Daily flights from **San José** with **Nature Air** (US$$70).

Bus and boat It is quite possible to travel to Tortuguero independently, but more challenging than the all-inclusive packages. There are a couple of options. From **Limón**, regular vessels leaves from the Tortuguero dock in **Moín**, north of Limón, US$50 return. It is a loosely run cooperative, with boats leaving at 1000. There is also a 1500 service that runs less frequently. If possible, book in advance through the Tortuguero Information Centre (check the times; they change frequently). If you are in a group you may be able to charter a boat for approximately US$200.

From **San José**, the bus/boat combination is the cheapest option and a mini-adventure in itself. Take the 0900 bus to Cariari from the Terminal Gran Caribe,

arriving around 1045. Walk 500 m north to the ticket booth behind the police station where you can buy you bus/boat ticket to Tortuguero. Take the 1200 bus to **La Pavona**, arriving around 1330. Take 1 of the boats to Tortuguero, which will arrive about 1500. The journey is about US$10 1-way. Don't be talked into a package if you're not interested – there are plenty of services to choose from in Tortuguero. The return service leaves at 0830 and 1330 giving you 1 or 2 nights in Tortuguero. (There appears to be an attempt to monopolize this service but for the time being at least, there are a couple of boats in operation.)

Alternative routes include the 1030 bus from San José to Cariari, changing to get the 1400 bus to La Geest and the 1530 boat to Tortuguero. Or 1300 bus San José–Cariari, 1500 bus Cariari to La Pavona, 1630 boat La Pavone to Tortuguero.

It is also possible to take a bus from Siquirres to **Freeman** (unpaved road), a Del Monte banana plantation, from where unscheduled boats go to Tortuguero; ask around at the bank of the Río Pacuare, or call the public phone office in Tortuguero (T2710-6716, open 0730-2000) and ask for **Johnny Velázquez** to come and pick you up, US$57, maximum 4 passengers, 4 hrs. Sometimes heavy rains block the canals, preventing passage there or back. Contact **Willis Rankin** (Apdo 1055, Limón, T2798-1556) an excellent captain who will negotiate rampaging rivers. All riverboats for the major lodges (see below) leave from Hamburgo or Freeman. If the excursion boats have a spare seat you may be allowed on.

Barra del Colorado *p183*
Air Flights to **San José** daily with **Sansa** (US$63).

Boat To **Tortuguero** takes 1½ hr and costs US$50. A motorized canoe can take 8 people and costs up to US$80, 2 hrs. Try and arrive in a group as boats are infrequent.

Cahuita and Parque Nacional
Cahuita *p185, map p184*

Bus Service direct from **San José**'s Terminal del Caribe, to **Cahuita** at 0600, 1000, 1200, 1400 and 1600, return 0700, 0800, 0930, 1130 and 1630, 3½ hrs, US$6.50, T2257-8129, **Trans Mepá**, 4 hrs, US$4.50, and from **Puerto Limón**, in front of Radio Casino, 0500-1800, return 0630-2000, 1 hr, US$0.80, T2758-1572, both continuing to Bribri, and Sixaola (dirt road) on the Panamanian border (US$1, 2 hrs). The bus drops you at the crossing of the 2 main roads in Cahuita.

Penshurst *p184*
Bus Small buses leave **Limón** (Calle 4, Av 6) for **Valle de Estrella/Pandora**, 7 a day from 0500, at 2-hourly intervals, last at 1800, 1½ hrs (returning from Pandora at similar times).

Puerto Viejo de Talamanca *p186, map p186*
Bus Daily services from **San José** from Gran Terminal del Caribe at 0600, 1000, 1200, 1400 and 1600, return at 0730. 0900. 1100 and 1600, 4 hrs, US$7.50; from **Limón** daily from Radio Casino, 0500-1800, return 0600-2000, 1½ hrs; 30 mins from **Cahuita**, US$0.45. To **Manzanillo** at 0700, 1530, 1900, returning 0500, 0830, 1700, ½ hr, US$0.80. To **Sixaola** 5 daily, 0545 until 1845, 2 hrs, US$1.80.

Around Puerto Viejo *p187*
Express bus to **Manzanillo** from Terminal Sixaola, **San José**, daily, 1600, return 0630. From **Limón** daily 0600, 1430, return 1130, 1900, 1½ hrs.

ⓘ Directory

Puerto Limón *p181, map p181*
Banks Usual hours and services, all with ATMs at **Banco de Costa Rica**, Av 2, Calle 1, Mon-Fri 0900-1400; **Banco Nacional**, Av 2, Calle 3, with ATM; **Banco Popular**, Calle 3, Av 1-2, with ATM. **Banco de San José**, Av 3, Calle 3-4, with ATM. **Internet** Edutec

Internet, on 2nd level above Plaza Caribe, US$2.30 per hr. Also 24-hour access at **Internet**, 1 block from Mas X Menos, US$1 per hr. **Laundry** Av 2, Calle 5-6, price per item, not that cheap, but 2-hr turnaround. **Medical services** Red Cross, Calle 3, Av 1-2, T2758-0125. **Hospital**, on road to Moin, T2758-2222. **Post office** Opposite central for international calls at Av 2, Calle 5-6 and at Calle 3, Av 4-5, Mon-Thu 0800-1700, Fri 0800-1600.

Cahuita and Parque Nacional
Cahuita *p185, map p184*

Banks There are none. Money exchange is difficult except occasionally for cash dollars (**Cahuita Tours** changes dollars and TCs). Take plenty of colones from Limón. Nearest banks are is in **Puerto Viejo** and **Bribri** (20 km) but several places accept credit cards. **Internet** Cyberbet, part of Cabinas Safari, US$1.60 per hr. **Willies Tours** has internet, opposite the bus station. **Post office** Next to police station at northern end of town.

Puerto Viejo de Talamanca *p186, map p186*
Banks Banco Nacional is 3 blocks south of ATEC, with ATM machine, but only take Visa or Plus (not MasterCard of Cirrus). The bank in Bribri does accept MasterCard credit card. You can change TCs and cash at **Manuel León's general store** on the beach. **Cabinas Los Almendros** changes TCs, euro and US dollars, and give credit card advance. **Internet** From **ATEC**, US$2.50 per hr. Also **Jungle Café**, fastest internet in town, but pricey and pre-pay cards only. **Books, Librería & Bazar Internet**, also fast, US$2.50 per hr. Internet next to Hot Rocks, slow, but open late. **Medical services** Chemist at the new shopping area by the bank. **Police** On sea front. **Post office** At the new shopping area by the bank. US$2 to send, US$1 to receive, atecmail@racsa.co.cr. **Telephone** There is a public telephone outside the ATEC office.

Contents

Footprint features

Border crossings

Nicaragua–Costa Rica
See pages 207 and 103
Nicaragua–Honduras
See pages 280 and 294

Nicaragua

At a glance

◉ **Getting around** Buses for the Pacific side; flights to reach the Caribbean; boats and ferries for Lake Nicaragua, Corn Islands and Río San Juan.

⏱ **Time required** 2-3 weeks.

☀ **Weather** The wet season, Jun-Dec, is when the Pacific Basin is bright green and it is warm and clear.

✖ **When not to go** The dry season, Feb-May, is very hot. Avoid unless diving or birdwatching.

★ Don't miss ...

1 Isla Ometepe, page 209.
2 Volcanoes, pages 211, 243 and 288.
3 Río San Juan, page 229.
4 Laguna de Apoyo, page 256.
5 Managua, page 259.
6 León, page 289.
7 Autonomous Atlantic Regions, page 302.

Caribbean Sea
HONDURAS
Pacific Ocean
COSTA RICA
Living Creek
Kampa
Cabo Viejo
Tuskru Sirpe
Laguna de Bismuna
Waspám
Leimus
Río Coco
Sandy Bay
Pahra
Auastara
Reserva Biosfera Bosawás
Sangni Laya
Yulu Tingne
Manu Watla
Musawas
Kukalaya
Sahsa
Susun
Puerto Cabezas/Bilwi
Bonanza
El Encanto
La Rosita
Banacruz
Haulover Creek
Siuna
El Empalme
Cordillera Isabela
Saslaya
Wani
Alamikamba
Limbaika
Las Manos
Ocotal
El Garrobo
El Porvenir
Company Creek
Somoto
Condega
Siawás
Sandy Bay Sirpi
El Espino
Estelí
La Cruz de Río Grande
Lago de Apanás
Jinotega
Pauta Dimon
Río Kurinwás
Kara
San Juan de Limay
San Isidro
Río Blanco
Tortuguero
Gulf of Fonseca
Guasaule
Matagalpa
Potosí
Somotillo
Matiguás
Sébaco
Volcán Cosigüina
Puerto Morazán
Ciudad Darío
Laguna de Perlas
Chichigalpa
V Momotombo
Santa Lucía
To Islas de Maíz/Corn Islands
Chinandega
La Libertad
Rama
Sisi
Corinto
León
Lago de Managua
La Gateada
Río Escondido
Bluefields
V Momotombito
Poneloya
Juigalpa
MANAGUA
Masaya
Cara del Moro
Nueva Guinea
Granada
Puerto Díaz
Acoyapa
Isla Zapatera
Diriamba
Pochomil
Jinotepe
Altagracia
La Boquita
Isla Ometepe
Volcán Concepción
Astillero
San Miguelito
Las Salinas
Rivas
Peñas Blancas
Lago de Nicaragua
San Juan del Norte
San Carlos
El Castillo
Islas Solentiname
San Juan del Sur
Los Ciutasos Wildlife Reserve
Río San Juan
N
50 km
50 miles

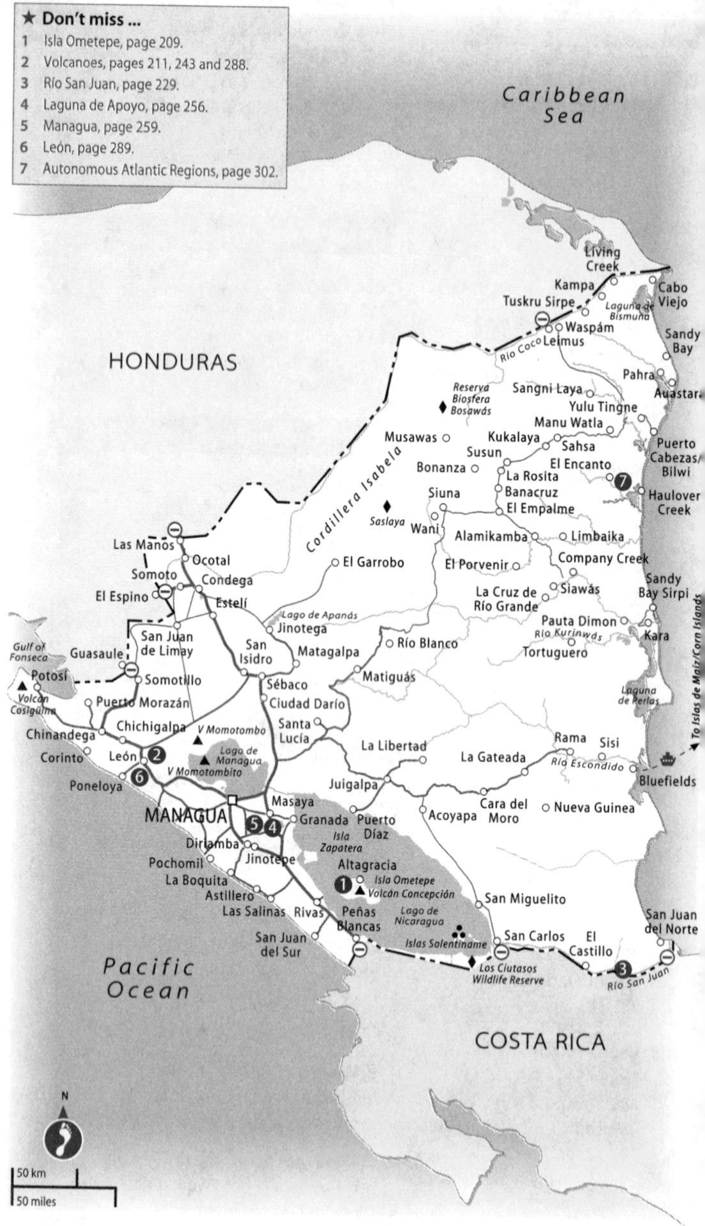

Nicaragua is a nation born out of poetry, fire and indomitable, revolutionary spirit. It is a land of tempestuous geological foundations and equally tempestuous history; a land where great heroism meets wild poetic struggle. The 1979 Sandinista revolution is indelibly etched on the national psyche, and Nicaraguans are living proof that political destiny can be commandeered by the people, in spite of the US government, who sponsored years of counter-revolutionary violence during the notorious Contra War.

Those years of brutal unrest, natural disasters and economic mismanagement have effectively crippled the country's infrastructure. Today, in spite of lasting peace and burgeoning foreign investment, Nicaragua suffers blackouts and water shortages. Many towns lack paved roads, horse and cart are widely used, and wood remains the principal source of fuel. Meanwhile, the ever-rising costs of petrol and staple foods mean the sting of poverty is bound to remain for some time.

Travelling in Nicaragua is a challenging, intensive adventure. It is at once beautiful, inspirational, amusing, saddening, grotesque, and replete with endless anarchic charms. Through it all, the people – eternally decent and good humoured – are the country's finest asset. To the north, you'll find dark, entrancing mountains and an endearing Campo culture irrevocably tied to the land.

To the south, the vigorous Río San Juan courses through verdant rainforest reserves, offering some of the best wildlife viewing in Central America. To the west, the Pacific coast is enticing tourists and foreign investors with its gorgeous, sandy beaches. To the east, a host of less-visited shores possess an English-speaking culture that is more Caribbean than Nicaraguan. Add the fine colonial towns of Granada and León, the magical island of Ometepe, the largest freshwater lake in Central America, remote indigenous villages, mysterious archaeological relics and endless smoking volcanoes, and you have some compelling reasons to visit this captivating country, very much on its way up.

The Rivas Isthmus

For many, their first encounter with Nicaragua is the slender isthmus of Rivas, an exciting region of transition and international activity. Bordering Costa Rica to the south, the isthmus separates the pounding Pacific Ocean from expansive Lake Nicaragua and its serene, rustic islands, including Isla Ometepe – an archetype of volcanic beauty. The Rivas Isthmus is the youngest part of the country, having emerged from the ocean four or five million years ago to fuse North and South America into a single continent. ►► *For listings, see page 208.*

Peñas Blancas to La Virgen

From Costa Rica, the Interamericana enters Nicaragua at the crossing of **Peñas Blancas**, where buses regularly depart to Rivas. The landscape changes dramatically as the rainforest ecosystem meets the tropical dry forests of the Pacific Basin. This stretch of land is rich pasture crossed by numerous streams.

The little windswept village of **La Virgen** has some less-than-clean beaches and a stunning view of the big lake and Ometepe. If you come early in the morning you may see men fishing in the lake while floating in the inner tube of a truck. This curious sight is particular to this small village. The fishermen arrive at the beach in the early morning and blow up the big tyre tubes, tie bait to a thick nylon cord and wade out, seated in the tubes, as far as 3 km from the coast. When they get out of the water, often fully clothed, the cord can have 15 or more fish hanging from it.

Rivas ⬤❶❷❸❹ ►► *p208.*

The capital of the department that carries its name, Rivas is a pleasant city with two beautiful churches, a happy, friendly population and lots of horse-drawn carriages with car tyres, unique to this area. It carries the nickname 'city of mangos' for the trees that grow seemingly everywhere around the city. Founded in 1720 and named after a high-level Spanish diplomat in Guatemala, Rivas was, and still is, a ranching centre. Rivas is a transportation hub and there are frequent bus services from Managua, Granada, San Juan del Sur and the border with Costa Rica at Peñas Blancas. The **tourist office** ① *de Texaco, ½ c abajo, T563-4914, rivas@intur.gob.ni*, has good maps of Nicaragua.

Rivas also has some modest and mildly diverting attractions. **Templo Parroquial de San Pedro** on Parque Central dates from 1863 and is the city's principal church, with a design reminiscent of the cathedral in León. Inside there is a famous fresco depicting the heroic forces of Catholicism defeating a withered Communism in a rather one-sided looking sea battle. **Museo de Antropología e Historia** ① *1½ c norte, Mon-Fri 0900-1200, 1400-1700, Sat 0900-1200, US$1*, has a dwindling, poorly labelled, but precious, collection of archaeological pieces, taxidermic displays and some ecological information. The main attraction is the beautiful old **Hacienda Santa Ursula** in which the museum is housed.

ATC Rivas is famous throughout Nicaragua for the production of finely crafted indigenous drinking cups called *jícaras*, made from the dried, hard case of the fruit that grows on the native *jícaro* tree.

Border essentials: Nicaragua–Costa Rica

Peñas Blancas → See also page 118.

Nicaraguan immigration Opens daily 0800-1200 and 1300-1745. When entering Nicaragua, complete Costa Rican exit formalities and then walk the 500 m to the new border controls. International bus passengers have to disembark and queue for immigration to stamp their passports. Then unload your baggage and wait in a line for the customs official to arrive. You will be asked to open your bags, the official will give them a cursory glance and you reload. Passports and tickets will be checked again back on the bus. If you are not on a bus, there are plenty of helpers on hand. Allow 45 minutes to complete the formalities. You will have to pay US$5-8 to enter Nicaragua plus a US$1 Alcaldía charge. If you arrive Monday-Friday before 0800 or after 1700, or at any time at the weekend, you will have to pay US$12 plus the Alcaldía charge.

When leaving Nicaragua, pay US$1 Alcaldía charge to enter the customs area and then complete formalities where you pay US$2 to have your passport checked Monday-Friday 0800-1700, US$4, 0600-0800 and after 1700, or any time on Saturday and Sunday. Then walk the 500 m to the Costa Rican border and simply have your passport stamped.

Transport Buses to Rivas, every 30 minutes, 0600-1800, US$0.75, 1 hour. From here buses connect to Managua, every 30 minutes, 0330-1800, US$2.50, 2 hours 45 minutes or to Granada, every 45 minutes, 0530-1625, US$2, 1 hour 45 minutes, try to board an express bus from Rivas to your destination. Express buses from Peñas Blancas to Managua, every 30 minutes, 0700-1800, US$3.50, 3½ hours. There can be long waits when international buses are passing through. If you are travelling independently, a good time to cross is around 0900, before the buses arrive.

If crossing by private vehicle, be aware there is no fuel going into Nicaragua until Rivas (37 km). After you have been through Migración, find an inspector who will fill out the preliminary form to be taken to Aduana. At the Vehículo Entrando window, the vehicle permit is typed up and the vehicle stamp is put in your passport. Next, go to Tránsito to pay for the car permit. Finally, ask the inspector to give a final check.

San Jorge 😊😊 ➤➤ p208.

It may seem like an extension of Rivas, but San Jorge is actually a separate town, one that most visitors see only on their way to the ferry for Ometepe. To catch the **ferry**, head east from the roundabout on the highway towards the lake, as far as the Parque Central. Here you will pass the **Iglesia de San Jorge**, a little Gothic-Mudéjar (a mixture of Christian and Muslim architecture from Spain) church, with the ruins of an ancient convent behind. From the church it is two blocks north, then east again all the way to el muelle (the dock). The cross over the road between the highway and the church is known as **La Cruz de España** and, together with a small mural painting and a few plaques, commemorates the fateful arrival of the Spanish.

For Sleeping and Eating price codes and other relevant information, see pages 43-46.

◉ Sleeping

Rivas *p206*
A Nicarao Inn Hotel, Parque Central, 2 c abajo, T563-3836, www.hotelnicaroinn.com.ni. The finest hotel here with 18 tastefully decorated, comfortable rooms, a/c, cable TV and Wi-Fi. Restaurant and bar. Breakfast included.
C Español, behind Iglesia San Pedro, T563-0006. 5 basic rooms, with bath and fan. Restaurant attached.
D Hospedaje Lidia, Texaco, ½ c abajo, near bus stop, T563-3477. 12 rooms, clean, family atmosphere, some with private bath, noisy, helpful, recommended.

San Jorge *p207*
There are a few ultra-cheap *hospedajes* scattered around the port.
B Hotel Dalinky, the port, 200 vrs abajo, T563-4990. Large, clean double rooms with a/c, cable TV and bath. Breakfast included and parking available. There's a handful of cheaper rooms too (**D**).
B Hotel Hamacas, the port, 100 vrs abajo, 25 vrs sur, T563-1709. As the name suggests, lots of hammocks, mostly slung across porches. The rooms are large and clean with a/c and cable TV. Breakfast included. **D** with fan.

❼ Eating

Rivas *p206*
♈♈ **El Mesón**, Iglesia San Francisco, ½ c abajo, T563-4535, Mon-Sat 1100-1500. Very good, try *pollo a la plancha* or *bistec encebollado*.
♈♈ **Rancho Cocteleró Mariscazo**, 800 m south of Rivas stadium on best side of Interamericana. One of the best seafood restaurants in Nicaragua. Simple decor, friendly service, very good value. Highly recommended.

◉ Transport

Rivas *p206*
Bus Express bus to **Managua**, every ½ hr, 0630-1700, US$2.50, 2 hrs. To **Granada**, every 45 mins, 0530-1625, US$2, 1 hr 45 mins. To **Jinotepe**, every ½ hr, 0540-1710, US$1, 1 hr 45 mins. To **San Juan del Sur**, every ½ hr, 0600-1830, US$1, 45 mins. To **Peñas Blancas**, every ½ hr, 0500-1600, US$0.75, 1 hr.

Taxi From centre of Rivas to the dock at **San Jorge**, US$1.50. Beware overcharging.

San Jorge *p207*
Boat To **Ometepe**, 12 daily, 0730-1830, 1 hr, US$2-3. Return journeys 0530-1600. Services are greatly reduced on Sun to 3 daily ferries.

Taxi From San Jorge a road runs from the shore through Rivas to the port of San Juan del Sur. Taxi to **Rivas**, US$1.50 (per person), beware overcharging, *colectivos* US$0.50. Direct from San Jorge to **San Juan del Sur** costs US$15. It is a lot cheaper to take a taxi to Rivas and another one from Rivas to San Juan.

◉ Directory

Rivas *p206*
Banks The plaza has 2 banks: a **Banpro** on the west side, and a **Banco Procredit** with a Visa ATM on the northwest corner. There's also a **BAC** ATM, plaza, 2 c oeste.
Western Union, 1 block from the market, Mon-Fri 0830-1600, Sat 0830-1200.
Internet Gaby Cyber, from bus terminal 5 blocks south, ½ block east, US$1 per hr, Mon-Sat 0800-2000, Sun 0900-1900.
Telephone Enitel is 3 blocks south of Parque Central, or 7 blocks south and 3 blocks east from bus terminal.

Isla Ometepe

The ancient Nahuas of Mexico were delivered to Ometepe by a dream, so the legend goes, after many years of fruitless wandering. Rising from the waters, there is an enchanted, other-worldly feel to the island; her forests and slopes hide mystical secrets, ancient relics and the remnants of long-lost jaguar cults. Two perfectly symmetrical volcanoes comprise this mysterious realm: Concepción is larger, active and periodically spews ash; Maderas is smaller, extinct and swathed in cloudforest. Each evening at dusk, their green slopes erupt with the chattering of exotic birds. Ometepe's pre-Columbian heritage survives in the form of bizarre petroglyphs and a statuary that is testament to a shamanic reverence for animal spirits. The island's inhabitants, descended from these cultures, are mostly fishing and farming communities, and some of Nicaragua's kindest people. This is a fine place for volunteering or learning about organic farming. The rich volcanic soil means agriculture here has always been organic, but a wave of foreigners are introducing more sophisticated, ecologically aware permaculture techniques. Thus far, tourist development has kept within the style and scale of the island, although there are now murmurings of larger, less sympathetic construction projects. Although you can hike, swim, cycle and kayak here, much of Ometepe's pleasure comes from simply lazing in a hammock. ▸▸ *For listings, see pages 216-218.*

Ins and outs

Getting there Boat connections from Granada and San Carlos are possible, but the most user-friendly are the one-hour boats and ferries from San Jorge to Moyogalpa, running almost hourly throughout the day, with reduced services on Sunday. The ferry costs US$2 per person each way; other boats cost US$1.50. The best choice is the ferry, which has three levels, a toilet, snack bar, television (with *telenovelas* blasted through concert speakers over the noise of the motors) and room for six cars. It's worth timing your crossing to use it, both for its facilities and for the great viewing deck, which offers a panoramic view of the lake and islands. If it's a clear day, the Zapatera archipelago is visible to the north, with Volcán Mombacho rising up behind it; on really clear days you'll see the smoke surging out of Volcán Masaya. A *lancha* called the *Mozorola* travels between Altagracia and San Jorge four times a week. If you are prone to seasickness buy Nausil from the *farmacia* before the crossing.

If you have a high-clearance 4WD you may want to take it across on the ferry (US$20 each way). Arrive at least one hour before departure to reserve a spot (if possible call the day before, T278-8190 to make an initial reservation). You will need to fill out some paperwork and buy a boarding ticket for each person travelling. Make sure you reserve your spot as close to the ferry ramp as possible, but leave room for trucks and cars coming off the ferry.

Getting around Taxis (vans and pick-ups) wait for the boat arrivals, as do buses. Most of the island is linked by a bus service, otherwise trucks are used. Walking, cycling or horse riding are the best ways to see the island; however, it can be dusty in the dry season.

Best time to visit The dry season is normally less harsh here, but after February everything is brown. The end of May is a happy, optimistic time, especially for farmers, but there can be a lot of gnats in the air. The rainy season is much prettier as the countryside becomes lush and green. The windy season from November to February can make the ferry crossing unsettling.

Tourist information **Ometepe Expeditions** ① *20 m from the port in Moyogalpa*, are the island's best tour operator and a good source of information. There's usually someone there who speaks English.

Background

Ceramic evidence shows that the island has been inhabited for at least 3500 years, although some believe this figure could be 12,000 years or more. Little is known about the pre-Conquest cultures of the island. From ceramic analysis carried out by US archaeologist Frederick W Lange (published in 1992), it appears the people of 1500 BC came from South America as part of a northern immigration that continued to Mexico. They lived in a settlement in what is today the town of Los Angeles and were followed by waves of settlement to both the western and eastern sides of the island.

Mystery also surrounds the people who inhabited the island at the time of the Conquest. A visiting priest reported in 1586 that the natives of the island spoke a language different from any of those spoken on the mainland. Yet the large basalt statues found on Ometepe appear to be of the same school as the ones found on Zapatera and attributed to the Chorotegas. Dr J F Bransford, a medical officer for a US Navy, came to Nicaragua in 1872 as part of an inter-oceanic exploratory team. His observations (published in 1881 by the Smithsonian Institute) remain one of the few sources of information about this mysterious place. During his digs in 1876 and 1877, near Moyogalpa, he noted that the Concepción volcano was forested to the top and 'extinct' (it would become very much alive five years later) and that the isthmus between the two volcanoes was passable by canoe during the rainy season. The island's population was estimated at 3000, with most living in Altagracia and some 500 others scattered around the island. Most people he described fitted the description of an Ometepino today – basically Chorotega in appearance; however, on the very sparsely populated Maderas side of the island lived a tall people – many of the men were over 6 ft – with decidedly unusual facial features. These people were more suspicious by nature and reluctant to talk or share the location of the big basalt idols of the islands. From this, Bransford concluded that they still worshipped the gods represented in the statues (by contrast, the other inhabitants of the island had happily revealed the location of their statues). There is little evidence of these people today, but their religious statues can be found next to the church in Altagracia and in the National Museum in Managua.

During the colonial period, Ometepe was used as a refuge for pirates, en route to or returning from a pillaging raid on Granada. The bandits would steal food supplies, livestock, even women, forcing some of the population to move inland. During William Walker's occupation of Granada, Moyogalpa was used as a temporary medical field hospital for retreating troops and would-be colonizers, until the local population attacked and they were forced to escape in canoes to the mainland.

In the 1870s the indigenous population rioted against a pact between Conservative and Liberal politicians during local elections. More problems arose in 1908 when *mestizo* migrants from Chontales fought to appropriate 4653 acres of indigenous communal lands that stretched from Urbaite to Maderas. The mainlanders eventually succeeded, but not without a long struggle that was still being fought in 1942, when the indigenous community rioted against the National Guard removing Indians from their land. The riot killed 23 indigenous and three soldiers. However, the island was spared involvement in the bloody battles of the Revolution and the Contra War and for this reason the Ometepinos call their island the 'Oasis of Peace'.

Volcán Concepción and Volcán Maderas

Ometepe's two volcanoes rising out of Lake Nicaragua appear prehistoric and almost other-worldly. The two cones are nature reserves and they are connected by a 5-km wide lava-flow isthmus. The island is always in the shadow of one of its two Olympian volcanic cones. The dominant mountain, one of the most symmetrical cones in the world and covered by 2200 ha of protected forest, is **Volcán Concepción** (1610 m high, 36.5 km wide). It is an active volcano that last blew ash in February 2007 and had its most recent major lava flow in 1957. The volcano was inactive for many years before it burst into life in 1883 with a series of eruptions continuing until 1887. Concepción also erupted from 1908 until 1910, with further significant activity in 1921 and 1948-1972. Thanks to its hot lava outbursts, one of the cone's indigenous names was *Mestlitepe* (mountain that menstruates). The other well-known name is *Choncotecihuatepe* (brother of the moon); an evening moonrise above the volcano is an unforgettable sight.

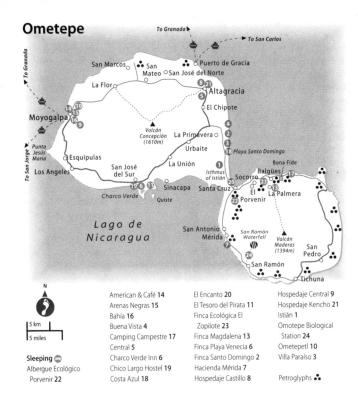

Ometepe

American & Café **14**
Arenas Negras **15**
Bahía **16**
Buena Vista **4**
Camping Campestre **17**
Central **5**
Charco Verde Inn **6**
Chico Largo Hostel **19**
Costa Azul **18**

El Encanto **20**
El Tesoro del Pirata **11**
Finca Ecológica El
Zopilote **23**
Finca Magdalena **13**
Finca Playa Venecia **6**
Finca Santo Domingo **2**
Hacienda Mérida **7**
Hospedaje Castillo **8**

Hospedaje Central **9**
Hospedaje Kencho **21**
Istián **1**
Ometepe Biological
Station **24**
Ometepetl **10**
Villa Paraíso **3**

Petroglyphs **∴**

Sleeping ⊜
Albergue Ecológico
Porvenir **22**

5 km
5 miles

Climbing the volcanoes

Volcán Concepción

There are two main trails leading to the summit. One of the paths is best accessed from Moyogalpa, where there is lots of accommodation; the other is from Altagracia. Climbing the volcano without a local guide is not advised and can be very dangerous: a climber died here in 2004 after falling into a ravine. Ask your hotel about recommended guides; many locals know the trail well but that doesn't make them reliable guides. See page 218 for recommended guides. The view from Concepción is breathtaking. The cone is very steep near the summit and loose footing and high winds are common. Follow the guide's advice if winds are deemed too strong for the summit.

From **Moyogalpa** the trail begins near the village of La Flor and the north side of the active cone. You should allow eight hours for the climb. Bring plenty of water and breathable, strong and flexible hiking shoes. From **Altagracia** the hike starts 2 km away and travels through a cinder gully, between forested slopes and a lava flow. The ascent takes five hours (3½ hours if you are very fit). Take water and sunscreen. Tropical dry and wet forest, heat from the crater and howler monkeys are added attractions.

Volcán Maderas

Three trails ascend Maderas. One departs from Hotel La Omaja near **Mérida**, another from Finca El Porvenir near **Santa Cruz**, and the last from Finca Magdelena near **Balgües**. Presently, the trail from Finca Magdelena is the only one fit enough to follow, but check locally. You should allow five hours up and three hours down, though relatively dry trail conditions could cut down hiking time considerably. Expect to get very muddy in any case. Ropes are necessary if you want to climb down into the Laguna de Maderas. Swimming in the laguna is not recommended as a tourist got stuck in the mud after jumping in and to be pulled out with a rope. Following the deaths of British and American hikers, hiking Maderas can no longer be done without a guide. Paying a local guide is a cheap life insurance.

policy and helps the very humble local economy. Guides are also useful in pointing out animals and petroglyphs that outsiders may miss. There is an entrance fee of US$2 to climb Maderas. The trail leads through farms, fences and gets steeper and rockier with elevation. The forest changes with altitude from tropical dry, to tropical wet and finally cloudforest, with howler monkeys accompanying your journey. Guides can be found for this climb in Moyogalpa, Altagracia and Santo Domingo or at Finca Magdelena where the hike begins.

Volcán Maderas (1394 m high, 24.5 km maximal diameter) last erupted about 800 years ago and is now believed to be extinct. The mountain is wrapped in thick forest and is home to the only cloudforest in Nicaragua's Pacific Basin other than Volcán Mombacho. The Nicaraguans called the mountain *Coatlán* (land of the sun). The 400 m by 150 m cold, misty crater lake, **Laguna de Maderas**, was only discovered by the non-indigenous population in 1930 and has a lovely waterfall on the western face of the cone. Maderas has 4100 ha of forest set aside and protected in a reserve.

Both cones have monkey populations, with the Maderas residents being almost impossible to miss on a full-day hike on the cone. The forest of Maderas also has a great diversity of butterfly and flower species, as well as a dwarf forest and the island is home to numerous parrots and magpie jays; the latter are almost as common as the pigeons in the squares of European cities. The **Isthmus of Istián**, the centre of the island's figure-of-eight shape and a fertile lowland finger that connects the two volcanoes' round bases, has several lagoons and creeks that are good for birdwatching. Off the northeast side of the isthmus are a couple of islands that also shelter rich bird life, in addition to the legendary **Charco Verde** on the southern coast of Concepción (see page 214).

Petroglyph sites
Ometepe has much to offer the culturally curious as well, with numerous pre-Columbian sites. A six-year survey in the mid-1990s revealed 73 sites with 1700 petroglyph panels and that is just the tip of the iceberg. A guided visit is recommended to one of the petroglyph sites, which are known according to the name of the farm they are found on. To list but a few: **San Marcos** has an eagle with outstretched wings; **Hacienda San Antonio** has geometric figures; **Altagracia**, in the house of Domingo Gutiérrez, shows a rock with an 'x' and a cross used to make sacrifices to the cult of the sun; **Hacienda La Primavera** has various images; **La Cigueña** shows the southern cross and various animals; and **El Porvenir** has a sundial and what some believe to be an alien being and a representation of the god of death. **La Palmera**, **Magdalena**, **San Ramón** and **Mérida** all have interesting petroglyph sites and **Socorro** has some sun calendars.

Moyogalpa
Moyogalpa is the port of entry for arrivals from San Jorge. It is a bustling town of commerce and travel, with a decidedly less indigenous population than the rest of the island. There is little of cultural or natural interest here but because it's a port it does have a lot of hotels. You may decide to spend the night if leaving on an early boat or if climbing Concepción from the western route, otherwise Altagracia, Santo Domingo and San Ramón are all more attractive options.

One interesting excursion (dry season only) is to walk or rent a bicycle to visit **Punta Jesús María**, 4-5 km away. It is well signposted from the road: just before Esquipulas head straight towards the lake. Jesús María has a good beach, a panoramic view of the island and a small café. In the mornings you can watch the fishermen on the long sandbar that extends into the lake. During the end of the dry season there are temporary places to eat and drink.

There is a small museum, cybercafé and artisan store called **Museo Ometepe** ① *up the street that runs from the dock to the church, ½ block from the Pro Credit office, T569-4225, 0800-2000*. The artisan crafts available here are hard to find anywhere else in Nicaragua. There are plantain rope hats from Pul, *jícaras* from La Concepción, oil paintings by local artists from Esquipulas and Moyogalpa, seed necklaces from Moyogalpa, wood sculptures from Altagracia, and pottery from San Marcos. You can also buy beautiful all-natural canteens known as a *calabazos* – a big round *jícaro* fruit, hollowed and smartly decorated, with a rope strap attached and drinking hole plugged with a corn cob.

Moyogalpa to Altagracia
Most transport uses the southern route to Altagracia as it is faster and in much better condition. The northern route is very rough but is more natural and scenic; it runs east from Moyogalpa along the north shores through the tiny villages of **La Concepción**, **La Flor** and **San Mateo**. There are commanding views of the volcano with its forests and 1957 lava flow visible beyond rock-strewn pasture and highland banana plantations. To

the north lies the deep blue of Lake Nicaragua. A fork to the left leads to the coast and the small, indigenous settlement of **San Marcos**; to the right it leads to **Altagracia**, past a baseball field (matches on Sundays) and a school. A tiny chapel marks your arrival in Altagracia. The town entrance is just southeast of the cemetery, and is perhaps the most scenic in all Nicaragua with its backdrop of Volcán Concepción.

The southern route, which is more heavily populated and completely paved with cement cobblestones, is the quickest route to Altagracia, Playa Santo Domingo and the Maderas side of Ometepe. The road passes the town of **Esquipulas**, where it is rumoured that the great Chief Niqueragua may have been buried, and the village of **Los Angeles**, which has some of the oldest known evidence of ancient settlers on the island, dated at 1500 BC. Between Los Angeles and the next settlement, San José del Sur, a turning leads to the **Numismatic Museum** ① *0800-1730*, which has a collection of bills and coins, some very old. At the fairly developed **San José del Sur**, evacuated in 1998 under threat of massive mudslides from Concepción, the road rises to spectacular views of Volcán Maderas across the lake.

Just past San José del Sur is the rough, narrow access road to **Charco Verde**, a big pond with a popular legend of a wicked sorcerer, Chico Largo, who was said to have shape-shifting powers. Today his discarnate spirit guards the pond, ruling all those who have sold their soul to him. In the rainy season this is one of the most scenic parts of the island. At the end of the road are a petrol storage tank and a twig-covered beach. There is some interesting lodging near the legendary pond (see Sleeping). Just east is the **Bahía de Sinacapa**, which hides an ancient volcanic cone under its waters, along with an island called **Quiste**. There is a good lookout nearby, **Mirador del Diablo**, where you can breathe in the best sunset on the island. **La Unión** is the highway's closest pass to the active cone and a good place to see howler monkeys. The road then passes through the indigenous village of **Urbaite** where the church's bell tower, typical of a design peculiar to the island, is separate from the church, built alongside it so as to ride out the island's frequent seismic events. After Urbaite, there is a right turn to the isthmus and Maderas volcano (see below). The road to Altagracia then passes the delightful little church at **El Chipote** (this is the entrance to the climb of the eastern face of Volcán Concepción) and enters the south of Altagracia.

Altagracia

This calm, unpretentious town is the most important on the island and it hides its population of around 20,000 well – except at weekends (there is usually dancing on Saturday nights, not to mention the odd fight among the local cowboys) and during festivals and holidays. Altagracia predates the arrival of the Spanish and was once home to two tribes who named their villages **Aztagalpa** (egrets' nest) and **Cosonigalpa**. The tribes were divided by what is now the road from Parque Central to the cemetery. Their less than amicable relationship forced the people of Cosonigalpa to flee to what is now San José del Sur and to the bay of Sinacapa. The Spanish renamed the village, but the population remains largely indigenous. In the shade of the trees next to Altagracia's crumbling old church, built in 1924 to replace a much older colonial temple, is a **sculpture park** which contains some of the most famous pre-Columbian statues in Nicaragua. They are estimated to date from AD 800 and represent human forms and their alter egos or animal protectors. The most famous are the eagle and the jaguar, which is believed to have been the symbol of power. West of the plaza, the **Museo de Ometepe** ① *Tue-Sun 0900-1200, 1400-1600, US$2*, has displays of archaeology and covers local ethnographic and environmental themes (in Spanish only).

Playa Santo Domingo

The sweeping sandy beach at Santo Domingo is reached via the southern road from Moyogalpa or from Altagracia's southern exit. Signs mark the turning on to a dirt road that can be very difficult in sections during the rainy season. The road winds through plantain plantations, past a miniature church, down a steep paved section and across a tiny bridge where women do laundry in the creek. The water is very clean upstream from here and great for swimming at its source, **El Ojo de Agua** ① *0700-1800, US$$1*, where you'll find a small ranch and some gentle walking trails. The road rises over a pass that allows a view of both cones and then dips into beautiful tropical dry forest and Santo Domingo.

This long sandy coastline is one of the prettiest freshwater beaches in Nicaragua and, with the forest-covered Volcán Maderas looming at the beach's end, it is truly exotic. The warm water, gentle waves and gradual shelf make it a great swimming beach. If you wade out you'll be able to see the cone of Concepción over the forest. The lake here is reminiscent of a sea (visitors are often surprised to see horses going down to drink from its shores, forgetting that it is fresh water). On this side of the island the trade winds blow nearly all year round and keep the heat and insects at bay. During the early rainy season there can be many gnats if the wind dies. The width of the beach depends on the time of year: at the end of the dry season there's a broad swathe of sand and at the end of the rainy season bathers are pushed up to the edge of the small drop-off that backs the beach. It is not unusual to see a school of freshwater sardines (silversides) bubbling out of the water being chased by a predator. Around the beach there are many magpie jays, parrots, vultures and hawks.

Santo Domingo can be used as a jumping-off point for the ultra-tranquil Maderas side of the island or for climbing either volcano. Facilities in Santo Domingo are limited to the hotels (see page 217), a micro-store and one bar; there is no town.

Balgües and around

The sand road towards Maderas ends at Santa Cruz; a fork leads left to Balgües or right to San Ramón. The road to Balgües is rocky and scenic although the village itself is a little sad in appearance. The people are very friendly, however, especially if you're travelling with a local; the feeling that everyone knows everybody on Ometepe is magnified here. This village is the entrance to the trailhead for the climb to the summit of Maderas. There are several interesting **organic farms** in the area, including the famous **Finca Magdelena**, **Finca Campestre** and **Michael's Farm**, where you can study permaculture techniques.

Mérida

From the fork at Santa Cruz the road goes south past small homes and ranches and through the towering palms of the attractive village of Mérida, in an area that was once an expansive farm belonging to the Somoza family. The road drops down to lake level and curves east past an old pier where Somoza's coffee production used to be shipped out to the mainland. There are some good places to stay here (see page 217). From the old dock you can kayak the canals of Istián and observe bird and mammal life.

San Ramón

Further along the eastern shores of Maderas is the affluent town San Ramón. Some foreigners and wealthy Nicaraguans have built vacation homes here and there is a private dock for their boats. The 'biological station' is the starting point for a once-gorgeous hike up the west face of **Volcán Maderas** to a lovely 40-m cascade, also called San Ramón. The forest here is home to white-face and howler monkeys and many parrots and trogons come to nest. This is a much less athletic climb than the hike to the summit, but sadly it has lost much of its charm. The path to the cascade has been largely destroyed by the deforestation of the middle slopes that once protected the forest reserve from erosion and landslides. The forest has been cleared in order to plant fruit trees and create grazing land for cattle. What's more, big hissing pipes now follow the trail all the way up to the cascade. The pipes are used to siphon off water that used to feed a precious mountain stream; it is now channelled to irrigate the biological station's plantain, avocado and other cash crops. The forest is lovely and the cascade is still pretty, but most of the wildlife is now forced to go elsewhere to look for shelter and water. In addition, at the entrance to the biological station you have to pay an entrance fee (said to go towards trail maintenance) in order to enter the trail.

Transport is not as frequent on this side of the island and you may have a long walk if you are not on a tour. Hotels and Moyogalpa tour companies offer packages that are reasonable if you can get together at least two other hikers.

◉ Isla Ometepe listings

For Sleeping and Eating price codes and other relevant information, see pages 43-46.

● Sleeping

Moyogalpa *p213*

B-C American Café and Hotel, the dock, 100 vrs up the hill, T645-7193. Excellent value, comfortable and immaculately clean rooms, cheaper without a/c (**C**). All have good, new mattresses and hot water. Italian, German, Spanish and English spoken. Recommended.
C-D Ometepetl, on main street from dock, T569-4276, ometepetlng@hotmail.com (reservations for Istián, Santo Domingo also). This longstanding Moyogalpa favourite has rooms with a/c (**D** without) and bath. There's a pool and a popular restaurant attached, vehicle rental and tours on request.
D-F Hospedaje Central, from dock, 1 block right, 3 blocks uphill, T569-4262, hospedaje-centralometepe@hotmail.com. This brightly coloured cheapie has dorms (**F**) and private rooms (**D**). Keep an eye on your stuff.
E Arenas Negras, opposite **Hotel Ometepetl**, T883-6167. 10 simple rooms, small but clean, 9 with private bath and fan. Friendly and basic.

Moyogalpa to Altagracia *p213*

A-B Hotel Charco Verde Inn, almost next to the lagoon, San José del Sur, T887-9302, www.charcoverde.com.ni. Pleasant cabañas with private bath, a/c, terrace (**A**); doubles with private bath and fan (**B**). Good reports. Watch out for the mythical Chico Largo.
B-D Finca Playa Venecia, 250 m from the main road, San José del Sur, T872-7668, www.hotelfincavenecia.com.ni. Very chilled out, comfortable lodgings and a lovely lakeside garden. Cabañas overlooking the water are best (**B**), but regular cabañas (**C**) and rooms (**D**) are good too. Recommended.
C El Tesoro del Pirata, Playa Valle Verde, near Charco Verde, Km 15, Carretera a Altagracia, turn towards the lake, T832-2429. Next to a good beach, cabins with private bath and a/c, dorms and rooms with fan and shared bath. Rustic restaurant attached.
D-F Chico Largo Hostel, San José del Sur, next to **Finca Playa Venecia**, T886-4069. Hostel with dorms (**F**) or private rooms (**D**), friendly ambience, poor beds.

Altagracia *p214*

D-E Hospedaje Castillo, Parque Central, 1 c sur, ½ c oeste, T552-8744, www.elcastillo.com. Pleasant, friendly hotel with 19 rooms, most have bath outside (**E**). There's a good restaurant, bar and internet facilities attached, credit cards are accepted and TCs changed. Tours to the volcanoes. Recommended.

D-E Hotel Central, Iglesia, 2 c sur, T552-8770. 19 rooms (**E**) and 6 cabañas (**D**) around a pretty courtyard, all with private bath and fan. There's a restaurant and bar, bicycle rental, tours and hammocks. Friendly and recommended.

Playa Santo Domingo *p215*

A-D Villa Paraíso, beachfront, T563-4675, www.villaparaiso.com.ni. Ometepe's most expensive and luxurious lodging has a beautiful, peaceful setting with 13 cute, stone cabañas (**A**) and 5 rooms (**D**). Most have a/c, private bath, hot water, cable TV, minibar and internet. Some of the rooms have a patio and lake view.

B Hotel Costa Azul, 50 vrs sur, T644-0327. A new hotel with 7 big, clean rooms. They have a/c, private bath and TV with DVD. There's a restaurant serving *comida típica* and breakfasts. Bike and motorbike rental, guides available.

B-D Finca Santo Domingo, Playa Santo Domingo, north side of Villa Paraíso, T485-6177, www.hotelfincasantodomingo.com. Friendly lakeside hotel with a range of rooms (**C-D**) and bungalows (**B**), all with private bath. There's an *artesanía* store, bicycle rental and various tours. The restaurant serves *comida típica* and has good views.

D Hotel Buena Vista, Playa Santo Domingo, Villa Paraíso, 150 m norte. Great views, you really feel the lake from here. 10 rooms have private bath and fan, there's a restaurant, a pleasant terrace and hammocks.

D Hotel Istiám, Villa Paraíso, 2 km sur, T887-9891, across the road from the beach, reservations through **Ometepetl** in Moyogalpa. Basic and often seemingly abandoned, friendly, family-run place. Rooms are simple but clean, with fan and bath, cheaper shared (**E**). Good swimming. Restaurant, tours and bike rental.

Balgües and around *p215*

B-F Finca Magdalena, Balgües, www.fincamagdalena.com, T880-2041. Famous cooperative farm run by 26 families, with accommodation in a small cottages, cabañas (**B**) doubles (**E**), singles, dorms (**F**) and hammocks. Camping possible. Stunning views across lake and to Concepción, good

meals around US$2, friendly, basic, wildly popular on the budget highway.

D Albergue Ecológico Porvenir, Santa Cruz, T855-1426. Stunning views at this tranquil, secluded lodge at the foot of Maderas. Rooms are clean, tidy and comfortable, with private bath and fan. Nearby trails run to the crater lake and miradors.

D El Encanto, Santa Cruz, T867-7128, www.goelencanto.com. An experimental finca comprising 4 ha of land. The rooms are good, clean and comfortable, and a there's very pleasant, chilled out garden. Various tours are available.

E-F Finca Ecológica El Zopilote, about 1 km uphill from Balgües. Funky hostel with dormitory, hammocks, camping and cabañas. Full moon parties, use of kitchen and free track up to the volcano.

F Camping Campestre, 500 m east of Balgües, T695-2071, www.fincacampestre.googlepages.com. English-owned organic farm with camping space near the banana plantation. Opportunities to volunteer, outdoor kitchen and camping equipment provided.

Mérida *p215*

B-F Hacienda Mérida, at the old Somoza dock in lower Mérida, T868-8973, www.h merida.com. Popular hostel with a beautiful setting by the lake. Lodgings have wheelchair access and include a mixture of dorms (**F**) and rooms (**C**), some with views (**B**). There's a children's school on-site where you can volunteer, kayak rental, good-quality mountain bikes, internet and a range of tours available, including sailing. The restaurant serves fresh, hygienically prepared food, good for vegetarians. Recommended.

San Ramón *p215*

E Ometepe Biological Station, T883-1107, for groups of students only. The station claims to 'manage' 325 ha of conservation land, partly consumed by cash crops. Rooms are simple with shared bath outside. Services include mountain bikes, kayaks, meals.

🍴 Eating

Moyogalpa *p213*

🍴 **Los Ranchitos**, muelle municipal, 2 c arriba, ½ c sur, T569-4112. Excellent food, including vegetarian pasta, vegetable soup, chicken in garlic butter. Recommended.

🍴 **The American Café**, the pier, 100 vrs arriba. This is the place for home-made food, like chilli con carne, pancakes and waffles. Also has a small second-hand book collection.

🍴 **Yogi's Café and Bar**, **Hospedaje Central**, ½ c sur. A great place for American food, beer and big-screen movies. **Yogi** is a big, but gentle, black labrador, not to be confused with the owner, Jerry, who is a very decent fellow, always open to philosophical conversation.

🔺 Activities and tours

Canopy tour

Canopy Sendero Los Monos, Playa Santo Domingo. A baby canopy tour, very much for beginners, with 4 cables and 6 platforms, US$10. Suitable for children 4 and up.

Organic farming

Bona Fide, Balgües, www.projectbonafide. com. Also known as Michael's farm, **Bona Fide** offer innovative courses in permaculture as well as volunteer opportunities for those wishing to learn more about the science and work of organic farming. An interesting project.

Tour operators

Ometepe Expeditions, 75 m from the port in Moyogalpa (in front of **Hotel Ometepetl**), T664-6910, ometepexpeditions@hotmail.com. A highly reputable agency that worked with the BBC to guide a group of disabled people to the summit of Concepción. Offer a range of tours including half- and full day hikes to the volcanoes and cloudforests. Experienced and helpful. English-speaking guides include **Bermán Gómez**, T836-8360, and **Eduardo Manzanares**, T873-7714. Recommended.

🚌 Transport

Boat

The lake can have very big swells. The best access route to the island is from San Jorge to Moyogalpa. The ferry and boat offer regular services. Cars are transported with the ferry.

From Moyogalpa to **San Jorge**, 12 daily boats and ferries, hourly 0530-1600, US$2. Reduced services on Sun, 3 ferries only.

The port of Altagracia is called San Antonio and is 2 km north of the town; pick-ups meet the boat that passes between Granada and San Carlos. To **San Carlos**, Mon and Thu 1800-1900, US$8, 11 hrs. To **Granada**, Tue and Fri, around 0000, US$4, 3½ hrs.

Bus

Buses wait for the boats in Moyogalpa and run to **Altagracia** hourly, 0530-1830, US$1, 1 hr. To **San Ramón** 0815, US$1.25, 3 hrs. To **Mérida**, 0830, 1430, 1630, US$2, 2½ hrs. To **Balgües**, 1030, 1530, US$2, 2 hrs. For **Charco Verde**, take any bus to Altagracia that uses the southern route.

Car and bike hire

Toyota Rent a Car, Hotel Ometepet, T459-4276. A strong 4WD is a must, US$35-50 for 12 hrs, US$60 for 24 hrs. A driver can also be provided, with advance notice.

Bicycle and motorbikes are widely available from hotels. **Hacienda Mérida** has some particularly good mountain bikes. Be careful on the northern road, it's rocky and dangerous.

📖 Directory

Banks Banco Procredit, pier, 500 vrs uphill, Visa ATM and dollar-changing facility. Western Union attached. Money changing (no TCs) in the 2 biggest grocery stores (1 opposite Hotel Bahía) or in hotels. Best to bring all the cash you need from Rivas. **Internet** Crushingly slow at most places; expect time-outs. **Hotel Central** in Altagracia, US$2 per hr. **Comercial Arcia** in Moyogalpa, US$2 per hr.

San Juan del Sur and around

West of Lake Nicaragua, the entrancing beauty of the Pacific Coast is complemented by one of nature's most vivid spectacles – the annual arrival of thousands of nesting sea turtles who have been coming to this stretch of coast for thousands of years; sometimes as many as 20,000 over a four-night period. But the region's rugged splendour has not been overlooked by international developers, who are constructing a host of beachfront retirement homes and grotesque gated communities around San Juan del Sur. Once a quiet fishing town, this vital destination is now swollen with foreign prospectors, surfers and party-goers. Still, the sunsets are immense, development is in its early stages, and a poor infrastructure means much of the coast has been spared, for now. The dry season along Nicaragua's Pacific Coast is very parched and brown, but most of the year the landscape is fluorescent green, shaded by rows of mango trees and dotted with small, attractive ranches with flower-festooned front gardens. Roadside stalls offer many fruits, such as watermelon, mango, níspero and some of the biggest papaya you'll see anywhere.
▸▸ *For listings, see pages 225-228.*

San Juan del Sur ⊜🏤🏩🏪⊖⊕ ▸▸ *pp225-228.*

Not long ago this was a secret place, a tiny coastal paradise on Nicaragua's Pacific Coast. In recent years, however, this little town on a big bay has become very popular, first as an escape from the built-up beaches across the international border in Costa Rica to the south, then as a magnet for real estate developers, US retirees and the international wave-hunting crowd. In addition, cruise ships now anchor in its deeper waters and tourists have begun to arrive in quantity. San Juan del Sur is a major destination, increasingly buzzing with activity. And although it has retained its character, it is increasingly starting to resemble Costa Rica. Fortunately, the recently elected Sandinista government has put a damper on the land grab, slowing, if not stopping, the destruction of the coast. It's no longer the place to experience a country off the beaten path, but there are still plenty of empty beaches and there is no doubt that the coast here is among the most beautiful stretches in Central America.

Ins and outs

Getting there Most of the buses come from Rivas, though a few leave direct from Managua. If coming from the border with Costa Rica take any bus towards Rivas and step down at the entrance to the Carretera a San Juan del Sur in La Virgen. A taxi is also a possibility from the border with Costa Rica and some hotels will pick you up at the border if you warn them well in advance. If driving, it is very straightforward: look for the turning in La Virgen from the Interamericana and head west until the road ends in San Juan del Sur.

Getting around You can get anywhere in San Juan by walking; if you are visiting outlying beaches you can arrange transport with local hotels or the ones at your destination. Additionally, there are many new shuttle services making frequent trips north and south of the town. For the wilder and truly untamed stretches further away from town you will need a decent 4WD or even a boat.

Best time to visit This is one of the driest parts of Nicaragua, with rains coming in late afternoon and blowing over quickly in the wet season and the land looking rather parched half-way through the dry season. Winds from December to March can make exposed beaches uncomfortable with blowing sand and boat excursions a wet experience. For surfing, April to December are the best months. To avoid the crowds don't come at Christmas time or Holy Week; the quietest months are May to June and September to October.

Safety Under no circumstances walk to Yankee or Remanso, the beaches north of San Juan del Sur, as this road is a long-time haunt of thieves. There have also been reports of unpleasant robberies on the beaches themselves, so check the security situation before heading over. Don't linger on the sand after dark in San Juan del Sur.

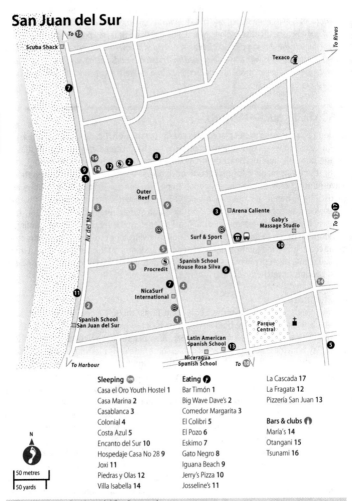

San Juan del Sur

Sleeping	Eating	La Cascada 17
Casa el Oro Youth Hostel 1	Bar Timón 1	La Fragata 12
Casa Marina 2	Big Wave Dave's 2	Pizzería San Juan 13
Casablanca 3	Comedor Margarita 3	
Colonial 4	El Colibrí 5	**Bars & clubs**
Costa Azul 5	El Pozo 6	María's 14
Encanto del Sur 10	Eskimo 7	Otangani 15
Hospedaje Casa No 28 9	Gato Negro 8	Tsunami 16
Joxi 11	Iguana Beach 9	
Piedras y Olas 12	Jerry's Pizza 10	
Villa Isabella 14	Josseline's 11	

Background

Andrés Niño, the first European to navigate the Pacific Coast of Nicaragua, entered the bay of San Juan del Sur in 1523 while looking in vain for a possible passage to Lake Nicaragua or the Caribbean. San Juan del Sur remained a sleepy fishing village until after Nicaragua's independence from Spain. It began working as a commercial port in 1827, and in 1830 took the name Puerto Independencia. Its claim to fame came during the California gold rush when thousands of North Americans, anxious to reach California (in the days before the North American railroad was finished), found the shortest route to be by boat from the Caribbean, up the Río San Juan, across Lake Nicaragua, overland for only 18 km from La Virgen (see page 206) and then by boat again from San Juan to California. It is estimated that some 84,880 passengers passed through the town en route to California, and some 75,000 on their way to New York. In 1854 the local lodge, El United States Hotel, charged a whopping US$14 per day for one night's lodging and food of bread, rice, oranges and coffee made from purified water. But as soon as the railway in the USA was completed, the trip through Central America was no longer necessary. The final crossing was made on 8 May 1868 with 541 passengers en route to San Francisco. The steamship was taken over for a while by William Walker to re-supply his invasion forces in the mid-1850s. In 1857, Walker escaped to Panama and later to New Orleans via San Juan. There was some very tough fighting here during 1979 Revolution in the hills behind San Juan, as Somoza sent his best troops to take on Commandante Zero, Edén Pastora, and his rebel southern front. As victory approached, a ragged group of Somoza's National Guard managed to escape out of San Juan (threatening to burn it down), just as southern Rivas was being taken by Pastora-led rebels.

Sights

Mark Twain described San Juan as "a few tumble-down frame shanties" in 1866, and said the town was "crowded with horses, mules and ambulances (horse carriages) and half-clad yellow natives". Today there are plenty of half-clad people, though less and less are natives and most are enjoying the sun and sea. Most of the horses and all of the mules have been replaced by bicycles, which is the preferred form of transport.

What makes San Juan del Sur different from other Nicaraguan beach towns is the growing ex-patriot crowd that has migrated here from across Europe and North America. San Juan is a natural bay of light brown sand, clear waters and 200 m cliffs that mark its borders. The sunsets are placed perfectly out over the Pacific, framed by the boats bobbing in the bay. The beach is lined by numerous small restaurants that offer the fresh catch of the day, along with lobster and shrimp. Surfers can climb in a boat and find access to very good breaks along the same coastline, one that has a year-round offshore breeze. Deep-sea fishing is also possible. Swimming is best at the northern end of the beach. See Activities and tours, page 227.

South of San Juan del Sur ⬤▲◉ ▸▸ pp225-228.

Be aware when visiting these beaches that there are real concerns about the treatment of locals, who are being denied access to the coast. Nicaraguan law stipulates that all Nicaraguan beaches must be open to the public (the term 'private beach' is either a hollow promise or they are breaking the law), but the law does not clarify how access must be granted. The beaches are rapidly being shut down to people of lower economic status (90% of the population), creating hard feeling among the Nicaraguans whose families have been visiting these beaches for generations.

A well-kept earth and rock road runs south from the bridge at the entrance to San Juan del Sur. Signs mark the way to a housing and apartment development called Parque Marítimo El Coco and also serve as directions to the superb beach and turtle nesting site of **La Flor** (see below). There are also signs for **Playa Remanso**, the first beach with lodgings south of San Juan. There are big houses being built here above a pretty beach which is good for swimming. Both **Remanso** and the beautiful **Playa El Yankee**, to the south, are good surfing beaches. The road is rough here and you will have to cross streams that are small during the dry season, but will require high-clearance and 4WD vehicles from June to November. The drive is over a beautifully scenic country road with many elevation changes and vistas of the ocean and the northern coast of Costa Rica.

Playa El Coco is a long copper-coloured beach with strong surf most of the year. Much of it is backed by forest and there are several families of howler monkeys that live between here and **La Flor**, two beaches to the south. There is a growing development at the north end of the beach with a mixture of condos, bungalows and homes for rent. This is the closest lodging to La Flor without camping. The housing complex at Playa El Coco is involved in community projects which includes free schooling for local children and the beach is open to the public. Prices for rental range from one night in a one-room apartment for US$85-1900 for one week in a big house.

Refugio de Vida Silvestre La Flor ① *US$10, US$2.50 student discount, access by 4WD or on foot*, just past Playa El Coco and 18 km from the highway at San Juan del Sur, protects tropical dry forest, mangroves, estuary and 800 m of beachfront. This particular bit of beachfront is a beautiful, sweeping cove with light tan sand and the spot where hundreds of nesting sea turtles (see box, page 224) choose to come each year. The best time to come is between August and November. Rangers protect the multitudinous arrivals during high season and are very happy to explain, in Spanish, about the animals' reproductive habits. Sometimes turtles arrive in their thousands, usually over a period of four days. Even if you don't manage to see the turtles, there is plenty of other wildlife. Many birds live in small, protected mangroves at the south end of the beach and you may witness a sunset migration of hundreds of hermit crabs at the north end, all hobbling back to the beach in their infinitely diverse shells. Camping can be provided (limited number of tents) during the turtle season, US$25 per night. Bring a hammock and mosquito netting as insects are vicious at dusk. The ranger station sells soft drinks and will let you use their outhouse; improved facilities are planned.

North of San Juan del Sur ●▲● ›› *pp225-228*.

There is an unpaved access road to beaches north of San Juan del Sur at the entrance to the town. It is possible to travel the entire length of the Rivas coast to Chacocente from here, though it is quite a trip as the road does not follow the coast but moves inland to **Tola** (west of Rivas) and then back to the ocean, and the surface is changeable from hard pack dirt to sand, stone and mud. Some of the beaches in this part of Rivas are spectacular with white sand and rugged forested hillsides and, like the coastline south of San Juan del Sur, they are being quickly cordoned off. This area is seeing big development and building projects, including gated communities and retirement resorts, and Tola itself has become a service town for the growing numbers of constructions workers.

Playa Marsella has plenty of signs that mark the exit to the beach. It is a slowly growing resort set on a pleasant beach, but not one of the most impressive in the region. North of here, **Los Playones** is playing host to ever-increasing crowds of surfers with a scruffy beer

Border essentials: Nicaragua–Costa Rica

The Nicaragua-Costa Rica border runs along the southern bank of the Río San Juan but has been the subject of much government tension and debate. The Costa Rican border reaches the south banks of the Río San Juan 2 km downriver from El Castillo but the river in its length is Nicaraguan territory. Officially Costa Rican boats are only allowed to navigate the river for commercial purposes. It is best to travel in Nicaraguan boats on the river, as Costa Rican ones could be detained or turned back depending on the political climate.

San Carlos to Los Chiles → *See also page 103.*

This is a frequently used crossing point between Nicaragua and Costa Rica. Crossing from the Río San Juan to other parts of Costa Rica is not legal, though this could change; ask in San Carlos if any other official points of entry or departure have opened up.

Nicaraguan immigration The border is open seven days a week 0800-1600. Exit stamps, costing US$2, must be obtained in San Carlos Mon-Fri only. Entrance stamps into Costa Rica (US$8) are only available via Los Chiles. Check with the police in advance for the latest situation.

Transport There are the boats per day from San Carlos to Los Chiles, 1030, 1300, 1500, US$8, two hours.

San Juan del Norte

Crossing to Costa Rica here is not legally permitted at time of printing, nor is entering Nicaragua without passing through San Carlos; the exception are package customers of the Río Indio Lodge, which has special permission for its clients.

Nicaraguan immigration There is no official immigration in San Juan del Norte. Projections suggest that the new San Juan del Norte airport, as yet unbuilt, will include immigrations and customs for international arrivals and departures. Whether this will open up the legality of boat arrivals and departures remains to be seen. See page 231.

shack and hordes of daily shuttle trucks. The waves are good for beginners, but are often heavily oversubscribed. **Maderas** is the next beach along, where many shuttles claim to take you (they don't, they drop you at the car park at Los Playones). This is a pleasant, tranquil spot, good for swimming and host to some affordable lodgings, best booked in advance. **Bahía Majagual** is the next bay north, a lovely white sand beach tucked into a cove. There was once a famous backpackers lodge here, but this has closed and something new (and no doubt upmarket) is being constructed in its place.

On the road to Majagual before reaching the beach is the private entrance to **Morgan's Rock**, a multimillion dollar private nature reserve and reforestation project with tree farming, incorporating more than 800 ha of rare tropical dry coastal forest and the stunningly beautiful Playa Ocotal. Don't even think about dropping by to check it out without first digging deep in your wallet as this is the most expensive place to sleep in Nicaragua and, most reports say, worth every *peso*. While the hotel may not win awards for social consciousness, it is on the progressive edge of conservation and sustainable tourism in ecological terms. If you can afford a few nights here, it is one of the prettiest places on the Central American coast and the cabins are set up high on a bluff wrapped in forest overlooking the ocean and beach (see Sleeping, page 226).

Sea turtles – the miracle of life

Every year between July and February thousands of beautiful olive ridley turtles (Lepidochelys olivacea) arrive at La Flor and Chacocente, two wildlife refuges set aside to aid in their age-old battle against predators with wings, pincers, four legs and two.

The sea turtles, measuring up to 80 cm and weighing more than 90 kg, come in waves. Between August and November as many as 20,000 arrive to nest in a four-night period, just one of many arrivals during the nesting season. Each turtle digs a hole with her rear flippers and patiently lays up to 100 eggs, covers them and returns to the water: mission complete. For 45 days the eggs incubate under the tropical Nicaraguan sand. The temperature in the sand will determine the gender of the turtle: temperatures below 29°C will result in males and 30°C and above will be females, though very high temperatures will kill the hatchlings. After incubation in the sand, they hatch all at once and the little turtles run down to the sea. If they survive they will travel as far as the Galapagos Islands.

The huge leatherback turtle (Dermochelys coriacea), which can grow up to 2 m and weigh over 300 kg, is less common than the olive ridley and arrives alone to lay her eggs.

Turtle eggs are a traditional food for the Nicaraguans, and although they are not eaten in large quantities, poaching is always a threat. Park rangers and, during peak times, armed soldiers protect the turtles from animal and human threats in both Chacocente and La Flor wildlife refuges. If you have the chance to witness it, don't miss out and get talking to the rangers who have a great passion for their work. Extreme caution must be exercised during nesting season as, even if you see no turtles on the beach, you are most likely to be walking over nests. Limit flash photography to a minimum and never aim a flash camera at turtles coming out of the water.

Camping is the best way to see the turtles in Chacocente or La Flor, but a pre-dawn trip from either San Juan del Sur or Playa El Coco to La Flor, or from Las Salinas to Chacocente is also possible.

To the north of Morgan's are more pristine beaches, such as **Manzanillo** and **El Gigante**, and all have development projects. One that has really got off the ground is **Rancho Santana** ⓘ www.ranchosantana.com. This is a massive housing and resort project located on the west side of the earthen highway between Tola and Las Salinas, behind a large ostentatious gate and a grimacing armed guard. Rancho Santana is a very organized and well developed project for luxury homes built by foreigner investors and retirees. The popular surf spot Playa Rosada is included in the complex's claim of four 'private' beaches. California-style hilltop luxury homes are being built here with stunning Pacific views and the 'state within a state' ambience includes a slick clubhouse called **Oxford** and a private helipad.

Further north from Rancho Santana is the legendary surf spot **Popoyo**. This place is getting crowded with surfers from around the world and with good reason. The surf here is very big with a good swell and still has waves when the rest of the ocean looks like a swimming pool. There is also lodging at a surf camp here. See www.surfnicaragua.com for information.

One of the prettiest beaches on the northern Rivas coast is **Playa Conejo**, now taken over by **Hotel Punta Teonoste**. It is located near Las Salinas with very funky and creative bungalows along the beach and a memorable circular bar right above the sand. Sadly the land behind the bungalows is completely treeless and the sun and wind are ferocious here in the dry season. Having said that, this is the nearest decent accommodation to Chacocente Wildlife Refuge, 7 km north of the hotel, and access via the highway from Ochomogo is year round.

Refugio de Vida Silvestre Río Escalante Chacocente ① *www.chacocente.info, US$4,* is an area of tropical dry forest and a beach most famous for the **sea turtles** that come to nest every year. This is one of the four most important sea turtle nesting sites on the entire Pacific seaboard of the American continent (another of the four, the **La Flor Wildlife Refuge**, is further south, see page 222). The park is also a critical tropical dry forest reserve for the Nicaraguan Pacific and a good place to see giant iguanas and varied bird life during the dry season, when visibility in the forest is at its best. The beach itself is lovely too, with a long open stretch of sand that runs back into the forest, perfect for stringing up a hammock. Camping is permitted – and it may be the most beautiful camping spot along the coast – but no facilities are provided and you will need to come well stocked with water and supplies. The Nicaraguan environmental protection agency **MARENA** has built attractive cabins for park rangers and scientists and it is possible that they will rent them to visitors in the future. At the moment the rangers seem surprised to see visitors but they are very sincere in their efforts to protect the wildlife and diversity of the reserve.

There is no public transport to the park and a 4WD is necessary during the turtle-laying season from August to November. There are two entrances to the area, one from Santa Teresa south of Jinotepe. Follow that road until the pavement ends and then turn left to the coast and El Astillero. Before you reach the bay of Astillero you will see a turning to the right with a sign for Chacocente. At Km 80 from the Interamericana is the bridge over the Río Ochomogo that separates the province of Granada from Rivas; the Interamericana is in excellent condition here as it continues south to Rivas. On the south side of the bridge a rough dirt road runs west to the Pacific Ocean. This is a 40-km journey through small friendly settlements to the same turning for the reserve.

---

⑤ San Juan del Sur and around listings

For Sleeping and Eating price codes and other relevant information, see pages 43-46.

⊜ Sleeping

San Juan del Sur *p219, map p220*
Hotel prices in San Juan del Sur double for Semana Santa, Christmas and New Year.
LL Casa Marina, opposite **Josselin's** on the beach road, T568-2677. For better or worse, these high-rise timeshare condos are a sign of the times. Apartments have 2 bedrooms, 2 bathrooms, kitchen, living room, fine views.
LL-L Piedras y Olas, Parroquia, 1½ c arriba, T568-2110, www.piedrasyolas.com. Beautiful luxurious homes (**L**) and hotel suites with great

furnishings, style and views of the bay. Sailing trips on the *Pelican Eyes* can be arranged.
AL Casablanca, opposite **Bar Timón** on the beach road, T568-2135, www.sanjuandel sur.org.ni/casablanca. Clean, comfortable rooms with a/c, cable TV, private bath, refrigerator. A small pool, parking, free internet, continental breakfast included. Friendly and relaxed.
AL Villa Isabella, behind church to the left, T568-2568, www.sanjuandelsur.org.ni/ isabella. Lovely, well-decorated wooden house with 17 clean rooms, private bath, a/c, disabled access, large windows. There's a pool, garage parking, internet, video library and breakfast included in the price. English spoken, very helpful.

A Colonial, del Mercado 1 c al mar, ½ c sur, T568-2539, www.hotel-nicaragua.com. This well-managed hotel has a pleasant, relaxing garden, and 12 comfortable rooms with a/c, cable TV, hot water. Continental breakfast included, bikes and tours can be arranged.

C-D Hotel Encanto del Sur, Iglesia, 100 m sur, T568-2222. 18 clean, tidy, comfortable rooms with private bath and a/c, cheaper with fan (**D**). Quiet, away from the action, good value.

C-E Costa Azul, mercado, 1c al mar, T568-2294. Comfortable, economical rooms with good mattresses and a/c, cheaper with fan (**D**) or shared bath (**E**). There's internet, hammocks, parking and kitchen.

C-E Hospedaje Casa No 28, mercado, 1c al mar, 1c norte, T568-2441. Good clean budget option with basic rooms and shared bath. Some rooms have private bath, a/c and hot water (**C**).

D Joxi, mercado, 1½ c al mar, T568-2348, casajoxi@ibw.com.ni. Friendly, Norwegian-run, bunk beds, a/c, cable TV, restaurant, bar.

D-F Casa el Oro Youth Hostel, Hotel Colonial, 20 vrs sur, T568-2415, www.casae loro.com. Young, popular hostel with dorm beds (**E-F**), private rooms (**D**) and a plethora of services, shuttles, tours and lessons. Good kitchen and garden. Plenty of hammocks.

South of San Juan del Sur *p221*

LL-AL Parque Marítimo El Coco, 18 km south of San Juan del Sur, T892-0124, www. playaelcoco.com.ni. Very nice apartments, bungalows and houses for 4-10 people, some on beach, others with ocean view. Closest lodging to La Flor Wildlife Refuge.

North of San Juan del Sur *p222*

LL Morgan's Rock, Playa Ocotal, T296-9442, www.morgansrock.com. Luxury hacienda on a secluded beach with options for activities and wildlife trips in the surrounding area.

A Marsella Beach Resort, Playa Marsella, T887-1337, www.marsellabeachresort.com. Independent cabins with private bath, a/c, great views, restaurant, house for rent (**LL**) too.

C-E Camping Matilda, Playa Maderas, T456-3461. The best lodgings on the beach. They have 8 rooms with private bath (**C**), 2 small dormitories (**D**), and some little 'camping houses' that look like dog kennels (**E**). Very friendly, relaxed and pleasant. Often full.

🍴 Eating

San Juan del Sur *p219, map p220*
There's many popular, but overpriced restaurants lining the beach, where your tourist dollars buy excellent sea views and mediocre food. Only the better ones are listed.

† †† - †† Bar Timón, across from **Hotel Casablanca**, T568-82243, daily 0800-2200. Probably the best of the beachfront eateries, serving lobster, prawns and a host of other seafood dishes. No plastic furniture. Popular and Nicaraguan.

††† - †† Big Wave Dave's, Texaco, 200 m al mar, T568-2203, www.bigwavedaves.net, Tue-Sun 0830-2400. Popular with foreigners out to party and hook up with others. Whole-some pub food and a buzzing, boozy atmosphere.

††† - †† La Cascada, Piedras y Olas, parque, 1½ c arriba. Palm-thatched restaurant, excellent location overlooking the harbour, good sandwiches.

††† - †† El Colibrí, mercado, 1 c este, 2½ sur. The best restaurant in town, with an excellent and eclectic Mediterranean menu, great decor, ambience, fine wines and really good food, much of it organic. Pleasant, hospitable and highly recommended.

††† - †† El Pozo, mercado, ½ c sur. Smart and stylish, with a robust international menu and an attractive, young clientele. This interesting little restaurant almost belongs in London or New York.

††† - † Pizzería San Juan, Tue-Sun 1700-2130. Good pizza and pasta, but a rather plain interior and not much of a dining experience.

†† Iguana Beach, next door to Timón. Sandwiches, burgers, beer and cheese-drenched nachos, as well as seafood. Popular with tourists, often buzzing and a good place to drink.

Josseline's, on the beach. One of the better beachside eateries, offering the usual seafood fare like shrimps, fillets and lobster. Some limited meat and chicken dishes too.

Comedor Margarita, mercado, ½ c norte.

Jerry's Pizza, mercado, ½ c este. American-owned pizza joint serving reasonable fast food and breakfasts. A nice, airy, open-front space, good for people-watching.

La Fragata, Texaco, 250 m al mar. The place for cheap and cheerful fast food, roast chicken.

Cafés and ice cream parlours

Eskimo, seafront, 2½ c north of **Hotel Estrella**. Sweet, cold cones, sundaes and banana splits. Another branch just south of Banco Procredit.

Gato Negro, mercado, 1c al mar, 1 c norte. Popular gringo café with good coffee, reading space and snacks. This is also one of the best bookshops in the country, with what they claim is the largest collection of English-language books on Nicaragua, in Nicaragua.

🎭 Entertainment

San Juan del Sur *p219, map p220*
The action revolves around **Iguana Beach**, **Maria's** and **Big Dave's Waves**, all located close to each other. You could also try: **Otangani**, north on the seafront, next to **Gallo de Oro**, T878-8384, Thu-Sun 1800-0100. Good fun dancing to techno and salsa. Female travellers should not walk here at night. Catch a cab, especially to return. **Tsunami**, seafront, next to **Maria's**. Loud reggae shakes bamboo walls draped with fairy lights and rasta flags. There's a big screen TV and movies on Mon and Wed night.

🥾 Activities and tours

San Juan del Sur *p219, map p220*
Canopy tour
Da' Flying Frog, located just off road to Marsella, T568-2351, tiguacal@ibw.com.ni,

US$25. Close to San Juan del Sur with 17 platforms, great views from the canopy.

Diving
The waters around San Juan del Sur are home to a wrecked Russian trawler and sea creatures including rays, turtles and eels. **Scuba Shack**, seafront, 3 c north of **Hotel Estrella**, T568-2502, www.scubashack-nicaragua.com. This friendly, professional PADI centre offers 1 tank dives (US$46), 2 tank dives (US$86), and open water certification (US$345), including equipment. Training to assistant instructor level, technical training. Also rents out equipment, runs snorkelling tours (US$92 for 4), and surfing lessons (US$30 per hr).

Fishing
Many hotels and surf shops also offer fishing. **Super Fly Sport Fishing**, advance reservation only, T884-8444, www.superflynica.com. Fly fishing and light tackle, deep-sea fishing, Captain Gabriel Fernández, fluent in English with lots of experience, also fishes north Pacific Coast and Lake Nicaragua.

Massage
Gaby's Massage Studio, mercado, ½ este, T568-2654, estrelladeluna@hotmail.com. Professionally trained in Managua, Gaby has 7 years' experience and combines techniques from Shiatsu, reflexology and aromatherapy. US$25 for 1 hr.

Sailing
Pelican Eyes Sailing Adventures, Parroquia 1½ c arriba, T568-2110, sailing@ piedrasyolas.com. Sails to the beach at Brasilito, US$70 per person, min 10 people, leaves San Juan at 0900, return 1700.

Surfing
The coast north and south of San Juan del Sur is among the best in Central America for surfing. Access to the best areas are by boat or long treks in 4WD. Board rental costs US$10 per day; lessons US$30 per hr.

Arena Caliente, mercado, ½ c norte, T815-3247, www.arenacaliente.com. Friendly surf shop with board rental, surfing lessons (with transport and rash vest) and fishing trips. Also run transport to the beaches.

NicaSurf International, mercado, 1c al mar, ½ c sur, T568-2626, www.nicasurfint.com. Board rental, classes, trips and tons of merchandise.

Outer Reed, mercado, 1 c al mar, ½ c norte. Specializes in supplying the right board for the right person. Tours include a 4-day odyssey to surf hard-to-reach waves in the north.

Surf and Sport, Mercado, ½ c al mar, T402-2973. Board rental, fishing equipment, tours, lessons and transportation to the beaches.

◉ Transport

San Juan del Sur *p219, map p220*
Boat **Rana Tours**, kiosk opposite **Hotel Estrella**, on the seafront, run transport to the northern beaches such as **Michal**, **Marsella** and **Madera**, US$10 per person. They depart at 1100 and return at 1630.

Bus Several companies run shuttles to the beaches north and south of **San Juan del Sur**, including **Casa Oro Youth Hostel**, **Arena Caliente** surf shop and **Indian Face Tours**. Each has at least 3 daily departures to **Las Playones**, the beach next to Maderas, US$5.

To **Managua**, every hr 0500-1530, 3½ hrs, US$2.50. Or take a bus/taxi to Rivas and change here. To **Rivas**, every ½ hr, 0500-1700, 40 mins, US$1. For **La Flor** or **Playa El Coco** use bus to **El Ostional**, 1600, 1700, US$ 0.70, 1½ hrs. Return from El Coco at 0600, 0730 and 1630.

For the **border**, take any bus to Rivas, get off when it hits the Interamericana (this crossing is also know as 'La Virgen'); all buses heading south from here will go to

Peñas Blancas (every 30 mins). Taxi to the border is US$10-15.

◉ Directory

San Juan del Sur *p219, map p220*
Banks **Banco Procredit**, mercado, 1 c al mar, will change dollars. There is a single ATM in town, Visa only, Mercado, 1 c al mar, 1 c norte, ½ c al mar. Some hotels might change dollars too. **Internet** Several places in town, most charge US$1 per hr. **Language schools** Karla Cruz, Parque Central, 1½ c sur (3rd house to the right after the road turns right), T657-1658, karlacruzsjds@yahoo.com. Private instructor who also gives classes, US$5 per hr, discount for longer periods, additional US$50 for homestay in her house, recommended. **Latin American Spanish School**, southwest corner of Parque Central, ½ c al mar, www.latinamericanspanish school.com, T820-2252. Professionally led, intensive classes, activities and homestay. **Nicaragua Language School**, southwest corner of Parque Central, ½ c al mar, T568-2142, www.nicaspanish.com. One-to-one immersion classes, volunteer opportunities and customized classes. Free internet. **Spanish School House Rosa Silva**, mercado, 50 m al mar, T682-2938, www.spanishsilva.com. 20 hrs of 'dynamic' classes cost US$120, student accommodation or homestay are extra. Activities include swimming, hiking and cooking. All teachers are English-speaking. Teaching by the hour, US$7. **Spanish School San Juan del Sur**, T568-2432, www.sjdsspanish.com. Regular morning classes, tutoring with flexible hours. **Laundry** Lavandería Gaby, mercado, ½ c arriba, around US$3 for a medium-sized load. **Post** 150 m left (south) along the seafront from the main junction.

Río San Juan and Solentiname Archipelago

The Río San Juan, a natural canal between the Pacific and Atlantic oceans, is one of the great natural attractions of Central America – a mini Amazonas, which runs through deep jungles, and is replete with surreal, uniquely adapted biological forms. Over 190 km long and with more than 17 tributaries, it runs the length of the southern border of the Indio Maíz Biological Reserve and connects Lake Nicaragua to the Atlantic Ocean. It is the best area in Nicaragua to spot wildlife. This great river has played an integral part in Nicaragua's colonial and post-colonial history and is one of the most accessible of the country's many pristine nature-viewing areas. Intrepid travellers can cross the international border here too. The department's capital, San Carlos, is perched on the shores of Lake Nicaragua, providing access to the wonderful Solentiname Archipelago. These idyllic islands are home to various artistic communities, where families practise a type of primitivist art that has reached galleries in New York and Paris. The archipelago has a fascinating history, and was the subject of a famous social experiment in Utopianism. ▸▸ *For listings, see pages 232-234.*

Background
First sailed by the Spanish in 1525, the complete length of the river was navigated on 24 June 1539, the day of San Juan Bautista, hence its name. In colonial times it was a vital link between the Spanish Caribbean and the port of Granada. After three attacks by Caribbean pirates on Granada, the Spanish built a fortress at El Castillo in 1675. The English tried to take the fort twice in the 18th century, failing the first time thanks to the teenage Nicaraguan national heroine Rafaela Herrera, and then succeeding with Lord (then Captain) Nelson, who later had to withdraw owing to tropical diseases. Later it became the site of many aborted canal projects. It is still a most rewarding boat journey.

San Carlos
Like a ragged vulture, San Carlos is perched between several transportation arteries. It is the jumping-off point for excursions west to the Islas Solentiname; south along the Río Frío to Los Chiles in Costa Rica; north across the lake to Isla Ometepe and Granada; and east to the Río San Juan itself. It's a reasonably ugly town, but not overly offensive. Nearby are the two great nature reserves of Los Guatusos and Indio Maíz, where it is very muddy at all times of the year (purchase rubber boots if you wish to explore these forests). At San Carlos there are the ruins of a fortress built for defence against pirates.

Solentiname Archipelago
On **Isla San Fernando**, many locals carve and paint balsa wood figures. The diet on the island is somewhat limited but there is lots of fresh fruit. Ask for Julio Pineda or his sister Rosa, one of the local artists. The island has a new **museum** ① *US$1*, with a variety of natural and cultural history exhibits as well as a spectacular view of the archipelago, especially at sunset; if closed ask in the village if it can be opened. Apart from at the hotel, there is no electricity on the island, so take a torch.

   Isla La Venada, named for its plentiful population of *venado* (deer), is also home to artists, in particular the house of Rodolpho Arellano who lives on the south side of the island. He is one of the region's best painters and his wife, daughters and grandson all paint tropical scenes and welcome visitors to see and purchase their works. On the north side of the island is a series of semi-submerged caves with some of the best examples of petroglyphs from the pre-Columbian Guatuso tribe.

Isla El Padre is privately owned and the only island inhabited by howler monkeys. If you circle the island in a boat they can usually be spotted in the trees.

Isla Mancarrón is the largest in the chain, with the highest hill at 250 m. This is where the famous revolutionary/poet/sculptor/Catholic priest/Minister of Culture, Ernesto Cardenal, made his name by founding a school of painting, poetry and sculpture, and even decorating the local parish church in naïve art. He preached a kind of Marxist liberation theology, where the trials of Christ were likened to the trials of poor Nicaraguans. There is a monument to the Sandinista flag outside the church. Hiking is possible on the island where many parrots and *Moctezuma oropendolas* make their home. The island's hotel of the same name is part of the local folklore as its founder Alejandro Guevara was a hero of the Sandinista Revolution; his widow Nubia and her brother Peter now look after the place.

Los Guatusos Wildlife Reserve

Known as the cradle of wildlife for Lake Nicaragua, Los Guatusos is home to many exotic and varied species of bird and reptile. It is also heavily populated by monkeys, especially howlers. The reserve is crossed by three rivers, Guacalito, Zapote and Papaturro, which are popular for boat touring. It is essential to be at the park for sunrise to see the best of the wildlife. After 1030 the river often becomes busier with the immigration traffic of labourers heading to Costa Rica. A new **research centre** ⓘ *explanations in Spanish only, US$4, ask for Armando who is an enthusiastic expert on orchids*, built by Friends of the Earth and the Spanish Government has a collection of over 90 orchids native to the region and a butterfly farm. Visitors are welcome. Lodging is also possible in the research centre (**E** per person, bunkbeds with mosquito netting and shared bath). There is a public boat from San Carlos to Papaturro (Monday to Saturday 1100 and 1400, US$1, 1½ hours; check the return schedule locally).

Sábalos and El Castillo

East of San Carlos, the first settlement of any real size you'll encounter is **Sábalos**. It has a handful of very basic, budget accommodations and is also the site of a more upmarket lodging, **Hotel Sábalos**, located slightly downstream on the opposite bank. This is a great place to see the comings and goings of everyday life on the river.

Continue east though, and around 15-30 minutes later you'll arrive at **El Castillo**, some 60 km from San Carlos, built around the restored ruins of the 18th-century Spanish fort called **La Fortaleza de la Inmaculada Concepción**. The old fort has a good history **museum** ⓘ *closes at 1200 for lunch, US$1.50*. The **tourist office** on the quay has a leaflet about the fort and town. It was here that Nelson did battle with the Spanish forces. There are great views of the river from the fortress. The town is on a wide bend in the river where some shallow but tricky rapids run the whole width. Horse riding is possible (about US$6 per hour). El Castillo is a good place to pick up food on the river.

Reserva Biológica Indio Maíz

A few kilometres downstream is the Río Bartola and the beginning of the Reserva Biológica Indio Maíz, 3000 sq km of mostly primary rainforest and home to more than 600 species of bird, 300 species of reptile and 200 species of mammal including many big cats and howler, white-faced and spider monkeys. Sleeping is possible in **Refugio Bartola**, a research station and training ground for biologists; it has a labyrinth of well-mapped trails behind the lodge. The hotel guides are very knowledgeable. They will also take you down the Río Bartola in a canoe for great wildlife viewing and birding. Neglect in recent years has made turning up without booking a bit of a gamble, so do book in advance. Camping is possible; ask the park ranger (his house is across the Río Bartola from the **Refugio Bartola** lodge).

Bartola and further east

The river past **Bartola** becomes more beautiful and the Costa Rican border reaches to the south bank of the river. The Costa Rican side is partially deforested; the Nicaraguan side with the Indio Maíz Reserve is almost entirely intact. Watch out for turtles, birds and crocodiles. Two hours downriver is the **Río Sarapiquí** and immigration check-points for both Costa Rica and Nicaragua (no stamps available though).

If coming from the Río San Juan to Río Sarapiquí you will need to check in with the Costa Rican guard station if you want to spend the night, or even if you want to pick up something at the store. If continuing down the river without stopping you only need to check in at the Nicaraguan station on the Río San Juan.

Past the Sarapiquí, the San Juan branches north, and both sides of the river (heavily forested) become part of Nicaragua again as the Río Colorado heads into Costa Rica. Two hours or so later, the San Juan reaches the Caribbean via a series of magnificent forest-wrapped lagoons. The Río Indio must be taken to reach the isolated but surprisingly wealthy village of San Juan del Norte.

San Juan del Norte

One of the wettest places on the American continent with more than 5000 mm of rain each year, San Juan del Norte (also called Santa Isabel) is also one of the most beautiful, with primary rainforest, lagoons, rivers and the Caribbean Sea. It is settled by a small population (estimated at 275), though it was once a boom town in the 19th century, when the American industrialist Cornelius Vanderbilt was running his steamship line between New York and San Francisco. Then called Greytown, San Juan del Norte was the pick-up point for the steamship journey to the Pacific via the Río San Juan, Lake Nicaragua to La Virgen and then by mule overland to San Juan del Sur. This service was quite popular during the 'gold rush' of San Francisco and a young Mark Twain made the crossing, later recounting his journey in the book *Travels with Mr Brown*. The town remained in its location on the Bahía San Juan del Norte, actually a coastal lagoon, until the 1980s, when fighting caused its population to flee. Re-established in its current location on the east bank of the Río Indio, the village is separated from the Caribbean Sea by 400 m of rainforest. The population is a mix of Miskito, Creole, Rama and Hispanic. There is no land route from here to Bluefields and the boat takes about three hours, US$600. Due to its proximity to Limón, in Costa Rica, colones are the standard currency here as all the food and supplies are bought easier there than in San Carlos. In Sarapiquí and San Juan del Norte córdobas, colones and dollars are all accepted.

If in your own boat (chartered), a trip further down the **Río Indio** is recommended, with lots of wildlife, virgin forest and Rama (please respect their culture and privacy). A visit to the ruins of old **Greytown** is also interesting, with a well-marked trail that leads through various cemeteries buried in the forest and to the town centre where only foundations and the church bell remain. It has been described as 'incredibly atmospheric' with amazing wildlife and is great for birding in the morning. Note the names on some of the tombstones, which include sailors from around the world. Most of the year the entrance is underwater so rubber boots are of great use here, as for the rest of the region. Swimming is best in the **Blue Lagoon**, as there are many sharks in the Caribbean. If coming on the public boat from San Carlos, Melvin can arrange tours with one of his *pangas* (expect to pay around US$15-20 for a boat).

◉ Río San Juan and Solentiname Archipelago listings

For Sleeping and Eating price codes and other relevant information, see pages 43-46.

● Sleeping

San Carlos *p229*
D Cabinas Leyko, Policía Nacional, 2 c abajo, T583-0354. The best place in town has clean, comfortable rooms with good mattresses, private bath and a/c. Cheaper with fan (**E**).
D Carelhy's Hotel, Iglesia católica, ½ c sur, T583-0389. 10 rooms with private bath, fan and cable TV. Can help arrange tours and transport, breakfasts for large groups.
E Cocibolca, in San Miguelito north of San Carlos, at the end of the jetty, T552-8803. Colonial-style hotel with hard beds. Ask for a room with a balcony. Horse riding arranged by the owner, Franklin, as well as day trips to El Boquete and El Morro Islands. The Granada–San Carlos boat stops here.
E Costa Sur, Consejo Supremo Electoral 50 m sur, T583-0224. 10 rooms, shared or private bath and fan, meals. Some have a/c (**C**).

Solentiname Archipelago *p229*
It's possible to stay in basic but generally very clean private homes.
L Refugio Mancarrón, Mancarrón, up the hill from the dock and church, T265-2716 (Managua). Includes 3 good meals per day. Fine spot, ideal for wildlife/hiking. Good rooms.
B-C Hotel Celentiname or Doña María, San Fernando, T893-1977. This hotel has pretty grounds and owners Daniel and María are friendly and helpful. Tiny rooms have shared bath, weak beds and no windows. The cabins have private bath and spectacular lake views. No advance booking.
D Albergue de la Comunidad de Solentiname/Doña Esperanza, Mancarrón, T283-0083. Turn right before church and call

out at the gate (¡*Buenas*!). Low-ceiling cabins in need of care, big grassy grounds, food available, library. Some with private bath, some with shared. Owned by the famed priest Ernesto Cardenal (can be booked through his **Galería de Los Tres Mundos**, in Managua, T278-5781).

Sábalo and El Castillo *p230*
AL Posada del Río, 100 m north from the dock, T616-3528. The best place in town, with very comfortable, pleasant rooms, hot water, a/c, private bath and balconies. Breakfast included.
B-E Hotel Victoria, north from the dock and at the end of the end road, T583-0188, hotelvictoria01@yahoo.es. 9 rooms with fan, private bath and hot water, 3 with a/c and 2 with shared bath (**E**). There's lots of turtles and caimans nearby, but they seem to feeding on waste from the hotel. Breakfast included.
C Albergue El Castillo, next to fortress above city dock, T583-0195. Comfortable, if simple wooden rooms and great views from a shared balcony overlooking the river. Only 1 room has a private bath, best rooms are 1 and 10 for extra side ventilation, but noisy bats for company in 10. Good food: try the *camarones del río* (river shrimp) in garlic butter. Noisy in the early morning as the public boats warm up (0500) motors. Breakfast included.
D Hotel Sábalos, on confluence of San Juan and Sábalo rivers, T894-9377, www.hotel sabalos.com.ni. This simple, wooden hotel has a great location, with views up and down the river, great for watching locals pass in canoes. Friendly and recommended.
E Universal, main dock, 50 m downriver. Friendly owners, pleasant views and small, clean, wooden rooms. A good budget choice.

Bartola and further east *p231*

LL Río Indio Lodge, between Río Indio and Río San Juan, Bahía de San Juan, near San Juan del Norte, T(506) 296-0095, www.rio indiolodge.com. Multi-million dollar lodge, designed for upmarket fishing packages but excellent for wildlife safaris, birdwatching and rainforest walks. Nicaragua's finest rainforest jungle lodge, recently named one of the top 10 jungle lodges in the world.

D Cabinas La Trinidad or **Doña Adilia's**, at confluence of Río San Juan and Río Sarapiquí on Costa Rican bank, mobile T(506) 391-7120, hurbinacom@yahoo.com. Little rooms with private bath, fan, not terribly clean, bring mosquito net. You need to check in with the Costa Rican guard station across from the lodge on the Río Sarapiquí.

San Juan del Norte *p231*

E Hotel Lost Paradise or **Melvin's Place**, on the river at the south end of town. Ceiling fan, private bath, screened windows but bring coils or mosquito netting. Bar, restaurant (order well in advance), night-time generated power, gazebo on the river, bottled water is sometimes for sale, becoming neglected.

⏶ Eating

San Carlos *p229*

ⵍⵍ-ⵍ Granadino, opposite Alejandro Granja playing field, T583-0386, daily 0900-0200. Considered the best in town, with a relaxed ambience, good murals, pleasant river views, *Camarones en salsa*, steak and hamburgers.

ⵍⵍ-ⵍ Kaoma, across from Western Union, T583- 0293. Daily from 0900 until the last customer collapses in a pool of rum. Funky place, decorated with dozens of oropendula nests, attracts a hard-drinking, friendly clientele.

ⵍ El Mirador, Iglesia católica, 1½ c sur, T583-0377, daily 0700-2000. Superb view from patio of Lake Nicaragua, Solentiname, Río Frío and Río San Juan and the jumbled roofs of the city. Decent chicken, fish and beef dishes starting at US$3 with friendly service.

ⵍ Mirasol, next to the Roman lake dock where the river meets the lake. Good grilled meats and decent salads, fried chicken, good place to sit in the daytime to watch life on the river and lake with nice views, ruthless mosquitoes in the evening.

El Castillo *p230*

ⵍ Bar Cofalito, on the jetty. Good view and even better *camarones de río* (crayfish), considered by many the best in town, occasional fresh fish. Owner has river kayaks and can organize expeditions on the Río San Juan, rents motorboat (US$10 per hr) for tarpon and snook fishing.

ⵍ Vanessa's, north of the dock. Great spot by the rapids, with excellent fish and river shrimp.

San Juan del Norte *p231*

Simple food, fresh lobster if in season, if not the fried snook is recommended. There is a pleasant bar upriver from **Doña Ester's Place** with a big palm ranch and cold beer, card-playing locals and friendly Rama. It can be hard to find someone in San Juan to cook a meal, so bring snacks and arrange meals at **Doña Ester's** or **Melvin's Place** in advance.

⏶ Entertainment

San Juan del Norte *p231*
Bars and clubs
There is a disco which is full of festive locals at weekends dancing to reggae, salsa, rap and merengue. If staying at **Melvin's Place** he will take you to the disco to make sure you have a good time and get home safely. It's a short walk but a ride in his *super-panga*, if offered, is not to be missed. There are no police in San Juan and while the locals are very honest, be aware that this is border country and care should be taken, particularly at night.

⊖ Transport

San Carlos *p229*

Air To **Managua**, La Costeña, 0925, 1425, US$120 return (see Managua for outgoing schedules). Sit on the left for the best views. There is a maximum weight for flights – you will be asked your body weight. Flights land and take off within 5 mins, so early arrival is advised. Taxi from airstrip to dock US$1.

Boat *Pangas* are small motor boats; *botes*, long, narrow ones; *planos*, big broad ones. All schedules are subject to change, check locally before planning a journey. To **Granada**, Tue and Fri, 1400, 15 hrs, US$7. Bring a hammock and expect an exhausting journey. To **Solentiname Archipelago**, stopping at islands La Venada, San Fernando and Mancarrón, Tue and Fri 1200, 2½ hrs, US$4. To **Los Guatuzos Wildlife Refuge**, stopping at village of Papaturro, Tue, Wed, Thu, 0700, 5½ hrs, US$5. To **El Castillo** (and Sábalos), 0800, 1100 (express), 1300 (slow boat), 1430, 1530, 1630, 1½ (express) – 2½ hrs, US$4, US$5 (express), US$2 (slow boat), reduced services on Sun when only first 2 boats run. Avoid the slow boat if you can, it's a gruelling 6-hr ride. To **Los Chiles (Costa Rica)**, 1000, 1600, 2 hrs, US$8. To **San Juan del Norte**, Tue, Fri, 0600, 8 hrs, US$15.

Private boats are expensive but are faster. Ask at docks, restaurants, taxi drivers or at tourism office. Average round-trip rates: **El Castillo** US$190-250, **Solentiname** US$100-150. Group tours are available from tour operators in Managua.

Bus Managua–San Carlos is a brutal ride, but locals prefer it to the ferry trip. There are some lovely views during the early part and pure pain in the kidneys at the end. San Carlos– **Managua**, daily at 0200, 0600, 0800 and 1100, 9½ hrs, US$7. Returning from Mercado El Mayoreo at 0500, 0600, 0700 and 1300.

Solentiname Archipelago *p229*

Boat Private transfers from San Carlos to **Solentiname** 1-1½ hrs, US$55-85 per boat. Public boat to **San Carlos**, Tue and Fri, 0430, 2-3 hrs, US$4

El Castillo *p230*

To **San Carlos**: 0500 (slow boat), 0520 (express), 0600, 0700, 1100 (express), 1400, 1½-2½ hrs, US$2.75, US$3.75 (express), US$2 (slow boat), reduced services on Sun when only first 2 boats run. Avoid the slow boat if you can, reduced services on Sunday. To **San Juan del Norte**, Tues, Fri, 0930, 5 hrs, US$10.

San Juan del Norte *p231*

To **San Carlos**, stopping at El Castillo, Thu and Sun, 0430, US$15. There's little chance of connecting with Bluefields, north on the Caribbean coast, unless you have lots of patience, cash and a strong, sea-faring stomach. You might hitch a ride on a fishing boat if you're lucky, otherwise expect a challenging trip.

ⓘ Directory

San Carlos *p229*

Banks BDF, next to dock for Solentiname. No exchange for TCs and you can only change cash with street changers. Bring all the cash you need, as there's no ATM for miles.

Granada

A bastion of old money and conservatism, Granada is Nicaragua's most handsome and romantic city. Plied by horse-drawn carriages and home to a wealth of grandiose Spanish houses, it's an achingly picturesque, beautifully preserved colonial masterpiece. But all its grandeur is mere artifice. Repeatedly sacked by pirates and burned to the ground by marauding North Americans, few original features remain, and today, tourism is undermining Granada's backward-looking obsession with authenticity. The city's centre is prettified and endlessly photogenic, but real estate prices have soared here, making it unaffordable for the average Nicaraguan. Slowly but surely, it is becoming a city of foreigners, like Guatemala's Antigua, whose very soul has been devoured by the intensity of outside interest. But for now, Granada remains fascinating: between the carefully crafted colonial façades, there is still plenty of local colour – often supplied by the inhabitants of the city's impoverished and ramshackle barrios, places where gringos fear to tread. The challenge of the future is a balancing act between authenticity and pretence, substance and form, progress and identity. The current King of Spain summed it up during a visit here: "don't touch anything", he remarked. ➤➤ For listings, see pages 245-251.

Ins and outs

Getting there There is a ferry service from San Carlos, a challenging 12- to 14-hour journey across Lake Nicaragua that connects with river boats from Río San Juan and Los Chiles, Costa Rica. En route it stops at Altagracia, Isla Ometepe.

There are express buses from Managua's Roberto Huembes market as well as La UCA. International bus companies **Transnica**, King Quality and **Ticabus** stop in Granada on some of their routes north from Costa Rica.

If coming from the north, take the Carretera a Masaya, turn right at the Esso station upon entering the city and then left up Calle Real towards the centre. If coming from the south, use the Carretera a Granada. You will enter at the cemetery; continue north to the Calle Real and turn east towards the lake to reach the centre.

Getting around Granada's city centre is small and manageable on foot. Parque Central is the best reference point and the cathedral is visible from most of the city. There are three main streets: **Calle Real** runs east (*al lago*) past several churches to the central square, continuing as Calle El Calmito east of the park past the city's two Spanish restaurants and on to the lake. Running perpendicular is **Calle Atravesada**, one block west of Parque Central, which runs from the old railway station in the north, south to Granada market. It has most of the cheap eating and night entertainment. The other important route, **Calle Calzada**, which starts at the big cross on Parque Central and runs east towards the lake, past many beautiful homes, colourful restaurants and small *hospedajes*, ending at Lake Nicaragua and the city port. Much of the city's beauty can be appreciated within an area of five blocks around the centre. The east side of the Parque Central is generally much quieter with far fewer cars and trucks. ➤➤ For further details, see Transport, page 250.

Best time to visit Granada is hot year round but due to it lakefront location it does not suffer from as much dust and smoke during the dry season as some other towns. If planning a trip on the lake avoid the windy months from November to March; the prettiest time of year is the rainy season from June to October. The main day of Granada's patron saint festival is 15 August with horse parades, bulls in the streets and processions. Holy Week celebrations in Las Isletas include interesting boat processions.

Tourist office INTUR ① *Iglesia San Fransisco, opposite the southwest corner, on Calle Arsenal, T552-6858.* Possibly the best INTUR office in the country, with a healthy supply of brochures, maps and English-speaking staff.

Safety The centre of Granada is generally safe, but can become very empty after 2100 and some thefts have been reported. Police presence is almost non-existent on week nights so always be careful to take precautions. Avoid walking alone at night, avoid the barrios outside the centre. Take care along the waterfront at any time of day and avoid it completely after dark.

Background
The Chorotega population encountered by the first Spanish explorer, Captain Gil González Dávila, inhabited important settlements on both north and south sides of the Volcán Mombacho. Nochari, on the south side of the volcano, was later moved further southeast and became modern-day Nandaime (see page 244). Today's Granada was in the northern Lake Nicaragua Chorotega province of Nequecheri, and was dominated by the heavily populated settlement of Xalteva. Granada was founded by Captain Francisco

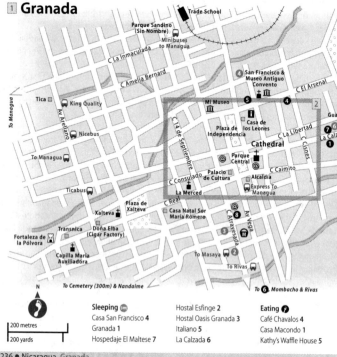

1 Granada

Sleeping
Casa San Francisco 4
Granada 1
Hospedaje El Maltese 7
Hostal Esfinge 2
Hostal Oasis Granada 3
Italiano 5
La Calzada 6

Eating
Café Chavalos 4
Casa Macondo 1
Kathy's Waffle House 5

Hernández de Córdoba around 21 April 1524 (the same year as León, and Nicaraguan historians have been arguing ever since to establish which was the first city of Nicaragua). The original wall, which divided the Spanish and Indian sectors of Granada, can be seen today just southeast of the Xalteva church. In 1585, a French chronicler described a religious procession in the city as rich in gold and emeralds, with Indian dances that lasted for the duration of the procession and a line of very well-dressed Spaniards, although the total Spanish population was estimated at only 200. Granada became a major commercial centre and when the Irish friar Thomas Gage visited in 1633 he marvelled at the city's wealth, most of which came from trade with Peru, Guatemala and Colombia.

Thanks to the lake and San Juan's river's access to the Atlantic, Granada flourished as an inter-oceanic port and trading centre, soon becoming one of the wealthiest, most opulent cities in the New World. But it wasn't long before reports of Granadino wealth reached the ears of English pirates occupying the recently acquired possession of Jamaica, which they wrested from Spain in 1665. Edward Davis and Henry Morgan sailed up the Río San Juan and took the city by surprise on 29 June 1665 at 0200 in the morning. With a group of 40 men they sacked the churches and houses before escaping to Las Isletas. In 1670 another band of pirates led by Gallardillo visited Granada via the same route. After destroying the fort at San Carlos, they sacked Granada and took with them men and women hostages.

In 1685, a force of 345 British and French pirates, led by the accomplished French pirate William Dampier, came from the Pacific, entering near where the Chacocente wildlife refuge is today (see page 225). The local population were armed and waiting to fight off the pirates but were easily overwhelmed by the size of the pirate army. They had, however, taken the precaution of hiding all their valuables on Isla Zapatera. The pirates burned the Iglesia San Francisco and 18 big houses, then retreated to the Pacific with the loss of only three men.

Granada saw even more burning and destruction in what were the biggest nationalist uprisings for Independence from Spain in 1811-1812 and during persistent post-Independence battles between León and Granada. When León's Liberal Party suffered defeat in 1854 they invited the North American filibuster William Walker to fight the Conservatives, thus initiating the darkest days of Granada's post-colonial history. Walker declared himself president of Nicaragua with the *cede* in Granada, but after losing his grip on power (which was regional at best) he absconded to Lake Nicaragua, giving orders to burn Granada, which once again went up in flames.

Since the days of William Walker, Granada has lost its importance as a commercial centre for inter-oceanic shipment of goods, but its Conservative Party supplied the country with presidents from 1869-1893 who brought modernization to the city with public lighting (1872), telephones (1879), running water (1880) and train travel (1886). The 20th century saw little action for the city other than continued economic growth for its landed aristocracy. In 1929 US journalist Carlton Beals described Granada as a town that "drowses in forgotten isolation". The old city was spared significant damage during the Revolution of 1978-1979, but Granada has undergone many facelifts in recent years. It is rapidly becoming an international city with its numerous foreign residents having a profound effect on the city's economy and culture.

Sights ⬤⬤⬤⬤⬤▲⬤⬤ ▸▸pp245-251.

The architectural style has been described as a mixture of Nicaraguan baroque and neoclassical. Having been rebuilt on a number of occasions, the city has a fascinating visual mix of Spanish adobe tile roof structures and Italian-inspired neoclassical homes with some ornate ceiling work and balconies. Italian architects such as Andrés Zapatta were contracted by the Granada elite to reconstruct the city after the many foreign-led assaults. The 20th-century writer Carlton Beals described Granada as "a haphazard picturesque little place, faintly reminiscent of Italian towns". However, most of the houses maintain the southern Spanish trademark interior gardens and large, airy corridors. It is interesting to compare the architecture of Granada with that of León, which was spared much of the looting and burning that the wealthier city of Granada suffered over the centuries.

Catedral Nuestra Señora de la Asunción
As a result of Granada's troubled history, its churches have all been rebuilt several times. Sadly, most have not retained much in the way of architectural interest or beauty. Last rebuilt and extended after William Walker's flaming departure in November 1856, the Catedral de Granada on Parque Central has become a symbol for Granada. The original church was erected in 1583 and rebuilt in 1633 and 1751. After Walker was shot and buried in Honduras in 1860, reconstruction began again on the cathedral, but was held up by lack of funds in 1891. The work in progress was later demolished and restarted to become today's church, finally opened in 1915. The cathedral has neoclassic and Gothic touches and its impressive size and towers make it a beautiful backdrop to the city, but the interior is plain. An icon of the Virgin, patron saint of Granada, is housed over the main altar. Mary has been proclaimed several times by the Nicaraguan government as the supreme ruler of Nicaragua's armed forces, responsible for defending the city against numerous attacks.

ATC Next to the cathedral is a big cross, erected in 1899, with a time capsule buried underneath. It was hoped that by burying common artefacts and personal belongings from the 19th century, it might ensure a peaceful 20th century. Despite the fairly violent period that followed, Granada did enjoy a reasonable amount of peace.

Parque Central
Parque Central is officially called Parque Colón (Columbus Park), though no one uses that name. Its tall trees and benches make it a good place to while away some time. There are food stalls selling the famous and tremendously popular Granada dish *vigorón*, which consists of a big banana leaf filled with cabbage salad, fried pork skins, yucca, tomato, hot chilli and lemon juice.

Calle Real

The most attractive of the Granada churches is **Iglesia La Merced**, which can be seen as part of a very nice walk from Parque Central down the Calle Real to the old Spanish Fortaleza de la Pólvora (see below). La Merced, built between 1751 and 1781 and also damaged by William Walker, has maintained much of its colonial charm and part of the original bell towers and façade. The pretty interior, painted an unusual tropical green colour, has an attractive altar and a painting of the Virgin on its north side. In front of the church is a cross constructed in 1999 as a symbol of hope for peace in the 21st century.

Further down the street is **Plaza de Xalteva**, which has unusual stone lanterns and walls, said to be a tribute to ancient Indian constructions. Unlike León and Masaya, Granada no longer has an Indian *barrio* of any kind, yet you can see the remains of the walls from the colonial period that separated the Spanish and indigenous sectors marked by a small tile plaque. The church on the plaza, **Iglesia Xalteva**, was yet another victim of William Walker. It was rebuilt at the end of the 19th century and is reminiscent of a New England church – a bit lacking in flair.

Just off the Calle Real, in between La Merced and Xalteva is the **Casa Natal Sor María Romero** ① *Tue-Sun 0800-1200, 1400-1700, free,* a small chapel and humble collection of artefacts and books from the life of María Romero Meneses (born in Granada 1902, died in Las Peñitas, León 1977). María was a local girl who became a Salesian nun at 28 and spent the rest of her life caring for the poor and ill, founding both a heathcare centre for the

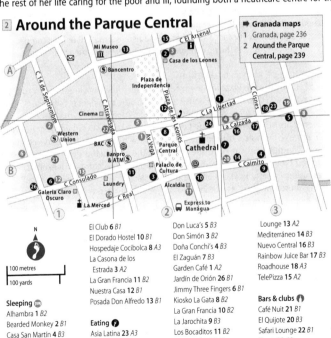

② **Around the Parque Central**

➡ **Granada maps**
1 Granada, page 236
2 **Around the Parque Central, page 239**

N
100 metres
100 yards

Sleeping 🛏
Alhambra **1** B2
Bearded Monkey **2** B1
Casa San Martín **4** B3
Colonial **5** B2
Darío **9** B3
El Club **6** B1
El Dorado Hostel **10** B1
Hospedaje Cocibolca **8** A3
La Casona de los Estrada **3** A2
La Gran Francia **11** B2
Nuestra Casa **12** B1
Posada Don Alfredo **13** B1

Eating 🍴
Asia Latina **23** A3
Café Dec Arte **24** B2
Café Mail **2** A2
Don Luca's **5** B3
Don Simón **3** B2
Doña Conchi's **4** B3
El Zaguán **7** B3
Garden Café **1** A2
Jardín de Orión **26** B1
Jimmy Three Fingers **6** B1
Kiosko La Gata **8** B2
La Gran Francia **10** B2
La Jarochita **9** B3
Los Bocaditos **11** B2
Los Portales **12** A2
Maverick Reading
Lounge **13** A2
Mediterráneo **14** B3
Nuevo Central **16** B3
Rainbow Juice Bar **17** B3
Roadhouse **18** A3
TelePizza **15** A2

Bars & clubs 🍸
Café Nuit **21** B1
El Quijote **20** B3
Safari Lounge **22** B1
Zoom **19** A3

poor and a home for street children in Costa Rica. She is said to have assisted in various miracles and may become the first saint in the history of Central America – her beatification was approved in Rome on 14 April 2002 by Pope John Paul II.

Further west along the Calle Real is the charming little **Capilla María Auxiliadora**. This church has some interesting features on its façade and some lovely detail work inside and is worth a visit. At the end of the street is the 18th-century fort and ammunitions hold, **Fortaleza de la Pólvora** ① *open during daylight hours, US$1-2 donation to the caretaker*. The fort was built in 1749 and used primarily as an ammunitions hold, then as a military base and finally a prison. You can climb up inside the southeastern turret on a flimsy ladder to have a good view down the Calle Real.

Calle Atravesada

There are a few sights of interest along the Calle Atravesada. Dating from 1886 and beautifully restored, the **old train station**, is now a trade school. Next to it is the 'Parque Sin Nombre' (park with no name). This little park was called Parque Somoza until the Revolution, when it was changed to **Parque Sandino**. When the Sandinistas lost in the 1990 elections, the park once again needed a new name. Some wise locals have since decided it best to allow the park to remain anonymous, though Parque Sandino remains its official name. Several blocks south and opposite Calle Arsenal is **Mi Museo** ① *Mon-Fri, 0800-1200, 1330-1700*. This new museum has an array of well-presented archaeological relics, including many rotund funerary pots that were once 'pregnant' with lovingly prepared human remains. Past Parque Central on the same street towards the volcano is the bustle and hustle of Granada's **market**. A visit here is a must, if only to compare the noisy, pungent chaos with the relative order of the more well-tended tourist drags.

Plaza de Independencia and around

Next to Parque Central is Plaza de Independencia, which has a movie-set quality to it. The bishop of Granada lives in the red house, at one time the presidential palace for William Walker. The telephone office is next door and just a few doors down is the historic **Casa de Los Leones** (its NGO name is **Casa de Los Tres Mundos**) ① *www.c3mundos.org, daytime exhibitions free*, with its 17th-century Moorish stone door frame that survived all the burning. The building was once the municipal theatre, then a private house where poet/priest Ernesto Cardenal was born. Now it is a cultural centre, with exhibits, music and occasional poetry readings and it's a good place to see the inside of a traditional Granada house. The plaza is occasionally home to folkloric acts on weekend nights.

One block east from the northeast corner of Plaza de la Independencia is the bright blue **Iglesia San Francisco** (1524), Nicaragua's oldest standing church with original steps. It was burnt down in 1685 by the group of pirates led by William Dampier, rebuilt, then modified in 1836 before being reduced to flames in 1856 on Walker's departure. It was finally rebuilt in 1868 with a fine restoration of the interior and a controversial decoration of the façade – some complain that it looks like a birthday cake. The legendary human rights priest Fray Bartolomé de las Casas preached here while visiting Granada in the 1530s.

Connected to the church is the mustard yellow **Museo Antiguo Convento de San Francisco** ① *T552-5535, daily 0830-1730, US$2, US$2.50 extra to photograph*. Originally founded as a convent in 1529, it was also burnt down in 1685 by Dampier. In 1836, after the religious orders of Central America had been forced to leave by the Central American Federation, it became a university, and then, in 1856, it was used as a garrison by William Walker, who burned it down once again before leaving the country. The old convent was rebuilt and became the most important secondary school in town, the Colegio de Granada, which later became the Instituto Nacional de Oriente until it closed in 1975. Restoration began in 1989 with help from the Swedish government. There is a mural in the entrance that leads to a small shop and café. The interior garden is dominated by towering 100-year-old palms, often full of squawking parakeets. In the east wing of the building is one of the country's most interesting pre-Columbian museums, housing large religious sculptures from the island of Zapatera in Lake Nicaragua (see page 242). The sculptures date from AD 800-1200; of particular note are the double standing or seated figures bearing huge animals, or doubles, on their heads and shoulders. The museum also has temporary exhibitions, historic photographs of Granada, some colonial period religious art and a gallery of Solentiname naïve painting.

Calle Calzada

East from the Parque Central, the brightly coloured and well-manicured Calle Calzada contains the city's highest concentration of restaurants and foreign tourists. This is the place for people-watching and enjoying a cold beer. The parade of gringo eateries peters out about halfway towards the lake, where you'll find the **Iglesia Guadalupe**. This church has seen plenty of action, thanks to its location near the water. Walker's forces used it as a final stronghold before escaping to the lake where Walker was keeping well away from the fighting, on a steamship. Originally constructed in 1626, its exterior has a melancholy, rustic charm, although the post-Walker interior lacks character. Beyond the church you'll pass the red cross and a baseball field before arriving at the lake and ferry port. Head south along the shore and you'll reach the fortress-like gates of the **complejo turístico**, a large recreation area of restaurants, discos and cafés, popular with the locals, particularly over Christmas and New Year.

Around Granada

Archipiélago Las Isletas

Just five minutes outside Granada, in the warm waters of Lake Nicaragua, is the chain of 354 islands called Las Isletas. The islands are big piles of basalt rock covered in lush vegetation growing in the fertile soil that fills in the islands' rocky surface. The number of mango trees on the archipelago is staggering (the abundance of fruit in general is an important part of the local diet along with fish) and magnificent giant ceiba and guanacaste trees dominate the landscape. Bird life is rich, with plenty of egrets, cormorants, ospreys, magpie jays, kingfishers, Montezuma oropendulas and various species of swallows, flycatchers, parrots and parakeets, as well as the occasional mot-mot. A great way to appreciate the bird life is to head out for a dawn kayaking expedition with **Iniuit Kayaks** or **Mombotour**, see page 249 for further details.

The islands were created by a massive eruption of the Mombacho Volcano that watches over the lake and islands to the west. You can see from the tranquillity of Las Isletas' waters how much of the mountain was blown into the water during the eruption. The islands' population consists mainly of humble fishermen and boatmen, though many of the islands are now privately owned by wealthy Nicaraguans and a handful of foreigners who build second homes and use them for weekend and holiday escapes. The school, cemetery, restaurants and bars are all on different islands and the locals commute mostly by rowing boat or by hitching rides from the tour boats that circulate in the calm waters. Fishing is the main source of income and you may well see the fishermen in the water laying nets for the lake's delicious *guapote* or *mojarra*. Many also find work building walls or caretaking on the islands owned by the weekenders.

The peninsula that jets out between the islands has small docks and restaurants on both sides. The immediate (north) side of the islands is accessed by the road that runs through the tourist centre of Granada and finishes at the docks. This is the more popular side of the archipelago and boat rides around the islands are cheaper from here (US$13 per hour per boat). In addition to the many luxurious homes on this part of the islands, is the tiny, late 17th-century Spanish fort, **San Pablo**, on the extreme northeast of the chain; it can be visited from the north side of the peninsula. Real estate companies have moved into this side of the archipelago and it is not unusual to see 'For Sale' signs in English.

There is a turning before the road ends with big signs for **Puerto Asese** ① *T552-2269, www.aseselasisletas.com*, which is a larger, more luxurious marina with a big restaurant. The boats from Puerto Asese also offer one-hour rides around the islands. Despite the fact that there are fewer canals you will have a better chance to see normal island life since this part southern part of the archipelago is populated by more locals, some of them quite impoverished. An hour on this side is normally US$15 with both sides charging US$1.50 for parking. A taxi or horse-drawn carriage to the docks costs US$4 or less. You will also be able to find transport to Las Isletas from nearby **Marina Cocibolca** ① *T228-1223, www.marinacocibolca.net*, which has public boat schedules at its administrative office.

Parque Nacional Archipiélago Zapatera

① *Some 40 km south of Granada, the journey to the islands takes about one hour from Granada by panga (skiff). Public boats depart irregularly from Puerto Asese and the average cost of hiring a private boat is US$100-150. Several tour companies offer trips including Oro Travel, see page 250; Tours Nicaragua in Managua (a sophisticated week-long archaeological trip), see page 271; and UCA Tierra y Agua, see page 249. There have been some reports of park rangers turning away visitors who do not have permission from MARENA, so it is best to use a tour operator to avoid disappointment. All hiking on Zapatera is guided. Beyond a simple restaurant and rustic lodgings, there are no facilities on the island. Bring all the supplies you need, including food and water.*

Although most important relics have been taken to museums, this archipelago of 11 islands remains one of the country's most interesting pre-Columbian sites. Isla Zapatera, the centrepiece and Lake Nicaragua's second largest island, is a very old and extinct volcano that has been eroded over the centuries and covered in forest.

Isla Zapatera has both tropical dry and wet forest ecosystems depending on elevation, which reaches a maximum height of 625 m. It is a beautiful island for hiking, with varied wildlife and an accessible crater lake, close to the northwest shore of the island. The main island is best known for what must have been an enormous religious infrastructure when the Spanish arrived, though many of the artefacts were not 'discovered' until the mid-19th century. There are conflicting reports on the island's indigenous name, ranging from *Xomotename* (duck village) to *Mazagalpan* (the houses with nets). Archaeological evidence dating from 500 BC to AD 1515 has been documented from more than 20 sites on the island. Massive basalt images attributed to the Chorotega people were found at three of these sites and some can be seen in the Museo Convento San Francisco in Granada and the Museo Nacional in Managua. US diplomat and amateur archaeologist Ephraim George Squier, on his visit to the island in 1849, uncovered 15 statues, some of which he had shipped to the US where they are in a collection at the Smithsonian Museum in Washington, DC. Another 25 statues were found by the Swedish naturalist Carl Bovallius in 1883, in what is the most interesting site, Zonzapote, which appears to have been part of an ancient ritual amphitheatre. In 1926, the US archaeologist Samuel Kirkland Lothrop theorized that Bovallius had uncovered a Chorotega temple consisting of several sacred buildings each with a separate entrance, idols and sacrificial mounds. But the evidence is not conclusive and further studies are needed. Equally impressive is the broad, flat rock that sits on the highest point of a small island to the north, **Isla el Muerto**. This 100 m x 25 m rock is one of the most interesting of Nicaragua's hundreds of petroglyph sites. The extraordinary range of rock drawings is believed to have been part of a very important burial site (hence the name 'Death Island').

Isla Zapatera has several hundred inhabitants who arrived during the 1980s from the northern extremes of Nicaragua to escape the violence of the Contra War. They are not legally allowed on the island, which enjoys national park status, so they may appear shy or suspicious. However, you can visit and stay at their community at Sonzapote through **UCA Tierra y Agua** in Granada, from where you can also hire guides to visit the petroglyphs or surrounding forests. Trails lead up Banderas Hill with great views of Ometepe and the lake, but the most demanding trail ascends Zapatera Hill (also known as Cerro Grande), the island's highest peak, for which you should allow six hours.

Reserva Natural Volcán Mombacho

ⓘ *To get to the reserve take a bus between Nandaime or Rivas and Granada or Masaya. Get off at the Empalme Guanacaste and walk (or take a taxi) 1 km to the car park. From here you can take a truck to the top of the volcano (great view), 25 mins; they leave every couple of hours from the parking area. The last trip is at 1500, although if there are enough people they will make another trip. It is also possible to walk the 5.5 km to the top using the steep cobblestone road (see below). Bring water, hiking shoes and a light sweater or better still a rain jacket or poncho. Park administration is in Granada, T552-5858, www.mombacho.org, Thu-Sun, 0830-1700, US$9 adult, US$3.25 children, which includes transfer to the reserve from the parking area and the aid of a park guide. Tickets are sold at the parking area at the base, along with purified water and snacks.*

Just 10 km outside Granada is one of only two cloudforests found in Nicaragua's Pacific lowlands. As well as the forest reserve, the volcano is home to coffee plantations and some ranches. The summit has five craters: four small ones – three covered in vegetation and one along the trails of the nature park – and one large one that lost one of its walls in a tragic mudslide in 1570 (see Nandaime, below).

The nature reserve is administered by the non-profit Cocibolca Foundation and is one of the best organized in Nicaragua. It's home to many species of butterfly and the famous Mombacho salamander (*Bolitoglossa mombachoensis*) which is found nowhere else in the world. Among other resident fauna, the biologists have counted some 60 species of mammal, 28 species of reptile, 10 species of amphibian, 119 species of bird and a further 49 species that are migratory visitors. More than 30,000 insect species are thought to exist, though only 300 have been identified to date. The volcano has terrific views of extinct craters and, if cloud cover permits, of Granada, Lake Nicaragua and Las Isletas. The cloud often clears for a few hours in the afternoon (1400-1530 best bet for a good view).

Paths are excellently maintained and labelled. For those who want to see a pristine, protected cloudforest the easy way, this is the perfect place. Most visitors opt for a one or two-hour stroll along the **Sendero Crater**, an easy trail that leads through magnificent cloudforest full of ferns, bromeliads and orchids (752 species of flora have been documented so far), has various lookout points and a micro-desert on the cone where you'll encounter steaming *fumaroles* and a stunning view of Cocibolca, Granada, Laguna de Apoyo and Volcán Masaya. An optional guide costs US$5 per group. Hardcore hikers may be disappointed by this relatively tame and well-tended trail, but there is an opportunity for a more challenging excursion too. The **Sendero El Puma** is only 4 km in length but takes around four hours to cover because of the elevation changes. This is the best walk for seeing wildlife, which can be very elusive during the daytime. A guide is obligatory, some speak English and they cost US$15 per group.

The main beauty of the park is its vegetation; if you wish to examine the amphibian, reptile and bird life of the reserve, you will have to sleep in the research station itself and go hiking at night and in the early morning. They have one big room with several beds, shared baths, kitchen and an outhouse. Cost per person with meals and a night tour is US$30. The research station offers simple, cheap sandwiches and drinks to visitors and has a good model of the volcano and historical explanations.

Canopy tours are not designed for nature watching, but to give you a bit of a rush and a sense of what it's like to live like the birds and monkeys up in the trees. Most people find it takes a long time for their smile to wear off. Mombacho has two canopy tours. On the forest reserve (west face) is the **Mombacho Canopy Tour**, see page 249, which includes lessons on a practice cable at ground level, assistance of one of the company guides, and all gear, and has 15 platforms from which you can buzz along a cable from platform to platform, high up in the trees and a suspended 1500-m long bridge. The Mombacho tour is over coffee plants and has some very big trees and the service includes refreshments in a little viewpoint overlooking the valley after your adventure. The views are not as spectacular as the Mombotour (see below) but are fun, and cheaper. The other canopy tour is on the east face of the mountain and is run by **Mombotour**, see page 249. This is a world-class canopy tour designed by the inventor of the sport, with 17 platforms 3-20 m above the ground on the lake side of Volcán Mombacho. The tour concludes with a faint inducing vertical descent on a rappel line.

Nandaime

Travelling south from Granada, the highway joins the Interamericana, which travels north to Los Pueblos and on to Managua. To the south, the highway continues to the departments of Granada and Rivas and on to the border with Costa Rica. A few kilometres south of the junction is the ranching town, Nandaime, which lies just west of the highway.

Nandaime (which translates roughly as 'well-irrigated lands') has an interesting history. It was the most important town for the Chorotega southern federation and could have been responsible for administering the religious sites on Isla Zapatera. The city was then moved for unknown reasons to a second location further west along the base of the Mombacho volcano and could have grown to be a sister city to Granada – had it survived. It was reported to have been a town with the same classic colonial design as Granada, home to a "formal and solid Catholic church". However, in 1570 an earthquake caused the rim of the Volcán Mombacho crater lake to collapse and the village was annihilated in a massive landslide. A third settlement was established at Nandaime's current position.

At the time of the Spanish arrival, it was a place for cultivation of the cacao fruit, the raw ingredient from which chocolate is made. During the 19th century much of the cacao was destined for the chocolate factories of Menier in France and the area became known as Valle de Menier. Today the area is home to big ranches and sugar cane and rice farms.

Nandaime has two pretty churches, **El Calvario** and **La Parroquia** (1859-1872). It is a peaceful cowboy town for most of the year, but becomes a raucous party town for the patron saint festival of Santa Ana in the last week of July (the most important day is 26 July). The festival includes the dance of the *Diablos de al Orilla*, which is a colourful, spectacular display of more than 40 men, who accompany the saint on an annual pilgrimage to the tiny settlement of **La Orilla**, closer to the southern face of Volcán Mombacho. There is a bullfight in La Orilla and much dancing and drinking, and the following days in Nandaime include more dancing in colonial period costume, cross-dressing, more drinking and some parading around on horseback.

Reserva Silvestre Privada Domitila

ⓘ *María José Mejía (the owner), Calle Amelia Benard, Casa Dr Francisco Barbarena, Granada, T881-1786, www.domitila.org or Amigo Tours, Hotel Colonial, Granada, T552-4080, who act as agents, arrange reservations. To get to Domitila you will need to hire a taxi or car, though a 4WD is needed in the rainy season. Entrance to the park is US$5 and guides cost from US$10-40. Reservations to stay or visit the reserve must be made at least three days in advance. Prices are overvalued so negotiate. The forest is quite bare at the end of the dry season; ideal months to visit would be Nov-Jan.*

Five kilometres south of Nandaime is the turning to an 8-km unpaved road that heads towards the lake and private nature reserve of Domitila. Just south of this turning, the Interamericana passes over the region's most important river, Río Ochomogo, the ancient border between the worlds of the Chorotega and that of the indigenous Nicaraguans to the south. Today it marks the end of Granada and the beginning of the isthmus department of Rivas (see page 206). Most of the pristine low-altitude tropical dry forest that has not been cut for grazing is located at the back of the Mombacho Volcano. However, further south there is a small swatch of it at this private wildlife reserve. Entry to the reserve is expensive, but it is home to more than 100 howler monkey species and 165 birds, 65 mammal and 62 butterfly species have been documented on their land. Due the small size of the reserve, nature watching is a more rewarding experience.

Lodging is available in eco-friendly rustic and attractive thatched huts at US$65 per person with three meals included, although food is average at best. The reserve management also offers horse riding and sailing excursions.

◉ Granada listings

For Sleeping and Eating price codes and other relevant information, see pages 43-46.

◉ Sleeping

L La Gran Francia, southeast corner of Parque Central, T552-6000, www.lagran francia.com. This traditional colonial building has some charming rooms with private bath, hot water, cable TV, a/c, minibar and internet access. Standard rooms are dark and face a wall. Suites have big wooden doors that lead on to small balcony with a lovely view and lots of light; worth the extra money. There's a swimming pool and staff are friendly.

L Hotel Darío, Calle La Calzada, de la Catedral, 150 vrs al lago, T552-3400, www.hoteldario.com. Right in the heart of town and housed by the smart, green and

white neoclassical building you can't fail to notice. The interior is handsome, with comfortable rooms and beautiful grounds. There's a gym, and a kidney shaped swimming pool for cooling off.

L-A Hotel Alhambra, Parque Central, T552-4486, www.alhambra.com.ni. Granada's landmark hotel has a stunning location on the plaza. Rooms vary dramatically in quality and price. The ones overlooking the park are best. There's a pool and terrace for drinks, and a restaurant – not owned by the hotel – that receives a lot of criticism for poor service. Often full with groups.

AL La Casona de los Estrada, Iglesia San Francisco, ½ c abajo, T552-7393, www.cas ona losestrada.com.ni. Decorated with fine furnishings, this small, homely hotel has 6 pleasant, well-lit rooms with private bath, hot water, a/c and cable TV. There's a pleasant plant-filled courtyard, English and French are spoken, and prices include breakfast.

AL-A Hotel Colonial, Calle La Libertad, Parque Central, 25 vrs al norte, T552-7581, www.hotelcolonialgranada.com. This centrally located, colonial-style hotel has a range of pleasant, comfortable lodgings, including heavily decorated rooms with 4-poster beds and 10 luxury suites with jacuzzi; all have hot water, a/c, cable TV and Wi-Fi. There's 2 pools, and the restaurant serves breakfast only.

A Casa San Francisco, Corrales 207, T552-8235, www.casasanfrancisco.com. This attractive, tranquil hotel comprises 2 colonial houses with 13 lodgings that vary greatly. One house has 2 suites and 2 comfortable rooms with private bath, cable TV, a/c, pool and a modern kitchen. The other has 8 rooms and 1 suite, a pool and restaurant. The friendly and helpful staff speak English.

A Casa San Martín, Calle La Calzada, catedral, 1 c lago, T552-6185, javier_sanchez _a@yahoo.com. 7 rooms in a beautiful colonial home, with cable TV, private bath, a/c or fan. Pleasant decor and garden terrace, very authentic Granada. Staff speak English.

A El Club, Parque Central, 3½ c abajo, T552-4245, www.elclub-nicaragua.com. This Dutch-owned hotel has 10 small, modern rooms with private bath, a/c, cable TV and Wi-Fi. There's a restaurant and bar downstairs, which can be noisy at times. The staff and friendly and helpful.

B Hospedaje El Maltese, Plaza España, 50 m sur, opposite *malecón* in Complejo Turístico, T552-7641, www.nicatour.net. 8 very clean rooms with private bath, nice furnishings, Italian spoken, restaurant **La Corte Del Maltese**, Mon-Fri 1600-2200. Don't walk here at night alone.

B Hotel Granada, opposite Iglesia Guadalupe, T552-2974, www.hotelgranada nicaragua.com. This recently renovated hotel has smart, clean, comfortable rooms with cable TV, Wi-Fi, a/c and hot water. A pool is being constructed, and there's a lovely view from the balcony and restaurant.

B Italiano, next to Iglesia Guadalupe, T552-7047, italianriky@latinmail.com. Rooms have bath and a/c, nice patio, drinks available, good value, Italian spoken.

B-D Nuestra Casa, La Merced, 1 c al norte, ½ abajo, T552-8115, www.hotelnuestracasa. com. Simple rooms with and without bath, cable TV and a/c (**B** with bath, TV and a/c). There's a pleasant honeymoon suite and the owner, an ordained minister in the Universal Life Church, will marry you on request. There's a popular bar and restaurant attached.

C Posada Don Alfredo, La Merced, 1 c norte, T552-4455, alfredpaulbaganz@hotmail.com. This interesting old hotel is housed in a historic building with many original features such as high, wooden ceilings and slatted windows. The rooms are dark and simple, some with a/c and hot water (**B**). The German management is hospitable and friendly.

C-F Dorado Hostel, southwest corner of Parque Central, 1½ c abajo, T552-6932, www.hostaldorado.com. Housed in a lovely colonial building, this new hostel has a relaxing patio, free Wi-Fi and DVD movies. Lodgings include single (**D**) and double rooms (**C**), and dormitories (**E**) of various sizes, cheaper with shared bath (**F**).

D Hospedaje Cocibolca, Calle La Cazada, T552-7223, www.hospedajecocibolca.com. A friendly, family house with 24 clean, simple rooms. There's a kitchen and internet access.

D Hostal Esfinge, opposite market, T552-4826, esfingegra@hotmail.com.ni. Lots of character at this friendly old hotel near the market. Rooms in the newer building are smaller, but some have bath and cable TV. Friendly and clean, with motorcycle parking.

D-F Bearded Monkey, Calle 14 de Septiembre, T552-4028, www.thebeardedmonkey.com. A sociable, popular hostel with dormitories (**F**), private rooms (**D**), and hammocks for those terribly impoverished backpackers. There's a plethora of services including restaurant, bar, cable TV, internet access, cheap calls, evening films, bike rentals, and free tea and coffee. Use lockers, as everybody is free to walk in and out. Runs trips to Laguna de Apoyo.

D-F Hostal Oasis Granada, Calle Estrada 109, south of the centre, T552-8006. Mix of dorms, shared and private rooms (**C-D** with all mod-cons), food available, laundry service and washing facilities. Full range of entertainment from book exchange and pool, through to free internet (and internet calls to Canada and USA) and DVDs – popular, gets good reports. Daily transit to Laguna Apoyo.

E La Calzada, near Iglesia Guadalupe, T475-9229, guesthouselacalzada@yahoo.com. This family-run guesthouse has 8 big, simple rooms with fan and bath; cheaper with shared bath.

🍴 Eating

¶¶¶ Casa Maconda, Calle La Calzada, 3½ c al lago, T680-6420. Closed Mon. This Spanish restaurant serves *paella*, tapas and the strongest Sangría in Granada. There's a happy hour from 1700-2000, a musical ambience, dance classes and exhibitions.

¶¶¶ El Jardín de Orión, northwest corner of Parque Central, 4 c abajo, ½ c al sur, T552-1220. This buzzing French restaurant has a fabulous garden terrace and a changing menu of sophisticated European cuisine. Great atmosphere and friendly service.

¶¶¶ La Gran Francia, corner of Parque Central. Daily 1100-2300. This beautiful restaurant is the epitome of colonial grandeur, with high ceiling dining rooms and a plethora of elegant, antique furniture. It serves expensive French-Nicaraguan cuisine, and has pleasant views from the upper floor balcony.

¶¶¶ Mediterráneo, Calle Caimito, T552-6764. Daily 0800-2300. Mediterranean cuisine served in a Spanish-owned colonial house with a tranquil garden setting. Mixed reviews; good seafood, bad paella. Popular with foreigners.

¶¶¶-¶¶ Doña Conchi's, Calle Caimito, T552-7376. Wed-Mon 1100-2300. A very beautiful restaurant, completely illuminated by candles and adorned with rustic

decorations like wood piles and bunches of dried flowers. They serve quality dishes such as grilled salmon, sea bass and lobster. Recommended.

¶¶¶-¶¶ El Zaguán, on road behind cathedral, T552-2522. Mon-Fri 1200-1500 and 1800-2200, Sat and Sun1200-2200. Incredible, succulent grilled meats and steaks, cooked on a wood fire and served impeccably. Undoubtedly the best beef cuts in Granada, if not Nicaragua. Highly recommended.

¶¶ Asia Latina, Calle La Calzada, 2½ c al lago. Thai and Asian fusion, with a touch of Latin. Great curries and vegetarian dishes, served in a friendly, atmospheric setting. Recommended.

¶¶ Café Chavalos, corner of calle Arsenal and Matirio, T852-0210, www.cafechavalos.com. An interesting training programme for 'would-be gang members', who, under supervision of chef Sergio, now learn to prepare international cuisine. Best to book in advance. Recommended.

¶¶ Don Luca's, Calle La Calzada, catedral, 2 c al lago, T552-7822. Excellent wood-oven pizza, *calzone*, and pasta. Pleasant setting.

¶¶ Jimmy Three Fingers, La Merced, 1 c al norte, ½ al abajo, T552-8115, www.jimmythreefingers.com. Famous rib-shack serving lovingly prepared, slow-cooked baby back ribs, seafood, Italian cuisine, gourmet soups and comfort food for Granada's homesick expats. Celebrated and reassuringly creative.

¶¶ La Jarochita, Alcaldía, 2 c al lago, T552-8304. Quite possibly Nicaragua's finest Mexican restaurant, serving *tacos*, *burritos* and *quesadillas con mole*, among other national staples. Colourful and friendly. Also has a branch in Masaya.

¶¶ La Terrazza La Playa, Complejo Turístico. Great *cerdo asado* and *filete de guapote*.

¶¶ Las Colinas del Sur, Shell Palmira, 1 c sur, T552-3492. Daily 1200-2200, Tue lunch only 1200-1500. Seafood specialities, excellent lake fish, try the *guapote* fried whole, boneless fillets, avocado salad. Far from centre, but worth it, take a taxi.

Los Chocoyos, Calle Corrales, north corner of the Convent, inside Casa San Fransisco, T552-8235. Daily 1200-2300. A range of tasty international cuisine including Mexican, Italian and French, served in a colonial setting.

Mona Lisa, Calle La Calzada, 3½ c al lago, T552-8187. Undoubtedly the best pizzas in Granada; stone-baked, tasty and authentic.

Roadhouse, Calle La Calzada, 2 c al lago. Popular with Nicaraguans, this rocking American-style restaurant serves a range of wholesome burgers. The fries, flavoured with cajun spices, are the real stand-out dish.

Los Bocaditos, Calle el Comercio. Mon-Sat 0800-2200, Sun 0800-1600. A bustling but clean locals' joint with buffet from 1100-1500, breakfast and dinner menu.

Los Portales, opposite Cafemail on Plaza de los Leones, T552-4115. Daily 0700-2200. Simple Mexican food, sometimes overpriced, but a great place for people-watching.

Nuevo Central, Calle La Calzada, 1½ c al lago. An unassuming little place, and just one of many terraced restaurants along this stretch. They do unpretentious, cheapish chicken and meat dishes with enormous portions. Popular with locals.

Kiosko La Gata, Parque Central. Daily 1000-1900. Offers traditional Nica drinks such as *chicha* and *cacao con leche*.

Restaurant Querube's, Calle el Comercio, opposite Tiangue 1. Clean and popular locals' joint near the market. Offers Nicaraguan and Chinese fare from a buffet, as well as set lunches and breakfasts.

TelePizza, Bancentro, 1½ c al lago. T552-4219. Daily 1000-2200. Good, tasty pizzas; but not outstanding. Popular with Nicaraguans or those that have had enough of the gringo places. Delivery service.

Cafés

Café de Arte, Calle Calzada, near the cathedral, T552-6461. Tue-Sun 1100-2200. This charming café hosts exhibitions of local artists. The desserts are 'to die for'. Recommended.

Café Isabella, 108 Calle Corrales, Bancentro, 1 c norte, ½ c abajo. Breakfast is served on a large covered balcony on the street or in the interior garden, also has vegetarian dishes.

Café Mail, next to Casa de Tres Mundos, T552-6847. Daily 0700-2200. Check your email while sipping a cappucino; offers breakfasts and light meals too. Good for people-watching on the patio outside.

Don Simón, Parque Central, T884-1393. Daily 0700-2100. Great views over the plaza. Simple breakfasts, good pastries, coffee, espresso, cappuccino, sandwiches.

Garden Café, Enitel, 1 c al lago. A very relaxed, breezey café with a lovely leafy garden and patio space. Good breakfasts, sandwiches, coffees, muffins and cookies. Friendly and pleasant. Recommended.

Kathy's Waffle House, opposite Iglesia San Francisco, 0730-1400. Kathy does the best breakfasts in town, and it's always busy here in the morning. You'll find everything from waffles to pancakes to *huevos rancheros*, all with free coffee refills. Highly recommended.

Maverick Reading Lounge, Telepizza, 1 c abajo. Fair trade gourmet coffee, hot tea, good selection of magazines in English and Spanish, second-hand books, cigars.

Rainbow Juice Bar, Calle La Calzade, 2 c al lago. Sweet, tasty juices and *licuados* – great for a nutrient boost.

Entertainment

Bars and clubs

Café Nuit, northwest corner of Parque Central, 2½ c abajo. Wed-Mon 1900-0200. Great live music venue, with acts on Fri and Sat performing inside a pleasant colonial courtyard. Very cool and popular.

César, on waterfront (Complejo Turístico). Fri and Sat only. Recommended for dancing and drinking, very popular, inexpensive bar with merengue and salsa music.

El Club, northwest corner of Parque Central, 3 c abajo. Mon-Thu until 2400, Fri-Sun until

0200. Clean, modern bar with Euro-ambience, dance music and a mixture of locals and foreigners. Stylish and a cut above the rest.
Jimmy Three Fingers, La Merced, 1 c norte. Fri-Sun 1800-0200. A renowned expat bar, also popular with Nicas and the local Harley Davidson chapter. The boss is an interesting and entertaining character. Live music and good, cold beer.
Safari Lounge, northwest corner of Parque Central, 1 c abajo. Complete with mock-Zebra skin upholstery, this modern bar is popular with foreigners and a great spot for people-watching over a rum or 2. The bar upstairs is more of a local affair.
El Quijote, southeast corner of Parque Central, 1 c al lago. Loud, boozy pub with a fun, foreign and mostly beer swilling crowd.

Cinema
1 block behind **Hotel Alhambra**, good, modern, 2 screens.

⊛ Festivals and events

Mar Folklore, Artesanía and Food Festival for 3 days (check locally for dates).
Mar/Apr Holy Week.
14-30 Aug Assumption of the Virgin.
Aug La Hípica takes place 2nd weekend of Aug. The Sun preceding La Hípica is **La Fiesta de Toros** with bulls running in the streets.
25 Dec Christmas celebrated with masked and costumed performers.

O Shopping

The **market** (large green building south of Parque Central) is dark, dirty and packed, but there are lots of stalls on the streets outside, as well as a horse cab rank and taxis. The main shopping street runs north-south, west of plaza.
Supermercado Pali, next to the outdoor market, is also dark and dirty, but marginally less chaotic for shopping.

▲ Activities and tours

Canopy tours
Mombacho Canopy Tour, on the road up to the Mombacho cloudforest reserve, T888-2566. Tue-Sun 0830-1730. Not as spectacular or professional as the **Mombotour** canopy, but fun, cheaper at US$30, US$10 student discount and combines better with a visit to the cloud-forest reserve on this side of the volcano.
Mombotour, Centro Comercial Granada No 2, T552-4548, www.mombotour.com. This is a world-class canopy tour designed by the inventor canopy tours, with 17 platforms 3-20 m above the ground on the lake side of Volcán Mombacho. The tour concludes with a vertical descent on a rappel line. 2 trips daily, US$38, including 4WD transfers.

Cultural and community tourism
La UCA Tierra y Agua, Shell Palmira, 75 vrs abajo, T552-0238, www.ucatierrayagua.org, Mon, Wed, Fri, 0830-1400. This organization will help you organize a visit to rural communities around Granada including Isla Sonzapaota, La Granadilla, Albergue Nicaragua Libre and Aguas Agrias. Very interesting and highly recommended for a perspective on local life and the land. Roll up your sleeves and muck in, if you wish.

Horse riding
Blue Mountain, southwest corner of Parque Central, 1½ c abajo, T552-5323, www.blue mountainnicaragua.com. Offer daily cowboy-style tours of the region, with birdwatching, swimming and fishing options. You can bottle-feed some calves too.

Kayaking
Inuit Kayaks, entrance to the touristic centre, 400 m sur on the lake, T608-3646, www.inuit kayak.com. Kayak rental, sales and tours of the Isletas. Sailing, catamarans and windsurfing too.
Mombotour, Central Comercial Granada No2, T552-4548, www.mombotour.com. Having overtaken the reputable 'Island

Kayaks' agency, Mombotour offer kayak lessons and guided tours of the Isletas, which can be combined with longer birding expeditions.

Massage
Seeing Hands, inside **EuroCafe**, off the northwest corner of Parque Central. This excellent organization offers blind people an opportunity to earn a living as masseurs. A range of effective, professional massages are available, from a 15-min back, neck and shoulder massage, US$2.50, to a 1-hr table massage, US$12.50.

Sailing
Marina Cocibolca, www.marinacocibolca. net. Check the marina's administrative offices for information for visits to the Isletas, Zapatera and nearby private reserves.
Puerto Asese, www.aseselasisletas.com. 3 km from Granada, this low-key dock is the place to find transport to Las Isletas or Zapatera.
Zapatera Tours, Calle Palmira contiguo a la Cancha, T842-2587, www.zapateratours.com. This company specializes in lake tours with trips to las Isletas, Zapatera, Ometepe and the Solentiname archipelago. It also offers biking, hiking and windsurfing.

Tour operators
JB Fun Tours, on Parque Central inside artisan shop at cultural centre, T552-6732, www.jbfun tours.com. Lots of options including fishing, manager Christian Quintanilla speaks English and is a good guide.
Oro Travel, Convento San Francisco, ½ c norte, T552-4568, www.orotravel.com. Granada's best tour operator offers quality, specialized tours, many including transfers and hotels. Owner Pascal speaks French, English and German. Friendly and helpful.
Tierra Tour, Calle la Calzada, catedral, 2 c lago, T0862-9580, www.tierratour.com. This well-established Dutch-Nicaraguan agency offers a wide range of services including economical trips to Las Isletas, cloudforest tours, birding expeditions and shuttles. Helpful and friendly.

Va Pues, Parque central, blue house next to the cathedral, T552-8291, www.vapues.com. This award-winning agency offers canopy tours, turtle expeditions, car rental, domestic flights and a 'romantic getaway' tour to a private island.

⊕ Transport

Bus
Local For the border with Costa Rica use **Rivas** bus to connect to **Peñas Blancas** service or use international buses.

Express minibuses to La UCA in **Managua** from a small lot just south of Parque Central on Calle Vega, every 20 mins, 0500-2000, 45 mins, US$1.20. Ask to be dropped on the highway exit to **Masaya**, US$0.60, from where it's a 20-min walk or 5-min taxi ride to the centre. Buses to Mercado Roberto Huembes, Managua, also leave from a station near the old hospital in Granada, west of centre, but they're slower and only marginally cheaper.

Leaving from the Shell station, Mercado, 1 c al lago: to **Rivas**, 7 daily, 0540-1510, 1½ hrs, US$1.50; to **Nandaime**, every 20 mins, 0500-1800, 20 mins, US0.70; to **Niquinohomo**, every 20 mins, 0550-1800, 45 mins, US$1, use this bus for visits to **Diriá**, **Diriomo**, **San Juan de Oriente**, **Catarina**; to **Jinotepe**, 0550, 0610, 0830, 1110, 1210 and 1710, 1½ hrs, US$1, for visits to **Los Pueblos**, including **Masatepe** and **San Marcos**. There's a 2nd terminal nearby, Shell station, 1 c abajo, 1 c norte, serving **Masaya**, every 30 mins, 0500-1800, 40 mins, US$0.50.

There are **shuttles** to Laguna Apoyo, 2 daily leave from Hostal Oasis, Calle Estrada 109, south of the centre, T552-8006, www. nicaraguahostel.com, to Crater's Edge hostel at the lake, 1000, 1600, 30 mins, US$2. They return at 1100 and 1700. **Paxeos**, Parque Central, blue house next to cathedral, T552-8291, www.paxeos.com. Daily shuttles to **Managua airport**, **León**, **San Juan del Sur** and **San Jorge**.

Long distance International buses to **San José**, **Costa Rica**, pass through Granada each day. See individual offices for schedules: **King Quality**, Shell Guapinol, 1½ c al Sur, opposite Ticabus, www.kingqualityca.com. **Ticabus**, Shell Guapinol, 1½ c al Sur, T552-2899, www.ticabus.com. **Transnica**, Calle Xalteva, Frente de Iglesia Auxiliadora, T552-6619, www.transnica.com.

Ferry

Schedules are subject to change.
The ferry to **San Carlos** leaves the main dock on Mon and Thu at 1400, and stops at **Altagracia**, **Ometepe** after 4 hrs (US$4 1st class, US$2 2nd class), **Morrito** (8 hrs, US$5 1st class, US$3, 2nd class) and **San Miguelito** (10 hrs, US$5.50 1st class, US$3 2nd class). It stops in **San Carlos** after 14 hrs (US$8 1st class, US$4 2nd class). This journey is tedious, take your own food and water, and a hammock, if you have one. The ferry returns from San Carlos on Tue and Fri following the same route. For **Altagracia** you can also take a cargo boat with passenger seats on Wed and Sat (1200, 4½ hrs, US$2). It is faster (and less scary) to go overland to **San Jorge** and catch a 1-hr ferry to **Ometepe**, see San Jorge page 208, for more details.

Taxi

Granada taxi drivers are useful for finding places away from the centre, US$0.50 during the day, US$1 at night. To **Managua** US$25, but check taxi looks strong enough to make the journey.

Directory

Banks Banco de Centro América (**BAC**) Parque Central, 1 c abajo, on Calle La Libertad, has an ATM and will change TCs and US dollars. ATM at Esso Station (15-min walk from town centre) accepts Cirrus, Maestro, MasterCard as well. **Banpro**, BAC, 1 c al sur, has a less reliable ATM and money changing facilities. Bancentro, BAC, 1 c al norte, has a Visa ATM. **Western Union**, from fire station ½ block south, Mon-Sat 0800-1300, 1400-1700. **Doctor** Dr Francisco Martínez Blanco, Clínica de Especialidades Piedra Bocona, ½ block west of Cine Karawale, T552-5989, f_mblanco@ yahoo.com, general practitioner, speaks good English, consultation US$10. **Internet** Internet cafés can be found all over town, while most *hostales* and hotels also offer internet access, including international calls. **Language schools** APC Spanish School, west side of Parque Central, T552-4203, www.spanish granada.com. Flexible immersion classes in this centrally located language school. There are volunteer opportunities with local NGOs. **Casa Xalteva**, Iglesia Xalteva, ½ c al norte, T552-2436, www.casaxalteva.com. Small Spanish classes for beginners and advanced students, 1 week to several months. Home stays arranged, and voluntary work with children, recommended. **Nicaragua Mía Spanish School**, inside Maverick's reading lounge, Calle Arsenal, T552-2755, www.nicara gua-mia-spanish school.com. An established and professional language school with various learning options, from hourly to weekly tuition. The school takes an ethical approach and contributes to local causes. **One on One**, Calle La Calzada 450, T552-6771, www.1on1 tutoring.net. One on One uses a unique teaching system where each student has 4 different tutors, thus encouraging greater aural comprehension. Instruction is flexible, by the hour or week, with homestay and activities available. There's an evening restaurant too, where you can practise your Spanish with locals. Recommended. **Laundry** Parque Central, 1½ c abajo, around US$3 for a medium-sized load, daily 0700-1900. **Post office** From fire station ½ block east, ½ block north. **Telephone** (Enitel) on corner northeast of Parque Central.

Masaya

Archaic folklore and vibrant craftwork are the distinguishing features of Masaya and the surrounding Pueblos de la Meseta, just 30 minutes from Granada. Irresistibly sleepy until fiesta time, these ancient settlements are home to bustling workshops and friendly communities whose inhabitants are directly descended from the ancient Chorotega peoples. Dramatic geological features complement the region's rich cultural assets with an intensely sulphuric and other-worldly volcano complex. The perpetually smoking, tempestuous Santiago Crater has been threatening cataclysm for centuries, whilst sedate Laguna Apoyo is the country's most attractive crater lake, with eternally warm, soothing waters heated by underwater vents. ▸▸ *For listings, see pages 257-258.*

Ins and outs

Getting there and around There are frequent bus services from Managua's Roberto Huembes market and La UCA bus station, as well as Granada's bus terminals. Taxis are available in Masaya, both the motorized and horse-drawn variety.

Best time to visit Most of the region remains green year round, though Masaya, Nindirí and the national park are much more enjoyable in the rainy season. From November to January, the upper rim villages of Laguna de Apoyo, such as Catarina and San Juan de Oriente, can be chilly by Nicaraguan standards.

Tourist information **INTUR** ⓘ *Banpro, ½ c sur, just south of the artisans' market, T522-7651, masaya@intur.gob.ni*, have a branch office in Masaya. They have maps of the city and information on events.

Background

Masaya has always been home to very hard-working and skilled craftsmen. The first tribute assessments of 1548 for the Spanish crown stipulated that Masaya was to produce hammocks and *alpargatas* (cloth shoes). Around 300 years later, when US diplomat and amateur archaeologist EG Squier visited Masaya, he noted that, along with Sutiava (León), Masaya was a thriving centre of native handicraft production. Composed of at least three pre-Columbian villages – Masaya, Diriega and Monimbó – Masaya was briefly the colonial capital of Nicaragua when Granada rose up in rebellion, and it has always been involved in major political events in Nicaragua. In November 1856, William Walker's occupying troops lost a critical and bloody battle here to combined Central American forces, triggering his eventual retreat from Granada and Nicaragua. In September 1912, Masaya was the scene of battles between Liberal army forces and the US Marines. The insurrection against Somoza was particularly intense here, with the indigenous community of Monimbó showing legendary bravery during popular rebellions in February and September 1978. Finally in June 1979, the Revolution took control of Masaya and it was used by retreating Managuan rebels as a refuge before the final victory a month later. Since the war years, Masaya has returned to making fine crafts, serving as the commercial centre for Los Pueblos de la Meseta and the heart of Nicaragua's Pacific culture.

Sights

Shaken by an earthquake in 2000, this attractive town suffered damage to around 80 houses and most of its churches. However, some attractive homes remain and the city is full of bicycles and traditional horse-drawn carriages, the latter used as taxis by the local population.

Mercado Nacional de Artesanías

Most people come to Masaya to shop, and the country's best craft market is here in the 19th-century Mercado Nacional de Artesanías, one block east of the south side of Parque Central. The late Gothic walls of the original market were damaged by shelling and the inside of the market burned during the Revolution of 1978-1979. Work to repair the walls began in 1992 and the interior was also restored for its grand opening in May 1997. After two decades of sitting in ruin it was reopened and is now dedicated exclusively to handmade crafts. There are 80 exhibition booths and several restaurants inside the market and it's a great place to shop without the cramped conditions or hard sell of a normal Latin American market. Every Thursday night from 1900 to 2200 there is a live

Ciudad de Masaya

Sleeping
Cailagua **1**
Maderas Inn **3**
Monimbó **2**
Regis **5**
Volcán Masaya **6**

Eating
Cafetín Criolla **12**
Che Gris **1**
Comedor Criolla **5**
Comidas Criollas **13**
El Bucanero **9**
Fruti Fruti **14**
La Cazuela de
  Don Nacho **10**
La Jarochita **2**
Panadería Norma **15**

Plaza Pedro Joaquin
  Chamorro **4**
Telepizza **3**

Bars & clubs
Coco Jambo **6**
Disco Ritmo de Noche **7**
La Ronda **8**

500 metres
500 yards

performance on the stage in the market, usually including one of Masaya's more than 100 folkloric dance groups with beautifully costumed performers and live marimba music.

The market sells local leather, wood, ceramic, stone and fabric goods, as well as some crafts from around Nicaragua. Although most vendors try to keep a broad variety to guarantee steady income, there are some stalls that specialize. One of them is **Grupo Raíces**, at the south side, which has a fine selection of ceramics from Condega, San Juan de Oriente and Jinotega, as well as soapstone sculptures. Nearby, on the outside of the southern block of stalls, is a stall that has the finest examples of *primitivista* paintings from Solentiname and Masaya artists. Just north of the main entrance is a special stall that has a selection of festival **masks** and **costumes**; made for festival participants, not tourists. Boys will greet you at the market with the handful of English words; they can help you find what you are looking for and will translate with the merchants for a tip of US$1-2.

Masaya's most famous craft is its cotton **hammocks**, which are perhaps the finest in the world and a tradition that pre-dates the arrival of the Spanish. The density of weave and quality of materials help determine the hammock's quality; stretching the hammock will reveal the density of the weave. The highest concentration of hammock weavers is one block east from the stadium on the *malecón* and one block north of the *viejo hospital*. With a deposit and 48-hours' notice, you can also custom-order a hammock in the workshops.

Laguna de Masaya and el Malecón

The best view of the deep-blue 27 sq km Laguna de Masaya and the Masaya volcanic complex is from the *malecón*, or waterfront, usually populated with romantic couples. There is also a **baseball stadium**, named after the Puerto Rican baseball star Roberto Clemente, who died in a flying accident in Florida while en route to Nicaragua with earthquake relief aid in 1972. The lake is 300 m below, down a steep wall. Before the pump was installed in the late 19th century, all of the town's water was brought up from the lake in ceramic vases on women's heads – a 24-hour-a-day activity according to British naturalist Thomas Belt who marvelled at the ease with which the Masaya women dropped down into the crater and glided back out with a full load of water. The lake has suffered from city run-off for the last few decades and the city is looking for funding to clean its waters, which are not good for swimming at the moment. There are more than 200 petroglyphs on the walls of the descent to the lake that can also be seen reproduced in the Museo Nacional in Managua. There are no official guides to take you to the petroglyph sites, but you can try the INTUR office near the market, or ask around locally.

La Parroquia de Nuestra Señora de la Asunción

Nearly every *barrio* in Masaya has its own little church, but two dominate the city. In Masaya's leafy Parque Central is La Parroquia de Nuestra Señora de la Asunción, a late-baroque church that dates from 1750. It was modified in 1830 and has undergone a complete restoration with financial help from Spain. The clean lines and simple elegance of its interior make it one of the most attractive churches in Nicaragua and well worth a visit. There is a subtle balance to its design, particularly inside, and its extensive use of precious woods and native tile floor add to its charm.

Iglesia de San Jerónimo

San Jerónimo is the spiritual heart of Masaya. This attractive domed church, visible from kilometres around, is home to the city's patron Saint Jerome (whose translation of the bible was the standard for more than a millennium) and a focal point for his more than two-month long festival. The celebration begins on 30 September and continues until early December, making it by far the longest patron saint festival in Nicaragua and perhaps in Latin America. The church of San Jerónimo was badly damaged by the earthquake in 2000. The walls survive with four sets of temporary exterior supports, however it is awaiting proper funding to restore it.

Comunidad Indígena de Monimbó

The indigenous *barrio* of Monimbó is possibly the richest artisan centre on the isthmus with many of its handmade goods being offered for sale across Central America. It remains the heart and soul of Masaya. During Spanish rule the Spanish and Indian sections of major cities were clearly defined. Today, nearly all the lines have now been blurred, yet in Monimbó (and in the León barrio of Sutiava) the traditions and indigenous way of life have been maintained to some extent. The Council of Elders, a surviving form of native government, still exists here and the beating of drums of deerskin stretched over an avocado trunk still calls people to festival and meetings and, in times of trouble, to war. In 1978, the people of Monimbó rebelled against Somoza's repressive Guardia Nacional. They achieved this entirely on their own, holding the barrio for one week using home-made contact bombs and other revolutionary handicrafts to hold off what was then a mighty army of modern weapons and tanks.

This neighbourhood should be the most famous artisan barrio in Central America, yet curiously commerce dictates otherwise. A visit to some of the workshops around Monimbó will quickly reveal why: here you will see leather goods with 'Honduras' written on them, flowery embroidered dresses that say 'Panama' and ceramics with 'Costa Rica' painted in bright letters. Even Guatemala, which has perhaps the finest native textiles in the western hemisphere, imports crafts from Monimbó – of course with their country's name on it. It is possible to do an artisan workshop tour independently, though hiring a local guide will make it much easier. The highest concentrations of workshops are located between the unattractive Iglesia Magdalena and the cemetery.

Around Masaya

Pueblos de la Meseta

A network of intriguing villages known as *Los Pueblos de la Meseta* occupy the region around Masaya. Fifteen minutes from Masaya is **Nindirí**, named after its former chief represented by a statue in the Parque Central. Known as the city of myths and legends, it is one of the oldest settlements in Nicaragua with evidence of over 3000 consecutive years of habitation. It is so rich in ceramic history that its small museum, the privately owned **Museo Nindirí** ① *1 block north of the Rubén Darío library, Tue-Sat, donation of US$1-2 requested*, has one of the country's most impressive pre-Columbian collections and Spanish colonial relics. It is run by the wife of the founder who will show you around.

Just outside Masaya to the north, on the road from Managua, is an old hilltop fortress, **Coyotepe**, also called La Fortaleza, built in the 19th century to protect Masaya. Once a torture centre used first by the Somozistas, later by the Sandinistas, it is now a clubhouse for the boy scouts. It is deserted and eerie (take a torch or offer a boy scout US$1-2 to show you around). Even if you don't want to see the fort, the view from the top of the hill is spectacular.

The nearby village of **Niquinohomo** is Sandino's birthplace (see Background, page 435), and the house where he lived from the age of 12 is opposite the church in the main plaza.

San Juan de Oriente is a charming colonial village with an interesting school of pottery (products are for sale). Nearly 80% of the inhabitants are engaged in the ceramic arts. To visit an artisan family workshop walk from north entrance of the village towards the church. Just before the church and next to the women's co-op is the house of Dulio Jiménez, who is very happy to show visitors his operation. It is a short walk to neighbouring **Catarina** (famous for ornamental plants), and a 1-km walk or drive uphill to **El Mirador**, with a wonderful view of Laguna de Apoyo (Granada and Volcán Mombacho too on a clear day).

Laguna de Apoyo

Laguna de Apoyo is very clean, beautiful for swimming and well worth a visit. The waters are kept warm by underwater vents and the sulphur content keeps mosquitos away. It's quiet during the week but busy at weekends. Without your own transport it's probably easiest to visit the lagoon from Granada with transport provided by **Hostal Oasis**, see page 247. There is also accommodation on the lake shore.

Parque Nacional Volcán Masaya

① *Daily 0900-1700, US$4. The visitor centre is 1.5 km from the entrance at Km 23 on the Managua–Masaya road. There are picnic facilities, toilets and barbecues nearby. It's possible to camp, but there are no facilities after the centre closes. If arriving by bus, ask the driver to drop you off at Km 23. At the entrance, park rangers might be available to drive you up to the summit, US$0.70.*

Created in 1979, Parque Nacional Volcán Masaya is the country's oldest national park. It covers an area of 54 sq km, and contains 20 km of trails leading to and around two volcanoes rising to around 400 m. **Volcán Nindirí** last erupted in 1670. The more active **Volcán Masaya** burst forth in 1772 and again in 1852, forming the Santiago crater between the two peaks; this in turn erupted in 1932, 1946, 1959 and 1965 before collapsing in 1985, and the resulting pall of sulphurous smoke made the soil uncultivable in a broad belt to the Pacific. Take fluids, a hat and hiking boots if you're planning on doing much walking. If walking to the summit, leave early as there is little shade along the road.

Santiago's most recent eruption was on 23 April 2001. Debris pelted the parking area of the park with flaming rocks at 1427 in the afternoon, shooting tubes of lava onto the hillside just east of the parking area and setting it ablaze. Today the cone remains highly irregular with large funnels of sulphuric acid being followed by periods of little or no smoke. On 4 October 2003 Santiago emitted an eruption cloud 4.6 km in length, but no actual eruption was forthcoming. A real eruption is expected soon.

ATC Although research into the activity of Volcán Masaya is limited, gaseous emissions range from 500 to 3000 tonnes a day, making the volcano one of the largest natural polluters in the world.

Volcán Masaya was called *Popogatepe* or 'mountain that burns' by the Chorotega people who believed that eruptions were a sign of anger from the goddess of fire, Chacitutique. To appease her they made sacrifices to the lava pit, which often included children and young women. In the 16th century Father Francisco de Bobadilla planted a cross on the summit of Masaya to exorcize the *Boca del Infierno* (Mouth of Hell); the cross visible today commemorates the event.

The biggest natural heroes of the park are the unique **parakeets** (*chocoyos*) who nest in the active Santiago crater. These orange- or crimson-fronted parakeets are best spotted just before the park closes between March and October. They lay two to four eggs per nest in the interior cliffs of the crater in July and after incubation and rearing lasting roughly three months, leave their highly toxic home for the first time.

From the visitor centre, a short path leads up to Cerro El Comalito, with good views of Mombacho, the lakes and the extraordinary volcanic landscapes of the park; longer trails continue to Lake Masaya and the San Fernando crater.

Masaya listings

For Sleeping and Eating price codes and other relevant information, see pages 43-46.

Sleeping

Masaya *p252, map p253*

B Hotel Monimbó, Iglesia San Sebastián, 1 c arriba, 1½ c norte, T522-6867, hotelmonimbo 04@hotmail.com. 7 good quality rooms with private bath, hot water, a/c and cable TV. There's a pleasant patio space and services include internet and transport.

B Maderas Inn, Bomberos, 2 c sur, T522-5825. Small rooms with private bath, a/c, cable TV and continental breakfast in the price. Cheaper without breakfast and a/c (**C**). Internet, tours, laundry service and airport transportation available.

C Cailagua, Km 30, T522-4435. Comfortable hotel with 22 rooms with private bath, a/c and cable TV, swimming pool, restaurant. In a noisy location, quite a way from centre. Good for the exhausted driver; secure parking.

E Hotel Regis, La Parroquia, 3½ c norte, T522-2300. Very friendly and helpful owner. Rooms are clean, with shared bath and fan. The best budget option.

Around Masaya *p255*

B Hotel Volcán Masaya, Km 23, Carretera a Masaya, T522-7114. Great location in front of the volcano at Parque Nacional Volcán Masaya, with spectacular views from the shared patio. Rooms have private bath, a/c, fridge and cable TV. Lobby area is good for relaxing.

B San Simian, Laguna Apoyo, beyond **Norome Resort**, T813-6866, www.san simian.com. A peaceful spot with 5 great cabañas and outdoor bathtubs, perfect for soaking under the starry sky. Facilities include bar, restaurant, hammocks, kayaks and a catamaran (US$15 per hr). Day use US$5. Recommended.

D-F Crater's Edge, Laguna Apoyo, access road, 500 m west, T860-8689, www.craters-edge.com. A friendly and hospitable hostel with dorm beds (**F**), private rooms (**D**) and plenty of facilities including kayaks, restaurant/bar, Wi-Fi, book exchange and a floating platform. Day use US$7. Daily transport to/from **Oasis** hostel in Granada. Recommended.

Eating

Masaya *p252, map p253*

† El Bucanero, Km 26.5, Carretera a Masaya. A Cuban-owned favourite with sweeping views of Laguna Masaya and a loud, party atmosphere. International and Nicaraguan menu including good beef dishes. Worth it for the views.

† La Cazuela de Don Nacho, artisan market, northeast side of stage, T522-7731. Fri-Wed 1000-1800, Thu 1000-0000. There's a jaunty atmosphere at this pleasant market-place eaterie, usually buzzing with diners. They serve *comida típica* and à la carte food such as *filete mignon*, *filete de pollo* and *churrasco* steak.

† La Jarochita, La Parroquia, 75 vrs norte, T522-4831. Daily 1100-2200. The 'best Mexican in Nicaragua; some drive from Managua just to eat here. Try *sopa de tortilla*, and chicken *enchilada* in *mole* sauce, *chimichangas* and Mexican beer.

† Restaurante Che Gris, Hotel Regis, ½ c sur. good food in huge portions, including excellent *comida típica*, *comida corriente* and à la carte. A branch at the southeast corner of the market.

†-† Telepizza, Parque Central, ½ c norte, T522-0170. Good wholesome pizza.

† Cafetín Criolla, southwest corner of the artisan market. Cheap, filling, greasy food, popular with the locals and often bustling.

† Comedor Criolla, northeast corner of Parque Central, 5 c al norte. Popular locals' haunt serving economical Nica fare, buffet food, breakfasts and lunch.

♥ **Comedor Criollas**, Parque Central, south side. Yet another local eaterie with the 'criolla' namesake. This large, clean, buffet restaurant serves up healthy portions of Nica fare.

♥ **Plaza Pedro Joaquin Chamorro**, in front of Iglesia San Sebastián in Monimbó. Good *fritangas* with grilled meats, *gallo pinto* and other traditional Masaya food, very cheap.

Cafés, juice bars and bakeries

Fruti Fruti, northeast corner of Parque Central, 3½ c norte. Sweet, fresh smoothies, including delicious, alcohol-free piña coladas.

Panadería Norma, northwest corner of the artisan market, ½ c norte. Good, fresh-brewed coffee, bread, cakes and pastries.

⊙ Entertainment

Masaya *p252, map p253*
Every Thu folkloric dances are performed behind the Mercado Artesanía.

Casino Pharaoh's, 3 blocks north of the park, T522-5222.

Chapo's, Bomberos 2½ c al sur. Mon-Fri 1200-0 200, Sat and Sun 1400-0300. A trendy bar/club, good for a beer and hamburger with cable TV.

Coco Jambo, 4-5 blocks west of the Parque Central on the Malecón Masaya. Busy Sat/Sun.

El Delfín Azul, 1½ calle south of the fire department. Fri-Sun.

La Ronda, south side of the Parque Central. Locals also gather here.

⊙ Transport

Masaya *p252, map p253*
Bus Buses leave from the new market or you can also catch a non-express bus from the Carretera a Masaya towards **Granada** or **Managua**. **Express** buses leave from Parque San Miguel to La UCA in **Managua** when full or after 20 mins, 0600-2000, US$0.60.

Granada, every 30 mins, 0600-1800, 45 mins, US$0.60. **Jinotepe**, every 30 mins, 0500-1800, 1½ hrs, US$0.50. **Managua**, every 30 mins, 0400-1800, 1 hr, US$0.50. **Express** to **Managua**, every 30 mins, 0400-2100, 40 mins, US$0.80. **Matagalpa**, 0600 and 0700, 4 hrs, US$2.25. Or take a bus to **Tipitapa**, 0300-1800, 45 mins, US$2, change for Matagalpa.

Buses run to Valle de Apoyo for **Lago de Apoyo** from Masaya 2 times a day (1000, 1600, 45 mins, US$0.50) then walk down the road that drops into the crater. The bus returns to Masaya at 1130 and 1650. You will have to get off at Km 37.5 and walk down the 5-km access road (it's very dusty in the dry season, so bring a bandana).

Taxi Fares around **Masaya** are US$0.30-0.80. **Granada**, US$15; **Managua** US$20; **airport** US$25. Horse-drawn carriages US$0.30.

From **Granada** to Laguna de Apoyo, US$15-20, or from **Managua**, US$35-40.

⊙ Directory

Masaya *p252, map p253*
Banks All banks will change dollars. The **BAC**, opposite the northwest corner of the artisan market, has an ATM; as does **Banpro**, opposite the southwest corner. There's a **Bancentro** on the west side of the plaza with a Visa ATM. You'll also find street changers around the plaza. **Doctor** Dr Gerardo Sánchez, next to town hall, speaks some English. **Internet** Intecomp, south of the main plaza. Also try **Mi PC a colores**, on Sergio Delgadillo. **Post office** Sergio Delgadillo. **Telephone** Enitel office on Parque Central.

Around Masaya *p255*
Language schools Apoyo Intensive Spanish School, Laguna de Apoyo, T882-3992, www.gaianicaragua.org, groups of 4, 5 hrs' tuition per day. 5-day programme, US$220 for a week/US$710 per month with food and accommodation; family stays available.

Managua

If, as the local saying goes, Nicaragua is the country where 'lead floats and cork sinks', Managua is its perfect capital. Managua has 20% of the country's population, yet there is little overcrowding; it has no geographic centre and when directions are given, they refer to buildings that haven't existed for over 30 years. And yet, despite having no centre, no skyline and no logic, it is full of energy: the heartbeat of the Nicaraguan economy and psyche. It has been the capital and commercial centre since 1852, but was destroyed by an earthquake in March 1931 and then partially razed by fire five years later. Rebuilt as a modern, commercial city, the centre was again decimated by an earthquake in December 1972. Severe damage from the Revolution of 1978-1979 and flooding of the lakeside areas as a result of Hurricane Mitch in 1998 added to the problems. It's a tribute to the city's resilience that it still has the energy to carry on. ▸▸ *For listings, see pages 265-275.*

Ins and outs

Getting there The airport is 12 km east of the city, near the lake. Buses and taxis (US$15 to Barrio Martha Quezada, half the price if hailed from the main road) run from the airport to the city. International bus services arrive at several terminals throughout the city. **Ticabus** and **King Quality** are in Barrio Martha Quezada, close to most of the cheap hotels. **Transnica** is in Metrocentro. Provincial bus services have three main arrival/departure points. City buses and taxis serve the provincial terminals. ▸▸ *See also Transport, page 271.*

Getting around Managua is on the southern shores of Lake Managua. Instead of cardinal points, the following are used: *al lago* (north), *arriba* (east), *al sur* (south), *abajo* (west). The old centre is a garden monument consisting of open spaces, ageing buildings, lakeside restaurants. Despite lying over 14 seismic faults and the warnings of seismologists, important new buildings have been built here including a presidential palace between the ruins of the cathedral and the lakefront, the epicentre of the 1972 earthquake.

Two areas now lay claim to being the heart of Managua. The older of the two is based around the **Hotel Crown Plaza** (formerly the Hotel Intercontinental and still referred to as the 'viejo Intercontinental'), with a shopping and cinema complex, complete with US-style 'food court' and, to the west, **Barrio Martha Quezada** with many mid-range and budget hotels, and international bus services. Nearby, to the south, **Plaza España** has the country's best supermarket and numerous shops, banks, travel agents, tour companies and nearly every airline office in the country. The other heart of the city is based on the **Carretera a Masaya**, running from the new cathedral to Camino de Oriente. This stretch of four-lane highway includes the **Rotonda Rubén Darío**, the **Metrocentro** shopping complex and numerous restaurants. You'll need to take a bus or taxi to get there or to the provincial bus terminals.

Buses are cheap, crowded and infamous for pickpockets. Their routes can be hard to fathom. **Taxis** must have red number plates. Taxi-sharing in Managua is standard.

Tourist information **Instituto Nicaragüense de Turismo** (**INTUR**) ① *Hotel Crown Plaza, 1 c al sur, 1 c abajo, enter by the side door, T254-5191, www.visitanicaragua.com, www.intur.gob.ni, Mon-Sat 0800-1700,* provides limited information about Managua and other parts of the country. Information on national parks and conservation should be obtained from **Sistema Nacional de Areas Protegidas** (**Sinap**) ① *Ministerio de Medio Ambiente y Recursos Naturales (Marena), Km 12.5 Carretera Norte, T263-2617.*

Safety Nicaraguans are incredibly friendly and Managua is one of the safest cities in Latin America, but you should still take sensible precautions. Never walk at night unless you are in a good area or shopping centre zone. Arriving in Managua after dark is not a problem, but it's best to book your hotel in advance and take a taxi. Long-distance buses are fine, but be careful in the market when you arrive to take the bus. If you prefer to avoid the bus terminals all together, get off the bus before you reach the market. When you arrive at the **Ticabus** station, make sure you know where you want to go before setting out. The **Mercado Oriental** (not to be confused with the Camino de Oriente which is safe and fun), said to be the largest informal market in Latin America, and its barrio, Ciudad Jardín, should be avoided at all costs.

Sights ⛪🔵🟡🟢❇️⭕️🔺🔵🔵 ➡️ pp265-275.

In the old centre of Managua near the lake shore, the attractive neoclassical **Palacio Nacional de la Cultura**, previously the Palacio de los Héroes de la Revolución, has been beautifully restored and houses the **Museo Nacional de Nicaragua** ① *Mon-Fri 0800-1700, Sat and Sun 0900-1600, US$2.25, includes a 20-min introductory guided tour in English and French*, as well as the Archivo Nacional and the Biblioteca Nacional.

Damaged by earthquake, the **Catedral Vieja** (old cathedral) now has a roof of narrow steel girders and side-window support bars to keep it standing, the atmosphere is of a sad, old building past its prime, left in ruins, but still worth a look. The **Centro Cultural Managua**, next to the Palacio Nacional de Cultura, has a good selection of before and

① **Managua**

| Sleeping 🛏️ | Crowne Plaza **2** | Hostal Real **4** |
| Best Western Las Mercedes **1** | Holiday Inn Select **3** | |

after photos of quake-struck Managua in 1972. The centre is also home to the national art school and the national music school. There are some art exhibits in galleries downstairs.

The garishly painted **Palacio Presidencial** is in front of the Palacio de la Cultura on the opposite corner to the old cathedral. These buildings are situated on the **Parque Central** and provide a striking contrast with the modern **Teatro Rubén Darío** ① *on the lake shore, www.tnrubendario.gob.ni, US$1.50-20 depending on show*, which hosts good plays, folkloric dances and musical events. There are usually temporary exhibitions in the theatre so, during the day, ask at the window to view the exhibit and you can probably look at the auditorium as well. The **Parque de la Paz**, just southeast of the Parque Central, is part of the rebuilding programme for the old centre. The park is a graveyard for weapons and a few dozen truckloads of AK-47s are buried there, some seen sticking out of the cement; take care here, the neighbourhood on the other side is of bad repute. Three blocks south of the Parque Central are the offices of the **Asamblea Nacional** (Nicaraguan parliament), which include the city's only high-rise building, once the Bank of America, now the offices of the *diputados* (parliamentary members).

A significant landmark is the **Hotel Crown Plaza**, which has a distinctive design similar to a Maya pyramid. From the hilltop behind the Hotel Crown Plaza the **Parque Nacional de la Loma de Tiscapa** provides the best views of the capital and of the **Laguna de Tiscapa** on the south side of the hill. From the top, a giant black silhouette of **Sandino** stands looking out over the city. The spot has historical significance as it is the site of the former presidential palace; it was here that Sandino signed a peace treaty with Somoza and was abducted (and later killed) at the entrance to the access road. Underneath the park facing the *laguna* (now blocked by a fence) are the former **prison cells of the** Somoza regime ① *daily 0800-1630*, where inmates were said to have been tortured before being tossed into the lake. To get there, take the road behind the Crown Plaza to the top of the hill using an access road for the Nicaraguan military headquarters. Guards at the park are nervous about photography; ask permission and photograph only downtown and towards the stadium – do not take photos on the access road up to the park.

From Tiscapa Hill, the **Catedral Nueva** (new cathedral), inaugurated in 1993, can be seen 500 m to the south of the lake. Designed by the Mexican architect Ricardo Legoreto, comments on the exterior range from 'strikingly beautiful' to 'sacreligious'. The interior, which is mostly unadorned concrete, has been described as 'post-nuclear, with an altar resembling a futuristic UN Security Council meeting room'. Many visitors are fascinated by the Sangre de Cristo room, where a life-size bleeding Christ is encased in a glass and

Nuevo Diario

Carretera Norte

To Airport &

Bello Horizonte
Shopping Centre

Ciudad
Xolotlán

Pista Portezuelo

Blvd Buenos Aires

To Mercado El Mayoreo Bus Station

Mercado Iván
Montenegro

Pista Sábana Grande

Buses to Masaya,
Granada & Rivas

Puerto Huembes/
Mercado Central

Centro Comercial
Managua

➡ Managua maps
1 Managua, page 260
2 Metrocentro, page 262
3 Marta Quesada and Bolonia, page 263

Bars & clubs ①
Rhumba & Z Bar 1

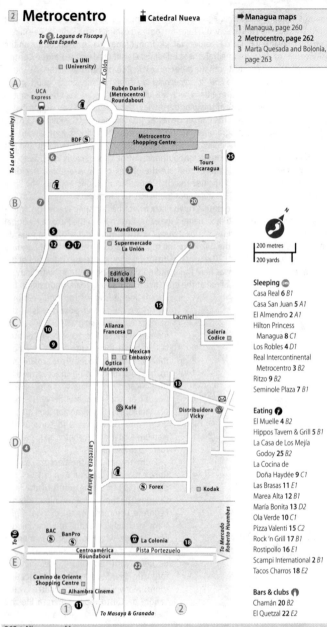

2 Metrocentro

✝ Catedral Nueva

➡ Managua maps
1 Managua, page 260
2 Metrocentro, page 262
3 Marta Quesada and Bolonia, page 263

To Ⓢ, Laguna de Tiscapa & Plaza España

La UNI (University)

Av Colón

UCA Express

Rubén Darío (Metrocentro) Roundabout

To UCA (University)

BDF Ⓢ

Metrocentro Shopping Centre

Tours Nicaragua

Munditours

Supermercado La Unión

Edificio Pellas & BAC Ⓢ

Lacmiel

Alianza Francesa

Galería Codice

Mexican Embassy

Optica Matamoros

Carretera a Masaya

@ Kafé

Distribuidora Vicky

María Bonita

Ⓢ Forex

Kodak

BAC Ⓢ

BanPro Ⓢ

Ⓜ La Colonia

To Ⓢ

Centroamérica Roundabout

Pista Portezuelo

To Mercado Roberto Huembes

Camino de Oriente Shopping Centre

Alhambra Cinema

To Masaya & Granada

N

200 metres
200 yards

Sleeping 🛏
Casa Real 6 *B1*
Casa San Juan 5 *A1*
El Almendro 2 *A1*
Hilton Princess
  Managua 8 *C1*
Los Robles 4 *D1*
Real Intercontinental
  Metrocentro 3 *B2*
Ritzo 9 *B2*
Seminole Plaza 7 *B1*

Eating 🍴
El Muelle 4 *B2*
Hippos Tavern & Grill 5 *B1*
La Casa de Los Mejía
  Godoy 25 *B2*
La Cocina de
  Doña Haydée 9 *C1*
Las Brasas 11 *E1*
Marea Alta 12 *B1*
María Bonita 13 *D2*
Ola Verde 10 *C1*
Pizza Valenti 15 *C2*
Rock 'n Grill 17 *B1*
Rostipollo 16 *E1*
Scampi International 2 *B1*
Tacos Charros 18 *E2*

Bars & clubs 🍸
Chamán 20 *B2*
El Quetzal 22 *E2*

steel dome, illuminated by a domed roof with hundreds of holes for the sun to filter through. At night, the dome sparkles with the glow of light bulbs in the holes. Pedestrian access is possible from the Metrocentro junction, while vehicles need to approach from the east.

Barrio Martha Quezada, a mixture of well-to-do housing alongside poorer dwellings, is to the west of the Crown Plaza. South again, through the Bolonia district, is **Plaza España** by the Rotondo El Güengüense roundabout. Plaza España is reached either by continuing over the hill behind the Crown Plaza and branching right at the major junction, or by going south on Williams Romero, the avenue at the western edge of Barrio Martha Quezada (bus No 118).

Around Managua 😑 ⇢ *pp265-275.*

Laguna de Xiloá

① *US$1.60 for cars, US$0.30 for pedestrians; or take bus No 113 to Las Piedrecitas for Xiloá.*
There are several volcanic crater lakes close to Managua, some of which have become centres of residential development, with swimming, boating, fishing and picnicking facilities for the public. Among the more attractive of these lakes is Laguna de Xiloá, 16 km

3 Martha Quezada & Bolonia

To Catedral Vieja & Parque Central/Al Lago
To Arriba

Streets labelled: Colón, 27 de Mayo, CST, To Abajo, Rotonda La Fuente, Taxis, Plaza Inter, Kafé, Santos Vanegas, Williams Romero/Av Monumental, King Quality, Ticabus, Médecins Sans Frontières, DHL, Av Bolívar, Spanish Chamber of Commerce, Ministry of Tourism, Galería Epikentro, Plaza El Carmen, Mini-Super Bolonia, San Francisco, To Catedral Nueva/Al Sur, Canal 2, Galería Siena, Galería Añil, To Plaza España

➡ **Managua maps**
1 Managua, page 260
2 Metrocentro, page 262
3 Marta Quesada and Bolonia, page 263

N
200 metres
200 yards

Sleeping 😴
Casa de Huéspedes Santos **4**
Casa Gabrinma **5**
Crowne Plaza **16**
El Conquistador **7**
Estancia La Casona **3**
Europeo **6**
Hospedaje Carlos **12**
Hostal Real **13**
La Posada del Angel **19**
Los Cisneros **20**
Los Felipes **21**
Mansión Teodolinda **1**
María La Gorda **2**
Posadita de Bolonia **11**

Eating 🍴
Aderezo **11**
Cocinarte **6**
Comida a la Vista **4**
Las Cazuelas **3**
Mirna's **7**
Panadería Tonalli **9**

Bars & clubs 🍸
Changó **13**
Shannon Irlandés **10**

Directions in Managua and beyond

How do you find anything in a country without street names or numbers? Sometimes visitors feel as if they are going round in circles, quite literally in the case of Managua with its epidemic of dizzying rotondas (roundabouts). The Nicaraguan system is foolproof – as long as you know every landmark that exists, or used to exist, in the city which means that, more often than not, foreigners spend most of their time completely lost.

In Managua, directions are based around the lake, so it is essential to know where the lake is and keep a bird's eye view of the city in your mind. With the location of Lake Managua you have north (al lago); away from the lake is south (al sur). Then you need to use basic Spanish and the sun. Where the sun comes up (arriba) is east and where it goes down (abajo) is west. City blocks are cuadras (abbreviated in this book as 'c'), and metres are better known here by their old Spanish approximation – varas (vrs). The key element once you fix your compass is the landmark from which directions begin, which can be a hotel, park, pharmacy, factory or, in worst-case scenarios, where a factory used to be before the earthquake in 1972! Once you find the landmark, getting to your ultimate destination is simple. For example, take Bar Changó, Plaza Inter, 2 c sur, 15 vrs abajo; to sip Nicaraguan rum here first you need to locate Plaza Inter, then go two blocks south and continue 15 m west.

Outside Managua you may also hear the standard orientation points of norte, sur, oeste and este. In Granada, al lago refers to the east; on the Pacific Coast al mar refers to the west, on the Caribbean side it means east. In mountainous areas, arriba and abajo may also indicate the rise and fall of the land, so it can get confusing. In smaller towns, many directions are given from the Parque Central or Iglesia (central church). It is useful to remember that nearly all the façades of Catholic churches in Nicaragua face west; so when stepping out of the church the north is to your right, south to the left, etc. If the worst comes to worst, hire a taxi, give the driver the coordinates and let him figure it out.

---

from Managua just off the new road to León. On Saturday and Sunday, the only days when buses run, Xiloá gets very crowded. It is quiet during the week and you can camp there, but without public transport you will have to walk or take a taxi.

Museo Las Huellas de Acahualinca

ⓘ *Along the lake, 2 km west of Museo Nacional, T266-5774, Mon-Fri 0800-1700, Sat and Sun 0900-1600, US$2.50; explanations in Spanish; taxi recommended as hard to find and in an unsafe neighbourhood.*

These ancient prehistoric animal and human footprints, preserved in the sedimentary tufa and discovered when stone was being quarried to build homes in the area, represent some of the oldest evidence of human occupation in Nicaragua. A museum has been created around the original site and the 6000-year-old footprints have been left exactly as they were found in excavation. The museum also has a small display of ceramic artefacts found at the site (the oldest ceramics date from 1000 BC, 3000 years later than the footprints) and an illustration of the estimated height of the people who made the footprints.

Mateare and Momotombito

Thirty kilometres northwest of Managua, **Mateare** is a pleasant fishing and agricultural town with some of the finest lake fish in Lake Managua (eat at your own risk). Distanced from the capital by a large peninsula, the lake is much cleaner here than on the Managua side. The fishermen can take you to the small volcanic island of **Momotombito** (US$60 for a day trip). The best time of year to visit is during the rainy season, when the island is green and the swell on the lake small. Beware of snakes when hiking around the island. There are other small islands in the shadow of the smoking Volcán Momotombo, which appears to loom over the lake from the mainland shore. Momotombito is a nature reserve, and has much bird and reptile life and a legendary family of albino crocodiles. There is a small military outpost on the calm side of the island. Stop there to check in if you wish to hike on the islands. Bring drinks or food as gifts for the (non-uniformed) guards, who are very friendly and usually quite bored. They might take you hiking for a small fee.

Pacific beaches near Managua

There are several beaches about an hour's drive from Managua. Because of their proximity to the capital, they get very crowded during the high season (January to April).

Pochomil beach (54 km from Managua, buses leave hourly from Mercado Lewites) is deserted in the week out of season. It gets cleaner the further south you go, but there are rocks and strong waves here so swim with care. It is a tourist centre with a few hotels and many small family-owned restaurants. At the entrance to **Masachapa** is the access road to the **Montelimar Resort**. Just before the gates of the resort is the dirt road to the area's nicest public beach, **Montelimar Gratis** or **El Muelle de Somoza**, which is a long deserted stretch of clean sand running from the crumbling Somoza family pier to the rocky point that separates the resort from the rest of Masachapa.

La Boquita is the nearest beach to the villages south of Managua and is visited by turtles from August to November. At **Casares** (69 km from Managua), south of La Boquita, the beaches are just south of the village. Access is a long hike or journey by 4WD and lodgings are available.

Heading north from Managua, a visit to the broad sandy **El Velero beach** ① *US$3.50*, is recommended, despite the entry fee and poor road. Facilities are controlled by the INSSBI (**Instituto Nicaragüense de Seguridad Social y Bienestar**) for the benefit of state employees and weekends are fully booked for weeks in advance. The beach is beautiful, and the sea is ideal for surfing and swimming. To get there, turn off at Km 60 on the old road to León and follow signs. **El Tránsito** is another lovely, undeveloped Pacific beach. Buses from Managua leave at 1200, 1315 and 1500 (from Mercado Lewites) and return at 0600 or 0700, US$0.70.

◉ Managua listings

Hotel and guesthouse prices

LL over US$150	L US$100-150	AL US$66-99
A US$46-65	B US$31-45	C US$21-30
D US$12-20	E US$7-11	F under US$7

Restaurant prices

₮₮₮ over US$15	₮₮ US$8-15	₮ under US$8

See pages 43-45 for further information.

● Sleeping

Managua *p259, map p260, p262 and p263*
Accommodation is generally expensive in Managua. Martha Quezada has the best budget options, but it's unsafe to walk around at night, particularly near the bus station where down-and-outs hang out. Bolonia has good mid-range hotels, while

Metrocentro is the place for business and high-end travellers. A 15% tax is supposed to be added to hotel bills.

Metrocentro

LL Hilton Princess Managua, Km 4.5, Carretera a Masaya, T255-5777, www.managua. hilton.com. Managua's **Hilton** has classy decor and plenty of facilities including bar, laundry and internet. Ask for a room facing the pool. The restaurant is good, if expensive.

LL-AL Real Intercontinental Metrocentro, Metrocentro shopping plaza, T278-4545, www.realhotelsandresorts.com. Nicaragua's finest international hotel, popular with business travellers. It has 157 rooms with hot water, a/c, telephone and cable TV. Facilities include pool, restaurant, bar and secretary service. Special weekend and multi-day rates with some tour operators. Certain rooms can be noisy on weekend nights. Recommended.

L Hotel Seminole Plaza, Intercontinental Metrocentro, 1 c abajo, 1 c al sur, T270-0061, www.seminoleplaza.com. Somewhat generic, if comfortable rooms, with private bath, hot water, cable TV, a/c, telephone. There's a small pool, restaurant and bar, and 1st-floor rooms are for disabled travellers. Pleasant location within walking distance of numerous bars and restaurants, rooms on the pool side are quieter. Good value, recommended.

AL Casa Real, Rotonda Rubén Darío, 2 c al sur, ½ c arriba, T278-3838, www.hcasareal.com. This business and NGO hotel has a quiet, central location. Spacious, ambient rooms have private bath, hot water, a/c, telephone, cable TV. French, German and English spoken.

AL Hotel Los Robles, Restaurante La Marseillaise, 30 vrs al sur, T267-3008, www.hotellos robles.com. Managua's best B&B offers comfortable rooms with classy furnishings, cable TV, a/c, hot water, Wi-Fi and luxurious bath tubs. The beautiful colonial interior is complemented by a lush, cool garden, complete with bubbling fountain. It's often full, so book in advance. Recommended.

A Casa San Juan, Reparto San Juan, Calle Esperanza 560, T278-3220, www.hotelcasasan juan.com. Rooms in this friendly, family-run hotel are clean, fresh and comfortable. They have a/c, bath and cable TV. Other services include internet, airport transfer, vehicle rental, laundry and ticket reservation.

A Hotel Ritzo, Lacmiel, 3 c arriba, 25 vrs al sur, T277-5616, www.hotelritzo.net. 10 sparse, comfortable rooms, decorated with Nicaraguan art. There's 24-hr room service, cable TV, internet, hot water and a/c. Good coffee and close to restaurants.

A Royal Inn Bed & Breakfast, Reparto San Juan, Calle Esperanza, No 553, T278-1414, www.hroyalinn.com/en. This personal hotel has cosy rooms and good attention to detail. Services include hot water, a/c, cable TV, radio, internet, garden, breakfast and very good coffee. The Nicaraguan touch.

Bolonia

AL Hostal Real, opposite German Embassy, T266-8133, www.hostalreal.com.ni. A very interesting and unusual hotel laden with exuberant antiques and art. The rooms vary greatly, and some of the interiors are exceptionally beautiful, particularly near the reception area. Very popular, so book in advance.

A Estancia La Casona, Canal 2, 1 c lago, ½ c abajo, T266-1685, www.estancialacasona. com. Located on a quiet street close to galleries, this family-run hotel has 9 rooms with private bath, hot water, a/c, cable TV. Breakfast is included, English and French are spoken, internet services available.

A Hotel Europeo, Canal 2, 75 vrs abajo, T268-2130, www.hoteleuropeo.com.ni. Each room is different, and some have interesting furnishings. Rooms at the back are best. All rooms have a/c, private bath with hot water, cable TV. There's a restaurant, bar, fax, secure parking, laundry service, free internet in lobby and pool. Price includes continental breakfast. Staff are friendly and helpful. A quiet location.

A La Posada del Angel, opposite Iglesia San Francisco, T268-7228, www.hotelposadadel angel.com.ni. This hotel, filled with interesting art work and antique furniture, has lots of personality. Good, clean rooms, private bath, hot water, cable TV, a/c, minibar, Wi-Fi and telephone. Pool, laundry service. Book ahead.

A Posadita de Bolonia, Canal 2, 3 c abajo, 75 m al sur, casa 12, T268-6692, www.posaditadebolonia.com.ni. This intimate hotel has 8 rooms with private bath, cable TV, internet. It's in a quiet area, close to several galleries. Friendly owner speaks English and is helpful. Full breakfast included.

Martha Quezada

L-LL Hotel Crowne Plaza, 'el viejo Hotel Inter', T228-3530, www.crowneplaza.com. This is one of the most historic buildings in Managua, home to the foreign press for more than a decade, as well as Howard Hughes when he was already off the deep end. The new Sandinista government also ran the country from here briefly in the early 1980s. Some rooms have a lake view, but are small for the price. Use of swimming pool for non-residents on Sun for US$18.

AL Mansión Teodolinda, INTUR, 1 c al sur, ½ c abajo, T228-1060, www.teodolinda. com.ni. This hotel, popular with business people, has good-quality, unpretentious rooms, all with private bath, hot water, kitchenette, cable TV, telephone. There's also a pool, bar, restaurant and laundry service.

A El Conquistador, Plaza Inter, 1 c al sur, 1 c abajo, T222-4789, www.hotelelconquistador.com. 11 airy rooms with a/c, hot water, cable TV, telephone and Wi-Fi. Pleasant courtyard patio, and a range of services including tours, business centre and laundry.

B María La Gorda, Iglesia El Carmen, 1 c al sur, ½ c arriba, ½ c al sur, T268-2455. Good value. 8 simple, secure rooms with a/c, private bath, hot water and cable TV. There's internet, laundry services, airport transfer, breakfast included and free local calls.

B-C Los Cisneros, Ticabus, 1c al Norte, 1½ c abajo, T222-3535, www.hotelloscisneros.com. Apartments and rooms with hot water, cable TV and Wi-Fi overlook a lush garden with hammock space. They can organize transit to the airport, serve breakfast, and speak English. Cheaper with fan (**C**). Recommended.

C Hospedaje Carlos, Ticabus, ½ c al lago, T222-2554. Secure, family-run place with 8 clean good value rooms, some have private bath. Rooms on left at the back better than on right.

C-D Los Felipes, Ticabus, 1½ c abajo, T222-6501, www.hotellosfelipe.com.ni. This pleasant hotel has a lovely garden filled with a plethora of coloured parrots. The 28 rooms have private bath, cable TV, Wi-Fi and telephone. There's a pool and staff are friendly. Cheaper with fan (**D**).

D Casa Gabrinma, Ticabus 1 c al sur, ½ c arriba, opposite radio *La Primerísima*, T222-6650. This family hotel has 4 basic rooms with fan and cable TV. Cheap food, group discounts, friendly and quiet.

E Casa de Huéspedes Santos, Ticabus, 1 c al lago, 1½ c abajo, T222-3713. Ramshackle cheapie with interesting courtyard space and basic rooms. Some have bath, others have washbasins outside. Breakfast is served and internet available. Friendly, popular and a good place to meet travellers.

Managua airport

AL Best Western Las Mercedes, Km 11 Carretera Norte, across from international terminal, T263-1011, www.lasmercedes.com. ni. Convenient for flights, with large tree-filled grounds, tennis court, pool and barber shop. Rooms are comfortable, but check before accepting one. There can be noise and fumes from the airport during peak hours. The outdoor café is the best place to kill time.

Pacific beaches near Managua *p265*

LL Montelimar Resort, near Pochomil and Masachapa, T269-6769, www.barcelomonte limarbeach.com. This expensive resort is becoming popular with package tours and is often booked solid Nov-Apr. It has a broad, unspoilt sandy beach ideal for bathing and surfing. The nearest public transport is 3 km away at Masachapa, taxi from Managua US$30 (70 km), or hire a car.

A Ticomo Mar, on the nicest part of Pochomil beach, T265-0210. Best hotel in the region

but still poor value. Bungalows have private porches, kitchens, hot water, a/c, private bath.
B Hotel Palmas del Mar, La Boquita, centre of beach, T552-8715. Beach front, private bath, a/c or fan, a bit noisy.
C-E Centro Vacacional de Trabajadores, El Tránsito. Has good value beach flats for 4-6 people at north end, normally available mid-week. Good meals available from Sra Pérez on the beach; possible accommodation too.
D Suleyka, Centro Turístico, La Boquita, T552-8717. Shared baths and fan, 6 rooms, good restaurant with fresh fish dishes.

🍴 Eating

Managua p259, map p260, p262 and p263
The Metrocentro shopping centre has several good 🍴-🍸 restaurants in its food court. It has cheaper versions of good restaurants such as **Doña Haydée** and **María Bonita**. Most restaurants will make a big salad or a rice, banana and bean dish for vegetarians.

Metrocentro
🍴 **Lo Stradivari**, Lacmiel, ½ c abajo, T277-2277. Low-key no-frills ambience at this Italian restaurant. Excellent home-made pastas, good salads, outdoor seating and good wine sauces. Recommended.
🍴 **Marea Alta**, Colonial los Robles 75, T278-2459, daily 1200-2200. Has good fresh fish, including sushi. Skip the shellfish but try grilled dorado fish or tuna. There's outdoor seating and a relaxed ambience.
🍴 **María Bonita**, Altamira, la Vicky, 1½ c abajo, T270-4326. Mexican and Nicaraguan food, including a lunchtime buffet during the week. Most popular on weekend nights, with live music and a noisy, happy crowd. Pleasant ambience, friendly staff.
🍴 **Rock 'n Grill**, next to Marea Alta, T278-6906. Filled with rock memorabilia, this fun restaurant serves steaks, ribs, burgers and shrimps. Music on Thu night. Popular with Nicaraguans and foreigners.

🍴 **Scampi International**, ALKE 1 ½ c abajo, T270-6013. Big, club-like space that attracts a mostly young clientele. They serve sushi and lobster, and keep live fish in a giant tank near the entrance. Seafood as fresh as it gets.
🍴 **El Muelle**, Intercontinental Metrocentro, 1½ c arriba, T278-0056. Managua's best seafood. There's excellent *pargo al vapor* (steamed red snapper), *dorado a la parilla*, *cocktail de pulpo* (octopus), and great *ceviche*. It's a crowded, informal setting with outdoor seating. Highly recommended.
🍴 **Hippos Tavern and Grill**, Colonial los Robles, ½ c al sur, T267-1346. Tavern-style place serving grilled food and good salads. Nice ambience and music. A popular spot for people-watching and after-work cocktails.
🍴 **La Cocina de Doña Haydée**, opposite Pastelería Aurami, Planes de Altamira, T270-6100, www.lacocina.com.ni, daily 0730-2230. Once a popular family kitchen eatery that has gone upmarket. Traditional Nicaraguan food. Try the *surtido* dish for 2, the *nacatamales* and the traditional *Pío V* dessert, a sumptuous rum cake. Popular with foreign residents.
🍴 **La Hora del Taco**, Monte de los Olivos, 1 c al lago, on Calle Los Robles. Good Mexican dishes including *fajitas* and *burritos*. A warm, relaxed atmosphere.
🍴 **Las Brasas**, in front of Cine Alhambra, Camino Oriente. The best value in town, serving decent, traditional Nicaraguan fare in an outdoor setting. It's a good place to come with friends and order a half bottle of rum; it comes with a bowl of ice, limes, coke and 2 plates of food. Great atmosphere.
🍴 **Ola Verde**, Doña Haydée, 1 c abajo, ½ c lago, T270-3048, www.olaverde.info. All organic menu of mostly veggie food, but some organic meat dishes too. Servings can be small and service mediocre, but there's a good store with organic coffee to keep you busy while you wait.
🍴 **Rostipollo**, just west of Centroamérica roundabout, T277-1968. Headquarters for the Nicaraguan chain that is franchised right across Central America and Mexico. Delicious chicken cooked over a wood fire, Caesar

salad, lunch specials and combo dishes. You'll find it next to McDonald's inside the Metrocentro food court.

Casa de Café, Lacmiel, 1 c arriba, 1½ c sur, T278-0605. Daily 0700-2200. The mother of all cafés in Managua, with airy upstairs seating area that makes the average coffee taste much better. Good turkey sandwiches, dess- erts, pies and *empanadas*. Recommended.

El Guapinol, Metrocentro. From 1100 daily. The best of the food court eateries with very good grilled meat dishes, chicken, fish and a hearty veggie dish (US$4.50). Try *Copinol* dish with grilled beef, avocado, fried cheese, salad, tortilla and *gallo pinto* US$4.

La Casa de los Mejía Godoy, Plaza el Sol, 2 c sur, T270-4928. This famous terraced restaurant regularly hosts live music acts (see Bars and clubs). It serves Nicaraguan cuisine, and good, economical lunch buffets. Very popular and recommended.

Pizza Valenti, Colonial Los Robles, T278-7474. Best cheap pizza in town, packed on Sun nights – national 'eating out with the family' night. They do home delivery.

Tacos Charros, Plaza el Café, 1 c abajo. The place for cold beer and tasty *tacos*. Check out the great photos of Pancho Villa, Mexico's most enigmatic revolutionary hero.

Martha Quezada

Anada, Estatua de Montoya 10 vrs arriba, T228-4140, daily 0700-2100. Nicaragua's original non-meat eatery and still one of the best. They serve wholesome vegetarian food, juices, smoothies, breakfasts and soups.

Cocinarte, INTUR, 1 c sur, closed Sun. International and vegetarian cuisine in a rancho-style setting.

Rancho Tiscapa, gate at Military Hospital, 300 vrs sur, T268-4290. Laid-back ranch-style eatery and bar serving traditional dishes such as *indio viejo*, *gallo pinto* and *cuajada con tortilla*. Good food and a great, breezey view of new Managua and Las Sierras. Recommended.

Aderezo, Ticabus 2 c arriba, ½ c sur. Clean, pleasant, serving home-cooked *comida típica*

Comida a la Vista Buffet, Ticabus, 2 c abajo. Often packed at lunch. Economical buffet.

Las Cazuelas, CST, 2 c sur, 1 c arriba, T228-6090. Always music on here. Great value breakfasts (US$1.50) with big portions, lunch and dinner too.

Mirna's, near **Pensión Norma**. 0700-1500. Good-value breakfasts and *comidas*, lunch buffet 1200-1500, popular with travellers and Nicaraguans, friendly service.

Panadería Tonalli, Ticabus, 3 c arriba, ½ c al sur. Pleasant little bakery serving nutritious wholemeal breads, cakes, cookies and coffee. Proceeds go to social projects.

Bolonia

El Churrasco, Rotonda El Güegüence. This is where the Nicaraguan president and parliamentary members decide the country's future over a big steak. Try the restaurant's namesake which is an Argentine-style cut with garlic and parsley sauce. Recommended.

Santa Fe, across from Plaza Bolonia, T268-9344. Tex-Mex style with walls covered in stuffed animal heads. It does a pretty good beef grill and *taco* salad, but bad *burritos*. Noisy and festive at lunchtime.

Rincón Cuscalteco, behind Plaza Bolonia, T266-4209, daily 1200-2200. Good cheap *pupusas salvadoreñas*, also *vigorón* and *quesillos*. Cheap beer and very relaxed.

Entertainment

Managua *p259, map p260, p262 and p263*
Bars and clubs

There are several god places on Lacmiel (and it's safe to walk at night as well).

Bar Chaman, Colonial Los Robles. A young, wild crowd, with lots of dancing and sweating to salsa, rock and disco on tape.

Bar Changó, Plaza Inter, 2 c sur, 15 vrs abajo. Where the terminally hip enjoy salsa, reggae, Brazilian hip-hop, rock, pop, jazz and world music. Lovely setting under a large tree.

La Casa de los Mejía Godoy, Plaza el Sol, 2 c sur, T278-4913, www.losmejiagodoy.org,

Thu-Sat, opens 2100. This is a chance to see 2 of Nicaragua's most famous folk singers. A very intimate setting, check with programme to make sure either Carlos or Luis Enrique is playing. Fri is a good bet, entrance US$15.

El Quelite, Entitel Villa Fontana 5 c abajo, T267-0126. Open-air, typical Nicaraguan dance bar with good food; try the *corvina a la plancha* (sea bass) US$5. Lots of dancing and live acts Thu-Sun.

El Quetzal, Rotonda Centro América, 1 c arriba, opposite Galería Simón, T278-1733. Fun crowd who fill the big dance floor and dance non-stop. Free entry, live music, ranchera, salsa, merengue.

Rhumba & Z Bar, Carretera a Masaya Km 3.5, opposite **Galería Simón**, T278-1733. Lots of dancing, popular, weekends only.

Shannon Bar Irlandés, 1 block east and 1 block south of **Ticabus**, T222-6683, open 1700-0200. Excellent food, whisky and Guinness (which often runs dry due to popularity). Recommended. Some rooms with shared bath (**F**) with breakfast available for those early-morning **Ticabus** departures.

Cinema

Alhambra 1, 2 & 3, Camino de Oriente, T270-3835. US films, Spanish subtitles, US$3, bring sweater for polar a/c.

Alianza Francesa, Altamira, 1 block north of Mexican Embassy. Shows French films and has art exhibits during the day.

Cinemas Inter, Plaza Inter, T222-5122. American films with Spanish subtitles. Book in advance on weekend evenings.

Metrocentro Cinemark, Metrocentro. Small, crowded theatre with 6 screens and steep seating.

Dance and theatre

Ballet Tepenahuatl, folkloric dances at the Teatro Rubén Darío.

Doña Haydée, opposite **Pastelería Aurami**, Planes de Altamira, T270-6100. Folkloric dance on Tue.

Intermezzo del Bosque, Colegio Centroamericano 5 Km al sur, T088-30071. On Wed,

food, dances, US$40, check with **Grayline Tours**, www.graylinenicaragua.com.

Teatro Nacional Rubén Darío, Frente al Malecón de Managua, T222-7426.

⊛ Festivals and events

Managua *p259, map p260, p262 and p263*

1-10 Aug The **Festival de Santo Domingo** (Managua's patron saint) is held at El Malecón church: ceremonies, horse racing, bullfights, cockfights, a lively carnival; proceeds go to the General Hospital.

1 Aug (½ day) and **10 Aug** are local holidays.

7 Dec **La Purísima** is held nationwide and is particularly celebrated in Managua. Altars are erected to the Virgin Mary, with singing, processions, fireworks and offerings of food.

◎ Shopping

Managua *p259, map p260, p262 and p263*

Bookshops

Hispamer, UCA, 1 c arriba, 1 c al sur. Best Spanish-language bookstore in the country, with maps, postcards and tourist items.

Handicrafts

Mercado Oriental is not recommended, see Safety, page 260.

Mercado Ricardo Huembes (also called **Mercado Central**), Pista Portezuelo, take bus No 110 or 119. The best place to buy handicrafts, and just about anything else. *Artesanía* from all parts of the country at the northeast end of the car park.

Metrocentro, in Plaza Inter and in Centro Comercial Managua. Some handicrafts (goldwork, embroidery) and good general shopping.

Mi Pueblo at Km 9.5 on Carretera Sur, T882-5650. Handicrafts and plants and there's also a good restaurant.

Takesa, del Intercontinental 2 c al sur, ½ abajo, Edif Bolívar 203, T268-3301. A smart shop selling Nicaraguan arts and crafts, high quality and high prices.

Imported goods
Galería Simón, opposite **Z-Bar** on Carretera a Masaya. Imported goods, take your passport, accepts US$ and TCs (to the value of items).

▲ Activities and tours

Managua *p259, map p260, p262 and p263*
Canopy tour
Tiscapa Canopy Tour, T893-5017, Tue-Sun 0900-1630, US$13. A breathtaking zip-line ride that is operated using 3 long metal cables and 4 platforms to traverse Tiscapa lake, at times more than 70 m in the air.

Spectator sports
The national sport and passion is **baseball**, with games on Sun mornings at the Estadio Denis Martínez. The season runs Nov-Feb and tickets cost US$1-5. Other popular sports include **basketball** and **football** although none have a regular venue and season. Nicaragua has had 4 lightweight world champion **boxers** but the big fights are staged outside the country. There is also **cockfighting** and **bullfighting** (but no kill).

Tour operators
Careli Tours, Edificio Invercasa, Planes de Altamira, Frente al Colegio Pedagógico La Salle, T278-6919, www.carelitours.com. One of Nicaragua's oldest tour operators with a professional service, very good English-speaking guides and traditional tours to all parts of Nicaragua.
Grayline Nicaragua, Rotunda El Güegüense, 250 m al sur, contiguo a **Viajes América**, PO Box 91, Edificio Central Correos de Nicaragua, T268-2412, www.grayline nicaragua.com. Day trips, tours packages, hotels, car rentals.
Otec, Antigua Cine Cabrera, Calle 27 de Mayo, 3 c arriba, T222-2619, www.otectours.com.
Schuvar Tours, Plaza España Edif Bamer No 4, T266-3588, www.schuvartours.com. Various cultural and adventure tours, transportation, car rental and flights.

Tours Nicaragua, Shell Plaza el Sol 110, 1 c al sur, 120 vrs abajo, 110, T252-4035, www.tours nicaragua.com. One of the best, offering captivating tours with a cultural, historical or ecological emphasis. A wide variety of tours to all parts of the country in vans, 4WD, boats and small plane. English-, German- and French-speaking guides. Contact Mike Newton, helpful. Guides, transfers, accommodation and admissions are included in the price.
Va Pues Tours, T606-2276, Apdo Postal LM-297, www.vapues.com. Dutch owner, multilingual guides (English, French, German, Dutch, Italian), helpful, reservations for domestic flights, car rental, specializes in half- to 1-day tours (US$20-30) around León.

⊕ Transport

Managua *p259, map p260, p262 and p263*
Air
For **Managua International Airport (MGA)**, take any bus marked 'Tipitapa' from Mercado Huembes, Mercado San Miguel or Mercado Oriental (near Victoria brewery), US$0.25. Alternatively, take a taxi (US$7-15). Be early for international flights – formalities are slow and thorough. Artisan stalls and cheap food in between arrivals and departures. Duty-free shops, café, toilets through immigration. You are not allowed to stay overnight in the airport. ATMs and money changing facilities.
   Tickets for domestic flights can be bought at the domestic terminal, located just west of the exit for arriving international passengers, or from city travel agents or tour operators. Keep luggage to a minimum, as there isn't much capacity on these little planes. Be aware that schedules are subject to change at any time. To **Bilwi**, La Costeña, 0630, 1030, 1430, US$148 return, 1½ hrs. To **Bluefields**, La Costeña, 0600, 0630, 1000, 1400, US$128 return, 1 hr; **Atlantic Airlines**, 0645, 1410. To **Corn Islands**, La Costeña, 0630, 1400, US$165 return, 1½ hrs; **Atlantic Airlines**, 0645, 1410. To **Minas**, La Costeña,

0900, US$139 return, 1 hr. To **San Carlos**, **La Costeña**, 0925, 1425, US$120 return. To **Waspam**, **La Costeña**, 1000, US$155 return, 1½ hrs. For return times see individual destinations.

Airline offices AeroMéxico, Óptica Visión, 75 vrs arriba, 25 vrs al lago, T266-6997, www.aeromexico.com. **American Airlines**, Rotunda El Güegüense 300 vrs al sur, T255-9090, www.aa.com. **Atlantic Airlines**, T270-5355, www.atlanticairlines int.com. **Continental Airlines**, Edificio Ofiplaza, p 2 edificio 5, T278-7033, www.continental.com. **Copa Airlines**, Carretera a Masaya Km 4 y medio edificio CAR No 6, T233-1624, www.copaair.com. **Delta Airlines**, Rotunda El Güegüense 100 m arriba, T254-8130, www.delta.com. **La Costeña**, T263-2142. **Spirit Airlines**, airport, T233-2884, www.spiritair.com. **Taca Airlines**, Edificio Barcelona, Plaza España, T266-3136, www.taca.com.

Bus

Local Beware of pickpockets on the crowded urban buses, particularly on tourist routes. City buses run every 10 mins 0530-1800, every 15 mins 1800-2200, when last services begin their routes; buses are frequent but routes are difficult to fathom. Tickets cost about US$0.20. The main bus routes are: **No 101** from Las Brisas, passing CST, Hotel Intercontinental, Mercado Oriental, then on to **Mercado San Miguel** and **El Mayoreo**. **No 103** from 7 Sur to Mercado Lewites, Plaza 19 de Julio, Metrocentro, **Mercado San Miguel** and **Villa Libertad**. **No 109** from Teatro Darío to the Bolívar/Buitrago junction just before Intercontinental turns east, then southeast to **Mercado Huembes/bus station**; **No 110** from 7 Sur to **Villa San Jacinto** passing en route Mercado Lewites, Plaza 19 de Julio, Metrocentro, Mercado Huembes/bus station and Mercado San Miguel. **No 113** from Ciudad Sandino, Las Piedrecitas, CST, Intercontinental, to **Mercado Oriental**.

No 116 runs east-west below Intercontinental, on Buitrago, also passing CST. **No 118** takes a similar route but turns south on Williams Romero to Plaza España, thence to **Israel Lewites bus station**. **No 119** runs from Plaza España to **Mercado Huembes/bus station** via Plaza 19 de Julio. **No 123** runs from Mercado Lewites via 7 Sur and Linda Vista to near Palacio Nacional de Cultura, and **Nuevo Diario**.

Long distance Bus Expresos are dramatically faster than regular routes. Check with terminal to confirm when the next express will leave. Payment is required in advance and seat reservations are becoming more common. There are also microbuses serving some of the major destinations. These are comparatively speedy and as comfortable as it gets.

La UCA serve just a few destinations close to Managua. *Expresos* and microbuses are cheap, fast and particularly recommended if travelling to Granada, León or Masaya. To **Granada**, every 15 mins or when full, 0530-2100, US$1.10, 1 hr. To **Jinotepe**, 0600-2100, every 20 mins or when full, US$1.10, 1 hr. To **León**, every ½ hr, 0730- 2100, US$1.75, 1½ hrs. To **Masaya**, every 15 mins or when full, 0530-2100, US$0.65, 40 mins.

Mercado Roberto Huembes, also called Mercado Central, is used for destinations southwest. To **Granada**, every 15 mins, 0520-2200, Sun 0610-2100, US$1, 1½ hrs. To **Masaya**, every 20 mins, 0625-1930, Sun until 1600, US$0.50, 50 mins. To **Peñas Blancas**, express bus, 0400, US$3, 3½ hrs; or go to Rivas for connections. To **Rivas**, every 30 mins, 0400-1800, US$1.75, 2½ hrs; express buses, US$2.50, 2 hrs; microbuses, US$3, 1½ hrs. To **San Juan del Sur**, express bus, 0900, 1600, US$3.25, 2½ hrs; or go to Rivas for connections.

Mercado Mayoreo, for destinations east and then north or south. To **Boaco**, every 30 mins, 0500-1800, US$1.75, 2 hrs. To **Camoapa**, 8 daily, 0630-1700, US$2.25, 3 hrs. To **El Rama**, 8 daily, 0500-2200, US$8,

9 hrs. To **Estelí**, every 30 mins, 0400-1800, US$3, 3½ hrs; express buses, 12 daily, US$3.50, 2½ hrs. To **Jinotega**, express buses, 11 daily, 0400-1730, US$3.50, 3½ hrs. To **Juigalpa**, every 20 mins, 0500-1730, US$3, 2½ hrs. To **Matagalpa** every 30 mins, 0330-1800, US$2.50, 2½ hrs; express buses, 12 daily, US$3, 2 hrs. To **Ocotal**, express buses, 12 daily, 0545-1745, US$5.50, 3½ hrs. To **San Rafael del Norte**, express bus, 1500, US$6, 4 hrs. To **San Carlos**, 0500, 0600, 0700, US$9, 9½ hrs. To **Somoto**, express buses, Mon-Sat 0715, 0945, 1245, 1345, 1545, 1645, Sun no express after 1345, US$4.50, 3½ hrs.

Mercado Israel Lewites, also called Mercado Boer, for destinations west and northwest. Microbuses leave from here, particularly recommended for journeys to León. To **Chinandega**, express buses, every 30 mins, 0600-1915, US$2.50, 2½ hrs. To **Corinto**, every hr, 0500-1715, US$3.50, 3 hrs. To **Diriamba**, every 20 mins, 0530-1930, US$1.25, 1 hr 15 mins. To **El Sauce**, express buses, 0745, 1445, US$3.25, 3½ hrs. To **Guasaule**, 0430, 0530, 1530, US$3.25, 4 hrs. To **Jinotepe**, every 20 mins, 0530- 1930, US$1.25, 1 hr 30 mins. To **León**, every 30 mins, 0545-1645, US$1.25, 2½ hrs; express buses, every 30 mins, 0500-1645, US$1.50, 2 hrs; microbuses, every 30 mins or when full, 0600-1700, US$1.75, 1½ hrs. To **Pochomil**, hourly, 0600-1920, US$1, 2 hrs.

International buses The cheap and efficient international buses are often booked up many days in advance and tickets will not be sold until all passport/visa documentation is complete. The best known is **Ticabus**, which parks in Barrio Martha Quezada, from Cine Dorado, 2 c arriba, T222-6094, www.tica bus.com, with services throughout Central America. Other operators include **King Quality**, end of Calle 27 de Mayo, opposite Plaza Inter, T228-1454, www.kingquality ca.com and **Transnica**, la Rotonda de Metrocentro 300 m al lago, 50 m arriba, T277-3133, www.transnica.com.

To **Costa Rica** Ticabus, 0600, 0700, 1200, US$15, 8hrs; King Quality, 1330, US$21, 8½ hrs; Transnica, 0530, 0700, 1000, 1200 (executive), US$13, executive service US$22, 8½ hrs.

To **El Salvador** Ticabus, 0500, US$30, 11 hrs; King Quality, 0330 (quality), 0530 (cruceros), 1100 (King), 'Cruceros class', US$25, 'Quality Class' US$35, 'King Class' US$51, 11 hrs; Transnica, 0500, US$18, 11 hrs.

To **Guatemala** Ticabus, 0500, US$46, 30 hrs including an overnight stay in El Salvador; King Quality, 0230 (cruceros), 1530 (quality/king), 'Cruceros class' US$52, 'Quality Class' US$62, 'King Class' US$86, 15 hrs.

To **Honduras (Tegucigalpa)** Ticabus, 0500, US$23, 8 hrs, then continues to San Pedro Sula, US$37, 10 hrs; King Quality, 0330 (king), 1130 (quality), 'Quality Class' US$30, 'King Class' US$42, 8½ hrs; Transnica, 0500, 8 hrs, US$20.

To **Mexico (Tapachula)** Ticabus, 0500, US$63, 36 hrs, including overnight stay in El Salvador; King Quality, 'Quality Class' US$74, 'King Class' US$96.

To **Panama** Ticabus, 0600, 0700, 1200, US$44, 28-32 hrs, including a 2- to 6-hr stopover in Costa Rica.

Car
All car hire agencies have rental desks at the international airport arrivals terminal. It is not a good idea to rent a car for getting around Managua, as it is a confusing city and fender benders are common and an injury accident means you could go to jail, even if not at fault. Outside the capital main roads are better marked and a rental car means you can get around more freely. (Taxis can also be hired by the hour or by the day, see below.)

Car hire For good service and 24-hr roadside assistance, the best rental agency is **Budget**, www.budget.com.ni, airport, T263-1222, **Holiday Inn**, T270-9669, and just off Carretera Sur at Montoya, 1 c abajo, 1 c sur,

T255-9000 (main office). Average cost of a small Toyota is US$50 per day while a 4WD (a good idea if exploring) is around US$100 per day with insurance and 200 km a day included; 4WD weekly rental rates range from US$600-750. Also at the airport is **Avis**, T233-3011, www.avis.com.ni, and **Hertz**, T266-8399. Another reliable agency is **Toyota Rent a Car**, www.toyotarentacar.com, which has cars to match its name and is at the airport, T266-3620, the Hotel Princess, T270-4937, and the Camino Real, T263-2358.

Taxi

Taxis (the best method of transport for foreigners) can be flagged down on the street. Fares range from US$1.50-2 for a short trip, US$2-3.50 across town, US$10 to airport. Fares are always per person, not per car. Taxi drivers may decide not to take you if your destination is in a different direction to other passengers. If they agree, ask how much (*¿por cuánto me lleva?*) before getting in. If the front seat is empty take it as the back seat will be filled en route. Street names and numbers are not universal in the city and the taxi driver may not know your destination; have the telephone number of your hotel with you. If heading for Barrio Martha Quezada, ask for the **Ticabus** if you do not know your exact destination. Taxis from the airport are 50% cheaper from the main road beyond the car park.

Radio taxis are recommended for early flights or late night transport. Companies include: **Co-op 25 de Febrero**, T222-5218, or **Co-op 2 de Agosto**, T263-1512, get price quote on the phone (normally 80-100% more expensive).

⊙ Directory

Managua *p259, map p260, p262 and p263*
Banks

Any bank in Nicaragua will change US$ to córdobas and vice-versa. TC purchase receipts may be required in banks when changing TCs. The best 2 banks for foreigners are **Banco de América Central (BAC)** and **Banco de Finanzas (BDF)**. BAC offers credit card advances, uses the Cirrus debit system and changes all TCs with a 5% commission. BDF changes American Express TCs only, also with a 5% commission. In Managua ATM machines are found in the airport, at the Metrocentro and Plaza Inter shopping malls and in many gas station convenience stores ('Red Total'). There are several money changers at the road junction in Altamira by the restaurant **Casa del Pomodoro** and outside **La Colonia** shopping centre in Plaza España. After 1800 and on Sun they are usually tricksters. On Sun you can change money at the **Intercontinental**, major hotels or banks inside **Metrocentro**.

Embassies and consulates

Austria, Rotonda El Guenguense, 1 c al norte, T266-3316. **Canada**, Bolonia Los Pipitos, 2 c abajo, T264-2723, Mon-Thu 0900-1200. **Costa Rica**, Los Robles, Tip Top, 25 vrs abajo, T270-3799, 0900-1500. **Denmark**, Bolonia Salud Integral, 2 c al lago, 50 vrs abajo, T254-5059. **Finland**, Hospital Militar, 1 c north, 1½ c abajo, T264-1137, 0800-1200, 1300-1500. **France**, Iglesia El Carmen, 1½ c abajo, T222-6210, 0800-1600. **Germany**, Plaza España, 200 m lago, T266-3917, Mon-Fri 0900-1200. **Guatemala**, just after Km 11 on Carretera a Masaya, T279-9834, fast service, 0900-1200 only. **Honduras**, Las Colinas No. 298, T276-2406. **Italy**, Rotonda El Güegüence, 1 c lago, T266-6486, 0900-1200. **Mexico**, Km 4.5, Carretera a Masaya, 1 c arriba, T277-5886. **Panama**, Col Mantica, el Cuartel General de Bomberos, 1 c abajo, No 93, T/F266-8633, 0830-1300. **Spain**, Las Colinas Ave, Central No. 13, T276-0968. **Sweden**, Plaza España, 1 c abajo, 2 c lago, ½ c abajo, Apdo Postal 2307, T266-0085, 0800-1200. **Switzerland**, Banpro Las Palmas, 1 c abajo, T266-3010. **UK**, Reparto Los Robles, Primera Etapa, main entrance from Carretera a Masaya, 4th house on right, T278-0014, Apdo Aéreo 169, 0900-1200. **USA**, Km 4.5, Carretera del Sur, T266-6010,

0730-0900. **Venezuela**, Km 10.5, Carretera a Masaya, T276-0267.

Emergencies
Police: T118 in an emergency; the local police station number will depend on what *distrito* you are in. Start with the Metrocentro area number, T265-0651. **Fire**: T115 in an emergency; the central number is T265-0162. **Red Cross**: T128 in an emergency.

Immigration and customs
Immigration: near Ciudad Jardín, Antiguo Edif del Seguro Social (bus No 101, 108) Mon-Fri 0800-1600, T244-3989. **Customs**: Km 5 Carretera del Norte (bus No 108).

Internet
Lots of places, especially in and around Plaza Inter, María Quezada and Metrocentro. Most internet cafés are open daily, charge around US$0.60 per hr and also offer internet calls.

Language schools
Casa Nicaragüense de Español, Km 11.5 Carretera Sur, Spanish classes and a thorough introduction to Nicaragua, accommodation with families. **Huellas**, Col Centroamérica, Callejón El Ceibo G-414, T277-2079, intensive classes, private classes and regular classes (0880-1200). **Nicaragua Spanish School**, Rotonda Bello Horizonte, 2 c al sur, 2 c arriba, T244-4512, regular and private classes. **Universidad Americana**, Centro de Idiomas Extranjeros, T278-3800 ext 301, open course with flexible hrs and regular 5-month course. **Universidad Centroamericana (UCA)**, Centro de Idiomas Extranjeros, T278-3923, ext 242-351, 5-week regular classes of all levels and open classes with flexible hours.

Libraries
Casa Ben Linder Library, Estatua Monseñor Lezcano 3 c al sur, 1½ c arriba, also good book exchange, T266-4373.

Medical services
Dentists Dr Claudia Bendaña, T277-1842, and Dr Mario Sánchez Ramos, T278-1409, T278-5588 (home). **Doctors** Internal medicine, Dr Enrique Sánchez Delgado, T278-1031; Dr Mauricio Barrios, T255-6900. **Hospitals** Generally crowded, with very long queues. The best are **Hospital Bautista**, near Mercado Oriental, T249-7070; **Hospital Militar**, south from Intercontinental and take 2nd turning on left, T222-2763; and **Hospital Alemán- Nicaragüense**, Km 6 Carretera Norte Siemens, 3 c al sur, 249-0701, operated with German aid. Phone for appointment first if possible. **Private clinics** These are an alternative. **Policlínica Nicaragüense**, consultation US$30. **Med-Lab**, Plaza España 300 m al sur, recommended for tests on stool samples, the director speaks English.

Post office
21 locations around Managua, the main office for the country is 1 block west of Parque Central. Wide selection of beautiful stamps. Poste Restante (*Lista de Correos*) keeps mail for 45 days, US$0.20 per letter. There is another post office in the Centro Comercial Managua and at the airport.

Telephone
Enitel, same building as post office, open 0700-2230. There is a small office in the international airport. Telephone offices are spreading around Managua.

The Northern Highlands

Nicaragua's ruggedly beautiful northern mountains and valleys have staged much of the history that has given the country its dubious international reputation. This is where Sandino fought the US occupation of Nicaragua from 1927 to 1933 and where the rebel Sandinistas launched their first attacks against the Somoza administration in the 1960s. Then, in the 1980s, the Contras waged war against the Sandinista Government in these mountains. Today, most visitors would be hard pressed to see where all this aggression came from. Most of the northern ranges and plains are full of sleepy villages with ancient churches, rustic cowboys and smiling children. This is where the soil and the homes blend into a single palette: the red-brown clay earth reflected in the adobe walls and red-tile roofs. Nothing is rushed here and many of the region's villages are evidence that time travel is indeed possible, with the 21st century in no danger of showing itself around here anytime soon.

North of Lake Managua, a couple of routes use the Interamericana on their way to the Honduran border. The road rises and winds through hilly country, with fields set aside for agriculture and coffee-growing, before giving way to mines and pine forests. At Sébaco, a turning heads east to good walking and wildlife country in Matagalpa and Jinotega. North of Sébaco, the highway continues to Estelí, a former FSLN hotbed. Beyond here the road splits, leading to Somoto and Ocotal before crossing the border and continuing to the capital of Honduras. ▶▶ *For listings, see pages 281-287.*

North from Managua ◉❼❽ ▶▶ *pp281-287.*

Heading east out of Managua along the southern shore of the lake is **Tipitapa** (21 km). The resort has reopened and you can swim in clean water in the baths. The air-conditioned restaurant attached to the thermal baths is good. There is a colourful market, and the **Fiesta del Señor de Esquipulas** takes place on 13-16 January.

The Interamericana goes north through Tipitapa to **Sébaco**, passing through **Ciudad Darío**, where the poet Rubén Darío was born. You can see the house, which is maintained as a **museum** ① *Mon-Fri 0800-1200, 1400-1700.* There is an arts festival for the week of his birthday, 18 January. Sébaco and the surrounding area was badly affected by Hurricane Mitch. East of the highway is **Esquipula**, 2½ hours by bus, a good place for hiking, fishing and riding. From Sébaco, a 134-km journey to the border at **El Espino** takes you through sharp hills with steep climbs and descents, but it's smooth and quite well banked. A reasonable road leads off the Interamericana 10 km northwest of Sébaco to join the Pacific Highway to León (110 km).

Matagalpa and around ◉❼❽◯▲❻❼ ▶▶ *pp281-287.*

Matagalpa, with its beautiful mountains and diverse scenery, is one of the best hiking areas of Nicaragua. A coffee boom in the late 1990s benefited the region greatly, but the crash in coffee prices in 2001 has subsequently decimated the fragile local economy. The local festival and holiday on 26 September celebrates the **Virgen de las Mercedes**.

In the small town there are a few sights, and while the old church is about the only colonial-style building left, the town retains a simple agrarian charm. It was badly damaged in the Revolution but all war damage has now been repaired. It is also the birthplace of Carlos Fonseca, one of the founder members of the FSLN. The house he was born in, now the **Museo Carlos Fonseca**, one block east of Parque San José, looks certain to remain closed for the foreseeable future. It's a busy town with just the **cathedral** and the **Galería de los Héroes y Mártires**, in the main square to the north, to consider as sights. **Matagalpa Tours** ① *Banpro, ½ c arriba, T772-0108*, are an excellent source of information, with a thorough knowledge of the city and the surrounding mountains; staff speak Dutch and English. Coffee, the region's main source of employment, is harvested from November to February and can be seen drying in the sun at the southern edge of town. There is a **coffee museum** ① *alcaldía, 1½ c norte, daily 0800-1230, 1400-1900, free*, devoted to its history and cultivation.

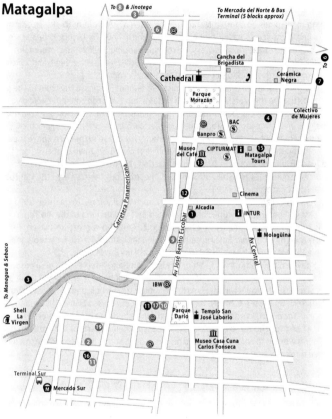

Matagalpa

To ⑧ & Jinotega

To Mercado del Norte & Bus Terminal (5 blocks approx)

To ⑥

Cancha del Brigadista

Cathedral

Cerámica Negra

Parque Morazán

Colectivo de Mujeres

BAC

Banpro

Museo del Café   CIPTURMAT   Matagalpa Tours

Carretera Panamericana

Cinema

Alcaldía

INTUR

Molagüina

Av José Benito Escobar

Av Central

To Managua & Sebaco

IBW

Shell La Virgen

Parque Darío   Templo San José Laborío

Museo Casa Cuna Carlos Fonseca

Terminal Sur

Mercado Sur

N

100 metres
100 yards

Sleeping	Eating	
Apante **10**	Alejandrina Buffet **1**	Pique's **4**
Fountain Blue **3**	Artesanos Café-Bar **15**	Rostisería La Casona **12**
Ideal **6**	Cafetería Don Chaco **13**	Rostisería La Posada **11**
La Profe **11**	La Pradera **3**	
La Siesta **2**	La Vida es Bella **6**	**Bars & clubs**
Selva Negra **8**	Madre Tierra **16**	Crazy Horse **17**
Soza del Río **9**	Pesca Mar **7**	Disco Rancho Escondido **19**

A nice way to discover the area on your own is with *Treasures of Matagalpa*, a brochure describing five one-day hikes ranging from four to eight hours, including a detailed map, instructions and a description of the history of the area. You can buy the brochure (US$1.75) at **Centro Girasol** ① *2 blocks south, 1 block west of Terminal Sur, T612-6030*. All profit goes to supporting families with disabled children. You should also visit the centre if you're interested in volunteering.

Jinotega and around ●●●● ▶▶ *pp281-287*.

A rough road spirals north from Matagalpa to Jinotega rising out of the valley and into one of the most scenic paved highways in the north, lined by highland farms, virgin cloudforest and breathtaking views of the surrounding valleys and mountains. At Km 143, **Diparate de Potter** ① *T612-6228, daily 0900-2100*, serves beef and chicken dishes and is worth a stop to sit down and enjoy the scenery.

Jinotega is a pleasant, friendly town which has famous images in the church. The jail, which was used in the years of the Somoza dictatorship, has been converted into a youth centre. There are several banks near the main plaza. **Alianza Turística** ① *Alcaldía, 2 c arriba, 1½ al sur*, has good information on the town but staff speak Spanish only. A beautiful hike, which starts from behind the cemetery, leads up to the cross above the city (1½-hour round trip). As with Matagalpa, excellent coffee is grown in the region. One road leads from Jinotega to El Tuma power station (18 km); another, which is unpaved and picturesque, goes to Estelí, through La Concordia, but there's very little transport between La Concordia and Estelí.

The beautiful **Lago de Apanás** (buses every hour from Jinotega, 20 minutes, US$0.35), 8 km east of Jinotega, is an artificial lake created by the damming of the Río Tuma. The lake is used to produce energy in a hydroelectric plant and is great for fishing, full of *guapote* (perch) and *tilapia*. Small enterprises lining the lake will fry fish for visitors and it's possible to rent a small boat and fish on the lake; ask the locals.

The paved highway north of Jinotega leads to **San Rafael del Norte**. There are some good murals in the local church, and a chapel on the hill behind, at Tepeyak, built as a spiritual retreat. The town was involved in the Sandinista struggle and its recent history is very interesting. **Museo General Sandino** ① *in the Casa Museo Ejército Defensor de La Soberanía Nacional; if locked, ask for the key at the mayor's house across the street*, is where Sandino used to send off telegrams to his troops in different parts of the northern hills. The young woman to whom he dictated his messages became his wife and the town has claimed him as their native son ever since.

Estelí ●●●●▲●● ▶▶ *pp281-287*.

This is a rapidly developing departmental capital, heavily damaged during the Revolution of 1978 to 1979. It's not especially attractive, but it is energetic, with a large student population injecting life into an otherwise humdrum agricultural centre. Worth visiting is the **Casa de Cultura**, which has a small exhibition of petroglyphs found in the area and of military memorabilia, and the **Galería de los Héroes y Mártires**, next door, with mementos and photographs of those killed defending the Revolution and moving paintings on the outside walls. Many cooperatives and support organizations were developed in the aftermath of the Revolution. One of them, the **Asociación de ex-combatientes históricos 18 de mayo** ① *C Principal, ½ c south of the Plaza de la*

Estelí

To Somoto & Honduras

To ② & Cigar Factory (Segovia Cigars)

C 4 NE
C 2 NE
C 1 NE
C Perú
C 1 SE
C 2 SE
C 3 SE
C 5 SE
C 7 SE
C 9 SE
C 11 SE

Carretera Panamericana

M ⑤ Crafts ③
⑫ ④ ④ ②
@ Computer Soluciones
Parque Central
✝ Cathedral ⑨
$ⓘ ⑨ ① ♩
$⊗ ⑦ ⑦ ⊡ Artesanía Sorpresa
$ ⑥
Supermercado Palí
□ Ministry of Health Information Centre
El Salvador Cooperative
⑥ⓘ
⑩
🍴 Craft
Parque Infantil
⑯ ⑯ Buses South & Managua
🏨
Shell Amniae Women's Centre
⑰
⑱
Cenac Language School
Shell 🏨 ①
Bús Station North

To ⑩⑯, Buses South & Managua

N
100 metres
200 yards

Sleeping 🛏
Alameda 1
Alpino 10
Barlop 2
Casa Nicarao 7
El Mesón 3
Hospedaje Luna 4
Los Arcos 12
Miraflor 5
Moderno 6
Panorama 2 9

Eating 🍴
Ananda 1
Café Luz 2
Cafetería El Rincón Pinareño 7
Cohifer 3
Don Pollo 2 4
Ixcotelli 6
Koma Rico 8
La Carreta 9
La Casita 10

Bars & clubs 🍸
Semáforo Rancho 16
Studio 54 18
Zona Zero 17

Cathedral, is good and has some crafts and a café with posters all over the walls. The **Ministry of Health Information Centre** ① *C Principal, 4 blocks from the plaza*, is involved with projects to revive traditional medicine and healing and offers advice on a wide range of herbal remedies. The **INTUR tourist office** ① *Parque Central, ½ c sur, on Calle Principal, T713-6799*, has information in Spanish on the city and its surroundings. If you are interested in visiting rural communities, La UCA Miraflor is the best organization to approach (see Miraflor, below).

Around Estelí 🛏🍴🍸① ▶▶ pp281-287.

Miraflor

Miraflor is a 5675-ha nature reserve 28 km northeast of Estelí in the Department of Jinotega. It contains the **Laguna de Miraflor** and has a wide range of flora and fauna (including the quetzal). **Unión de Cooperativas Agropecuarias (UCA) Miraflor** ① *costado noreste de la catedral 2 c arriba, ½ c sur, T713-2971, www.miraflor. org*, operates in the reserve, has a tourism project and is in charge of environmental protection. The cooperative can provide wooden huts, basic facilities and accommodation (**E-G**), meals, horse hire (US$7 per day) and guided walks (US$10 per person). A visit is recommended to see rural life and is a beautiful area for riding. Travelling to the region at night is not recommended due to crime, although police have been installed at the entrance to the Miraflor reserve.

El Sauce and around

A very poor gravel road just north of Estelí runs to El Sauce where there is a large 16th-century church (burnt down in 1997 and refurbished in 2002). It's a place of pilgrimage and people come from all over Central America to visit the black **Christ of Esquipulas**, celebrated in a giant festival

Border essentials: Nicaragua–Honduras

El Espino
Immigration Nicaraguan immigration is in El Espino, 5 km from the Honduran border at La Playa. The Nicaraguan side is open 24 hours.

Money changing There are no money changing facilities; locals will oblige. Motorists leaving Nicaragua should enquire in Somoto if an exit permit has to be obtained there or at El Espino. This applies to cyclists too.

Transport Minibuses run between Somoto and the border every hour 0615-1710, US$1. Buses to Estelí are hourly, 2½ hours, US$1.65, express buses are Managua-bound, 1½ hours, US$1.65, and will drop you off at the Shell station, just east of central Estelí. There are six daily buses to Managua, 3½ hours, US$4. On the Nicaraguan side, taxis wait to take you to Somoto, they may try to overcharge; pay no more than US$8. On the Honduran side, taxis go between the border and the Mi Esperanza bus stops, when full, US$1 for foreigners, less for locals.

Ocotal
This is recommended as the best route from Tegucigalpa to Managua (see page 281).

Immigration Nicaraguan immigration is open 24 hours. Arrivals must fill in an immigration card, present their luggage to the customs authorities and obtain a receipt, and then present these to the immigration authorities with passport and entry fees. When leaving the country, fill out a card, pay the tax and get your passport stamped.

Money changing Money changers operate on both sides. Rates for cash and TCs are usually better in Estelí.

Transport Las Manos–Ocotal bus, every 30 minutes or when full, 0500-1645, US$0.80, 45 minutes. Taxis also available, US$7-8, set fare before boarding.

that culminates 15-18 January. After 20 km, an equally rough road branches north to **Achuapa**, beyond which an unmade road continues through the *artesanía* town of **San Juan de Limay** (one *hospedaje*), famous thoughout Nicaragua for its great **soapstone carvings**. The artists are happy to invite you into their house to watch them carve (average sculpture costs US$8 or less). Further on, **Pueblo Nuevo** (two basic *hospedajes*) is near an archaeological site. From here the road goes on to join the Interamericana just east of Somoto.

Condega
From Estelí, the Pan-American goes north to Condega, a quiet town producing agricultural goods. Its name means 'pottery makers' and the indigenous village was once known for its ceramics. Some of the country's most beautiful pottery is still made here and visitors are welcome at the **Ducuale Grande Ceramic Co-operative** ① *opposite Colegio Ana Velia de Guillén, T752-2374,* a women's co-op that makes attractive red-clay earthenware; there's a small shop attached. Condega has a small and well-kept **archaeological museum** ① *Casa de Cultura de Condega, Plaza Central, Julio C Salgado, opposite the Policía Nacional, T752-2221, Tue-Sun 0800-1200, 1400-1800,* with permanent expositions of discoveries from the region.

Somoto

Continuing along the highway you reach Somoto, a pleasant town in a lovely setting. Recent excavations have uncovered unusual pre-Columbian remains which are on display at the **Museo Arqueológico de Somoto** ① *on the Parque Central, Mon-Fri 0800-1200*. The town is also famous for the best *rosquillas* (a traditional toasted food, dry but tasty, made of egg, cheese, cornmeal and butter) in Nicaragua. Try the *viejita* which also has pure cane sugar in the centre. Fifteen kilometres north of Somoto is one of Nicaragua's most impressive canyons, a national monument well worth visiting. It's a moderate and slippery 3-km hike from a highway exit, best reached by taxi (US$4). A guide is recommended, but not essential.

Ocotal

From Somoto a road turns off right to Ocotal (18 km), a clean, cool, whitewashed town on a sandy plain and well worth a visit. It is near the Honduran border, to which a road runs north (bus marked Las Manos), and the scenery is wonderful. From Ciudad Sandino – formerly Jícaro – 50 km east from Ocotal, you can get to **San Albino**, where there are many gold mines and the nearby Río Coco is used to wash the gold.

◉ The Northern Highlands listings

For Sleeping and Eating price codes and other relevant information, see pages 43-46.

◉ Sleeping

North from Managua *p276*
E El Valle, Sébaco, on the highway 1.5 km south of town, T775-2209. Small, simple rooms with fans and TV at this quiet, motel-style place on the highway. Some have a/c.
F Casa Agricultor, Ciudad Darío, bus station, 1½ c al norte, T776-2379. Simple, dark rooms; 3 with bath, 5 without, all have a fan, and there's secure parking. The owner, Emma López, is hospitable and friendly.
F Hotel Oscar Morales, Esquipula. Clean, with shower.

Matagalpa and around *p276, map p277*
LL-E Selva Negra, 10 km on road to Jinotega at Km 139.5, at 1200 m, T772-3883, www. selva negra.com. Set in a gorgeous private rainforest reserve, Selva Negra has a range of mostly extravagant accommodation including Germanic cottages (**LL-A**), double rooms (**B**) and dorm beds (**E**). There's a good, if expensive, restaurant serving organic food

farmed on the premises. Entrance is US$3 if you just want to hike the surrounding trails – ask for a map at the hotel.
A Lomas de San Thomas, Escuela Guanuca 400 m arriba, T772-4189. The most luxurious in the region. 26 spacious rooms with private bath, hot water, cable TV, telephone, minibar. Away from the centre.
C Hacienda San Rafael, on the road to La Dalia, T612-2229. This lovely organic coffee farm is the producer of the fine **Café de los Reyes**. Lodging is in an attractive wooden lodge with spectacular views of surrounding mountains above well-manicured gardens. The 270-ha farm has short nature paths, 1 leading to a small waterfall. Rooms have shared bath, meals available, must reserve.
C-F Esperanza Verde lodge, www.finca esperanzaverde.org. This famous eco-lodge, built for the observation of butterflies, has handsome wood and brick cabins (**B**) with covered patios, solar power, private bath and bunk beds. There are also dorm rooms (**E**) and camping at US$6 per person.
D Hotel Apante, west side of Parque Darío, T772-6890. Clean rooms with private bath, hot water and cable TV. The management's friendly and there's free coffee 24 hrs a day.

D Hotel Fountain Blue, catedral, 3 c al norte, 2 c abajo, T772-2733. Comfortable rooms with private bath, cable TV, hot water and fan. A simple breakfast of coffee and bread is included, and laundry service is available.

D Hotel La Siesta, Texaco, 1½ abajo, T772-2476. Clean, tidy, good value hotel with friendly management. Rooms have hot water, cable TV and fan. There's internet facilities, international call centre and a café, too.

D Hotel Soza del Río, Av Río Grande, T772-3030, opposite the river. 17 economical rooms with bath, fan and cable TV. Breakfasts, buffet lunches and dinner served.

E Hotel La Profe, Shell el Progreso, 20 vrs al norte, T772-2506. A pleasant, family-run place. Tidy rooms have cable TV, fan, private bath and hot water.

Jinotega and around *p278*

A Hotel Café and Restaurant Borbon, Texaco, 1 c abajo, ½ c norte, T782 2710. Well-appointed and very nice. 25 comfortable rooms with private bath, hot water, a/c, cable TV. Quiet, friendly, best in province, good restaurant ♥♥ with traditional dishes.

C Hotel Solentuna Hem, Esso, 1 c arriba, 2½ c norte, T782-2334. Clean, safe, family hotel with 17 rooms. The owner lived in Sweden for many years, and offers a range of beauty treatments including massage and pedicure. Breakfast and dinner are served, and coffee tours are available. Pleasant and professional.

D Hotel Central, catedral, ½ c norte, T782-2063. 20 rooms of varying quality. Rooms upstairs have private bath, cable TV and a great mountain view. Cheaper rooms (**F**) are without bath or view. There's also a communal TV and purified water dispenser downstairs, and a restaurant with very cheap food. Great location, very friendly.

E Primavera, Esso station, 4 c norte, T782-2400. This economical hotel has 28 clean, plain rooms, cheaper without cable TV and bath (**F**). Breakfast is served but not included in the price. Good local atmosphere.

F Hospedaje Rocío, just south of the petrol station, San Rafael del Norte, T652-2313. Small, homely and very clean, good value, with bath and set meals.

Estelí *p278, map p279*

A Alameda, Shell Esquipulas, 1 c al arriba, 1½ c sur, T713-6292, www.alamedaesteli.com. Clean, large hotel with clean, bright rooms. Services include internet, pool, parking and restaurant. Very comfortable and decent, but far from the centre; use a taxi or car.

A Hotel Los Arcos, Catedral, 1 c norte, www.familiasunidas.org/hotelosarcos.htm. This brightly painted, professionally managed and comfortable hotel has 18 rooms with private bath, a/c or fan, and cable TV. The attached restaurant, **Vuela Vuela**, is also reputable, and profits go to social projects.

A-D Alpino, Almacén Sony, ½ c arriba, T713-2828, halpino@hotmail.com. A wide range of lodgings with differing features and prices, from apartments with cable TV and a/c (**A**), to basic, economical rooms with fan (**C-D**)

C Casa Hotel Nicarao, central plaza, 1½ c sur, T713-2490. Clean, comfortable rooms set around a relaxing courtyard filled with plants, paintings and sitting space. Very friendly management and a nice atmosphere, but the walls are thin and let lots of noise through. There are cheaper rooms without bath (**E**).

C El Mesón, Av Bolívar, central plaza, 1 c norte, T713-2655, barlan@ibw.com.ni. Clean, comfortable rooms at this friendly, helpful hotel, all with hot water and cable TV. There's a travel agency attached, and an *artesanía* shop over the road. Recommended.

D Hotel Miraflor, Parque Central, ½ c norte, T713-2003. Popular with Nicas. 7 rooms with hot water, cable TV and private bath. The attached restaurant serves *comida típica*.

D Hotel Panorama 2, catedral, 1 c sur, ½ c arriba, T713-5023. Same features as **Hotel Panorama 1** (on the Interamericana), but much quieter at night, with good access to centre restaurants, secure parking, rooms upstairs nicer. If leaving on early bus pay in advance, ask for receipt.

D Moderno, catedral, 2½ c sur, T713-2378. Clean, comfortable rooms with a/c, hot water and cable TV. There's a restaurant for guests, where breakfast and dinner are served.

E Barlop, Parque Central, 6 c norte, T713-2486. This hotel has 12 rooms, 6 of which are good, 6 basic. The former have showers and cable TV. Parking available.

E Hospedaje Luna, catedral, 1 c al norte, 1 c arriba, T441-8466, www.cafeluzyluna.com. Brand new hostel with 2 dorms and 2 private rooms. There's hammock space, an activities board, tourist information, DVDs, tours and drinking water. Volunteer work in Miraflor can be arranged here – 3 months' commitment and Spanish speakers are preferred. Discounts for longer stays and groups.

Condega p280

D Hotel Restaurante Gualca, T715-2431. 6 rooms with shared baths, clean, noisy at weekends.

E Hospedaje Framar, on main plaza, T715-2393. 14 very clean and pleasant rooms, cold showers, nice garden, safe, friendly, English spoken, excellent value. Parking for motorbikes.

E Pensión Baldovinos, opposite the park, T715-2222. 20 rooms, cheaper with shared bath. Fan, group discounts, good food.

Somoto p281

D Hotel Colonial, Iglesia, ½ c al sur, T722-2040. An attractive, professionally managed hotel with decent rooms; all have private bath, cable TV and fan. Popular with businessmen and NGOs.

D Hotel Panamericano, north side of Parque Central, T722-2355. Good-value rooms at this interesting hotel, where you'll find an orchid collection, a craft shop and a menagerie of animals. The annexed section, a few roads away, has a lovely garden and recreation area. The owners run trips to the canyon and surrounding countryside. Highly recommended.

F El Bambú, Policía Nacional, 2 c norte, T722-2330. Close to the highway and bus station. 20 simple, economical rooms with cable TV. Some have bath, some don't.

F Hospedaje La Provedencia, Intel, 2½ c norte, T722-2089. Offer 6 simple rooms with 2 shared baths inside a house. Friendly, family-run and basic.

Ocotal p281

A-C Hotel Frontera, behind the Shell station on the highway to Las Manos, T732-2668, hosfrosa@turbonett.com. This is the best hotel in town, even if it looks like a prison compound from outside. It has an inviting swimming pool, bar, restaurant and events room. The rooms are clean and comfortable, if uninspiring, and cheaper without a/c (**C**). Internet, laundry and international call facility.

C-D Hotel Benmoral, at south entrance to city, T732-2824. 20 dark, clean rooms with a/c or fan (**D**), cable TV, hot water. Food is available, and parking spaces. Friendly and helpful.

D-E Hotel Belrive, Shell station on the highway, 1 c abajo. Motel-style with rooms with bath, hot water and cable TV. There's parking and a restaurant. Pleasant and friendly.

E Hotel El Viajero, Esso station, 3½ c abajo, T732-2040. Clean, pleasant, economical place with 15 rooms. All have fan, most with bath (cheaper without). Breakfast and lunch are served, there's internet service and cable TV.

🍴 Eating

North from Managua p276

🍴 **Los Gemelos**, Sébaco, Monumento de la Virgen, 1½ c abajo. Regular buffets and a variety of meat and chicken dishes served. There's a disco on Sat and Sun evenings, playing hip-hop, salsa and dance.

🍴 **El Sesteo**, Sébaco, Del BDF, 1½ c abajo. Clean, wonderfully airconditioned and well staffed. The menu boasts a fine selection of steaks, chicken, soup and shrimp dishes.

🍴 **El Buen Gusto**, Ciudad Darío, bus station, 3½ c al norte. This new, clean *comedor* serves home-cooked Nicaraguan fare and some good-looking fairy cakes.

Matagalpa and around p276, map p277

♨ Restaurant La Pradera, Shell la Virgen, 2 c al norte, T772-2543. One of the best in town, ideal for 'meat lovers', also serves good seafood.

♨ Restaurante Pesca Mar, Cancha del Brigadista, 3 c arriba, T772-3548. Open until 2200. Seafood specialities, shrimp in garlic butter, red snapper in onions.

♨-♨ La Vida es Bella, T772-5476, Col Lainez. An Italian-run restaurant, has received strong praise from a couple of readers.

♨-♨ Restaurante Pique's, T772-2723, Casa Pellas, 1c arriba. Atmospheric Mexican restaurant serving tacos, tequila, tostados and chiliquilas. Popular and friendly.

♨-♨ Rosticería La Posada, T772-2330, Parque Darío, ½ c abajo. Very fine eatery serving roasted chicken and fish a la tipitapa.

♨ Alejandrina Buffet, Alcadía, ½ c al sur. Economical buffet serving freshly cooked Nica fare. Clean, tasty and friendly.

♨ Rosticería La Casona, Museo del Café, 1½ al sur, T772-3901. Local haunt serving a range of chicken and beef dishes, cold beer and refreshments. Not bad, and economical.

Cafés

♨ Artesanos Café Bar, Banpro, ½ c arriba. This pleasant café-bar has a wooden, rancho-style interior. They do breakfasts, light lunches, and hot and cold drinks including licuados, iced coffee and really excellent cappuccinos. Popular with both locals and tourists, and a good night spot too.

♨ Madre Tierra, Texaco, 1½ abajo. Adorned with political photography, peace flags, outsider art, and iconic, revolutionary portraits, this new café-bar has an alternative, intellectual feel. They serve tasty home-made burgers, light meals and cold beer. The action hots up at night, with regular live music and documentary films.

Jinotega and around p278

♨ Roca Rancho, Esso, 1 c sur, 2½ c arriba. Tue-Sun 1200-0000. This fun, friendly restaurant looks a bit like a beach bar. Serves up comida típica, shrimps, burgers, bocas, beer and liquors. Live music on Thu.

♨ Jinocuba No 1, Alcaldía, 5 c norte, T782-2607. Daily 1200-1200. Widely recommended cuban restaurant serving Mojito cubano and pollo habanero among other things.

♨ Las Marías, Esso, 2½ c sur. Good locals' lunch buffet with pork, chicken and beef-based Nica dishes. Family-run and friendly.

Estelí p278, map p279

♨♨-♨ Cohifer, Cohifer, catedral, 1 c arriba, ½ c al sur. A very decent establishment that promises a fulfilling gastronomic experience. Excellent steaks, chicken and fish dishes. Well established and recommended.

♨ Ixcotelli, Almacén Sony, ½ c arriba, T714-2212. Fine Nicaraguan cuisine in a pleasant, ranch-style setting.

♨ Las Brasas, just off northeast corner of central park, T713-4985, Tue-Sun 1130-2400. Popular, lively place, with stacks of booze and bottles lining the walls. They serve Nicaraguan food and a range of beef dishes, inlcuding steak fillets, brochetas and mixtas. Try the cerdo asado. Recommended.

♨ Cafetería El Rincón Pinareño, Enitel, ½ c sur. Cuban and Nicaraguan dishes and home-made pastries, try vaca frita (shredded fried beef with onions and bell peppers), sandwich cubano, very good service and food, crowded for lunch, recommended.

♨ Don Pollo 2, catedral, 1 c norte, ½ c arriba. This popular roast chicken place is great for a cheap, tasty fill and a bottle or 2 of cold beer. Mariachis on some evenings.

♨ Koma Rico, Enitel, 1 c norte, 1½ c arriba. Some of the best street food in the city. They serve tasty grilled meats and chicken. Very popular with locals.

Cafés, juice bars and bakeries

♨ Ananda, Enitel, 10 vrs abajo. Chilled-out yoga centre filled with healthy plants. They serve delicious and healthy fresh fruit licuados – the perfect boost if you're feeling run down. Highly recommended.

† Café Luz, catedral, 1 c al norte, 1 c arriba. This new, English-owned café supports communities in Miraflor. They serve a range of breakfasts, including fruit salads with yogurt and granola, pancakes with honey, and – for homesick Brits – egg and bacon buttie. They also sell *artesanías*, light lunches, and have a liquor licence for evenings.

† La Casita, opposite la Barranca, at south entrance to Estelí on Interamericana, T713-4917, casita@sdnnic.org.ni. Nicaragua's best home-made yogurt in tropical fruit flavours. Very cute place with pleasant outdoor seating underneath trees on back patio.

Condega *p280*

† La Cocina de Virfrank, Km 191, Carretera Panamericana, T715-2391. Daily 0630-2000. Very cute roadside eatery set in a little garden with excellent food and economical prices.

Somoto *p281*

††-† Restaurante Almendro, Iglesia, ½ c al sur. Famous for its steaks, good *comida corriente*. Big tree in the centre gives the restaurant its name and is a famous Mejía Godoy song.

††-† Restaurante Somoteño, Parque Central, 2 c abajo, 75 vrs al norte, on Interamericana, T722-2518. Cheery outdoor seating with bamboo walls, great beef grill with friendly service and monumental portions: *corriente* (normal), *semi à la carte* (too big) and *à la carte* (way too big). Recommended.

† Cafetería Bambi, Enitel, 2½ c sur, T722-2231. Tue-Sun 0900-2200. Surprisingly no deer on the menu, just sandwiches, hamburgers, hot dogs, *tacos* and fruit juices.

Ocotal *p281*

††-† Llamarada del Bosque, south side of Parque Central, T732-2643. Popular locals' joint that serves tasty and economical buffet food and *comida típica*.

††-† Restaurante La Cabaña, next to **Hotel Benmoral**, T732-2415. Daily 1000-2300. Good steak dishes such as *filete a l a cabaña* or *jalapeño*. Lovely garden setting with banana trees and separate gazebos for the tables.

† Comedor la Esquinita, Esso, 1 c al sur. Clean, pleasant *comedor* with tables set around a leafy courtyard. Economical Nica fare.

● Entertainment

Matagalpa and around *p276, map p277*
Bars and clubs
Crazy Horse, Parque Darío, 10 vrs abajo. Wild West-style drinking hole with log cabin exterior and an inside filled with cartwheels, Stetson hats and other cowboy memorabilia. They serve cold beer and Flor de Caña.

Disco Rancho Escondido, Parque Darío, 2 c abajo. Popular place for a dance and a drink.

La Posada Restaurant and Disco, Parque Darío, ½ c abajo. Another good place for dancing, popular with families.

Estelí *p278, map p279*
Bars and clubs
Rincón Legal, Textiles Kanan, 1 c abajo. This classic, must-see Sandinista bar is filled with revolutionary memorabilia and managed by an FSLN comrade. They often stage live music and play rousing Sandinista tunes.

Semáforo Rancho Bar, Hospital San Juan de Dios, 400 m al sur. Don your dancing shoes for Estelí's quintessential night spot. It hosts some of the best live music in the country, with nationally and internationally renowned acts performing regularly.

Studio 54, next to Casa Pellas. A great place for a dance, with bright, young, boisterous crowds descending en masse.

○ Shopping

Matagalpa and around *p276, map p277*
Cerámica Negra, Parque Darío. This kiosk, open irregularly, sells black pottery in the northern tradition – a style found only in parts of Chile, Nicaragua and Mexico. For more information contact Estela Rodríguez, T772-4812.

Estelí *p278, map p279*
Mocha Nana Café, La Casa de la Mujere, 1½ c abajo, have a selection of English-language books, including Footprint guides. *Artesanías* can be found opposite **Hotel Mesón**.

▲ Activities and tours

Matagalpa and around *p276, map p277*
Tour operators
Matagalpa Tours, Banpro, ½ c arriba, T772-0108, www.matagalpatours.com. Trekking, hiking, birdwatching and rural community tours are among their well-established repertoire. Dutch- and English-speaking, helpful and friendly. The best in town for all your adventuring needs.

Estelí *p278, map p279*
Cigars
The country's finest cigars are manufactured in Estelí. Contact **INTUR** for a factory list. All visits must be arranged in advance.

Tour operators
Tisey, Apdo Postal No 63, T713-2655, next to **Hotel El Mesón**. Run by the hotel.

☉ Transport

North from Managua *p276*
Sébaco is a major transportation hub with northbound traffic to **Matagalpa** and **Jinotega** and northwest to **Estelí**, **Ocotal** and **Somoto**. Buses pass every 15 mins to/from **Estelí** US$1.20, **Matagalpa** US$1.10 and **Managua** US$1.50. Buses between Matagalpa and Sébaco pass the highway just outside **Chagüitillo** every 15 mins.

Matagalpa and around *p276, map p277*
Terminal Sur (Cotransur) is located near Mercado del Sur and used for all destinations outside the department of Matagalpa.

To **Jinotega**, every ½ hr, 0500-1900, US$1.40, 1½ hrs. To **Managua**, every ½ hr,

0335-1805, US$2.20, 3-4 hrs; express buses, every hr, 0520-1720, US$2.75, 2½ hrs. To **Estelí**, every ½ hr, 0515-1745, US$1.40, 2-3 hrs; express buses, 1000, 1630, US$1.50, 1½ hrs. Express bus to **León**, 0600, US$2.75, 3 hrs. Express bus to **Masaya**, 0700, 1400, 1530, US$2.75, 4 hrs.

Terminal Norte, by Mercado del Norte (Guanuca), is for all destinations within the province of Matagalpa including **San Ramón** and **El Tuma**. Taxi between terminals US$0.50.

Jinotega and around *p278*
Most destinations will require a change of bus in Matagalpa. To **Matagalpa**, every ½ hr, 0500-1800, US$1.50, 1½ hrs. To **Managua**, express buses, 10 daily, 0400-1600, US$4, 3½ hrs. To **San Rafael del Norte**, 10 daily, 0600-1730 US$1, 1 hr. Average local fare for a taxi in Jinotega is US$0.50.

Estelí *p278, map p279*
Estelí has 2 terminals, both located on the Interamericana. The north terminal deals with northern destinations, the south terminal, southern destinations. A handful of Managua express buses also stop at the Shell station, east of the centre on the Interamericana.

North station To **Somoto**, every hr, 0530-1810, US$1.10, 2½ hrs, use this service to connect to El Espino border bus. To **Ocotal**, every hr, 0600-1730, US$1.40, 2 hrs, use this for bus to Las Manos crossing. To **Jinotega**, every hr, 0445, 0730, 0830, 1330, 1600, US$2.25, 2 hrs. To **El Sauce**, 0900, US$1.25, 3 hrs. To **San Juan de Limay**, 0530, 0700, 1000, 1215, 1400, 1500, US$2.25, 3 hrs. To **Miraflor**, take a bus heading towards **San Sebastián de Yalí** (not one that goes to Condega first), 3 daily 0600, 1200, 1600, US$2, 1½ hrs. Return bus passes at 0700, 1100 and 1620. You can also come in 4WD; there are 2 rental agencies in Estelí.

South station Express bus to **León**, 0645, 3 hrs, US$2.75 To **Managua**, every ½ hr, 0330-1800, US$2, 3 hrs; express buses, roughly every hr, 0545-1515, US$2.75, 2 hrs.

To **Matagalpa**, every ½ hr, 0520-1650, US$1.40, 2 hrs; express buses, 0805, 1435, US$1.50, 1½ hrs.

Ocotal p281
The bus station is on the highway, 1 km south of the town centre, 15-20 mins' walk from Parque Central. Buses to **Las Manos/Honduras border** every 30 mins, 0500-1645, US$0.80, 45 mins. To **Somoto**, every 45 mins, 0545-1830, US$0.75, 2½ hrs. Express bus to **Managua**, 10 daily, 0400-1530, US$4.50, 4 hrs. To **Ciudad Antigua**, 0500, 1200, US$1.25, 1½ hrs. To **Estelí**, leaves the city market every hr, 0445-1800, US$1.30, 2½ hrs; express buses are Managua-bound, 2 hrs, US$1.65, they will drop you off at the Shell station, just east of central Estelí.

● Directory

Matagalpa and around p276, map p277
Banks Banco de América Central (BAC and Credomatic), Parque Morazán, 1 c al sur, on Av Central, changes all TCs and cash on Visa and MC and has ATM for most credit and debit cards with Cirrus logo. **Banpro**, opposite **BAC**, offers similar services.
Internet Many around town, particularly along Av José Benito Escobar, US$0.50 per hr.

Estelí p278, map p279
Banks Almost every bank in the city is located in one city block. If you go 1 block south and 1 block east from the central park you will find the 2 banks that change TCs, **Banco de América Central** (**BAC**), T713-7101, which changes all brands of TCs. **Internet** Cafés all over, try **Computer Soluciones**, Parque Central, US$0.50 per hr. **Language schools** Centro Nicaragüense de Aprendizaje y Cultura (**CENAC**), Apdo 40, Estelí, T713-5437, cenac@tmx.com.ni. 20 hrs of Spanish classes, living with a family, full board, travelling to countryside, meetings and seminars, opportunities to work on community projects, US$140 per week. Teaches Nicaraguans, and welcomes volunteers. **Horizonte Nica**, INISER, 2 c arriba, ½ c al norte, T713-4117, www.ibw.com.ni/horizont. Intensive Spanish courses with a programme of activities and home stay. Excursions and voluntary work offered, as well as education about local communities as well as the language. US$165 for 20 hrs and homestay. **Los Pipitos-Sacuanjoche Escuela de Español**, Costado Noreste Catedral, 1 c norte, ½ c abajo, T713-3830, www.lospipitosesteli.org.ni. Social projects are a part of the course and all profits go to disabled children and their families. Excursions to local cooperatives and homestay available. US$120-170, flexible options.

Ocotal p281
Bank Bancentro, Parque Central, 1 c norte, 1 c abajo, have a Visa ATM and money-changing facility; as does **Banco Procredit**, Parque Central, 1 c abajo.

León and the Pacific Northwest

Nicaragua's sweltering northwestern provinces are the setting for immense and extraordinary panoramas, scorched skies and violently shifting geological tempers. This a land born of fire, home to one of the most densely active volcanic chains in the world: the Cordillera Los Maribios. Within this tempestuous terrain lies León, one of Central America's finest colonial cities. The former home Nicaragua's most accomplished poets, León is the artistic and intellectual heart of the country. As a former hotbed for Sandinista activity, a wealth of satirical murals, commemorative sites, bombed-out ruins and bullet-marked buildings are evidence of the city's turbulent revolutionary history. Today, its student population gives it a vibrant edge and an active nightlife. For the adventurous traveller, León is a good base to climb one of the volcanoes: Momotombo is known for its perfect shape and incredible views; Cerro Negro is the youngest volcano in Central America, erupting every four to five years; Volcán Telica has bubbling mudholes at the base and glowing lava in the crater; San Cristóbal is the tallest volcano in Nicaragua and highly active; while Cosigüina is surrounded by beautiful nature and famous for its huge crater lake and spectacular views. Back down on the coast are the beaches at Poneloya and the major port of Corinto. ➤➤ *For listings, see pages 295-300.*

Towards León

From Managua, the old paved road to León crosses the Sierra de Managua, offering fine views of the lake. It is longer than the new Pacific Highway and not in good condition. About 60 km down the new road to León lies the village of **La Paz Centro**, with several truck-stop restaurants and accommodation. There is a good range of cheap, handmade pottery here, and you can ask to see the potters' ovens and production of bricks. Try the local speciality *quesillo* (mozzarella cheese, onions and cream wrapped in tortilla), available all along the highway.

From La Paz Centro, you can reach **Volcán Momotombo**, which dominates the Managua skyline from the west. It is possible to camp on the lakeside with great views of the volcano. You need a permit to climb Momotombo from the south as a geothermal power station has been built on the volcano's slopes. At the time of writing, no permit was required to climb the volcano from the north but one reader has reported it as being a gruelling 11-hour climb. Take local advice and use a professional guide – ask at **Va Pues** or **Quetzaltrekkers** (see Activities and tours, page 299) in León.

At the foot of the volcano lies **León Viejo**, destroyed by earthquake and volcanic eruption on 31 December 1609 and now being excavated. It was here that the brutal first Spanish governor of Nicaragua Pedrarias and his wife were buried in La Merced church, next to Francisco Hernández de Córdoba, the country's founder who had been beheaded under order of Pedrarias. Archaeological excavations have revealed the cathedral, the Convento de la Merced, the Casa del Gobernador, as well as the bodies of Hernández de Córdoba and Pedrarias, which have been placed in a special tomb in the Plaza Mayor. The ruins themselves are little more than low walls and probably only of serious interest to archaeologists, but you can see the ground plan of the old Spanish town and from the ruins of the old fortress there are breathtaking views of Volcán Mombotombo, Lake Managua and Momotombito Island and the Maribios Volcanoes range. You would need to take a bus to from Managua to La Paz Centro (US$1, 45 minutes), and then catch or bus or take a taxi to Puerto Momotombo, and walk 10 minutes to the site.

León has a colonial charm unmatched elsewhere in Nicaragua, except perhaps by Granada. It is typified by narrow streets, red-tile roofs, low adobe houses and time-worn buildings. In recent years, economic factors have taken precedence over the cleaning up of old buildings, but the work continues slowly. Founded by Hernández de Córdoba in 1524 at León Viejo, 32 km from its present site, it was moved here after the devastating earthquake of 1609. The existing city was founded in 1610. As the capital, León was the dominant force in Nicaragua until Managua took control in 1852. Today, it is still thought of as the 'intellectual' capital, with a university founded in 1804, religious colleges, the largest cathedral in Central America, and several colonial churches.

ATC It is said that Managua became the capital, although at the time it was no more than an indigenous settlement, because it was halfway between violently Liberal León and equally violently Conservative Granada.

Ins and outs

Getting there Regular buses to León run from Managua and Chinandega, with frequent routes from Estelí and Matagalpa. International buses will drop you off, if asked, at the entrance to town. The bus terminal is at the northeastern end of town, a 20-minute walk, or short taxi ride from the centre.

Getting around Most attractions are within a few blocks of the centre so choosing a fairly central hotel will make it an easy city to explore on foot. Local buses will take you to the terminal and a network of *colectivos* work as cheap taxis (US$0.15). Taxis cost US$0.60 during the day, US$0.80 at night.

Tourist information INTUR ① *Parque Rubén Darío 2½ c al norte, T311-1325, www.leonon line.net*, has maps for sale, reference books and friendly staff.

Sights

Legend has it that the plans for the **Basílica de la Asunción** (to give the cathedral its full name) ① *open to visitors 0700-0900, 1600-1800*, were switched with those of Lima (Peru) by mistake. However, the enormous size of the building, designed by Guatemalan architects, may be explained by the need to withstand the area's heavy seismic activity. Construction was begun in 1746 and was not completed for 113 years. Its famous shrine – 145 cm high, covered by white topazes from India given by Felipe II of Spain – is, sadly, kept in a safe in the vestry, to which the bishop holds the key. The cathedral also houses a very fine ivory Christ, the consecrated Altar of Sacrifices and the Choir of Córdoba, the great Christ of Esquipulas (in bronze with a cross of very fine silver) and statues of the 12 Apostles. At the foot of one of these statues is the tomb of Rubén Darío, the 19th-century Nicaraguan poet, and one of the greatest in Latin America, guarded by a sorrowful lion. All the entrances to the cathedral are guarded by lions said to come alive after midnight to patrol the old church.

León has the finest **colonial churches** in Nicaragua, more than 12 in all, and they are the city's most significant attraction. **La Recolección**, with a beautiful baroque Mexican façade, built in 1786, has a neoclassical interior with mahogany woodwork. **La Merced**, which was built in 1615 and burned by pirates in 1685, is notable for its seven different altars. It is one of the oldest churches in León and has fine woodwork inside and a restored exterior. **San Felipe** was built at the end of the 16th century for the religious services of the black and mulatto population of the city. It was rebuilt in the 18th century in a manner

León

A

San Felipe

Av Central

5 C

4 C N

B

Honorary Spanish Consul

③ ⑯ Tierra Tours

⑧

⑩

⑳

⑫ 3 C NE

⑩

La Recolec

⑪

INTUR

④ UNAN (University)

⑤

C

✠ Zaragoza

⑬

Centro Popular de la Cultura

@

1 AV NO

La Merced

BA AT S

To Comunidad Indígena de Sutiava & Poneloya

6 AV NO

5 AV NO

4 AV NO

3 AV NO

⑮

2 AV NO

Pool Tables

UNAN

㉑

⑥

S S

Mausoleo Héroe y Mártires

Museo-Archivo Alfonso Cortés

San Francisco ✠

D

Museo-Archivo Rubén Darío

Museo Ortiz-Gurdián

C Central/Rubén Darío

Parque Rubén Darío

Parque Central ✠ Cathedral

⑦

San Juan de Dios ✠

@ Teatro Municipal José de la Cruz Mena

③

C Jorge de Marcoleta

⑤

⑦

@

⑱

② Museo de Leyendas y Tradiciones

⑬

E

⑤ & Va Pues Tours

San Nicolás de Laborio ✠

②

To Guadalupe

④ To 1

① ② ③

N

200 metres
200 yards

290 ● Nicaragua León & the Pacific Northwest

Sleeping 😴
América **1** *D5*
Austria **2** *D4*
Bigfoot Hostel **17** *C5*
Calle de los Poetas **7** *D1*
Casa Vieja **4** *B5*
El Cedro **10** *B3*
Europa **8** *B6*
Hostal Clínica **18** *D3*

Hostal La Casa
Leonesa **12** *B4*
La Casona **13** *E3*
La Casona Colonial **14** *B5*
La Perla **11** *C3*
La Posada del Doctor **15** *B4*
Lazybones Hostel **3** *B3*
Los Balcones **16** *C5*
Tortuga Boluda **5** *D1*

Via Via **20** *C5*

Eating 🍴
Café Pizza Roma **10** *B4*
Caña Brava **25** *A5*
Cocinarte **5** *E2*
Comedor Lucía **11** *C5*
Como No **16** *B3*
Delicias Tropicales **15** *C3*

To 25, Chinandega & San Jacinto

6 C NE

To Bus Terminal (3 blocks) & Market

TSA Tours Travel

San Juan
Bautista

Parque
San Juan

Mercado
San Juan

Museo
Entomológico   Quetzaltrekkers

2 C NE
Western
Union
@
11
17 20
La Unión
Supermarket
1 Cinemas
16
1 C NE

El Calvario

1 C SE

2 C SE

3 C SE

Cimac

4 C SE

5   6

El Mississippi **12** D6
El Sesteo **6** D4
La Buena Cuchara **2** E3
La Casa Vieja **13** C2
Lacmiel **14** E4
Mediterraneo **8** B3
Puerto Café
 Benjamin Linder **4** C3
Venivé **7** D2

Bars & clubs
Café Taquezal **3** D3
Divino Castigo **20** B3
Don Señor **21** C3
La Pasarela **5** C4

true to its original form, a mixture of baroque and neoclassical. **El Calvario**, constructed during the same period, has a notable neoclassical façade attributed to the growing French influence in Spain at the time. **Iglesia y Convento de San Francisco** ① *US$1.50*, founded in 1639, is the oldest convent with a church in León. It still has two plateresque altars from Spain and its original pillars. In 1830, after the expulsion of the Franciscans from Nicaragua, it was used by various civic organizations and is now a gallery. **Iglesia de San Nicolás de Laborío**, founded in 1618 for the local indigenous population, is the most modest of the León churches, constructed of wood and tiles over adobe walls with an unostentatious façade and a simple altar, 10 m tall. The celebration for San Nicolás is 10 September. **Iglesia de Nuestra Señora Pilar de Zaragoza** was built from 1884-1934 and has two unusual octagonal turrets and an arched doorway with tower above. There is a pleasant walk south across the bridge, past the church of **Guadalupe**, to the cemetery.

The house of poet Rubén Darío, the famous 'Four Corners' in Calle Rubén Darío, is now the **Museo-Archivo Rubén Darío** ① *Tue-Sat 0900-1200, 1400-1700, Sun 0900-1200, entry and guided tour free but donations accepted.* It has an interesting collection of personal possessions, photographs, portraits and a library with a wide range of books of poetry in Spanish, English and French. Darío died in 1916 in another house in the northwest sector (marked with a plaque). Alfonso Cortés – another of Nicaragua's finest poets who wrote a famous poem while chained to the bars in front of Rubén's old bed – went insane while living in Darío's house in 1927 and spent the rest of his years in a Managuan asylum until his death in 1969, leaving behind the *museo-archivo*.

Two blocks west of La Merced church is the **Centro Popular de la Cultura** which has frequent exhibitions and events, and is the only place in León to see live folk concerts (schedule on the front door). **Museo de Leyendas y Tradiciones** ① *Parque Central, 3 c sur, Tue-Sat 0800-1200, 1400-1700, US$0.50*, has handcrafted life-size models depicting the rich legends of León. **Museo Ortiz Guardián** ① *Mon- Fri 1100-1900, US$1*, is a colonial home and art museum. **Museo Archivo Alfonso Cortés** ① *Mon-Sat 0800-1200, 1400-1700*, has dusty displays of the great poet's manuscripts. **CIMAC** ① *Costado sur del Puente Martínez, ½ c arriba, 1 c al norte, T311-0752, cimac@ibw.com.ni, Mon-Fri 0800-1100, 1400-1700, Sat 0800-1100, US$1*, which used to be a garbage plant, has been transformed into a centre for urban environmental initiatives, with a self-guided trail.

The western end of the city, **Sutiava**, is the oldest, and here is the oldest of all the churches, the parish church of **San Juan Bautista** (1530). Las Casas, the Apostle of the Indies, preached here several times. It has a fine façade, the best colonial altar in the country and an interesting representation of *El Sol* (the sun), carved in wood on the ceiling. The church has been beautifully reconstructed. Also in the suburb of Sutiava is the **Casa de Cultura** with several interesting murals adorning the walls. Inside there are a few cafés, information about prominent Nicaraguan cultural figures and the offer of a free history and cultural lesson on Thursdays (1500) in basic Spanish.

Around León ⊖⊕⊕⊕ ›› *pp295-300.*

Poneloya and Las Peñitas beaches

A bumpy road from León heads west to Poneloya and Peñitas, a couple of relaxed and very friendly beach communities 19 km from León. Both contain long beautiful stretches of sand and a mixture of humble houses and rich vacation homes. Most of the coast has big waves and strong currents (swim here with great caution – there are drownings every

León & Los Maribios volcanic chain

year). The south end of Las Peñitas and Puerto Mántica, at the north end of Poneloya, are the best for swimming, with good surfing in between, but there are no boards available to rent. During the week you will have the beaches to yourself so be prepared to fend for yourself; at weekends people come from León and in Semana Santa it's sardine time. It is possible to rent quadbikes from the *pulpería* at the intersection of the road to Las Peñitas and Poneloya, called **Licorería Estela de los Mares** (US$10 per hour, you must also show a driving licence, sign a release form and pay a US$10 deposit).

San Jacinto

On the road to Estelí, 12 km north of the intersection with the Chinandega–León road, is San Jacinto. About 200 m to the west of the road is a field of steaming, bubbling **mud holes**, which is worth visiting. You should approach carefully, the ground may give and scald your legs; follow other footmarks for safety, avoiding walking on the crystallized white sulphur, and listen for hissing. It is recommended to hire a guide (ask tour operators in León) or trust one of the local children (US$0.25 tip) to show you where it is safe to walk. A visit can be combined with a hike to the edge of the spectacular crater of Telica with glowing lava inside. The climb is fairly easy but trails can be hard to find. It's best to use a professional guide and make an excursion from León – ask at **Va Pues** or **Quetzaltrekkers**.

Chinandega

About 40 km beyond León, Chinandega is one of the hottest, driest towns in Nicaragua. Agriculturally, this is one of the richest areas in Central America. Once upon a time, the whole region was filled with orange and lemon groves, but sadly, these have been replaced with bananas, peanuts, sugar cane and this is partly the reason why it's so blistering. Most people come to Chinandega to plan forays into the surrounding Maribios volcano range. There's a good market by the bus terminal and you can hire horse-drawn cabs. The local fiesta is on 26 July.

Chichigalpa

Not far away, near Chichigalpa, is the **Ingenio San Antonio**, the largest sugar mill in Nicaragua, with a railway between the town and the mill (five trains a day each way May-November, passengers taken, US$0.10; also bus US$0.30). While there are no official tours of the installations, you can apply at Gate (*Portón*) 14 to be shown around. On the edge of Chichigalpa itself is the **Flor de Caña distillery**, maker of what many believe to be the finest rum in the world, aged up to 21 years and made in over 15 flavours. On leaving you will recognize the picture on the bottle labels, a palm-shaded railway leading towards Chichigalpa with volcanoes in the background.

Border essentials: Nicaragua–Honduras

Guasaule

Immigration The distance between the border posts is 500 m. The border is open 24 hours. To enter Nicaragua costs are US$7 plus a US$1 Alcaldía charge; to exit it is US$2 plus the US$1 immigration charge.

Money changing Money changers offer the same rates for córdobas to lempiras as on the Honduran side. Banco de Crédito Centroamericano, beside immigration, is recommended, good rates, no commission, and will accept photocopy of passport if yours is being checked by immigration.

Transport Buses run every 30 minutes from the border to Chinandega, US$1.40. Express bus to Managua, 1130, 1230 and 1700, four hours, US$3.50 via Somotillo and León. From Managua to Río Guasaule at 1810.

Corinto

Twenty-one kilometres from Chinandega, Corinto is the main port in Nicaragua and the only one at which vessels of any considerable size can berth. About 60% of the country's commerce passes through here. The town itself is on a sandy island, **Punto Icaco**, connected to the mainland by long railway and road bridges. There are beautiful old wooden buildings with verandas, especially by the port. Entry to the port is barred to those without a permit.

On the Corinto–Chinandega road is **Paseo Cavallo beach**. The sea is treacherous here and people drown every year. There are no facilities in Corinto's barrier islands, but they are beautiful with crashing surf on one side, calm and warm swimming water on the other. The journey can be negotiated with any fisherman. A *panga* can be rented for the whole day for US$40 so you can explore the numerous islands and mangroves. You'll see lots of birdlife but also lots of sandflies, so be sure to bring repellent.

North of Chinandega

The road north to Puerto Morazán passes through the village of **El Viejo**, where there is an old church, **La Basílica del Viejo**, famous throughout the country for its celebration on 6 December called La Lavada de la Plata, which consists of devotees washing all silver parts of the altar. The Basílica has la Virgen del Hato, which leaves the altar every December in a major pilgrimage to visit Corinto, Chinandega, León and Managua.

From Chinandega there are six buses a day to **Potosí** (at least three hours, US$1.20). In the centre of the village there are warm thermal springs in which people congregate to relax each afternoon. There are also pleasant black-sand beaches; the sea, although the colour of coffee, is clean. The passenger ferry from Potosí to La Unión (El Salvador) has been suspended. Ask around for an ad hoc service or ask in Chinandega before setting out.

It is a four-hour hike to the cone of **Volcán Cosigüina**. The path is overgrown and very difficult to follow, so you may need a guide (see Tour operators, page 299). There is plenty of wildlife in the area, including poisonous snakes. On 23 January 1835, one of the biggest eruptions in history blew off most of the cone, reducing it from 3000 m to its present height of 800 m, throwing ash as far as Colombia, and leaving an enormous crater lake. From the cone there are beautiful views of the Golfo de Fonseca shared by Nicaragua, Honduras and

El Salvador. The volcano and the surrounding dry tropical forest are a Reserva Natural, administered by the Ministry of the Environment and Natural Resources in Managua.

Jiquilillo beach, 42 km from Chinandega, is reached by a mostly paved road branching off the El Viejo-Potosí road. Lying on a long peninsula, there are a few lodgings and small restaurants. From Chinandega a rough paved road goes to the Honduran border on the **Río Guasaule** near **Somotillo** (where the road improves) heading to Choluteca, Honduras. The bus from Chinandega takes 1¾ hours (US$1.25).

◉ León and the Pacific Northwest listings

For Sleeping and Eating price codes and other relevant information, see pages 43-46.

⊜ Sleeping

León *p289 map p290*
L La Perla, Iglesia La Merced, 1 c norte, T311-3125, www.laperlaleon.com. This handsome old colonial building has been remodelled recently and now houses elegant rooms, suites, bar, restaurant and pool.
A Hostal La Casa Leonesa, catedral, 3 c norte, 15 vrs arriba, T311-0551, www.lacasaleonesa.com. This typical León house has a lovely elegant interior, a swimming pool and 10 rooms of varying size, all with private bath, hot water, cable TV, telephone. Breakfast included. Rooms upstairs are cheaper (**B**).
A Hotel Austria, catedral, 1 c sur, T311-1206, www.hotelaustria.com.ni. Very clean and comfortable rooms surrounding a lush central courtyard. They have hot water, a/c, cable TV and telephone. Internet and laundry service available. Continental breakfast is included in the price. Friendly and oftenfully booked.
A La Posada del Doctor, Parque San Juan, 25 vrs abajo, T311-4343, www.laposadadeldoctor.com. Very clean and nicely furnished rooms with private bath, hot water, cable TV, a/c. Services include laundry, parking and Wi-Fi. Pleasant little patio and relaxed atmosphere. Breakfast included.
A Los Balcones, esq de los bancos, 1 c arriba, T311-0250, www.hotelbalcones.com. A handsome colonial building with an attractive courtyard, bar and restaurant. The 20 rooms have private bath, hot water, a/c and cable

TV; some have a good view. Breakfast included. Tasteful, professional, comfortable.
B La Casona Colonial, Parque San Juan, ½ c abajo, T311-3178. This pleasant colonial house has 5 good value homely rooms with private bath and a/c. Management is friendly and hospitable, and there's a lovely green garden, too. Cheaper with fan (**C**).
B-C Europa, 3 C NE, 4 Av, T311-6040, www.hoteleuropaleon.com.ni. Pleasant patios and quiet, clean comfortable rooms with Wi-Fi, safe, telephone, a/c, hot water. Services include restaurant, bar and parking.
C América, catedral, 2 c arriba, T311-5533, www.vianica.com/hoteles/leon/hotelamerica. Plain, comfortable rooms in a friendly old house. There's a pleasant patio and garden, internet, parking and meals on request.
C-F Lazybones Hostal, Parque de los Poetas, 2½ c norte, T311-3472, www.lazybonesleon.com. Managed by a friendly English-Colombian couple, this quality hostel has a great pool and lots of extras including free coffee and tea, pool table, internet, rental and a daily 10 min long-distance phone call. Dorms (**F**) are clean, some private rooms have private bath (**C**), cheaper without (**D**). Check out the mural by one of Managua's finest graffiti artists. Recommended.
D Calle de los Poetas, Calle Rubén Darío, Museo Darío, 1½ c abajo, T311-3306, rsampson@ibw.com.ni. This comfortable good value guesthouse has a relaxed homely ambience, spacious rooms with private and shared bath, a beautiful garden and friendly hosts. It's also the base for **Sampson Expeditions** (page 299). Often full, arrive early. Discounts for longer stays. Recommended.

D Hostal Clínica, 1 Av NO, Parque Central, 1½ c sur, T311-2031, marymergalo2000@ yahoo.com. Family-run and very Nicaraguan. Single and double rooms with private or shared bathroom, breakfast and drinks available. Very friendly, good reports.

D-F Vía Vía, Banco ProCredit, ½ c sur, T311-6142, www.viaviacafe.com. Part of a worldwide network of Belgian cafés, this excellent and professionally managed hostel offers clean dorm beds (**F**) and a range of private rooms (**D-E**), some with TV. There's a tranquil garden, a well-stocked and socially aware information centre, popular restaurant-bar, community tours and classes. 'A meeting place for cultures'. Recommended.

E Casa Vieja, Parque San Juan, 1½ c sur, 311-4235. Sociable Nica hotel with some long-term residents and a family feel. It has 9 large rooms with fan, communal bath and kitchen, cooking on request, laundry service and telephone. Friendly.

E El Cedro, T311-4643, northwest corner of Parque Central, 2½ c norte. 9 clean, comfortable, good value rooms with private bath and cable TV. Café and bar attached; the friendly management speak English. Recommended.

E La Casona, Teatro González, 2 c sur, T311-5282, lacasonahostal@hotmail.com. This spacious house has lots of places to relax, a garden with hammocks, pool (sometimes empty), use of kitchen and washing facilities. The rooms have private and shared bath, poor mattresses and fan. Economical and popular with volunteers. Lovely hosts.

F Bigfoot Hostel, Banco ProCredit, ½ c sur, www.bigfootadventure.com. Sociable, buzzing and popular with a younger crowd. This Australian-run backpackers' joint has lots of dorm space, a handful of private rooms (**E**), pool, sandboarding tours, TV, pool table, and a popular restaurant serving everything from cappuccinos to wholesome Nica fare.

F Tortuga Booluda, Iglesia San Juan de Dios, 1½ c abajo, T311-4653, www.tortugabool uda.com. Pleasant Nica-run hostel with links to social projects, dorms, chill-out spaces, hammocks, kitchen and notice board.

Poneloya and Las Peñitas beaches *p292*

B Suyapa Beach Hotel, Las Peñitas, T885-8345 www.suyapabeach.com. A well-kept and professional hotel with a pool and 20 clean rooms, all with poor beds and private bath, some with a/c. Rooms on 2nd and 3rd floor have ocean views and a breeze. Often full with groups. Cheaper with fan (**D**).

C Oasis, Terminal de Buses, 200 vrs norte, Las Peñitas, T839-5344, www.oasislaspenitas. com. 7 large rooms with poor mattresses; some rooms have phenomenal views. Lots of chill-out spaces with hammocks. Services include rental of surf boards, horse riding and laundry service. The restaurant has great views but the toilets are nasty.

C Posada de Poneloya, Playa Poneloya, from the intersection of Las Peñitas and Poneloya, 150 m to the right, T317-1378. 19 rooms with private bath, hot water, a/c, room service and nanny service, parking, not a great part of the beach, but lively on weekends.

D Samaki, overlooking the bay, Las Peñitas, T640-2058, www.lasamaki.net. 4 tasteful rooms with good mattresses, safes, mosquito nets and private bath. Canadian owned, very relaxed, friendly and hospitable, and home to Nicaragua's only kite-surfing operation. Fresh food made to order, including delicious, real Asian curries. Recommended.

D-F Barca de Oro, Las Peñitas, at the end of the beach facing Isla Juan Venado Wildlife Refuge, www.barcadeoro.com.ni. Friendly, funky hotel with dorm beds (**F**) and private rooms (**D**), all with fan and bath. Services include kayaking, horse riding, body boarding, book exchange, hammocks, tours of the area and beauty treatments.

Chinandega *p293*

AL Los Volcanes, Km 129.5, Carretera a Chinandega, at southern entrance to city, T341-1000, www.losvolcaneshotel.com. Very pleasant, comfortable rooms with private bath, hot water, a/c, cable TV. There's a smart restaurant and bar, service is professional.

B Hotel Pacífico, Iglesia San Antonio, 1½ c sur, T341-1418, hotelpac@ibw.com.ni.

Comfortable, friendly hotel with decent, modern rooms, all have a/c, cable TV, private bath and hot water. Recommended.
C Hotel San José, esq de los Bancos, 2½ c norte, T341-2723. Clean, comfortable and friendly. 10 small, plain rooms have private bath, a/c, cable TV. Breakfast included. Laundry service and internet available.
D Don Mario's, Enitel, 170 vrs norte, T341-4054. Great value rooms and friendly hosts at this homely lodging. Rooms have a/c, private bath and cable TV. The owners speak excellent English. Recommended.

🍴 Eating

León *p289 map p290*
₦₦₦-₦₦ Caña Brava, on bypass road, T311-5666, daily 1100-2200. For many locals the best food in town, with excellent beef dishes, large portions and attentive service. It has little charm though, and is far from the centre.
₦₦ Café Pizza Roma, catedral, 2½ c norte, T311-3568, 1200-2300. Closed Tue. Average pizzas, good meat dishes. Popular with Nicas.
₦₦ Cocinarte, Costardo norte Iglesia el Laborío, T325-4099. Quality vegetarian restaurant with an intriguing international menu of Eastern, Middle Eastern and Nicaraguan cuisine. Lots of fresh and organic produce used, and it holds a monthly organic market. Fri evenings are romantic music nights and Sun afternoon sees chess matches with free coffee. Recommended.
₦₦ El Sesteo, next to cathedral, on Parque Central, T311-5327. The place for watching the world go by, particularly in the late afternoon. Good pork dishes, *nacatamales*, fruit drinks and *cacao con leche*. Portraits of Nicaraguan cultural greats on the wall. Begging can be frequent if you sit outside.
₦₦ Lacmiel, catedral, 5 c sur. Good meat dishes and onion soup. Occasional live music. Recommended.
₦₦ Mediterráneo, Parque Rubén Darío, 2½ c norte, T895-9392,.Tue-Sun 1200-2300. French and Mediterranean cuisine, including pasta

and Italian wines. It has a wide range of meat and chicken dishes, and takeaway pizza too. Popular with foreigners, recommended.
₦₦ Venivé, Iglesia de San Juan de Dios, 1 c sur. León's finest Spanish tapas restaurant. Smart, stylish and sadly neglected by the locals.
₦₦-₦ La Casa Vieja, Iglesia San Francisco, 1½ c norte, Mon-Sat 1600-2300. Intimate little restaurant-bar with a vaguely rustic feel. Serves quality meat and chicken dishes, beer and home-made lemonade. Recommended.
₦₦-₦ Vía Vía, Banco Procredit ½ c sur. A very popular place for breakfast, lunch or dinner. The gringo-friendly menu has food glossaries and descriptions of some classic Nicaraguan dishes. It also serves favourites from other Central American countries and has live music. See also under Bars and clubs.
₦ Casa Popular de Cultura, Plaza Central, 1 c norte, 2½ c abajo. Friendly little locals' spot, sometimes with passing musicians. Serves sandwiches and burgers. Good atmosphere.
₦ Comedor Lucía, Banco Procredit, ½ c sur. Reputable *comedor* serving good but slightly pricey *comida típica* and buffet food, popular with locals. Lunch only.
₦ El Mississippi, southeast corner of the cathedral, 1 c sur, 2½ c arriba. Also known as, perhaps unfortunately, '*la cucaracha*' (the cockroach), everyone raves about the bean soup here. Simple, unpretentious dining at this locals' haunt.
₦ La Buena Cuchara, Parque Rubén Darío, 3½ c sur. Friendly, homely little *comedor* with tasty and economical buffet food. Lunch only. Recommended.

Cafés, bakeries and juice bars
Como No, Parque Rubén Darío, ½ c norte. Delicious-smelling wholemeal bread, juices, shakes, economical breakfasts and sandwiches.
Delicias Tropicales, next to the Casa de Cultura. Tasty fresh fruit juices and smoothies, very refreshing after the heat of León's streets.
Puerto Café Benjamín Linder, next to UNAN (northern corner), T311-0548. Daily 0800-2400. Fresh-roasted coffee at this café named after a social worker who

was killed by Contras in 1980s. Profits go to the prosthetic clinic in León. Massage and high-speed internet access.

Sutiava

Los Pescaditos, Iglesia de San Juan, 1 c sur, 1 c abajo. Daily 1200-2230. Excellent seafood at reasonable prices, go with the waiter to choose your fish from the ice box.

El Capote, Billares Lacayo, 3 c sur, ½ c arriba, T315-3918. Mon-Sat 1100-2300, Sun 1000-1700. No frills bar and eatery with very good food, seafood, cow's tail soup, a massive *surtido* (sampler) dish for US$7.

Poneloya and Las Peñitas beaches *p292*

Most of the best restaurants are found at the hotels and hostels.

Chinandega *p293*

Frank's Bar and Grill, southeast corner of Iglesia El Calvario, 1 c sur. One of the best in town, with good beef cuts and fine wine. Smart, clean interior.

Gerry's Seafood, Shell central, 1½ c norte. Reportedly very good fish and seafood.

Corona de Oro, Iglesia San Antonio, 1½ c arriba, T341-2539. Chinese food with flavour. The chicken curry and shrimp skewers are especially tasty.

El Mondongazo, south side of Colegio San Luis, T341-4255. Traditional Nicaraguan foods like *sopa mondongo* (tripe soup), beef, chicken and meatball soup.

Las Tejitas, Parque Central, 7 c arriba. Cheap and cheerful. They serve buffet food, grilled meats and *comida típica*. Very popular and always packed out. A Chinandega institution.

⏏ Entertainment

León *p289 map p290*
Bars and clubs

León has a vibrant nightlife, owed to its large student population. The action moves between different places depending on the night of the week.

Café Taquezal, southwest corner of Parque Central, ½ c abajo, T311-7282. Mon-Sat 1800-0200. Pleasant atmosphere with good live folk music on Thu nights. Classic León decor. Food served.

El Cedro, T311-4643, northwest corner of Parque Central, 2½ c norte. Thu night is rock night, the only place in town to catch some decent guitar riffs. The friendly management is worldly and English-speaking. Lots of beer and popular with Nicas.

Discoteca Dilectus, southern entrance to the city. Wed-Sun. Inconveniently located, but probably the best disco in town. Upmarket crowd.

Divino Castigo, UNAN, 1 c norte, daily 1700-0100. Good atmosphere, 'bohemian nights' on Tue and Sat. Look at the *mesa maldita* (cursed table) where old newspaper articles tell you the cruel history of this house. Or ask for Sergio Ramírez's book from which the bar derives its name.

Don Señor, opposite Parque La Merced. Tue- Sun. Popular with students and young Nicas on Fri nights, with liberal doses of karaoke, dancing and beer. A good place to see the locals cut loose.

Olla Quemada, Museo Rubén Darío, ½ c abajo. Popular on Wed nights with live music acts and lots of beer. Great, friendly atmosphere.

La Pasarela, UNAN, 1 c arriba. Great outdoor student venue, best in the dry season.

Vía Vía, Banco ProCredit, ½ c sur. Good on most nights, but best on Fri when live music performs. There's salsa on Sat, free pool on Tue and quiz night on Mon. Good, warm atmosphere. Popular with foreigners.

Cinema

Next to **La Unión** supermarket, 1 block north and 1 block east of El Sesteo in Plaza Siglo Nuevo, T311-7080/83. Films shown in English with Spanish subtitles.

☻ Festivals and events

León *p289 map p290*
Mar/Apr Holy Week ceremonies are outstanding with sawdust street-carpet, similar to those in Guatemala, especially in Sutiava on Good Fri after 1500.
20 Jun Liberation by Sandinistas.
1 Nov All Saints' Day.
Dec Santa Lucía is celebrated in Sutiava; there are processions, religious and cultural events, sports and Pepe Cabezón (a giant head on legs) accompanies La Gigantona (an impossibly tall princess) through the city.
7 Dec Día de la Concepción, festivities including singing, dancing and fireworks.

○ Shopping

León *p289 map p290*
The old **market** (dirty) is near the centre, behind the cathedral, and the **new market** is at the bus terminal, which is now **Mercado San Juan,** not touristy, good local atmosphere. **Libro Centro Don Quijote,** by **Hotelito Calle Real,** sell 2nd-hand books, some in English.

▲ Activities and tours

León *p289 map p290*
Cultural and community tourism
Casa de Cultura, Iglesia La Merced, 1½ c abajo. Offer a range of courses including traditional and contemporary dance, music and painting. Ask inside for a schedule.
Vía Vía, Banco ProCredit, ½ c sur, T311-6142, www.viaviacafe.com. Cultural tours include 'cowboy for a day' where you milk a cow and prepare an ox cart; 'gallera', where you attend a cockfight; and 'workshop cooking', which includes trips to markets and tortilla-making.

Sandboarding
Bigfoot adventures, Banco ProCredit, ½ c sur, www.bigfootadventure.com. Fancy descending the slopes of an active volcano at high speed? The most professional outfit in town will kit you out with a sandboard and safety gear, and transport you to the top of Cerro Negro. The fastest boards have been clocked at 70 kph.

Tour operators
Tierra Tour, La Merced, 1½ c norte, T311-0599, www.tierratour.com. Dutch-owned outfit with good information and affordable tours of León, the Maribios volcanoes and Isla Juan Venado reserve. Runs shuttles direct to Granada and other places.
Va Pues, North side of El Laborio church, inside Cocinarte restaurant, T315-4099, wwwvapues.com. Popular tours include Cerro Negro, León Viejo, night turtle tours, kayaking and city tours. English, French and Spanish spoken. Also has an office in Granada and organizes trips all over the country.

Trekking
Flavio Parajón, Texaco Guadalupe, 1 c abajo, ½ c sur, T880-8673, fparajon2003@ yahoo.es. Good, friendly, honest and experienced mountain guide for Maribios volcanoes. He has his own 4WD, speaks Spanish and basic English.
Quetzaltrekkers, Iglesia Recolección, 1½ c arriba, T843-7647, www.quetzaltrekkers.com. Non-profit organization, proceeds go to street kids. Multi-day hikes to Los Maribios US$20-70 including transport, food, water, camping equipment. Guides are foreign volunteers, check your guide's experience before trip, be sure to climb with at least one local guide who knows the volcanoes well.
Sampson Expeditions, Calle Rubén Darío, 1½ c abajo, inside **Hostal Calle de Los Poetas,** T311-3306, rsampson@ibw.com.ni. Kayaking in Juan Venado and Laguna El Tigre, volcano expeditions, poetry tours. Rigo Sampson comes from a family of devout hikers and climbers and is Nicaragua's foremost expert on climbing the Maribios volcanoes. He also works closely with social organizations to help local kids into schools. Professional and highly recommended.

🚌 Transport

León *p289 map p290*
Bus

The bus terminal is in the far eastern part of town, a long walk or short taxi ride from the centre. Small trucks also ferry people between the bus terminal and town for US$0.25. Besides the regular and express buses, *compartidos* (small vans) go to most places below, often faster than the bus. To **Managua**, express bus, every 30 mins, 0500-1600, US$1.50, 1 hr 45 mins. To **Chinandega**, every 15 mins, 0500-1800, US$1, 1 hr 45 mins. To **Corinto**, every 30 mins, 0500-1800, US$1, 2 hrs. To **Chichigalpa**, every 15 mins, US$0400-1800, US$0.75, 1 hr. To **Estelí**, express bus, 0520, 1245, 1315, 1515, US$2.50, 3 hrs; or go to San Isidro for connections. To **Matagalpa**, express bus, 0400, 0700, 1400, US$2.75, 3 hrs; or go to San Isidro for connections. To **San Isidro**, every 30 mins, 0420-1730, US$1.50, 2½ hrs. To **El Sauce**, every hr, 0800-1600, US$1.50, 2½ hrs. To **El Guasaule**, 0500, US$2, 2½ hrs. To **Salinas Grandes**, 0600,1200, US$0.40, 1½ hrs.

Taxi

Taxis around town charge US$0.60 in the day and US$0.80 at night.

Around León *p292, map p292*
Bus

Take No 101 from **León**'s Terminal Interurbana, or the central market west to the bus stop near Sutiava church on Calle Rubén Darío, **Poneloya**, then walk 3 mins to Terminal Poneloya outside the market, from where a small bus leaves every hr or so for **Las Peñitas** (0600-1700, 45 mins, US$0.60) at the south end of Poneloya beach.

Taxi

From León to Las Peñitas costs around US$10.

Chinandega *p293*

Most buses leave from the new market at the southeast edge of town. To **Corinto**, every 20 mins, 0600-2100, 30 mins, US$0.40. To **Guasaule**, every 2 hrs, 0600-1600, 2 hrs, US$2.25. To **León**, every 15 mins, 0600-1700, 1¼ hr, US$1. To **Managua**, every 30 mins, 0600-1600, 3 hrs, US$2.50. To **Somotillo**, every 3 hrs, 0900-1500, 2 hrs, US$2. Buses for **Potosí**, **El Viejo** and **Puerto Morazán** leave from the Mercadito at northwest of town. A local bus connects Terminal, Mercado and Mercadito.

🛈 Directory

León *p289 map p290*

Banks There are many banks on the 2 roads that lead from the front and back of the cathedral to the north. Next to the La Unión Supermarket is **BAC (Banco de América Central)** T311-7247, for TCs of any kind and cash from credit cards. Cash can be changed with the *coyotes* 1 block north of the back of the cathedral or at any bank. **Hospital** Hospital at catedral, 1 c sur, T311-6990. **Internet** At nearly every hotel and almost every street in León, best high-speed hook-up at **Puerto Café Benjamín Linder**, next to UNAN (northern corner), T311-0548, 0800-0000. **Language schools** León Spanish School, Casa de Cultura, Iglesia La Merced, 1½ c abajo, www.apc-spanish schools.com, T311-2116. Flexible weekly or hourly 1-on-1 tuition with activities, volunteering and homestay options. Pleasant location inside the casa de cultura. **Metropolis Academy**, www.metropolis spanish.com, La Merced, 2 c norte, 875-9325. A range of programmes from simple hourly tuition to full-time courses with daily activities and family homestay. 20 hrs of tuition costs US$115. **Vía Vía**, Banco ProCredit, ½ c sur, T311-6142, www.viaviacafe.com. This growing cultural centre has good ties to local communities. A convenient, sociable option with bar-restaurant-hostel on site. **Police** T311-3137. **Post office** Correos de Nicaragua, Banco Mercantil 1 c norte, T311-2102. **Telephone** Enitel is on Parque Central at the west side, T311-7377. Also at bus terminal.

Corn Islands and the Caribbean Coast

A rich cultural melting pot characterizes Nicaragua's Caribbean Coast, where lilting Creole English is the lingua franca, lightly peppered with Spanish. British buccaneers, Jamaican labourers, Chinese immigrants and indigenous tribes have all contributed to the evolution of the region's exotic flavours. Politically, culturally and historically, The Costa Atlántica is a world apart. Take the single-propeller plane over here and you'll soon see why. Vast tracts of virgin rainforest divide Nicaragua from its Caribbean cousin, an unrelenting carpet of green treetops punctuated only by meandering, toffee-coloured rivers and swollen coastal lagoons. Few roads – or Spanish colonists – have ever penetrated this wilderness.

The Corn Islands are the region's principal attraction: two islands with white-sand beaches, scintillating coral reefs and turquoise waters. Little Corn is a low-key dive centre, Big Corn is home to diverse fishing communities and a good place to sample authentic Caribbean life while it lasts. On the mainland, Bluefields is the nearest city of any size, a decaying and shambolic spectre, but ripe with all the sights, sounds and smells of any bustling tropical port. This is the place to drink rum and watch the tropical storms roll in. The coast's isolation has allowed the Miskito peoples to thrive here, asserting their political will through the Yatama political party and controlling municipal governments since 2004. Bilwi is the administrative capital of the Miskito world, but Waspam is its spiritual heart. Located on the banks of the formidable Río Coco, only the truly brave and adventurous will get this far. Surrounded by impenetrable rainforest, a sturdy boat and a trustworthy guide will be necessary to navigate the river, its complex network of tributaries and the many isolated communities that comprise the Miskito nation. ▸▸ *For listings, see pages 309-314.*

Managua to El Rama ⊖🚌🚉 ▸▸ pp309-314.

At **San Benito**, 35 km from Managua on the Interamericana going north, the Atlantic Highway branches east, paved all the way to Rama on the Río Escondido. Shortly after Teustepe, a paved road goes northeast to Boaco. A turn-off, unpaved, goes to **Santa Lucía**, a village inside a crater, with a women's handicraft shop. There is also a cooperative here with an organic farming programme (information from Unag in Matagalpa). **Boaco** (84 km from Managua) is called the city of two floors because of its split-level nature. The upper floor has a nice square with good views of the countryside.

The Atlantic Highway continues through **Juigalpa**, a pleasant town with one of the best museums in Nicaragua, **Museo Gregorio Aguilar Barea** ① *T812-0784, Mon-Fri, US$0.25*, housing a collection of idols resembling those at San Agustín, Colombia. The bus terminal is in the town centre near the market, up the hill.

The main road continues east to **Santo Tomás** and smaller villages (including La Gateada, connected by air from Managua via San Carlos on Friday with **La Costeña**), then to **Cara de Mono**, on the Río Mico, and finally to El Rama, 290 km from Managua.

There is not much to see in **El Rama**, a godforsaken transport hub for overland traffic heading between Nicaragua's interior and the central Caribbean coast. The village was an ancient trading centre of Rama Indians and has been settled by Europeans since at least 1747, but there is no surviving evidence of this. El Rama's greatest asset is also its worst: water. The Río Siquia, Río Mico and Río Rama converge on the little port, and the Río Escondido that drains into the Bay of Bluefields. In the last 20 years the village has been erased three times by hurricanes – the worst of which left El Rama beneath 15 m of water. The level was so high that Army rescue boats tangled their propellers on power cables.

Once upon a time, El Rama was literally the end of the road. Apart from a marginal dirt road that allows passage from Managua to Bilwi for a brief part of the dry season, the only reliable way to get to the central and northern Caribbean coast without boarding an aeroplane was via land to El Rama, then by boat to Bluefields. But all that has changed with a new road that connects El Rama to Pearl Lagoon. At present, only a single daily bus plies this modest byway at 1600, the journey time is three hours (you may find trucks that leave sooner). From Pearl Lagoon you can easily catch a *panga* south along the coast to Bluefields, but not until the next day. This route is longer, but it is far more scenic and interesting, affording the chance to experience the Caribbean warmth and hospitality that is so characteristic of the region's rural stretches. The regular route to Bluefields (from Managua via El Rama) is now a 12- to 13-hour trip with improvements to the highway; the bus from Managua to El Rama takes nine to 10 hours (express bus seven hours), the boat from El Rama to Bluefields takes two hours, as long as you arrive early enough to find a seat. If necessary there is accommodation in El Rama, but most will want to be on their way quickly. ▸▸ *See Transport, page 313, for boat and bus schedules.*

Bluefields and around ●❼❹❺❻ ▸▸ *pp309-314.*

Dirty and chaotic but curiously inviting, Bluefields is the heart and soul of Nicaragua's Caribbean world and the capital of Southern Atlantic Autonomous Region, known by its acronym RAAS. It is located at the mouth of the Río Escondido, which opens into Bluefields Bay in front of the city. The majority of the population is Afro-Caribbean, though the other ethnic groups of the region are represented and the main attraction of the town is its ethnic diversity and west Caribbean demeanour. The main church of the city is Moravian, the language is Creole English and the music is calypso and reggae. Bluefields is a good jumping-off point to visit Pearl Lagoon and other less explored areas of the wide-open region.

Ins and outs

Getting there and around La Costeña and Atlantic Airlines fly twice daily from Managua's domestic terminal and the Corn Islands, and once a day except Sundays from Bilwi. Getting there by land is more complicated. The classic route uses a long-distance bus from Managua to connect with boats at El Rama, from where you travel downstream to the coast. However, an alternative route follows a new road from El Rama to Pearl Lagoon, from where you catch a *panga* to Bluefields. Most of Bluefields can be seen on foot, though taxis are recommended at night. All visits to surrounding attractions are by boat. ▸▸ *For further details, see Transport, page 313.*

Best time to visit May is the most festive time thanks to Palo de Mayo (maypole) events. Rain is common year-round, but January to April is driest.

Tourist information INTUR ① *opposite Salón Siu, Barrio Central, T572-0221, bluefields@ intur.gob.ni,* has friendly staff and some limited information on local sights and activities.

Background

Bluefields is named after the Dutch pirate Henry Bluefeldt (or Blauvedlt) who hid in the bay's waters in 1610. The native Kukra Indians were hired by Dutch and British pirates to help them with boat repairs and small time trade began with the Europeans. The first permanent European settlers arrived at the end of the 18th century and the ethnic mix of the area began to change. The 19th century saw a healthy trade in bananas and an influx of Afro-Caribbeans from Jamaica to work in the plantations and administer the Anglican and Moravian churches. During the 20th century Chinese immigrants also came to Bluefields creating what was thought to be the largest Chinese community in Central America. The fighting of the Revolution did not affect the area much, but the Contras of the 1980s used the eastern coast to harass Sandinista positions and many of the Chinese left during these years.

Bluefields was nearly wiped off the map by Hurricane Joan in October 1988. Some 25,000 residents were evacuated and most of the structures were destroyed. An army member arriving the day after the hurricane described the city as appearing trampled by a giant, with nothing left of the buildings but wooden footprints. The famous Bluefields Express boat that worked the 96-km journey from Rama to Bluefields was later found wrecked inside thick forest – 4 km from the riverbanks.

The town, like the entire region, is struggling against the Colombian drug runners. Bluefields is used as a landing and strategic post, and the recent murders of honest local police is a symptom of the Colombians stamping their authority. Most of the merchandise is cocaine and Nicaragua is one of the highways north from the producer, Colombia, to the world's biggest cocaine market, the USA. Local dealers are also getting involved and, although consumption is well below US and European rates, slowly the corruption of the Bluefields/eastern Chontales corridor is being consolidated.

Bluefields

Within Nicaragua, Bluefields is best known for its dancing and it is the **reggae** capital of the country. The best time to see the locals dance is at the annual **Palo de Mayo** (maypole) celebrations (also known as ¡Mayo Ya!). The festival is celebrated throughout May and there are countless dance contests between different neighbourhoods. The only rule is to hang on to the ribbon connected to the maypole and move. There is also some interesting local music and poetry in the festival.

Although Bluefields is doing its part to pollute the bay that surrounds it, the sheer expanse of water (30 km from north to south and 6 km wide) means that it is still beautiful. If you have some time in Bluefields, a boat excursion to see some of the bay provides a different perspective on the tired city waterfront.

Rama Cay

ⓘ *A boat ride to the island will cost US$15-50 depending on the number of passengers. Check at the southern dock next to the market to see if any boats are going; if you hitch a ride, returning could be a problem.*

This island in the Bay of Bluefields, only 20-30 minutes by *panga* from Bluefields, is home to the last tribe of Rama Indians, led by an elderly woman chief. The Rama, calm and friendly people who are renowned for their kindness and generosity, are pretty accustomed to visitors but sadly this is the least studied group of all the indigenous peoples in Nicaragua and the most likely to lose its language. They may have been the dominant group on the coast before the arrival of the Europeans but their reluctance to support the British in their pirate attacks against the Spanish led to the rise of the Miskitos, who allied with the British (and were given muskets, hence their name). With the help of firepower and economic support, the Miskitos eventually took over almost all of the Rama territory and much of the Mayagna, an area comprising the Caribbean coast from Cape Camarón in Honduras to Río Grande in Nicaragua. The exception is the little island of Rama Cay and the Río San Juan, where the Rama are making a comeback.

The Rama are highly skilled at languages, often speaking Rama, Creole English, Spanish and some even Miskito, despite receiving little or no formal schooling. The Rama language is related to that of the northern Amazonian peoples and it is believed they migrated from that area. There is a small **community tourism project** ① *contact Oscar Omier, Martina Thomas or Sonia Omier, T628 1112, etnoram@yahoo.com, or speak to INTUR in Bluefields,* on the island with accommodation and guides, if you're interested in learning more.

El Bluff

El Bluff is a peninsula that separates the sea from the Bay of Bluefields. In happier days it was a busy port, but now the beach is dirty and not very appealing. There is a good walk to the lighthouse with a fine view of the bay and the sea, and the locals are happy to see visitors. Boats leave from the southern dock in Bluefields next to the market. The boat costs US$3 and leaves when full.

Reserva Silvestre Privada Greenfields

① *T268-1897, www.greenfields.com.ni. The reserve at Kukra Hill can be reached by a regular pangafrom Bluefields, or an infrequent bus from El Rama or Pearl Lagoon. US$15 entrance.* Greenfields is a 284-ha, privately managed nature reserve of mangroves, rivers and forests. There's a botanical park and 30 km of paths snaking through the Swiss-owned wildlife sanctuary, sometimes visited by scientists and home to jaguars, tapirs, monkeys caymans and otters. There are pricey eco-lodgings (US$250 for a two-day all inclusive stay) and camping facilities.

Laguna de Perlas

This oval-shaped coastal lagoon, 80 km north of Bluefields, covers 518 sq km and is one of the most beautiful places on the coast. The lagoon is fed principally by the jungle-lined Río Kurinwás but also by the rivers Wawashán, Patch, Orinoco and Ñari. The shores range from pine forests and mangroves to savanna and rainforest. The cultural diversity is equally broad with Afro-Caribbean, Miskito and Garífuna settlements at different points around the lagoon. To get the most out of a trip, hire a guide or use a tour operator; try **Hotelito Casa Blanca** (see page 309), who have extensive contacts and offer tours to the wonderfully tranquil Pearl Keys, wildlife viewing on the Wawashán river and fishing trips.

The village of **Pearl Lagoon**, in the far southwest of the estuary, is the most developed and is a good place to start when planning a trip. The village is well organized, clean and welcoming with an Afro-Caribbean community and interesting Moravian church. All the best accommodation for the lagoon is based here and there are regular boat services to Bluefields.

Between Pearl Lagoon and the Caribbean Sea is the Miskito village of **Tasbapauni**. One hour from the village of Pearl Lagoon, it has around 2000 inhabitants living on a strip of land less than 1 km wide between the sea and the lagoon. Though it can have debris, the beach here is pleasant and the locals have started to clean it up. The village is worth a visit and is also an ideal jumping-off spot to explore the more remote white sand paradise of Pearl Keys.

Also north of the Pearl Lagoon village is **Orinoco**, Nicaragua's most significant population of Garífuna peoples. This group has been studied by anthropologists in Honduras, but went unnoticed in Nicaragua until finally being recognized by the government in 1987 – after more than 150 years of settlement. The language and many of the dances and culinary customs of the Garífuna remain intact, in a curious mixture of old

African and Caribbean indigenous influences that has taken on a life of its own. They have an annual cultural festival from 17-19 November.

The **Río Kurinwás** area is a fascinating, largely uninhabited jungle where it is possible to see monkeys and much other wildlife. It might occasionally be possible to get a boat to the town of **Tortuguero** (also called **Nuevo Amanecer**), a mestizo town that will really give you a taste of the frontier. Tortuguero is about a six-hour speedboat ride from Bluefields up Río Kurinwás, or several days by regular boat.

Río Grande is the next river north of Río Kurinwás, connected to the Pearl Lagoon by the Top-Lock Canal. At its mouth are five interesting villages: the four Miskito communities of **Kara**, **Karawala**, **Sandy Bay Sirpi** and **Walpa**, and the Creole village of **La Barra**. Sandy Bay Sirpi is on both the river and the Caribbean, and has a good beach.

Travelling upriver, the Río Grande is a noticeable contrast to the Río Kurinwás; it is much more settled, dotted with farms and cattle grazing. Some distance upriver (about a six-hour speedboat ride from Bluefields, several days by regular boat), you reach the mestizo town of **La Cruz de Río Grande**. It was founded around 1922 by Chinese traders to serve workers from a banana plantation (now defunct). La Cruz has a very pretty church, and there are resident expatriate (US) monks of the Capuchin order in the town. The truly adventurous can walk between La Cruz and Tortuguero; each way takes about 10 hours in the dry season, 12 in the rainy.

Corn Islands ⊜🐟🏵▲⊖🛈 ⤵ *pp309-314.*

The Corn Islands are a portrait of Caribbean indolence with their languid palm trees, colourful clapboard houses and easy, rum-soaked dilapidation. Divorced from the mainland by 70 km of turquoise sea, many islanders are incurable eccentrics. Few, if any, pay much mind to the world outside, concerning themselves only with the friendships, feuds and often entertaining gossip that is the staple diet of island life. But a burgeoning tourist trade and Colombian 'business interests' mean the islands are no longer the place to experience the authentic Caribbean life of days gone by. Outsiders are steadily infiltrating, bringing tourists, foreign-owned hotels and crime. But like everything else here, the pace of change has been slow. For now, the islands remain distinctly low-key, staunchly individualistic, and governed by a handful of families who have been here for generations. Scratch the surface and you'll discover that many things are as they have always been: rains come and go, mangoes fall, and waves lap the sugar-white beaches in perpetuity.

Ins and outs

Getting there The islands are 70 km off the mainland of Nicaragua. The big island is 13 sq km and the little one is 3.5 sq km. About 7 km of Caribbean Sea separates them. Two Nicaraguan airlines fly daily to Big Corn and there are boat services three times a week from Bluefields. Transportation to Little Corn is on a twice-daily skiff with two big outboards and good native navigators. The boat has no roofing to protect from rain and sun and it can be a wet ride if it's rough – not for the weak-hearted. ⤵ *For further details, see Transport, page 313.*

Getting around The big island has one paved road that does a lap of the island with two buses and nearly 100 taxis. The small island has no roads; walking or boating are the only way of getting around.

Best time to visit Unlike most of Nicaragua's tourist destinations the dry season is by far the best time to visit the islands, with better visibility in the water and more sunshine. The best and driest months are February to April, or September to October when the waters are normally calm (unless a hurricane passes). Holy Week and Christmas are very crowded, as is 27-28 August when the festival takes place. June and September have the fewest foreigners.

Tourist information There is no tourist office on the Corn Islands. A good online source of information is www.bigcornisland.com.

Safety Paradise has a dark side and you should use common sense at all times. On Big Corn, take care at the commercial dock area near Brigg Bay and at Queen's Hill. Avoid walking at night on the island anywhere, always use a taxi to get between bars and your hotel. Theoretically, there is now a police force on Little Corn, but they may be hard to find. It's better not to walk alone in the bush, and don't walk there at night at all. Don't go out with locals unless recommended by your hotel; thieves, known as 'pirates', sometimes pose as informal tour guides.

Background
During his fourth and final exploratory voyage, Columbus encountered the islands and named them *Islas Limonares*. At the time, they were inhabited by Kukra Indians, of which little is known today except for a reported tendency towards cannibalism. During the 18th century the islands became a haven for pirates resting in between pillages. Eventually they were settled by Afro-Caribbeans, mostly Jamaicans, who arrived from the neighbouring islands of San Andrés. The local economy was based on the production of palm oil until the devastating winds of Hurricane Joan in 1988, which reached over 200 kph and destroyed most of the palm trees on the island. Lobster fishing took over as the biggest industry, but supplies are being depleted rapidly. Tourism and 'white lobster' (cocaine) are taking over as the biggest sources of income for the islanders. Thanks to their proximity to the San Andrés Islands, which come under Colombian jurisdiction (although located inside Nicaragua's ocean platform), drug traffickers have had a lot of involvement here, using Little Corn as a refuelling stop for many years. Today there's a meagre police presence, frequently rotated to keep hands (and noses) clean. But there is still a lot of drug money on both islands, and parcels of coke are still dumped at sea (albeit less and less frequently), allowing locals to fish for the lucrative 'white lobster'. Meanwhile, there has been a migration of Miskito communities from the mainland to the islands to dive for real lobster, although dwindling supplies have created unemployment in both native and migrant populations, with some desperate people turning to crime. Yet there is a surprising affluence to both islands that can probably only be explained by tourism or drugs. Either way, the Corn Island natives remain some of the most hospitable, polite and welcoming people in Nicaragua; a people with a profound understanding of the word 'relaxed'.

Big Corn

Big Corn has a good landing strip, airport terminal and quite a few decent hotels. Around Waula Point is **Picnic Centre**, a fine beach for swimming and sunbathing. On the sparsely populated southeastern part of the island is the long and tranquil **Long Beach** in Long Bay. With Queen Hill rising above the western part of the bay it is also very scenic. The most interesting nature is to be found beneath the water, with beautiful reefs and rich marine life. Bird life, however, is disappointing. Snorkelling is best on the northern coast of Big Corn, just west of **Sally Peaches**, in front of the Hotel Bayside. The eastern side of the island is the most rustic and quieter. Facing the Atlantic, it has good waves for most of the year and plenty of rocks. There are numerous estuaries and wetlands all around the island, containing a startling amount of fresh water.

Part of the attraction of the place is the locals, who are very friendly and happy to return a smile and a wave. Big Corn does not offer the natural beauty of Little Corn, but it is more lively and those who bore easily or are not into snorkelling or diving might prefer the big island. The northeastern part of the island has a lovely community called **South End**, the most idyllic example of Afro-Caribbean culture on the islands. There is also some nightlife with a reggae bar and several restaurants. To celebrate the abolition of slavery in 1841, Big Corn holds an annual festival, culminating on the anniversary of the decree on 27 August (book accommodation well in advance for this week) with the **Crab Festival**. Various activities take place, including the election of a Crab Festival Queen, and copious amounts of crab soup are served.

Little Corn

The small island has some of the finest coral reefs in Nicaragua and is a superb place for snorkelling and diving. *National Geographic Explorer* gave the reefs nine out of 10. Little Corn is more relaxed and less developed than its larger neighbour, although it now suffers from crime. The locals on the island are keenly aware of the beauty of their home and most of the development here is carried out by natives.

The island has good opportunities for walking, with the north end of the island a mixture of scrub forest and grazing land leading down to the brilliant turquoise sea. The prettiest side of the island is also the windward side; visiting during a windy period can be disappointing for snorkellers but helps calm mosquitoes and the heat. The most developed areas are along the western shores of the narrow southern part of the island, separated from the windswept east coast by a large swamp. This is where the boats arrive and there are numerous options for sleeping and eating. The water is calm and good for swimming and there is a good sense of community spirit here.

There are lovely highlands at both southern and northern tips of the island. The highlands of the southeast have been cordoned off by the **Casa Iguana** (see page 310), but the northern ones are open to all and have great beaches and only a few foreign settlers. South of an attractive Southeast Asian-style lodge called **Derek's**, there is a long spectacular beach that runs the entire length of the island, broken only by some small rocky points. Near the southern end of this beach there are good places to eat right on the sand and simple lodges. All the beaches have sugar-white sand, although it disappears at high tide. There is some very interesting and unique artisan jewellery sold south of **Hotel Los Delphines**, near the village at the 'bottle house' of Vice Mayor 'Tall Boy' Robert Knight, which also sells shoes, sandals and T-shirts.

Puerto Cabezas (Bilwi)

Puerto Cabezas, capital of the Región Autonomista Atlántico Norte, has a distinctly different atmosphere from Bluefields. It is principally a large Miskito village and offers an excellent introduction to the Miskito area. You can arrange to stay in small Miskito villages, for example near Haulover, a few hours by boat south of town. There are significant minorities of *mestizos* (referred to on the coast as *españoles* or the Spanish) and Creoles, many of whom came to 'Port' by way of Las Minas. Spanish is a second language for the majority of residents; many speak at least some English, and for some, English is their native language. The local name for Puerto Cabezas is **Bilwi**, although the name is of Sumo origin. The Miskitos conquered the Sumos to obtain the town some time in the last century. There are two main roads, the only paved streets, which run parallel to each other and to the sea. At the southern end of the town is the port area; a walk along the pier at sunset is highly recommended. The airport is at the northern end. The main market occupies the central part of town.

Waspám and the Río Coco

The Coco River (called *Waspán* in Spanish and *Wanghi* in Miskito) is the heart of Miskito country. There is a road from Puerto to Waspám; during the dry season the 130-km trip should take about three hours by 4WD vehicle, several hours longer by public bus (leaves Puerto at 0700, Monday to Saturday and, with luck, returns from Waspám at 1200). The bus can be boarded at several points in Puerto along the road out of town, US$5 to Waspám. The trip takes you through the pine forests, red earth, and north of Puerto towards the Coco River (the border with Honduras), and you will pass through two Miskito villages, **Sisin** and **Santa Marta**. Hitching is possible; if you cannot get all the way to Waspám, make sure you are left at Sisin, Santa Marta or La Tranquera. You can take lifts from the military; never travel at night.

Parque Nacional Saslaya

Saslaya was the first national park in Nicaragua, located within the **Reserva Biósfera Bosawás**, which contains the largest tropical cloudforest in Central America. The **Proyecto Ecoturístico Rosa Grande**, supported by Nature Conservancy and the Peace Corps, involves the community of **Rosa Grande**, 25 km from Siuna, near an area of virgin forest with a trail, waterfall on the River Labú and lots of wildlife including monkeys and large cats. One path leads to a lookout with a view over the **Cerro Saslaya**; another circular path to the northwest goes to **Rancho Alegre Falls**. Guides can be hired for US$7 a day plus food. Excursions cost US$13 per person for guide, food and camping equipment. You may have to pay for a camp guard while hiking. Tourism is in its infancy here and you may find little things 'added on' to your bill. Be certain you have enough supplies for your stay. In Siuna, contact **Proyecto Bosawás** ① *200 m east of airstrip; Mon-Fri 0800-1700.* Groups of five or more must reserve in advance; contact the **Amigos de Saslaya** ① *c/o Proyecto Bosawás, Siuna, RAAN,* by post.

For Sleeping and Eating price codes and other relevant information, see pages 43-46.

⦿ Sleeping

Bluefields *p303*

Most hotels in Bluefields are quite basic and run down.

AL Hotel Oasis, 150 m from Bluefields Bay, T572-2812, www.oasishotelcasino.net. The best hotel in town with spacious modern rooms, comfortable furnishings and professional service. There's a casino downstairs with a handful of gaming tables, should you fancy a low-key punt. Breakfast included.

B Bluefields Bay Hotel, Barrio Pointeen, T572-2838, www.geocities.com/bluefields bay/hotel. Owned by the region's university, this hotel has clean, simple rooms with private bath and hot water. The rooms upstairs are better and less damp. Excursions are offered to surrounding areas.

C Caribbean Dreams, Barrio Punta Fría, opposite market, T572-1943. With 27 rooms, private bath, a/c or fan and cable TV. Services include a restaurant with home-cooking and à la carte menu, Wi-Fi and laundry. Clean and often booked, call ahead. Helpful owners.

C Mini Hotel Central, Barrio Punta Fría, T572-2362. Has 9 simple rooms with private bath, a/c, TV. Cheaper with fan (**D**).

D Los Pipitos, Punta Fria, 50 m from **Caribbean Dreams** (above). 4 rooms with private bath and a/c, cheaper with fan (**E**), simple but good; bakery on premises.

E Hotel Costa Sur, Barrio Central, across from Lotería, T572-2452. Lots of rooms, all with shared bath and fans. Bar and restaurant attached.

E Hotel Kaora View, Entrada a Las Carmelitas, ½ c norte, Barrio Teodoro Martínez, T572-0488. 10 rooms with 1 shared bath, new, very clean, friendly, good service.

Laguna de Perlas *p304*

D Casa Blanca, in May 4 sector, T572-0508, casa_blanca_lp@yahoo.com. The best hotel in town, with clean, light, comfortable rooms; all but 1 have shared bath. The owners are very hospitable and friendly, and offer fishing expeditions, trips to the cays and community tours. They're happy to answer questions by email, and prefer reservations in advance. Good restaurant attached. Recommended.

E Green Lodge, next to Enitel, from dock, 1 c sur, T572-0507. This basic, homely and friendly hotel has 8 tiny, narrow rooms with shared bath, The owner, Wesley, is very knowledgeable about the area, has good contacts and can help arrange tours. They cook cheap grub too.

Corn Islands *p305*
Big Corn

AL Casa Canada, South End, T644-0925, www.casa-canada.com. Sophisticated, luxurious rooms with ocean views. Each is splendidly equipped with a DVD player, minibar, coffee-maker, leather chairs and mahogany furniture. A beautiful infinity pool overlooks the waves. Friendly and hospitable management. Recommended.

A Hotel Paraíso, Brig Bay, T575-5111, www.paraisoclub.com. A friendly hotel, run by 2 Dutch men who contribute to local social projects. They offer a range of clean, comfortable cabañas, all with hammocks and mosquito nets. It's right on the beach, and there's good snorkelling at the wreck off-shore.

B Anastasia's, North End, T425-9589. Located by the best snorkelling reef on the island, this hotel offers a marine park with 'snorkel trails'. The restaurant is on stilts, and all rooms have private bath, cable TV and a/c.

B Picnic Centre, Picnic Centre Beach, T575-5204. Great location, 8 average rooms with private bath, some with a/c. There's a very popular mid-priced ranch on the beach for eating and drinking, and worth a visit if sleeping elsewhere. Good ambience.

C Panorama, Iglesia Católica, ½ c al este, T575-5065. Motel-style place by the beach offering simple, economical rooms with mosquito nets. Cheaper without a/c (**D**).

D Silver Sand, Sally Peaches, south of rocky point, T575-5005. Managed by the enigmatic Ira Gómez, who alone is worth a visit. Rustic fishermen's cabins in a gorgeous, secluded setting. Ira can organize fishing trips, and cook up the catch in his bar-restaurant on the beach. Look out for the happy neighbours playing reggae through their enormous speakers.

Little Corn

AL-B Casa Iguana, on southeastern bluff, www.casaiguana.net. This is a famous, popular lodging, beautifully located with stunning views of the beaches. It has 4 cabañas with shared bath (**B**), 9 *casitas* with private bath (**A**), and 1 'luxury' *casita* (**AL**). Food is grown in the lush, attractive gardens, great breakfasts, sociable dining and an expensive internet café (US$10 per hr). An impressive outfit, even if it is a bit of a gringo summer camp. Book in advance, especially in high season.

B Ensueños, Otto Beach, www.ensuenos-littlecornisland.com. Trippy, rustic cabins with sculpted *Lord of the Rings*-style interiors; some have electricity, some don't (**C**). The grounds are wonderfully lush and filled with exuberant fruit trees, and naturalist owner Ramón Gil is an interesting and friendly host. There are comfortable houses too (**A**), and meals are available. Recommended.

B Los Delfines, in the village just south of the boat landing, T820-2242, www.hotellosdelfines.com.ni. Little Corn's most upmarket hotel, popular with Colombian businessmen. The rooms are average for the price, comfortable, clean with a/c. Hot water is sporadic. The restaurant has nice views, but service is annoyingly slack.

C Derek's, at northernmost point of east coast, T419-0600, www.dereksplacelittle corn.com. Southeast Asian-style cabins on stilts, all equipped with renewable energy, mosquito nets, orthopaedic mattresses and hammocks. It's a tranquil, social spot, and the cabins are very clean in spite of the backpacker clientele. Meals, snorkelling gear and bicycle rental available to guests.

C-E Sunrise Paradise, on the east coast just north of *Grace's*. Also known as Carlito's, and managed by the head of informal security, who is a real gentleman. It offers a range of simple cabins all with fan and electricity. There's also food, beer and hammocks, and the grounds are pleasant.

Puerto Cabezas (Bilwi) *p308*

B Liwa-Mairin, enitel, 2c este, 20 vrs norte, T792-2315. The best in town. This new hotel has great big, airy double rooms with lots of light, balconies, sea views, a/c, cable TV and tasteful, comfortable furnishings. Good value.

C-D Miss Judy's, next to Centro de Computación Ansell, T792-2225. Also known as Casa Museo, this lovely house has lots of interesting art and artefacts in the attached museum and gallery. Rooms have private bath, cheaper with fan (**D**). Friendly and interesting, with lots of family history.

D Hospedaje Bilwi, in front of pier. Tucked away from the paved road, this large, basic hotel has 19 rooms, some with fan, some with a/c. Good view of the dock from the back balcony. There's a seafood restaurant downstairs.

Parque Nacional Saslaya *p308*

E Chino, Siuna. The best and most expensive place in town.

F Bosawás Field Station, on the river Labú. Has a few hammocks, clean but simple, locally produced and cooked food, US$1.25.

F Costeño, Siuna,100 m east of airstrip. Basic.

Eating

Managua to El Rama p301

Boaco is cattle country and there are many good places to enjoy a local steak.

† La Casona, Boaco, next to Texaco, T842-2421, daily 0800-2300. Try their *lomo de costilla* or *plato típico*.

† La Cueva, Boaco, south side of the Parroquia Santiago church, T842-2438. Very good steaks.

Bluefields p303

†††-†† Chez Marcel, alcaldía, 1 c sur, ½ c abajo, T572-2347. The best place in town, serving *filete mignon*, shrimp in garlic butter and grilled lobster. Often recommended.

†† Bella Vista, Barrio Punta Fría, T572-2385. Daily 1000-2300. On the water's edge, overlooking the tired old boats and bay, this seafood restaurant serves shrimp, lobster, meat and *comida economica*.

†† El Flotante, Barrio Punta Fría, T572-2988. Daily 1000-2200. Built over the water at the end of the main street with a great view of the fishing boats and islets. They serve good shrimp and lobster, but service is slow. Dancing at weekends.

†† Salmar, alcaldía, 1 c sur, ½ c abajo, T572-2128. Daily 1600-2400. This restaurant with a tasteful interior is often recommended as a quality dining establishment. Serves seafood and meat including chicken in wine sauce.

††-† La Loma, Barrio San Pedro, opposite University BICU, T572-2875. Open-air ranch with a great view from the top of a hill.

††-† Tex Mex house, alcaldía, 1 c sur, ½ c abajo. Tex-Mex restaurant above Salmar serving fajitas, tacos, mixed plates, margueritas and, of course, tequila.

††-† Twins, alcaldía, 2 c al mar, 2½ c sur. This seafood restaurant above the 'lobster pot' is one of the better ones.

† Cafetín Central, opposite Bancentro, inside Mini Hotel. Centrally located café serving reliable and cheap fare including breakfasts and chicken dishes.

† Luna Ranch, Santa Matilde opposite URACAN. Fast food and full plates in this interesting cultural centre.

† Pizza Martinuzi, alcaldía, 1 c sur, ½ c abajo. Very reasonable pizza, chicken and burgers.

Corn Islands p305
Big Corn

††-† Fisherman's Cave, next to dock. This great little seafood restaurant overlooks the water and fishing boats. A relaxing spot. Check out the pools filled with live fish.

††-† Nautilus Dive Centre, North Point, T575-5077. Fabulously eclectic menu with Caribbean curry and classic dishes such as rondon soup, containing vegetables, coconut milk and seafood. They also do pizza and will deliver.

††-† Seva's Place, 500 m east of Anastasia's in Sally Peaches, T575-5058. Quite possibly the island's best restaurant. They serve great seafood, meat and chicken from a fine location with rooftop seats and ocean views. Try the lobster *a la plancha*.

† Relax, South End. 0800-2000. Also known as **Virgil's Place**, they do the best ice cream on the island and some light meals too, including fried chicken.

Little Corn

See Sleeping for most of the eating options.

†† Habana Libre, just north of boat landing, T848-5412. Really tasty, flavourful dishes including succulent veal, fish and lobster served with interesting sauces. There's terraced seating, good music and amiable staff. Cuban specialities are available on request and in advance. Be sure to try a *mojito* – they're outstanding.

† Miss Bridgette's, in the village, north of the dock. A lovely little *comedor* serving wholesome, home-cooked fare. Service is very Caribbean, so be prepared to wait.

Puerto Cabezas (Bilwi) p308

In addition to those below, there are numerous *comedores* in the **San Jerónimo Market**.

¥-¥ Crisfa, Enitel, 2½ c norte, 1 c oeste. Tasty *comida típica*, meat and chicken dishes. Not bad, one of the better ones.

¥-¥ Kabu Payaska, hospital, 200 vrs al mar. Often recommended by the locals, this restaurant overlooking the water serves some of the best seafood and *comida típica* in town.

¥-¥ Miramar, Enitel, 3 c norte, 2 c al mar. At the end of a road leading to the sea, this seafood restaurant overlooks the waves and has a disco at weekends.

¥ Comedor Avril, opposite Banpro. Cheap homemade fare, *comida típica* and breakfast.

⊕ Entertainment

Bluefields *p303*
Some of the bars are quite shady, but the ones below are safe for gringos.

Cima Club, Banpro, 1 c abajo. It's hard to miss this centrally located dance hall with 2 floors and a large sign. Popular and often recommended by locals.

Four Brothers, Cotton tree, from alcaldía, 1 c al mar, 4½ c sur. The best reggae spot in Nicaragua, a big ranch full of great dancing. Usually open Tue-Sun, ask around to see what kind of music is playing. US$1 admission.

Garibaldi, alcaldía, 2 c sur, 1 c al mar. Rum, beer and reggae at this darkened joint for dancing and drinking.

Corn Islands *p305*
Big Corn
After dark, always use taxis to get between your hotel and the bars, even if they're close to each other.

Marvin and Myers bar, next to the dock. Chill out with a beer while waiting for the boat to Little Corn. Good for people-watching.

Nancy's Bar, Brigg Bay. 1900-0200. Head here on a Fri night for cold beer, reggae and raucous dancing.

Nico's, South end, 1900-0200. The action kicks off on Sun, with wall-to-wall drinking

and dancing by the waves. They serve beef soup when you need perking up.

Reggae Palace, Brigg Bay. 1900-0200. Sat night is the big night here. As usual, reggae, salsa and rum in heavy doses.

▲▲ Activities and tours

Corn Islands *p305*
Diving
Dive Little Corn, boat landing in village, Little Corn, T823-1154, www.divelittlecorn.com. There's a strong PADI ethos at this 5-star, gold palm centre, with training right up to assistant instructor level. They also offer night dives, single and 2-tank dives, snorkelling tours, and 5 or 10 dive packages – trips leave several times daily. Open-water training is US$320 including materials, and packages can combine with Casa Iguana stays.

Dolphin Dive, in the village, south of the dock, Little Corn, T690-0225, www.cornislands scubadiving.com. Operated by islander Sandy Herman, a passionate and friendly instructor with many years diving experience. She offers PADI instruction to dive master level, and a range of customized trips for diving, fishing or snorkelling. Open water training is US$320, a 2-tank dive is US$65. Packages are available, including discounts at Delphines. Groups are kept small. Recommended.

Nautilus Resort & Dive Centre, North Point, Big Corn, T575-5077, www.divebigcorn.com. Diving and snorkelling tours with Guatemalan NASE-certified training instructor include trips to see the cannon of the old Spanish Galleon, blowing rock, PADI certification from US$275, night dives and 2-tank dives from US$60-90 per person, snorkelling trips and glass-bottom boat tours at US$15 per person.

Fishing
Ira Gómez, Silver Sand hotel, Sally Peaches, south of rocky point, Big Corn, T575-5005. One of those irresistible local characters, Ira is an enthusiastic fishing man and can organize your trip.

⊕ Transport

Managua to El Rama p301
Boat

From **El Rama**, to **Bluefields**, *pangas* depart when full, several daily, 0530-1600, US$10, 2 hrs. The ferry is slightly cheaper and much slower. It departs Mon, Wed and Fri in the early morning (around 0800 when the bus has arrived), US$8, 5-8 hrs.

Bus

2 trucks a day to **Santa Lucía** from **Boaco**, US$1, 1 bus a day to and from **Managua**. From **Boaco**, unpaved roads go north to **Muy Muy** and **Matagalpa**, and south to **Comoapa**. **Managua**-Boaco goes every 40 mins from Plaza Mayoreo (2 hrs 10 mins, US$1.50).

From Managua buses leave from the Mercado Mayoreo to **El Rama**. Managua–Rama, every hr, 0400-1130, 8 hrs, US$7. From **El Rama** to **Managua**, hourly from 0400-1130; to **Juigalpa**, every hr, 0800-1500, 6 hrs, US$3.75. **Juigalpa–El Rama**, hourly from 0800-1500. To **Laguna de Perlas** from **El Rama**, 1600, 3 hrs, US$7.50. **Laguna de Perlas** to Rama, 0600.

Bluefields p303
Air

The airport is 3 km south of the city centre, either walk (30 mins) or take a taxi US$2. **La Costeña** office, T572-2500; also on Managua and the Corn Islands route with similar times and costs is **Atlantic Airlines** T572-1299.

La Costeña to **Managua**, daily 0710, 0840, 1120, 1610, US$128 return, 1 hr. To **Corn Islands**, daily 0740, 1510, US$98 return, 20 mins. To **Bilwi**, daily except Sun 1210, US$148 return, 1 hr.

Boat

Pangas (motorboats) depart when full. The early ones are more reliable, and services on Sun are restricted. To **Laguna de Perlas**, from 0830, several daily, US$6, 1½ hrs, continues to **Tasbapauni**, US$12, 2½ hrs. To **El Rama**,

0530-1600, several daily, US$10, 2 hrs. To **Corn Islands**, ferry, 0900, every Wed, US$12, 5-6 hrs; cargo ferry, Sun, 0600.

Laguna de Perlas p304
To **Bluefields**, boat schedules are irregular; boats leave when full. The first of the day, 0630, US$6, 1½ hrs, is the only one guaranteed, although one usually leaves soon after. Get to the dock at 0600 to get your name on the passenger list. Services are restricted on Sun when it may be quicker to go via Kukra Hill. Bus to **El Rama**, 0600, US$7.50, 3 hrs.

Corn Islands p305
Air

La Costeña flies from Big Corn to **Managua** with a stop in **Bluefields**, daily at 0810 and 1540, US$165 round trip, 90 mins with stop. Re-confirm seats before travelling. **La Costeña** office is on Big Corn, T575-5131.

Boat

Inter-island boats Big Corn to Little Corn, daily 1000, 1630, US$6.50, 40 mins. Little Corn to Big Corn, daily 0700, 1400, US$6.50, 40 mins. Boats leave from main dock, first come, first served. US$0.20 charge to get into the dock area. Buy big blue trash bags to keep luggage dry at shop across from dock entrance, best to sit near the back.

Mainland boats Subject to change, check locally; Corn Islands to **Bluefields** leaves Tue, 0900, US$12, 5-6 hrs; and Fri and Sun 1200. To **Bilwi**, daytime departure, 1 per month, US$30, 3 days.

Bus

2 buses circle the paved island road on Big Corn every 20 mins, US$0.50.

Taxi

Taxis charge US$2 for trips to and from the airport or any trip after 2000. Any other trip is US$1. Hourly taxi rates are US$6 per hr, poor value, as there are many taxis and trip fares are cheap.

Puerto Cabezas (Bilwi) *p308*
Air

The airstrip is 3 km north of town. From the airport, taxis charge US$2 to anywhere in Bilwi. To **Bluefields**, La Costeña, Mon-Sat, 1110, US$60 1-way, US$110 round-trip. To **Managua**, La Costeña, daily 0820, 1220, Mon-Sat 1610, US$96 1-way, US$148 round-trip; **Atlantic Airlines**, daily 1210, US$96 1-way, US$148 round trip. To **Minas**, La Costeña, Mon, Wed, Fri, 1315.

Bring your passport as there are immigration checks by the police in Bilwi and sometimes in the waiting lounge in Managua. All bags are x-rayed coming into the domestic terminal from any destination.

Boat

To **Corn Islands**, once a month, night departure, US$30, 3 days. It is recommended that you do not hire a boat with fewer than 2 people.

Independent travel to the **Cayos Miskitos** is not recommended due to problems with drug runners from Colombia using the islands as a refuge. Contact an agency such as AMICA to arrange a guided visit.

A good boat trip is to **Laguna Bismuna** on the northern coast, reportedly one of the most beautiful in Nicaragua, though easiest access is via Waspam.

Bus

Express bus to **Managua**, Thu and Sat, 0800, US$15 from Enitel, 20 hrs. There are also buses to **Rosita** and **Siuna** that connect to buses to Managua. To **Waspam**, 0700, Mon-Sat, returns from Waspam 1200, US$5.

⊕ Directory

Bluefields *p303*
Banks There are banks for money-changing, no ATMs, bring all the cash you need when visiting the Carribbean coast. Possibility of a Visa advance if stuck.

Corn Islands *p305*
'Bucks' are córdobas in island speak.
Banks The only bank is **BanPro** on southwest bay on Big Corn, T575-5109. No ATM, and credit card advance for VISA only. TCs are not accepted or changed anywhere. Dollars are widely used on the islands; be safe and take all the cash you need with you. If stuck, you might get a credit card advance at the airport. **Hospital** Brig Bay T575-5236. **Internet** Big Corn has a café near Nautilus, US$1.50 per hour. Little Corn has extortionate cafés at **Los Delfines** and **Casa Iguana**, US$10 per hr. **Police** T575-5201. There are few, if any police on the Little Corn – ask around.
Telephone Enitel, T575-5061.

Puerto Cabezas (Bilwi) *p308*
Banks There is **Banpro** for changing dollars, no ATMs. Bring all the cash you need.
Hospital On the outskirts of town.

Contents

Footprint features

Border crossing

Panama–Costa Rica
See page 337

Panama

At a glance

⊖ **Getting around** Buses up to a point; flights at times; taxis best in Panama City and cheap for groups.

◉ **Time required** Time required 2-3 weeks.

☼ **Weather** Temperatures in the high 20°Cs from Dec-Apr, the dry season.

✖ **When not to go** The wettest months are Oct and Nov.

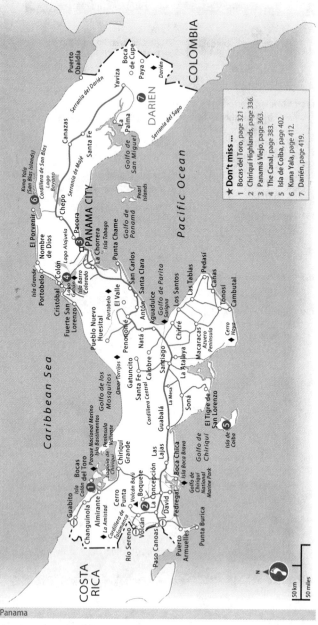

COSTA RICA

COLOMBIA

Caribbean Sea

Pacific Ocean

DARIÉN

PANAMA CITY

Puerto Obaldía
Boca de Cupe
Paya
Darién
Yaviza
La Palma
Serranía del Darién
Serranía del Darién
Serranía del Sapo
Golfo de San Miguel
Canazas
Santa Fe
Serranía de Majé
Lago Bayano
Cordillera de San Blas
Kuna Yala (San Blas Islands)
El Porvenir
Nombre de Dios
El Valle
Chepo
Pacora
Lago Alajuela
La Chorrera
Punta Chame
Isla Taboga
Golfo de Panamá
Pearl Islands
Portobelo
Colón
Cristóbal
Fuerte San Lorenzo
Isla Barro Colorado
Lago Gatún
Portobelo
Isla Grande
San Carlos
Santa Clara
Antón
Aguadulce
Sariná
Golfo de Parita
Los Santos
Pedasí
Las Tablas
Cañas
Tonosí
Cambutal
Cerro Hoya
Azuero Peninsula
Macaracas
Chitré
La Villa
Santiago
Calobre
Pueblo Nuevo Huesital
Penonomé
Natá
Omar Torrijos
Gatuncito
Santa Fe
Cordillera Central
La Mesa
Soná
Guabalá
El Tigre de San Lorenzo
Isla de Coiba
Golfo de Chiriquí
Las Lajas
Boca Chica
Golfo de Chiriquí National Marine Park
David
Pedregal
Golfo de Boca Brava
La Concepción
Boquete
Volcán
Volcán Barú
Cerro Punta
La Amistad
Cordillera Talamanca
Río Sereno
Paso Canoas
Puerto Armuelles
Punta Burica
Changuinola
Guabito
Almirante
Bocas del Toro
Isla Colón del Toro
Laguna de Chiriquí
Parque Nacional Marino Isla Bastimentos
Península Valiente
Chiriquí Grande
Golfo de los Mosquitos

★ Don't miss ...

N

50 km
50 miles

The isthmus of Panama owes much to its fortuitous geographic position. Over 1000 species of bird, 10,000 species of plant and scores of rare animals make their home on this sinuous snake-like land mass, a vital biological corridor between the Americas. Its scintillating natural diversity is matched only by an eclectic social heritage. As a historic meeting point for global cultures, a vibrant patchwork of ethnicities colours the land: European, Afro-Caribbean, North and South American influences are strongly evident, but it is the nation's indigenous peoples who supply the most colour and intrigue.

Today, Panama is a place of great dynamism and change, fast emerging as one of Latin America's most powerful nations. No single element has been more critical in driving the nation's development than the Panama Canal, a key component in the world trade system. Plans to expand the 'big ditch' signal an evermore prominent role for this tiny nation, and Panama's fate as the crossroads of the world is sealed. Fortunately, the mood is optimistic. Panameños are proud of their country and its accomplishments and some politicians are boasting, perhaps over-optimistically, that Panama will achieve First-World status in a single generation.

But all this development comes at a price. In the aftermath of a frenzied and somewhat dubious land grab, the integrity of Panama's fragile natural environment is in peril. Rainforests are being cleared for gated communities and foreign-owned housing projects; ancient tribal lands face obliteration from grandiose hydroelectric schemes; and many of the country's most beautiful coastal habitats have already been wrecked by luxury hotels hoping to profit from tourism. But as the world awakens to Panama's intense natural beauty, there's increased pressure to protect it. National parks, nature reserves and conservation projects are springing up everywhere. Panama may just choose sustainability yet.

Bocas del Toro

Isolated from the rest of Panama until the 1980s, Bocas del Toro Province owes much of its distinct Afro-Caribbean character to the 19th-century banana boom, which brought the wealth, plantations and migrant workers so crucial to its independent development. Today, ramshackle communities cling to the shores of rum-soaked islands. Indolent beaches flank verdant rainforests, home to scores of colourful birds, butterflies and tiny psychedelic frogs. World-class waves pound the sands, while delicate coral gardens and eerie underwater caverns occupy the protected waters just offshore. The archipelago's superlative natural attractions are partially protected by the Parque Nacional Bastimentos – part rainforest, part marine park, home to populations of dolphins and sea turtles. But all this natural beauty has brought unprecedented attention to Bocas del Toro and its islands are now under threat from over-development.

Fortunately, tourism on the mainland is much less advanced, with dense banana plantations and a single road skirting the coast. Beyond here lies the Kingdom of the Naso with its impenetrable jungles, crocodile-infested waterways and vivid indigenous culture.

Come prepared. Bocas del Toro has its own micro-climate that can see heavy rain at all times of the year. » For listings, see pages 326-333.

Mainland Bocas del Toro ●● » pp326-333.

Mainland Bocas del Toro is an expanse of steamy banana plantations and dense rainforests, experienced by most travellers as mere passing scenery on their way to the islands. Vestiges of 19th-century infrastructure are slowly decaying along the coastal highway and around Laguna Chiriquí, where sadly declining ports, plantation buildings and a still functioning railway hark back to the glory days of the United Fruit Company. Nearby, the coastal wetlands are fascinating and teeming natural habitats, home to peaceful manatees and scores of elegant water birds. Inland, the Naso tribe is struggling to survive along a network of darkened, jungle-shrouded rivers, where a new hydro-electric project is threatening their ancient lands and culture. You can make contact with the Naso through the Wekso project, who can also set you up with guides. If you're lucky, you might meet the King.

Changuinola

Coming from Costa Rica, the first place of any real size you'll encounter is Changuinola. Hot and sprawling, this is the main commercial centre and largest urban settlement in Bocas del Toro province. Although largely uninteresting and equally unattractive, it has an airport and lively nightlife with local bars. It's also good for shopping (the food markets are great) and there are several banks where you can change traveller's cheques and use ATMs. Like most port towns, Changuinola can be quite rough, so you should take care going out after dark. Lone women should take particular care.

Changuinola's main interest to travellers is as a departure or arrival point for fast water taxis to the Bocas del Toro archipelago. They depart every one to two hours from Finca 60 just outside town (US$7), and navigate the historic Snyder Canal, constructed in the 1903 to transport bananas from the plantations to cargo ships awaiting in the bay. It's a fun, high-speed ride, rushing past walls of tangled jungle foliage en route to the ocean. Buses run regularly from the border to Changuinola; a taxi costs US$15-20, and a taxi from Changuinola to Finca 60 costs around US$5.

Around Changuinola

If you'd like to explore the coastal wetlands at your own pace, you can visit the **Humedal San San Pond Sak**, around 5 km north of Changuinola, on the edge of an old plantation. Here, wooden walkways snake through the teeming wetlands, home to water birds and crocodiles. To get there, take a 4WD taxi and arrange a return time. It can get seriously wet and muddy, so don appropriate footwear. You can also explore the wetlands in a kayak by taking a tour with **Starfleet Scuba** in Bocas del Toro Town, Isla Colón (see Activities and tours, page 331). The waters are home to a large manatee population.

Since ancient times, the lands around Changuinola have been occupied by the **Naso tribe** (also known as the Teribe), who retain many elements of their pre-Columbian culture. In 2004, their 3500-strong community was divided over plans for a new Colombian hydroelectric power plant, supported by the now-exiled King Tito in exchange for much-needed social and education funds. The plant does not actually encroach on Naso lands, but it is significant enough to flood their traditional hunting grounds. Tragically, a much larger government project is now planned for the banks of the Bonyic River, a major waterway running right through their territory. You can visit the Naso, if you wish, by staying at the rustic **Wekso Ecolodge**. The lodge will be able to arrange visits to local communities and guides for treks in the Parque La Amistad, a vast, beautiful, but hard-to-reach national park that extends into neighbouring Costa Rica. You should organize your stay in advance through **ODESEN** (National Organization for Sustainable Ecotourism Development) ① *T6569-3869, www.bocas.com/odesen.htm. To get to Wekso, take a taxi to El Silencio and then a boat down the Río Teribe.*

Almirante and the Banana Coast

South of Changuinola, the old banana railway advances through one of Central America's most important banana-growing regions, concluding at the small commercial port of Almirante. In the early 20th century, disease virtually wiped out the banana business here and plantations were converted to *abacá* and cacao. However, with the development of disease resistant strains, bananas are once again thriving. The main players in the industry are large multinational companies, including **Cobanat**, who export through **Chiquirí Land Company** (a subsidiary of **Chiquita Brands**) and Dole (a subsidiary of **Standard Brands**), who export bananas to Europe and the US from Almirante. Almirante is a common transit point for tourists travelling between Panama's interior and the Bocas del Toro archipelago. Water taxis to the latter depart hourly, 0600-1830, US$4, crossing the bay of Almirante at high speed. An island in the bay which sank during the 1991 earthquake now shows as nothing more than a patch of shallow turquoise water.

South to Chiriquí Province

Chiriquí Grande, located on the shores of Laguna de Chiriquí, was once the embarkation point for travellers catching the ferry to Almirante and beyond to the Bocas del Toro archipelago. But now, with a paved road connecting Almirante, Changuinola and Costa Rica with the interior, it is rarely visited and today, rather depressed. Most travellers bypass it completely on their way to Panama's interior, south of Laguna de Chiriquí, where a road climbs up through virgin rainforest into the mountains. About 2.5 km before the continental divide you'll encounter a 10-m waterfall. Soon after, you'll start descending steeply, pass the Fortuna hydro-electric plant and enter Chiriquí Province. If you're travelling under your own steam, you can stop to admire the views. As you descend further into the sweltering Chiriquí lowlands, the road eventually connects with

Diving and snorkelling in Bocas del Toro

The teeming Caribbean waters around Bocas del Toro are home to a impressive array of marine life including dolphins, sea turtles, rays and nurse sharks, to name a few. But the real joy of diving in Bocas is in the details, with some wonderful intact coral gardens (74 out of 79 Caribbean species exist here) that play host to a multitude of little gems. Brittle stars, spotted morays, arrow crabs, toadfish and squid are just some of the inhabitants you expect to see, along with most of most of the common Caribbean reef fish.

A trip to observe these awesome sea creatures is obligatory. If you've never dived before, the waters around Bocas del Toro are particularly calm and sheltered, making it a great place to learn. PADI Open Water Diver courses are reasonably priced at US$250-300. They last three to four days. Be warned, the course is as demanding as it is rewarding, and you won't get much beach time. When you're not in the water learning and practicing skills, you'll need to study your textbook and watch cheesy PADI DVDs. Four to five dives will be included in your training package and there's a multiple-choice exam at the end. Once you've passed, you'll be qualified to dive all over the world and take your skills in new directions – underwater naturalist, photographer and deep diver are some of the immediate possibilities.

Bocas dive sites are as varied as they are vivid and there are many more than mentioned here. Some of them known only to a handful of people, some are waiting to be discovered. **Hospital** point is a popular location at the northern side of Isla Solarte with a gently sloping shelf of corals that suddenly drops to a depth of 16 m. On the western side of Isla Solarte lies **Coral Garden** with its profusion of colourful corals and depths from 4 to 18 m. **The Wreck** is a popular dive where a small ferry was deliberately sunk in 2000 to create an artificial reef. The bay in front of Bocas town is the site of **The Playground**, a circle reef where turtles are often spotted. **Cayo Crawl**, at the southern end of Isla Bastimentos, is a popular site full of great corals and often frequented by tour boats. A handful of really excellent sites lie further afield, but are only accessible during the calm months of March, April, September and October. **La Gruta** del Polo has spooky underwater caverns and swim-throughs. **Tiger Rock** is widely renowned as one of the best dives in Bocas, with underwater pinnacles and an abundance of marine life. **Cayos Zapatillas** is highly regarded, with its swim-throughs and corals. If you don't have the time or inclination to dive, snorkeling is a simple way to get close to the action. Most tour operators run snorkel trips to the major sites, including Hospital point and Cayo Crawl, but it might be worth going with a reputable dive shop to avoid second rate service.

the Interamericana, also known as the Pan-American highway, 14 km east of David, with connections to Panama City. If you're travelling in the opposite direction, towards Bocas del Toro, descending from the continental divide to Chiriquí Grande is a cyclist's delight – good road, spectacular views, little traffic and downhill all the way (but nowhere to eat until Punta Pena, just outside Chiriquí Grande).

Bocas del Toro Archipelago ⬤🅿➕▲🆘 ↠ *pp326-333.*

Once upon a time, this archipelago was the great backpackers' secret, but this is no more. Several years ago, large numbers of foreigners starting arriving to retire, open small businesses or otherwise bask in the idyllic Caribbean lifestyle. Sadly, this flurry of international activity has attracted a frenzy of less benign forces, including large-scale developers with plans for gated communities and high-rise condos. All this mercenary ambition has resulted in a rather venal land grab, sky-high property prices and the destruction of local ecosystems. Tread carefully, life is fragile.

Fortunately, most of the action is concentrated on Isla Colón, the archipelago's largest island and site of the provincial capital, Bocas del Toro Town. Here, you can expect all the amenities, bustle and fakery associated with a booming tourist scene. Still, it's a sunny place that plays host to a friendly community, fine restaurants and raucous night life. Across the water, Isla Bastimentos is the laid-back and authentic alternative with a thoroughly indolent disposition, dilapidated clapboard housing and wealth of colourful, talkative characters. Either of these islands make a good base for exploring the archipelago's rich natural world, now marketed, perhaps too hopefully, as 'the Galapagos of the 21st century'.

Background

The scattering of islands and keys that comprise the Bocas del Toro archipelago have historic links with Columbus' fourth voyage in 1502, when he landed, serviced and re-supplied his ships in the protected waters of the Bahía Almirante. Later, pirates and buccaneers sought refuge here, followed years afterwards by the fruit companies. North

1 Bocas del Toro Archipelago

➡**Bocas del Toro maps**
1 Bocas del Toro Archipelago, page 321
2 Bocas del Toro, page 323

To Changuinola ▼

Swan Cay (Isla del Cisne)

Boca del Drago — Isla Colón — Playa Bluff

Caribbean Sea

Punta Toro — Red Frog Beach

Isla Toro Carenero

To Guabito, Sixaola & Changuinola ◀

Bahía Almirante — Bocas del Toro — Bastimentos

Playa Larga — ◆ National Marine Park

Almirante

Cayo Nancy (Solarte)

Punta Coco

Isla Bastimentos

Punta Vieja

Zapatilla Norte

Zapatilla Sur

Isla San Cristóbal

Cayo Crawl

Laguna Bocatorito

Isla Popa

Cayo del Agua

N

5 km
5 miles

▶ To Chiriquí Grande, David & Panama City

Riding the rapids: whitewater rafting in Chiriquí

Chiriquí's rugged, mountainous terrain is home to some of the most accessible and challenging whitewater rapids in Central America. The **Río Chiriquí** and **Río Chiriquí Viejo** offer experiences of differing ferocity, from relatively gentle Grade 2 jaunts to adrenalin-charged encounters with violent Grade 5 monsters.

The **Río Chiriquí Viejo** offers the best year-round rafting in the province, although this fantastic river is currently under threat from new plans for a hydroelectric dam. Grade 3 and 4 rapids course through the **Palon section**; Grade 2 and 3 rapids in the tamer **Sabo section**. The **Jaguar section** is a Grade 4 stretch with 73 rapids and 16 km of canyons and waterfalls. There are other more technical Grade 5 and 6 rapids that require experience and preparation to reach, most notable the **Puma section**, near Volcán. All of the Río Chiriquí rapids become more

difficult in the rainy season, June to December, rising a Grade or even two Grades during the especially wet months of October and November. The wet season also supplies enough water for some more subdued rapids, including the Grade 3 **Witches section** of the Río Chiriquí. Beyond here, the Río Gariche, Río Majagua and Río Esti have Grade 2 and 3 rapids, suitable for beginners, families and children.

Be sure to discuss your options thoroughly with your chosen tour operator and check your insurance cover before embarking. Two very reputable and long-standing whitewater specialists can be found in Boquete: **Chiriquí River Rafting**, Avenida Central, next to Lourdes, T720-1505, www.panama-rafting.com; and **Panama Rafters**, just below the square on Avenida Central, T/F720-2712, www.panama rafters.com.

American and European expats are the most recent arrivals to these broadly multi-cultural isles, where a mixture of Mestizo, Afro-Caribbean and Ngöbe-Buglé communities make their home. English is widely spoken, as is Spanish, and to a lesser extent Ngöbére, the native tongue of the Ngöbe-Buglé. The local Creole dialect, Guari-Guari, is derived from all three languages.

Isla Colón

Scores of hotels, waterfront restaurants and moneyed gringos beset the island's principal settlement and port of entry, **Bocas del Toro Town**, known simply as 'Bocas' by the locals. Those expecting the authentic Caribbean of times gone-by will be sorely disappointed. But in spite of the crowds and good-natured hustle, Bocas does manage to retain a certain small-town charm – for now, at least. A handful of historic buildings recall the early 20th century, when Bocas was again booming, this time with bananas, not tourism. As the former Headquarters of the United Fruit Company, the town was one of the most prosperous in Panama and home to a population of 20,000. It was hit particularly hard by the banana blight of the 1930s, and when the fruit companies moved out, they didn't return.

Main Street, also known as Calle 3, is the town's principal road and the site of many amenities. It runs past a shady central plaza before connecting with the lazy waterfront road, also known as Calle 1, home to a wealth of colourful clapboard houses, bars, restaurants and hotels. The **tourist office** ① *Calle 1, T757-9642, www.bocas.com, Mon-Fri 0830-1630*, has a permanent exhibition, with English translations, about Columbus' landfall, indigenous peoples and the United Fruit Company years. For up-to-date information, you can check out the monthly *Bocas Breeze*, also online at www.thebocasbreeze.com. There isn't much to do in Bocas itself except sample the freshly caught fish, imbibe the local rum and partake in the night life. Nearby there's a new butterfly conservation project, **Bocas Butterfly garden** ① *0900-1500, US$5; take a water taxi to get there.*

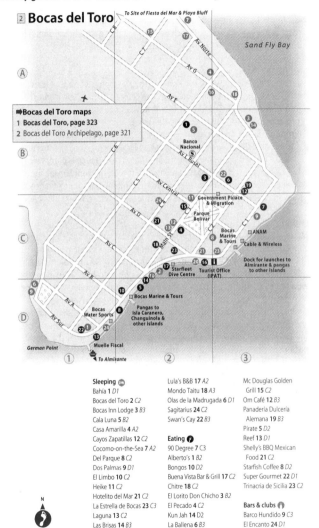

2 Bocas del Toro

Bocas del Toro maps
1 Bocas del Toro, page 323
2 Bocas del Toro Archipelago, page 321

Sleeping
Bahía **1** *D1*
Bocas del Toro **2** *C2*
Bocas Inn Lodge **3** *B3*
Cala Luna **5** *B2*
Casa Amarilla **4** *A2*
Cayos Zapatillas **12** *C2*
Cocomo-on-the-Sea **7** *A2*
Del Parque **8** *C2*
Dos Palmas **9** *D1*
El Limbo **10** *C2*
Heike **11** *C2*
Hotelito del Mar **21** *C2*
La Estrella de Bocas **23** *C3*
Laguna **13** *C2*
Las Brisas **14** *B3*
La Veranda **15** *A2*
Los Delfines **16** *A2*

Lula's B&B **17** *A2*
Mondo Taitu **18** *A3*
Olas de la Madrugada **6** *D1*
Sagitarius **24** *C2*
Swan's Cay **22** *B3*

Eating
90 Degree **7** *C3*
Alberto's **1** *B2*
Bongos **10** *D2*
Buena Vista Bar & Grill **17** *C2*
Chitre **18** *C2*
El Lorito Don Chicho **3** *B2*
El Pecado **4** *C2*
Kun Jah **14** *D2*
La Ballena **6** *B3*
Lemongrass **17** *C2*
Lily's Café **16** *C2*

Mc Douglas Golden
  Grill **15** *C2*
Om Café **12** *B3*
Panadería Dulcería
  Alemana **19** *B3*
Pirate **5** *D2*
Reef **13** *D1*
Shelly's BBQ Mexican
  Food **21** *C2*
Starfish Coffee **8** *D2*
Super Gourmet **22** *D1*
Trinacria de Sicilia **23** *C2*

Bars & clubs
Barco Hundido **9** *C3*
El Encanto **24** *D1*
Iguana **20** *C2*

Beyond Bocas, there are plenty of beaches, but you'll need some sort of transport to get to them. The best swimming beach is **Boca del Drago**, 25 km away and served by regular buses, although there isn't much sand to enjoy, particularly at high tide. If travelling by bicycle, there's a bat cave on the way known simply as *La Gruta*; stop at the village of Colonia Santeña and ask directions. The most attractive beach on the island is **Bluff Beach**, 7 km from Bocas, but the waters are fraught with rip-tides and unsuitable for swimming; surfers will fare much better with its waves. **Punch Beach** is another good surfing spot. There are also many unnamed beaches in the area that a good taxi driver will know about.

Isla Caranero

Isla Caranero, or Careening Cay, is the site where Christopher Columbus careened his vessels (ie tilted them on their side for the purposes of cleaning or repair) during his fourth exploration of the Americas. The closest island to Isla Colón, Isla Caranero is a tranquil alternative for those who want to be close to the action, but not completely immersed in it. A string of mostly mid-range accommodation flanks the shores of this tiny island, visible from the waterfront in Bocas and two minutes away by water taxi (US$1). Most taxis don't run after around 2200 without prior arrangement. There's also a raucous party twice weekly at the **Aqua Lounge**, so it's not all peace and quiet. A few highly popular surf spots can be found on the island with reef point breaks suitable for intermediate and advanced surfers. There also are some less challenging waves in the nearby bays, including **Black Rock**.

Isla Bastimentos

Named after an old Spanish word for 'supply', Isla Bastimentos is the island where Christopher Columbus re-stocked his ships with provisions in 1502. It's the second largest island in the archipelago and a welcome relief from the bustle of Isla Colón. **Bastimentos Town** is the main settlement, clinging to a steep slope with half-fallen structures and rickety wooden stilts. The population is friendly, Afro-Caribbean and English-speaking. They seem to be thoroughly engaged with life's more civilized pursuits – idle conversation, smoking and drinking rum. Other communities on the island include Bahía Honda and Salt Creek, both indigenous Ngöbe-Buglé. The former is located close to an interesting bat cave and home to a new eco-tourism project, '**Trail of the Sloth**', which involves a dugout canoe trip and hike through the rainforest. On the southeastern corner of the island is **Cayo Crawl**, also known as **Coral Cay**, which has excellent snorkelling in the coral garden. It's also the site of a famous local restaurant on the water.

The island's coastline is the site of several good surfing beaches, including the best in the region, **Silverbacks**, with legendary and occasionally terrifying 25-ft Hawaiian-style waves, suitable only for advanced boarders (peaks December to February). Take a water taxi to get there. **Playa Wizard**, also known as Playa Primera or First Beach, is an easy 20-minute hike from Bastimentos Town. Ask locally for the path or just follow signs from the road (note, if you find yourself passing through a cemetery, you've taken a wrong turn). The waves are good and strong, but there are also lots of powerful rip-tides, so it's not really suitable for swimming. East of Playa Wizard lies another good surfing spot, **Red Frog Beach**, named after the strawberry-coloured poison dart frogs that inhabit the forests skirting its white-sand shores. You can reach it via a path at the end of Playa Wizard, but if you're carrying a board, it might be better to take a water taxi. Red Frog Beach is also the site of a hideous new residential development, www.redfrogbeach.com, presently under construction and soon to ruin the island's peaceful ambience. From Red Frog, the trail continues to **Magic Bay** and then to the sheltered waters of **Playa Polo**, good for snorkelling. **Playa Larga** lies another half hour away and is an important nesting site for leatherback and hawksbill turtles. Sea access to this final stretch of coast is generally restricted to the calm months of March, April, September and October.

Around half the island's land is protected by the **Parque Nacional Marino Isla Bastimentos**, which reaches over the island and surrounding waters in a strange r-shape. You'll definitely need a guide if you want to explore the park's rainforests, as the trails are poor and overgrown. Offshore, the marine element of the park promises superlative diving and snorkelling, accessible with many tour operators based in Bocas del Toro Town (see page 331). The magical Cayos Zapatillas are within the park's boundaries (see below).

Isla Solarte

Isla Solarte, also known as Nancy Cay, is a quiet, verdant island inhabited by a small community of Ngöble-Buglé fishermen and a handful of wealthy foreigners. At its westernmost tip lies Hospital point, named after the old United Fruit Company medical facilities, now decommissioned and removed to Almirante on the mainland. A local historian, Clyde Stephens, owns the plot where it once stood. There are a couple of walking trails that snake Isla Solarte's length, and the surrounding waters are sheltered and particularly good for snorkelling.

Isla del Cisne

Opposite Boca del Drago is a small island and wildlife sanctuary, Isla del Cisne (or Swan Cay), home to large populations of seabirds, including frigates and boobies. You'll need to join a tour or a hire a boat to get up close. As there's a risk of disturbing the nests and other important elements of the habitat, you'll need ANAM permission to go ashore. You should definitely be accompanied by a qualified naturalist if you choose to do so.

Cayos Zapatillas

The Cayos Zapatillas comprise two small islands protected by the Parque Nacional Marino Isla Bastimentos. The snorkelling and diving around these two islands is widely regarded as the best in the archipelago, with coral reefs, dolphins and diverse fish species. Their white-sand shores are an important turtle-nesting site and the westernmost island is home to an easy walking trail. You must pay the ranger US$10 to land; access to the islands is only during the calm months of March, April, September and October.

Isla Popa and Cayo Agua

Isla Popa is one of the largest islands in the archipelago and home to two rustic Ngöble-Buglé fishing communities: Popa 1 and Popa 2. Few tourists make it out here, but if you do, you'll be able to encounter Ngöble-Buglé culture firsthand, purchase attractive handicrafts or hunt out the legendary blue frogs that are unique to the island. Cayo Agua lies just beyond Isla Popa, also very remote and home to interesting communities.

Isla San Cristóbal

Mostly stripped of its tropical forests, Isla San Cristóbal is a home to a sizeable Ngöble-Buglé fishing and farming community. Its southeastern shores embrace Laguna Bocatorito or Dolphin Bay, a bottlenose dolphin breeding ground that's very popular with tourists. June to September are the best months to observe the clever creatures, who often enjoy splashing and frolicking near the surface. It's not a good idea to go diving with them – the bubbles from the regulator tend to freak them out.

Bocas del Toro listings

For Sleeping and Eating price codes, and other relevant information, see pages 43-46.

Sleeping

Changuinola *p318*

C Alhambra, on the main street (Calle 17 de Abril), T758-9819. Large rooms, hot water, TV, a/c and telephone.

C Semiramis, diagonally opposite the **Alhambra**, T758-6006. Dark rooms with outstandingly kitsch pictures, a/c and TV. The restaurant serves Chinese plus standard Panamanian food.

D Taliali, 150 m from bus station, set back from Calle 17 de Abril. Simple quarters with a/c, TV and hot water.

D-E Carol, T758-8731, 200 m from bus station. Small dark rooms with bath, hot water, TV and a/c (cheaper rooms without), The restaurant next door is under the same ownership.

Almirante and the Banana Coast *p319*

D-E San Francisco, Almirante. Small dark rooms with a/c or fan. Overpriced.

E Albergue Bahía, Almirante, T778-9211. Clean lodgings. Friendly owner will store belongings.

South to Chiriquí Province *p319*

For nature lovers and those looking for a fantastic location, the **Cloudforest Jungle Lodge** can be found just inside the Fortuna Forest Reserve.

B Finca La Suiza, southern side of the Fortuna Reserve, Quadrifoglio, T6615-3774 (in David), www.panama.net.tc. From Gualaca, pass the sign to Los Planes (16.4 km) and the turning to Chiriquicito; 300 m after this junction is the sign for the Fortuna Reserve, 1 km beyond the sign is the gate to the finca on the right. Owned by a Swiss couple, Herbert Brüllmann and Monika Kohler, excellent for birdwatching on 20 km of forest trails, very good food, comfortable accommodation with bath and hot water, breakfast US$5, dinner US$14.50.

D Pensión Emperador, Chiriquí Grande, T757-9656. With balconies overlooking the wharf. Clean and friendly.

Isla Colón *p322, map p323*

LL Punta Caracol, western side of the island, T757-9410, www.puntacaracol.com. Located in a secluded enclave on the western side of the island, **Punta Caracol** is an exclusive and famous eco-resort consisting of a string of thatched luxury bungalows arcing over the water on their own private pier. The most expensive lodgings in the area, first-class and very attentive.

LL-L Bocas del Toro, Calle 2 y Av C, T/F757-9018, www.hotelbocasdeltoro.com. This attractive wooden hotel on the seafront has large clean rooms, some with excellent sea views. There's a good restaurant downstairs, kayak rental and Wi-Fi. The rooms are very comfortable and well-equipped with flat screen TVs, a/c and coffee-makers.

LL-L El Limbo, on the front street next to **Bocas del Toro**, T757-9062, www.ellimbo. com. This hotel has a great location overlooking the channel between Isla Colón and Caranero. The business-like rooms have nice wooden floors and walls, a/c, TV and fridge. Those with balconies and sea views are better, and more expensive. The restaurant is good but pricey. They also have a place on Isla Bastamientos (**AL**).

L-B La Estrella de Bocas, Calle 1, T757-9011, www.bocas.com/estrella.htm. Big apartment complex with a range of options including standard rooms (**B**), small apartments (**A**) and luxury apartments with sea views, fully equipped kitchen, a/c, cable TV and private bath (**L**). There's an exclusive bar and restaurant upstairs, for guests only.

AL Bahía, south end of main street, Bocas del Toro, T757-9626, www.hotelbahia.biz. Built in 1905, this interesting historic building was the former HQ of the **United Fruit Company**. All rooms have hot water, TV and a/c. The remodelled rooms with balcony are more expensive. Laundry service available and restaurant in front. Helpful.

AL Bocas Inn Lodge, north end of Main St, Bocas, T757-9600, bocasinn@ancon expeditions.com. Run by tour operator **Ancon Expeditions** (see page 377). Comfortable and simple with pleasant, spacious bar and terrace, communal veranda upstairs and platform for swimming. The water is heated with solar panels. Crab and lobster off the menu due to overfishing concerns. Prices include breakfast. Good reviews.

AL Cocomo-on-the-Sea, Av Norte y Calle 6, Bocas del Toro, T/F757-9259, www.coco moonthesea.com. A lovely place on the seafront with a lush garden, sundeck and 4 clean, simple rooms with a/c and private bathroom. A huge breakfast is included, home-cooked meals available, book swap and free use of kayaks. US owner Douglas is very helpful. Recommended.

AL Swan's Cay, opposite the municipal building on main street, Bocas del Toro, T757-9090, www.swanscayhotel.com. A smart, upmarket hotel on the seafront with an elegant lobby, 2 pools, 2 restaurants, Wi-Fi and comfortable rooms with hot water, a/c, cable TV and the usual amenities. Perhaps not quite as luxurious as it would like to be.

A Cala Luna, behind **Alberto's Restaurant**, Calle 5 and Av E, Bocas del Toro, T757-9066, www.calalunabocas.com. A hidden gem in the backstreets. Rooms are spacious with a very appealing, sparse, almost Japanese style. Same owners as **Alberto's**.

A Hotelito del Mar, Calle 1, T757-9861, www.hotelitodelmar.com. Rooms here are sparklingly clean and adorned with lovely vibrant art work. They all have private bath, hot water and a/c. Tourist information is available and tours by arrangement. The owner is friendly. Good central location.

A Lula's B&B, Av Norte, across street from **Cocomo-on-the-Sea**, T757-9057, www.lulabb.com. Old style, family-run place with a huge kitchen and living area downstairs. This is the base of operations for Bocas Surf School. All rooms come with a/c,

private bath and hot water; Wi-Fi and full breakfast are included. Owners Bryan and Jana Hudson are friendly and helpful. Homely, clean and recommended.

A-B Laguna, on main street with Av D, T757-9091, hlaguna@cwp.net.pa. This centrally located 3-star hotel has 17 attractive wooden rooms with a/c, hot water, cable TV and orthopaedic mattresses. There's a breakfast terrace and bar downstairs.

A-B Los Delfines, Av G y Calle 5, Bocas del Toro, T/F757-9963, www.bocasdelfines.com. A big, blue Caribbean clap-board house with clean, reasonably sized rooms with cable TV, Wi-Fi, hot water and a/c.

A-B Punta Manglar (formerly **Mangrove Point**), T/F757-9541. Set among the mangroves and accessible by boat, this hotel has cabins sleeping 2-8 persons. They also offer PADI courses up to dive master and fun dives.

A-B La Veranda, Calle 7y Av G, T757-9211, laverandapanama.tripod.com. Beautiful wooden, original Bocas-style house with history. Rooms come with private (**A**) or shared bath (**B**). Large veranda on 1st floor has a communal kitchen and an area to eat or relax. The pricing system is slightly confusing.

A-E Hotel La Rumba, 1.5 km out of town at Big Creek, T757-9961, www.hotellarumba. com. Rooms of varying sizes and facilities in a round, thatched hotel, with restaurant and bar overlooking the sea. Games, happy hours and satellite showing sport. Dorms are available and ocean-view rooms cost more.

B Las Brisas, on the sea at north end of the main street, Bocas del Toro, T/F757-9549, www.brisasbocas.com. Marketed as a surf 'n' sports lodge, this wooden building on stilts has a nice veranda over the sea. All rooms have a/c and private bath, although those upstairs have thin walls. Outdoor activities are offered, including surfing, snorkelling and cycling. Friendly and English-speaking.

B Casa Amarilla, Calle 5 y Av G, T757-9938, www.casaamarilla.org. 4 large airy rooms with good beds, a/c, fridge, digital safe and large cable TVs. Owner Dennis Fischer lives upstairs and is a very sound fellow – helpful and interesting to chat to. Fruit breakfast in the morning, free coffee and tea all day. Good value and highly recommended. Space is limited, so book in advance.

B Dos Palmas, Av Sur y Calle 6, Bocas, T757-9906, dospalmas@bocasmail.com. A quaint hotel with lots of local charm. Clean rooms have hot water and a/c, cheaper with fan. Built over the water with a swim off platform at back. Free coffee before midday.

B Hotel Olas de la Madrugada, Av Sur, T757-9930, www.hotelolas.com. New and already popular hotel built over the water. Clean and bright rooms, all with a/c, cable TV and private hot water shower. Friendly owners are opening a bar and restaurant, they also have jet-ski and wakeboard rental. Wi-Fi and breakfast included.

C Del Parque, seaward side of square, Bocas del Toro, T757-9008, delparque35@hotmail. com. Well-kept old town house with light rooms and good beds, hot water, free coffee and fruit. Discounts in low season, can help arrange tours.

C Hotel Cayos Zapatillas, on the High St, odd-looking building overlooking the park. Very reasonably priced for the central location. Rooms have private hot water shower and cable TV. Simple and economical.

D Sagitarius, 1 block from main street on Calle 4, Bocas del Toro, T757-9578. Simple rooms with hot water, bath, a/c, cheaper with fan, TV. Clean and good.

D-E Heike, on main square, Bocas del Toro, T757- 9708, www.bocas.com/heike.htm. A friendly, inexpensive backpackers' hostel with rooms (**D**), dorms (**E**), shared bathrooms, kitchen, communal veranda and a cosy sun terrace complete with hammocks and sofas. Surfboards are available for rent, free use of the guitars, filtered water and pancake breakfast included. Recommended.

E Mondo Taitu, Bocas del Toro, T757-9425, mondotaituhostel@yahoo.com. Buzzing party hostel that's popular with surfers and backpackers. A good place to meet other travellers, hang out and get groups for trips. The bar is busy (and noisy) in the evenings,

happy hour 1900-2000. Amenities include kitchen, bikes (including tandems!), guitars, surf boards, free coffee and tea, and a pancake breakfast. 'Tree house rooms' and dorms available. Friendly.

Isla Caranero p324

LL-AL Buccaneer Resort, east side, T/F757-9042, www.bocasbuccaneer.com. A range of high-end suites and attractive cabañas on the beach, all with a/c. Breakfast included.

LL-AL Careening Cay Resort, north side of the island, T757-9157, www.careeningcay. com. Very attractive wooden cabañas in a tranquil, well-manicured location, some are equipped with stove, microwave and fridge, all have a/c, TV, DVD and bath. The family suite is particularly good, with a 10-person capacity, sofas, kitchen, loft and hammocks. Their restaurant, the **Cosmic Crab Café**, is excellent, and the *artesanía* store has some interesting international crafts. There are also plans for a butterfly garden. Recommended.

AL Acuario, T757-9565, www.bocas.com/ casa-acuario.htm. An attractive clapboard house, nicely situated on a pontoon over the water. Rooms come with direct TV, a/c and balconies. There is also a kitchen and bar. American owned.

AL Doña Mara, T757-9551, www.donamara. com. Located by a small white-sand beach, this comfortable hotel offers 7 clean, quiet rooms with hot water, a/c and cable TV. Prices include breakfast. The attached restaurant does very good Caribbean seafood, good music, and happy hour 1600-1900. Prices drop by US$20-30 in low season.

AL Hotel Tierra Verde, T757-9903, www.hotel tierraverde.com. A well-maintained hotel situated among the palms, a stone's throw from the shore. Rooms have private showers, hot water and Wi-Fi. Those with ocean-view cost more. Continental breakfast included. Comfortable and friendly.

E Aqua Lounge Hostel and Bar, T6734-2550, bocasqualounge@yahoo.com. A very cool party hostel that flies in DJs for the famous Wed and Sat night parties. There's a chill-out terrace on the water, swimming area, hammocks, restaurant, kitchen, bar, water trampoline and internet. Lodgings consist of large dorms and prices include buffet breakfast. Happy hour 1000-1900.

Isla Bastimentos *p324*
LL Al Natural, Old Point, T/F757-9004, www.alnaturalresort.com. Belgian-owned eco-lodge bungalows using traditional techniques and native fallen trees; electricity is provided by solar power. Bungalows consist of 3 walls, leaving 1 side open and exposed to a spectacular view of the ocean and Zapatillas in the distance – a truly natural experience. Price includes transport from Isla Colón, 3 lovingly prepared meals with wine, use of kayaks and snorkelling gear. Email reservations in advance. Highly recommended.
LL Eclypse del Mar, offshore, near Bastimentos town, T6611-4581, www.eclypse demar.com. Attractive 'Acqua-Lodge' in the same vein as the famous **Punta Caracol**. Secluded bungalows built over the water, all ully equipped and with stunning sunset views.
AL Coral Cay, east of Isla Bastimentos, T6626-1919, www.bocas.com/coralcay.htm. Peaceful, rustic cabins built over the water. Beautiful surroundings and outstanding seafood. Price includes 2 meals per day, snorkelling equipment and the use of a traditional dugout canoe. Watch out for the sandflies.
A Caribbean View Hotel, Bastimentos Town, T757-9442, hotelcaribbeanview@yahoo.com. Wooden, traditional-style hotel, with lovely local owners, upmarket for rustic Bastimentos Town. Rooms available with a/c or fan, all have private shower, hot water and TV. Wi-Fi, kayaks, boat and cave tours also available. There is a communal deck over the water.
A El Limbo, T757-9062, www.ellimbo.com. Close to the national park with a handsome beach-front location. Rooms are clean and comfortable. They offer a good mix of activities. However, it's a little pricey for the package.
C-D Hostel Bastimentos, Bastimentos Town, T757-9053. An elevated position overlooking the town, islands and surrounding waters.

Attractive budget accommodation, with shared dorms and private rooms with showers, communal kitchen and TV. Friendly owners.
D Pensión Tío Tom, Bastimentos Town, T757-9831, www.tio-tom.com. This rustic, budget accommodation on the water has rooms with mosquito nets and private bath. Chilled vibe, friendly and helpful owners who also run the internet café a couple of doors down. Lots of personality. Recommended.
D-E Yellow Jack, Bastimentos Town, T6753-2954, viajeros81@yahoo.com. A small, new hostel with dorms (**E**), private rooms (**D**) and a chilled out communal area built over the water. You can also rent a house/ apartment for US$400 /month or US$150/week. The friendly Argentine owner, Manu, is an experienced dive instructor and offers PADI training, snorkelling, diving and fishing tours. He'll also sell you delicious fresh fish to cook up in the shared kitchen. Very friendly, tranquil and highly recommended.

Isla Solarte *p325*
AL Solarte del Caribe, T6593-2245, www.solarteinn.com. B&B on the southern side of the island. Comfortable beds, colourful, tropical surroundings and good food. Breakfast and roundtrip transport included.

❼ Eating

Isla Colón *p322, map p323*
Note that local lobster and crab populations are dwindling due to tourist demand.
♈♈♈ 90 Degree, Calle 1, inside the Tropical Market. Upmarket restaurant that might appeal to moneyed urban types. Creative dishes include prawn penne and Indonesian pork tenderloin. Smart, sophisticated and overlooking the water.
♈♈♈ La Ballena, next to **Swan Cay Hotel**, Bocas del Toro. Delicious Italian seafood pastas and cappuccinos, good for breakfast with tables outside. A bit pricey though.
♈♈♈-♈♈ El Pecado, on southwest corner of parque, Bocas del Toro. Panamanian and

international food including Lebanese. One of the best restaurants in town, and not too expensive. Great drinks and good wines worth splashing out on, also try their early evening hummous with warm Johnny Cakes (coconut bread). Highly recommended.

♛ **Alberto's Restaurant**, Calle 5, Bocas del Toro. Authentic Italian cuisine including great pizza, pasta and lasagne. There's also BBQ meat and fish. Wine is served. Reasonable prices.

♛ **Bar y Restaurante The Pirate**, Calle 3, next to **El Limbo Hotel**, Bocas del Toro. Long-standing wooden restaurant built over the water. They serve good seafood, breakfasts, smoothies and wine. There's also a full bar and happy hour.

♛ **Bongos**, Main St. Slightly overpriced American-style food including hot dogs and burgers. Plastic seats and a cheery gringo crowd, but nothing special. Occasional live music, shut Mon.

♛ **Buena Vista Bar and Grill**, Bocas. Long-standing restaurant-bar run by a very friendly Panamanian and his American girlfriend. Good menu for both bar snacks and main meals, grills, tacos, fish and veggie options. Nice spot over the water to relax and chat with a beer or cocktail.

♛ **Lemongrass**, Calle 2, next to **Buena Vista**, upstairs. Owner here has experience of cooking in Asia so expect good, authentic Thai curries and lots of seafood. Good views over the bay and excellent bar for cocktails.

♛ **The Reef**, end of Main St, opposite **Super Gourmet**. Big wooden structure with a terrace over the water. They serve local food, seafood specials and cocktails. Popular with Panamanians.

♛ **Restaurant Claudios**, at **Hotel Laguna**, opposite the park in Main St. Reasonably priced, good Italian food, pizzas and home-made pastas. Big breakfast menu.

♛ **Shelly's BBQ Mexican Food**, behind **Claudios**, T757-9779. First Mexican eatery in Bocas, with enchiladas, mole, guacamole and barbecued meats. They also do home delivery (plus taxi cost) and sell a range of frozen specials in Bocas's **Super Gourmet** store.

♛♛ **Trinacria de Sicilia**, Av D, between Calle 1 and 3. Really excellent, authentic Italian pizzas with delicious wafer-thin crusts. Recommended.

♛♛-♛ **Lily's Café**, next to **Tropical Suites Hotel**. Chilled out and friendly café on the water serving Caribbean cuisine with a health food twist. A good range of breakfasts and mains, including pastas, soups, salads and sandwiches. Open for breakfast and lunch only.

♛ **El Lorito Don Chicho**, Main St. Most popular – and oldest – local café in town, serving cheap, good dishes and cakes. Ask for the delicious pudding – unique to Bocas – and their malted milkshakes.

♛ **Kun Jah**, close to **Hotel Limbo**. Chinese food in vast, cheap and greasy portions. Probably quite tasty – if you're drunk, starving or on a budget. They have a relaxing terrace on the water. Only just OK.

♛ **McDouglas Golden Grill**, opposite the park, Main St. The fast-food emporium of Bocas – cheap burgers, chips and hot dogs. Also pizzas with loads of cheese, and breakfast eggs and pancakes – good for those on a budget, but not on a diet.

♛ **Om Café**, now located over **Flow Surf Shop**, close to **La Ballena**. Closed Wed. Excellent, home-made Indian food served in very relaxing and ambient surroundings. Tables are available on the balcony or private rooms for larger parties. **Om** also serves good breakfasts with home-made granola and yoghurt, lassis, fruit salads and bagels. Recommended.

♛ **Restaurant Chitre**, Main St. The best *fonda* in town. Nice owners, and a good spot for watching street traffic.

Cafés and bakeries

Panadería Dulcería Alemana, Calle 2. This small bakery does cakes, bread, coffee and economical breakfasts.

Starfish Coffee, Calle 3, just before **Bocas Water Sports**, Bocas del Toro. Cappuccino, pastries, croissants and brownies. Excellent breakfast deals at reasonable prices. Owner offers yoga classes in the morning and tours of their environmentally friendly coffee plantation on the mainland on request.

Super Gourmet, Calle 1, near the ferry for Almirante. Deli and gourmet supermarket that does very good, if pricey, sandwiches, pastas and salads. You'll also find some locally produced chocolate on sale here – very tasty.

Isla Caranero *p324*

¶¶¶-¶¶ **Cosmic Crab Café**, north side of the island, facing Isla Colón. Managed by a friendly American couple, Joan and Steve, who offer a very creative menu with diverse international influences including Greek, Thai, Indian and Caribbean. Dishes include seafood lasagne, baby back ribs in mango chutney sauce, seafood bisque and Key Lime pie. Their cocktails and fresh fruit smoothies are exceptional, and they have an entire menu devoted just to Martinis. Highly recommended.
¶¶ **The Pickled Parrot**, facing Isla Basti-mentos. Draft beers and American BBQs, with a daily happy hour 1500-1700. Lovely at sunset.
¶¶ **Restaurant Doña Mara**, facing Isla Colón. Excellent Caribbean seafood including octopus, shrimp and conch meat. The house speciality is Caribbean whole fish. Good music and happy hour 1600-1900. They also do typical Panamanian food.

Isla Bastimentos *p324*

¶ **Red Rooster**, Bastimentos Town. A wooden restaurant over the water serving breakfast, lunches and dinners. There are veggie options, including lasagne and falafel. Closed Sun.
¶ **Roots**, Bastimentos Town. Bar and restaurant with a nice terrace, run by Oscar who will also guide tourists to the lake in the middle of the island. It hasn't been open for a while, but no indication it's closed for good.

⊕ Entertainment

Isla Colón *p322, map p323*
Barco Hundido, Calle 1, next to Cable & Wireless office, Bocas del Toro. Thatched-roof watering hole, affectionately known as the **Wreck Deck** (its original name) built over the water and above a wrecked, sunken boat.

Lights illuminate the boat at night making it a perfect spot to watch the local marine life and the thumping local nightlife. The place to hang out; dancing, Caribbean scene, mixed drinks, 3 dance floors, good music and on occasion – at the owners whim – 'pizza and movie night'.
El Encanto, Main St, Bocas del Toro. The only truly local spot. Salsa is played at volume and there is a pool hall. An interesting change from the gringo haunts.
Iguana Bar, Bocas del Toro. New, smart establishment with surf videos, gringos and good music. Another pre-**Barco** spot.
Lemongrass, Calle 2, next to **Buena Vista**, upstairs, Bocas del Toro. Excellent bar for cocktails and moonlit views over the bay. Occasionally hosts live music.
Mondo Taitu, at the north end of Bocas, T757-9425. Relaxed and often buzzing bar in a backpackers' hostel. Good for beer and cocktails and for warming up for the **Barco Hundido**.

Isla Caranero *p324*
Aqua Lounge, 2 min from Bocas. An estimated 350 people turn up here for the famous parties on Wed and Sat nights. DJs are flown in from Panama City and Costa Rica, and free drinks are supplied for ladies. Happy hour runs 1000-1900, giving you plenty of warm-up time. There's an entertaining water trampoline that attracts drunken revellers.

Isla Bastimentos *p324*
Every Mon anyone who wants to party heads over to Isla Bastimentos for **Blue Mondays**, a largely local event with live Calypso music and the full Caribbean vibe. Hugely popular.

▲ Activities and tours

Isla Colón *p322, map p323*
Diving and snorkelling
Bocas Watersports, Main St, T757-9541, www.bocaswatersports.com. Dive courses, waterskiing and kayak rental. Local 2-tank dives cost US$50, with longer 2-tank trips to

Tiger Rock and the Zapatilla Cayes running at around US$75. Snorkelling gear costs US$5 a day. They offer a day-long snorkelling tour to Dolphin Bay, Crawl Cay, Red Frog and Hospital Point, snacks included, US$20. Training from Open Water Diver to Dive Master.

La Buga Dive Center, Barrio Sur, next to the **El Ultimo Refugio** restaurant, T757-9534, www.labugapanama.com. This is a new outfit. They offer training from Open Water Diver, US$245, to Dive Master. Specialities include Deep Diver, Night Diver and Underwater Naturalist. They claim to have the biggest, fastest boat in the area, and know special dive sites their competitors don't.

Starfleet, near tourist office, T/F757-9630, www.starfleetscuba.com. A very professional, PADI Gold Palm 5-star dive centre, managed by Tony Sanders from England. They offer training from Open Water Diver, US$250, right up to Instructor level. A 2-tank dive is US$60, a day-long snorkel tour, US$20. They have over 14 years' experience in Bocas waters. Safe, with good instructors and equipment. Recommended.

Surfing
You can rent boards from a small shop next to **The Yellow House** or in **Mondo Taitu**. There are 2 surf shops in town, **Tropix**, on Main St (T757-9415) who make custom boards and **Flow**, located under **Om Café**. **Bocas Surf School** operates from Lula's B&B, Av H, T6482-4166, www.bocassurfschool.com.

Tour operators
There are now numerous tour operators, most have maps and pictures of the surrounding islands to help plan your own day if you have a big enough group. Usual tours visit either Dolphin Bay, Hospital Point, Coral Cay and Red Frog Beach (Bastimentos), or Boca del Drago and Swans Cay (Bird Island). For a little extra you can add Cayos Zapatilla to the first tour.

Cap'n Don's, T6487-8460. Private boat rental, windsurfing equipment, kayaks, hobie cats, pedal boats and snorkelling.

Catamaran Sailing Adventures, 3rd St, beside Almacén Rosa Blanca, T757-9710 or T6464-4242, www.bocassailing.com. Owner Marcel offers popular day sailing tours on his 12-m catamaran around the Bocas Islands for US$40, including lunch and snorkelling gear. Very knowledgeable when it comes to finding the best reef areas – you can also hire the whole boat for an overnight trip for US$350 and do a customized trip. Trips leave daily, but you will need advance reservation. Environmentally aware and recommended.

J&J Transparente Tours, main st beside **The Pirate**, T757-9915, transparentetours@ hotmail.com. Boat tours of the islands and major sights, including Laguna Bocatorito, Coral Cay, Zapatillas, Red Frog Beach and Hospital Point.

⊖ Transport

Changuinola *p318*
Air To **Bocas del Toro**, with **Aeroperlas**, Mon-Fri 0805, 1000, 1640; Sat 0950, 1650; and Sun 0815, 1650, 10 mins, US$37. Fares and schedules subject to change.

Boat If you're coming from or going to Costa Rica, the best route between Bocas del Toro and the mainland is a fast water taxi along the historic Snyder Canal – a 15-km canal built in the late 1800s to transport bananas from Changuinola to awaiting ships in the open sea. Today, it's a great way to zip through the narrow canals at speed. **Bocas Marine Tours**, T758-9859, Calle 3 next to The Pirate, offer 7 daily services between **Bocas and Changuinola**, 0830-1730, US$7 each way.

Bus To **Almirante**, every 30 mins till 2000, 30 mins, US$1.50. To **San José** 1 daily, 1000 (no office, pay on bus) US$10, 6-7 hrs, 1 stop for refreshments in Limón, but many police checks (note this bus may not always run). You can also cross the border and catch a more regular service from **Sixaola** to Limón and then onto San José. Bus to **David**, 4 hrs, US$7.

Train The banana railways provide links between **Guabito** on the Costa Rican border,

Changuinola and **Almirante**. There are no passenger trains, and banana trains are incredibly slow, although passage can be negotiated with officials. Schedules and fares should be checked with the **Chiriquí Land Company**, Almirante T758-3215. Should leave for border every day.

Almirante and the Banana Coast *p319*
Boat Water taxi from Almirante to **Bocas** US$3. To get to the muelle from the bus station, cross over railway line, bear left following far side of fence across scrub land to road, head left along road 2 blocks to the quay.
Bus To **David**, every 40 mins, 4 hrs, US$7; **Changuinola**, every 30 mins, 30 mins, US$1.50
Car The road between Chiriquí Grande and Almirante is in excellent condition for the 74-km length of the new road.

Isla Colón *p322, map p323*
Air Bocas del Toro can be reached with **Aeroperlas** or **Air Panama** twice daily from Albrook Airport, US$103 one-way. To **David** Mon, Wed and Fri, US$65; to Changuinola, twice daily, US$37. **Nature Air** (Costa Rica, www.nature air.com) now operate flights between Bocas del Toro and San José; Costa Rica, US$140 one-way. Call **Bocas International Airport** for details, T757-9841.
Boat From Isla Colón to the other islands, including **Caranero**, **Bastimentos** and **Solarte**, water taxis depart from various points along the waterfront – ask around The Pirate, Taxi 25, near IPAT or the dock for Bocas Marine Tours. Fares are US$1-3 one-way, and always rising with the cost of petrol. From Caranero or Bastimentos Town it's easy to flag down a passing boat. If you're going to remote beaches, don't forget to arrange a time to be picked up. If hiring a boat, try to arrange it the day before, at least US$60 per day, depending on the boatman (4 hrs minimum, can take 9 people or more, depending on boat size).
To **Almirante**, water taxis run daily 0530-1830, 30 mins, US$3. *Palanga*, the

car ferry, runs between **Almirante** and Bocas every day, leaving at 0900 and returning from Bocas at 1200. US$15 per car (more for large vehicles), US$1 for foot passengers. To **Changuinola**, 7 daily services with **Bocas Marine Tours**, 0700-1730, US$7 one-way.
If going to Costa Rica, catch the 0700 departure for early connections at Sixaola, see page 337. A bus leaves Changuinola direct for **San José** at 1000. However, if you are simply going to **Puerto Viejo** or **Cahuita**, you can leave any time before lunch.

❸ Directory

Changuinola *p318*
Banks Bancistmo Mon-Fri 0800-1500, Sat 0900-1200, changes AMEX Tcs. Cash advances on Visa and MasterCard. **Immigration** Oficina de Migración, renewal of visas and tourist cards.

Isla Colón *p322, map p323*
Banks Banco Nacional de Panamá, Calle 4 and Av E, T757-5948, Mon-Fri 0800-1500, Sat 0900-1200, 24-hr ATM machine. **Immigration** Migración office, at the back of the Palacio, is for visitors arriving by air or boat. Official waits at the airport to stamp passports of those arriving nationals covered by the '*convenio*' and to provide tourist cards for others (eg US citizens arriving from Costa Rica). Those requiring visas must go to the **Banco Nacional** to purchase the relevant documentation (US$10) and then go to the office in the Palacio. This office does not renew tourist cards or visas. **Internet** Bocas Internet Café, next to the M/S Isla Colón Supermarket on Main St, US$2 per hr; **Don Chicho's Internet**, next to **El Lorito** restaurant, US$2 per hr. **Bravo Centre** is fast and has an international call centre US$2 per hr. **Laundry** Lavamático, on the right, just beyond **Hostal Ancón** at north end of town, US$3 per load, pick up following day.

Chiriquí

South of Bocas del Toro, the land rises sharply as it enters Chiriquí Province and the Cordillera de Talamanca – a spine of rugged, alpine-like mountains that reaches west into Costa Rica and east into the cordillera central. Extraordinary cloudforests flourish at this sublime elevation, home to diverse bird and mammal species, delicate mosses, orchids and a host of ethereal plant life. But the land is fertile as it is entrancing. Beyond the wilderness of fog-drenched peaks, rich volcanic soil supports a scattering of diminutive farming communities, highland fincas and crops of coffee, cold vegetables, strawberries and citrus fruit. The mingling of Atlantic and Pacific winds in the Chiriquí Highlands which creates the so-called bajareque *(literally 'falling down'), the fine mist that shrouds the area, has also drawn large numbers of North American retirees, who find the cool climate, agreeable scenery and low cost of living an irresistible combination. Fortunately, the region's rugged topography has help to soften the impact of foreign developments.*

This is the place for great outdoor adventures, where you can hike between flower-festooned villages, bike through the hills or brave ferocious whitewater rapids. But descend into the steamy lowlands and you'll find yet more diversions: remote wind-swept beaches, dazzling coral reefs and utterly unspoilt islands. Chiriquí has it all, just as its inhabitants like to boast.

Most international activity is concentrated in Boquete, an agreeable mountain town that's home to a sizeable expat community. Less-visited settlements lie to the west of Boquete, including Volcán and Cerro Punta, which offer access to the Parque Internacional Amistad and a host of other natural attractions. The lowland areas of Chiriquí are somewhat sweltering year round. David is the provincial capital, a largely uninteresting but not unpleasant city. Beyond it lies several remote locales, including the Parque Nacional Marino Golfo de Chiriquí. ➤➤ *For listings, see pages 343-350.*

David and the Lowlands ⊕⊘⊛▲⊙⊙ ➤➤ *pp343-350.*

David, capital of Chiriquí Province, is Panama's second city. It is hot and humid, rich in timber, coffee, cacao, sugar, rice, bananas and cattle. Founded in colonial times as San José de David, it has managed to keep its traditions intact while modernizing itself. The attractive city is safe and friendly and a gateway to the Chiriquí Highlands and the Caribbean province of Bocas del Toro. With a wide selection of hotels and restaurants, it is a good place to break the trip from Costa Rica, rest, resupply and become acquainted with Panama and its people.

Ins and outs

David presents a significant navigational challenge to the visitor: it is perfectly flat with no prominent landmarks, the central plaza is not central, there are few street signs, some streets have two names and the locals use neither, preferring nostalgic points of reference (eg across the street from where the old oak used to be) to genuinely useful guidance. City bus routes are circuitous and generate additional confusion. When you get hopelessly lost take a taxi – for US$1 it's not such a bad idea. The **IPAT tourist office** ⓘ *Calle Central, between Av 5 Este and Av 6 Este, T775-4120, Mon-Fri, 0730-1530,* is friendly enough, but they don't have a wealth of information.

Sights

The city of Davis focuses on the fine central plaza, **Parque Cervantes**, which teems with birds in the early morning, providing good birdwatching from the balconies of the Hotel

Occidental or Iris. The colonial-style **Iglesia de San José** is on the west side of the park. The bell tower in Barrio Bolívar was built separately as a defence against tribal attacks. The Palacio Municipal is opposite Hotel Nacional on Avenida and Calle Central. The **Museo José de Obaldía** ① *Av 8 Este 5067 y Calle A, Norte, 4 blocks from plaza, Mon-Sat 0830-1630, US$0.25*, is a museum of history and art in the house of the founder of Chiriquí Province.

A few kilometres north of David on the Boquete road is **Balneario Majagua**, where you can swim in a river under a waterfall (cold drinks for sale). There is another bathing place on the right 10 km further on. Take a Dolega or Boquete bus and ask the driver to drop you off. About 2 km along the main road to the border is the **Carta Vieja rum factory** ① *Mon-Fri 0800-1600*, offering free tours and something to take away with you. Also heading towards the Costa Rican border, a dirt road turns to the left to **Las Palmas**, a pleasant orange-growing village which welcomes tourists. Just before the village is a **waterfall** where a single column of water falls into a pool, delightful for swimming and camping. Ask directions in David.

About 10 km east of David is the small town of **Chiriquí**. A paved road through Gualaca leads north to the mountains and over the divide to Chiriquí Grande (see page 319).

David

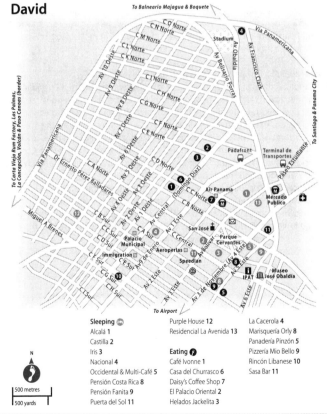

Sleeping 🛏
Alcalá **1**
Castilla **2**
Iris **3**
Nacional **4**
Occidental & Multi-Café **5**
Pensión Costa Rica **8**
Pensión Fanita **9**
Puerta del Sol **11**

Purple House **12**
Residencial La Avenida **13**

Eating 🍴
Café Ivonne **1**
Casa del Churrasco **6**
Daisy's Coffee Shop **7**
El Palacio Oriental **2**
Helados Jackelita **3**

La Cacerola **4**
Marisquería Orly **8**
Panadería Pinzón **5**
Pizzería Mio Bello **9**
Rincón Libanese **10**
Sasa Bar **11**

Chiriquí Lowlands

You'll find the black-sand beaches of **Playa Barqueta**, 30 minutes west of David, good for surfing and home to a burgeoning development project. This is also the site of the **Refugio de Vida Silvestre de Playa La Barqueta**, a turtle-nesting site that's close to the resort of **Las Olas**. To reach Playa Barqueta from David, head west along the Interamericana then south along the turning to Alanje.

East of David, the Interamericana advances through the lowlands, flanking the Pacific Coast and several turn-offs to some remote and lesser visited locales. The **Parque Nacional Marino Golfo de Chiriquí** is a protected area of coral reefs, islands and mangrove swamps. To get there, travel 38 km east on the highway and take the turning to Horconcitos. Travel down the peninsula all the way to **Boca Chica**, a small fishing village with access to the national park and the verdant island of **Boca Brava**, good for birding. Frequent bus services run to Horconcitos, but services to Boca Chica are less frequent, so you should allow a lot of time to get here and be prepared to hitch, spend the night or take a taxi. Many sports fishers are drawn to this area and there are a handful of hotels, including some expensive options. Back on the Interamericana, 70 km east of David, lies the Pacific beaches of **Las Lajas**. Facilities are limited with a couple of small, sparse restaurants, so remember to bring your own food and drink from town. Watch out for strong waves and sharks. To get there, take the southbound turn-off at San Félix, or take a morning bus from David to Las Lajas, US$4. From there it's a short taxi trip to the beach (taxis US$3).

Paso Canoas, La Concepción and the Costa Rican border

Paso Canoas is the principal point of entry for travellers coming from Costa Rica. It's a busy border town with many good eating places, especially open-front restaurants opposite Costa Rican Customs. Informally crossing back and forth between shops and business areas is easy, but travellers intending to leave one country for the other must submit to formalities before proceeding. At **Jacú**, east of Paso Canoas, there is a secondary check-point, where most often only cars and buses coming from Costa Rica are checked. Have passport, tourist card, vehicle permit and driver's licence handy in case they are asked for (usually hassle free).

La Concepción lies roughly half-way between David and the border, 30 km east of Paso Canoas on the Interamericana. It is an important agricultural shipping point, also widely known for its handmade saddles. There are several decent hotels, but better can be found in Volcán, Cerro Punta or David. The **Fiesta de la Candelaria** is at the end of January. La Concepción is the gateway to the town of **Volcán**, see page 340, and the western section of the Chiriquí Highlands. From here you can travel to the much quieter border town of Río Sereno and cross the border into Costa Rica. Note that Río Sereno does not hand out Panamanian tourist cards, making it hard to enter Panama from here.

Boquete and the Eastern Highlands ⬤🚻🏨🏕️⛺🏧⛰️🌐 » pp343-350.

David to Boquete

Heading north towards Boquete in the heart of the cool Eastern Highlands, a well-paved road climbs gently from David, passing (after 10 km) a waterfall with a swimming hole, open-air restaurant/bar and space for wild camping. It passes through **Dolega** (swimming pool, one *pensión*, notable for its carnival four days before Ash Wednesday) before reaching (after 40 km) the popular mountain resort of Boquete.

Border essentials: Panama–Costa Rica

Paso Canoas → *See also page 161.*
Panamanian immigration Panamanian customs are open 24 hours; the Costa Rican side is open 0500-2100 Panama time. After checking in at Entrada, buy a tourist card from the IPAT tourist office around the corner of the building to the left. Return to Entrada for an entry stamp. All relatively quick and painless, unless an international bus has arrived just before you. Free maps of Panama available at IPAT.
Currency exchange Money changers will change colones into dollars at a good rate; the Banco Nacional de Panama cashes TCs and also has Visa ATM.
Sleeping Palace, basic but clean bathroom. There is a reasonable restaurant at the border. Greater choice, although n ot necessarily better, on the Costa Rican side.
Time Panama is one hour ahead.
Transport Buses to Panama City via La Concepción and David with Padafront, T775-8913, there are 11 daily every 1½-two hours, from terminal on northeast corner of main intersection. Fare to Panama City, US$14; express 2300, 2400, US$17. Regular buses run to David for US$1.50, 1½ hours.

Río Sereno → *See also page 342.*
Crossing to Costa Rica This is a minor international crossing post, recommended because the area is prettier and cooler than Paso Canoas (see above), but only for those using public transport. Private vehicles cannot complete formalities here, and Panamanian tourist cards are not available.
Panamanian immigration Immigration and customs are in the wooden police station visible on the hill north of the main Panamanian street. Departing travellers who have been in Panama for over 30 days should see Essentials for details on exit permits. Those entering Panama with a visa, or from countries which require neither visa nor tourist card, will be admitted; those requiring a tourist card or a visa will be directed to Paso Canoas.
Costa Rican immigration The office is in a new white building at Río Sereno, open 0800-1600 Costa Rican time, Sunday till 1400. Departing travellers who have overstayed their 90-day permit will be directed to Paso Canoas for the required tax payments and fines.
Transport There is a frequent bus service dawn to dusk from David to Río Sereno, three hours, via La Concepción, Volcán, Santa Clara; several minibuses daily Río Sereno-Paso Canoas, 2½ hours. On the Costa Rican side bus from San Vito via Sabalito to the border.

Boquete

At 1060 m in the valley of the Río Caldera, with the slopes of Volcán Barú to the west, Boquete is a beautiful panorama of coffee plantations and orange groves, strawberry fields and gardens. Good lodging and facilities make the town an excellent base for fishing, riding, river rafting and hiking in the area, see Activities and tours page 348. It is a slow-paced, predominantly wood-built town with several attractive landscaped parks, including the main plaza and the nearby **Parque de las Madres**.

The fairground east of the river is the site for the annual **Feria de las Flores y del Café**, usually held mid-January. In April, a **Feria de las Orquídeas** is held with many varieties of local and exotic orchids, as well as other flowers. The **cemetery** ① *Mon-Sat 0930-1300, 1400-1800*, is worth a visit, and there is a small museum of *huacas* (funerary sculptures) in the centre and a fine panoramic view from the 'Bienvenidos a Boquete' arch at the entrance to the town.

Boquete has gained international recognition as a producer of fine coffees and there are some excellent tours, see Activities and tours, page 349. **Coffee Adventures** run very comprehensive, informative 2½- to three-hour tours that cover everything from plant to production, harvesting to roasting to a tasting of the final product.

There is a **tourist office** (CEFATI) ① *T720-4060, daily 0900-1800*, at the entrance to town. Helpful staff provide information about the area and there is a café, shop and small museum upstairs.

Volcán Barú

The highest point in the country, Volcán Barú rises to an altitude of 3475 m and is reached easily from Boquete, 21 km to the east, and not so easily from Volcán to the west. The summit lies within the boundaries of **Parque Nacional Volcán Barú** which covers some 14,000 ha and borders the vast La Amistad International Park to the north, which itself spans the Panamanian-Costa Rican border covering much of the Cordillera Talamanca. Rainfall in the park ranges between 3000 and 4000 mm a year, and temperatures range from a subtropical 17°C to a distinctly chilly 7°C. Rich cloudforest makes ideal conditions for reptiles, amphibians and birds, with around 40 species endemic to the park.

From Boquete it is 21 km to the summit. The first 7 km is paved, sometimes lined with aromatic pines, goes through coffee groves, most numerous in the area during the year-end harvest season, mainly tended by Ngöbe-Buglé (Guaymí) people. The paved road ends at a small, usually unmanned, ANAM office, from where the track winds up from the office through tall,

Boquete

Sleeping 🛏
Cabañas Isla Verde 11
Fundadores 1
Hostal Boquete 2
Hostal Mozart 12
Hostal Nomba 13
Hostal Palacios 3
La Casa de Doña Cata 7
La Montaña y el Valle 10
Panamonte 4
Pensión Marilós 5
Pensión Topas 6
Rebequet 8
Villa Lorena Cabañas 9

Eating 🍴
Art Café La Crêpe 10
Bistro Boquete 14
Casona Mexicana 1
Delicias del Perú 9
El Explorador 2
Lourdes 3
Machu Picchu 11
Palo Alto 6
Papa Ricco's 13
Pizzería La Volcánica 4
Punto de Encuentro 8
Roxanne's 12
Sabrosón 5

Bars & clubs 🍸
Zanzibar 16

100 metres
100 yards

impressive cloudforest, thick with hanging creepers, lichen and bromeliads. The steep cuttings are carpeted with a glorious array of ferns and colourful flowers. Many birds can be seen, including bee hummingbirds, as well as wild turkeys and squirrels. The perfume from the flowers, especially in the wet season when there are many more blooms, is magnificent.

As the road rises, increasingly steeply, there are wonderful views of the Boquete Valley, the Río Caldera running through a steep gorge, and the misty plain beyond stretching to the Pacific. Some 9 km from the park entrance is a sign on the right, 'La Nevera' (the ice-box). A small side-trail here leads to a cool mossy gully where there is a stream for water, but no flat ground to camp. This is the only reliable water source during the dry season, so take plenty with you.

At the summit the cloudforest is replaced by a forest of TV and radio aerials in fenced-off enclosures. A short path leads to a small cross and a trigonometric point, from where the best views of dusty craters and the valleys of Volcán, Bambito and Cerro Punta stretch out below. The high-altitude brush contrasts spectacularly with the dark green forest, wisps of mist and cloud clinging to the treetops. Occasionally horizontal rainbows can be seen in the haze, formed in the *bajareque* drizzle. There are many craters around the main summit, with dwarf vegetation, lichens and orchids. Even in the dry season, you will be lucky to have a clear view of both oceans.

In a suitable vehicle it takes about two hours to the top (depending on the weather); or it's a 4½- to six-hour hike up, three hours down, from the park office. Zona Urbana minibuses (US$1) go to El Salto, 4 km from Boquete and 3 km from the end of the asphalt. Vehicles which service the antenna installations often go up to the summit. Officially they are not allowed to take passengers, but drivers may give you a lift. A taxi to the end of the paved road costs US$4 (recommended during the wet season as there is little chance of hitching and because the mountain summit usually clouds over in the afternoon making an early start your best option). Hiking from the summit all the way back to Boquete takes at least six hours. For those wishing to continue over Barú to Volcán on the mountain's west side, a trail begins 50 m before the cross, descending steeply over loose sand and scree before entering the forest. It's eight to 12 hours to Volcán, and there's no water until you are halfway down; a challenging and rewarding hike (see page 341).

The managers of the **Hotel Panamonte** in Boquete own **Finca Lérida**, on the slopes of Volcán Barú, and can arrange tours. Ask at the hotel's front desk.

Other hikes and excursions
Twenty-seven kilometres north of the Interamericana (13 km south of Boquete) is a turn-off east to Caldera (14 km), from where a 25- to 30-minute walk leads to **Los Pozos de Caldera** ① *no facilities, options for camping, entry US$1*, a well-known series of hot springs said to be good for rheumatism sufferers. River-rafting trips on the Chiriquí start from Caldera (see Activities and tours). There are six buses a day from David to Caldera, four a day from Boquete to Caldera, and pick-ups from the main road to the village.

Across the suspension bridge, **Conservas de Antaño** ① *T720-1539*, is a very friendly family-owned business that makes old-fashioned fruit preserves. **Café Ruiz** ① *2 km north of Boquete, T720-1392*, is a small factory known for its premium-grade roasted coffees. They welcome visitors for a guided tour starting at 0900 and lasting three hours (Don José Ruiz speaks English), explaining the whole process from harvesting to hand selecting only the best beans and vacuum packing the product. Next door is **Villa Marta**, a private mansion with a huge landscaped garden open to the public, and a sign: *'Mi jardín es su jardín'*. **Los Ladrillos**, a few kilometres further up the Caldera Valley, is a small area of basalt cliffs with octagonal fingers of rock in clusters. Beyond is **Horqueta**, a picturesque hillside area of coffee groves, with a roadside waterfall and banks of pink impatiens; beautiful views to the south.

Volcán and the Western Highlands ⊖🅿🅿❄🄲 ▶ *pp343-350.*

The western section of the Highlands is bounded on the north by the Cordillera and on the west by the Costa Rican border, a prosperous and dynamic agricultural region renowned for vegetables, flowers, superb coffees, and the brown Swiss and Holstein dairy herds that thrive in the cool highland pastures. The area is a birdwatchers' Mecca and is also popular with residents of Panama City wishing to cool off for a few days.

Heading away from La Concepción there is a very good paved road north, rising 1200 m in 32 km to Volcán. From Cuesta de Piedra, a turning to the right will take you to the canyons of the **Macho de Monte**, a rather small river which has worn deep and narrow gorges. Further on, to the left, is the **Mirador Alan Her** ⓘ *US$0.10*, with good views from the purpose-built tower to the sea, and on a clear day, the Punto Burica peninsula which marks the Panama–Costa Rica border. Local cheeses on sale are very good, especially the mozzarella. Near Volcán, you can get excellent wood carvings at **Artes Cruz** where Don Cruz, who speaks English, will make charming souvenirs to order and have them ready on your return trip.

Around Boquete

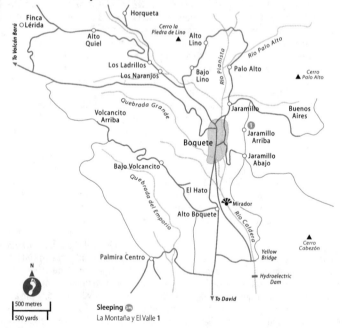

Sleeping 🛏
La Montaña y El Valle 1

Volcán and around

Volcán sits on a broad 1450-m-high plateau formed by an ancient eruption of Volcán Barú. The pumice soil is extremely porous and dries within minutes of the frequent torrential downpours in the rainy season; in summer the area is tinder dry.

The town is very spread out. The centre (with police station, gas station, supermarket and bakery) clusters around the crossroads to Cerro Punta and Río Sereno. Volcán is a rapidly growing farming town, with nurseries cultivating ferns for export, the **Beneficio Café Volcán Barú** (interesting tours during October-February harvest season), and a small factory owned by the Swiss Bérard family producing excellent European-style sausages. San Benito school is noted for hardwood furniture, woodcarvings using *cocobolo* hardwood and hand-painted ceramics sold for the benefit of the school. Brother Alfred will let you browse through his warehouse full of English books from the now-closed Canal Zone libraries and you can take away what you will. **Cerámica Beija-Flor** is run by local women who market their own wares.

Southwest of town is the **Las Lagunas de Volcán** nature reserve, with two beautiful lakes, abundant aquatic and other birdlife. High vehicles or 4WDs are required in the wet season. **Sitio Barriles**, 6 km from town on the road to Caizán (several buses daily, US$0.50), has interesting petroglyphs; also past Fina Palo Santo, 5 km from town on the road to Río Sereno. **La Fuente Park** ① *US$0.25* (signed from the main road) has playing fields and a spring-fed swimming hole (source of Río Gariché) that's excellent for children.

Volcán is a good jumping-off place for the ascent of **Volcán Barú**. It is possible to climb the west side in one or two days, camping about halfway by a small spring (the only reliable water in the dry season) or in a crater near the top (no water), descending the following day to Boquete on the vehicle road. The trail is beautiful, climbing gently at first through lush cloudforest (many birds, butterflies and orchids), then scrambling steeply over loose volcanic sand and scree – a challenging but rewarding hike. Guides can be arranged in Volcán; climbers sometimes get lost. For **tourist information**, Angel Rodríguez at Hotel Don Tavo speaks fluent English and is very knowledgeable about the area.

The road divides at the police station in Volcán. The right branch continues north to tiny **Bambito** and **Cerro Punta** (22 km), following the Chiriquí Viejo river valley up the northwest foothills of Volcán Barú and across the dry plain known as **Paso Ancho**, with coffee farms in the hill to the west.

Cerro Punta ⊜⊘ ⏵ pp343-350.

Heading north from Volcán, at the end of the road is Cerro Punta sitting at an altitude of 2130 m. Set in a beautiful valley, it is at the heart of a vegetable- and flower-growing zone, and a region of dairy farms and racehorse stables. It is sometimes called 'Little Switzerland' because of its Alpine-style houses and the influence of Swiss and former-Yugoslav settlers (there is a settlement called **Nueva Suiza** just south of town). The countryside, full of orchids, is beautiful, though economic pressures push the potato fields ever higher up the hillsides, to the cost of the wooded areas, and sadly encourage the extensive use of agro-chemicals. There are many fine walks in the crisp mountain air. Continue through Cerro Punta to follow the main street as it curves to the left. **Haras Cerro Punta** (topiary initials clipped in the hedge) and **Haras Carinthia** (name visible on stable roof) are well-known thoroughbred farms who will usually receive visitors and show them round. Further on is the small bridge at Bajo Grande. The right fork leads to **Respingo**, where there is a small forest ranger station. Buses depart from David via La Concepción and Volcán taking a couple of hours (US$2.65).

Camino Los Quetzales Trek

Continuing along the main road in Cerro Punta through town is the starting point of the easy six-hour hike, mostly downhill after an initial climb, to Boquete. The track is clear in places and there are a few signs showing the direction and time to Boquete, with the last section following the Río Caldera canyon. It is easier in the dry season (December-April), but can be enjoyed throughout the year. Take food, insect repellent and waterproofs. This hike is also recommended for birdwatching; quetzales and many other species may be seen. Take a taxi (4WD) from Cerro Punta to the Respingo ranger station, US$10. You can stay overnight here in the rangers' quarters (**F** per person), clean, shared bath and kitchen. The Camino Los Quetzales leads to **Bajo Mono**, from where there are irregular local buses to Boquete (20 minutes, US$1). The walk can also be done in the opposite direction (uphill). It is possible to set out from and return to Boquete in one (very long) day.

Parque La Amistad

① *7 km from the centre of Cerro Punta (signposted at road junction, entrance fee US$1, payable at Las Nubes).*

This park has been open since 1991. It has two trails, both good for birdwatching, including quetzales. Nature buffs should also visit Los Quetzales Reserve inside Parque La Amistad. See also Sleeping, page 346.

Volcán to the border

From the fork at the police station in Volcán, the left branch loops 48 very scenic kilometres west, climbing over the Cerro Pando, and passing through beautiful cattle country and coffee plantations on a well-paved, little-travelled, winding road to the Costa Rican border. **Los Pozos**, an area of small thermal pools beside a rushing river, is a good campsite, but accessible only by 4WD vehicles and hard to find as the turn-off from Volcán-Río Sereno road is unmarked. Enquire at **Panadería Mollek** (good espresso and pastries), opposite the police station in Volcán. Sr Juan Mollek has a farm at Los Pozos and can provide information. At **Río Colorado**, 15 km from Volcán, **Beneficio Café Durán**, a coffee processing plant whose delicious aroma of fermenting pulp and drying beans will announce its proximity from kilometres away, is hospitable to visitors. At **Santa Clara**, 25 km from Volcán, is the **Finca Hartmann**, 1300-1800 m, where the US **Smithsonian Tropical Research Institute** maintains a biological research station devoted to ecological studies. Enter the unmarked drive 50 m west of petrol station, next to a green house with 'Ab Santa Clara No 2' sign and proceed 1 km on a dirt road. Latest birdwatching checklist compiled by researchers lists 277 species observable on the densely wooded coffee and cattle farm which borders La Amistad International Park to the north. Biologists and the Hartmann family welcome visitors and have information in Spanish and English.

Border with Costa Rica – Río Sereno → *See box, page 337.*

The village of Río Sereno has the air of a cowboy town. The Panamanian businesses are centred around the plaza (including **Banco Nacional** – changes traveller's cheques), and the Costa Rican businesses along a street right on the border. Approaching the village from Volcán, abandoned installations from the era of military government are visible on the right. The bus station is just to the right of the *alto* (stop) sign. Follow the main street left along the plaza to where it ends at a steep road crossing diagonally. This is the border with Costa Rica, otherwise unmarked with numerous vendors' stalls, especially Sundays during coffee harvest (October to December or January). It is safe to park (and lock) your vehicle in the open area of **Almacén Universal**. Costa Rican shops selling leather goods, a few crafts, clothing, gladly accept US dollars at current rates. Do not miss the upper floor of **Super Universal** and **Supermercado Xenia**. If crossing into Panama, sell your colones here; it will be much more difficult in Volcán or David and rates are worse in Panama City.

Río Sereno to Paso Canoas
A paved winding road runs 50 km south along the Panama side of the border to Paso Canoas, about two to 2½ hours by bus. At Km 41 an impressive cascade over 100 m high pours over a cliff on the left of the Río Chiriquí Viejo below. For information on whitewater rafting on the Río Chiriquí Viejo from Breñón during the dry season, see Acitivities and tours (Boquete), page 348. There is a good view of the river valley at Km 47, with Volcán Barú visible to the northeast.

◉ Chiriquí listings

For Sleeping and Eating price codes, and other relevant information, see pages 43-46.

◉ Sleeping

David *p334, map p335*
Most cheap hotels are on Av 5 Este.
AL Nacional, Av and Calle Central, T775-2221, www.hotelnacionalpanama.com. The best hotel in David, just as their promotional material shamelessly declares. 75 rooms and suites, all predictably comfortable, but perhaps a little generic and overpriced. The amenities are excellent, including garden, pool, casino and 3 restaurants. Excellent lunch buffet, US$7.
B Alcalá, Av 3 Este between Calle D and E Norte, T774-9018, hotelalcala@cwpanama.net. Rooms are clean, pleasant and functional, if unexciting. There's Wi-Fi, restaurant, bar, parking and room service.
B Castilla, Calle A Norte between Av 2 and 3 Este, T774-5260, www.hotelcastilla panama.com. A clean, quiet hotel with well-appointed rooms. There's Wi-Fi in reception, parking, room service, a/c, cable TV and hot water. Modern, comfortable and central.
B Fiesta, on the Interamericana, T775-5454, hotelfiestamef@mef.gob.pa. Comfortable rooms with the usual features, including a/c and hot water, restaurant, and a good pool.
B Puerta del Sol, Av 3 Este y Calle Central, T774-8422, puertadelsol@cwpnama.net. A large, professional hotel with 86 comfortable

rooms, a/c, Wi-Fi, parking and restaurant. Clean, tidy, helpful and respectable. Not bad.
C Iris, Calle A Norte, on Parque Cervantes T775-2251, hotel_irispanama@hotmail.com. This hotel has a range of rooms, both bath, a/c, hot water and cable TV; cheaper with fan (**D**). Friendly, clean and comfortable enough. Restaurant attached.
C Occidental, Av 4 Este on Parque Cervantes, T775-4695. This large, centrally located hotel is very good value. Sizeable, comfortable rooms with bath, cable TV, hot water and a/c. Some have nice balconies overlooking the plaza. Recommended.
C-E Bambú Hostel, Calle de La Virgencita, San Mateo District, T730-2961. Mix of dormitories and private rooms, with use of kitchen, lounge, films and swimming pool.
C-E The Purple House, Calle C Sur and Av 6 Oeste, Barrio San Mateo, T774-4059, www.purplehousehostel.com. Hostel close to town centre with private (**C-D**) and dormitory rooms (**E**) and orthopaedic mattresses. A wealth of amenities include book exchange, *artesanías*, DVD rental, kitchen, Wi-Fi, free internet and stacks of information on travel throughout the country. Good reports. Taxi from bus terminal is around US$3, shops and restaurants within striking distance.
D Pensión Costa Rica, Av 5 Este, Calle A Sur, T775-1241. A bit run-down and noisy, but friendly. They have a variety of clean, basic rooms, with shower and/or a/c.

D Residencial La Avenida, Av 3 Este between Calle D and E Norte, T774-0451, residencialavenida@hotmail.com. Simple economical rooms with bath and a/c, cheaper with fan (**E**). Parking, good value.

D-F Pensión Fanita, Calle 5 between 5 Este and 6 Este, pensionfanita@hotmail.com. Friendly, family-run pensión in an old wooden house. They have a range of lodgings, including private rooms with a/c, bath and cable TV (**D**) and very basic quarters without fan or bath (**F**). Euros accepted. Recommended for budget travellers.

Boquete and the Eastern Highlands *p336, map p338*

Accommodation is difficult to find during *feria*.

L La Montaña y el Valle – The Coffee Estate Inn, Jaramillo Arriba, T/F720-2211, www.coffee estateinn.com. 2.5 km from San Juan Bautista church in Boquete (pass church, turn right at fork, cross river, turn left at intersection, then follow signs). De-luxe cottages in gorgeous, verdant grounds. The 3 spacious units are fully equipped with kitchen and living area, and deliver great views of the countryside. Delicious gourmet food is available, including freshly roasted coffee from their farm. They also offer good information on the surroundings, including natural attractions. Recommended.

L-AL Panamonte, Av Central, north of town, T720-1324, www.panamonte.com. Built in 1919, this highly attractive hotel is today managed by the Collins family (Swedish-American). The rooms here are elegant and comfortable, while the garden is home to over 200 varieties of orchid. New developments include a day spa, and various tours are also available. Charming and highly recommended.

AL-A Boquete Country Inn, Av Central, T720-2470, www.boquetecountryinn.com. Well restored B&B in the centre of town, owned by a long-established Panamanian local and her north American husband who can organize tours on the couple's yacht. Rooms are homely and smart and set among flowered grounds with idyllic streams.

A Tinamou Cottage, 10 mins from town, T720-3852, habbusdekwie@cwpanama.net. Perfect for nature lovers, this cottage is set on a private coffee finca and has capacity for up to 3 people (1 double, 1 single). Cost includes breakfast. Can arrange pick up in town.

A-C Cabañas Isla Verde, on main street, follow signs posted just before the **Casona Mexi** restaurant, T/F720-2533, www.islaverde panama.com. This is a good-value lodging conveniently located with lots of space and a relaxing atmosphere. 6 2-storey 'roundhouse' cabañas and 2 'suites' overlook a small stream (there's also a cheaper room with an outside bathroom). German owner Eva Kipp is friendly and knowledgeable. Discounts available in the low season.

B Pensión Topas, behind Texaco station at south end of town, T/F720-1005, www. pension-topas.com. Brightly coloured hotel run by the Schöb family. The garden has views of Volcán Barú, a small pool and volley ball court. The comfortable rooms have bath, cheaper without (**E**). Good breakfasts, tours are arranged, and there's a beer garden at the family finca during the dry season.

B Villa Lorena Cabañas, by bridge near **Panamonte**, T/F720-1848. Comfortable whitewashed cottages for 4-6 persons, overlooking the Río Caldera.

B-C Rebequet, Av A Este y Calle 6 Sur, T720-1365, rebequet@hotmail.com. Excellent spacious rooms (**B**) and a handful of comfortable cabins around the garden (**C**). The rooms are wellequipped with nice furniture, TV, fridge and bath. Tours are available. Popular, friendly and helpful. Recommended.

C Fundadores, Av Central at south end of town, T720-1298, hotfundland@cwp.net.pa. Pleasant lodging with comfortable rooms, restaurant, beautiful lush grounds and a stream. Cabañas are also available (A).

C Hostal Mozart, on the Volcancito road, 5 mins' drive from central Boquete, T720-3764. Charming, brightly decorated house with an outside patio offering nice views. Friendly owner Lorenza speaks German,

English and Spanish. Breakfast and dinners are delicious. Camping also available.

C La Casa de Doña Cata, main plaza, T720-1260. Formerly **Pensión Virginia**, this slightly faded wooden house on the plaza has good balconies and functional rooms. Use of kitchen, laundry, tourist information is available. OK for a single person (**D**), but overpriced for 2.

C-E Hostal Boquete, just off Calle 4 Sur to left of bridge, T720-2573, www.hostalboq uete.com. This lovely hostel has great views of the river and a pleasant, sociable atmosphere. Brightly coloured private rooms (**C**) and dorm beds (**D-E**) are available. Services include Wi-Fi, laundry, *artesanías*, BBQ pit, tours, community kitchen and satellite TV. Suite rental for $75.

C-E Hostal Nomba, 100 m from Parque Central, behind **Bistro Boquete**, T6497-5672, Brand new hostel already becoming very popular with backpackers, offers simple but comfortable dorms and private rooms, communal kitchen, library, in-room security lockers and bike rental.

D Hostal Palacios, Av Central on main plaza, T720-1653. A family-run hostel owned and operated by a friendly and enthusiastic former basketball star. Quite basic, with bath and hot water (cheaper without), and use of kitchen. Good information on hiking. Recommended for backpackers.

D Pensión Marilós, Av A Este y Calle 6 Sur, opposite **Rebequet**, T720-1380. A friendly, economical place with an agreeable home ambience. Rooms are very clean and comfortable with bath and hot water. Guests have use of the kitchen and living areas. The English-speaking management can also organise tours or store luggage. Often full but sharing is permitted. Excellent value and recommended.

Volcán and the Western Highlands *p340*
Hotels are often fully booked during holidays. Price categories shown for cottages are for 1 or 2 persons, but most for larger groups for the same price or slightly more.

LL-AL Cabañas Dr Esquivel, on the road behind **Supermercado Bérard**, Volcán, T771-4770, www.cabanasdresquivel.com. Several large houses in a compound, all fully equipped with kitchen, living room and bedrooms. Clean, comfortable and a good option for families.

LL-AL Hotel Bambito Resort, Bambito, T771-4373, www.hotelbambito.com. This luxury resort has a stunning countryside setting at the edge of a lake. Rooms are very comfortable, predictably, with a host of services including pool, guided tours and restaurant. Attractive and attentive.

AL Hostal Cielito Sur B&B, 9 km from Volcán, past **Hotel Bambito** but before Cerro Punta, T/F771-2038, www.cielitosur. com. A lovely place to stay with lots of personal attention. Each room is decorated with artwork from Panama's indigenous groups, and a delicious country-style breakfast is included. Good information about the area from owners Janet and Glenn Lee. Recommended.

A Las Huacas, main street at west end of Volcán, T771-4363. Comfortable cottages with hot water, clubhouse, elaborate gardens and interesting aviaries. English spoken.

B Cabañas Las Reinas, signed from main road, Volcán, T771-4338. Self-contained units with a kitchen in a lawn setting.

B Don Tavo, main road, Volcán, T/F771-5144, www.volcanbaru.com/hoteldontavo. Clean, comfortable rooms with private baths and hot water, all set around a pleasant, leafy garden. Services include restaurant and internet. Friendly and recommended.

B Dos Ríos, Via Río Sereno, T771-4271, www.dosrios.com.pa. Rooms here are clean, comfortable and colourful, set in well-tended grounds with a stream. Services include restaurant, bar and butterfly garden.

D Cabañas Señorial, main road at entrance to Volcán, T771-4239. Basic lodgings, for short-stay couples.

D El Oasis, behind restaurant **Calle La Fuente**, El Valle, T771-4644. Simple quarters. The owner also rents rooms in her home by **La Fuente** pool. Bar can be noisy.

D La Nona, Calle La Fuente, El Valle, T771-4284. Cabins for up to 5. Friendly, good value.
D Motel California, on main street, Volcán, T771-4272. Quiet, simple rooms, including larger units for up to 7, with clean private baths and hot water. Services include parking, restaurant and bar. Good but check beds, some are very old and soft. Friendly Croatian owner (Sr Zizic Jr) speaks English.

Cerro Punta *p341*
LL-A Los Quetzales Lodge & Spa, T771-2182, www.losquetzales.com, at Guadalupe. A true forest hideaway, with 5 self-contained cabins, 3 dormitories or 5 separate chalets to choose from. Los Quetzales is located in Volcán Barú National Park, a cloudforest reserve at 2020 m. Nearly 100 bird species are visible from the porches and the grounds are also home to streams, a trout hatchery and primeval forest. 4WD vehicles only and a bit of a hike from parking area, but worth it. Owner Carlos Alfaro is fluent in English and can arrange transport or daily cook.
AL The Hartmanns, 1 km beyond the end of the dirt road, Santa Clara, T/F775-5223, www.fincahartmann.com. This working coffee finca has comfortable wooden cabins in the woods, no electricity but bath and hot water. They're also excellent auto mechanics.
C Hotel Cerro Punta, just before the turning to La Amistad, T720-2020. 9 simple rooms, comfortable and economical enough, and a quite good restaurant.
D Pensión Eterna Primavera, in Cerro Punta town. Basic quarter for budget travellers.

🍴 Eating

David *p334, map p335*
🍴 Casa del Churrasco, Av Central, between D and C Norte. This open-front restaurant lays on an excellent lunch buffet and serves stone-baked pizzas in the evening. Recommended.
🍴 Restaurant and Marisqueria Orly, Av 5 Este, between Calle Central and Calle A Norte. An open-air wooden structure adorned with

nets and other nautical accessories. They serve seafood. Karoke on Fri and Sat evenings.
🍴 Rincón Libanese, Calle F Sur, between Av Central and Av 1 Este. Arabic and Lebanese cuisine, including kebabs and other grilled meat specialities.
🍴-🍴 Multi-Café, in Hotel Occidental, Av 4 Este on Parque Cervantes. A variety of passable buffet fare, including breakfasts. Popular with locals and good value. Open all day.
🍴-🍴 El Palacio Oriental, Av Domingo Díaz (Central) y Calle E Norte. Long-standing and reliable Chinese restaurant serving the usual Eastern fare. Economical.
🍴 Café Ivonne, Calle C Norte, between Av Central and Av 1 Oeste. Popular little open-air locals' café, serving breakfasts, burgers and economical *comida corriente*.
🍴 La Cacerola, Av Obaldía behind **Super Barú**, just off the Interamericana. Self-service joint serving clean, fresh Panamanian dishes all day. Good value. Highly recommended.
🍴 Pizzería Mio Bello, Calle A Sur y Av 5 Este. Economical pizzas and Italian fare. Popular with David's youth, but has probably seen better days.
🍴 Restaurant Sasa Bar, Calle C Norte, between Av 4 Este and Av 5 Este. Popular locals' haunt with a wide range of ultra-cheap meals. Busy at lunch-time.

Cafés, bakeries, juice bars and ice cream parlours
Daisy's Coffee Shop, Av 2 Este and Calle C Norte. For your caffeine fix. Coffee, pies, snacks and ice creams.
Helados Jackelita, Calle E Norte y Av Domingo Díaz. Very good fresh fruit ice cream and smoothies.
Panadería Pinzón, Av 5 Este, Calle A Sur, opposite **Pensión Costa Rica**. Excellent bakery/café with sandwiches, breads and cakes.

Boquete and the Eastern Highlands *p336, map p338*
🍴🍴-🍴 Art Café La Crepe, Av Central, near San Juan Batista. A range of French crêpes are served at this jazzy, continental eatery,

including some very creative ones. Province cooking is the house speciality, and dishes include fresh rainbow trout and crayfish in brandy and liqueur. The attached art gallery displays work by international artists.

†††-†† Hibiscus, Calle A Este, Boquete. Intimate French restaurant serving escargot and chicken cordon bleu. Popular among Boquette's burgeoning expat community.

†††-†† Restaurante Hotel Panamonte, Av Central, north end of Boquete. This restaurant is quaint and charming and the meals are fantastic – pricey, but worth the treat. Open for breakfast, lunch and dinner, serving succulent trout, fresh juices and delicious desserts, among others.

†† Bistro Boquete, Av Central, Boquete. US owner Loretta once cooked for a US president in her previous establishment in Colorado. Her bistro here is renowned for excellent filet mignon at very reasonable prices, good breakfasts, tasty lunches and dinners. Highly recommended.

†† Delicias del Peru, Av Central, Boquete. Good place to take in Boquete's gorgeous verdant forests and garden views. This is a popular spot for pisco sour and ceviche. Everything is nicely presented.

†† El Explorador, a 45-min walk from Boquete (past **Hotel Panamonte**) across from La Montaña and El Valle. This restaurant has a beautiful location with a picnic area, children's playground and hammocks. Entrance to area is US$1, but free to restaurant diners. Excellent local food is served, including breakfast and dinner. Open weekends and holidays only.

†† Machu Picchu, Av Belisario, Porras. Fantastic Peruvian food cooked by a very friendly Peruvian. Impressive menu, mostly meat, fish and seafood.

†† Palo Alto, past the **Hotel Panamonte**, cross bridge, take left and 400 m after that on the left. Beautiful country-style decor set beside the gurgling Río Caldera. Lunch, dinner, international fare and good coffee.

†† Roxanne's, Av Central, south over the bridge. Smart wooden steakhouse serving a range of grilled meats, for all your carnivorous needs.

†† Snoopy's, over bridge on Calle 4, opposite flower fair grounds. Run by English man Roy Knight, **Snoopy's** has become a very popular spot for laid-back eating with good views, burgers, snacks and some main meals.

††-† Casona Mexicana, Av Central, south past the library. Tasty Mexican food dished up by a Panamanian lady who used to live in Mexico.

††-† Papa Ricco's, Av Belisario Porras. Real Italian pizzas, reportedly very tasty and good value. Open Fri-Sun, 1200-2000.

† Java Juice, Av Central. Cheap smoothies, burgers, sandwiches and snacks.

† Lourdes, Av Central. Good spot with an outside terrace, but mixed reports on the food.

† Pizzería La Volcánica, Av Central, ½ block from main plaza. Good pizzas and pasta at reasonable prices. Economical and popular.

† Punto de Encuentro, Av A Este, near **Pensión Marilo's**. Cosy little café with a garden and notice board. Breakfast only; pancakes, fruit salad and juices.

† Sabrosón, on Av Central near church. High-carb Panamanian fare. Good quality and value – the best place for budget dining.

Bakeries

King's, Av B Este near Parque a las Madres, is a particularly good bakery.

Pastelería Alemana, south of the arch at the entrance to town. Delicious coffee and pastries.

Volcán and the Western Highlands *p340*

† La Hacienda Restaurant, Bambito, T771-4152. Tasty dishes include fresh trout and barbecued chicken. Recommended.

† Hotel Don Tavo, Av Central, Volcán. The restaurant in the hotel serves pizza and local dishes.

† Lizzy's, near post office, Volcán. Fast food, English spoken.

† Lorena, on road to Río Sereno. Good fish brought from coast daily. Tables on the porch.

† La Luna, 4 km on the road to Cerro Punta in Paso Ancho. Good Chinese food.

† Marisquería El Pacífico, main road east of main intersection. Good seafood. Recommended.

Border with Costa Rica – Río Sereno *p342*
🍴 **Bar Universal**. Recommended for fried chicken and plantain chips (family atmosphere during the day, more raucous Sat evenings and on pay day during the coffee harvest).
🍴 **Sr Eli**, top end of the Costa Rican street. Unnamed restaurant, serving good food, friendly and helpful.

🎭 Entertainment

Boquete and the Eastern Highlands *p336, map p338*
Not renowned for nightlife Boquete is usually a ghost-town after 2200, however, the recent influx of tourists and expats are obviously having some impact. African themed **Zanzibar**, Av Central, is open till 2400 and serves cocktails (closed Mon) and **Snoopy's**, over the bridge on Calle 4, opposite the flower fair grounds, has a large hall and hosts various events.

Volcán and the Western Highlands *p340*
Weekend discos at **Eruption** and **Kalahari**, rustic, good places to meet young locals.

🎉 Festivals and events

David *p334, map p335*
Mid-Mar Major week-long international fair and fiesta.

Boquete and the Eastern Highlands *p336, map p338*
Jan Feria de las Flores y del Café is a 2-week-long festival (starts 2nd week of Jan) highlighting Boquete's abundance of exotic and colorful flowers. This time of year coffee-harvesting season is in full swing and the fair exhibits coffee and coffee-based products. Vendors come from all over Central America to sell their wares. Lodgings fill up, so make reservations in advance.
28 Nov Independence from Spain Boquete erupts in a day-long parade hosting marching bands from schools from all over Panama.

Volcán and the Western Highlands *p340*
Dec Feria de las Tierras Altas is held during the 2nd week of Dec in La Fuente Park. Rodeo, dancing, crafts fair and many other attractions.

🔺 Activities and tours

David *p334, map p335*
Servicios Turísticos, Calle Central, T775-4644. Regional tours.
Travesías, Calle B Norte between Av 5 and 6 Este, T/F774-5352, travesias@mixmail.com. Regional tours.

Boquete and the Eastern Highlands *p336, map p338*
River rafting
Chiriquí River Rafting, Av Central, next to **Lourdes**, T720-1505, www.panama-rafting.com. Open 0830-1730. Bilingual father-and-son team Héctor and Ian Sánchez, offer 2- to 4-hr Grade II, III and IV trips with modern equipment on Río Chiriquí and surrounding area, US$60-105 per person. They can arrange lodging and transport to starting-point or vehicle delivery to landing point. Offer trips during dry season, Dec-Apr, as well on Río Chiriquí Viejo (Grade III/IV Technical, US$90-100) and Río Esti (Grade II and III). Recommended.
Panama Rafters, just below the square on Av Central, T/F720-2712, www.panama rafters.com. Good, solid rafting operation with quality gear, guides and a strong emphasis on safety. Kayak and multi-day trips are available, but most trips are run on the excellent Río Chiriquí Viejo. ½-day on the Grade III Harpia section US$75, full day on the Grade IV Jaguar section US$90.

Tour operators
Aventurist, T720-1635, www.aventurist. com. Mountain bike hire, hiking, coffee tours.
Boquete Mountain Safari Tours, T627-8829, www.boquetemountainsafaritours.com. Good selection of ½- and full-day tours, from hikes to full on adventures.

Coffee Adventures , T720-3852, www.coffee adventures.net. Freelance tour guides Terry van Niekerk and Hans van der Vooren provide tours of fine local coffee operations. Daily 0900, US$25 per person. Tours in English, Spanish and Dutch, minimum people. The tours visit **Café Kotowa**, T720-1430. The same company offer Boquette Tree Trek canopy tours, www.canopypanama.com, and visits to local indigenous villages.
Feliciano Tours, T624-9940, provide tours and transport of the area US$20-US$60. Good for those needing guidance on trails of the area, some English spoken.
Hiking/birdwatching tours, T720-3852. Run by Terry Van Niekerk, who speaks English, Spanish and Dutch, and provides hiking and birdwatching tours of the area surrounding Boquete. Highly recommended for the **Los Quetzales** hike (5 hrs) which also includes transport back from Cerro Punta to Boquete (2 hrs). Tours include fresh coffee and snacks and some include a light breakfast. Prices from US$20-60 per person depending on tour.
Hiking tours, Av A Ote on road to cemetery, T/F720-2726. Friendly and helpful owner Sr Bouttet arranges guided tours in the area including Volcán Barú, Cerro Punta (around US$50 per day for a group of up to 3) and can give advice on where to stay overnight.
Hotel Panamonte, Av Central, north end of town, organizes day trips to Volcán Barú, birdwatching and coffee plantations, US$150 for a group of up to 4.
Sr Frank Glavas at **Pensión Marilo's**, Av A Este y Calle 6 Sur, organizes guides and trips throughout the area.

☉ Transport

David *p334, map p335*
Air
There are two airline offices in David: **Air Panama**, Av 2 Este and Calle D Norte, which flies 2-3 times daily to Panama City; and **Aeroperlas**, Calle Central, between Av 2 Este and Av 3 Este, which flies 2-3 times daily to

Panama City and 3-5 times a week to **Bocas del Toro**, depending on the season. To **Panama City**, US$104; to **Bocas del Toro**, US$65. Daily service to **San José**, Costa Rica, US$110, one way.

Bus
Local Around US$0.20 for a ticket.
Long distance The main bus terminal is at Av 2 Este, 1 block north of Av Obaldía. Taxi to centre US$1. All companies use this except **Padafront**, whose terminal is nearby at Av 2 Este y Av Obaldía, T775-8913.

To **Panama City** regular buses US$10.60, express US$15, 3 hrs, 10 daily with **Padafront**. To **Paso Canoas** (border with Costa Rica), US$1.50, 1½ hrs, every 15 mins 0500-1830. Direct to **San José** with **Tracopa**, 0830 daily, US$12, 8 hrs, with stop in San Isidro.

Regular buses go to **Boquete** every 25 mins, 0600-2145, 1 hr, US$1.20; **Volcán**, every 15 mins, 0700-1800, 1½ hrs, US$2.30; **Chiriquí** Grande, every 90 mins, 0630-1600, 3 hrs, US$7; buses to **Almirante** every 40 mins, 0500-1900, 4 hrs, US$8; **Cerro Punto**, 2¼ hrs, US$3.

Car
Budget, T775-5597; **Hertz**, T775-6828; **Mike's**, T775-4963. Rent a 4WD vehicle in David if going to Volcán Barú.

Taxi
Taxi into the city from the bus station costs around US$1-2. US$0.65 for a ride in the city.

Paso Canoas, La Concepción and the Costa Rican border *p336*
Bus
From David via **Concepción** and **Paso Canoas** buses run every 15 mins, 0500-2000, 2½ hr, US$3.

Train
Chiriquí Railway: passenger service Puerto Armuelles-**Progreso** (halfway to Paso Canoas), twice a day each way, 2 hr, US$1. There is also a 'Finca Train', 4 decrepit, converted banana trucks, leaving at 1500 for

the banana fincas, returning, by a different route, at 1800. No charge for passengers. Minibuses also leave all day for the fincas.

Boquete and the Eastern Highlands *p336, map p338*

Bike and scooter
Estate Office-Gringo's Scooter Hire, Av Central near park. Infomation on hiking, bike hire (US$2.50 per hr, US$10 day 8 hrs), scooter hire (US$6.50 per hr, US$20 day), pay deposit.

Bus
Local buses depart in Boquete from the main plaza, called El Parque, old fashioned and pretty, every 20 mins to **Volcán** (US$1.65), **David** (US$0.50), and **Paso Canoas** (US$0.75). 10 buses daily to **Panama City** via David with **Padafront**, US$11, 7 hr; terminal beside Delta petrol station next to **El Sótano** restaurant, east of Volcán intersection on Interamericana Highway, T770-4485.

◑ Directory

David *p334, map p335*
Banks Banistmo, Av 2 Este y Calle A Norte, also on Av Obaldía, for Visa cash advances, changes AMEX TCs without commission. **Banco Nacional de Panamá**, 0800-1330 (generally very convenient, but guards have been known to turn away travellers wearing shorts), changes Amex TCs, 1% commission plus US$0.10 tax per cheque. **Banco General**, Av 3 Este y Calle C Norte, changes TCs, 1% commission, Visa ATM. **Caja de Ahorro** (Caja Pronto), Av 2 Este y Calle Central, for Master-Card and Amex TCs. **Embassies and consulates** Costa Rica, Urbanización El Bosque, 2 blocks west of clinic, best take a taxi, T774-1923. **Immigration** Immigration office, Calle C Sur between Av Central and 1 Este, T775-4515, Mon-Fri 0800-1500. **Ministerio de Hacienda y Tesoro**, Calle C Norte, 1 block from Parque Cervantes, near the post office. **Internet** Sinfonet, Calle E Norte y Av Domingo Díaz, daily 0800-0000, US$1 per

hr; **Speedlan**, Av 3 Este y Calle A Sur, beside Panamá Rey hotel, T777-2438, US$1 per hr. **Instituto OTEIMA**, C D N between Av 1 and 2 Este, daily 0800-1200, 1330-2000, US$1 per hr; **Electrónica Nacional**, Av Obaldía, opposite Domino's Pizza, US$1.50 per hr. **Laundry** Lavandería One, Av Centenario Central y 1A Sur; Lavafast, 1 Av Obaldia. **Post office** Calle C Norte y Av 3 Este.

Boquete and the Eastern Highlands *p336, map p338*
Banks Global Bank, Mon-Fri, 0800-1500, Sat 0800-1500 changes TCs with a commission of US$1 per cheque and has an ATM. Same hours at **Banco Nacional** and Banolar, on the main street, who will both cash TCs. **Internet** Oasis Internet, near Pastelería Alemán; Kelnix, beside Chiriquí River Rafting, T720-2803, daily 0800-2000, US$1.80 per hr. **Language schools** Habla Ya, Central Avenue, Los Establos Plaza 20-22, Boquete, T720-1294, www.hablaya panama.com. Recommended by one traveller for great Spanish tuition with homestay options. US$220 for 1 week, US$700 for 4. Can also provide excursion advice. **Spanish by the River**, Alto Boquete, Entrada a Palmira, 180mts a mano izquierda, T720-3456, www.spanishbytheriver.com, offer a mixture of group and private tuition, accommodations and homestay. **Laundry** Lavomático Las Burbujas, south of church, very friendly, US$1 to wash. **Post office** In the Palacio Municipal.

Volcán and the Western Highlands *p340*
Banks Banco Nacional and Banco de Istmo, Mon-Fri 0800-1500, Sat 0800-1200, both change dollar TCs. **Internet** Sinfonet, in Hotel Don Tavo, US$1 per hr, friendly and helpful. Hardware store **Ferremax**, main road opposite police station, T771-4461, sends and receives international faxes, 0700-1200, 1400-1800, US$1.50 per page plus telephone charge, English spoken. **Laundry** Lava-mático Volcán, main road opposite Jardín Alegría dancehall. Service only US$2.50, wash, dry and fold, reliable, Doña Miriam will have washing ready when promised.

Panama City

Shaped and sustained by intense international activity, Panama City is a place where sweltering tropical exuberance meets soaring fiscal ambitions. Transnational cargo, commerce and capital flow through this city's institutions like incessant life-force. Throughout its evolution, waves of immigrants have arrived from east and west, north and south. Today, Panama City's multi-ethnic society is a striking affirmation of all that is foreign, bustling and transitory. But it is a deeply polarized society too. As the construction boom advances with an almost religious zeal, scores of new skyscrapers, tower blocks and luxury condos compete for a piece of the already crowded horizon. Higher and higher they reach, leaving many everyday Panamanians wondering what the view must be like from way up there.

Panama City's cultural diversity asserts itself most vividly in the day-to-day hustle of its working-class population. The districts of Santa Ana and Calidonia throng with busy market stalls and a frenetic street life where people of disparate ancestries – Chinese, Afro-Caribbean, mestizo and indigenous among them – jostle and barter and hawk. Casco Viejo offers glimpses of Old Spain with its wonderful colonial architecture, and 19th-century France, too, with a handful of elegant French mansions constructed during the first failed attempt to build a canal. Where the French failed, the Americans succeeded, and the districts of Ancón, Balboa and Amador – part of the former US-occupied Canal Zone – reveal a penchant for order and mall-style shopping experiences. Bella Vista and the financial district are a truly international effort, with a host of foreign banks, posh restaurants and chic fashion boutiques. But it is the Colombians, particularly, who helped raise these towers of glass and steel. Undoubtedly, Panama City offers an endlessly fascinating journey for those willing to unravel the many complex threads of its social fabric.

And when the relentless energy of this urban powerhouse gets too much, you can always escape to nearby beaches and gentle Pacific islands. ▶▶ *For listings, see pages 366-382.*

Ins and outs

Getting there Tocumen International Airport is 27 km from the city centre. For flights see page 378. Set price taxis (US$25), shared taxis (*compartido*) and buses are available for getting into Panama City. The bus journey should take 1 hr but can take up to three in the rush hour. Car rental companies also have offices at the airport. If arriving by air from another part of the country, the domestic airport is Marcos A Gelabert airport, located in Albrook; a taxi to the city centre costs US$2-3. The city is also well served by international buses from countries throughout Central America, with offices in the centre of town and at the bus terminal, also in Albrook; US$2 taxi into the city centre. ▶▶ *For further details, see Transport, page 378.*

Getting around The old part of the city, Casco Viejo, can easily be toured on foot. There are old, usually crowded and very cheap buses for getting to other districts. The reasonably priced taxis charge on a zone system and can be shared if you wish to economize. Taxis can be hired by the hour for a city tour. At night, radio taxis are preferable. Many *avenidas* have both names and numbers, although locals are most likely to use the names, so asking for directions can be a bit complicated. Also, because there is no postal delivery to homes or businesses, few buildings display their numbers, so try to find out the nearest cross street.

The wider metropolitan area has a population of approximately 720,000. Adjacent to the city, but constituting a separate administrative district, is the town of San Miguelito, a residential area for over 330,000 people. Once a squatter community, every available square inch of hillside has been built on and it is increasingly considered to be a part of greater Panama City.

Tourist offices The main office for the **Instituto Panameño de Turismo (IPAT)** ① *Av Samuel Lewis y Calle Gerardo Ortega, Edif Central, T526-7000, www.visitpanama.com, or www.ipat.gob.pa,* has good lists of lodgings and other services, but is generally not geared towards the visiting public. There are other **IPAT kiosks** ① *Tocumen Airport in Panamá Viejo, Tue-Sun 0800-2200; on the pedestrian mall on Av Central, Mon-Fri 0900-1700; and opposite Hotel Continental on España.* and in all regions of the country. The tourist police are good for directions and general enquiries; many of their offices have free maps to hand out.

Safety Tourist police on mountain bikes are present in the downtown areas of the city, recognizable by their broad armbands. Panamanians are generally very friendly and helpful. Accustomed to foreigners, they are casual about tourists. However, as in any large city with many poor people, certain areas can be dangerous after dark and reasonable

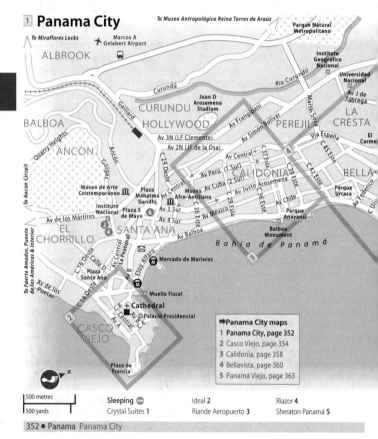

1 Panama City

➡ **Panama City maps**
1 Panama City, page 352
2 Casco Viejo, page 354
3 Calidonia, page 358
4 Bellavista, page 360
5 Panamá Viejo, page 363

Sleeping 🛏
Crystal Suites 1   Ideal 2   Riazor 4
   Riande Aeropuerto 3   Sheraton Panamá 5

precautions should be taken at all times. Attacks have been reported in Casco Viejo (although this area is now well patrolled by police during the daytime) and Panamá Viejo. Marañón (around the market), San Miguelito (on the way in from Tocumen Airport) and Calidonia can all be dangerous; never walk there at night and take care in daylight, too. Poor districts such as Chorillo, Curundú and Hollywood are best avoided altogether. Probably the safest area for budget travellers to stay is Bella Vista, although it is deserted after dark and street crime can take place here at any hour. Taxis are the safest way to travel around the city and drivers will give you good advice on where not to go. If concerned, lock the doors of the taxi.

History

Panama City was founded in 1519 by Pedro Aria Dávila, thus establishing a Pacific base for the conquest of Peru. Spanish troops and plundered Inca gold flowed in and out, bringing unprecedented wealth to the city – and unprecedented attention from pirates. In 1671, Henry Morgan raised it to the ground. Fortunately, Panama City rose from its ashes three years later at the strategically advantageous location of present-day Casco Viejo, several kilometres away.

To Betania & Colón
Via Transistmica
Tumba Muerto
Via Venetto
La Batista
EL CARMEN
Via Argentina
Av 2 N Eusebio Morales
EL CANGREJO
Calle D
Via España
Via Brasil
To O & Tocumen International Airport
Main Banking District
Av Samuel Lewis
OBARRIO
San Gabriel
CAMPO ALEGRE
Aquilino de la Guardia (49)
Av 4 Sur
Av Nicanor de Obarrio (C 50)
To O
To Panamá Viejo
MARBELLA
Via Israel
Balboa
Paitilla Airport (closed) ✈
Via Italia
To Atlapa Convention Centre, Tourist Office & Panamá Viejo
PUNTA PAITILLA
To Tocumen International Airport

Stanford 6

In 1855, the transcontinental railroad was opened, adjoining Panama City with its Caribbean cousin, Colón. Crowds of gold prospectors poured across the isthmus en route to California. By then, Panama City's ethnic make-up had changed irrevocably, with Chinese and Afro-Caribbean railroad labourers settled into permanent communities. In 1882, the French arrived on the scene to much fanfare and jubilation. They constructed several elegant mansions and commenced work on the Panama Canal, expending many thousands of employees and nearly bankrupting France in the process. The US took over the project and initiated a new phase of efficiency. They drastically improved the city's sanitation, eradicated yellow fever and brought malaria under control. New waves of immigrant workers arrived from all over the world, but the Caribbean especially, and racial tensions were high. The canal company operated out of a US-governed 16-km wide Canal Zone stipulated in their treaty with Panama, a 'country within a country', to which belonged the thoroughly ordered districts of Ancón, Balboa and Amador. The Canal Zone would be a source of ongoing resentments, and, in 1964, rioting.

In the 1970s and 1980s, the city's skyline mushroomed as it gained prominence as a centre of international banking, cocaine trafficking and money laundering. President Manuel Noriega and the Colombians enjoyed several years of criminal prosperity until George Bush decided to initiate a full-blown invasion on 20 December 1989. Many historical buildings were damaged or destroyed during 'Operation Just Cause'. Today the city is experiencing exceptionally high levels of growth, partly fuelled by plans to expand the Canal. Soaring energy demands and high levels of traffic are placing particular strain on the infrastructure.

Sights

Casco Viejo

Casco Viejo (the 'Old Compound' or San Felipe), which occupies the narrow peninsula east of Calle 11, is an unusual combination of beautifully restored public buildings, churches, plazas, monuments and museums alongside inner-city decay which, after

2 Casco Viejo

Bahía de Panamá

Mercado San Felipe

Av Eloy Alfar
Palacio Presidencial

Av Central
C Colón
Av B
C 13 Este
C 12
C 11 Este
Salsipuedes

Plaza Santa
Santa Ana
C 12
San Felipe Neri
Former Archbishop Palace

Municipalidad
La Merced
Av B
Cathedral
Plaza Catedral (Plaza Independencia)

Av Central
SAN FELIPE

Palacio Municipal & Museo de Historiá de Panamá
Museo del Canal Interoceánico

Plaza Herrera

Av A

C 15 Oeste
C 14 Oeste
C 13 Oeste
C 12 Oeste
C 11 Oeste
Tiger's Hand Bulwark

San José

→ Panama City maps
1 Panama City, page 352
2 Casco Viejo, page 354
3 Calidonia, page 358
4 Bellavista, page 360
5 Panamá Viejo, page 363

N

| 100 metres |

Sleeping
Caracas 2
Casa Grande 3

Hospedaje Casco Viejo 5
Luna's Castle 4

Eating
Café Coca Cola 1
Café de Niri 9

decades of neglect, is now gradually being gentrified. Several budget hotels are found here, some very badly run down but not without their faded glory. Created in 1673 after the sacking of old Panama, Casco Viejo is a treasure trove of architectural delights, some restored, others in a desperate state of repair, but most demanding a gentle meander through the shady streets. In 1992 local authorities began reviving some of the area's past glory by painting the post-colonial houses in soft pastels and their decorations and beautiful wrought-iron railings in relief. New shops, art galleries and restaurants are moving into restored buildings in an attempt to make Casco Viejo a tourist attraction.

At the walled tip of the peninsula is the picturesque **Plaza de Francia**, with its bright red poinciana trees and obelisk topped by a cockerel (symbol of the Gallic nation), which has a document with 5000 signatures buried beneath it. Twelve large narrative plaques and many statues recall the French Canal's construction history and personalities; the work of Cuban doctor Carlos Finlay in establishing the cause of yellow fever is commemorated on one tablet. Facing the plaza is the French Embassy, housed in a pleasant early 20th-century building; it stubbornly refused to relocate during the years when the neighbourhood declined and is now one of the main focus points in the area's renaissance. Built flush under the old seawalls around the plaza are **Las Bóvedas** ('The Vaults'), the thick-walled colonial dungeons where prisoners in tiny barred cells were immersed up to their necks during high tides. Nine 'vaults' were restored by the Instituto Panameño de Turismo (IPAT) in 1982 and converted into an art gallery – **Galería Las Bóvedas** ① *Tue-Sun 1100-1900; students offer walking tours of the Casco Viejo from here during these hours, copies of* Focus on Panama *are available here* – and a handicraft centre. The French restaurant **Las Bóvedas** occupies another two 'vaults' next to the former Palacio de Justicia, partly burned during 'Operation Just Cause' and now housing the **Instituto Nacional de Cultura** (INC), with an interesting mural by Esteban Palomino on the ground floor.

Steps lead up from the Plaza de Francia to the **Paseo de las Bóvedas** promenade along the top of the defensive walls surrounding the peninsula on three sides. This is a popular place for an evening stroll; it is ablaze with bougainvillea and affords good views of the Bahía de Panamá, the Serranía de Majé on the Panama/Darién provincial border (on a clear day), Calzada Amador (known during the Canal Zone era as the Causeway) and the islands beyond.

Map labels:
Instituto Bolívar
Salón Bolívar
Plaza Bolívar
San Francisco
Teatro Nacional
Palacio Nacional de Gobierno
9
8
4
Tourist Police
Av Central
Santo Domingo (Ruins) & Museo de Arte Colonial Religioso
7
Roberto Chiari
French Embassy
Instituto Nacional de Cultura
3
Plaza de Francia
Las Bóvedas

Dulcería Panadería La Gran Vida **2**
Granclement **4**
Monolo Caracol **8**
Mostaza **7**
Panadería Azukitar **5**

Two blocks northwest of the plaza (Avenida A and Calle 3) are the restored ruins of the impressive **Church and Convent of Santo Domingo** (1673, later destroyed by fires in 1737 and 1756), both with paired columns and brick inlaying on their façades. The famous 15-m-long flat arch, **Arco Chato**, which formed the base of the choir was built entirely of bricks and mortar with no internal support. When the great debate as to where the canal should be built was going on in the US Congress, a Nicaraguan postage stamp showing a volcano, with all its implications of earthquakes, and the stability of this arch – a supposed proof of no earthquakes – are said to have played a large part in determining the choice in Panama's favour. A chapel on the site has been converted into the interesting **Museo de Arte Colonial Religioso** ① *Tue-Sat 0830-1630, US$0.75, students and seniors US$0.25, T228-2897*, whose treasures include a precious Golden Altar, a delicate snail staircase, silver relics and wooden sculptures from Lima and Mexico, 19th-century engravings of the city, and the skeleton of a woman found during excavation of the church.

Not far from Santo Domingo, across Avenida Central, the neoclassical **Teatro Nacional** ① *T262-3525, Mon-Fri 0800-1600, US$0.50*, with 850-seat capacity, opened in 1908 with Verdi's *Aida* being performed in what was then considered the state of the art in acoustics. French-influenced sculptures and friezes enliven the façade, while Roberto Lewis' paintings depicting the birth of the nation adorn the theatre's dome. The ballerina Dame Margot Fonteyn, who married a member of the prominent Arias family and was a long-time resident of Panama until her death in 1991, danced at the theatre's re-inauguration in 1974.

Diagonally opposite the Teatro Nacional (Avenida B and Calle 3) is the peaceful **Plaza Bolívar**, with a statue of the liberator Simón Bolívar, draped in robes, standing below a large condor surrounded by plaques of his deeds. Around the square are the former **Hotel Colombia**, the **Church of San Felipe Neri**, and many 19th-century houses still displaying roofs of red-clay tiles bearing the stamp 'Marseilles 1880'. On the east side stand **San Francisco Church** ① *Mon-Sat 1430-1800, Sun all day*, colonial but 'modified' in 1917 and modernized in 1983, and the **San Francisco Convent** (1678), the largest of all the religious buildings, which was restored by Peruvian architect Leonardo Villanueva. The Bolivarian Congress of June 1826, at which Bolívar proposed a United States of South America, was also held in the Chapter Room of the Convent, now known as the **Salón Bolívar**, and the 1904 Constitution was also drafted here. This northern wing was dedicated as the **Instituto Bolívar** in 1956; its wood panelling, embossed leather benches and paintings (restored in part by the government of Ecuador) may be viewed with an authorized guide from the Bolivarian Society (T262-2947). The adjacent Colegio Bolívar, built on a pier over the water, is due to become the new Cancillería (Ministry of Foreign Affairs).

Another long block west of Plaza Bolívar, and one block north on the seafront (Avenida Eloy Alfaro) between Calles 5 y 6, is the **Palacio Presidencial**, the most impressive building in the city, built as an opulent residence in 1673 for successive colonial auditors and governors, enlarged and restored under President Belisario Porras in 1922.

A few blocks west, Avenida Alfaro curves north around the waterfront to the colourful **Central Market, Mercado San Felipe** (see Shopping, page 376) and the **Muelle Fiscal** wharf where coastal vessels anchor and small cargo boats leave for Darién and sometimes Colombia. Two blocks further north, where Avenida Alfaro meets Avenida Balboa by the pier, is the modern **Mercado de Mariscos** (fish and seafood market), where fishermen land their catch.

Returning to Casco Viejo, two blocks south of the Palacio Presidencial is the heart of the old town, the **Plaza Catedral** or **Independencia**, with busts of the Republic's founders, and surrounding public buildings. On the west is the **cathedral** (1688-1794, refurbished in 1999), its twin towers, domes, classical façade encrusted with mother-of-pearl and three of the tower bells brought from the Old Panama Cathedral. To the right of the main altar is a subterranean passage which leads to other *conventos* and the sea. On the southwest corner with Calle 7 is the neoclassical **Palacio Municipal** (City Hall), on the first floor of which is the **Museo de Historia de Panamá** ① *Mon-Fri 0800-1600, US$0.50*, which covers the nation's history since European landfall, and includes highlights of the treaty between Panama and the US which led to the construction of the Canal. The former post office next door, originally built in 1875 as the **Grand Hotel** ("the largest edifice of that kind between San Francisco and Cape Horn" according to a contemporary newspaper), is the city's best example of French architecture. It became de Lesseps' headquarters during canal excavations in the 1880s and was sold back to Panama in 1912. It has been entirely gutted and converted into the **Museo del Canal Interoceánico** ('Museum of the Panama Canal') ① *Plaza Catedral, T/F211-1650, Tue-Sun 0900 -1700, US$2.50, concessions US$0.75, www.museodelcanal.com, photography is not allowed, English- and French-speaking guides are available, other languages available if booked in advance, hand-held English audio commentaries cost US$5*. It has a comprehensive and interesting history of Panama – mainly the central provinces – as shaped by its pass route, recommended.

The east side of the plaza is dominated by the former **Archbishop's Palace**, which was later occupied by a university, was a shelter for runaway kids and then spent a period as the **Central Hotel** (1884), once the most luxurious in Central America. The interior featured a palm garden, restaurants, barber's shop, 100 rooms with private baths and a wooden staircase imported from New York, and it was the centre of Panama's social life for decades. Today it is decrepit and may, in time, benefit from the creeping regeneration of the old city.

There are a number of other interesting religious structures within two or three blocks of the cathedral, but the most-visited is the **Church of San José** ① *Av A and Calle 8, 1 block west and 2 south of the Plaza Catedral, T228-0190*, with its famous Altar de Oro, a massive baroque altar carved from mahogany and, according to common belief, veneered with gold. This was one of the few treasures saved from Henry Morgan's attack on Old Panama in 1671 and legend records different versions of how it was concealed from the buccaneers: whitewashed by the priest, or even covered in mud by nuns; however, a remark attributed to Morgan hints that he was not deceived!

A block to the south on Calle 9 is the run-down **Plaza Herrera**. French influence is evident in the windows and flower-filled cast-iron balconies of the green and pale pink houses and *pensiones*. Behind Plaza Herrera are the ruins of the **Tiger's Hand Bulwark**, where the defensive wall ended and the landward-side moat began. The strongpoint held a 50-man military post and 13 cannon; it was demolished in 1856 as the town expanded but restored in 1983. Portions of the moat can still be detected.

Santa Ana and Calidonia

As Avenida Central emerges from Casco Viejo and strikes west into the mainland, it enters the bustling and unpretentious district of Santa Ana, marked by a busy plaza complete with elderly gents, shoe-shiners and a small colonial church. This is a favorite locale for political meetings and a good place to catch buses to other parts of the city. Nearby, running towards the Central Market between Avenida Central and Avenida B (officially known as Carrera de Chiriquí), is an exotic, narrow alley called **Salsipuedes** ('Get out if you can') where crowded stalls sell everything from fruit to old books and medicinal plants. In 1892, over 75 of the street's residents were Chinese merchants, but the city's Chinatown (**Barrio Chino**) is now largely confined to nearby Calle Juan Mendoza and adjacent Calle B with a typical Chinese archway at the entrance, good Chinese restaurants and general shops.

South of plaza Santa Ana lies the slummy district of **El Chorillo** with its rotten clapboard housing and visibly impoverished population. North of the plaza, Avenida Central continues its journey into a pedestrianized precent called **La Peatonal**. This is a popular commercial sector with a profusion of fast-food outlets and vast open-front stores selling cut-price clothes. You'll see lots of nattering women selling lottery tickets, as well as the occasional Kuna drifting through in colourful traditional garb. La Peatonal concludes at the busy Plaza 5 de Mayo at Calle 22 Este, an important junction full of roaring traffic and chaotic activity. Buses leave for the Canal at a small station just west of here. In the centre of the plaza is an obelisk honouring the firemen who died in a gunpowder magazine explosion on the site in May 1914. The former quarters of the

③ Calidonia

⇒Panama City maps
1 Panama City, page 352
2 Casco Viejo, page 354
3 **Calidonia, page 358**
4 Bellavista, page 360
5 Panamá Viejo, page 363

Museo Antropológico Reina Torres de Araúz is also on the plaza, now empty and slightly sad-looking since the museum's relocation to Curundú. There's a good *artesanía* market just behind the building. One block east of Plaza 5 de Mayo is the **Museo Afro-Antillano** ① *Justo Arosemena and Calle 24, T262-5348, Tue-Sat 0830-1530, US$1,* which features an illustrated history of Panama's West Indian community and their work on the Canal. There's a small library.

As Avenida Central continues north, it enters the district of Calidonia and grows increasingly hectic. A helter-skelter profusion of stalls and kiosks teeters beneath crumbling apartment blocks, while vociferous street vendors flog pirated DVDs, tend to vast simmering pots or mountains of sweltering tropical fruit. Expect sensory overload and watch your pockets. East of Avenida Central and running parallel to it are several slightly calmer roads with lots of economical hotels and several gloomy casinos. Keep heading east and you'll soon reach the bay of Panama, skirted by Avenida Balboa, a popular stretch for jogging. The building sites and enormous piles of rubble everywhere are part of plans for new sky-scrapers, including a 100-storey affair with a restaurant on top. The bay of Panama is a good place to contemplate the city, with colonial Casco Viejo, the soaring financial sector and transitting ships all visible from its rather smelly shores. On a semi-circular promontory jutting out into the water by Calle 34 is a great monument to **Vasco Núñez de Balboa**, who stands sword aloft as he did when he strode into the Pacific on 15 September 1513. The 1924 statue stands on a white marble globe poised on the shoulders of a supporting group representing the four races of Man.

There are two museums nearby: **Museo de Ciencias Naturales** ① *Av Cuba y Calle 30, T225-0645, Tue-Sat 0900-1530, Sun 1300-1630, US$1, students and seniors US$0.25,* which has good sections on geology, palaeontology, entomology and marine biology, and **Museo Casa del Banco Nacional** ① *Calle 34 between Av Cuba and Av Justo Arosemena, Mon-Fri 0800-1230, 1330-1630, free,* which, although not widely known, is worth a visit. It contains a large numismatic and stamp collection and a history of banking from the 19th century, old postal and telephone items, and historic photos.

Bella Vista and the Banking District

North of Calle 42 Este, Avenida Central turns into Vía España and enters the neighbourhood of Bella Vista. Once an attractive residential district, it still exudes an air of middle-class contentment despite the recent intrusion of upmarket hotels, bars and restaurants. This is the city's Zona Rosa, or entertainment district, and it borders several other moneyed neighbourhoods including El Cangrejo, Campo Alegre and Obarrio. Together, these form a much larger administrative department, also called Bella Vista, which is home to Panama City's fabled Banking District as well. Coming from the working-class quarters of Santa Ana and Calidonia, the difference is striking. This is 'New Panama', replete with five-star hotels and trendy restaurants, where the burgeoning elite window-shop at Porsche showrooms and international boutiques. The majority of Panama City's 87 banks find their home here, in sleek, skyward-reaching structures of glass and steel – the 'Cocaine towers' – testament to the profitability of the Colombian drug trade as much as the international finance sector. Beyond Bella Vista, ever higher towers rise up from ever more exclusive neighbourhoods, including the soulless waterfront condos of Punta Paitilla and Punta Pacífica, little more than upmarket ghettos for foreign retirees and dubious 'businessmen'.

④ Bella Vista

Panama City maps
1 Panama City, page 352
2 Casco Viejo, page 354
3 Calidonia, page 358
4 **Bellavista, page 360**
5 Panamá Viejo, page 363

N

200 metres
200 yards

Sleeping
Bella Vista **1** *D1*
California **2** *D1*
El Panamá **3** *B2*
Euro **4** *D1*
Hostal La Casa
   de Carmen **5** *A3*
Mamallena **8** *B2*
Marbella **6** *B2*
Miramar
   Intercontinental **9** *D2*
Riande Continental **10** *B2*
Vía España **7** *D1*
Zulys Backpackers **11** *C2*

Eating
Angel **1** *A2*
Athens **2** *C2*
Bar Restaurante 1985 **3** *B2*
Caffé Pomodoro **4** *B2*
El Patio Mexicano **6** *A3*
El Trapiche **7** *A2*
Gauchos Steak House **8** *D2*
Greenhouse **9** *A2*
Jimmy's **10** *B2*
La Novena **11** *A1*
Las Costillitas **12** *A2*
Las Tinajas **13** *D2*
Madame Chang **14** *D3*
Manolo **16** *A2*
Matsui **15** *A2*

Niko's Café **17** *B3*
Ozone Café **18** *D2*
Parillada Martín Fierro **19** *A2*
Pavo Real **20** *A2*
Petit Paris **21** *A2*
Pizzeria Sorrento **22** *B3*
Rincón Suizo **3** *B2*
Rockin Gorrilla **23** *A2*
Sushi Itto **24** *B3*
Taj Mahal **25** *D1*

Curundú

West of Calidonia lies the department of Curundú with its run-down apartment blocks, brazen street life and dangerous, dilapidated slums. The atmosphere can be sketchy and uncomfortable, so you should avoid exploring this area on foot. If you want to see it, a taxi ride to the bus station or Albrook airport will afford brief glimpses, as will trips to either of Curundú's two major attractions, which are both worth venturing into the area for. The 265-ha **Parque Natural Metropolitano** ① *between Av Juan Pablo II and the Camino de la Amistad, along the Río Curundú, T232-5552, www.parquemetropolitano.org, visitor centre open Mon-Fri, 1030-1630, park open Mon-Sun, 0600-1700, US$2*, has a mirador (150 m) with a great view over the city and a glimpse of the Canal, as well as two interpretive walking trails from which *tití* monkeys, agoutis, coatis, white-tailed deer, sloths, turtles and up to 200 species of bird may be glimpsed (go early morning for best viewing); green iguanas sun themselves on every available branch. The **Smithsonian Institute** has installed a unique construction crane for studying the little- known fauna in the canopy of this remnant of tropical semi-deciduous lowland forest, which can be visited while walking the paths of the Metropolitan Park. Researchers and students wishing to use the crane need to apply through the Smithsonian Institute. The visitor centre also runs guided one-hour tours and holds regular slide shows. No ANAM permit is required; it's a recommended, easy excursion. A taxi from the city centre costs US$3-4. Nearby, the **Museo Antropológico Reina Torres de Araúz** ① *Av Ascanio Villalaz, Mon-Fri 0900-1600, T262-8338, free*, have displays on Panamanian history, anthropology and archaeology. Their collection includes rare pre-Columbian gold and jewellery, ceramics and surreal stone figures. They also have a reconstructed tomb excavation, complete with skeletal remains. This is a new location for the museum, and much of the interesting collection may not yet be on display.

Ancón

Ancón curves round the hill of the same name north and east and merges into Panama City. It has picturesque views of the palm-fringed shore. Take care on Ancón Hill, as robberies sometimes occur. The following walk takes in the sights of Ancón: walk to the top of the hill in the morning for views of the city, Balboa and the Canal (toilets and water fountain at the top – you may have to climb part of the radio tower to see anything); the entrance is on Avenida de los Mártires (formerly Avenida de Julio and briefly Avenida Presidente Kennedy). From Avenida de los Mártires take a clockwise route around the hill, bearing right on to Balboa Road (Avenida Estado de Jamaica), you will soon come upon the **Kuna Artesans** market on your left where the Kuna sell their multicolored *molas*. Further on, down and to the left, is the **Mercado Artesanal** where a wider variety of handicrafts, woven baskets from the Wounaan-Embera people, as well as Ecuadorian sweaters can be found. You will come upon **Chase Manhattan** and **Citibank** shortly after passing the Mercado Artesanal. The post office and a café follow. Then walk down the Prado lined with royal palms to the **Goethals Memorial** ① *free, ID must be shown to the guards*, in honour of the engineer George Washington Goethals, behind the building of the Canal. The steps lead to the administration building to see the restored murals of the construction of the Canal. Follow Heights Road until it becomes Gorgas Road where you will pass the headquarters of the **Smithsonian Tropical Research Institute** ① *opposite Plaza 5 de Mayo, Mon-Fri 0900-1700, Sat 0900-1200, café Mon-Fri 1000-0430, T212-8113, www.stri.org*, an English-language scientific research library where applications to visit Barro Colorado Island are made. The café/bookshop sells environmental books and nature guides, including national park maps.

A little further, among trees and flowers, is the former **Gorgas Army Community Hospital**. Named after William Crawford Gorgas, the physician who is credited with clearing the Canal Zone of the more malignant tropical diseases before construction began in the beginning of the 20th century. Gorgas Road leads back to Avenida de los Mártires, but look out for the sign to the **Museo de Arte Contemporáneo** ① *Av de los Mártires, entrance on Av San Blas, T262-8012, Tue-Sun 0900-1700, US$1.* Housed in a former Masonic Lodge (1936), the permanent collection of national and international modern paintings and sculptures has special exhibitions from time to time, with marquetry, silkscreen and engraving workshops, and a library of contemporary visual art open to students. At the foot of Ancón Hill the **Instituto Nacional** stands on the four-lane Avenida de los Mártires. At **Mi Pueblito** ① *north of Av de los Mártires, east of the Quarry Heights entrance, open till 2200, small admission charge,* you'll find nostalgic replicas of three different villages: one colonial from the Central Provinces, one Afro-Antillian and one indigenous. It's on a busy road so best to take a taxi. To continue further west into Balboa, see page 379.

Balboa

The town and docks of Balboa are just over 3 km west of Panama City (10 minutes by taxi, US$5) and stand attractively between the Canal quays and Ancón Hill. It has been described as efficient, planned and sterilized – a typical American answer to the wilfulness and riot of the tropics. The Canal administration building (with fine murals on the ground floor) and a few other official residences are on Balboa Heights. At the foot of the Heights is the town of Balboa, with a small park, a reflecting pool and marble shaft commemorating Goethals, as well as a long palm-flanked parkway known as the Prado. At its eastern end is a theatre, a service centre building, post office and bank.

Fuerte Amador

Before the Puente de las Américas crosses the Panama Canal the long peninsula of Fuerte Amador stretches into the Pacific, formerly the HQ of the Panamanian Defence Force, seized by US forces in 1989 and returned to Panama in 1994. Beyond Fuerte Amador are the formerly fortified islands of Naos, Perico and Flamenco, linked by the 4-km causeway (**Calzada Amador**) built of rubble excavated from the Canal. There are many interesting buildings in this area bearing the marks of the conflict, and some attractive lawns and parkland. The Calzada has been extensively developed over recent years. As you enter the Causeway you pass the Figali Convention Centre, built and inaugurated in 2003 for the Miss Universe competition and centennial celebrations. The Figali Centre now hosts major music and sports events. It has fine views of the Puente de las Américas and the ships lined up to enter the Canal. The bridge was built between 1958 and 1962 by the US to replace the ferry crossing. It is 1653 m long and, with a road surface to seaway distance of 117 m, there is ample room for all ships to pass below. The bridge, which has three lanes, is the only vehicular crossing on the Pacific side of the Canal. There is also a pedestrian walkway for the length of the bridge, but muggings have occurred on the bridge even in broad daylight so take care. There are small charges for entry and for swimming at Solidaridad Beach on **Naos** (crowded at weekends and the water is polluted – not recommended). There is a small marine park with local marine life on show. At Punta Culebra on Naos is the new **Marine Exhibition Center** ① *T212-8793, Tue-Fri 1300-1800, Sat-Sun 1000-1800, US$2* (of the Smithsonian Tropical Research Institute), with interesting aquaria and exhibitions on marine fauna. As the road reaches **Isla Perico**, there is a newly built block of restaurants, bars and some shops underneath what is set to be an apartment-style hotel. A 'mega resort' is in process at Naos Harbour – a 300-room hotel, 114-room apartment-hotel, casino, shops, condos and new beach, and there is a proposal for a cable car to the Causeway descending from the top of Ancón Hill. **Flamenco**, the last of the islands, is the headquarters for the National Maritime Service and home to the Flamenco Yacht Club, a large duty-free store and a pristine mall of boutiques, expensive souvenir shops and lively range of restaurants, bars and clubs. Most popular between Wednesday and Saturday nights.

The **Bridge of Life Biodiversity Museum** ① *T314-1395, www.biomuseopanama.org*, currently being developed on the Causeway, is designed by architect Frank O.Gehry with botanical gardens designed by New York specialist Edwina von Gal. Labelled a learning centre and 'hub of an interchange of nature, culture, the economy and life' the museum is an impressive and modern testament to Panama's location as a major ecological crossroads.

Panamá Viejo

① *Tue-Sun 0900-1700, US$3, T226-8915, www.panamaviejo.org. Getting there: taxi from the city centre, US$10; buses from Vía España or Av Balboa, US$0.80. Panamá Viejo also makes a good excursion for passengers with a little time to kill at nearby Tocumen Airport; taxis can be as much as US$5 but still reasonable, especially if this is the only chance you'll have to see Panama. Alternatively, take any bus marked Vía España, get off at Vía Cincuentario, then take a bus to Panamá Viejo.*

5 Panamá Viejo

➡**Panama City maps**
1 Panama City, page 352
2 Casco Viejo, page 354
3 Calidonia, page 358
4 Bellavista, page 360
5 **Panamá Viejo, page 363**

Colonial road to Portobelo

Pacific Ocean

N — Not to scale

King's Bridge **1**
Convento de San José **2**
Main Plaza **3**
Cathedral **4**
Cabildo **5**
Convento de Santo Domingo **6**
Bishop's Residence **7**
Slave's House/ House of the Genovese **8**

Royal Houses **9**
Emperor's Bridge **10**
Dungeons **11**
Kitchens **12**
Meat Market **13**
Convento de Compañía de Jesús **14**
Convento La Concepción **15**
Church of La Concepción **16**

Hospital de San Juan de Dios **17**
Convento de San Francisco **18**
Convento de la Merced **19**
La Navidad Fort **20**
Matadero/ Slaughterhouse Bridge **21**

A recommended short trip is to the ruins of Panamá Viejo, 6.5 km northeast along the coast. A wander among the ruins still gives an idea of the site's former glory, although many of the structures have been worn by time, fungus and the sea. The narrow **King's Bridge** (1620) at the north end of the town's limits is a good starting point; it marked the beginning of the three trails across the isthmus and took seven years to build. Walking south brings you to the **Convento de San José**, where the Golden Altar originally stood (see page 356); it was spared by the great fire that swept the town during Morgan's attack (which side started the fire is still debated). Several blocks further south is the main plaza, where the square stone tower of the **cathedral** (1535-1580) is a prominent feature (US$4 extra). In the immediate vicinity are the Cabildo, with imposing arches and columns, the remnants of **Convento de Santo Domingo**, the **Bishop's Residence**, and the **Slave Market** (or House of the Genovese), whose jail-like structure was the hub of the American slave trade. There were about 4000 African slaves in 1610, valued at about 300 pesos apiece. Beyond the plazas to the south, on a rocky eminence overlooking the bay, stand the **Royal Houses**, the administrative stronghold including the **Quartermaster's House**, the **Court** and **Chancellery**, the **Real Audiencia** and the **Governor's Residence**.

Further west along the Pacific strand are the dungeons, kitchens and meat market (now almost obliterated by the sea); a store and refreshment stands cluster here on the south side of the plaza, and handicrafts from the Darién are sold along the beach. Across Calle de la Carrera stands another great complex of religious convents: **La Concepción** (1598) and the **Compañía de Jesús** (1621). These too were outside the area destroyed by the 1671 fire but are today little more than rubble. Only a wall remains of the Franciscan **Hospital de San Juan de Dios**, once a huge structure encompassing wards, courtyards and a church. Another block west can be seen part of the **Convento de San Francisco** and its gardens, facing the rocky beach. About 100 m west is the beautiful **Convento de La Merced**, where Pizarro, Almagro and their men attended Mass on the morning they sailed on their final and momentous expedition to Peru. Decades later Morgan stored his plunder here until it could be counted, divided up and sent back to the Atlantic side. At the western limit of Panamá Viejo stands **La Navidad Fort** (1658). Its purpose was merely to defend the **Matadero (Slaughterhouse) Bridge** across the Río Agarroba but its 50-man garrison and half-dozen cannon were no match for the determined force of privateers; it is also known as Morgan's Bridge because it was here that the attack began.

There is a new **visitor centre**, with exhibitions in Spanish, as well as maps, pictures and models of how Panama's first city would have looked. There are also opportunities for students to volunteer in future excavations (check www.panamaviejo.org). By the ruins is **Museo de Panamá Viejo** ① *Vía Cincuentenario, T226-89156, Mon-Sun 0900-1700, US$2.*

The whole area (unfenced) is attractively landscaped, with plenty of benches to rest on, and floodlit at night. Late afternoon when the sun is low is an especially nice time to visit, although at least two hours should be allowed to appreciate the site fully. The main ruins are patrolled by police and reasonably safe. **Dame Margot Fonteyn**, the ballerina, is buried alongside her husband Roberto Arias Guardia in the Jardín de la Paz cemetery behind Panamá Viejo. IPAT organizes free folklore events and local dance displays on Saturdays in the dry season (*verano*), which are worth seeing. The tourist office in Panama City (T226-7000) has a list of programmes and can supply professional guides if required.

Playa Kobbe to San Carlos

A string of Pacific beaches west of Panama City offers easy respite from the capital's frenetic pace. These beaches are invariably crowded with Panamanian day-trippers at weekends and holidays, but quiet in the week. **Playa Kobbe** (also known as Playa Bonita) is the first and nearest with a large intercontinental hotel and golf course. There is a charge to use the beach. Continue west on the Interamericana and you'll reach a turning at Bejuco with a road reaching 28 km down a peninsula to **Punta Chame**. You'll find a white-sand beach, a few houses and just one hotel/restaurant. It's quite windy here, attracting lots of wind- and kitesurfers between December and April. At low tide the sand is alive with legions of small pink crabs and there's a splendid view northeast to Taboga Island and the entrance to the Canal in the distance. Food is prepared by the beach and there are several bars. A pick-up runs between the highway and the beach, US$1, linking you to the outside world.

Beyond Chame are two beaches: **Nueva Gorgona**, 3 to 4 km long, waves increasing in size from west to east, and a well-stocked grocery store. A little further along the Interamericana is **Playa Coronado**, the most popular beach in Panama, but rarely crowded. Homeowners from Playa Coronado have installed a checkpoint at the turning, unaffiliated with the police station opposite. Be polite, but do not be deterred from using the public beach. Opposite the turning to Playa Coronado is a road inland to Las Lajas and beyond to the hills and **Lagunas del Valle**, about one hour from the highway. Ten kilometres beyond Playa Coronado is the town of **San Carlos**, where there's a good river and sea bathing (beware of jelly fish and do not bathe in the estuarine lake). There are not many restaurants in San Carlos, but there are plenty of food shops. The beaches of **El Palmar** and **Río Mar** are within striking distance. Beyond San Carlos, the Interamericana enters the province of **Coclé**, home to the famous beaches of **Santa Clara** and **Farallón** (see Coclé, page 398).

Isla Taboga

Tobaga island – dubbed 'Island of Flowers' – is a favourite year-round resort. It produces delicious pineapples and mangoes, and has one of the oldest churches in the Western hemisphere. Admission to the beach at **Hotel Taboga** is US$10, redeemable in tokens to buy food and drink (covered picnic huts cost extra). There are other good places to swim around the island, but its south side is rocky and sharks visit regularly.

Calypso Queen (T314-1730) provide ferry services to Tobaga island from Isla Naos Pier on Amador Causeway. The trip outis very interesting. You pass the naval installations at the Pacific end of the Canal, the great bridge linking the Americas, tuna boats and shrimp fishers in for supplies, and visiting yachts from all over the world. Part of the route follows the channel of the Canal, with its busy traffic. Taboga itself, with a promontory rising to 488 m, is carpeted with flowers at certain times of year. There are few cars in the meandering, helter-skelter streets and just one footpath as a road. All items are expensive on the island, so make sure you bring plenty of cash as there is no bank.

Islas Perlas

Some 75 km southeast of the city are the Islas Perlas ('Pearl Islands'), where you will find beautiful beaches with crystal-clear water, good snorkelling, diving and sailing, and lots of shark. The islands are so-named for the prolific pearl fishing in colonial days; today, these waters are rich in Pacific mackerel, red snapper, corvina, sailfish, marlin and other species, drawing lots of sea anglers. High mountains rise from the sea, and there is a little fishing village on a shelf of land at the water's edge. **Contadora**, one of the smallest Pearl Islands, has become quite famous since its name became associated with a Central American peace initiative. It was also where the last Shah of Iran, Mohammed Rezá Pahlaví, was exiled, in a house called 'Puntalara', after the Iranian Revolution. Contadora is popular with Canadian, Spanish and Italian holidaymakers and is becoming crowded, built-up and consequently not as peaceful as it once was.

You'll find no less than 13 powdery white beaches flanking its shores and a growing number of luxury hotels. Nearby, **Isla San José** is a private island with waters rich in marine life, particularly black marlin, drawing sports fishers keen to snag a catch, and perhaps a world record – no less than 16 have been bagged here already. This is the second largest island in the archipelago, home to exceptionally fertile soils and abundant plant species. **Isla Viveros** is a particularly idyllic spot filled with turquoise lagoons and white sand beaches. It's a good place to watch flocks of Great Frigates, but unfortunately you'll also have to share the paradise with a hideous new housing development, www.islaviveros.com. One of the more pristine islands in the archipelago is **Isla San Telmo**, the site of lush primary forests, prolific bird species and nesting turtles. Whales also visit the region is great numbers during the month of September.

◉ Panama City listings

Hotel and guesthouse prices

LL over US$150	L US$100-150	AL US$66-99
A US$46-65	B US$31-45	C US$21-30
D US$12-20	E US$7-11	F under US$7

Restaurant prices

††† over US$15   †† US$8-15   † under US$8

See pages 43-45 for further information.

◉ Sleeping

Tocumen International Airport
LL-L Sheraton Panama , Vía Israel y Calle 77, T305-5100, www.starwoodhotels.com. This excellent and reputable hotel has 4 restaurants, 1 with an excellent view over bay, another offering Southeast Asian cuisine. Other facilities include casino, sports bar and outdoor swimming pool. Located 10-15 mins from Tocumen airport.
L-AL Riande Aeropuerto, near Tocumen Airport (5 mins), T290-3333, www.hoteles riande.com. Conveniently located for fliers, with free transport to the airport. Rooms are predictably well appointed. Amenities include pool (loud music all day), tennis courts and casino.

Casco Viejo *p354, map p354*
D Hotel Colón, just off Calle 12, 1 block from the Plaza Santa Ana, T228-8510, elhotelcolon @pa.inter.net. This colonial building is well maintained and has lovely tiling downstairs. It's located on the edge of El Chorillo, so take care, especially at night. Most rooms have fan and cold water, cheaper with shared bath (**E**), some have a/c (**C**). Beds are soft but clean.
D Luna's Castle, 9na este, between Av B and Av Alfaro, T262-1540, lunascastle@yahoo. com. Undoubtedly the best hostel in Panama City. You'll find a wealth of amenities here including comfortable communal spaces, Wi-Fi, table tennis, guitars, book exchange and a kitchen. There's even a cosy movie theatre showing films until midnight. At the time of research there were only dorm beds, but plans for rooms were in the works (**C**). Slightly sketchy area. Book ahead.
D-E Hospedaje Casco Viejo Calle 8, in front of San José church, T211-2027, www.hospedajecascoviejo.com. A mix of rooms (**D**) at this backpackers' hostel, with private and shared bathrooms, and dorms (**E**) too. A safe, quiet spot with outdoor terrace, kitchen and internet access. They have good travel advice for Panama and moving on.

E Caracas, Calle 12 on Plaza Santa Ana, T228-7229. This big, dark old building has seen better days. The interior is gloomy, but rooms are large and clean, and some overlook the action on the plaza (but note that outside windows are a security issue here). Most rooms have fan, some have a/c (**D**).

F Casa Grande, Av Central, Calle 8-9, T211-3316, 1 block behind the cathedral. Slummy, smelly and definitely scary, this sad old hotel has fallen into almost total disrepair. Lone females should avoid it; others should come only if they really like to rough it. Bathrooms are shared, water is cold, rooms with a balcony cost a dollar extra. Take care.

Santa Ana and Calidonia *p357, map p358*
AL Costa Inn, Av Perú y Calle 39, T227-1522, www.hotelcostainn.com. A sparklingly clean and comfortable hotel right on the edge with Bella Vista. Double rooms feature 2 bathrooms, and the rooftop pool has great views of the city. Scheduled transport to the airport and other places. Breakfast included.

AL Roma Plaza, Av Justo Arosemena y Calle 33, T227-3844, www.hotelromaplaza.com. A range of rooms and suites, all clean and airy, but expensive given stiff competition in the area. The rooftop pool has panoramic views, and there are a couple of restaurants. **Italian Garden** offers a good-value buffet breakfast for US$5.25. Wi-Fi enabled.

B Acapulco, Calle 30 Este y Av Perú, T225-3832, F227-2032. There are 55 rooms here, some are a little musty, but those with balconies are better. All have a/c, cable TV, telephone, hot water and room service. There's an excellent restaurant and safe parking. Conveniently located and recommended.

B Caribe, Av Perú y Calle 28, T225-0404, caribehotel@hotmail.com. One of the city's older hotels, with 153 very large rooms, rooftop pool and bar, casino and restaurant. In the heart of Calidonia.

B Centro Americano, Av Justo Arosemena y Av Ecuador, T227-4555, www.hotelcentro americano.com. The 61 rooms here are very clean and well appointed, with Wi-Fi, hot water, good reading lights and cable TV. Some have balconies and views of the bay. Restaurant, beauty salon and parking available.

B Discovery, Av Ecuador, T225-1140, h_discovery@cwpanama.net. A clean, modern, economical hotel. Rooms are comfortable, with a/c, hot water and cable TV; some have jacuzzis. There's a restaurant/ bar downstairs, and internet, private parking, tours and airport pickup are also available.

B Dos Mares, Calle 30 between Perú and Cuba, T/F227-6149, dosmares@cwpanama. net. This hotel has a good rooftop pool with views across the city. Some rooms are more 'renovated' than others, so ask to see a few. Otherwise generally clean and comfortable, with a/c, hot water, cable TV and phone as standard. There's internet service a restaurant.

B Latino, Av Cuba y Calle 36 Este, T227-2994, hlatino@cableonda.net. Rooms here are clean, functional and rather straightforward – if small for the price. Cable TV and a/c as standard. There's also a restaurant and pool.

B Lisboa, Av Cuba y Calle 31, T227-5916. The rooms at this hotel are nice and big, and some have good views over the bay. The usual amenities include a/c, hot water and cable TV, with a restaurant downstairs. The decor is very 'red', so if you like your accommodation fiery, you'll love this place.

B Residencial Alameda, Calle 30 Este, Av Cuba, T225-1758, residencialalameda@hot mail.com. A big, modern building. Rooms here are comfortable, with ill-matching furniture, a/c, clean bathrooms, hot water, cable TV and telephone.

B Stanford, Plaza 5 de Mayo, T262-4933, hotelstanford@cwpanama.net. Formerly Hotel Internacional, this tower on the plaza has spacious rooms with hot water, a/c and cable TV. Although a little tatty for the price, the views of the city and ocean are almost worth it.

B Veracruz, Av Perú y Calle 30, T227-3022, www.hotelveracruz.com.pa. This hotel sports an elegant reception area, but some of the rooms are noisy and in need of renovation.

It has a very good restaurant, helpful staff, sea views, Wi-Fi, jacuzzi and sauna.

C Andino, Calle 35 y Av Perú, beside Parque Parades, T225-1162, www.hotelandino.net. This excellent value hotel has large rooms with all mod cons including cable TV, fridge, telephone and Wi-Fi access. Highly recommended, especially for groups.

C Arenteiro, Calle 30 Este y Av Cuba, T227-5883, F225-2971. Some of these simple, functional rooms are on the small side, but they're all clean and have hot water, cable TV, telephone and a/c. There's a popular bar/restaurant downstairs.

C Covadonga, Calle 29, Av Perú, T225-5275, marit@sinfo.net. This hotel has a good rooftop terrace with a pool and views over the city. Rooms are clean and comfortable, with cable TV, sometimes noisy a/c, and powerful, hot showers. Ecotours, including birdwatching and hiking, are soon to be available. There's a restaurant and internet terminal downstairs.

C Pensión Monaco, Av Cuba y Calle 29, T225-2573. This large, slightly soulless place has big, comfortable rooms; some have views. Cable TV, hot water and a/c are standard, private parking available.

C Residencial Jamaica, Av Cuba and Calle 38, T225-9870. Smart-looking building with very clean if unexciting rooms, all with colour TV, hot water and a/c.

C Residencial Turístico Compostela, Av Cuba and Calle 29, T227-6394. Rooms are smallish, simple and also comfortable, with good beds and dimmer switches on the lights. A good deal for the price.

C Riazor, Calle 16 Oeste, T228-0777, wwwhotelriazorpanama.com. This hotel has 46 cool, clean rooms, most with a/c, some cheaper ones with fan (**D**); all have hot water and cable TV. There's a restaurant downstairs, 24-hr taxi service and laundry.

C Venecia, Av Perú, between Calle 36 and 37, T227-7881, www.hotelvenecia. cjb.net. This hotel is fading, but still going strong. Some rooms are better than others; ask to see a few. The good ones are large

and have a fridge. All have cable TV, bath, hot water and a/c.

D Ideal, Calle 17 Oeste, off Av Central, between Plaza Santa Ana y Plaza 5 de Mayo, T262-2400. This faded old hotel – complete with gaudy decor – certainly hasn't forgotten its heyday in the 1970s. Rooms are clean and tidy with hot water, a/c and cable TV. There's a pool. Hectic location and brusque management.

D Las Tablas, Av Perú 2830 y Calle 29 Este, T227-3699. Rooms here are equipped with fan and cable TV. They're a good deal for budget travellers, although the hotel interior is slightly dark and gloomy. Opposite is **El Machetazo** supermarket, food for cheap meals.

D Residencial Turístico El Edén, Calle 29 Este between Av Cuba and Justo Arosemena, T225-2946. Simple, economical rooms with a/c, hot water and cable TV. Staff are pleasant.

D Residencial Volcán, Calle 29 and Av Perú, T225-5263, opposite Migración, next to Museo de Ciencias Naturales. A very good option for budget travellers and backpackers. Rooms have a/c or fan, and cable TV. Guests have access to the rooftop pool at **Covadonga**, next door. Friendly, safe, clean and recommended.

Bella Vista and the Banking District *p359, map p360*

LL Miramar Intercontinental, Av Balboa, T250-3000, www.miramarpanama.com. Former guests of this classy hotel include President Bush, who hired 120 rooms here during his visit to Panama. This illustrious lodging has a wealth of amenities, including 3 restaurants, a huge pool, gym, Wi-Fi and exclusive marina.

LL Riande Continental, Vía España and Ricardo Arias, T263-9999, www.hoteles riande.com. Sister hotel to the **Riande Aeropuerto** and a landmark in the modern city centre. Tasteful and modern lodgings, with gym, jacuzzi, business services, casino, travel agency and panoramic views. Prices including buffet breakfast.

LL-L El Panamá, Vía España 111, T215-9000, www.elpanama.com. This hotel sports a tropical art-deco style, huge rooms, good pool and a vast 'Vegas' style casino. A bit inefficient, but generally good.

A Euro Hotel, Vía España 33, opposite the **Bella Vista**, T263-0802, www.eurohotel panama.com. Located on a busy street, this hotel has large, comfortable rooms with a/c, hot water and cable TV. There's also a pool, restaurant and bar.

A Hostal La Casa de Carmen, Calle 1, Urbanización El Carmen Casa 32, Vía Brasil, 1 block back from Vía España, T/F263-4366, www.lacasadecarmen.net. A good value option, close to the banking sector. Rooms have hot water, cable TV and a/c as standard.

A Hotel Vía España, Calle Martín Sosa (on the corner of Vía España), T264-0800. This large hotel has clean rooms with comfy beds, a/c, private bath, telephone, TV with cable. A few suites have a jacuzzi for a very good price. Restaurant on-site and internet available. Friendly and recommended.

A Marbella, Calle D (between Calle 55 and Calle Eusebio A Morales), El Cangrejo, T263-2220, www.hmarbella.com. Plush rooms with a/c, cable TV and private bath in a safe, central area of town.

B California, Vía España y Calle 43, T263-7736, www.hotel-california.ws. A good, clean, professional hotel with friendly, English-speaking staff. Rooms are modern, with a/c, cable TV, Wi-Fi and hot water. There's a good restaurant attached.

C Bella Vista, Vía España N 31 y Calle 42, T264-4029. Located on a busy road, this hotel has affordable, good-value rooms with fan or a/c, hot water, cable TV and telephone. Secure parking, bar and restaurant available.

C-E Mamallena, Calle Manuel Maria Ycaza, opposite **Restaurante Jimmy**, T6676-6163, www.mamallena.com. A newish hostel with private rooms and dorms, kitchen and plenty of places to hang out. Often full with backpackers. They've done their research, and have details about sail boats to Colombia on the website.

E-F Zulys Backpackers, Calle Ricardo Arias 8, between **Hotel Continental** and **Mariott**,

T269-2665. Dorms and private rooms with a/c, free coffee, internet and security lockers. They offer numerous tours around the country and boat trips to Colombia.

Apartments

A Crystal Suites Hotel, Vía Brasil y Samuel Lewis, T263-2644, www.crystalsuites.com. Luxury suites with restaurant, bar, business centre and swimming pool.

Camping

There are no official sites but it is possible to camp on some beaches or, if in great need, in the **Balboa Yacht Club** car park. It is also possible to camp in the **Hipódromo** grounds (11 km east of the city, on Vía España) but there are no facilities; this is allowed if you are waiting to ship your vehicle out of the country. Also possible, by previous arrangement, at **La Patria** swimming pool nearby, and at the **Chorrera** (La Herradura) and **La Siesta** beaches on the Interamericana.

Playa Kobbe to San Carlos *p365*

A Palmar Surf Camp, Playa El Palmar, T240-8004, palmarsurfcamp@hotmail.com. Simple but pleasant lodgings offering surf lessons, board rental and 'surfari' tours. Breaks of varying difficulty can be found on the beach near the hotel.

B Cabañas de Playa Gorgona, San Carlos, T269-2433. Simple self-catering cabins, popular and busy at the weekend when there's a 2-night minimum stay. There's a communal BBQ area and simple meals available.

B Gorgona Hayes, San Carlos, T223-7775. A good hotel with a pleasant pool, fountain, tennis court and restaurant.

B Hostal Chiquito, Lagunas del Valle information T236-4632 (Panama City). A 160-ha farm with 8 guest rooms, 2 double rooms in separate units, meals included, riding, hiking, lake swimming. Electricity evenings only, transport provided from Panama City.

B Hotel Canadian, Chame, T240-6066, www.hotelcanadianpanama.com. A pleasant hill-top retreat with good views, pool, bar, restaurant and lazy hammocks. Hospitable owners and plenty of interesting tours on offer. Away from the beach, but transit is available.

B Playa Río Mar, beyond San Carlos on the Río Mar Beach, T240-8027. Comfortable rooms with a/c and hot water. Has a good seafood restaurant too.

B Río Mar Surf Camp, San Carlos, T6516-5031. Accommodation consists of simple rooms with hot water and a/c, slightly cheaper with fan. Backpackers can share rooms for US$10 per person. They offer surf tours on both coasts, classes, board rental and repair. There are facilities for skate-boarders too.

Isla Taboga *p365*

You may be able to find locals to stay with.
AL-A Cerrito Tropical, north end of town, T390-8999, www.cerritotropicalpanama.com. Small B&B overlooking the bay leading to the Canal. It has 6 comfortable rooms, all with a/c. Price includes breakfast.

A Taboga, T250-2122, htaboga@sinfo.net. Apdo 550357, Paitilla, Panamá, 300 m east of wharf. Rooms here have a/c, and cable TV. There's also a restaurant, café, pool and beach.

C Chu, on main street, 200 m left of wharf, T250-2036. A wooden colonial style building with beautiful views, own beach and terraced restaurant serving traditional fish and chicken dishes. The walls are thin and bathroom is shared.

Islas Perlas *p365*

L Contadora Resort, T214-3719, www. hotelcontadora.com. Same ownership as **El Panamá** in Panama City, this chalet complex has a nice location on beach, but it's a little run down.

A Contadora Island Inn, T6699-6414, www.contadoraislandinn.com. A selection of rooms here, all with private bath and B&B service. There's also a good range of relaxation and adventure acitivities – take your pick.

🍴 Eating

Casco Viejo *p354, map p354*
As Casco Viejo slowly gentrifies, more and more good restaurants are popping up. Wander around to see what's new.

♦♦♦-♦♦ Casablanca, Plaza Bolívar. Long-established restaurant with tables al fresco in the picturesque plaza. The food is pretty good, but not fantastic. They serve meat, pasta, salad and seafood.

♦♦♦-♦♦ Monolo Caracol, Av Central, across from Palacio Nacional de Gobierno y Justicia. This widely respected restaurant serves excellent tapas and seafood, uses the freshest ingredients and is often recommended. It is popular and can get noisy. Closed Sun.

♦♦♦-♦♦ Las Bóvedas, Plaza Francia. Located in the converted dungeons at the seaward end of Casco Viejo, this atmospheric restaurant serves up French cuisine beneath intimate, arched stone ceilings. An interesting spot, with an adjoining art gallery and live jazz Fri-Sat. Closed Sun.

♦♦♦-♦♦ Mostaza, Calle A opposite Arco Chato. This is one of the best restaurants in Casco Viejo, often visited by the president. It's an intimate spot with an Argentine-inspired menu of excellent beef cuts, steaks and grilled fish. Live music at the weekends.

♦♦ Café de Niri, Av Central y Calle 3. A popular place with tables outside, although the food is reportedly average.

Cafés, bakeries and ice cream parlours
Café Coca Cola, Av Central and Plaza Santa Ana. A bustling, friendly little locals' haunt with reasonably priced set lunches.

Dulcería Panadería La Gran Vida, Av Central 11-64 (between Calle 11 y 12). Good *chicha* juice, cheap ice cream, *empanadas* and cakes. Good for food on the go.

Granclement, Calle 3 between Av Central and Roberto Chiari. Fantastic gourmet ice cream to take your taste buds to another level. Not cheap, but delicious.

Santa Ana and Calidonia *p357, map p358*
Dining in these districts isn't fantastic, but it is economical. Most hotels have passable restaurants, otherwise eateries here are mostly simple affairs, geared towards locals.

¶¶ **Marbella**, Av Balboa y Calle 39. This well-established and popular eatery serves fine paella, shellfish and other lovingly prepared seafood including conch, squid and fresh oysters. Lobster is the house speciality.

¶¶-¶ **Café Boulevard Balboa**, Calle 33 and Av Balboa. One of the few bay-side eateries that hasn't been demolished for new skyscrapers. This Panamanian diner has been around since the 1950s and continues to serve good breakfasts, lunches and dinners. Popular with Panamanians. Closed Sun. Recommended.

¶¶-¶ **Romanaccio Pizza**, Calle 29, between Av Cuba and Av Peru. Good, tasty Italian-style pizzas with authentic crusts. Forget the burgers. Closed Sun.

¶ **El Sabor Interiorano**, Calle 37, between Av Central and Av Perú. A cosy, unassuming little locals' haunt serving affordable staples and Panamanian fare.

¶ **Parillada El Establo**, Av Peru and Calle 37. Unpretentious, open-air eatery where you can you dine on grilled meats.

¶ **Rincón Tableño**, Av Cuba No 5 y Calle 31. Panamanian fare. Several locations, this popular restaurant serves good *comida criolla* and is always bustling with working-class Panamanians. Lunchtimes only.

Cafés and bakeries
Panadería Azukitar, Av Central, near Plaza Santa Ana. Big, clean place with lots of sweet rolls, cakes and other sugary treats.
Rosca Dulce, Av Cuba and Calle 27. A well-stocked and friendly bakery where you can pick up cake and coffee for under a dollar. Good for a cheap breakfast on the go.

Bella Vista and the Banking District *p359, map p360*
The city's best restaurants are concentrated in Bella Vista, where you can find good-quality food and a wide range of international cuisine.

¶¶¶ **Bar Restaurante 1985**, Eusebio Morales and Calle 49B Oeste. Fine French cuisine from Chef Willy Diggelmann, including gourmet dishes for devoted foodies. Veal cutlets, filet mignon and seafood stews are among the offerings. A second restaurant, **Rincón Suizo**, adjoins this one and serves equally good (though slightly cheaper) Swiss food, including cheese fondues.

¶¶¶ **Gauchos Steak House**, Calle Uruguay y Calle 48. Choose your own cut at this often buzzing steakhouse in Marbella, a must for meat lovers.

¶¶¶ **Matsui**, Av Eusebio A Morales A-12. Excellent sushi and other Japanese fare, all you can eat 1200-2000.

¶¶¶ **Rendezvous**, at the **Riande Continental**. They serve a superb Sunday brunch here, although not cheap.

¶¶¶ **Sushi Itto**, Calle 55 and Samuel Lewis, at the back of Plaza Obarrio building, T265-1222. Widely renowned Mexican-owned sushi house that has mastered an intriguing fusion of Latin and Japanese cuisine, utilizing local ingredients in classic Oriental recipes.

¶¶¶-¶¶ **Madame Chang**, Av 5 Sur, between Calle 48 and Calle 49. Some claim this is the best Chinese restaurant in Latin America. It's a well-established haunt, with a calm, clean interior and a menu sporting Peking duck and other tasty fare.

¶¶¶-¶¶ **El Patio Mexicano**, Av 1RA B Norte, off Vía Argentina. Excellent Mexican cuisine from this authentic and atmospheric restaurant that serves delicious *mole*-renched peppers, tasty enchiladas and tequila cocktails. The best Mexican in the city, and reassuringly creative. Closed Mon.

¶¶ **Angel**, Vía Argentina 68, T263-6411. Spanish fare and seafood including imported mussels, eel and *bacalao* (cod). Closed Sun.

¶¶ **Athens**, corner of Av Uruguay and Av 4 Sur. A lively restaurant specializing in Greek and Middle Eastern cuisine, including tasty stuffed pittas, kebabs and salads. Good atmosphere.

¶¶ **Caffé Pomodoro**, Av Eusebio A Morales, north of Calle 55. Tasty and affordable Italian cuisine from renowned local restaurateur

Willy Diggelmann. Fresh, simple and served in hearty portions, the way Italian food should be.

El Trapiche, Vía Argentina 10, T221-5241. This popular restaurant specializes in classic Panamanian fare, serving dishes such as empanadas and *mondongo* (seasoned tripe). They often host traditional music and dance programmes; call for information. Also in Panamá Viejo, Vía Cincuentenario.

Jimmy's, Paseo Cincuentenario just beyond Atlapa Centre, T226-1096. Popular with Panamanian business people at lunch time, this often busy eatery serves good grills, meat and seafood. Also on Av Manuel M Icaza opposite **Riande Continental**.

Las Costillitas on Vía Argentina. This restaurant has a good range of meat, chicken and fish dishes, with a huge menu which takes 30 mins to read. Closed Sun.

Las Tinajas, on Calle 51, near **Ejecutivo Hotel**, T263-7890. Panamanian cuisine and traditional entertainment, including dance, music and costumes (Tue and Thu-Sat from 2100). A little touristy, but the food is very good and authentic. There's also a craft shop attached. Closed Sun.

Manolo, Vía Argentina, sidewalk terrace. A favourite for politicians and young people in evenings and Sun morning. They serve draught beer, Spanish tapas and *churros*. Also on Vía Venetto y Calle Eusebio A Morales.

Ozone Café, Calle Uruguay. Trendy little restaurant in the Marbella district, serving international food to a young crowd.

Parrillada Martín Fierro, Calle Eusebio A Morales, T264-1927. Carnivores will delight at the excellent beef cuts, Argentine steaks and other fine meat dishes served at this reputable steak house.

Pavo Real, Vía Argentina and Calle José Martí. This upmarket English pub and restaurant serves wholesome British fare for homesick expats, including fish and chips, and international food such as steak, burgers and salads. There's darts too.

Rockin Gorrilla, Vía Argentina. A fun, buzzing restaurant with a giant guitar-playing gorilla as its mascot. They serve North American and Tex

Mex such as burgers, nachos and club sandwiches. And beer, of course.

Taj Mahal, Calle 42 and Av Justo Arosemena. Over 100 items grace the menu of this reputable Indian restaurant, enough to satisfy the appetite of any curry lover. Tandoori dishes are the house speciality. Closed Mon.

La Novena, Vía Argentina. A lovely, unpretentious little restaurant serving wholesome vegetarian food and delicious, chocolate-filled desserts. Closed Tue.

Restaurant y Pizzeria Sorrento, Vía Ricardo Arias 11, T269-0055. One of best meal deals in this part of town. Excellent pizza, pasta and more traditional Panamanian dishes at good prices.

Niko's Café, with 4 locations at Vía España near **El Rey** supermarket, T264-0136; El Dorado Shopping Centre, T260-0022; Paitilla, past old airport T270-2555; and behind the former Balboa High School in the Canal Zone T228-8888. Cheap, reliable fast food, including burgers, subs and sodas.

Cafés and bakeries

Greenhouse, Vía Argentina and Av 4TA B Norte. Swamped in swathes of green foliage, this trendy café-lounge serves burgers, wraps and sandwiches and overlooks the Vía Argentina.

Petit Paris, Vía Argentina and Av 3RA B Norte. French-style café serving crunchy baguette sandwiches, cappuccinos and other Euro fare.

Betania

El Mesón del Prado, Edif Alcalá, Tumba Muerto, T260-9466. Spanish fare and seafood at this comfortable, popular restaurant.

La Tablita, Transisthmian Highway, Los Angeles neighbourhood, T260-1458. This landmark steakhouse serves decent cuts at reasonable prices.

Fuerte Amador p362

Café Barko, Calzado de Amador. One of the most established restaurants in Flamenco Mall, specializing in seafood and Panamanian dishes, beautifully prepared.

¶¶ **Crêpes and Waffles**, located upstairs at the Flamenco Mall. Pleasant, light dishes, including crêpes and waffles, as the name suggests.

¶¶ **Pencas**, Amador Causeway, in front of Plaza Iberoamericana, T211-3671, www.pencas.com. Panamanian food and live 'Panamanian Expressions' – folkloric nights with music and dancing on Wed nights. Call ahead and make a reservation as it gets busy.

¶¶-¶ **Mi Ranchito**, by Naos Isla, T228-4909. This charming, simple, outdoor restaurant is highly recommended in the evening for seeing the skyline, as well as for good, cheap traditional food and drink.

Islas Perlas *p365*

¶¶ **Gallo Nero**, by runway. Good seafood especially lobster, pizza and pasta, at reasonable prices. Run by a German couple, Gerald and Sabine.

¶ **Fonda Sagitario**, near **Gallo Nero**. A café offering cheap eats; also a supermarket and a duty-free shop.

¶ **Michael's**, opposite **Gallo Nero**. Good pizzas and ice cream.

⊙ Entertainment

Panama City *p351, maps p352, p354, p358 and p360*

Bars and clubs

Many late night haunts are concentrated in the Marbella district, particularly along and around Calle Uruguay (Calle 48).

La Chiva Parrandera. Is an open-sided bus that tours the hot-spots from 2000-2400. Call T263-3144, for information, US$25 per person.

Café Bolívar, Plaza Bolívar, Casco Viejo. Small, snug bar with outside tables.

Casablanca, Plaza Bolívar, Casco Viejo. Fancy, hip bar and restaurant offering Provençale/Thai cuisine. Mixed reports on the food.

Deep Room, Calle Uruguay area of Bella Vista. An excellent club. Tribal house and electronica. Late start, sometimes 0400.

La Parrillita, Av 11 de Octubre, Hato Pintado. Restaurant/disco in a railway carriage.

Las Bóvedas, Plaza de Francia, Casco Viejo, T228-8068. Jazz on the weekends from 2100-0100.

Liquid, Calle 50 and Calle José de la Cruz. A popular dance club that hosts electronic events and late night dance parties. If there's any big pop music names in town, they're likely to be playing here.

Moods, Calle Uruguay. Reggae, reggaeton, salsa and other Latin music. A slightly older crowd and occasional live music.

Next, Av Balboa, T265-8746. One of the biggest commercial discos in the city – sweaty, pricey and popular.

Oz Bar and Lounge , Calle 53 Este, Marbella. Well established chill-out lounge bar with house nights and good DJs. Ladies drink free on Fri.

Panamá Viejo, T221-1268. Colombian restaurant, bar and disco. Open 24 hrs.

Unplugged, Calle 48, Bella Vista. Mon-Sat, rock 'n' roll club.

Voodoo Lounge, Plaza Pacífica, Punta Pacífica, T215-1581. Fri house music, live DJs Sat electronic music.

Wasabi Sushi Lounge, Marbella, T264-1863, Electronic music, live DJs, occasional retro and sushi. Wed is ladies nights, when the sangria flows for free.

Cabarets, casinos and gambling

Panamanians are big gamblers and there are more than 20 state-managed casinos in Panama City, some in the main hotels. If you fancy a punt, most offer blackjack, baccarat, poker, roulette and slot machines. Winnings are tax-free and paid without deductions.

Cinema and theatre

La Prensa and other newspapers publish daily programming (*cartelera*) of cultural events. Good range of cinemas including **Cine Balboa** near Steven's Circle, **MultiPlaza Mall** at Punta Pacífica, modern multi-screen **Albrook Mall**, www.albrookmall.com, and **Multi Centro** in Paitilla, have large multi-screen cinemas.

Anayansi Theatre, in the Atlapa Convention Centre, Vía Israel, San Francisco. Has a 3000-seat capacity, good acoustics, regular recitals and concerts.

Balboa Theatre, near Steven's Circle and post office in Balboa. Folkloric groups and jazz concerts sponsored by National Institute of Culture.

Cine Universitario, in the National University, T264-2737. US$1.50 for general public, shows international and classic movies, daily (not holidays) at 1700, 1900 and 2100.

Guild Theatre, in the Canal Area at Ancón. Mounts amateur productions mainly in English.

Teatro Nacional, see page 356, occasionally has shows and performances. There are regular folklore sessions every other Sun and monthly National Ballet performances when not on tour. Check press for details.

Live music

Bar Platea, opposite the old Club Union building, Casco Viejo. Good jazz lounge and bar, open late – live music here starts around 2200.

Café El Aleph, Vía Argentina north of Vía España, T264-2844. Chilled out coffee house atmosphere here. They serve snacks and full meals, have internet facilities and host occasional art shows, as well as live jazz at weekends. Phone for programme.

Café Gardel, Vía Argentina, T269-3710. A small restaurant with a tiny bar. The perfect atmosphere for jazz.

Giorgio's, 1 block south of Vía Porras.

Hotels Granada and **Soloy** (Bar Maitai, T227-1133) are recommended for live Latin music at weekends.

Las Bóvedas, Plaza de Francia, T228-8068. Renowned jazz performances on weekends, 2100-0100.

Nottingham, Fernández de Córdoba, Vista Hermosa, T261-0314. This restaurant hosts live salsa at weekends. No cover charge.

Vino's Bar, Calle 51 y Colombia, Bella Vista, T264-0520. Another restaurant with weekend live salsa, cover charge.

✸ Festivals and events

Panama City *p351, maps p352, p354, p358 and p360*

Feb/Mar Carnival has become more elaborate in recent years. Activities include a parade on Shrove Tue.

3 Nov Independence Day, practically the whole city – or so it seems – marches in a colourful and noisy parade through the old part of the city lasting over 3 hrs. Another parade takes place the following day.

Dec Annual **Christmas parade**, with US influence much in evidence, rather than the Latin American emphasis on the *Nacimiento* and the Three Kings.

⬡ Shopping

Panama City *p351, maps p352, p354, p358 and p360*

Duty-free imported luxuries of all kinds are an attraction at the Zona Libre in Colón, but Panama City is a booming shopping centre where anything from crystal to cashmere may be cheaper than at their point of origin.

The smartest shops are along **Calle 50** (Av 4 Sur) in Campo Alegre, and **Vía España** in Bella Vista and El Cangrejo, but **Av Central** is cheaper, the best and the most popular.

Of the various commercial centres, with banking, entertainment and parking facilities, the largest is **Los Pueblos**, on Vía Tucumen, with buses leaving from 5 de Mayo, or take a taxi for US$5. It's a huge complex of mega-stores. **Multi Plaza** is a new mall located at Punta Pacífica, close to Atlapa, with department stores, shops, restaurants, banks and an 8-screen cinema. **Multi Centro** is at Punta Paitilla and easily accessible from the centre of town. **Albrook**, by the national bus terminal, have a mall that includes a large cinema.

Arts and crafts

Traditional Panamanian *artesanía* includes *molas*, eg Emma Vence, T261-8009; straw, leather and ceramic items; *chunga nawala* (palm fibre) canasters; the *pollera* circular dress, the *montuno* shirts (embroidered), the *chácara* (a popular bag or purse), the *chaquira* necklace made by Ngöbe-Buglé (Guaymí) people, and jewellery. Indigenous Darién (Embera) carvings of jungle birds and animals from cocobolo wood or *tagua* nut (small, extremely intricate, also *tagua* necklaces) make interesting souvenirs (from US$10 up to US$250 for the best, museum-quality pieces). The tourist office has a full list of *artesanía* shops, including those in the main hotels.

Artesanías Nacionales, indigenous co-ops selling a good selection direct from open-air outlets, can be found in Panamá Viejo, Canal Area at Balboa and along road to Miraflores Locks at Corozal (daily if not raining).

Colecciones, Vía Italia, opposite **Hotel Plaza Paitilla Inn**, have a wide selection. Plenty of straw articles available, including baskets, bags, traditional masks and Panama hats (US$150 for the best quality).

Flory Salzman on Vía Venetto at the back of **El Panamá Hotel**, T223-6963. The best place outside San Blas Islands for *molas*, huge selection, sorted by theme, ask for discounts.

Inovación, or **Indutípica**, Av A y Calle 8 Ote (opposite San José Church) for reproductions of pre-Columbian ceramics and jewellery, necklaces, Kuna *molas* (prices starting from US$2.50) from the Darién, and Ngöbe-Buglé dresses from Bocas del Toro.

Mercado Artesanal de Cinco de Mayo, behind the old Museo Antropológico Dra Reina. Stalls selling Kuna, Ngöbe-Buglé and Embera crafts as well as local Panamanian work. They also have a range of hammocks and artefacts from neighbouring countries.

Reprosa, Av Samuel Lewis y Calle 54, T269-0457. A unique collection of pre-Columbian gold artefacts reproduced in sterling silver vermeil; David and Norma Dickson make and sell excellent reproductions (**Panamá Guacas**, T266-6176).

La Ronda, Calle 1a, Casco Viejo, www.pana malaronda.com. An attractive little store that sells a range of Panamanian *artesanías*. Convenient if you can't get out to the markets.

Books and music

La Garza, Av José de Fábrega y Calle 47, near the university. Bookshop with good supply of Latin American literature (Spanish only).

Gran Morrison, Vía Espana, T269-2211, and 4 other locations around the city. Books, travel guides and magazines in English.

Legends, Calle 50, San Francisco, diagonal to the Iglesia de Guadalupe de Panamá, T270-0097. A cultural oasis – CDs, books, T-shirts and posters.

Librería Argosy, Vía Argentina north of Vía España, El Cangrejo, T223-5344. Very good selection in English, Spanish and French, also sells tickets for musical and cultural events. Recommended.

National University Bookshop, on campus between Av Manuel Espinosa Batista and Vía Simón Bolívar, T223-3155. For an excellent range of specialized books on Panama, national authors, social sciences and history, Mon-Fri 0800-1600. Highly recommended.

Simón Bolívar Library on campus has extensive Panamanian material, only for registered students but visitors engaged in special research can obtain a temporary permit from the director, Mon-Fri 0800-2000, Sat 0900-1300.

Librería Cultural Panameña, SA, Vía España y Calle 1, Perejil, T223-5628, www.libreria cultural.com. Mon-Fri 0900-1800, Sat 0900-1700. Excellent, mostly Spanish bookshop with obscure Panamanian prints as well as regular titles and very helpful staff.

Smithsonian Tropical Research Institute (see page 361), Edif Tupper, Av de los Mártires (opposite National Assembly), has a bookshop and the best English-language scientific library in the city, Mon-Fri 0800-1600.

Camping equipment

Army Force, east end of the pedestrianized section of Av Central, west of Plaza 5 de Mayo.

Army-Navy store, Av Central near Plaza 5 de Mayo, for various pieces of camping and hiking equipment.

Markets and supermarkets

Bargain hard as prices are extremely competitive. The central **Mercado San Felipe**, close to the docks and Palacio Presidencial, is the place for fresh produce (pigs, ducks, poultry and geese) and pets. The most interesting part is the chaotic shopping area along Calle 13 and the waterfront (Terraplen). It's the best place to buy second-hand jungle and military supplies (eg powerful insect repellents, machetes and cooking equipment) for a trek into the forested interior.

Supermercado El Rey has a branch on Vía España just east of **Hotel Continental**, at El Dorado, and at several other locations. **Super 99**, **Farmacias Arrocha**, **Casa de la Carne** (expensive) and **Machetazo**, also a department store (on Av Central, Calidonia), are said to be the city's best.

Newspapers and magazines

The international edition of the *Miami Herald* is widely available at news stands and hotels, as are leading US papers and magazines. Spanish and English magazines at branches of **Farmacias Arrocha**, **Super 99** and **Gago** supermarkets/drugstores.

Photography

There are many places for equipment such as **Foto Decor** and **Foto Enodi**, Vía Porras. **Relojería**, Calle Medusín, off Av Central in Calidonia. Watch shop for camera repairs.

▲ Activities and tours

Panama City *p351, maps p352, p354, p358 and p360*

Birding and wildlife

Advantage Tours, T6676-2466, www.advantagepanama.com. Founded by a group of biologists, this reputable operator offers a range of birding and wildlife tours, including expeditions to Darién. The guides are experienced and well-trained and often have a background in biology or tourism. Sponsors of the Audubon Society.

Ancon Expeditions, Calle Elvira Méndez, next to **Marriott Hotel**, T269-9415, www.anconexpeditions.com. This is the tour operator for the environmental agency ANCON. Excellent guides and service, with especially recommended programmes in the Darién region (Cana Valley and Punta Patiño). They can also arrange programmes to most of Panama's wilderness areas. Trans-Darién treks and specialist birding programmes available.

Panama Audubon, Casa 2006-B, Llanos de Curundu, T232-5977, www.panamaaudubon. org. The excellent Panama Audubon Society is the country's foremost avian authority. They have been involved in the study, protection and promotion of Panama's birds for 35 years. They host regular events including lectures, workshops, field trips and tours. See their website for schedules.

Diving

See also individual listings for Bocas del Toro and Veraguas, both endowed with excellent sites.

Panama Dive Adventure, Miguel Brostella Av, Edif. Don Manuel 2a, opposite TGI Fridays, El Dorado, T279-1467, www.panamadivead venture.com. Diving and technical courses, including deep diver. Tours to both coasts and sites including Portobelo, Bocas del Toro, Coiba and Isla Iguana. Equipment sales, rental, repair and service. They also have offices at **Coco Plum lodge** in Portobelo.

Panama Divers, T314-0817, www.panama divers.com. A very reputable dive operator that offers custom-made tours and promises 'Discovery Channel quality' underwater experiences. They travel to both Pacific and Caribbean coasts, including premier sites such as Isla Coiba. PADI certification to Divemaster level, with special photography and videography courses offered.

Scubapanama, Urbanización El Carmen, Av 6 Norte y Calle 62a No 29-B, T261-3841, www.scubapanama.com. Respected local dive operator. Offer dives in the Caribbean (near Portobelo), Pacific and the Canal.

One option includes all 3 areas in 1 day. Longer trips can be arranged on request, including options in Islas Perlas and Isla Coiba. Given sufficient numbers all-inclusive multi-day trips to Isla Coiba start at around US$450-500. Certification courses available. Additional offices in Portobelo.

Fishing

Exploration Panama, T720-2470, www.explorationpanama.net. Big game fishing in several different Pacific Coast locales. Various packages are available, including an adventurous long-distance trip to the less-visited waters around Darién.

Panama Canal Fishing, T669-0507, www.panamacanalfishing.com. Fishing trips on Lago Gatún, where you can catch world-class Peacock Bass and Snook. They claim to reel in 20-30 per person, as Peacock Bass is not native to the lake and their numbers are presently out of control.

Outdoor and adventure tourism

Adventuras Panama, Edificio Celma, Of 3, El Paical, T260-0044, www.adventuresin panama.com. Specialist in hiking, rock climbing and canyoning. Very knowledgeable about Darién and the old colonial roads, and very active on looking for new opportunities. Many trips focus on the nearby Chagres National Park including the 'Jungle Challenge' which involves rappelling off a series of waterfalls – great fun! Good store of equipment with the unusual option of naturist hiking if the mood takes you and weather suits.

Panama Pete Adventures, Av Miguel Brostella, Plaza Camino de Cruces No 35, bear Country Inn & Suites El Dorado, T/F6673-6436, www.panamapete adventures.com. All the adventure options available in Panama, including biking, hiking, caving, fishing and kayaking.

Sailing

Panama Yacht Tours, T263-5044, www.panamayachttours.com. Private charters, canal transit, sunset cruises, parties and fishing trips, including services to both coasts.

San Blas Sailing, T314-1800, www.sanblas sailing.com. The first and oldest San Blas sailing charter offers crewed yacht tours of the Kuna Yala archipelago lasting from 4 to 21 days. They have an impressive fleet of monohulls and catamarans.

Tour operators

Adventuras Panama, Edificio Celma, Of 3, El Paical, T260-0044, www.adventuresinpana ma.com. Specialist in hiking, rock climbing and canyoning. Very knowledgeable about Darién and the old colonial roads, and very active on looking for new opportunities. Many trips focus on the nearby Chagres National Park including the 'Jungle Challenge' which involves rappelling off a series of waterfalls.

Ancon Expeditions, PO Box 0832-1509 WTC, T269-9415, www.anconexpeditions.com. This is the tour operator for the environmental agency ANCON. Excellent guides and service, with especially recommended programmes in the Darién region. They can also arrange programmes to most of Panama's wilderness areas.

Arian's Tours, Vía España, Plaza Concordia, Oficina 143A, T213-1172, www.arianstours pty.com. This agency offers a wide range of cultural and ecological tours including birdwatching, visits to indigenous communities, night tours of Panama City, hiking in national parks and dolphin observation.

Eco Circuitos, T314-0068, Planta baja del Hotel Country Inn and Suites, Amador, www.ecocircuitos.com. Expertly run with conservation an utmost priority. Good range of creative tours include hiking, diving, cultural exchange and educational programs.

EcoMargo Tours, Calle 50 San Francisco, local 1, next to **Farmacias Arrocha**, T302-0390, www.margotours.com. Specializes in ecotourism for small groups with an emphasis on using local guides. Professional and well-established with over 30 years' experience. They can also book various lodges and excursions.

Panama Divers, T314-0817, www.panama divers.com. A very reputable dive operator that offers custom-made tours and promises 'Discovery Channel quality' underwater experiences. They travel to both Pacific and Caribbean coasts, including premier sites such as Isla Coiba. PADI certification to Divemaster level, with special photography and videography courses offered.

Panama Star Tours, Calle Ricardo Arias, Edif Comi PB, T265-7970, www.panamastar.com. Arranges itineraries and books accommodation throughout the country. Well-established and professional.

☉ Transport

Panama City *p351, maps p352, p354, p358 and p360*
Air
International flights Tocumen
International Airport (PTY), 27 km, www.tocumenpanama.aero. Official taxi fare is US$25 to or from Panama City, maximum 2 passengers in same party, US$14 each sharing with 1 other, or US$10 per person if you share making it a *colectivo*. US$2 extra if you go by the toll road – much quicker. Bargaining is possible with regular cabs but not with tourist taxis at the airport.

From airport to city, walk out of the terminal and across the main road to the bus shelter. Another option is to walk 300 m to the traffic circle where there is a bus shelter (safe but hot during the day). For about US$3 (should only be US$1.20) driver takes you by Panamá Viejo, just off the main airport road.

Buses to the airport are marked 'España-Tocumen', 1 hr, US$0.35, but if going at a busy time, eg in the morning rush hour, allow 1½-3 hrs.

There is a 24-hr **left-luggage** office near the **Budget** car rental desk for US$1 per article per day (worth it, since theft in the departure lounge is common). The official IPAT tourist office at the airport remains open to meet late flight arrivals. There are duty-free shops at the airport with a wide selection and good prices. Most facilities are found in upper level departure area **Banco Nacional de Panamá**, **Cable & Wireless** office for international phone, fax and internet access); car rental is downstairs at Arrivals.

Aerolíneas Argentinas, Vía Brasil y Av Ramón Arias, T269-3815; **AeroMéxico**, Av 1BNorte, El Cangrejo, T263-3033; **Air France**, Calle Abel Bravo y 59 Obarrio T269-7381; **Alitalia**, Calle Alberto Navarro, T269-2161; **American Airlines**, Calle 50 Plaza New York, T269-6022; **Avianca**, 223-5225; **Aviatur**, T315-0311; **Cathy Pacific**, Av 1-B Norte, El Cangrejo, T263-3033; **Continental**, Av Balboa y Av 4, Ed Galerías Balboa, Planta Baja, T263-9177; **Copa**, Av Justo Arosemena y Calle 39, T217-2672; **Cubana**, Av Justo Arosamena, T227-2291; **Delta**, Edif World Trade Centre, Calle 53E, Marbella, T214-8118; **Grupo Taca**, Centro Comercial Camino de Cruces, Local 2, Vía Ricardo J Alfaro, T360-2093; **Iberia**, Av Balboa y Calle 34, T227-3966; **KLM**, Av Balboa y Calle Uruguay, Edif Plaza Miramar, T264-6395; **LAB**, Calle 50 No 78, Ed Bolivia, T263-6771; **LanChile**, Calle 72, San Francisco, T226-7119; **Lufthansa**, Calle Abel Bravo y 59 Obarrio, Ed Eurocentro, T269-1549; **Mapiex Aéreo**, T315-0344; **Mexicana**, Vía Argentina, Ed Torre el Cangrejo oficina 64, T264-9855; **United Airlines**, Bella Vista, L-1, T225-6519
Domestic flights These operate from Marcos A Gelabert airport at Albrook in the Canal Area. There is no convenient bus service, taxis charge US$2-3. Good self-service café especially for fried breakfast before early flight to San Blas. **Aeroperlas**, reservations T315-7500, www.aeroperlas. com, operates daily flights to 17 destinations throughout the country. **Air Panama**, T316-9000, www.flyair panama.com, have flights to 22 destinations, including San Jose in Costa Rica. **Mapiex Aéreo**, sales T315-0344, www.mapiex.com, operates private charters to several

destinations throughout the country including many Darién outposts. Rodolfo Causadias of **Transpasa**, T226-0842, is an experienced pilot for photographic work.

Bus

Local The traditional small buses known as *chivas*, consisting of locally made wooden bodies grafted onto truck chassis, have all but disappeared. Most buses in urban areas are second-hand US school buses brightly painted in fanciful designs, but in poor condition. They are known as *diablos rojos* (red devils) and are notorious for roaring engines and aggressive drivers. Most outbound (east) buses travel along Av Perú, through Bella Vista, before fanning out to their various destinations. Inbound (west) buses travel along Vía España and Av Central through the Calidonia shopping district. The basic fare is US$0.25, usually paid to the driver upon descending; if there is a fare box, deposit upon entering. To stop at the next authorized stop, call out *'parada'* to the driver.

Long distance All buses apart from the Orange buses leave from the clean and efficient bus terminal in Albrook, near the domestic airport. Taxi US$1.50-2 to centre. Facilities at the vast terminal include ATMs, internet access, clothes shops, luggage shops, bakeries and basic restaurants.

Most long-distance buses are fairly modern and in good condition. Except for the longest routes, most are 24-seater 'Coaster'-type minibuses. Check if a/c on next bus out is functioning. Offices are arranged in long line from right to left in the terminal.

Orange buses to all **Canal Area** destinations (Balboa, Miraflores, Paraíso, Kobbe, etc) leave from SACA terminal near Plaza 5 de Mayo; from the Plaza, walk past the National Assembly tower and turn left.

From the Gran Terminal de Transporte, Albrook (T232-5803): **Bocas del Toro**, 0800 (Mon, Fri, Sat, Sun) and 2000, 12 hrs, US$24; Chame/San Carlos, every 15 mins, 0530-2000, US$2.70; **Chitre**, hourly, 0600-2300, 3½ hrs,

US$7.50; **Colon**, every ½ hr, 0330-2130, 2hrs, US$2-2.50; **David**, hourly, 0530-0000, US$12.50-15; Darién, 4 daily, US$14; El Valle, every ½ hr, 0445-2100, 2 hrs, US$3.50; **Las Tablas**, hourly, 0600-1900, 5 hrs, US$8; **Paso Canoas (border with Costa Rica)**, 10 daily, 8 hrs, US$14; **Penonomé**, every 15 mins, 0445-2245, 2¼ hrs, US$4.50; **Santiago**, every ½ hr, 0600-2300, 3½ hrs, US$7.50.

International Buses going north through Central America get booked up so reserve a seat in advance and never later than the night before departure. **Ticabus**, in the Gran Terminal de Transporte, Albrook, T314-6385, www.ticabus.com, run a/c buses to **San José**, daily at 1100, arriving at 0200 the next day, US$25 one-way (but check times and prices which change at regular intervals); continuing to **Managua**, US$45; **Tegucigalpa**, US$65, and on as far as **Tapachula** on the Mexico-Guatemala Pacific coast border, US$110, via **Guatemala City**, US$95 (3½ days, overnight in Managua and El Salvador). Tickets are refundable; they pay on the same day, minus 15%. **Panaline** to **San José** from the Albrook Gran Terminal, T314-6383, leaves daily at 2200 arriving at 1530 the following day, US$25. You can also travel with **Padafront** , T314-6263, www.padafront.com, Panama City-Paso Canoas then change to **Tracopa** or other Costa Rican buses for San José and other destinations en route to the Costa Rican capital.

Car

Several major downtown arteries become one-way during weekday rush hours, eg Av 4 Sur/Calle 50, one-way heading west 0600-0900, east 1600-1900. The Puente de las Américas can be used only to go into or out of town depending on time and day, mostly weekends; these directions are not always clearly signed.

Car rental At the airport: Avis, T238-4056; **Budget**, T238-4068; **Dollar**, T238-4032; **Hertz**, T238-4081 and **National**, T238-4144. **In El Cangrejo**: Avis, Vía Venetto, T264-0722; **Barriga**, Edif Wonaga 1 B, Calle D, T269-0221;

Budget, T263-9190; Dollar, T269-7542. Gold, Calle 55, T264-1711; Hertz, Hotel Sheraton, T226-4077 ext 6202, Calle 50, T264-1111, El Cangrejo T263-6663; International, Vía Venetto, T264-4540.

Cycling
Almacén The Bike, Calle 50 opposite Telemetro. Good selection of cycle parts.

Taxi
Service is generally good, but can be scarce during peak hours and many drivers have little clue where many streets are – it's good to have a rough idea of the address location; voluntary sharing is common but not recommended after dark. If a taxi already has a passenger, the driver will ask your destination to see if it coincides with the other passenger's. If you do not wish to share, waggle your index finger or say '*No, gracias*'. Similarly, if you are in a taxi and the driver stops for additional passengers, you may refuse politely. Overcharging is common and official fares are based on a zone system: US$1 for 1 passenger within 1 zone, US$0.25 for each additional zone.. Additional passengers US$0.25 each regardless of zones; sharing passengers each pay full fare. Panamanians rarely tip, but foreigners may add US$0.25-0.50 to the fare. Hourly hire, advised for touring dubious areas, US$10 per hr. Radio taxis summoned by telephone are highly recommended. They are listed in yellow pages under 'Taxis'. Add US$0.40 to fare for pick-up. 'Tourist taxis' at major hotels (aged, large American cars with 'SET' number plates) have a separate rate structure: they are more expensive than those you flag down.

Train
A luxury train now runs daily from Corozal Passenger Station in Panama City to **Colón** US$22 one way, US$44 return, 0715, returns 1715, 1¼ hrs. Turn up on the day or book in advance through tour operators. More details available at www.panarail.com. A cab to the station from Panama City costs about US2.50.

Playa Kobbe to San Carlos *p365*
Bus Buses ply the Interamericana with great frequency, picking up and dropping off passengers at beach towns en route to Panama City or the interior. In some cases, access roads to the actual beaches and resorts are too long to walk. You may need to take a taxi from the Interamericana.

Isla Taboga *p365*
Boat Taboga is reached in 1-1½ hrs with **Calypso Queen** services departing from Isla Naos on the Amador Causeway (check the times in advance, T314-1730); taxi from Panama City about US$4 per person. From Panama City to Taboga: Mon, Wed, Fri, 0830 and 1500; Tue and Thu, 0830; Sat and Sun, 0800, 1030 and 1600. From Taboga to Panama City: Mon, Wed, Fri 0930 and 1630; Tue and Thu 1630; Sat and Sun, 0900, 1500 and 1700. Return fare US$10.

Islas Perlas *p*
Aeroperlas and **Air Panama** operate daily services between **Contadora** and **Panama City** (see Domestic flights, above).

Directory

Panama City *p351, maps p352, p354, p358 and p360*

Banks
See also Money, page 52. Try to avoid 15th and last working day of the month – pay days. Panamanian banks' hours vary, but most open Mon-Fri 0800-1500, Sat 0800-1200. **Visa** T264-0988; **MasterCard** T263-5221; **Diners** T263-8195. **Algemene Bank Nederland** changes Thomas Cook TCs. **American Express**, Agencia de Viajes Fidanque, Av Balboa, Torre Banco BBVA, Piso 9, T225-5858, Mon-Fri 0800-1715, does not exchange TCs. **International Service Center**, T001-800-111-0006. ATM for withdrawals at **Banco Continental** near hotel of same name. **Banistmo**, Calle 50, Mon-Fri 0800-1530, Sat 0900-1200, changes TCs,

no commission on AMEX, US$5 per transaction for other TCs. **Banco General** takes American Express, Bank of America and Thomas Cook TCs, 1% commission, minimum US$2 per transaction. Branch at Av Central y 4 Sur (Balboa) can be used for cash advances from ATMs on Visa. **Bank of America**, Vía José de la Cruz Herrera, Calle 53 Este, no commission on own TCs, US$0.10 tax. You can buy AMEX TCs at **Banco Mercantil del Istmo** on Vía España (they also give cash advances on MasterCard). **Banco Nacional de Panamá**, Vía España opposite the Hotel Continental, T205-2000, changes AMEX TCs with 1% commision. **Banco Sudameris** will also change Thomas Cook TCs. **Chase Manhattan Bank**, US$0.65 commission on each TC, Visa advances. **Citibank** has plenty of ATMs for cash withdrawals for its own debit or credit card holders, also Visa cash advances. **Lloyds Bank**, Calle Aquilino de la Guardia y Calle 48, Bella Vista, T263-6277, T263-8693 for foreign exchange, offers good rates for sterling (the only bank which will change sterling cash, and only if its sterling limit has not been exhausted). It is possible to change South American currencies (poor rates) at **Panacambios**, ground floor, Plaza Regency, behind Adam's Store, Vía España, near the Banco Nacional de Panamá and opposite Hotel Riande Continental (it also has postage stamps for collectors).

Conservation
Asociación Nacional de Conservación de la Naturaleza (ANCON), Calle Amelia Dennis de Icaza, Ancón Hill, past Panama's Supreme Court, in former Quarry Heights, Casa 153, T314-0052, www.ancon.org, for comprehensive information on the country's natural attractions and environmental matters. They also run a chain of lodges throughout the country eg in Darién and Bocas.

Dentist
Balboa Dental Clinic, El Prado, Balboa, T228-0338, good, fair price. **Dr Daniel Wong**, **Clínica Dental Marbella**, Edif Alfil (ground floor), near Centro Comercial Marbella, T263-8998. **Dr D Lindo**, T223-8383, very good but fix price before treatment.

Embassies and consulates
Canada, World Trade Center, Galería Comercial, 1st floor, Calle 53e, Marbella, T264-9731; **Chile**, Vía España, Edif Banco de Boston, T223-9748, 0900-1200, 1400-1600; **Colombia**, World Trade Center, Calle 53e, Marbella, T264-9266, 0800-1300; **Costa Rica**, Calle Samuel Lewis, T264-2980, 0900-1600; **El Salvador**, Av Manuel Espinoza Batista, Edif Metropolis 4A, T223-3020, 0900-1300; **France**, Plaza de Francia, Zona 1, T211-6200; **Germany**, Edif Bank of America, Calle 50 y 53, T263-7733, 0900-1700; **Guatemala**, Edif Altamira, 9th floor, 9-25, Vía Argentina, T269-3475, 0800-1300; **Honduras**, Av Balboa, Bay Mall, T264-5513, 0900-1400; **Israel**, Edif Grobman, Calle MM Icaza, 5th floor, PO Box 6357, T264-8022; **Italy**, Av Balboa Edif Banco Exterior, T225-8948, 0900-1200; **Mexico**, Edif Credicorp, Calle 50, T263-4900, 0800-1200; **Netherlands**, Altos de Algemene Bank, Calle MM Icaza, 4, T264-7257, 0830-1300, 1400-1630; **Nicaragua**, Edif de Lessep's, 4th floor, Calle Manuel María Icaza, T264-8225; **Norway**, Calle La Boca, Balboa, T228-1103, 0900-1230, 1430-1630; **Spain**, Plaza Porras, entre Av Cuba y Av Perú, Calle 33A, T227-5472, 0900-1300; **Sweden**, consulate at Av Balboa y Calle Uruguay, T264-3748, 0900-1200, 1400-1600; **Switzerland**, Av Samuel Lewis y Calle Gerardo Ortega, Edif Banco Central Cancellería, 4th floor, T390-6330, PO Box 499 (Zona 9A), 0845-1145; **UK**, MMG Tower, Calle 53, Zona 1, T269-0866; **USA**, PAS Building 783, Demetrio Basilio Lakas Avenue Clayton, T207-7000, http://panama.us embassy.gov ; **Venezuela**, Edif HSBC, 5th floor, Av Samuel Lewis, T269-1244, 0830-1100.

Hospitals and clinics

The **US Gorgas Army Community Hospital** has closed and US medical facilities have moved to the Howard Air Force Base, across the Puente de Las Américas. Private clinics charge high prices; normally visitors are treated at either the **Clínica San Fernando**, T305-6300, or the **Clínica Paitilla**, T265-8800, which both have hospital annexes. For inoculations buy the vaccine at a chemist and ask them to recommend a clinic; plenty in La Exposición around Parque Belisario Porras.

Immigration

Migración y Naturalización, Av Cuba (2 Sur) y Calle 29, T225-8925; visa extensions and exit permits issued Mon-Fri 0800-1530. **Ministerio de Hacienda y Tesoro**, Av Perú/Calle 36, T227- 4879, for tax compliance certificate (*paz y salvo*) required for exit visa (*permiso de salida*) if you stay more than 30 days. **Customs** for renewal of permits and obtaining exit papers for vehicles at Paitilla airport.

Internet

Internet cafés are everywhere in Panama City, but are especially concentrated in the commercial centre around Vía España. Rates can be as low as US$0.50 per hr. New places are constantly opening, with many offering perks to clients, such as free coffee.

Language schools

ILERI , 42G Vía La Amistad, El Dorado T/F260-4424, www.ileripanama.com. Small school offering homestays, US$450 per week 1-to-1 tuition.

Laundry

Lavamático Lavarápido, Calle 7 Central No 7-45, ½ block from Plaza Catedral, Mon-Sat 0800-2000, Sun 0900-1400. Many around Plaza Catedral; wash and dry US$2. **Lavandería y Lavamático América**, Av Justo Arosemana and Calle 27. Self service wash and dry only US$1.50. Very convenient for the Calidonia hotels.

Post office

There is no home postal delivery service in Panama. Recipients either have a post office box (*apartado*), or receive mail via General Delivery/Poste Restante (*Entrega General*). The new main post office is close to Casco Viejo at the west end of Av Balboa at Av B, opposite the Mercado de Mariscos, Mon-Fri 0700-1745, Sat 0700-1645; 'Poste Restante' items are held for a month. Official name and zone must be included in the address: **Main Post office**: 'Zona 1, Central, Av Balboa opposite Mercado de Mariscos'; **Calle 30 East/Av Balboa**: 'Zona 5, La Exposición'; **El Dorado Shopping Centre**, Tumba Muerto: 'Zona 6A, El Dorado'; **Vía España, Bella Vista** (in front of Piex store): 'Zona 7, Bella Vista'. Parcels sent 'poste restante' are delivered either to **Encomiendas Postales Transístmicas** at the El Dorado Centro Comercial or the main post office if there is no duty to pay on the goods. The post office operates a courier system called **EMS** to most Central and South American countries, Europe, US and some Asian countries. Packages up to 20 kg: 2 to 3 days to USA (500 g documents to Miami US$13); 3 to 4 days Europe US$20; Asia US$25. Also private courier services, eg **UPS**, Edif Fina, Calle 49, El Cangrejo, ½ kg to London or Paris, 3-4 days, US$30; **Jet Express (Federal Express)**, Edif Helga, Vía España y Av 4 Sur/Calle 50, 500g to Miami, 2 days, US$19.

Telephone

Cable & Wireless has its main office in Vía España, on the ground floor of Banco Nacional building. They offer excellent but expensive international telephone, telex, fax and modem (use Bell 212A type) facilities. Collect calls to 21 countries, dial T106. For cost of phone cards and international calls, see Essentials, page 55. Local calls in Panama City, US$0.10 for 3 mins, US$0.05 for each additional min; anywhere else in the country, US$0.15 per min.

Panama Canal

Whether travelling through the Canal, or just standing at its side, watching the vast ocean-going vessels rise and fall as they pass through the locks, it's hard to not be impressed by this colossal engineering feat. Most Panameños will insist that you visit Miraflores Locks, with good reason, for the viewing platform here supplies unrivalled views of canal operations. But if it's scale you're after, the Gatún Locks near Colón are truly gigantic, with ships passing directly under the viewing platform. Traversing the canal by boat is another option for experiencing the awesome scale of this world wonder.

But the canal isn't all ships and locks. The immense quantities of water required for its day-to-day operation are supplied by the vast, verdant rainforests skirting its banks. Awesome rivers, fascinating indigenous tribes and scores of colourful birds find their home in these protected forests, which are some of the most accessible in the Americas. The Parque Nacional Camino de Cruces has several designated hiking trails, including the Camino de Cruces colonial gold route which runs north as far as the Río Chagres. The Parque Nacional Soberanía is home to 500 avian species and promises world-class birding. The more remote Parque Nacional Chagres is the place for intrepid jungle adventures, while the Parque Municipal Summit is a zoo and botanical gardens that's easily reached from the capital. More natural attractions lie close to the northern entrance of the canal. The excellent Isla Barro Colorado is an artificially created island on Lago Gatún, home to a Smithsonian Institute biological research station and many species of animals.

The forests flanking the canal belong to several national parks and are therefore quite vast and wild, so there are all sorts of beasts lurking in there. There are jaguars in the forests but you would be very lucky indeed to see one. For listings, see pages 387-388.

History

Dreams of a trans-isthmian canal began with the Spanish conquest, but it was not until the 19th century, when Panama was still a province of Colombia, that anyone possessed enough engineering savvy to begin to accomplish it. In 1878, Colombia signed the Salgar-Wise agreement, granting a 99-year concession to the French to build a canal. So began a tragic misadventure that ended swamped in tropical disease, corruption and debt. Ferdinand de Lesseps was the man responsible. Architect of the Suez Canal, his status as a national hero helped guarantee the future success of the enterprise and led many French families to invest their life-savings. By 1893, the sheer complexities of the project, the continual rains, land-slides and bouts of deadly infections brought the company, its share-holders and the entire French economy to its knees. De Lessep's obsession with building a technically impossible sea-level canal – and his stubborn insistence upon it – was particularly instrumental in their failure. Over 22,000 workers are believed to have died.

The US acquired the abortive project from the French but failed to secure rights to build from Colombia. They spurred Panama to secede and provided the military support necessary for their success. On 3 November 1903 the nation of Panama was born. Soon after, the US acquired the dubious rights to build and manage the canal 'in perpetuity'. In the following years, they surmounted many problems that had defeated the French. Most importantly, they eradicated yellow fever from Panama and incorporated a lock system into the canal's design. The Ancón was the first ship to sail transit the completed canal on 15 August 1914. In 1999, in accordance with the Torrijos-Carter treaty, the US relinquished all rights to the canal and the 16-km wide, US-Governed Canal Zone – formerly a source of great resentment among Panamanians. Today, the Panama Canal is managed by an independent corporation, the Panama Canal Authority, who are presently working to expand it.

Panama Canal Railway

The Panama Canal Railway (Corozal One West, T317-6070, www.panarail.com) first opened in 1855 under auspices of the Panama Rail-Road company. Its function was to carry California gold rush prospectors to the Pacific Coast. It was later employed by the French and American canal companies to transport personnel, equipment and tons of rubble during the arduous task of excavation. Today the railway runs parallel to the canal, carrying tourists and Free Zone executives between Panama City and the Caribbean port of Colón. This is a great way to experience the misty early morning canal, as you rush past walls of tangled jungle foliage and darkened lakes. You'll traverse the isthmus in just one hour, but the return service from Colón doesn't depart until several hours later, giving you time to briefly explore the coast (see Transport, page 388).

Parque Nacional Camino de Cruces

Skirting the eastern banks of the Panama Canal, the Parque Nacional Camino de Cruces, on the Gaillard Highway (www.anam.gob.pa) was established in 1992 to consolidate the protected areas of the Parque Nacional Soberanía to the north and the Parque Metropolitano to the south. The park derives its name, 'Way of Crosses', from the fragments of old Spanish gold trails hidden within its forest enclaves. Some of these old cobblestone paths are now partially restored and trails here are generally well maintained. They include the famous Las Cruces Trail, which travels north into Parque Nacional Soberanía and as far as the Río Chagres, where plundered treasure was once loaded onto boats and steered to the Caribbean. You will need a guide if you plan to traverse its entire length.

ATC The park is particularly resplendent during the flowering months of April and May. The landscape rises and falls with gentle hills, home to oak, cotton and palm trees.

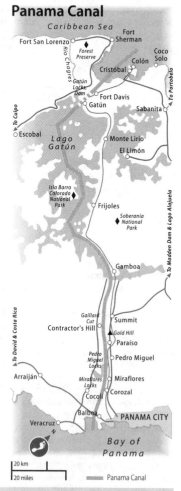

Panama Canal

Caribbean Sea

Fort San Lorenzo
Fort Sherman
Forest Preserve
Colón
Coco Solo
Cristóbal
To Portobelo
Río Chagres
Gatún Locks, Dam
Fort Davis
Gatún
Sabanita
To Cuipo
Escobal
Lago Gatún
Monte Lirio
El Limón
Isla Barro Colorado National Park
Frijoles
Soberanía National Park
To Madden Dam & Lago Alajuela
Gamboa
To David & Costa Rica
Gaillard Cut
Contractor's Hill
Summit
Gold Hill
Paraíso
Pedro Miguel Locks
Pedro Miguel
Arraiján
Miraflores Locks
Miraflores
Cocolí
Corozal
Balboa
PANAMA CITY
Veracruz
Bay of Panama

20 km
20 miles
Panama Canal

Miraflores Locks

Miraflores Visitor Centre ① *Mon–Sun, 0900-1600, www.pancanal.com, US$8 entrance to the museum and Canal viewing platform, US$5 for platform only*, was constructed as part of Centenial celebrations at a cost of US$6 million. As most Panamanians will tell you, a visit to Miraflores to watch the vast engineering operations is more or less obligatory. The large observation deck supplies superb views of transiting vessels and enthusiastic commentary in English and Spanish. The museum is spread over four floors with captivating exhibitions on global trade, local ecology, engineering and the history of the canal. The entrance price also includes a documentary film in English and Spanish. There is a café and restaurant on site, the latter, **The Miraflores**, was used in the movie *The Tailor of Panama*. This is the easiest and most popular way to experience the canal. To get there from Panama City, take the Gamboa bus from the SACA terminal behind Plaza 5 de Mayo, US$1, and ask the driver to stop at Miraflores. It's a 10-minute walk from the highway. A taxi will cost around US$10 one-way from Panama City.

Pedro Miguel Locks

These locks lie several kilometres north of Miraflores and offer a poor man's experience of the canal. It's free to watch the ships at these one-chamber locks, but you won't get anything like the views at Miraflores. A taxi from Panama City costs US$12 one-way.

Parque Municipal Summit

Parque Municipal Summit ① *Carretera Gaillard towards Gamboa, 20 mins from Panama City, T232-4854, www.summitpanama.org, 0900-1700, US$1*, is home to an impressive botanical collection with 150 species from Asia, Africa and the Americas, including the world's finest palm collection. Their zoo shelters 40 species of animals, all endemic to Panama, including the majestic Harpy Eagle – Panama's national bird. The park has been actively involved in conservation for many years, working closely with organizations such as the Smithsonian Tropical Research Institute and Houston zoo. Their visitors' centre contains information about their work and they sometimes need volunteers for environmental education and other tasks.

Parque Nacional Soberanía

The exuberant rainforest habitat of the Parque Nacional Soberanía contains over 1300 species of plants, 100 species of mammals, 55 species of amphibians, 79 species of reptiles and over 500 species of birds. Resident fauna include deer, agoutis, jaguars, peccaries, monkeys, sloths, snakes, caimans and abundant vociferous frogs.

Parque Nacional Soberanía ① *Carretera Gaillard, T232-4192, www.anam.gob.pa, 0600-1700, US$3*, is very popular with birdwatchers with over 500 species recorded to date. It is reputedly one of the finest bird observation areas in the world and once held the record for the most bird counted in a 24-hour period. The park has several fabulous trails. The Plantation Trail begins at the turn-off for the Canopy Tower (on the highway to Gamboa) and follows an old plantation road built in 1910. It's a moderate, 6.5-km trail that concludes at the intersection for the Camino de Cruces Trail. From here, the Camino de Cruces Trail follows the old Spanish gold route north to the Río Chagres, or south into the Parque Nacional Camino de Cruces (see Parque Nacional Camino de Cruces). A guide for this trail is recommended, as it becomes quite unkempt in parts. The park's most famous and popular trail is the Pipeline road, accessed from the Carretera Gaillard running along the canal, just north of Gamboa, the old American dredging port. The

Linehandling the Panama Canal

The best way to see the Panama Canal is by boat. If you don't have your own, it is possible to sail through as a linehandler on a yacht. Each yacht is required to have four onboard line-handlers plus the helmsman for what is normally a two-day journey. While many Panamanians work full-time as line-handlers, people with experience, or at least a modicum of common sense, may be able to get a position as a linehander and work their way through. One experienced captain in Costa Rica said the task is not difficult, but you do have to work when it is time to work – so don't expect to sunbathe all the way through.

An additional benefit is that in as well as getting to see the canal from the inside, the yacht's owners are required to feed linehandlers three meals a day and, if the journey takes more than one day (for most yachts transit requires two days) accommodation.

If you are interested go to the Panama Canal Yacht Club in Colón on the Caribbean side (email pcyachtclub@cwpanama.net), or the Balboa Yacht Club (www.balboayachtclub.com) on the Pacific side. Ask in the club or office for the best person to speak to. Don't expect to just turn up and get a job. Private yacht transits are seasonal and there may be competition for line-handling positions. But the number of private yachts in transit is on the increase. Transit obviously has its risks, and no yacht owner will put their vessel at risk when they can use professional and experienced Panamanians. But nevertheless, with all these caveats, it is still the best way to see the canal.

---

now-abandoned coast-to-coast pipeline was built during the Second World War by the US and hidden in the jungle as a guarantee of oil supply should the canal be sabotaged. Bird life here is very prolific, particularly early in the morning. If you're not an experienced birder, a well-qualified guide will really bring your experience of this world-class trail to life. The park has an information centre at the Summit Garden.

Parque Nacional Chagres

The Parque Nacional Chagres is particularly wild and rugged, punctuated by dramatic valleys, rocky mountains, rivers and dense tracts of forest. Jaguar, tapirs and anteaters occupy the park, although they are difficult to spot. You'll find rare elfin forests at the higher altitudes.

The park is also home to Lago Alajuela, formerly Madden Lake, an artificial reservoir formed by the damming of the Río Chagres. It is used to generate electricity as well as maintain the level of Lago Gatún, vital for the functioning of the canal. The entire Chagres area has great potential for jungle adventure. Multi-day trekking trips into wildlife rich parts of the forest can be arranged with some companies in Panama City, as can tubing, rafting and abseiling within the watershed – see Tour operators, page 377. The park can be reached by bus from Panama City, first to Las Cumbres and then a second bus to Caimitillo. After that it is a 3½- to four-hour walk to Nuevo Caimitillo. Dugout canoes offer transportation to Emberá indigenous villages at Parara Puru (15 minutes) and Embera Drua (30-40 minutes). The Emberá in this area are friendly and seem to be coping well with the impacts of tourism on their lives – they also make excellent quality crafts which are sold at very reasonable prices. It may be possible to stay within the village of

Parara Puro for a small fee and with the permission of community, giving a greater insight into village life. If visiting the villages on an organized tour, make sure your company pays the correct visitation fee to the community in question – there have been several incidents of payment being withheld. On a similar note, all trips made in the area should involve the employment of Emberá guides/assistants to ensure that these villages benefit from tourism on their lands. The Camino Real passes through the park if you want to follow in the footsteps of the old Spanish colonists. There is a refuge at Cerro Azul, marking the start of a challenging three-day hike to the north coast (guide essential). Take a bus for Chepo from Panama City and get off at Vista Hermosa, then walk the 6 km to the ranger hut.

Barro Colorado Nature Monument

Lago Gatún was created with the damming of the Río Chagres and now supplies the water necessary for the day-to-day functioning of the canal. Inside the lake is **Barro Colorado Island**, to which many animals fled as the basin slowly filled. The island is a formally protected area called the Barro Colorado Nature Monument and has been a site of scientific research for over 70 years. The Smithsonian Tropical Research Institute accept limited numbers of visitors to their research facilities, which are among the most utilized in the world. The excursion is highly recommended for seeing wildlife, especially monkeys, and includes transportation to the island, a lecture, buffet lunch and walk around a guided trail with over 50 points of interest. You must reserve your place at least two weeks in advance (see also page 388).

Gatún Locks

On the Caribbean side of the canal, 10 km southwest of Colón, are the Gatún Locks (*Esclusas de Gatún*) with their neat, attendant town. The **observation point** ① *daily 1000-1630*, is perhaps the best spot in the Canal area for photographing the passage of ships. The most magnificent of the Canal's locks, Gatún integrates all three lock 'steps' on the Atlantic side, raising or lowering ships to or from 26 m in one operation. The flights are in duplicate to allow ships to pass in opposite directions simultaneously. Passage of the locks takes about one hour. A bus from Colón to Gatún Locks costs US\$1.

◉ Panama Canal listings

For Sleeping and Eating price codes, and other relevant information, see pages 43-46.

◉ Sleeping

Parque Nacional Soberanía *p385*
LL-L Canopy Tower Ecolodge and Nature Observatory, signposted from just beyond Summit Gardens on the Transisthmus Highway, T264-5720, www.canopytower.com. A hotel and ecolodge that rises to the rainforest canopy in a converted old communications tower. 7 quirky little rooms, with private bath, price includes meals and guided walks. Some cheaper rooms available off season. Excellent for wildlife. Day trips and guided tours welcome.

LL-L Gamboa Rainforest Resort, on the hill above Gamboa overlooking the Río Chagres, T314-5000, www.gamboaresort.com. This looming green and white resort built on an old American golf course has a restaurant (a bit soulless) and swimming pool. There is an ancient tree dividing the complex. Cheapest rooms are in apartments formerly occupied by US dredging engineers. An aerial tramway runs silently through the canopy to a mirador with good views of the canal (at US$35 not cheap but an easy way to see monkeys, sloths and crocodiles). Tour available to non-residents.

AL Ivan's Bed and Breakfast, Jadwin Av 111, Gamboa, T314-9436, www.gamboaecotours. com. This comfortable little B&B in Gamboa is owned and operated by Ivan and Gladys Ortiz, both certified birding guides. They have 4 comfortable rooms and offer interesting tours of Lake Gatún and the surrounding national parks. Friendly and hospitable.

▲▲ Activities and tours

Canal tours
Several agencies in Panama City offer boat tours of the canal. Most find that a partial transit through Miraflores and Pedro Miguel locks is quite enough to appreciate the operation.

Canal and Bay Tours, T209-2000, www. canalandbaytours.com. Full transit of the canal on the first Sat of the month, 0730, adults US$165, children US$75. Partial transit every Sat, 0930, adults US$115, children US$75. They also run various tours to Panama Bay, including an evening tour with bar and calypso.

Panama Marine Adventures, T226-8917, www.pmatours.net. Full transit of the canal once a month, adults US$165, children US$75, call for schedule. Partial transit Thu, Fri and Sat, Jan-Mar; and Sat, Apr-Dec; adults US$115, children US$65.

Smithsonian Tropical Research Institute, at the Tupper Building in Ancón, T212-8026, www.stri.org. Captivating daily trips to the island last 4-6 hrs, US$70, including boat, audio-visual display and lunch (but take water). Take a Gamboa Summit bus from

next to Plaza 5 de Mayo (0600 and 0615) to the Dredging Division dock at Gamboa (US$0.65), from where the boat leaves. Make arrangements with the Institute in Ancón and book well in advance – several weeks if possible. Tours don't go Mon or Thu, max 12 people on Tue and Wed, 15 on Fri, 25-30 Sat and Sun. ID required when booking. Highly recommended.

Visitors without permits will be turned away on arrival. Don't be late for the boat, as they don't wait.

⊜ Transport

A good way to experience the Panama Canal area is to rent a car.

Bus
All the major Panama Canal destinations including Miraflores Locks, Summit, Gamboa and the Parque Nacional Soberanía are served by orange buses from Panama City, which regularly traverse the Gaillard highway. They depart from the SACA terminal next to Plaza 5 de Mayo, hourly, 0500-2230, US$0.35-1. For Miraflores, ask the drive to drop you at 'Las Esclusas de Miraflores', from where it's a 10-min walk. A taxi to the locks is US$10/hr.

Train
The famous Panama Canal Railway runs daily from Corozal Passenger Station in Panama City to **Colón**, US$22 one way, US$44 return, departs 0715, returns 1715, 1 hr. Turn up on the day or book in advance through tour operators. More details available at www.panarail.com. A cab to the station from Panama City costs about US2.50. The outdoor viewing platform is great for feeling the rush of wind and jungle scenery.

Central Caribbean Coast

Panama's central Caribbean coast has always been a vital port of call for goods and persons moving between the Old World and New. Waves of Spanish conquistadors, colonialists, gold prospectors and canal workers have all passed through this transitory and historically fascinating region. Tourism on the Central Caribbean coast is nascent. Economically, the region is far less developed than its Pacific cousin and few visitors venture beyond its colonial ruins. Press on though and you'll discover a swathe of protected forests and dive sites. The beaches are scant but pleasant nonetheless.

The ramshackle slum of Colón, with its attendant port of Cristóbal, forms the northern terminus of the Panama Canal and railroad, where tax-free goods are traded in an enormous Free Zone – just like the great gold fairs of colonial times. East and west of Colón, a string of handsome fortifications recall the era of piracy, when buccaneers such as Sir Francis Drake were drawn to the great wealth that passed through on its way to Spain. They include the UNESCO world heritage site of San Lorenzo, and the enigmatic Portobelo, with its old canons pointing wistfully over the sea. The central Caribbean coast has a strong Afro-Caribbean flavour, with interesting communities of Congos – the descendants of escaped African slaves – inhabiting the towns and villages along its shores. The population of Isla Grande are particularly welcoming and lay on a good party at the weekend.

▶▶ *For listings, see pages 394-397.*

Colón and Cristóbal ⊜❼❸❶ ▶▶ *pp394-397.*

Landfall on the Caribbean side for the passage of the Canal is made at the twin cities of Cristóbal and Colón, the one merging into the other almost imperceptibly and both built on Manzanillo Island at the entrance of the Canal in Bahía Limón. The island has now been connected with the mainland. Colón was founded in 1852 as the terminus of the railway across the isthmus; Cristóbal came into being as the port of entry for the supplies used in building the Canal.

Avenida del Frente is the main commercial street and is quite active but has lost its past splendour: the famous Bazar Francés closed in 1990, the curio shops are not noteworthy and the railway station stands virtually deserted except for the movement of a few freight trains. Nevertheless, there is talk of declaring the whole of Colón a free zone (the Zona Libre being the city's main attraction), the authorities are moving to give the city new housing and employment (residential estates such as 'Rainbow City' and 'Puerto Escondido' are being extended on the landward side to relocate entire neighbourhoods of slums), and the demands on Cristóbal's busy port facilities (200 million tons of cargo a year) continue to increase. It is to be hoped that, if these plans are realized, Colón may become a pleasant place again.

Ins and outs

Mugging, even in daylight, is a real threat in both Colón and Cristóbal. The situation has improved now that the two main streets and some of the connecting ones are guarded by police officers; you are still strongly recommended not to stray too far from their range of sight. Keep a few dollars handy for muggers if the worst happens.

Sights

The French-influenced **cathedral** ① C 5 y Av Herrera, 1400-1745 daily, has an attractive altar and good stained-glass windows. The **Washington Hotel** ① on the seafront at the north end of the town, is the town's most historic structure and is worth a look. The original

Colón

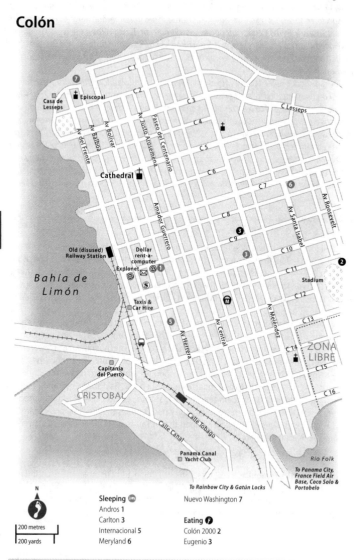

C 1
C 2
C 3
C 4
C Lesseps
C 5
C 6
C 7
C 8
C 9
C 10
C 11
C 12
C 13
C 14
C 15
C 16

Casa de Lesseps
Episcopal ❼
Av del Frente
Av Balboa
Av Bolívar
Paseo del Centenario
Justo Arosemena
Cathedral
Amador Guerrero
Old (disused) Railway Station
Dollar rent-a-computer
Explonet
Bahía de Limón
Taxis & Car Hire
Av Santa Isabel
Av Roosevelt
❻
❸
❸
❺
Av Herrera
Av Central
Av Meléndez
Stadium ❷
ZONA LIBRE
Capitanía del Puerto
CRISTOBAL
Calle Canal
Calle Tobago
Panamá Canal Yacht Club
Río Folk
To Panamá City, France Field Air Base, Coco Solo & Portobelo
To Rainbow City & Gatún Locks

N

200 metres
200 yards

Sleeping 🛏
Andros **1**
Carlton **3**
Internacional **5**
Meryland **6**
Nuevo Washington **7**

Eating 🍴
Colón 2000 **2**
Eugenio **3**

wooden hotel was built in 1850 for employees of the Railroad Company. President Taft ordered a new fireproof hotel to be built in 1912 and the old one was later razed. Although remodelled a number of times, today's building, with its broad verandas, waving palms, splendid chandelier, plush carpets and casino, still conjures up a past age, while the café provides an excellent view of ships waiting to enter the Canal.

Across from the **Washington** is the **Old Stone Episcopal Church**, built in 1865 for the railway workers; it was then the only Protestant church in Colombia (of which Panama was a province). Running north through the centre of Colón is the palm-lined **Avenida Central**, with many statues (including one of *Columbus and the Indian Girl*, a gift from the Empress of France). The public market is at the corner of Calle 11. **Avenida del Frente**, facing the Bahía de Limón, has many old wooden buildings with wide verandas.

The main reason to come to Colón is to shop at the **Zona Libre** ① *Mon-Fri 0800-1700 (a few places retail on Sat morning), if you have a car, pay a minder US$1 to watch it while in the zone*. It's the second-largest free zone in the world, an extensive compound of international stores and warehouses established in 1949 and surrounded by a huge wall – pick up a free map from hotels or tourist office showing who sells what. A passport or official ID must be shown to gain entry to the zone.

The 30-minute beach drive around Colón's perimeter is pleasant and cool in the evening; despite the slums at the south end there are some nice homes along the east shore of the peninsula. Permission from the Port Authority security officer is required to enter the port area, where agents for all the world's great shipping lines are located in colonial Caribbean-style buildings dating from 1914. Almost lost in a forest of containers is the **Panama Canal Yacht Club** ① *T441-5882*, whose open-air restaurant and historically decorated bar offer very good food (seafood and Chinese). This is the place to ask about sailing boat charters to the Kuna Yale (see page 412) or shorter trips aboard visiting yachts.

West of Colón ● ›› pp394-397.

Fuerte San Lorenzo
Perched on a cliff-top promontory overlooking the mouth of the Río Chagres with great views of the coast, Fort San Lorenzo is one of the oldest and best-preserved Spanish fortifications in the Americas. Construction had begun the year before Drake launched a 23-ship attack on the post (1596) and proceeded up the Chagres in an unsuccessful attempt to reach Panama City. The following century, Morgan fought a bloody 11-day battle to take the fort as a prelude to his decisive swoop on Panamá Viejo in 1671. Although new defences were then built, they were unable to prevent British Admiral Edward Vernon's successful attack in 1740 (one of Vernon's cannon with the 'GR' monogram can still be seen). Engineer Hernández then spent seven years strengthening the garrison (1760-1767), but the threat to San Lorenzo gradually receded as Spanish galleons were diverted to the Cape Horn route and the era of the freebooters approached its end. The last Royalist soldiers left the fort in 1821 as Colombia declared its Independence from Spain. The earliest artillery sheds can be seen on the lower cliff level but most of the bulwarks, arched stone rooms and lines of cannon are 18th century. The site has undergone an extensive UNESCO renovation programme and is well worth a visit. There is a picnic area and a tiny beach is accessible by a steep path down the cliff.

Costa Abajo

There is no crossing of the Chagres at San Lorenzo. To continue down the Costa Abajo you have to return to the Gatún Dam and take the gravel road along the west side of the river, which winds its way through pristine forest to the coastal village of **Piña** and its kilometre-long beach. The road runs west along a steep and rocky shore to **Nuevo Chagres** and **Palmas Bellas**, quiet fishing resorts in coconut palm groves, but with few facilities. You'll need a 4WD to continue to **Río Indio** and **Miguel de la Borda**, where the road comes to an end. The villages beyond, including historic **Río Belén** where one of Columbus's ships was abandoned in 1502, are still only accessible by sea.

If you want a real adventure you can travel from **Penonomé** in Coclé Province across the continental divide to **Coclecito**, and then, with collective boat transport, down the Coclé del Norte River to the coast and the town of the same name – a true jungle adventure for those prepared to rough it and get away from it all. For more information contact Sven and Vivi on T993-3620 or T674-1162 (mobile).

Portobelo and around 🏠🚐🌐🗓🎫 ⇝ *pp394-397*.

Parque Nacional Portobelo

The Parque Nacional Portobelo is a large protected area north of the Parque Nacional Chagres. It encompasses the Costa Arriba all the way from Buena Ventura to Isla Grande, including a strip of teeming protected water that can be dived. Two dive shops serve the area and both are located in **Buena Ventura**, nothing more than a handful of buildings and a few kilometres west of Portobelo. This is also the site of the best lodgings in the area. The national park can be hiked, with two forested hills – Cerro Cross and Cerro Brujas – and a trail that adjoins the famous Camino Real, which you'll need a few days to follow in entirety. You shouldn't venture into the forests without a trustworthy guide. There are no tour operators in the region, but any agency in Panama City should be able to set you up. Alternatively, enquire locally – your hotel will probably have contacts.

Portobelo

East of Colón along the Caribbean coastline is Portobelo, founded in 1519 on the protected bay in which **Columbus** sought shelter in 1502. Researchers believe they have now located the wreck of the *Vizcaína*, abandoned by Columbus, in shallow waters somewhere off the coast of Portobelo. Now little more than a large village, the 'Beautiful Port' was once the northern terminus of the **Camino Real**, where Peruvian treasure, carried on mule trains across the isthmus from Panama City, was stored in fortified warehouses. The gold moved on when the periodic arrival of the Spanish Armada created famed fairs where the wealth of the New World was exchanged for goods and supplies from Europe. The fair of 1637 saw so much material change hands that, according to the Englishman Thomas Gage, it took 30 days for the loading and unloading to be completed. In the **Royal Contaduría**, or Customs House, bars of gold and silver were piled up like firewood. Such riches could hardly fail to attract foreign pirates. Portobelo was one of **Francis Drake**'s favourite targets but it was also his downfall; he died here of dysentery in 1596 and was buried in a lead-lined coffin in the bay off Isla Drake. Divers are currently attempting to discover the exact spot, intending to return Drake's body to his home city of Plymouth. By the beginning of the 17th century several *castillos* (Santiago, San Gerónimo and San Fernando) had been built of coral stone quarried nearby to protect the harbour. Attacks continued, until in 1740 the treasure fleets were rerouted around the

Horn and the Portobelo Fairs ended. The fortifications were rebuilt after Vernon's attack in 1744 but they were no longer seriously challenged, leaving the fortresses visible today. The largest, the aptly named 'Iron Castle', was largely dismantled during Canal construction. But there are many other interesting ruined fortresses, walls, rows of cannon and remains of the town's 120 houses and public buildings still to be seen standing along the foreshore amid the present-day village. In 1980 the remains of the colonial structure, known as the **Monumental Complex** ① *US$1, closed Sun*, was declared a World Cultural Heritage monument by UNESCO. The Contaduría (1630) has been restored, with similar plans for the Plaza, Hospital Chapel and the Fernández House. There is a small museum with a collection of arms.

In **San Felipe Church** (1776) is the 17th-century cocobolo-wood statue of the Black Christ, about whose origin there are many legends. One tells of how fishermen found it floating in the sea during an epidemic of cholera in the town. It was brought ashore and immediately the epidemic began to wane. Another says that the life-size image was on its way to Cartagena when the ship put in to Portobelo for supplies. After being thwarted five times by rough weather to leave port, the crew decided the statue wished to remain in Panama. It was thrown overboard, floated ashore and was rescued by the locals.

The **tourist office (IPAT)** ① *just west of the square behind the Alcaldía, T448-2073, Mon-Fri 0830-1630*, can provide guides, schedules of Congos and other performances, as well as comprehensive information about the many local points of interest, including the surrounding 34,846-ha **Portobelo National Park**, which has 70 km of coast line with beautiful beaches, superb scuba-diving sites and boat rental to visit secluded beaches nearby, such as **La Huerta**. Services in town are limited with no bank or post office and just one minimart.

East to Isla Grande
A paved road continues northeast from Portobelo to Isla Grande, and another heads east to Nombre de Dios (25 km) and Palenque. Scuba-diving is offered at several places along the way. The road passes through **Garrote** and **La Guaira**, from where *lanchas* (motor boat) can be hired (US$1.50) at the car park to cross to Isla Grande.

Isla Grande
This island is a favourite on account of its dazzling white palm-fringed beaches, the fishing, scuba-diving, snorkelling and windsurfing, and the relaxed way of life. The best beaches are enclosed in front of the two expensive hotels, but you should be able to use them. A good, more public beach, is on a spit before Hotel Isla Grande. The island's 300 black inhabitants make a living from fishing and coconut cultivation. A powerful French-built lighthouse crowns the small island's northern point, where there is a mirador, reached by steep path. There are a number of colourful African-tinged festivals held here throughout the year. The part of the village to the right of the landing stage is more lively with competing salsa sounds.

Nombre de Dios and beyond
The beautiful, deserted mainland beaches continue as the 'road' heads east to Nombre de Dios. The historic town (1520) near the present village was once the thriving trading port which first hosted the famed fairs, located at the end of the stone-paved Camino Real from the capital. By the 1550s more than half the trade between Spain and its colonies was passing through its lightly defended harbour, but in 1594 the decision was made to

move operations to the more sheltered site of Portobelo. The Camino Real was diverted and Nombre de Dios was already dying when Drake captured and burnt it two years later, so that William Dampier could describe the site some years later as "only a name ... everything is covered by the jungle with no sign that it was ever populated". Excavations have taken place revealing the Spanish town, parts of the Camino Real, a broken cannon and other objects, most of which are now in the National Museum.

The modern village is built on either side of a freshwater channel, a footbridge links the two. The church is built on a plaza on the west side, the main square is on the east. It has few facilities, one hotel and a restaurant on the square, but there's a beautiful beach for the few who get this far. A *cayuco* (US$3 per person, 12 minutes) can be taken to **Playa Damas**, an unusual beach where alternating patches of red and white sand resemble a chess board. The beach is owned by an amateur ecologist who has built some rustic huts and a campsite, **Costa El Oro** (*T263-5955*), on a small island here, he also offers expert guidance on local fishing and diving spots. Buses come into the centre en route to Portobelo or Cuango; while most go as far as the main square before coming back the same way, some turn round before this at the little plaza beside the police station.

The track staggers on for another 25 km linking the peaceful fishing villages of the **Costa Arriba**. Locals eagerly await the paved road's eventual extension through the succession of seaside villages to the Golfo de San Blas opposite El Porvenir, the capital of the Kunas' self-governed area of Kuna Yala ('Kuna Earth').

Not far beyond Nombe de Dios, near **Viento Frío**, is **Diver's Haven**, which, as the name suggests, is recommended for diving tours. The next village is **Palenque**, unspoilt, with a good beach and very rudimentary huts being built for visitors. **Miramar** is the cleanest of all the *pueblitos* along this coastline. The occasional smuggling boat puts in here and a few Panama City tourists come to stay in the three houses on the tiny **Isla Bellavista** (ask Niano at **Bohio Miramar** bar/restaurant) – US$70 for house with three double beds, no beach but you can swim off the jetty). Boats can take you on to **Santa Isabel** (beyond the reach of the dirt road), US$35 for the boat, or to **Kuna Yale** US$25 each, minimum eight people (see page 412). The village at the end of the road is **Cuango**, a bit run down and dusty between rains, with a littered beach.

⊙ Central Caribbean Coast listings

For Sleeping and Eating price codes, and other relevant information, see pages 43-46.

⊜ Sleeping

Colón and Cristóbal *p389, map p390*
There are plenty of dirt-cheap *pensiones* in Colón, but safety is definitely an issue so none have been recommended here.
AL Meryland, Calle 7 y Santa Isabel, T441-7128. This new hotel is clean, secure and professional. It has 80 comfortable rooms, each with telephone, a/c and hot water. There's a good restaurant attached.

AL Nuevo Washington, Av del Frente Final, T441-7133, newwashingtonhotel@eveloz. com. An interesting old hotel with lots of history and character. The art-deco style building has a garden with good views of ships entering the canal. There's a restaurant, bar and casino on-site.
B Andros, Av Herrera, between Calle 9 y 10, T441-0477, www.hotelandros.com. This hotel is modern, clean and comfortable. It has 60 rooms with TV, a/c, hot water and Wi-Fi. Good restaurant attached.
B Carlton, Calle 10 y Av Meléndez, T447-0111, www.elhotelcarlton.com. Clean

professional and comfortable enough. Rooms have a/c, telephone, cable TV and hot water. There's also a restaurant, internet and laundry service. A good choice and one of the better hotels.

B Internacional, Av Bolívar, y Calle 11, T445-2930. Rooms here are clean, bright and tidy. The usual amenities include a/c, hot water, cable TV, free internet, restaurant, bar and garden terrace. Simple but comfortable.

Fuerte San Lorenzo *p391*

D Las Bahías, on the edge of the roadless Golfo de los Mosquitos, 4 km west of Coclé del Norte and 60 km from Colón. A small rustic lodge. 4 cabañas on the beach with 1 double and 2 single beds in each. **Las Bahías** is only accessible by boat, either by collective *cayuco* from Gobea or Río Indio (US$8) or from Muelle de Calle 5 in Colón.

Portobelo and around *p392*

Accommodation is limited in and around Portobelo.

A Coco Plum Cabañas, Buena Ventura, 5 km west on road to Colón, T264-1338, www.cocoplum-panama.com . Colourful, nautically themed cabins adorned with fishing nets and shells. There's a small dive shop attached and they offer snorkelling tours and transit to the beaches. A pretty, relaxing spot.

A Scuba Portobelo, Buena Ventura, T261-3841, www.scubapanama.com. Clean, pleasant, nautically themed rooms and cabins with a/c, fan and hot water. There's a common room for reading, restaurant-bar, and tours in *lancha* (motor boat) offered. Owned by **Scuba Panama**, who also do dive trips from here. Rates rise slightly at the weekends.

E Hospedaje Sangui, T448-2204, on the highway in Portobelo, close to the church. Economical and basic quarters with shared bath and cold water. For the impoverished traveller.

Isla Grande *p393*

During holidays and dry season weekends, make reservations in advance; prices often double during high season. All hotels have bars and simple restaurants.

LL-L Bananas Village Resort, north side of the island, usually accessed by boat but also by path over the steep hill, T263-9510, www.bananasresort.com. Relatively discreet luxury hotel, on the best beach on the island, with a good but expensive bar. Day use costs US$35 and includes a welcome cocktail.

A Isla Grande, T225-2798 (reservations), west of the main pier, at the end of the path. Colourful, if slightly run-down cabins overlooking the beach, popular with Panamanians. To keep you entertained, facilities include BBQ, volley ball, ping-pong, pool table, waterslide and restaurant. There's rooms too, slightly cheaper than the cabins. Rates rise over the weekend (**AL**).

B Villa Ensueño, east of the main pier, T/F448-2964, villaen@cwpanama.net. Big lawns (big enough to play football), colourful cabins and picnic tables overlooking the water. There's also hammocks, ping-pong and *artesanías*. Friendly and pleasant.

C Cabañas Jackson, immediately behind main landing stage, T441-5656. Clean, friendly and economical lodgings. Rooms have fan, cold water and spongy beds. Grocery shop attached.

D Cabañas Monte Carlos, La Guaira, T441-2054. Basic quarters on the mainland, if the island's booked out.

Nombre de Dios and beyond *p393*

C Diver's Haven, not far beyond Nombe de Dios, near Viento Frío, T448-2248. Recommended for diving tours.

E Bohio, to left of road, on beach 50 m before the quay. 2 small but light rooms with TV and fan; the restaurant at the back of the jetty rents out 2 dark rooms. Boats can take you on **Santa Isabel** (beyond the reach of the dirt road), US$35 for the boat, or to **San Blas** US$25 per person, minimum 8 people.

E Casa de Huéspedes, on main square. With restaurant. A beautiful beach can be enjoyed by those few who get this far. A *cayuco* (US$3 per person, 12 mins) can be taken to Playa Damas, an unusual beach where alternating patches of red and white sand resemble a chess board. The beach is owned by an amateur ecologist who has built some rustic huts and a campsite (**Costa El Oro**, T263-5955) on a small island here, also offers expert guidance on fishing and diving spots.
F Nameless hospedaje, Cuango. Ask for María Meneses at 1st house on the left on east side of square. There is also one restaurant and store here.

♦ La Torre, T448-2039, in La Escucha, 3 km west on the road to Colón. Large wooden structure serving good seafood.

Isla Grande *p393*
You'll find lots of good fresh fish at a host of places on the waterfront.
♦♦ Kiosco Milly Mar, just west of landing pier. A cute little place serving excellent fish dishes at moderate prices.
♦♦-♦ Bar-Restaurant Congo, west of the pier. This restaurant juts out over the water on its own small pier. They serve up the usual Caribbean treats, rum, beer and fresh fish.

❼ Eating

Colón and Cristóbal *p389, map p390*
Hotels **Carlton** and **Washington** have good restaurants (♦♦). There are also several fast-food outlets.
♦♦ Colón 2000, Calle 11 and Av Roosevelt. Big, clean restaurant at the ferry terminal. They serve reliable breakfasts and lunches.
♦♦ Hotel Andros, Av Herrera and Calle 9, T441-0477. Modern self-service outlet, open till 2000, except Sun – check out the mirrors.
♦ Eugenio, Calle 9 and Av Meléndez. Bustling locals' haunt with lots of cheap eats and wholesome home-cooking.

Portobelo and around *p392*
A number of small *fondas* serve coconut rice with fresh shrimps, spicy Caribbean food with octopus or fish, or *fufú* (fish soup cooked with coconut milk and vegetables).
♦♦ La Ancla, Buena Ventura, 5 km west on the road to Colón. **Coco Plum**'s restaurant is pleasant, brightly decorated and overlooks the waves. They serve breakfasts, lunches and seafood dinners.
♦♦ Los Cañones, in Buena Ventura, 5 km west on the road to Colón. Good food in a lovely setting by the water, but not cheap.

❀ Festivals and events

Portobelo and around *p392*
21 Oct The miraculous reputation of the **Black Christ** is celebrated annually; purple-clad pilgrims come from all over the country and the statue is paraded through the town at 1800 on a flower- and candle-covered litter carried by 80 men (who take 3 steps forward and 2 steps back to musical accompaniment); feasting and dancing till dawn.
Jan-Mar/Apr Other fiestas in the Portobelo region – for example **Carnival**, **Patron Saint's Day** (20 Mar) – are opportunities to experience the congos. Unlike the dance of the same name found elsewhere on the Caribbean coast, the congo here is the name given both to the main, male participants and a slowly unfolding ritual which lasts from the **Día de los Reyes** (6 Jan) to **Easter**. Among the various explanations of its symbolism are elements of the people's original African religions, their capture into slavery, their conversion to Catholicism and mockery of the colonial Spaniards. Members of the audience are often 'imprisoned' in a makeshift palisade and have to pay a 'ransom' to be freed.

⊖ Transport

Colón and Cristóbal *p389, map p390*
Air
Former US France Field AFB has replaced Colón's old airstrip as the busy local airport, on the mainland east of the city, taxi under US$1 but bargain. **Aeroperlas** have daily flights Mon-Thu to **Panama City**, T430-1038. Flights are hectic with Free Zone executives; no reservations so allow plenty of time or plan to stay the night in Colón.

Boat
For **San Blas** try asking at Coco Solo pier, T430-7327, or in Miramar, but be aware that services are less frequent than they were.

Bus
Bus station on Av del Frente and Calle 12. To **Panama City**, every 20 mins, express (a/c) US$2.50, regular buses, US$2, about 2 hrs; to **La Guaira**, 5 daily, 2 hrs, US$2.85; to **Portobelo**, hourly, US$2.50, 1 hr (note that Portobelo can be visited from Panama City in a day without going into Colón by taking an early bus to the Sabanitas turn-off (US$1) and waiting for a Colón–Portobelo service (US$1.50).

Taxi
Tariffs vary, US$0.75 in Colón, US$1.25 to outskirts, US$8-10 per hr. Taxis (and **car rental**) on Av del Frente facing Calle 11; most drivers speak some English and can advise on 'no-go' areas. You are advised to take a taxi between the train and bus stations.

Train
US$22, one way, US$35 return, to **Panama City**, leaves 1715, station on west side of town just off the centre.

Portobelo and around *p392*
Boat
Launch to **Santa Isabel** (beyond reach of Costa Arriba road), 2 hrs, to **San Blas** 3 hrs, but these services are increasingly infrequent.

Bus
To **Colón**, hourly, 0700-1800, 1 hr, US$2.50; to **María**, **Chiquita**, 40 mins, US$0.80; to **La Guaira**, 5 daily, US$1.25, 45 mins (taxi is also a possibility). To villages further east, take buses marked 'Costa Arriba' from stop at back of square: **Nombre de Dios**, 45 mins US$1; **Palenque**, 70 mins, US$1.50; **Miramar**, 80 mins US$3, **Cuango**, 1½ hrs, US$3.50. Road paved until just beyond Nombre de Dios.

Isla Grande *p393*
Buses drop you at La Guaira on the mainland from where *lanchas* (motor boat) nip across to the island, US$1.50. Tell the boatman if you need a particular locale, Bananas resort, for example. From La Guaira 5 buses per day go to Colón, hourly, 0530-0830, the last at 1300, US$2.85. There may be later buses on Sun and you should expect crowding at such times. Hitching with weekend Panamanians is also possible, all the way to **Panama City** if you're lucky!

⊕ Directory

Colón and Cristóbal *p389, map p390*
Banks Banco Nacional de Panamá. Caja de Ahorros. **Chase Manhattan Bank. Citibank. Lloyds Bank** agency in Colón Free Zone, at Av Santa Isabel y Calle 14, T445-2177. Mon-Fri 0800-1300. **Internet** **Explonet**, Frente, between Calle 9 y Calle 10, Mon-Sat 0800-2300, Sun 1300-2000, US$2.50 per hr. **Dollar Rent-a-Computer**, Calle 11 Y Av Guerrero, above Café Nacional, T441-7632, US$2.50 per hr, net phones US$0.61per min to England. **Post office** In Cristóbal Administration Building, on corner of Av Bolívar and Calle 9. **Telephone** Cable & Wireless in Cristóbal.

Isla Grande *p393*
Telephone There are 2 pay phones: 150 m to the left of the landing jetty, on a small plaza, to the right beside the basketball court.

Coclé and Veraguas

After the bustle and madness of the capital, the cleanliness and prosperity of Panama's interior comes as a welcome change. Coclé Province marks the geographic centre of the country, where more Panamanian presidents have been born than anywhere else. Ancient colonial churches, highland villages, rainforests, mountains and beaches are some of its attractions, all lying close to the Interamericana Highway. A popular stop for most visitors is El Valle, a cool mountain retreat with good hiking and a famous Sunday market.

West of Coclé, Veraguas is one of Panama's least populated, least developed and least visited provinces – and the only one to embrace both Caribbean and Pacific shores. The Caribbean side, isolated by the Corderilla Central, is an inhospitable wilderness of dense tropical forests. Conversely, the Pacific side has been sadly decimated with endless cattle ranches occupying the land where forests once stood. Santiago, the provincial capital, does no better, with its drab airs and wealth of banking facilities. But keep looking, for beyond the rolling pastures and faceless capital lie some exceptional and alternative sights. At the remote Pacific village of Santa Catalina, world-class 9-m waves break over the shores. At the Parque Nacional Cerro Hoya, historically isolated at the southwestern tip of the Azuero Peninsula, a wealth of endemic animal species make their home. But the real draw is Isla Coiba, a former penal colony turned national park and UNESCO World Heritage Site. This is the place to see really big marine life – humpback whales, bottlenose dolphins, sharks, rays and eels included. ⟩⟩ For listings, see pages 402-405.

West on the Interamericana ⬤❶❷ ⟩⟩ pp402-405.

From Panama City, the Interamericana heads westwards along a well graded and completely paved road to the Costa Rican border 489 km away. Lots of public transport plies up and down this road, making it easy to jump between attractions. Just look for the concrete bus shelters.

Panama City to Coclé

The well-plied Interamericana runs through western Panamá province before entering Coclé. Most visitors skip this understated locale on their way to bigger things, but stopping here offers a good introduction to the style and pace of the provinces. The first place of any note you'll reach is **La Chorrera**, 34 km from the capital, with an interesting *artesanía* store, **Artes de las Américas**, and a branch road (right) leading 1.5 km to **El Chorro**, the waterfall from which the town takes its name.

Around 20 km further, set among hills, is the old town of **Capira**. Just west of Capira is a sign indicating the turn-off to **Lídice**, 4 km north of the highway and at the foot of Cerro Trinidad, which local tradition calls 'the end of the Andes'. The town was the home of Czech immigrants who in 1945 succeeded in changing the town's name from Potero to commemorate Lídice in their homeland, which suffered heavily in the Second World War.

The Interamericana then passes through the orange groves of **Campana**, where a 4-km road climbs to the **Parque Nacional Altos de Campana**. Created in 1966, the 4816-ha park – the first in Panama – protects humid tropical forest growing on mountainous volcanic rock that forms picturesque cliffs ideal for walking and hiking. Beyond here, a string of Pacific beaches flanks the highway until it crosses the border into Coclé Province (see page 365).

El Valle

Several kilometres before the provincial border lies the turning to the comparatively cool, summer resort of El Valle, located just inside Coclé. The road heads north into the mountains, climbing through fine scenery to the summit of **Los Llanitos**, then down 200 m to a verdant plateau surrounded by dark, brooding peaks. El Valle is a pleasant and popular weekend retreat for Panameños hoping to escape the heat of the city. You can visit it as a day trip, but it's worth spending some time here to explore the natural surroundings, as the town itself is not terribly captivating. There's a popular Sunday market, visited by Panameños and tourists, where soapstone carvings of animals, straw birds, painted gourds (*totumas*), carved wood tableware, pottery and *molas* are sold. There is also a colourful flower market. The orchid nursery has a small zoo and Panama's best-known **petroglyphs** can be seen near the town. This is one of many good walks in the vicinity (ask directions); another is to the cross in the hills to the west of town. Four kilometres before the town is a parking spot with fine views of the village and a waterfall nearby. El Valle is also the place to buy Gruber's Jungle Oil, a specially formulated lotion that is reportedly very effective in deterring mosquitos, as well as treating a range of skin conditions. Its creator, Franklin Gruber, offers tours of the area and is has extensive knowledge of ethno-botany, herbalism and healing, for more information see botanicogruber.com.

Beyond El Valle is the **Canopy Adventure** ⓘ *T983-6547 (in El Valle, Spanish only), T264-5720 (in Panama City), 0600-1700, US$50*, with a series of cables and wires whizzing you through the forest; the last stage swoops across the face of a waterfall. It's good for all ages and the whole experience takes about 1½ hours and includes a short hike through the forest. To get there from El Valle take a bus to El Chorro Macho or taxi to La Mesa.

Santa Clara and Antón

Santa Clara, with its famous beach, 115 km from Panama City, is the usual target for motorists. The beach is about 20 minutes from the Interamericana, with fishing, launches for hire and riding. About 13 km beyond is Antón, which has a special local *manjar blanco* (a gooey fudge) and a crucifix reputed to be miraculous.

Penonomé

A further 20 km along the Interamericana is the capital of Coclé Province, Penonomé, an old town even when the Spaniards arrived. An advanced culture which once thrived here was overwhelmed by volcanic eruption. Objects revealed by archaeologists are now in Panama City, in the American Museum of Natural History in New York, and in the local **Museo Conte de Penonomé** ⓘ *Tue-Sat 0900-1230, 1330-1600, Sun 0830-1300*. The local university and the **Mercado de Artesanato** on the highway are worth a visit. There is a delightful central plaza with the air of a tiny provincial capital of times past. Penonomé is often a lunch stop for motorists making the trip from Panama City to the western border.

Balneario Las Mendozas and Churuquita Grande

Just under 1 km northwest of Penonomé is Balneario Las Mendozas, on a street of the same name, an excellent river pool for bathing in deep water. Further down the Río Zaratí, also known as the Santa María, is **La Angostura** where the river dives down a canyon. The dirt access road is usually suitable for ordinary cars. There are copper- and gold-mining activities in this area and further north, beyond La Pintada, where a new 35-km road has been built to Coclecito on the Caribbean side of the Continental Divide.

The operating mining company is also involved in conservation work including reforestation near La Angostura.

Northeast of Penonomé is Churuquita Grande (camping is possible near the river with a waterfall and swimming hole). There's a **Feria de la Naranja** (orange festival) held on the last weekend of January: the inauguration and dancing is on Saturday; the big day, Sunday, includes a colourful parade and huge displays of fruit. From Penonomé you can visit **La Pintada** (buses every 30 minutes), a mountain village that makes a quiet stopping-off point for hiking and horse riding.

El Caño, El Copé and Natá

El Caño is 24 km west of Penonomé, and 3.5 km from the main road is the **Parque Arqueológico del Caño** ① *Tue-Fri 0900-1600, Sat-Sun 1030-1300, US$1*, which has a small museum, some excavations (several human skeletons have been found in the burial site) and standing stones.

From El Caño (the ruins) you can take a *chiva* up into the mountains, changing to another at Río Grande, to the village of **El Copé** (direct buses from Panama City), which gives access to the **Parque Nacional Omar Torrijos**, a protected forest of rubber trees with some good trails.

A further 7 km along the Interamericana is **Natá**, one of the oldest towns in Panama and the Americas (1520). The early colonists fought constant attacks led by Urracá. The **Iglesia de Santiago Apóstol** (1522) is impressive, with interesting wood carvings. It is sadly run down now; donations gratefully received for restoration work.

Aguadulce and Calobre

Some 10 km beyond is Aguadulce, a prosperous supply centre, with local pottery for sale and *salinas* (saltworks) nearby.

Another 17 km further on, just after the large Santa Rosa sugar plantation, a road leads off right to the mountain spa of Calobre (31 km). The hot springs are, however, a good hour's drive away, on a very rough road, through great mountain scenery.

Santiago and around ⊜⊘▲⊝ ⇒ *pp402-405*.

Back on the Interamericana, the highway briefly dips into Herrera Province, passing the important junction of Divisa (from where a road heads south into the Azuero Peninsula), before crossing into neighbouring Veraguas Province. After 37 km it passes Santiago.

Santiago

Capital of the province, Santiago is one of the oldest towns in the country. It is situated in a grain-growing region that is very dry in summer, and here you can buy very good and cheap *chácaras* – macramé bags used by male *campesinos* as a convenient hold-all for lunch and other necessities in the fields – in the market here.

Just east of Santiago is the turn-off to **La Atalaya**, site of a major pilgrimage and festival in honour of a miraculous statue of Christ, and home of the **Instituto Jesús Nazareno** ① *open to visitors on Sun*, an important agricultural school for rural boys. West of Santiago is **La Mesa** (turn-off at Km 27), with a beautiful, white colonial church. The old rough road heads south through **Soná** and rejoins the Interamericana at **Guabalá**. The paved highway from Santiago to Guabalá saves a couple of hours.

San Fransisco

The peaceful town of San Fransisco lies 17 km north of Santiago and is the site of a famous church. Built in 1727, the church is widely considered as one of the oldest and finest examples of baroque art in the Americas. Often visited by pilgrims and widely revered as a national monument, its interior is home to colourful frescoes, ornate wood carvings and no less than nine altars. Around 200 m from the church lies **El Chorto del Espíritu Santo** – a rather pleasant waterfall and local swimming hole. Ask for directions.

Santa Fe

Continue north for another 40 km and you'll reach the remote highland town of Santa Fe, a centre of orchid cultivation that's drawing growing numbers of naturalists and hikers. The forests of **Cerro Tute** and **Alto Piedra** are the main attraction, with their rugged, mountainous terrain and large populations of birds. Santa Fe was historically important as a centre for the country's gold mining operations. It was founded by the Spaniards in 1557.

Parque Nacional Cerro Hoya

South of Santiago, a narrow strip of Veraguas Province reaches into the western half of the Azuero Peninsula, isolated and effectively cut off from the more developed eastern side by impassable mountains. From the Interamericana, a single road staggers down the peninsula's western coastline, newly paved and extended in 2006, opening up access to the highly secluded Parque Nacional Cerro Hoya. Protecting the southwest tip of the peninsula, the 32,557-ha park protects four life zones in a region that has been devastated by agriculture, over-grazing, season burning and human population pressure. More than 30 species of endemic plants have been recorded in the park and it is one of the last known sites to see the red macaw. One research trip in 1987 even found an endemic species of howler monkey. Turtles also use the coastal beaches for nesting from July to November.

You'll need a guide to explore the park, which can be arranged with Tanager Tourism, www.tanagertourism.com, an excellent new eco-tourism project located in the tiny coastal hamlet of Palmilla, close to the settlement of Mariato and on the road to the park. Run by two Dutch biologists, Loes Roos and Kees Groenendijk, Tanager Tourism has rustic accommodation and offers a range of interesting tours, including visits to local communities, birdwatching and transportation to nearby Isla Cébaco. There's also turtle-watching at the local beach, an area protected by an interesting local conservation initiative. Tourism in this part of the country is at its very earliest stages, making it a fascinating destination in itself, and a truly alternative one. To get there, take a bus to Mariato/Torio and ask the driver to let you out at 'La casa de los Holandeses'.

Santa Catalina

The up-and-coming surfers' town of Santa Catalina is located on the gulf of Montijo, southwest of Santiago and close to Isla Cébaco. Formerly little more than a scruffy fishing village, this remote site is hotly tipped to become one Central America's great surfing Meccas. First discovered by intrepid wave-seekers in the 1970s, a burgeoning expat community has since settled with an eye to the future, see www.santacatalinabeach.com for more information on the town and its services. Waves here average 5-20 ft, making it the preserve of more advanced surfers, although there are more gentle beaches nearby. Santa Catalina also provides access to the fantastic Isla de Coiba, with its famous diving and snorkelling. Big things are planned for this stretch of Pacific Coast, so you should try to experience it while it's still relatively unspoilt. To get to Santa Catalina, you will have to travel via Soná.

Isla de Coiba

Offshore lies the stunning UNESCO World Heritage Site of Isla de Coiba, which, at 503 sq km, is the largest island within Panamanian territory. A former penal colony, the limited interaction has ensured the protection of the plant, animal and marine life in the area which has been protected since 1992 as **Parque Nacional Coiba**. The park itself covers over 2700 sq km and includes areas of rich open ocean, Coiba and outlying islands and the second largest coral reef in the Eastern Pacific. On land the mostly untouched rainforest supports Panama's largest surviving colony of scarlet macaws, along with 146 other avian species. The marine environment, which in terms of pelagic life can only be rivalled by islands such as Cocos and the Galapagos, boasts 23 recorded species of whales and dolphins, including humpback, sperm and killer whales, some of which can spotted on dive trips to the island. Marine life of the fishy kind includes white-tip, bull, hammerhead and whale sharks in addition to manta and eagle rays.

◉ Coclé and Veraguas listings

For Sleeping and Eating price codes, and other relevant information, see pages 43-46.

◉ Sleeping

El Valle *p399*

The town has no real centre, although the market marks El Valle's commercial heart. Accommodation is hard to find at weekends, while budget lodgings are generally poor value and in short supply. Everyone cycles.

LL-L Canopy Lodge, on the road to Chorro el Macho, T264-5720, www.canopylodge.com. This is the sister hotel of the famous Canopy Tower near Gamboa and popular among birders. Very comfortable, well serviced and highly recommended by former guests, including Sir David Attenborough. Birdwatching packages are available and reservations required.

LL-L Casa de Lourdes, Calle El Ciclo, T983-6450, www.lacasadelourdes.com. Luxury Tuscan-style villas complete with elegant guest rooms, spa, fitness centre, pool and an excellent restaurant serving top-notch Panamanian cuisine. Personal services include tailor-made sports and leisure programmes.

L Crater Valley Adventure Spa, Vía Ranita Dorada, T983-6167, www.crater-valley.com. This small but comfortable hotel offers a range of adventure activities including horse riding, trekking, climbing, biking and rappelling. More sedate types might want to take advantage of the spa options, which include skin treatments, salon services and massage. Prices rise at the weekends.

AL Hotel Campestre, at the foot of Cara Coral Hill, T983-6146, www.hotelcampestre. com. This hotel has 20 comfortable rooms, all with fan, Wi-Fi, hot water and TV. It has a dramatic location at the foot of a mountain and there's a short nature walk that begins in the grounds. Prices include breakfast.

AL Los Capitanes, Calle de la Cooperativa, T983-6080, www.los-capitanes.com. Owned and operated by a retired German sea captain, Mr Manfred Koch. The hotel grounds are pretty and well-tended, home to 16 rooms including 2 suites with bath tubs. The restaurant serves German cuisine, à la carte food, wines and cocktails. Pleasant and relaxing lodgings.

B Hotel Don Pepe, Av Principal, T983-6425, www.hoteldonpepe.com. Owned and operated by the gregarious Don Pepe, who can often be found in the well-stocked *artesanía* store below. Rooms are clean and comfortable with hot water and TV. Additional services include internet, laundry and guide. Friendly and recommended.

C Pensión Niña Dalia, Av Central, T983-6425. Spartan quarters for backpackers and budget travellers. No towels or soap provided, but they will look after bags. The restaurant lays on a popular weekend lunch buffet – all you can eat for US$7. Private houses nearby may rent cheaper rooms.

Santa Clara and Antón *p399*
L Cabañas Las Sirenas, Santa Clara, T223-0132, www.lasirenas.com. Clean, comfortable and well-equipped cabañas for 5 or 8 people. The landscaped environment is swathed in colourful flowers and backs onto the beach, making this a very attractive and relaxing lodging.
C Hotel Rivera, Antón, Km 131, T987-2245. Clean, simple lodgings with bath and a/c or fan, located on the Interamericana. Cheaper without bath.

Penonomé *p399*
B Guacamaya, on the Interamericana, east side of town, T991-0117. Clean, comfortable and tidy rooms with hot water, a/c and cable TV. There's a restaurant, bar and casino too. Pleasant enough, if fairly unremarkable.
C Dos Continentes, Av Juan D Arosemena, T997-9325. Large, comfortable rooms with hot showers, cable TV and a/c. There's a good little restaurant downstairs, pool and an internet terminal. Clean and functional. Not bad.
D Pensión Los Pinos, on the Interamericana, towards Panama City. Basic rooms with bath and a/c (cheaper with fan). The owner is grumpy and unhelpful.

Balneario Las Mendozas and Churuquita Grande *p399*
AL Trinidad Spa and Lodge, Chiguirí Arriba, T983-8900, www.posadaecologica.com. An excellent purpose-built lodge for walkers and ecotourists. It offers guided treks on foot or mule, including through the mountains to El Valle, or across the isthmus to the Atlantic coast with the final stage by dugout canoe.
B La Iguana Eco-resort, Churuquite Grande, www.laiguanaresort.com. This hotel is nestled in verdant natural surroundings with hiking trails, rivers and waterfalls. There's also a pool, climbing tree and a host of outdoor

tours and activities on offer. The rooms are functional and have capacity for 5 persons. Pleasant and reasonably priced.
E Juan Cedeno's, La Pintada, in front of the church. Juan Cedeno has a house with a couple of large, clean rooms, a/c and hot water.

Aguadulce *p400*
C El Interamericano, on the Interamericana, T997-4363. Clean rooms with bath, a/c, TV and balcony. Also has a swimming pool.
D Pensión Sarita, T997-4437. Spartan quarters for the budget traveller.

Santiago *p400*
B Piramidal, on the Interamericana, T998-3123. A rather cold, grey building, but friendly inside, and conveniently located for the Panama City–David bus, which stops right by it. Rooms have a/c, TV, and shower. There's a good pool. Recommended.
C Gran David, on the Interamericana, T998-4510. A good deal for budget travellers. Rooms here are clean and functional with private bath, a/c and hot water (cheaper with fan and without TV, **D**). There's a pool and lots of weird walkways. The attached restaurant is OK – economical, but portions are stingy.
C Roselas Apartotel, Vía San Francisco, T998-7269. Good, secure apartments with kitchen, a/c and hot water. Clean and friendly with safe parking for motor-cycles, but a bit out of the way if you don't have transport.
D Santiago, Calle 2, near the cathedral, T998-4824. Quite shabby and run down, but friendly and economical. Rooms have a/c and private bath, but no TV. Rooms with fan are even cheaper (**E**).

Camping
Campamento Evagélico 'La Buena Esperanza', some 28 km west of Santiago, off the road to Canazas, T999-6237, www.elcampamento.net. A beautiful setting on a lake with a few cabins.

Santa Fe p401

C La Qhia Hostel, T954-0903, www.panama mountainhouse.com. This ecologically aware hostel is operated by a Belgian-Argentine couple and offers access to the surrounding natural attractions, including Santa Fe national park and various waterfalls. There's dorms (**E**) and private rooms, or you can rent the whole villa if you wish, a handsome structure reminiscent of a Swiss chalet, US$150 per night, 2-night minimum.

Parque Nacional Cerro Hoya p401

C Tanager Tourism, Palmilla, T6667-6447 (leave a message and contact number), www.tanagertourism.com. Offering easy access to alternative attractions such as the national park and Isla Cebaco, this excellent new eco-tourism project will interest naturalists, adventurists and anyone else who wants to get off the tourist trail. Presently, accommodations consist of large, but comfortable tent 'ranchos' (rooms are also in the works) and a great outdoor shower. Owned and operated by 2 Dutch biologists, Kees Groenedijk and Loes Roos, who also offer a range of nature and community tours (see Activities and tours, below).

Santa Catalina p401

A Punta Brava Surf Lodge, T6614-3868, www.puntabrava.com. Located right in front of the famous Santa Catalina break, this surfers' hotel has a mixture of rooms, suites and cabañas, internet access, kitchen and restaurant. Various promotional packages are available if you plan to stay a week or longer.

⊘ Eating

El Valle p399

You'll find a handful of functional eateries close to the market, otherwise most dining takes place in the hotels.

¶¶¶ La Casa de Lourdes, Calle El Ciclo, T983-6450, www.lacasadelourdes.com. This is the place for that special evening meal, where you'll find Panamanian cuisine at its finest. Interesting, exotic dishes include Yucca croquets, blackened fish in a tamarind sauce, and cashew fruit and nut tart. A real treat.

¶¶-¶ Don Pepe Wholesome, economical fare and a wide range of dishes to choose from, including burgers, chicken and Chinese.

¶¶-¶ Pensión Niña Dalia, Av Central, has an open-air eatery which lays on a good weekend lunch buffet popular with the locals.

Penonomé p399

¶¶-¶ Jin Foon, on the Interamericana, inside **Hotel Guacamaya**. Fairly good Chinese food and the usual meat, chicken and fish staples, for those who prefer less exciting flavours.

Santiago p400

¶¶¶-¶¶ Mar del Sur, Av Central. Reportedly one of Santiago's finest restaurants, serving Peruvian-style seafood.

¶¶-¶ Los Tucanes, on the Interamericana. Large, clean, buffet place that's economical and popular with the locals. There's a smarter, more expensive restaurant with the same name next door, and a bakery, too, for a cheap breakfast or snack.

▲ Activities and tours

Coclé and Veraguas p398
Community and eco-tourism
Tanager Tourism, Palmilla, T6715-7471 (evenings), www.tanagertourism.com. This socially and environmentally aware eco-tourism project is operated by 2 Dutch biologists and located in the lesser visited 'unspoiled side' of the Azuero Peninsula. They offer tours of local communities and natural attractions, including snorkelling trips to Isla Cebaco, hiking in Cerro Hoya national park, turtle watching on the beach and swimming in local waterfalls. Tourism in this region is embryonic, making it all the more fascinating to visit.

Diving and snorkelling
Excellent but expensive package trips to Coiba can be arranged with good dive centres in Panama City (see Panama City Activities and tours, page 376). Otherwise you should contact the local centres below (located in Santa Catalina) who can organize shorter and more cost-effective expeditions.
Scuba Charters, Santa Catalina, T938-0007, www.scuba-charters.com. A range of tours and packages. Excluding US$25 park entrance fees: 2-tank dives to Cobia National Park, US$105; 3-tank dives, US$135; full-day snorkel tour, US$65. They also dive other locations in the gulf of Chiriquí, including Islas Secas, Isla Montuoso and Islotes Cativo.
Scuba Coiba, Santa Catalina, T202-2171, www.scubacoiba.com. Professional outfit that offers multi-day trips to Isla Coiba and overnight accommodation in the ranger's station. Excluding US$35 entrance fee, a 2-day all-inclusive trip to Coiba costs US$450; 3 days, US$670. Excluding US$25 entrance fee, a regular 2-tank dive in Coiba national park costs US$115. PADI open water and advanced certification in the waters around Santa Catalina is US$250.

☉ Transport

El Valle p399
Bicycle The preferred mode of transport for the locals and a good way to get around. Various places rent them out. Try Don Pepe's, US$2 per hr, US$8 per day.
Bus To Panama City, hourly, 0700-1600, 2½ hrs, US$3.50.
Bus To Panama City, hourly, 0700-1600, 2½ hrs, US$3.50.

Santa Clara, Antón, Penonomé and Aguadulce p399
Bus Frequent and efficient buses travel in both directions along the Interamericana, passing through and between all the above towns. Locate a concrete bus shelter when you want to catch one and shout 'parada' when you want to get out.

From **Penonomé**, buses to **Panama City** pass every 15 mins, US$4.50, 2 ½ hrs. For **David**, go to Santiago and change.

Santiago p400
Bus To **Panama City**, every ½ hr, 0600-2300, 3½ hrs, US$7.50; for **David**, buses stop outside the **Hotel Piramidal**, hourly, 3½ hrs, US$7.50; to **Chitré**, every ½ hr, 0600-1700, 1½ hrs, US$3; to **San Fransisco**, every ½ hr, 0700-1600, 1 hr, US$1.75; to **Santa Fe**, every hr, 0700-1600, ½ hrs, US$2.50; to **Palmilla**, 10 daily, 0600-1730, 2 hrs, US$3.50; for **Santa Catalina** first go to Soná, then take connecting a bus, 0515, 1200, 1600, 2 hrs, US$4.

Parque Nacional Cerro Hoya p401
Bus From Palmilla to **Santiago**, 10 daily, 0530-1630, 2 hrs, US$3.50.

Santa Catalina p401
Bus Despite its burgeoning tourism infrastructure, Santa Catalina remains relatively remote and can only be reached via Soná. From **Soná**, infrequent buses connect with the coast, 0515, 1200, 1600, 2 hrs, US$4.

The Azuero Peninsula

One of the earliest parts of Panama to be settled, a network of prosperous villages extends throughout the Azuero Peninsula, many retaining their 400-year-old colonial traditions, costumes and charms. The small town of Divisa is the crossroads for a major paved road that branches south into the peninsula, an area composed of the densely inhabited provinces of Herrera and Los Santos, along with a narrow strip of Veraguas. Chitré, the colonial capital of Herrera, is the best base for exploring this fascinating land of rural villages frozen in time. There's a good chance you'll encounter a fiesta, or, at the very least, some bastions of Panamanian tradition: there's a seco factory in Pesé, a community of hat-makers in Ocú, potters in La Arena and mask-makers in Parita. The festivities here are the most spirited in all of Panama. Las Tablas, the capital of Los Santos province, hosts the country's most resplendent carnival, with floats, music, fireworks and unrestrained merriment. The small town of Guararé, also in Los Santos, hosts an important folkloric festival – the Festival Nacional de la Mejorana – which includes widespread singing and joyful mud fights. Nearby, Villa de Los Santos, from where Panama's first cry for independence came, is the site of stunning Corpus Christi celebrations, when the eternal battle between good and evil is enacted by hordes of dancing devils. ➤➤ *For listings, see pages 409-411.*

Chitré and around ⊜❼❀❸❻ ➤➤ *pp409-411.*

Chitré

Passing through **Parita**, with a church dating from 1556, the road reaches the cattle centre of Chitré, capital of Herrera Province and the best base for exploration. The cathedral (1578) is imposing and beautifully preserved. The small **Museo de Herrera** ① *C Manuel Correa, Tue-Sat 0900-1230, 1330-1500, Sun 0900-1200, US$1*, has historical exhibits, a few archaeological artefacts, and some local ethnographic displays. The town is known primarily for its red clay pottery, especially its roofing and floor tiles, which are exported, and for its woven mats and carpets.

Beaches around Chitré

There are some nice beaches close to Chitré served by local buses, for example **Playa Monagre** and **El Rompio** ① *take the Santa Ana bus from Chitré terminal, frequent services during the day, 30 mins, US$1 to Monagre*, which are busy at weekends and holidays. It is a 30-minute walk south along the beach from Monagre to El Rompío, where you can catch a bus back to Chitré or head further south at low tide for mangroves and solitude. There are a few restaurants at Monagre but no accommodation.

At **Puerto Agallito**, 15 minutes by bus from Chitré, many migratory birds congregate and are studied at the Humboldt Ecological Station.

Parque Nacional Sarigua

Along the swampy coast just to the north is the 8000-ha Parque Nacional Sarigua (US$3), established in 1984 to preserve the distinctive 'tropical desert' and mangrove margins of the Bahía de Parita. This is actually a man-made wasteland and a stark warning of the dangers of deforestation and over-farming. Much more interesting than its physical or natural features are the ancient artefacts that have been unearthed within the park's boundaries. The pre-Columbian site of **Monegrillo** is considered very significant but there is little for the non-specialist to appreciate.

La Arena

La Arena, the centre for Panamanian pottery, is 2 km west of Chitré. Large earthen flowerpots, colourful wind chimes and animal figurines are among the offerings. The Christmas festivities here, 22-25 December, are worth seeing, with music, dancing, bull running in the Plaza de Toros and cock fights (popular all over Panama). To get there, take a bus from Chitré (US$0.30; taxi US$1.50). Alternatively, tour operators in Panama City can arrange shopping tours here.

Pesé

Pesé, 22 km west of Chitré, is the birth place of Seco Herrerano, Panama's national drink. You can, with advance notice, visit the Varela Hermanos distillery, www.varelaher manos.com, observe the production process, tour the sugar cane plantations, take a tipple and stock up on supplies. More devout types will be pleased to hear that Pesé is also the setting for important religious ceremonies, with Christ's cruxifiction vividly re-enacted every year on Good Friday.

Ocú

About 45 km west of Chitré is Ocú, an old colonial town, whose inhabitants celebrate a few notable fiestas during the year with traditional dress, music, masks and dancing. One of their more unique traditional performances is the 'Duel of the Tamarind', basically a staged sword duel recalling the good old days when people could 'demand satisfaction' for their grievances and kill their debtors. Ocú is also known for its woven hats, which are cheaper than elsewhere in Panama. These days, the majority of Ocú's hats tend to be sold in stores along the Interamericana.

Los Santos

Los Santos, only 4 km across the Río La Villa from Chitré in Los Santos Province, is a charming old town with a fine 18th-century church (San Anastasio) containing many images. The first call for Independence came from here, recognized in the interesting **Museo de la Nacionalidad** ① *Plaza Bolívar, Tue-Sat 0900-1600, Sun 0900-1200, US$1*, set in a lovely house where the Declaration was signed on 10 November 1821. **Azuero regional IPAT office** ① *T966-8072, Mon-Fri 0830-1630*, is next door.

Guararé

The main road continues 22 km southeast through agricultural country to the tiny town of Guararé, notable only for its folkloric museum, the **Museo Manuel Zárate** ① *2 blocks behind the church, T996-2535*, where examples of Azuero's many traditional costumes, masks and crafts are exhibited in a turn-of-the-20th-century house. There is also a wealth of traditional dance, music and singing contests during the annual National Festival of La Mejorana.

Las Tablas and around ⬤🟡🟢🔵 ›› pp409-411.

Small paved roads fan out from Las Tablas to the beaches along the south coast and the small villages in the hills of the peninsula. A circular tour around the eastern mountain range can be done by continuing south to **Pocrí** and **Pedasí** (42 km), then west to **Tonosí**, all with their ancient churches and lack of spectacular sights, but typical of the Azuero Peninsula. Another 57 km of paved road runs directly over the hills from Tonosí to Las Tablas.

Las Tablas

Las Tablas is the capital of Los Santos Province and the peninsula's second-largest city, 67 km from the Divisa turn-off. The central **Iglesia de Santa Librada** with its gold-leaf altar and majestic carvings is one of the finest churches in this part of Panama and is now a National Historic Monument. **El Pausilipo**, former home of thrice-President Porras – known to Panamanians as 'the great man' – is in the process of being turned into a museum. Las Tablas is widely known for its **Fiesta de Santa Librada** (19-23 July, see Festivals and events, page 411).

The lovely and unspoilt beach of **El Uverito** is located about 10 km to the east of town but has no public transport (taxi US$4.50).

Pedasí and nearby beaches

Pedasí is a peaceful little town and the municipal library near the church has many old volumes. The local festival, on 29 June is **Patronales de San Pablo**. President Mireya Moscoso was born in Pedasí and the family figures prominently in the town's history. Beautiful empty beaches – **Playa del Toro**, **Playa La Garita** and **Playa Arena** – and crystal-clear seas are 3 km away, but beware of dangerous cross-currents when swimming. There is no public transport to the beaches but it is a pleasant walk early in the morning. You can also walk along the seashore from one beach to another, best at low tide. The local fishing craft are based at **Playa Arena** (also the safest for swimming) and boats can be hired for sport fishing, whale watching and visits to **Isla Iguana**, a wildlife sanctuary 8 km offshore, protecting the island's birdlife, reptiles (including turtles) and forest. Locally hired boats cost about US$50 for half a day. The **IPAT** office in Los Santos arranges tours with knowledgeable naturalist René Chan who lives locally.

Playa Venado to Cañas

About 31 km from Pedasí, and 12 km before Cañas, a small sign points to the black-sand beach of **Playa Venado**, a surfers' paradise. There are five cabañas for rent here. The road onwards goes to **Cañas** (no hotel), running near the Pacific Coast for a short distance, with a string of lovely coves and sandy beaches accessible by rough tracks.

Tonosí

The remote little cowboy town of Tonosí lies about 25 km west of Cañas. Picturesque as it is, the points of interest are outside of the town. A branch road leaves the town and goes 25 km further south to **Cambutal**, west of which begins **Parque Nacional Cerro Hoya**, where sea turtles come ashore to lay their eggs from July to November (see page 401). There is also a 20-km long beach at **Guánico Abajo**, 20 minutes' drive from Tonosí, but no public transport. You'll find rooms to rent, cabañas and camping on the beaches in the area. Ask around.

Heading north

An alternative to the main road returning to Las Tablas takes the inland road north following the Río Tonosí. Crossing a saddle between the two mountain ranges that occupy the centre of the peninsula (picturesque views of forested Cerro Quema, 950 m), the road arrives at **Macaracas**, another attractive but unremarkable colonial town, from where two paved roads return to Los Santos and Chitré (35 km).

⊙ The Azuero Peninsula listings

For Sleeping and Eating price codes, and other relevant information, see pages 43-46.

⊜ Sleeping

Chitré *p406*
Prices can rise by 50-100% during festivals.
A Hotel Los Guayacanes, Vía Circunvalación, T996-9758, www.losguayacanes.com. A large, comfortable 'country-club'-style hotel with generous grounds, casino, pool, tennis court, restaurants and artificial lagoon. Perhaps not as sophisticated as it pretends to be, but reasonably good value and quite secluded.
B Hong Kong, Av Carmelo Espadafora, T996-4483. This hotel is inconveniently located away from the city centre, but rooms are clean and comfortable, with a/c, cable TV and hot water. There's also a pool with water-slides and Chinese food served in the restaurant.
B Versalles, Paseo Enrique Grensier, near entry to Chitré, T996-4422, www.hotelver salles.com. An unsightly box-like exterior gives way to a rather pleasant interior complete with a cool, lush gardens and pool. Not bad, a little bland but good value. It's a 5- to 10-min walk from the city centre.
C Hotel Bali Panama, Av Herrera and Calle Correa, T996-4620, www.hotelbalipanama. com. Formerly **Hotel El Prado**, this friendly, helpful hotel has 28 clean, functional rooms with a/c, cable TV and hot water. There's Wi-Fi in lobby and a good restaurant attached.
C Rex, Calle Maliton Matín by main plaza, T/F996-4310, hotelrex6@hotmail.com. An excellent location on the plaza, with great views from a shared balcony. Rooms are smallish, have a/c and cable TV. Breakfast is included in the price and there's a good restaurant downstairs. Internet available. Recommended.
D Pensión Central, Av Herrera next to **Hotel Bali Panama**, T996-0059. Clean and basic with soft beds, but OK. Get a quieter room at the back. Rooms have a/c and cable TV but are a few dollars cheaper with fan.

D Santa Rita, Calle Manuel Correa y Av Herrera, T996-4610. Very simple, functional rooms with cable TV, a/c and hot water. The cheaper rooms have fan and no hot water. Friendly and clean, with restaurant attached.

Las Tablas *p408*
C Piamonte, Av Belisario Porras, T994-6372, hotelpiamonte@hotmail.com. A friendly, helpful hotel. Rooms are clean and comfortable with modern a/c units; the junior suites have big baths. They can help arrange tours, including transfers to Isla Iguana. The sign outside says 'Monolo'. Restaurant attached. Recommended.
C Pensión Mariela, Av Belisario Porras, opposite **Piamonte**, T994-6473. Small, functional rooms, but comfortable and spotlessly clean. Same owner as the Piamonte with the same tours and transfers available.

Pedasí *p408*
C Dim's hostel, Av Principal, T995-2303. A lovely hostel with a peaceful leafy garden, hammocks, restaurant, internet and good clean rooms. Transportation to Playa Venado and Isla Iguana available. Very friendly and recommended.
C Residencial Moscoso, T995-2203. Basic, family-run lodgings. Rooms with fan are cheaper (**D**). No hot water.
C Hotel Residencial Pedasí, Av Central, at the entrance to town, T995-2490, info@ residencialpedasi.com. This attractive terracotta building has comfortable rooms with hot water, a/c and cable TV. Secure parking, internet, restaurant and tours to Isla Iguana are also available. Friendly.

Playa Venado *p408*
D There are 5 cabañas for rent here (no electricity, very basic, overpriced), and plenty of idyllic **camping** spots (camping free, showers cost US$0.25), as well as a combined open-air restaurant.

🍴 Eating

Chitré p406

🍴 **El Mesón**, in the **Hotel Rex**, on the plaza. Good national and international dishes, including a barbeque platter of various grilled meats. The portions are generally quite generous and tasty, apart from the sandwiches which are poor. Recommended.
🍴-🍴 **Pizza Monolo**, Paseo Enrique Geenzier. Pizza joint that's popular with Panamanian families and quite buzzing on a Sat evening. Small bakery attached.
🍴 **El Aire Libre**, on the plaza. Popular little locals' place that's always busy at breakfast time.
🍴 **El Chitreano**, Calle Antonio Burgos. Charming little locals' haunt with checkered table cloths and *comida típica* served in large portions.
🍴 **La Estrella**, on the plaza, opposite the cathedral. Buffet fare and other economical eats.

Pedasí p407

🍴 **Turístico JR's**, T995-2176. Owner was formerly head chef at **El Panamá** (see page 368). Swiss/French dishes, good quality and variety, expensive. Recommended.
🍴 **Angela**. Local fare, good.

☸ Festivals and events

The Azuero Peninsula p406

Some of Panama's most fascinating and raucous festivals are celebrated in the Azuero Peninsula, giving you the chance to experience the region at its most expressive. Expect hotel rates to double during Carnaval, Semana Santa or the Feast of Corpus Christi. Some dates change annually and you should check with the tourist board to see what's on when. There are many settlements across the peninsula, each with a patron saint and a corresponding festival; ask around to see what's happening locally.

Chitré and around p406

16-22 Jan San Sebastían, the district's patron saint, is celebrated in Ocú with costumed folklore groups.
Mar/Apr Villas de Los Santos and Guararé are particularly renowned for their **Semana Santa** celebrations.
End Apr The Feria de Azuero. 'Little devil' (*diablito*) and other masks featuring in the *fiestas* are the local handicraft speciality and may be purchased from stalls or workshops around Los Santos and in Parita.
May/Jun Corpus Christi (40 days after Easter) is a 4-day feast celebrated in Los Santos with one of the country's most famous and popular festivals, a glorious distillation of the peninsula's strong Spanish roots and well worth attending.
24 Jun Chitre's patrion saint is honoured in the **Fiesta de San Juan Bautista**. Also in the preceding week.
3-6 Aug The town of Parita's patron saint, **Santo Domingo**, has a well-attended festival with lots of bullfighting.
Aug Festival del Manito and El Matrimonio Campesino is a 3-day festival in Ocú straight from medieval Spain and well worth witnessing. Dramatic performances include the Duelo del Tamarindo and the Pentiente de la Otra Vida.
18 Aug Processions commemorate Parita's founding in 1558.
23-28 Sep The Feria de la Mejorana is an important folk music festival that attracts great crowds to Guararé. A 'mejorana' is a type of string instrument, much like a guitar.
19 Oct Chitre's founding (1848) is celebrated with colourful performances and historically themed parades.
10 Nov Villa de Los Santos. Celebrations commemorate Panama's day of independence from Spain.

Las Tablas p408

Feb Commencing the Sat before Ash Wed, **Carnaval** is celebrated all over the Azuero Peninsula with great gusto, but Las Tablas takes the crown. Expect 4 days of spirited celebrations, with lots of dancing, drinking and water fights. Calle Arriba and Calle Abajo famously compete for the best floats and beauty queens.

29 Jun Celebrations with folkloric dancing honour the **patron saint of Pedasí**.

16 Jul Playa El Arenal, near Pedasí, is the site of an annual **fishing tournament**.

19-23 Jul **Fiesta de Santa Librada** and incorporated **Fiesta de la Pollera**. Las Tablas is widely known for this festival. The *pollera* is a ruffled, intricately embroidered in a single colour, off-the-shoulder dress based on colonial fashions and is now the national costume of Panama; *polleras* are made in villages near Las Tablas, the most beautiful coming from Santo Domingo (5 km east).

25 Nov More music and dancing in honour of the town Pedasí's patron saint.

⊖ Transport

Chitré and around *p406*
Bus Chitré is the transport hub of the peninsula. There is a bus terminal just outside town, take city bus **Las Arenas**.

To **Panama City** (250 km), hourly, 0600-2300, 4 hrs, US$7.50. To **Santiago**, every ½ hr, 0600-1800, 1 ½ hrs, US$2.50. There is no direct service to **David**, change at Santiago. To **Divisa**, 30 mins, US$1.30; same fare and time to **Las Tablas** (buses leave when full). To **Tonosí**, 3 hrs, US$4.50.

Ocú *p407*
Bus Several buses a day from Chitré, 1 hr, US$1.75, and buses on to **Panama City**, US$7.

Those with limited time can get a glimpse of the peninsula and villages by taking a bus from Chitré to **Pesé**, **Los Pozos** or **Las Minas**, all in the foothills of the western range, and then another to **Ocú**; staying the night and taking another bus on to Santiago to return to the Panama City–David Highway.

Car
Ocú can be reached directly from the Interamericana (19 km) by a paved turn-off south just past the Río Conaca bridge (11 km west of Divisa); *colectivos* run from here for US$0.80. Alternatively, a mostly gravel road runs west from Parita along the Río Parita valley, giving good views of the fertile landscapes of the northern peninsula.

Las Tablas and around *p408*
Bus To **Panama City**, hourly, 0600-1630, 5 hrs, US$8; to **Santo Domingo**, every ½ hr, 0600-1630, 10 mins, US$0.40; to **Tonosí**, every 45 mins, 0800-1600, 2½ hrs, US$4.25; to Pedasí, every 45 mins, 0500-1800, 1 hr, US$2; to Playa Venado,1400, 2 hrs, US$3.20 .

Pedasí *p408*
To **Las Tablas**, every 45 mins, 0500-1700, 1 hr, US$2.

Playa Venado and Tonosí *p408*
Hitching is difficult as there is little traffic.

Bus
1 a day to Playa Venado from **Las Tablas** at 1400, about 2 hrs, US$3.20, return at 0700. No direct bus Pedasí-Tonosí.

Pedasí–Cañas around 0700 and 1500, US$2; **Cañas–Tonosí** 1 a day. **Tonosí–Las Tablas**, 4 a day between 0700 and 1300, US$3, 1 hr, leave when full.

A milk truck leaves Tonosí at 0700 for **Chitré**, via Cañas, Playa Venado, Pedasí and Las Tablas, takes passengers, returns 1230.

Tonosí–**Chitré** via Macaracas, 4 a day before 1100, 3 hrs, US$4, mostly paved road.

⊙ Directory

Chitré and around *p406*
Internet Econoútiles stationary store, Av Herrera 1 block from cathedral, US$3 per hr. Also at **Abacus**, Belarmino Urriola, US$2.50 per hr.

Kuna Yala

Kuna Yala, also known as the Islas San Blas, is a land of kaleidoscopic coral reefs, sublime desert isles and fascinating indigenous villages where little has changed for hundreds of years. Men cast their fishing lines from dugout canoes, children scale coconut trees and groups of women chatter outside their cane-and-thatch houses, sewing molas and donning their traditional attire of red head scarves, vibrant blouses, colourful skirts and beads. This is the land of the Kuna, where family, community and tradition are the dominant social forces. Some 400 Caribbean islands and 200 km of coastline comprise this sparsely inhabited semi-autonomous province – and tourism is strictly controlled. No large-scale developments blight the landscape, no resorts or gated communities threaten the environment. Life here is wonderfully pure and simple. There are few places like this left on earth.

The typical Kuna village is a crowded, ramshackle affair, punctuated by a maze of teetering alleyways. Life here is based on egalitarian principles. Friends, relatives and neighbours often organize themselves into small entrepreneurial groups to co-operate in some shared venture – farming a plot, harvesting coconuts, running a hotel or fishing for lobster, for example. At the heart of the community lies the Casa de Congreso, the house of congress, where local issues are discussed, debated and voted to conclusion. The local chief, or sáhila, is responsible for the village and reports to the Congreso General Kuna, a unified political body that confers with Panama's national government.

For listings, see pages 417-418.

Ins and outs

Getting there

There are around 20 airstrips in the Kuna Yala archipelago and most are served by the two domestic airlines, Air Panama and Aeroperlas. Most people enter the *comarca* via El Porvenir, which has a small airstrip and access to several nearby accommodations. On a sailing journey, this is the place to obtain your final exit stamp from Panama, or to check in if coming from Colombia. Other popular points of entry include Cartí, Río Sidra, Corazon de Jesus, Playón Chico and Mamitupo. You will be required to pay a local tax when you land and for any subsequent island you visit, usually US$1-3. Carry lots of small notes.

It is also possible to reach Kuna Yala overland. From Panama City, head east along the Interamericana to the village of **El Llano**, then turn north and cross over the mountains until you reach the village of Cartí, from where boats depart to the islands. Hardcore adventurists can also walk over the continental divide from Cañita to Cartí. Take a bus from Panama City towards Darién and get off at Cañita, then walk two to three hours to the **EcoLodge** at Burbayar (there is also a lodge at Nusagrande). The following day camp on the coastal side of the Serranía de San Blas and on the third day make sure that you reach **Cartí** before 1600 when the last boat leaves for the islands – US$20-30 to El Porvenir, or US$10 (20 minutes) to Isla Naranjos. Before embarking on either of these journeys, contact your hotel to check the state of the roads, seasonal accessibility and frequency of transit from Cartí to the islands. You may also be able to reach the *comarca* by boat from Colón, or from less frequent sailings along the Central Caribbean coast.

Getting around

Without your own yacht, moving freely between the islands is not easily accomplished. It's sometimes possible to rent a *lancha* (motor boat) or dugout canoe for your own purposes, but usually your hotel will want to organize your daily excursions along with those of the other guests. This means that unless you're travelling in a group large enough to warrant your own vessel, you may have a limited say in which islands you visit and when. Public *lanchas* (motor boat) do depart between major settlements but there's no official schedule. If you have a specific journey in mind, you should discuss it with your hotel manager or guide. Note that you will have difficulty finding a boatman to travel to the more remote eastern islands, but you may be able to hitch a ride with a yacht. Otherwise, light plane remains the best way of travelling long-distance within the *comarca*.

Tourist information

There are no official tourist information offices in Kuna Yala. Your local hotel owner or guide will know about all the best attractions. Many of the hotels listed below have their own websites, which give a good indication of what to expect.

Local customs

The Kuna are very conservative and you should respect by their culture by dressing appropriately when visiting their villages. Not all islands are open to outsiders and you cannot land wherever you wish. Photography is an important issue. Never take a photo without permission and expect to pay US$1 for each you do snap. In Kuna Yala, visitors are generally treated hospitably, but also expected to act with the courtesy of guests in someone's home.

History

According to their own history, the Kuna arrived on Panama's Caribbean coast during the 16th century, having been driven from their Colombian homeland around the time of the Spanish conquest. However, recent evidence suggests that they did not properly settle on the islands until the mid-1800s, first inhabiting the jungles of Darién after fleeing the Gulf of Urabá in Colombia. It's likely that disease and conflicts with other indigenous groups spurred their migration to the coast and islands that are their present-day home.

Throughout history, the Kuna have been keen traders, exchanging coconuts for staples such as sugar, cacao and rice, as well as tools, cloth and weapons. Former business partners include the Scots, who established the ill-fated colony of New Edinburgh in Darién in 1698. By 1700, New Edinburgh had sunk beneath a barrage of tropical disease and Spanish hostility, never to return. Around 1740, promising relations were struck with the French, who were so admired that they were even permitted to marry Kuna women. But when they started growing cacao for export and using the local Kuna as a workforce, relations rapidly deteriorated. The French were violently expelled from the region. The British, with their well-established colony of Jamaica were the next trading partners, but it is the Colombians who proved most consistently loyal and profitable. Trade with Colombia continues today, protected by international treaty. Lobsters and coconuts are Kuna Yala's major export and much of it ends up in the Caribbean port of Colón, an international centre of commerce located at the northern entrance to the Panama Canal.

In 1903 the nation of Panama was born and the new government initiated a programme of 'national culture' which included the forced suppression of age-old Kuna traditions. The result was outright rebellion. In 1925, the Kuna attacked the local Panamanian police force with the backing and support of the US government. Each side suffered around 20 casualties and the Kuna subsequently established their own independent region, officially recognized as a semi-autonomous province or *comarca* in 1938. Their constitution was set out in *La Carta Orgánica de San Blas* in 1945, a document

Sailing to Colombia via the San Blas Islands

With the price of a plane ticket to Cartagena costing around US$170, an alternative, more adventurous route to Colombia could be spending several days travelling by boat. It's adventurous, a true travel experience and a chance to see part of the world normally reserved for those with very big budgets.

Two types of boat can take you to Colombia. The first are local trading vessels, which occasionally head to Colombia stopping at many of the more inhabited Kuna islands and settlements along the coast. These usually cost around US$200 per person, if heading all the way to Cartagena, Barranquilla or Santa Marta. You may be able to track one down at the port in Colón (see crossing the Darién by sea section, page 424, for further details of ports along the route).

A second option is recreational yachts, often foreign-owned and destined for Cartagena. Some boats are on round the world trips, but a small number make it their business to ferry adventurous travellers to and from Colombia. Price is between US$250-200, including basic food. These boats usually leave from Portobelo or Isla Grande. Ask in Hostel Voyager in Panama City, contact Sr Burgos at Hotel San Blas or Casa Viena, www.casa viena.com, in Cartagena if coming from Colombia.

Sailing vessels usually head along the coast using the most northerly islands of the San Blas, such as Cayos Holandés as overnight stops before the two- to three-day sail across the open sea to Colombia. Prevailing winds and currents make it a rougher ride from Panama to Colombia.

Choosing a boat and captain is important. Sailing is not a risk-free business as demonstrated by the multitude of wrecks in the San Blas area. Talk to your captain about previous experience and look at the boat. If in doubt, listen to your instincts. And as ever, when leaving a country, paperwork is important. Make sure you've completed exit formalities as directed by your captain.

which outlined the *comarca*'s unique self-governing structure and relationship to national government. In 1980, the Kuna elected their own representative to the national legislature. In 1999 Kuna-born Enrique Garrido was made head of Panama's general assembly, giving new voice and energy to the Kuna cause.

The islands ●●●●● ▶▶ *pp417-418*.

El Porvenir

El Porvenir is the western gateway to the archipelago and the usual point-of-entry for visitors to Kuna Yala. There's a small landing strip that sees early morning traffic from Air Panama and Aeroperlas, a simple grocery store, a basic hotel and a small beach. A Kuna museum has some modest but captivating displays on Kuna culture, including interesting old photos, descriptions of important ceremonies and a handful of Kuna crafts.

Nearby, the more bustling communities of **Isla Wichub-Huala** and **Isla Nalunega** offer the option of encountering village life first-hand. Each has its own *Casa de Congreso*, or house of congress, where local political decisions are made, as well as a range of simple accommodation, sparsely stocked general stores and basketball courts. Between Wichub-Huala and Nalunega lies the artificial island of **Ukuptupu**, the former home of a Smithsonian Institute research station, which operated here for 20 years until asked to leave in 1998. It's now the site of a popular hotel and a great place to watch the comings and goings of yachts, motorboats and dugout canoes. Around 15 to 30 minutes away lie several small islands, easily visited as a day excursion. They include **Isla Pelicano** with its gorgeous beach and colourful coral reef, and **Isla Perros**, with its teeming sunken ship that's rich in marine life and great for snorkelling. **Isla Ogobsibu** is a private island with its own lodgings.

Cayos Chichime

Not more than a couple of hours sail to the east of El Porvenir lie the idyllic islands of the Cayos Chichime, also known as Wichudup or Wichitupo in the Kuna language. The deep-water channel entering the harbour is only 30 m wide with reefs on both sides, and requires care even from experienced captains. Both islands are beautiful and inhabited by only a handful of Kuna who survive through a combination of fishing, harvesting coconuts and selling *molas* to passing boats. Many of the Kuna who live on the islands only do so for four to five months per year before returning to the more inhabited islands or moving on to another island. One of the islands' more permanent residents seems to be Umburto who, if he has space, will let you stay in a hut for US$5 per night – he might even throw in some food. And for a small fee the family will also cook locally caught seafood (through don't accept lobster or crab due to over-fishing, and certainly not the meat or eggs of sea turtles which are sometimes caught). Umburto has a boat with a motor and will take you to Porvenir for a negotiated price.

Cayos Holandés

To the east of Chichime lies a long chain of sparsely inhabited islands known as Cayos Holandés or Dutch Keys. Some of the islands have no permanent residents, but most have at least one family of Kuna harvesting coconuts. These cayos are the furthest from the mainland in Kuna Yala and have a rugged, remote feel. Washed by strong Caribbean swells the Cayos Holandés harbor abundant marine life along the barrier reef and in the deep-water channels at either end of the group – in these areas Caribbean reef sharks, tarpon and rays are often seen. Even on the sheltered southern side there exist some pristine patch reefs only metres from islands themselves. Towards the eastern end of the chain is an excellent protected anchorage know to local yacht types as 'the swimming pool', due to its clear, calm water and location surrounded on all sides by islands. As with Chichime, caution and good navigational charts are required when entering this area. One of the local reefs is called 'wreck reef' – for good reason.

Cartí

The community of Cartí, south of El Porvenir, consists of several densely inhabited island villages and a mainland settlement with a landing strip. **Cartí Sugtupu** is the usual port of call, with its interesting folkloric museum and crowds of *mola* vendors. There's lots of social amenities in this busy community, including a school, post office, library and medical centre. Sadly, it's also quite polluted, particularly around the port. If you're looking for an encounter with traditional Kuna culture, this isn't the best place. Many people here have exchanged their traditional clothing for Western-style attire and cruise ships frequently descend on the area bringing crowds of gawping tourists, which is actually the best time to see the locals dressed like Kunas, if you can stand the ambience. If you're looking for a more natural locale, the rather lovely **Isla Aguja** lies nearby, with its beaches, palm trees and handful of inhabitants. Some people get to this region by road, travelling north from the village of **El Llano**, which lies east of Panama City on the Interamericana (see page 412). It's also possible to reach Cartí by boat from El Porvenir, US$25, speak to your hotel about arranging the trip.

Río Sidra

The community of Río Sidra lies around 16 km east of Cartí, close to the mainland and with its own airstrip. Río Sidra has some basic amenities, including a telephone and general store, and is the jumping-off point for some rather splendid and secluded private islands, including **Isla Kuanidup** and **Isla Dup Askunikad**, which have rustic lodgings, blissful hammocks and beaches. Nearby, Isla Nusatupo is a lesser visited spot that offers access to the Cayos Los Grullos, with fine snorkelling around islands and coral reefs. **Isla Maquina** is a quiet, traditional island that's worth visiting as a day trip, but no tourist facilities exist for longer stays. It may be possible to reach the area by hired motorboat from Cartí; enquire locally.

Corazón de Jesús

Around 30 km east of Río Sidra, Corazón de Jesús is the archipelago's main trading centre and home to a large grocery store, airstrip and lots of built-up areas. Connected to Corazon de Jesús by a footbridge, **Narganá** is the *comarca*'s administrative centre, with the only courthouse, jail and bank for miles. Both communities are highly westernized with concrete being the preferred construction material. Although you won't encounter the kind of 'cane-and-thatch' culture that most people expect from the Kuna, a visit to these communities is still an intriguing experience, often giving fascinating insights into Kuna life. Some 7 km east of Narganá lies the more traditional community of **Isla Tigre**, reportedly very clean and friendly. **Isla Kwadule** is the home of a comfortable eco-lodge, while Río Azúcar is a very crowded island, close to the mainland and popular with yachters. There are lots of amenities here, including a hardware and grocery store.

Playón Chico

Playón Chico lies around 40 km east of Corazon de Jesús. It's a large, inhabited island, relatively modern and the jumping-off point for exploring the more remote eastern islands. Nearby, **Isla Iskardarp** is home to the **Sapibenega Kuna Lodge**, widely regarded as the archipelago's premier lodging. The waters are rough between here and Corazon de Jesús, making it hard to reach the area by motorboat; the best way is by plane.

Mamitupo

Mamitupo, 30 km east of Playón Chico, has an airstrip and gives access to some interesting sites for those who get this far. **Isla Uaguitupo**, also known as Dolphin Island, is home to an upmarket eco-lodge and neighboured by **Achutupu**, a very traditional, attractive island with lots of unspoilt culture. **Isla Ustupo**, 15 km away, is the largest island in the *comarca* with a population of 5000, lots of social amenities and a grocery store. **Isla Ailigandi** lies around 35 minutes from Mamitupo and has an array of murals and political statues devoted to the Kuna nation.

⦿ Kuna Yala listings

For Sleeping and Eating price codes, and other relevant information, see pages 43-46.

● Sleeping

It's a very good idea to book ahead, but if you just turn up at the airport you'll probably find a bed somewhere – ask around. Camping is possible on some of the islands, but you'll need permission; speak to the *sáhila* (the local chief) first. Point of entry is specified below for hotels on islands but you will still require transit by boat to reach most of them (this should be provided by the hotel, assuming you've booked ahead). All rates are per person and all but the lowest include meals, transport and excursions. Even the most expensive accommodation is very rustic.

LL Sapibenega Kuna Lodge, 5 mins from Playón Chico, T215-1406 or T6676-5548, www.sapibenega. com. Widely acknowledged as the best (and most expensive) lodgings in the entire *comarca*. Lodgings consist of beautiful, cane-and-thatch cabañas on stilts, all solar-powered with private baths, balconies and hammocks.

LL Uaguinega Ecoresort, Isla Uaguitupu (point of entry: Mamitupo), T263-7780, www.uaguinega.com. Also known as 'Dolphin Island Lodge'. A range of upmarket wooden cabins and cane-and-thatch cabañas. Amenities include bar-restaurant, hammocks and volley ball. This the only hotel in the *comarca* with satellite internet, if you strangely feel the need to contact the outside world.

L Cabañas Wailidup, Isla Wailidup (point of entry: El Porvenir), 25 mins from El Porvenir, T259-9136 (Panama City) or T6709-4484, www.kuna-niskua.com. Very exclusive cabañas on a private island, all powered by solar energy. Guests enjoy their own personal beach, bar-restaurant and pier. Sandflies may be an issue during certain months. The owner is Sr Juan Antonio Martínez, who also owns Kuna Niskua on Wichub-Huala.

L Kwadule, Isla Kwadule (point of entry: Corazon de Jesus). An exclusive private island with attractive cabañas on stilts overlooking the water. There's a very nice restaurant/bar and a nearby coral reef too. Rooms have private bath.

AL Cabañas Coco Blanco, Isla Ogobsibu (point of entry: El Porvenir), 15 mins from El Porvenir, T6706-7316, cabanascoco blanco@yahoo.it. Secluded private island with a handful of traditional cane-and-thatch cabañas right on the beach. Interestingly, they prepare a lot of Italian food.

A Kuanidup, Isla Kuanidup (point of entry: Río Sidra), 25 mins from Río Sidra, T6635-6737, kuani9@hotmail.com. An idyllic, isolated spot with rustic cabañas, swaying hammocks, lovely coral reef and achingly picturesque white-sand beaches. The perfect castaway desert island.

A Kuna Niskua, Isla Wichub-Huala (point of entry: El Porvenir), 5 mins from El Porvenir, T259-9136 (Panama City) or T6709-4484, www.kuna-niskua.com. Owned by the friendly and knowledgeable Sr Juan Antonio Martínez, who is reportedly an important player in Kuna politics. These are some of the most attractive rooms in the area, right in the heart of a thriving Kuna community. Most rooms have private bath and shower, but some cheaper ones have shared bath (**B**). Recommended.

B Cabañas Ukuptupu, Isla Ukuptupu (point of entry: El Porvenir), 5 mins from El Porvenir, T293-8709 (Panama City) or T6514-2788, www.ukuptupu.com. Housed in the former Smithsonian Institute research station, these wooden cabins are built on platforms over the water. Some walkways have hammocks and interesting views of the boats arriving at Wichub-Huala. The owner, Don Juan García, speaks some English and is very hospitable. The bathroom is shared with Kuna-style barrel and bucket showers. Highly recommended.

B Hotel El Porvenir, El Porvenir, T221-1397
(Panama City) or T6692-3542, hoteleporvenir
@hotmail.com. Managed by the friendly Miss
Oti. Simple, solid rooms close to the airstrip,
with a handy grocery store attached. Rates
include three meals, but lobster is extra. All
rooms have a private bathroom. For large
groups, call the Panama City number.
B Hotel San Blas, Isla Nalunega (point of
entry: El Porvernir), 5 mins from El Porvenir.
T344-1274 (Panama City) or T6749-9697.
Located inside a Kuna community. The
traditional cane and thatch cabañas here are
more interesting than the solid brick wall
rooms upstairs, which are simple and
smallish. The hotel's guide, Lucino, is very
friendly and scouts for guests at El Porvenir
airport; he speaks English and French.
There's a small beach out front.
D Alberto Vásquez's, Nalunega, 5 mins from
El Porvenir, T6772-5135. If you would like the
experience of staying in a Kuna house,
Alberto Vásquez has 2 rooms, each with a
2-person capacity, shared bath, bucket-and-
barrel shower. Reasonable rates include 3
meals, but excursions are US$5 extra, when
available. Alberto works for Juan García
(Cabañas Ukuptupu) and is a good guide.
D Narganá Lodge Hotel, Narganá (point of
entry: Corazón de Jesús). A basic hotel and
restaurant, **El Caprichito**, serving good
crab dishes.

✪ Festivals and events

All the following fiestas involve dances,
games, meals and speeches, and are
traditional. Those on Narganá have a stronger
Western element (but also typical dancing
and food).
Feb Anniversary of the Tule Revolution,
at Playón Chico, Tupile, Ailigandi and Ustupu.
19 Mar Fiesta patronal on Narganá.

8 Jul Anniversary of Inakiña on Mulatupo.
29-31 Jul Fiesta patronal on Fulipe.
20 Aug Charles Robinson anniversary
on Narganá.
3 Sep Anniversary of Nele-Kantule
on Ustupo.
11 Sep Anniversary of Yabilikiña
on Tuwala.

◎ Shopping

Molas ('reverse appliqué' blouses) cost
upwards of US$10 each. You can also try the
San Blas perfume *Kantule*. Both *molas* and
Kantule are also obtainable in many
Panama City and Colón shops.

◎ Transport

Air
Both Air Panama and Aeroperlas fly to Kuna
Yala, serving all of the major destinations. El
Porvenir is the entry point for most visitors,
US$58 one-way. All flights leave between
0600 and 0630, Mon-Sat, returning
0700-0830. Evening and Sun flights must be
booked privately. Baggage over 15 kg is
charged at US$0.50 per kg, so wear your
heavy stuff.

Boat
There are occasional boats to Kuna Yala from
Colón, but there is no scheduled service and
the trip can be rough. One ship that goes
from time to time is the *Almirante*; try to find
the captain, Figueres Cooper, who charges
US$30 for the trip. The port captain's office
at Coco Solo may have information on boat
departures, T441-5231 or T445-1055,
although most boats are not keen to take
gringos. Alternatively, go to the Costa Arriba
and try from there.

Darién

Southeast of Kuna Yala lies the similarly beautiful and less-visited province of Darién. Having traversed the entire North American continent from Alaska, the Interamericana Highway promptly ends here, in Panama's remote and edgy eastern frontier. Beyond it, an engulfing wilderness reaches into Colombia, the so-called Darién Gap, where notorious paramilitaries traffic arms and drugs.

Impenetrable rainforests punctuate this dark, magnificent and undeniably savage land, partly protected by the Parque Nacional Darién. Huge biodiversity, rich and differing ecosystems, and abundant animal life have earned the park 'World Biosphere' and 'World Heritage' status. For now, plans to extend the Interamericana eastwards have been halted in the face of Colombia's civil war. But when the highway does reach into Darién's forests, we should expect to see scenes like those in western half of the province, now a sad expanse of wasteland and unpleasant frontier towns. Experience the remaining wilderness of Darién while it lasts. ▶▶ *For listings, see page 426.*

Ins and outs

As one of the great impenetrable wildernesses of the world, crossing the Darién Gap is the dream of many, but not a trip to be undertaken lightly. By all accounts good Spanish, good guides, serious planning and lots of money are essential. If you're looking for an exciting route to Colombia, the river crossings and jungle treks of the Darién are one option; alternatively, you can use launches and canoes to skip along the Pacific or Caribbean coastline. But neither option is cheap.

East of Chepo the Darién stretches out over a third of the area of Panama and is almost undeveloped. Most villages are accessible only by air, river or on foot. The Interamericana ends at Yaviza; from there, if you want to cross by land to South America, it's on foot through the jungles of Darién.

At the end of 1992, Panama and Colombia revealed a plan to build a road through the Darién Gap, which includes environmental protection. Construction of a previous project had been halted in the 1970s by a lawsuit filed by US environmental groups who feared deforestation, soil erosion, endangerment of indigenous groups and the threat of foot-and- mouth disease reaching the US. Even if the plan is completed, the Darién Gap road linking Panama with Colombia will not be open for many years, so the usual way of getting to Colombia is by sea or air. It is possible to go overland, but the journey is in fact more expensive than by air – and considerably more dangerous.

Sights

The Interamericana runs east 60 km from Panama City to the sizeable town of **Chepo**. There are no hotels or *pensiones* in Chepo, but if you are stuck there, ask at the fire station, they will be able to find a place for you. There is a document check in Chepo and at one or two other places. From Chepo the highway has been completed as far as **Yaviza** (225 km). It is gravel from Chepo until the last 30 km which are of earth (often impassable in the rainy season).

From **El Llano**, 18 km east of Chepo, a road goes north to the Caribbean coast. After 27 km it passes the **Nusagandi Nature Lodge** in the Pemansky Nature Park. The lodge is in Kuna territory, in an area of mostly primary forest. The coast is reached at **Cartí**, 20 km from Nusagandi. From here there is access to the Kuna Yala (see page 412).

Thirty-five kilometres east of Chepo the Interamericana crosses the Lago Bayano dam by bridge (the land to the north of the highway as far as Cañazas is the **Reserva Indígena del Bayano**). Lago Bayano dam supplies a significant amount of Panama's electricity, and has been a source of friction with the Kuna people who occupy the land around the lake and especially above in the catchment area.

The main villages (Yaviza, Púcuro, Paya and Cristales) have electricity and radios; canned food (but no gasoline) is available in Yaviza, Pinogana, Unión de Chocó, Púcuro and Paya, only the Emberá-Wunan (also spelt Wunaan) of the Chocó and Kuna women retain traditional dress. Organized **jungle tours** to Kuna and Emberá-Wunan villages and the Río Bayano costing from US$65 to over US$300 can be purchased through **Extreme Tours** in Panama City. Two of the easiest villages to visit on your own are **Mogue**, 45 minutes upriver from La Palma (at high tide), US$10 (possible to see harpy eagles in this area), and **Puerto Lara** – an hour's walk from turning off the main road just south of Santa Fe (four-person huts, US$20 per person, including meals).

The private **Punta Patiño Nature Reserve** owned by the Panamanian NGO **ANCON** is 25 km southwest of La Palma. Covering some 260 sq km, the reserve protects diverse

Darién

habitats ranging from rare Pacific Dry forest through to mangroves. Punta Patiño is a good place to get a feel for the Darién and offers rewarding wildlife viewing, including 130 species of birds and the possibility of seeing a harpy eagle, marmosets, kinkajous, tamanduas and at times the big cats. Heading back from Punta Patiño you pass the small fishing village of **Punta Alegre**, known for frequent fiestas, with a population of Colombian immigrants and Emberá tribesmen. Access within the region is by collective boat (US$3.50 to Mogué, similar to Punto Alegre). Organized trips can be arranged through **Ancon Expeditions** (*T269-9415, www.anconexpeditions.com*), see page 377.

The bus service from Panama City (see page 426) has its problems; the road is bad and may be washed out after rains. Find out before you leave how far you can get. Alternatively there is an irregular boat to Yaviza, going about once a week, US$12 including meals, leaving from the harbour by the market in the old city, information from Muelle Fiscal, Calle 13, next to the Mercado Público. The only sleeping accommodation is the deck (take a hammock) and there is one primitive toilet for about 120 people. The advertised travel time is 16 hours, but it can take as long as two days.

Yaviza/El Real

Another possibility is to fly to La Palma and take the shorter boat trip to Yaviza, or direct to El Real (three a week, US$68 return), which is about 10 km from Yaviza. There is only one hotel at **Yaviza**; there is also a TB clinic and a hospital. Crossing the river in Yaviza costs US$0.25. From Yaviza it is an easy two hours' walk to **Pinogana** (small and primitive), where you have to cross the Río Tuira by dugout (US$1 per person). From Pinogana you can walk on, keeping the river to your left, to **Vista Alegre** (three hours). Recross the river and walk 30 minutes to **Unión de Chocó** (some provisions and you can hammock overnight; you can sleep in the village hall but use a net to protect against *vinchucas* – Chagas disease). It's 1-km upriver to Yape, on the tributary of the same name, then three to four hours' walk to **Boca de Cupe**. Alternatively, you can go by motor dugout from Pinogana to Boca de Cupe (about US$65 per boat). Or take a boat from Yaviza to El Real (US$10), where there is a basic place to stay (**E El Nazareno**, T228-3673). Opposite there is a lady who will prepare meals if given notice. From there, take a motor dugout to Boca de Cupe (about US$15-20 per person, five hours). A boat to Paya costs about US$35 per person for groups of four or five. Boats from El Real are infrequent and may only go to Unión de Chocó or Pinogana. A jeep track runs from El Real to Pinogana.

There are various other combinations of going on foot or by boat, prices for boat trips vary widely, so negotiate. They tend to be lower going downstream than up. It is wise to make payment always on arrival.

Boca de Cupe

You can stay overnight at Boca de Cupe with a family. Food and cold beer is on sale here (last chance if you are going through to Colombia), and **Restaurant Nena** (blue building near landing dock) serves meals for US$2 and is a good source of information. Lodging (**D**) in Boca de Cupe with Antonio (son of María who helped many hikers crossing Darién, but who died in 1989). Don Ramón will prepare meals for US$2 and let you sleep on his floor. You can go with Emberá-Wunan people to Unión de Chocó, stay one or two days with them and share some food (they won't charge for lodging). The Emberá-Wunan are very friendly and shy, and it's best not to take pictures. In Boca de Cupe get your exit stamp (though you may be told to get it at Púcuro) and keep an eye on your luggage. From Boca de Cupe to Púcuro by dugout (US$20-50), to Paya (if river level is high enough), US$80. The section Boca de Cupe-Púcuro is possible on foot.

Púcuro

Púcuro is a Kuna village and it is customary to ask the chief's permission to stay (he will ask to see your passport). Immigration here, if arriving from Colombia, can be very officious. The women wear colourful ornamented *molas* and gold rings through their noses. There is a small shop selling basic provisions, such as tinned meats and salted biscuits. Visitors usually stay in the assembly house. People show little interest in travellers. From Púcuro you can walk through lush jungle to Paya, six hours (guide costs US$20, not really necessary, do not pay in advance), which was the capital of the Kuna Empire. From Púcuro to Paya there are four river crossings. The path is clear after the first kilometre.

Paya

In Paya you may be able to stay in the assembly house at the village, but it is usual to stay 2 km away eastwards in the barracks (US$2.50 per person, recommended). There's a passport check, baggage search and, on entry into Panama at least, all gear is treated with a chemical which eats plastic and ruins leather – wash it off as soon as possible. For US$2-2.50 you will get meals. The Kuna people in Paya are more friendly than in Púcuro. From Paya there are two routes.

Paya to Turbo

Route one From Paya, the next step is four to six hours' walk to **Palo de las Letras**, the frontier stone, where you enter Los Katíos, one of Colombia's national parks (see below). The path is not difficult, but is frequently blocked up to the border. From there you go down until you reach the left bank of the Río Tulé (three hours, no water between these points), you follow it downstream, which involves seven crossings (at the third crossing the trail almost disappears, so walk along the river bed – if possible – to the next crossing). If any of these watercourses are dry, watch out for snakes. About 30 minutes after leaving this river you cross a small creek; 45 minutes further on is the abandoned camp of the Montadero, near where the Tulé and Pailón rivers meet to form the Río Cacarica. Cross the Cacarica and follow the trail to the MA (**Ministerio del Medio Ambiente** – Colombian

National Parks) abandoned rangers' hut at **Cristales** (seven hours from Palo de las Letras). Guides from Paya to Cristales (they work in a rota and always go in pairs), charge US$55-200. They each carry a gun and a small bag of provisions and travel very fast.

If you insist on walking beyond Montadero, a machete, compass and fishing gear (or extra food) are essential. The path is so overgrown that it is easier, when the river is low, to walk and swim down it (Cristales is on the left bank, so perhaps it would be better to stick to this side). Occasional dugouts will take you to **Bijao** (or Viajado), two hours, for around US$120 per boat. There is no village nearby, so arrive prepared. It is possible to walk to Bijao down the right (west) bank of the Río Cacarica (heavy going). From the bend to the east of the river the path improves and it is one hour to Bijao. At Bijao ask for the ANAM station, where you can eat and sleep (floor space, or camp). At the end of 1998 guerrillas seized Bijao, killing several people and driving out others, so it is unclear what facilities are available now.

From Bijao a motor dugout used to run to **Travesía** (also called Puerto América) for US$40 per person (two to five hours), from where motorboats go to Turbo for US$10 (in scheduled boat – if it stops; if not it'll cost you about US$250 to hire a boat). Travesía has some accommodation and provisions but has been reported as expensive and anti-gringo. Once again, there is a walking route south to Limón (two hours) and east to La Tapa (30 minutes). A cargo boat may be caught from here to Turbo. There is one *residencial* and a shop in Travesía. The last section from Travesía down the Atrato goes through an area full of birdlife including hummingbirds, kingfishers, herons and 'screamers', which are about the size of turkeys and are believed to be endemic to the Atrato Valley. The river enters the Great Atrato swamp and from there to the Bahía de Colombia. Turbo is on the opposite coast.

On arrival in Turbo, you must go to the **DAS office** (**Security Police**) ① *Postadero Naval, north along Carrera 13 near airport, 0800-1630*, to get your entrance stamp. If you fail to do this, you will have to wait until Cartagena, or elsewhere, and then explain yourself in great detail to DAS and quite likely you will be fined. If you arrive at the weekend and the DAS is closed, make sure you obtain a letter or document from the police in Turbo that states when you arrived in Colombia. The problems with this route are mostly on the Colombian side, where route finding is difficult, the undergrowth very hard to get through, and the terrain steep. Any rain adds to the difficulties though equally, when the water is low, boats need more pole assistance and the cost increases.

If you are coming into Panama from Colombia by these routes, and you have difficulty in obtaining entry stamps at Púcuro or Boca de Cupe, obtain a document from an official en route stating when you arrived in Panama. This may be equally hard to get. When you arrive in Panama City, go to the **Oficina Nacional de Migración** (who may send you to the port immigration) and explain the problem. One traveller reports hearing of several arrests of travellers caught without their entry stamp. Many of these 'illegals' stay arrested for weeks. It may help to be able to prove that you have sufficient money to cover your stay in Panama.

The **Parque Nacional Katios**, extending in Colombia to the Panamanian border, can be visited with mules from the MA headquarters in Sautatá. Entry by motorized vehicle is prohibited. Look out for the Tilupo Waterfall, 125 m high, where the water cascades down a series of rock staircases, surrounded by orchids and other fantastic plants. The Alto de la Guillermina is also in the park, a mountain behind which is a strange forest of palms called 'mil pesos', and the Ciénagas de Tumaradó, with red monkeys, waterfowl and alligators.

Route two The second route is a strenuous hike up the Río Paya valley through dense jungle (machete country) for about 16 hours to the last point on the Paya (fill up with

Cautions and notes on crossing the Darién Gap

When planning your trip by land or along the coast to Colombia, remember there are strict rules on entry into Colombia and you must aim for either Turbo or Buenaventura to obtain your entry stamp. Failure to do this will almost certainly involve you in significant fines, accusations of illegal entry, or worse in Colombia. Do not enter Darién without full details of which areas to avoid because of the activities of drug traffickers, bandits and guerrilla groups, mostly from Colombia, but operating on both sides of the border.

The best time to go is in the dry months (January to mid-April); the trip would be considerably harder in the wet season (May to December). Even when totally covered in mosquito repellent you will get bitten and run the risk of contracting dengue fever. Travel with a reliable companion or two. Talk to knowledgeable locals for the best advice. Hire at least one indigenous guide, but do it through the village corregidor, whose involvement may add to the reliability of the selected guides. (Budget up to US$10 per day for the guide and his food. Negotiate with the chief, but do not begrudge the cost.) Travel light and move fast. The journey described here takes about seven days to Turbo.

Maps of the Darién area can be purchased from the Ministerio de Obras Públicas, Instituto Geográfico Nacional Tommy Guardia, in Panama City (US$4, reported to contain serious mistakes). Information is also available from Asociación Nacional para la Conservación de la Naturaleza, Calle Amela Dennis de Icaza, Ancón Hill, T314-0060, www.ancon.org.

water), then a further three hours to the continental divide where you cross into Colombia. Down through easier country (three to four hours) brings you to **Unguía** where motor boats are available to take you down the Río Tarena, out into the Gulf of Urabá, across to Turbo. This trip should not be taken without a guide, though you may be lucky and find some local people making the journey and willing to take you along. They will appreciate a gift when you arrive in Unguía. Hazards include blood-sucking ticks, the inevitable mosquitoes and, if that weren't enough, thirst.

There are many other possible routes from Panama crossing the land border used by locals. Most involve river systems and are affected by water levels. There are few tracks and no reliable maps. We have heard of successful crossings using the Salaqui and Balsas rivers, and a land route Jaqué–Jurado–Río Sucio. Good Spanish and guides, serious planning and money are essential. See below for sea routes.

By sea: the Caribbean route via Puerto Obaldía

Boats leave, irregularly, from the Coco Solo wharf in Colón (minibus from Calle 12, 15 minutes, US$0.80, taxi US$4) for Puerto Obaldía, via Kuna Yala. These are small boats which give a rough ride in bad weather and cost around US$30 per person. Take your own food, water and shade; with stops, the journey takes two to four days. There are flights with **Ansa** ① *T226-7891/6881*, and **Transpasa** ① *T226-0932/0843*, at 0600-0630 from Panama City to Puerto Obaldía, daily except Sunday, for US$44 single (book well in advance). There are also flights with **Aerotaxi**. Puerto Obaldía is a few kilometres from the Colombian border. Arriving in Puerto Obaldía you have to pass through the military control for baggage search, immigration (proof of funds and onward ticket asked for) and malaria control. In Puerto Obaldía there are shops, **Colombian Consulate**, **Panamanian Immigration**, but nowhere to change traveller's cheques until well into Colombia (not Turbo); changing cash is possible. There are *expresos* (speedboats) from Puerto Obaldía (after clearing Customs) to Capurganá, and then another on to **Acandí** (**F** Hotel Central, clean, safe; **F** Hotel Pilar, safe). From Acandí you can go on to Turbo, on the Gulf of Urabá, no fixed schedule (you cannot get to Turbo in the same day; take shade and drinks and be prepared for seasickness). Medellín can be reached by road from Turbo. Walk from Puerto Obaldía to Zapzurro, just beyond the border, for a dugout to Turbo, US$15, where you must get your Colombia entry stamp. It seems that most vessels leaving Puerto Obaldía for Colombian ports are contraband boats. As in other parts of Darién seek security advice.

Capurganá (Colombia)

Alternatively you can get from Puerto Obaldía to Acandí on the Colombian side of the border, either by walking for nine hours or by hiring a dugout or a launch to Capurganá (US$8), and then another launch at 0715, which takes one hour and costs US$3. The snorkelling is good in Capurganá. There is a Panamanian consul (Roberto) who issues visas for Panama. There are **Twin Otter** flights to Medellín. To walk to Capurganá takes four hours, guide recommended (they charge US$10); first go to **La Miel** (two hours), then to **Zapzurro** (20 minutes), where there are shops and cabins for rent, then an hour to 90 minutes to Capurganá. Most of the time the path follows the coast, but there are some hills to cross (it's hot, take drinking water). From Acandí a daily boat is scheduled to go at 0800 to Turbo (US$15, three hours). Take pesos, if possible, to these Colombian places, the rate of exchange for dollars is poor.

The Pacific route

Although not quick, the Pacific coastline provides another relatively straightforward route across the Darién but a good knowledge of Spanish is essential. Take a bus from Panama City (Plaza 5 de Mayo) to **Metetí** (**D-E** Hospedaje Feliz, basic 'box' rooms), 50 km from Yaviza, the junction for transport to **Puerto Quimba**, where boats can be taken to La Palma. Alternatively, take a bus to **Santa Fe**, which is 75 km short of Yaviza and off to the south, a rough but scenic six to eight hours (US$8, three a day, check times). In Santa Fe it is possible to camp near the police post. Then hitch a ride on a truck (scarce), or walk two hours to the Río Sabanas at Puerto Larda (11 km) where you must take a dugout or launch to La Palma, or hire one (US$5, two hours). **La Palma** is also reached by boat from Yaviza (US$3, eight hours). It is the capital of Darién and you can change cash and traveller's cheques and stop overnight – it has one *pensión* (**F**, friendly, English-speaking owners, with cooking and laundry facilities), or you might be able to stay with the *guardia*). **Jaqué** is on the Pacific Coast, near Puerto Piña, 50 km north of the Colombian border (one hotel). **Bahía Piña** has a runway, used mainly by the expensive fishing resort. If you want to stay in the area, there are a range of options provided as part of the **Darién Paradise Trail** ① T226-7000, www.darientrail.tripod.com, a community-based ecotourism circuit with accommodation in Santa Fe, Boca Lara, La Palma, Sambu, Meteti-Canglón and Ipeti Embera. Hotels tend to be in the **E** category.

These isolated settlements on the Pacific Coast are close to the **Parque Nacional Darién**, Panama's largest and wildest protected area. Cana and Cerro Pirre are at its heart but at present it is not advisable to visit because of the various armed bands that use the jungle as cover. From Jaqué you can catch a launch to Jurado in Colombia (US$25, four 'murderous' hours, take something to sit on). The launch continues to Bahía Solano or there are weekly cargo boats to Buena Ventura (M/N Fronteras US$45 including food, 36 hours, bunks but OK), where there is a DAS office where you can sort out your paperwork.

Alternatively, at the Muelle Fiscal in Panama City (by the main waterfront market, near Calle 13), ask for a passenger boat going to Jaqué. The journey takes 18 hours, is cramped and passengers cook food themselves, but costs only US$12. Jaqué is only reached by sea or air (the airstrip is used mostly by wealthy visitors going sports fishing); there are small stores, a good *comedor*, and one *hospedaje*.

The guard post is open every day and gives exit stamps. Canoes from Jaqué go to Juradó (US$20, 4½ hours) or Bahía Solano (US$45, 160 km, with two overnight stops) in Chocó. The first night is in Jurado. There are flights from Jurado to Turbo, but you can get 'stuck' in Jurado for several days. Bahía Solano is a deep-sea fishing resort with an airport and *residencias*. Flights from Bahía Solano go to Quibdó, connecting to Cali, or Medellín (book in advance; the town is popular with Colombian tourists). On this journey, you sail past the lush, mountainous Pacific Coast of Darién and Chocó, with beautiful coves and beaches, and you'll see a variety of marine life.

◉ Darién listings

For Sleeping and Eating price codes, and other relevant information, see pages 43-46.

◉ Sleeping

Yavisa/El Real *p421*
E Tres Américas, pay in **Casa Indira** shop next door. Take mosquito coils – there isn't anywhere to hang a net – basic, but friendly.

Paya to Turbo *p422*
F Doña Julia, Unguia. With bath.
F Residencias Viajero, Unguia. With bath.

Puerto Obaldía *p424*
E Residencia Cande. A good *pensión*, nice and clean, which also serves very good meals for US$1.50, order meals in advance.

Capurganá (Colombia) *p425*
Several hotels including **B Calypso**, **D Náutico**, **E Uvita** and **E Al Mar**. Also *pensiones* or you can camp by the beach.

The Pacific route *p425*
It is easy to find accommodation with local families and camping is possible on the beach.
LL Cana Field Station, Cana, T269-9415 (Panama City), www.anconexpeditions.com. Mainly used by groups and ornithologists.

E Guacamaya, Santa Fe, T299-6727.
F Chavela, Jaqué. Clean, basic, friendly.

◉ Transport

Bus From bus terminal in Panama City, buses leave every 2 hrs 0630-1430 for **Pacora**, US$0.80, **Chepo**, US$1.60, **Cañitas**, 4 hrs, US$3.10, **Arretí**, 6 hrs, US$9, **Metetí** and **Canglón**, 8 hrs, US$11.20. Beyond, to **Yaviza**, in the dry season only (Jan-Apr), US$15, 10 hrs minimum. Plenty of pick-ups run on the last stretch to Yaviza, eg about 3 hrs from Metetí to Yaviza.

The Pacific route *p425*
Air and boat There are 2 daily **Aeroperlas** flights from Panama City to **La Palma**, US$40, and 1 a day to **Jaqué** on the Pacific shore, US$49; also to **Yaviza** 3 days a week, but check with the airline **Parsa**, T226-3883. They have an office at the domestic airport in Panama City. If you cannot get a plane from **La Palma** to **Jaqué**, there are boats, US$15. En route there is an Ancón Lodge at Punta Patino. Details from **Ancon Expediciones** in Panama City, page 377.

Contents

Background

Costa Rica

History

Pre-Columbian history

Population of the Americas began somewhere between 40,000 and 15,000 years ago, when mankind first crossed the Bering Straight from Asia. A slow southerly migration steadily peopled the continent, and evidence suggests that humans first appeared in what is now Costa Rica roughly 10,000 years ago.

Early human settlement developed in this intermediate zone without a single dominant cultural group. The region was very much at the boundary of a north-south divide, taking its influences from both the Maya civilizations of modern-day Mexico and from several smaller groups in South America.

Farming, which began in earnest around 1000 BC, is the greatest indicator of this division. The Chorotega people, who lived in the northwest of Costa Rica on the Nicoya Peninsula, present day Guanacaste, were the largest and most advanced tribe in the country at the time of conquest. Arriving from Chiapas in southern Mexico around the 13th century, they cultivated beans and maize and developed a tradition of ceramics influenced by the Mesoamerican cultures of the Maya and later the Aztec. However, people on the Caribbean coast and in southern regions were more influenced by South American cultures, leading to the dominance of tuber cultivation, in particular yucca or manioc. Likewise, the dominance of jade, an influence from the north, waned with the decline of the Maya between AD 500-800, allowing the influence of gold from cultures of the south to emerge.

With increased food supplies, social organization and hierarchy developed to manage the increased populations. Regions of Costa Rica were divided into *cacicazgos* which were the basis for exchange of goods within the country and further afield. Rivalry and competition were intrinsic to the hierarchy, and dominance of an area was directly related to military ability and population. Likewise, dominance relied on the creation and development of strategic alliances to overcome and dominate the enemy.

Archaeological evidence of early settlements in the country are scarce. The largest single pre-columbian site in the country is the Guayabo National Monument, close to Turrialba, which is believed to have been ruled by a *cacique* or shaman. Inhabited from 1000 BC to AD 1400, the economy of Guayabo was based on agriculture, hunting and fishing. The reasons for abandoning the site remain a mystery, as do explanations of the country's other main archaeological remains, the stone spheres found dotted around the Diquis Valley in the south of the country.

Population estimates for the country prior to the arrival of the Spaniards vary dramatically. Early studies put the population as low as 27,000, but these estimates are almost certainly made after the first wave of disease impacted on the region. More recent studies put the figure somewhere between 250,000 and 400,000.

Spanish settlement

The Genoese explorer Christopher Columbus introduced European influences to the country when he dropped anchor off the coast of Puerto Limón at Isla Uvita on 18 September 1502. After 17 days exploring the coastal area, teased by the prospect of locals decorated in gold, Columbus and his men moved south, calling this section of the coast of 'Veragua' *costa rica* – the rich coast. The precious metal never materialized in significant quantities but rumours travelled far and fast at the turn of the 16th century. The Spaniards settled in the Meseta Central, where the numbers of several thousand sedentary indigenous farmers were soon greatly diminished by the diseases brought by the settlers. Cártago was founded in 1563 by Juan Vásquez de Coronado, but there was almost no expansion for 145 years, when a small number left Cártago for the valleys of Aserrí and Escazú. They founded Heredia in 1717, and San José in 1737. Alajuela, not far from San José, was founded in 1782. The settlers were growing in numbers but they were still poor and raising only subsistence crops.

Independence and coffee
Independence from Spain was declared in 1821, whereupon Costa Rica, with the rest of Central America, immediately became part of Mexico. This led to a civil war during which, two years later, the capital was moved from Cártago to San José. After independence, the government sought anxiously for some product which could be exported and taxed for revenue and settled upon coffee, which had been successfully introduced from Cuba in 1808, making Costa Rica the first of the Central American countries to grow what was to become known as the golden bean. The Government offered free land to coffee growers, thus building up a peasant landowning class. In 1825 there was a trickle of exports, carried by mule to the ports and y 1846 there were ox-cart roads to Puntarenas. By 1850 there was a large flow of coffee to overseas markets, which was greatly increased by the opening of a railway in 1890 from San José and Cártago to Puerto Limón along the valley of the River Reventazón. From 1850, coffee prosperity began to affect the country profoundly: the birth rate grew, land for coffee was free and the peasant settlements started spreading, first down the Reventazón as far as Turrialba, then up the slopes of the volcanoes, then down the new railway from San José to the old Pacific port of Puntarenas.

The banana industry
Bananas were first introduced in 1878 and Costa Rica was the first Central American republic to grow them. It is now the second largest exporter in the world. Labour was brought in from Jamaica to clear the forest and work the plantations. The industry grew and in 1913, the peak year, the Caribbean coastlands provided 11 million bunches for export. The United Fruit Company (today known as Chiquita) then turned its attentions to the Pacific littoral, especially in the south around the port of Golfito. Although some of the Caribbean plantations were turned over to cacao, abacá (Manilla hemp) and African palm, the region regained its ascendancy over the Pacific littoral as a banana producer. By the end of the century over 50,000 ha were planted with bananas, mostly in the Atlantic lowlands.

In the 1990s Chiquita, Dole and Del Monte, the multinational fruit producers, came under international pressure over labour rights on their plantations. Two European campaign groups targeted working conditions in Costa Rica where, despite constitutional guarantees of union freedom, there was a poor record of labour rights abuse. Only 10% of Costa Rica's 50,000 banana workers were represented by unions. The rest preferred to join the less political *solidarista* associations, which provided cheap loans and promoted savings, and thus avoided being blacklisted or harassed. Del Monte agreed in 1998 to talk to the unions after a decade of silence, while Chiquita declared its workers free to choose trade union representation.

Democratic government

Costa Rica's long tradition of democracy began in 1889 and has continued to the present day, with only a few lapses. In 1917 the elected president, Alfredo González, was ousted by Federico Tinoco, who held power until 1919, when a counter-revolution and subsequent elections brought Julio Acosta to the presidency. Democratic and orderly government followed until the campaign of 1948, when violent protests and a general strike surrounded disputed results. A month of fighting broke out after the Legislative Assembly annulled the elections, leading to the abolition of the constitution and a junta being installed, led by José Figueres Ferrer. In 1949 a constituent assembly drew up a new constitution and abolished the army. The junta stepped down and Otilio Ulate Blanco, one of the candidates of the previous year, was inaugurated. In 1952, Figueres, a socialist, founded the Partido de Liberación Nacional (PLN), and was elected President in 1953. He dominated politics for the next two decades, serving as President from 1953-1958 and 1970-1974. The PLN introduced social welfare programmes and nationalization policies, while intervening conservative governments encouraged private enterprise. The PLN was again in power from 1974-1978 (Daniel Oduber Quirós), 1982-1986 (Luis Alberto Monge), 19861-1990 (Oscar Arias Sánchez) and 1994-1998 (José María Figueres).

President Arias drew up proposals for a peace pact in Central America and concentrated greatly on foreign policy initiatives. Efforts were made to expel Nicaraguan Contras resident in Costa Rica and the country's official proclamation of neutrality, made in 1983, was reinforced. The Central American Peace Plan, signed by the five Central American presidents in Guatemala in 1987, earned Arias the Nobel Peace Prize, although progress in implementing its recommendations was slow. In the 1990 general elections, Rafael Angel Calderón Fournier, a conservative lawyer and candidate for the Social Christian Unity Party (PUSC), won a narrow victory, with 51% of the vote over the PLN candidate. Calderón, the son of a former president who had been one of the candidates in the 1948 disputed elections, had previously stood for election in 1982 and 1986. The President's popularity slumped as the effects of his economic policies were felt on people's living standards, while his government was brought into disrepute by allegations of corruption and links with 'narco' traffickers.

PLN government (1994-1998)

In the February 1994 elections, another former president's son gained power by a narrow margin. José María Figueres of the PLN won 49.6% of the vote, 2.2% points ahead of his PUSC rival. In the Legislature, the PLN won 29 seats and the PUSC won 25 seats, while smaller parties won those that remained. The election was won on economic policies. Figueres argued against neo-liberal policies, claiming he would renegotiate agreements with the IMF and the World Bank, but in his first year of office a third Structural Adjustment Programme (backed by the international agencies and drawn up by the previous administration) was approved. A subsequent National Development Plan and a Plan to Fight Poverty contained a wide range of measures designed to promote economic stability and to improve the quality of life for many sectors of society. While the plans were partly responding to the protests that followed the approval of the Adjustment Programme, many of their proposals were at variance with the programme's policies.

Elections, 1998 and 2002

Elections were held in February 1998 and were won by the PUSC candidate, Miguel Angel Rodríguez, with 46.6% of the vote, 2% ahead of the PLN candidate. Thirty percent of voters abstained. The new president took office in May 1998, promising to make women, the young and the poor a priority for his government. Typically for Costa Rica, the elections of early 2002 ran on a frenzy of neutrality. President Pacheco, 68 years old, stimulated just enough support to win after the election went to a run-off when none of the three candidates won outright victory in the first round. The challenges to the candidates were to restimulate the economy, hit by the global downturn and the low coffee prices, and both claimed to be opposed to privatization of state-run industries.

Arias returns

Having successfully convinced Costa Rica's Congress to change the constitution and allow re-election, Oscar Arias was elected president in 2006, 16 years after serving his first term. The election was extremely close, and only decided after several recounts. President Arias, a strong supporter of the Central America Free Trade Agreement, has promised to stabilize the economy and to make Costa Rica one of the Latin America's most developed countries.

Economy

The country's agricultural economy is based on the export of coffee, bananas, meat, sugar and cocoa. The Meseta Central with its volcanic soil is the coffee-growing area and the staple crops are grown here too: beans, maize, potatoes and sugar cane. Dairy farming is efficient and lucrative here. More recently, diversification of exports has been successful, with non-traditional crops now accounting for about 60% of revenue. Costa Rica remains the second largest banana exporter in the world, with production dominated by US multinational companies. The country's timber industry is very small although deforestation has occurred at an alarming rate.

High growth in the industrial sector has led to considerable economic diversification, and manufacturing accounts for about 21% of GDP, compared with 8.7% in the case of agriculture. The port of Caldera, near Puntarenas on the Pacific coast, has been improved, and manufacturing for export is being encouraged. High education levels have successfully attracted a growing technology sector, including the US microprocessor Intel whose assembly plant near San José is expected to earn more in exports than bananas and coffee.

Tourism is a major industry and one of the main sources of foreign exchange revenue, with over 1.9 million visitors in 2007, providing revenue of US$1.9 billion. The construction of hotels and land prices have soared, driven up by foreign (mainly US) purchasers. Conservation groups have criticized larger developments due to environmental impact, the proximity of national parks and reserves, and the destruction of ecosystems.

Recent trends

The Costa Rican economy suffers from large public-sector deficits, partly because of a high level of government spending on social welfare. The country amassed a large foreign debt which, including accumulated arrears, amounted in 1989 to US$5 billion and was one of the highest per capita in the developing world. In the late 1980s, Costa Rica turned to the IMF and the World Bank for help in adjusting its economy, and was one of the first countries to take advantage of a US-sponsored debt reduction proposal.

In 1995, legislation was approved to liberalize the banking system, support privatization and end state monopolies. Labour unions opposed many of the economic measures, including the laying off of 8000 public sector workers. There were many strikes, including an extended protest by teachers. Implementation was delayed until 1999, allowing another round of elections in the interim. Despite record growth of 8.3% in 1999, budgetary pressures led the government to announce a privatization programme that has met with more public demonstrations and roadblocks. Resistance to reforming ICE, the state-owned electricity and telecommunications monopoly, which resulted in strikes in May 2003, has hindered the economic restructuring that is considered essential for continued investment in the high-tech industry. The move away from a reliance on coffee and banana exports is gaining pace, as historically low coffee prices and reduction in banana production continue to take their toll. While the economic downturn affected the economy overall, the shift towards technology based on high levels of education continue to reap rewards. In 2000 electrical manufacturing generated over US$2 billion for the economy – more than tourism at the time – however, this level of contribution has tailed off in recent years.

The last couple of years have seen a very public discussion on the merits of the Central America Free Trade Agreement (CAFTA), a regional organization designed to increase trade. Opposition rallies and campaigns set out the views that US products would undermine the Costa Rican economy. In October 2007 a national referendum narrowly decided in favour of ratifying the treaty.

Government

Costa Rica is a unitary multiparty republic with one legislative house, the Legislative Assembly of 57 deputies, elected by proportional representation for four years. Executive authority is in the hands of the president, elected for the same term by popular vote. Men and women over 18 have the right to vote. Voting is secret, direct and free. Judicial power is exercised by the Supreme Court of Justice.

Culture

People

In all provinces except Limón, over 98% of the population are white and mestizo. In Limón, 33.2% are black (many of whom speak Jamaican English as their native tongue) and 3.1% indigenous. There are only 5000 indigenous people in the whole country and they are separated into three groups: the Bribri (3500), Boruca (1000) and Guatuso. Although officially protected, the living conditions of the indigenous population are very poor. In 1992, Costa Rica became the first Central American country to ratify the International Labour Organization treaty on indigenous populations and tribes. However, even in Limón, the percentage of black people is falling, it was 57.1% in 1927. Much of the Caribbean coastland, especially in the north, remains unoccupied. On the Pacific coastlands a white minority owns the land on the hacienda system, which has been rejected in the uplands. About 46% of the people are mestizos. The population has risen sharply in the mountainous Peninsula of Nicoya, which is an important source of maize, rice and beans.

Music and dance

The regional music – if such a thing exists – is the staccatoed percussion of the marimba, a xylophone-type instrument which, despite being technically impressive, is rarely relaxing and almost intrusive as it struggles for harmony. The guitar is also a popular instrument for accompanying folk dances, while the chirimía and quijongo, have not yet totally died out in the Chorotega region of Guanacaste Province. This province is the heartland of Costa Rican folklore and the Punto Guanacasteco, a heel-and-toe dance for couples, has been officially decreed the 'typical national dance', although it is not in fact traditional but was composed at the turn of the last century by Leandro Cabalceta Brau during a brief sojourn in jail. There are other dances too, such as the Botijuela Tamborito and Cambute, but they are only really performed when outsiders need to be shown some native culture. Among the country's most popular native performers are the duet **Los Talolingas**, authors of *La Guaria Morada*, regarded as the 'second national anthem' and **Lorenzo 'Lencho' Salazar**, whose humorous songs in the vernacular style are considered quintessentially Tico.

Some of the Republic's indigenous groups have dances of their own, which are gradually disappearing: the *Danza de los Diablitos* of the Borucas; the *Danza del Sol* and *Danza de la Luna* of the Chorotegas; and the *Danza de los Huesos* of the Talamancas. A curious ocarina made of beeswax, the *dru mugata* is still played by the Guaymí people and is said to be the only truly pre-Columbian instrument still to be found. The drum and flute are traditional among various groups, but the guitar and accordion are moving in to replace them. As in the case of Nicaragua, the Caribbean coast of Costa Rica, centred on Puerto Limón, is inhabited by black people who came originally from the English-speaking islands and whose music reflects this origin. The sinkit seems to be a strictly local rhythm, but the calypso is popular, and the cuadrille, square dance and maypole dance are also found. There is also a kind of popular hymn called the saki and brass, percussion and string instruments are played, as well as the accordion.

Land and environment

Costa Rica lies between Nicaragua and Panama, with coastlines on the Caribbean (212 km) and the Pacific (1016 km). The distance from sea and sea ranges from 119 km to 282 km. A low, thin line of hills between Lake Nicaragua and the Pacific is prolonged into northern Costa Rica with several volcanoes (including the active Volcán Arenal), broadening and rising into high, rugged mountains and volcanoes in the centre and south. The highest peak, Chirripó Grande, southeast of the capital, reaches 3820 m. Within these highlands are certain structural depressions; one of them, the Meseta Central, is of paramount importance. To the southwest this basin is rimmed by the comb of the Cordillera; at the foot of its slopes, inside the basin, are the present capital San José and the old capital, Cártago. Northeast of these cities, about 30 km away, four volcano cones rise from a massive common pedestal. From northwest to southeast these are Poás (2704 m), Barva (2906 m), Irazú (3432 m) and Turrialba (3339 m). Irazú and Poás are intermittently active. Between the Cordillera and the volcanoes is the Meseta Central: an area of 5200 sq km at an altitude of between 900 m and 1800 m, where two-thirds of the population live. The northeastern part of the basin is drained by the Reventazón through turbulent gorges into the Caribbean; the Río Grande de Tárcoles drains the western part of it into the Pacific.

There are lowlands on both coasts. On the Caribbean coast, the Nicaraguan lowland along the Río San Juan continues into Costa Rica, wide and sparsely inhabited as far as Puerto Limón. A great deal of this land, particularly near the coast, is swampy; southeast of Puerto Limón the swamps continue as far as Panama in a narrow belt of lowland between sea and mountain.

The Gulf of Nicoya, on the Pacific side, thrusts some 65 km inland; its waters separate the mountains of the mainland from the 900-m-high mountains of the narrow Nicoya Peninsula. From a little to the south of the mouth of the Río Grande de Tercels, a lowland savannah stretches northwest past the port of Puntarenas and along the whole northeastern shore of the Gulf towards Nicaragua. Below the Río Grande de Tercels the savannah is pinched out by mountains, but there are other banana-growing lowlands to the south. Small quantities of African palm and cacao are now being grown in these lowlands. In the far south there are swampy lowlands again at the base of the Península de Osa, and between the Golfo Dulce and the borders of Panama. Here there are 12,000 ha planted with bananas. The Río General, which flows into the Río Grande de Térraba, runs through a southern structural depression almost as large as the Meseta Central.

Nicaragua

History

Nicaragua was at the crossroads of northern and southern prehispanic cultures. In Managua, near the crater lake of Acahualinca, there are some well-preserved human and animal footprints of what appears to be a mass flight from a volcanic eruption 6000 years ago. The best understood cultures are the Chorotegas, who came from Mexico around AD 800, and the Nicaraguas, from the same region who partially displaced the Chorotegas in the Pacific basin around AD 1200. The Nicaraguas set up a very successful society which traded with people from Mexico to Peru. The more primitive Chorotegas (Mangue speakers) remained in the areas not occupied by the Nicaraguas (Nahuat speakers), though some were pushed down into Guanacaste and the complete relationship between the two has yet to be fully explained. The most interesting pre-Columbian remains are the many petroglyphs left by unnamed pre-Chorotega cultures, and the Chorotegas' own large basalt figures found in and around Lake Nicaragua, in particular on the islands of Zapatera and Ometepe. Nicaragua is rich in ceramic history, with traces of 3000 years of continuous occupation being found in some areas. The Ramas and Sumos, of South American lowland origin, populated the eastern seaboard regions, but are almost extinct today. Other pre-Columbian cultures of note were the mountain Matagalpa people, thought to be related to the Lenca; the strangely primitive, understudied Chontales, who inhabited the eastern side of the two lakes; and, in the area that is now León, the Subtiava people who are perhaps from Baja California in Mexico.

Christopher Columbus arrived on the Caribbean shores of Nicaragua in 1502 on his fourth and final voyage. The Spanish explorer Gil González Dávila arrived in 1522 overland from Panama and, searching for the wealthiest chief of all, arrived on the western shores of Lake Nicaragua to meet the famous Nicaraguas chief, Niqueragua. The 16th-century Spanish chroniclers described the Nicaraguas' land as the most fertile and productive they had ever seen in the Americas. The chief Nicaragua and Dávila engaged in long philosophical conversations conducted through a translator and eventually the great chief agreed to accept Christianity. After the conversion to Christianity of more than 900 people, Dávila was chased out of Nicaragua by the fierce Chorotega chieftain Diriangen, whose troops decimated Dávila's small force. In 1524 a stronger army was sent and the populace was overcome by Francisco Hernández de Córdoba. Granada and León were founded on the shores of Lake Nicaragua and Lake Managua respectively. In 1570 both colonies were placed under the jurisdiction of Guatemala.

The local administrative centre was not rich Granada, with its profitable crops of sugar, cocoa and indigo, but impoverished León, then barely able to subsist on its crops of maize, beans and rice. This reversal of the Spanish policy of choosing the most successful settlement as capital was due to the ease with which León could be reached from the Pacific. In 1852, Managua was chosen as a new capital as a compromise, following violent rivalry between Granada and León.

Walker's expedition

The infamous expedition of William Walker is an important event in Nicaraguan and Costa Rican history. William Walker (1824-1860) was born in Nashville, Tennessee, graduated and then studied medicine at Edinburgh and Heidelberg, and was granted his MD in 1843. He then studied law and was called to the bar. On 5 October 1853, he sailed with a filibustering force to conquer Mexican territory, declared Lower California and Sonora an independent republic and was then driven out. In May 1855, with 56 followers armed with a new type of rifle, he sailed for Nicaragua, where Liberal Party leaders had invited him to help them in their struggle against the Conservatives. In October he seized a steamer on Lake Nicaragua belonging to the Accessory Transit Company, an American corporation controlled by Cornelius Vanderbilt. He was then able to surprise and capture Granada and make himself master of Nicaragua as Commander of the Forces. Two officials decided to use him to get control of the Transit Company; it was seized and handed over to his friends. A new government was formed, and in June 1856 Walker was elected President. On 22 September, to gain support from the southern states in America, he suspended the Nicaraguan laws against slavery. His Government was formally recognized by the USA that year. Walker attempted to take control of La Casona in the Guanacaste province of Costa Rica, only to be repelled by the southern nations forces. A coalition of Central American states, backed by Cornelius Vanderbilt, fought against him until he surrendered to the US Navy to avoid capture in May 1857. In November 1857, he sailed from Mobile with another expedition, but soon after landing near Greytown, Nicaragua, he was arrested and returned to the USA. In 1860 he sailed again from Mobile and landed in Honduras in his last attempt to conquer Central America. There he was taken prisoner by Captain Salmon of the British Navy, and handed over to the Honduran authorities who tried and executed him on 12 September 1860. Walker's own book, *The War in Nicaragua*, is a fascinating document.

US involvement

US involvement in Nicaraguan affairs stretches back a long way. In 1909, US Marines assisted Nicaraguan Conservative leaders in an uprising to overthrow the Liberal president, José Santos Zelaya. In 1911, the USA pledged help in securing a loan to be guaranteed through the control of Nicaraguan customs by an American board. In 1912 the United States sent marines into Nicaragua to enforce control. Apart from short intervals, they stayed there until 1933. During the last five years of occupation, nationalists under General **Augusto César Sandino** waged a relentless guerrilla war against the US Marines. American forces were finally withdrawn in 1933, when President Franklin Roosevelt announced the 'Good Neighbour' policy, pledging non-intervention. An American-trained force, the Nicaraguan National Guard, was left behind, commanded by **Anastasio Somoza García**. Somoza's men assassinated General Sandino in February 1934 and Somoza himself took over the presidency in 1936. From 1932, with brief intervals, Nicaraguan affairs were dominated by this tyrant until he was assassinated in 1956. His two sons both served a presidential term and the younger, General **Anastasio Somoza Debayle**, dominated the country from 1963 until his deposition in 1979; he was later assassinated in Paraguay.

Revolution (1978-1979)

The 1978-1979 revolution against the Somoza Government by the Sandinista guerrilla organization (loosely allied to a broad opposition movement) resulted in extensive damage and many casualties (estimated at over 30,000) in certain parts of the country, especially in Managua, Estelí, León, Masaya, Chinandega and Corinto. After heavy fighting, General Somoza resigned on 17 July 1979, and the Government was taken over by a junta representing the Sandinista guerrillas and their civilian allies. Real power was exercised by nine Sandinista *comandantes* whose chief short-term aim was reconstruction. A 47-member Council of State formally came into being in May 1980; supporters of the Frente Sandinista de Liberación Nacional (FSLN) had a majority. Elections were held on 4 November 1984 for an augmented National Constituent Assembly with 96 seats; the Sandinista Liberation Front won 61 seats, and **Daniel Ortega Saavedra**, who had headed the junta, was elected president. The Democratic Conservatives won 14 seats, the Independent Liberals nine seats and the Popular Social Christians six (the Socialists, Communists and Marxists/Leninists won two seats each). The failure of the Sandinista Government to meet the demands of a right-wing group, the Democratic Co-ordinating Board (CDN), led to this coalition boycotting the elections and to the US administration failing to recognize the democratically elected government.

The Sandinistas

Despite substantial official and private US support, anti-Sandinista guerrillas (the Contras) could boast no significant success in their war against the Government. In 1988, the Sandinistas and the Contras met for the first time to discuss the implementation of the Central American Peace Plan, drawn up by President Oscar Arias Sánchez of Costa Rica and signed in August 1987. To comply with the Plan, the Nicaraguan Government made a number of political concessions. By 1989 the Contras, lacking funds and with diminished numbers, following a stream of desertions, appeared to be a spent force. The Sandinista Government brought major improvements in health and education, but the demands of the war against the Contras and a complete US trade embargo did great damage to the economy as a whole. The electorate's desire for a higher standard of living was reflected in the outcome of the elections, when the US-supported candidate of the free market National Opposition Union (UNO), Señora **Violeta Chamorro**, won 55.2% of the vote, compared with 40.8% for President Ortega. The 14-party alliance, UNO, won 52 seats in the National Assembly, the FSLN won 38 and the Social Christian Party one seat. Señora Chamorro, widow of the proprietor of *La Prensa*, who was murdered by General Somoza's forces in 1978, took office on 25 April 1990. The USA was under considerable pressure to provide substantial aid for the alliance it created and promoted, but of the US$300 million promised for 1990 by the US Congress, only half had been distributed by May 1991. President Chamorro's refusal to dismiss the Sandinista General Humberto Ortega from his post as head of the armed forces (EPS), and to drop the Nicaraguan case against the USA at the International Court of Justice, were said to be hindrances to more rapid disbursement. In 1986 the Court in The Hague found the USA guilty of crimes against Nicaragua for mining its harbours.

The lack of foreign financial assistance prevented any quick rebuilding of the economy. The Government's scant resources did not permit it to give the disarmed Contra forces the land and services that had been promised to them. Demilitarized Sandinistas and landless peasants also pressed for land in 1991, with a consequent rise in tension. Factions of the two groups rearmed, to be known as recontras and recompas; there were

The Contra War

Then US President Ronald Reagan labelled the Contras the 'Freedom Fighters', and on one occasion even sported a T-shirt that read, 'I'm a Contra too'. His administration lobbied to maintain and increase military aid to the Nicaraguan Contras fighting the Sandinista Revolution during the 1980s. The first bands of Contras were organized shortly after the Sandinistas took power in 1979. The leaders were mainly ex-officials and soldiers loyal to the overthrown general Anastasio Somoza Debayle. Thanks to the United States, the Contras grew quickly and became the largest guerrilla army in Latin America. When they demobilized in May 1990, they had 15,000 troops.

The Contras divided Nicaragua in two: war zones and zones that were not at war. They also divided United States public opinion between those who supported President Reagan's policy and those who opposed it. The US House of Representatives and the Senate were likewise divided. The Contras are also associated with one of the biggest political scandals in the US after Watergate. The so-called 'Iran-Contra Affair' broke at the end of 1986, when a C-123 supply plane with a US flight crew was shot down over Nicaraguan territory. The scandal that followed caused some US government officials to resign, including Lieutenant Colonel Oliver North. The intellectual authors of the affair remained unscathed.

The most famous Contra leader was former Guardia Nacional Colonel Enrique Bermúdez, known in the war as 'Commander 3-80'. In February 1991, Bermúdez was shot dead in the parking lot of Managua's Intercontinental Hotel. The 'strange circumstances' surrounding his death were never clarified, and the killers were never apprehended. After agreeing to disarm in 1990, the majority of the Contra troops returned to a normal civilian life. However, most of them never received the land, credit, work implements, etc. they had been promised. The Contras live on today as the political party Partido Resistencia Nicaragüense (Nicaraguan Resistance Party), which has been ineffective due to internal disputes and divisions.

many bloody conflicts. Divisions within the UNO coalition, particularly between supporters of President Chamorro and those of vice-president Virgilio Godoy, added to the country's difficulties. Austerity measures introduced in early 1991, including a devaluation of the new córdoba, strained the relationship between the administration, Sandinista politicians and the National Workers' Front (FNT), the so-called 'concertación', a pact which the private sector refused to sign. Pacts signed in January 1992 between government, recontras and recompas failed to stop occasional heavy fighting over the next two years. In 1994, however, a series of bilateral meetings between previously entrenched parties and ceasefires announced by the EPS and the main recontra group, FN 3-80 (Northern Front 3-80) contributed to a disarmament accord, proposed by archbishop Miguel Obando y Bravo, between the Government and FN 3-80.

Movement towards a real and lasting peace

The achievement of a more peaceful state of affairs, if not reconciliation, did not remove other political tensions. After the UNO coalition realigned itself into new political groupings and returned to the National Assembly following a boycott in 1993, the FSLN began to fall apart in 1994. By early 1995, the Sandinistas had become irrevocably split between the orthodox wing, led by Daniel Ortega, and the Sandinista Renewal Movement (MRS), under Sergio Ramírez. The MRS accused the orthodox wing of betraying Sandinista principles by forming pacts with the technocrats and neo-liberals of the Government. The MRS was itself accused of opportunism. Linked to this was considerable manoeuvring over UNO-inspired constitutional reform. The National Assembly approved 67 amendments of the constitution, among which were the strengthening of the legislative branch of government at the expense of the executive, and the prohibition of relatives of the president from seeking that office. President Chamorro denied the validity of the reforms, but the National Assembly unilaterally adopted them in February 1995.

The 1996 elections

In 1995 the National Assembly approved legislation governing the 20 October 1996 presidential elections. The frontrunner was **Arnoldo Alemán**, former mayor of Managua, of the Liberal alliance. His main opponent was Daniel Ortega of the FSLN, who regarded Alemán's policies as a return to Somoza-style government. After reviewing the vote count because of allegations of fraud, the Supreme Electoral Council (CSE) declared Arnoldo Alemán had won by 51%, compared with 37.7% for Daniel Ortega. The FSLN called for new elections in Managua and Matagalpa, as the OAS declared the elections fair but flawed. Ortega announced he would respect the legality but not the legitimacy of the Government of Alemán.

Nature plays her hand

In 1998, two meteorological events caused even greater hardship for parts of the country: the drought (and related fires) from the El Niño phenomenon and, much more costly in terms of lives lost and property destroyed, the floods and storm damage from Hurricane Mitch. In July 2000 an earthquake measuring almost six points on the Richter scale hit western Nicaragua killing four people and causing damage near the epicentre at Laguna de Apoyo, near Masaya.

A new opportunity

In November 2001, Daniel Ortega of the FSLN lost to Enrique Bolaños of the ruling Liberal Party (PLC). Voters chose Enrique Bolaños by more than 15 points in what many believed to be a vote against Ortega rather than approval of the Liberal Party. In Enrique Bolaños' first three months of office in 2002, he shocked many by taking a very aggressive stance against corruption and his administration exposed several cases of embezzlement under the Alemán adminstration. The desire to cleanse the past and clear the way for the future was apparent when in December 2003, former president **Arnoldo Alemán** was sentenced to 25 years in prison, later transferred to house arrest, for corruption including money laundering and embezzlement to a value of nearly US$100 million.

President Bolaños' agreement to allow his predecessor to be investigated led to his alienation by some in the Liberal Party. The delicate balance of power in Congress restricted the president's powers, and further changes were only avoided at the last minute when Bolaños made a pact with Sandinista leader Ortega. Elections for the new president took an interesting turn in April 2006 when the US urged Nicaragua to shun Ortega's left-wing Sandinista party. He was returned to power in November 2006.

Economy

The World Bank classes Nicaragua among the world's poorest countries and its per capita income is the lowest in Latin America. The economy is based on agriculture, which contributes almost 20% of GDP. The principal export items are coffee, bananas, sugar, cotton, rice, corn, tobacco, sesame and soya beans. The main industries are food processing (sugar, meat and shrimps), textiles, wood, and chemical and mineral products. Mineral resources are scarce but there are gold, copper and silver deposits. Tourism has grown significantly in recent years, with 920,000 visitors in 2007, up from 579,000 in 2004.

Since the late 1970s, GDP has fallen, starting with a decline of 29% in 1979. In 1981-1990, it fell by an annual average of 2.4%, with only one year of positive growth. In the same period, income per capita fell by an average of 5.6% a year, a collapse caused by guerrilla insurgency, the US trade embargo, fluctuations in Central American Common Market trade, floods, drought and changing commodity prices. From 1996-2006 per capita GDP grew at an average of 2.3% (neighbouring Costa Rica's grew at 2.5%).

In 1990, the US-supported government of President Violeta Chamorro took office amid great optimism that the economy could be revived on the back of renewed trade with the USA. Trade sanctions were lifted and the US Congress was asked to provide US$300 million in aid immediately, to be followed by a further US$200 million.

President Alemán promised to continue the structural adjustment programme of the Chamorro government but Nicaragua's entire economic outlook was radically altered by Hurricane Mitch in 1998, which killed over 3000 and caused damage of over US$500 million. The extent of economic problems in Nicaragua was reinforced when in January 2004 the World Bank cleared 80% of Nicaragua's debt to the institution. Nicaragua also benefitted from the 2005 G8 summit which cleared 100% of international debt to Nicaragua. In 2006, Nicaragua joined El Salvador and Honduras as fully signed up members of the Central America Free Trade Agreement with the US.

Government

A new Constitution, approved by the 92-member National Constituent Assembly in 1986, was signed into effect on 9 January 1987. Legislative power is vested in a unicameral, directly elected National Assembly of 92 representatives, each with an alternate representative, with a six-year term. In addition, unelected presidential and vice presidential candidates become representatives and alternates respectively if they receive a certain percentage of the votes. Executive power is vested in the President, assisted by a Vice President and an appointed Cabinet. The Presidential term is five years. The next elections are scheduled for 2011.

Culture

People

With a population of 5.5 million, population density is low: 43 people per sq km, compared with El Salvador's 322. Nine out of 10 Nicaraguans live and work in the lowlands between the Pacific and the western shores of Lake Nicaragua, the southwestern shore of Lake Managua, and the southwestern sides of the row of volcanoes. In latter years settlers have taken to coffee-growing and cattle-rearing in the highlands of Matagalpa and Jinotega. Elsewhere, the highlands, save for an occasional mining camp, are very thinly settled.

The densely forested eastern lowlands fronting the Caribbean were neglected, because of the heavy rainfall and their consequent unhealthiness, until the British settled several colonies of Jamaicans in the 18th century at Bluefields and San Juan del Norte. But early this century the United Fruit Company of America opened banana plantations inland from Puerto Cabezas, worked by blacks from Jamaica. Other companies followed suit along the coast, but the bananas were later attacked by Panama disease and exports today are small. Along the Mosquito coast there are still English-speaking communities of African, or mixed African and indigenous, descent. Besides the mestizo intermixtures of Spanish and indigenous (69%), there are blacks (9%), indigenous (5%) and mixtures of the two (mostly along the Atlantic coast). A small proportion is of Spanish and European descent.

Music and dance

Nicaragua is 'marimba country' and the basic musical genre is the *son*, this time called the *Son Nica*. There are a number of popular dances for couples with the names of animals, like *La Vaca* (cow), *La Yeguita* (mare) and *El Toro* (bull). The folklore capital of Nicaragua is the city of Masaya and the musical heart of Masaya is the indigenous quarter of Monimbó. Here the marimba is king, but on increasingly rare occasions it may be supported by the *chirimía* (oboe), *quijada de asno* (donkey's jaw) and *quijongo*, a single-string bow with gourd resonator. Some of the most traditional *sones* are *El Zañate*, *Los Novios* and *La Perra Renca*, while the more popular dances still to be found are *Las Inditas*, *Las Negras*, *Los Diablitos* and *El Torovenado*, all involving masked characters. Diriamba is another centre of tradition, notable for the folk play known as *El Güegüense*, accompanied by violin, flute and drum, and the dance called *Toro Guaco*. The Caribbean coast is a totally different cultural region, home to the Miskito people and English-speaking black people of Jamaican origin concentrated around Bluefields. The latter have a maypole dance and their music is typically Afro-Caribbean, with banjos, accordions, guitars and drums as the preferred instruments.

Religion and education

Roman Catholicism is the prevailing religion, but there are Episcopal, Baptist, Methodist and other Protestant churches. Illiteracy was reduced by a determined campaign by the Sandinista government in the 1980s. Higher education at the Universidad Nacional Autónoma de Nicaragua at León, with three faculties at Managua, and the private Jesuit Universidad Centroamericana (UCA) at Managua is good. There are two separate Universidades Nacionales Autónomas de Nicaragua (UNAN).

Land and environment

There are three well-marked regions: **1** A large, triangular-shaped central mountain range beginning almost on the southern border with Costa Rica and broadening northwards; the prevailing moisture-laden northeast winds drench its eastern slopes, which are deeply forested with oak and pine on the drier, cooler heights; **2** A belt of lowland plains which run from the Gulf of Fonseca, on the Pacific, to the Costa Rican border south of Lake Nicaragua. Out of it, to the east, rise the lava cliffs of the mountains to a height of 1500-2100 m. Peninsulas of high land jut out into the lowland, which is generally from 65 km to 80 km wide along the Pacific, but is at its narrowest 20 km between La Virgen on Lake Nicaragua and San Juan del Sur. **3** A wide belt of eastern lowland through which a number of rivers flow from the mountains into the Atlantic. On the plains are the two largest sheets of water in Central America and 10 crater lakes. The capital, Managua, is on the shores of Lake Managua (Xolotlán), 52 km long, 15-25 km wide, and 39 m above sea-level. Its maximum depth is only 30 m. The Río Tipitapa drains it into Lake Nicaragua, 148 km long, about 55 km at its widest, and 32 m above sea level; Granada is on its shores. The 190-km Río San Juan drains both lakes into the Caribbean and is one of 96 principal rivers in the country. The longest at 680 km is the Río Coco, on the border with Honduras.

Volcanoes

Lying at the intersection of three continental plates, Nicaragua has a very unstable, changing landscape. A row of 28 major volcanoes runs through the Pacific basin, six of which have been active within the last century. The northernmost is Cosigüina, overlooking the Gulf of Fonseca, at 800 m with a lake in its crater. Its final eruption was in 1835. Northeast of Chinandega begins the Maribios volcanic chain, with Chonco (1105 m) and the country's highest, the cone of San Cristóbal (1745 m), which recommenced erupting in 1971 after a long period of inactivity. This volcano's lava discharge was used as a lighthouse by Pacific pirates in a very destructive raid on the colonial capital of León in 1685. Just south rises Volcán Casita, which is notable for its pine forest, the southernmost of its kind in the American continent's northern hemisphere. A side of Casita collapsed during the torrential rains of Hurricane Mitch (1998), burying numerous villages in Posoltega and killing hundreds of people. Further south, just before León, is the very active Telica (1061 m) with eruptions occurring every five years, and the extinct cones of little Santa Clara and Orata (836 m), which is believed to be the oldest in the chain. Just south of León is one of the youngest volcanoes on the planet, Cerro Negro, which was born in 1850 and has risen from sea level to 450 m in this short period. Its most recent eruptions occurred in 1992 and 1995 and it frequently coats León in a thick black layer. Volcán Pilas is formed of various craters, the highest of which rises to 1001 m and contains one active crater known as El Hoyo, which last erupted in 1954. Other extinct cones lie between Pilas and the majestic Momotombo (1300 m), which overlooks the shores of Lake Managua and last erupted in 1905, though a geothermal plant utilizes its energy daily. The chain ends with little Momotombito, which forms an island in Lake Managua. Managua's volcanoes are all extinct and six contain crater lakes. The Dirianes volcanic chain begins just north of Masaya with the complex of the same name, including the smoking, lava-filled Santiago crater, and four extinct craters and a lagoon. Masaya is the only volcano on the American continent with a consistent lava pool. The last eruptions occurred in 1965 and 1979 and, after a nine year period of calm, it began to smoke heavily again in 1995 with an eruption expected soon. South between Masaya and Granada is the extinct Apoyo, which died very violently 2000 years ago, leaving the deep blue Laguna de Apoyo, 6 km in diameter. Along the shores of Lake Nicaragua, and shadowing Granada, is Volcán Mombacho (1345 m), wrapped in cloudforest. Mobacho had a major structural collapse in 1570 and the resultant explosion not only wiped out an indigenous village at its base, but also fathered hundreds of Las Isletas in nearby Lake Nicaragua. The volcanoes of Lake Nicaragua include the Isla de Zapatera (600 m), a national park and pre-Columbian site, and the final two in the Nicaraguan chain which make up the stunning Isla de Ometepe: the symmetrical and active cone of Concepción (1610 m), which last erupted in 1956, and the cloudforest covered Maderas (1394 m), which holds a lake at its summit.

Climate

The wet, warm winds of the Caribbean pour heavy rain on the Atlantic coastal zone, especially in the southern basin of the Río San Juan, with more than 6 m annually.

While the dry season on the Atlantic coast is only short and not wholly dry, the Pacific dry season, or summer (November to April), becomes very dusty, especially when the winds begin to blow in February. There is a wide range of climates. According to altitude, average annual temperatures vary between 15°C and 35°C. Midday temperatures at Managua range from 30°C to 36°C, but readings of 38°C are not uncommon between March and May, or of 40°C in January and February in the west. It can get quite cold in the Caribbean lowlands, especially after rain. Maximum daily humidity ranges from 90% to 100%.

Panama

History

The history of Panama is the history of its pass-route; its fate was determined on 15 September 1513 when Vasco Núñez de Balboa first glimpsed the Pacific. Panama City was of paramount importance to the Spaniards: it was the focus of conquering expeditions both northwards and southwards along the Pacific coasts. All trade to and from these Pacific countries – including the fantastic gold of the Incas – passed across or around the isthmus. As part of Colombia and its predecessors, Panama was traditionally considered part of South America until recent years, when it has more and more been classed as a Central American republic. The distinction has political significance as international economic integration increases in importance.

The Camino Real

Panama City was founded in 1519 after a trail had been discovered and opened up between what is now the Bay of Panama on the Pacific and the Caribbean. The Royal Road, or the *Camino Real*, ran from Panama City to Nombre de Dios until it was re-routed to Portobelo. An alternative route was used later for bulkier, less-valuable merchandise; it ran from Panama City to Las Cruces, on the Chagres River but has now been swallowed up in the Gatún Lake. It ran near to Gamboa on the Gaillard/Culebra Cut and was navigable to the Caribbean, particularly during the rainy season. Vestiges of these trails are still in existence, although much of both routes was flooded by the artificial Gatún and Madden/Alajuela lakes created to feed the Canal. It was in these early years that crossing between the Atlantic and Pacific became part of a Panamanian tradition that ultimately led to the construction of the Canal.

Intruders were quickly attracted by the wealth passing over the Camino Real. Sir **Francis Drake** attacked Nombre de Dios, and in 1573 his men penetrated inland to Vera Cruz, further up the Chagres River on the Camino Real, plundering the town. Spain countered later attacks by building strongholds and forts to protect the route: among them San Felipe, at the entrances to Portobelo; and San Lorenzo, at the mouth of the Chagres. Spanish galleons, loaded with treasure and escorted against attack, left Portobelo once a year. They returned with European goods sold at great fairs held at Portobelo, Cartagena and Vera Cruz. Feverish activity either side of the loading and unloading of the galleons made it a favourite time for attack, especially for those with political as well as pecuniary motives. Perhaps the most famous was the attack by **Henry Morgan** in 1671. After capturing the fort of San Lorenzo, he pushed up the Chagres River to Las Cruces. From there he descended to Panama City, which he looted and burnt. A month later Morgan returned to the Caribbean with 195 mules loaded with booty.

Panama City was rebuilt on a new site, at the base of Ancón Hill, and fortified. With Britain and Spain at war, attacks reached their climax with Admiral Vernon's capture of Portobelo in 1739 and the fort of San Lorenzo the following year. Spain abandoned the route in 1746 and began trading round Cape Horn. San Lorenzo was rebuilt: it is still there, and has been tidied up and landscaped.

In 1821, Gran Colombia won independence from Spain. Panama, in an event celebrated annually on 28 November, declared its own independence and promptly joined Bolívar's Gran Colombia federation. Though known as the 'Sovereign State' of Panama it remained, even after the federation disintegrated, a province of Colombia.

The Panama railroad

Some 30 years after independence, streams of men were once more moving up the Chagres and down to Panama City: the forty-niners on their way to the newly discovered gold fields of California taking a quicker and safer route than the challenges of continental North America. Many perished on this 'road to hell', as it was called, and the gold rush brought into being a railway across the isthmus. The Panama Railroad from Colón (then only two streets) to Panama City took four years to build, with great loss of life. The first train ran on 26 November 1853. The railway was an enormous financial success until the re-routing of the Pacific Steam Navigation Company's ships round Cape Horn in 1867 and the opening of the first US transcontinental railroad in 1869 reduced its traffic. Having been out of operation for several years, a concession to operate the line was awarded to a Kansas rail company in 1998. Freight and a passenger service have now been restored.

Building of the canal

Ferdinand de Lesseps, builder of the Suez Canal, arrived in Panama in 1881 to a hero's welcome, having decided to build a sea-level canal along the Chagres River and the Río Grande. Work started in 1882. One of the diggers in 1886 and 1887 was the painter Gauguin, aged 39. About 30 km had been dug before the company crashed in 1893, defeated by extravagance, corruption, tropical diseases (22,000 people died, mostly of yellow fever and malaria) and by engineering difficulties inherent in the construction of a canal without lift-locks. Eventually the Colombian government authorized the company to sell all its rights and properties to the United States, but the Colombian Senate rejected the treaty and the inhabitants of Panama, encouraged by the United States, declared their independence on 3 November 1903. The United States intervened and, in spite of protests by Colombia, recognized the new republic. Colombia did not accept the severance until 1921.

Within two weeks of its independence, Panama, represented in Washington by the controversial Frenchman **Philippe Bunau-Varilla**, signed a treaty granting to the USA 'in perpetuity' a 16-km wide corridor across the isthmus over which the USA would exercise authority 'as if it were sovereign'. Bunau-Varilla, an official of the bankrupt French canal company, presented the revolutionary junta with the *fait accompli* of a signed treaty. The history of Panama then became that of two nations, with the Canal Zone governor, also a retired US general, responsible only to the President of the USA.

Before beginning the task of building the canal, the United States performed one of the greatest sanitary operations in history: the clearance from the area of the more malignant tropical diseases. The name of the physician William Crawford Gorgas will always be associated with this, just as the name of the engineer George Washington Goethals will always be associated with the building of the canal. On 15 August 1914, the first official passage was made by the ship *Ancón*. During this period, and until the military seized power in 1968, a small commercially orientated oligarchy dominated Panamanian politics, although presidential successions were not always smooth.

Treaty with the USA (1939)

As a result of bitter resentment, the USA ended Panama's protectorate status in 1939 with a treaty which limited US rights of intervention. However, the disparity in living standards continued to provoke anti-US feeling, culminating in riots that began on 9 January 1964 and resulted in the death of 23 Panamanians (the day is commemorated annually as Martyrs' Day), four US marines and the suspension of diplomatic relations for some months.

In 1968, **Arnulfo Arias Madrid** was elected president for the third time, having been ousted twice previously. After only 10 days in office he was forcibly removed by the National Guard, which installed a provisional junta. Brigadier General Omar Torrijos Herrera ultimately became Commander of the National Guard and principal power in the junta, dominating Panamanian politics for the next 13 years. Gradually, the theoretically civilian National Guard was converted into a full-scale army and renamed the Panama Defence Forces. Constitutional government was restored in 1972 after elections for a 505-member National Assembly of Community Representatives, which revised the 1946 constitution, elected Demetrio Basilio Lakas Bahas as president, and vested temporary extraordinary executive powers in General Torrijos for six years. Torrijos' rule was characterized by his pragmatic nationalism; he carried out limited agrarian reform and nationalized major industries, yet satisfied business interests; he had close links with left wing movements in Cuba, El Salvador and Nicaragua, yet reached agreement with the USA to restore sovereignty over the Canal Zone to Panama and to close the US military bases by the year 2000. In 1978, elections for a new National Assembly were held and the representatives elected Arístedes Royo Sánchez president of the country. General Torrijos resigned as Chief of Government but retained the powerful post of Commander of the National Guard until his death in a small plane air-crash in 1981. There followed several years of rapid governmental changes as tension rose between presidents and National Guard leaders.

General Noriega's administration

Following an election in May 1984, Nicolás Ardito Barletta was inaugurated in October for a six-year term, though the fairness of the elections was widely questioned. He was removed from office by military pressure in September 1985 as he attempted to assert some civilian control and was replaced by Eric Arturo Delvalle. His attempts to reduce military influence in government, by then concentrated principally in the hands of **General Manuel Antonio Noriega Moreno**, led to his own removal by General Noriega in February 1988. Manuel Solís Palma was named President in his place.

With the economy reeling and banks closed as a result of US economic sanctions, the campaign leading up to the election of May 1989 saw the growing influence of a movement called the **Civilista Crusade**, led by upper and middle-class figures. When their coalition candidate, Guillermo Endara Galimany, triumphed over Noriega's candidate, Carlos Duque Jaén, the election was annulled by the military. General Noriega appointed Francisco Rodríguez as provisional President in September, but by December, General Noriega had formally assumed power as Head of State. These events provoked the US military invasion **Operation 'Just Cause'** on 20 December to overthrow him. He finally surrendered in mid-January, having first taken refuge in the Papal Nunciature on Christmas Eve. He was taken to the USA for trial on charges of drugs trafficking and other offences, and sentenced to 30 years in prison. **Guillermo Endara** was installed as President. The Panamanian Defence Forces were immediately remodelled into a new public force whose largest component is the civilian National Police, with a compulsory retirement after 25 years' service. More than 150 senior officers were dismissed and many were arrested. Panama has not had a regular army since. Noriega was released in September 2007, to a long list of extradition appeals.

After 'Just Cause'

After the overthrow of General Noriega's administration, the US Senate approved a US$1 billion aid package including US$480 million in direct assistance to provide liquidity and get the economy moving again. A further US$540 million aid package was requested from the USA, Japan, Taiwan and the then EEC to enable Panama to help clear its US$610 million arrears with multilateral creditors and support the Panamanian banking system, but inevitably there were delays and little progress was made until 1991. The USA put Panama under considerable pressure to sign a Treaty of Mutual Legal Assistance, which would limit bank secrecy and enable investigation into suspected drug traffickers' bank accounts. Higher levels of crime and drugs trafficking led to the government passing a law to create the Technical Judicial Police (PTJ) to pursue criminals. While structural, economic and legal changes impacted Panama in the early 1990s, Panama was still not without problems. Charges of corruption at the highest level were made by Panamanians and US officials. President Endara himself was weakened by allegations that his law firm had been involved with companies owned by drugs traffickers. Though the economy grew under Endara, street crime increased, social problems continued, there were isolated bombings and pro-military elements failed in a coup attempt.

The 1994 elections and after

The 1994 elections took place with 2000 local and international observers, and polling was largely incident-free and open. **Ernesto Pérez Balladares** of the Partido Revolucionario Democrático (PRD), won with less than a third of the popular vote, with a campaign harking back to the record of the party's founder, Omar Torrijos, successfully avoiding any links with its more recent leader Noriega. The PRD also won a narrow majority in the Legislative Assembly. Pérez Balladares, who appointed a cabinet containing members of opposition parties as well as from the PRD, gave priority in his campaign to tackling the problems of social inequality, unemployment, deteriorating education standards and rising crime, which had all characterized the end of Endara's term.

In May 1999, Mireya Moscoso emerged victorious in presidential elections which saw a 78% voter turnout. Moscoso obtained 45% of the popular vote, ahead of her closest rival Martín Torrijos (son of General Omar Torrijos) with 38%. Moscoso took office on 1 September, becoming the first female president of Panama, enjoying the honour of receiving control of the Panama Canal from the US on 31 December 1999 and presiding over the nation's centennial celebrations in 2003.

Elections in May 2004 saw **Martin Torrijos**, son of former dictator Omar Torrijos, win the presidential elections. Commentators believe he gained support from his father's reputation, who was widely regarded as a hero for negotiating the handover of the Panama Canal. Torrijos Jnr has pledged to improve public finances, judicial reform and the predictable chant of any incoming Latin president, take a firm stance against crime and corruption.

Tax fraud and displaced dictators

Criticism from the international community in early 2000 suggested that Panama was 'inward looking' and that the country was suffering accordingly. Strong economic growth in 2000 was accompanied by the decision to analyze the past: President Moscoso announced his aim to investigate crimes committed while military goverments were in power between 1968 and 1989.

Two incidents in late 2000 also showed the country's willingness to play a more responsible international role. Discussions between Moscoso and the Colombian president Andrés Pastrana produced an agreement to strengthen security on their shared border in the Darién region, in an attempt to reduce violence by Colombian rebels and paramilitary groups, and to tackle arms and drugs smuggling in region.

The political crisis in Peru in September 2000 bought to the fore the country's reputation as the number one destination for politicians seeking exile. Peru's former intelligence chief, Vladimiro Montesinos, fled to Panama under cover of darkness and, while the Panamanian government was keen to reject his request for political asylum, pressure from Latin American leaders, the US and the Organization of American States led to his temporary political asylum in the interests of stability in Peru. While Panama racks up political points with its neighbours, the country is keen to move away from its image as a dumping ground for political criminals. This unenviable reputation has seen the shah of Iran, former Guatemalan President Jorge Serrano Elías, the Haitian military leader Raoul Cedras and the former Ecuadorean President Abdala Bucaram all seek asylum in Panama.

Canal area

The former Canal Zone was a ribbon of territory under US control extending 8 km on either side of the canal, including the cities of Cristóbal and Balboa. The price paid by the United States Government to Panama for construction rights was US$10 million. The French company received US$40 million for its rights and properties after the first attempt at constructing a canal finally ground to a halt in 1893 and US$25 million was given to Colombia in compensation. The total cost at completion was US$387 million. Panama long ago rejected the perpetuity clause of the original Canal Treaty, but in April 1978 a new treaty was ratified and on 1 October 1979. The Canal Zone, now known officially as the Canal Area, including the ports of Cristóbal and Balboa; the dry docks; and the trans-isthmus railway, was formally restored to Panamanian sovereignty. The US Southern Command moved to Miami in 1997, and by the end of 1999 the few remaining bases had closed.

Though polls indicated that many Panamanians supported retention of US military bases, largely because of their employment of civilians and direct governmental expenditures in Panama (about US$350 million a year in the last years of US operation), vocal minorities demanded their departure. In the run-up to the final handover however, there prevailed a curious mixture of national euphoria and apprehension over the country's ability to manage so vital an international resource. US phasing out of the bases was achieved ahead of schedule, though the two countries agreed in 1997 to create a Multilateral Anti-Drug Centre, which would occupy a former US base and would have some military components.

According to figures for 2007, 13,237 ocean-going ships passed through the Panama Canal raising revenues of US$1182 million. In 2006 the freight vessel *Maersk Dellys* established a new toll record by paying US$249,165 for transiting the canal. The Canal currently operates at 93% of capacity, and at current growth rates will have reached its limit by 2014. In October 2006 a referendum backed a US$5.2 billion investment programme to upgrade the canal, doubling its capacity. The expansion work began in September 2007.

Economy

Panama's economy has traditionally been founded on income derived from visitors taking advantage of its geographical position; its banking centre; and Canal employees and US military personnel spending money in the Republic. However, this contribution is lessening with the departure of the US military and Canal workers, so the country is developing new sources of income including tourism, agricultural exports and industry.

Apart from the Canal, the other traditional mainstay of the economy is agriculture, which contributes about 10% of GDP. The leading agricultural export crop is bananas, a large proportion of which are marketed by subsidiaries of the US multinationals Chiquita and Dole. Shrimp is another major export, having grown to about 12% of total earnings. Raw sugar is also an important export item, while smaller quantities of pineapples, coffee, and hides and skins are sold abroad. The main industry is food processing but there are also textile and clothing concerns, cement, chemicals, plastics and other light industries. Petroleum products, made from imported crude, are the only industrial export. The lowering of import tariffs in 1993, as a part of trade liberalization measures, contributed to a decline in manufacturing output.

Vast deposits of copper have been found. The mine at Cerro Colorado, if fully developed, could be one of the largest in the world with reserves said to exceed one billion tonnes. A 25-year concession granted to a Canadian company is being vigorously opposed by the Ngöbe-Buglé indigenous group. Large coal, gold and silver deposits have been found. So far no oil has been discovered but exploration is taking place. One of the most dynamic sectors of the economy is banking. There are currently over 100 banks from 32 countries in Panama.

Recent trends

The adoption of neo-liberal economic policies in the 1990s brought rising discontent as spending cuts caused job losses. Strikes and demonstrations became commonplace and poverty increased. The economic plan announced at the outset of Pérez Balladares' term gave priority to reducing poverty by 50%, though it achieved little. Steady inflation, the stable political situation and a growth in tourism are expected to stimulate the economy in the coming years. Panama also hopes to benefit from e-commerce, setting up a world-class communications system making the country an important hub in the e-commerce world. While prospects appear to be promising, growing social unrest became apparent in 2001 when general strikes over bus prices (and in 2003 over management of social security funds) paralyzed public services and revealed a greater disillusionment amongst those suffering from recession and increased unemployment.

The role of tourism in the economy continues to grow as Panama has many of the appeals of Costa Rica to the north, it is now the largest industry in the country.

Government

Constitutional reforms were adopted by referendum in April 1983. Legislative power is vested in a unicameral, 72-member Legislative Assembly which is elected by universal adult suffrage for a term of five years (and whose elections are hotly contested, in part because a five-year term yields members total compensation of US$600,000 each). Executive power is held by the President, assisted by two Vice Presidents and an appointed Cabinet. Panama is divided into nine provinces and two semi-autonomous indigenous reservations.

Culture

People

The population of 3.2 million is mostly of mixed descent but there are indigenous and black communities and a small Asian population. Most of the rural population live in the six provinces on the Pacific side, west of the Canal. There is only one rural population centre of any importance on the Caribbean: in Bocas del Toro, in the extreme northwest. Of the 60 indigenous tribes who inhabited the isthmus at the time of the Spanish conquest, only three have survived in any number: the Kunas (also spelt Cunas, particularly in Colombia) of the San Blas Islands (50,000); the Guaymíes, who prefer to be called Ngöbe-Buglé, of the western provinces (80,000); and the Emberá-Wunan, formerly known as Chocóes of Darién (10,000). These, and a few others, such as the Teribes, account for 6% of the total population. Indigenous opposition to the opening of copper mines at Cerro Colorado and demonstrations supporting greater autonomy for indigenous people in the area characterized 1996, but were inconclusive. However, an administrative enclave, the Comarca, providing for some Ngöbe-Buglé home rule, has been created. A number of African slaves escaped from their Spanish owners during the 16th century. They set up free communities in the Darién jungles and their Spanish-speaking descendants, known as *cimarrones*, still live there and in the Pearl Islands. The majority of Panama's blacks, often bilingual, are descended from English-speaking West Indians, brought in for the building of the railway in 1850, and later of the Canal. There are also a number of East Indians and Chinese, a few of whom, especially in the older generations, tend to cling to their own languages and customs.

Music and dance

Being at the crossroads of the Americas, where Central America meets South America and the Caribbean backs on to the Pacific, and being one of the smallest Latin American republics, Panama possesses an outstandingly rich and attractive musical culture. Albeit related to that of the Caribbean coast of Colombia and Venezuela, it is very different. The classic Panamanian folk dances are the *tambor* or *tamborito*, *cumbia*, *punto* and *mejorana*, largely centred on the central provinces of Coclé, and Veraguas and those of Herrera and Los Santos on the Península Azuero. Towns that are particularly noted for their musical traditions are Los Santos, Ocú, Las Tablas, Tonosí and Chorrera. The dances are for couples and groups of couples, and the rhythms are lively and graceful, the man often dancing close to his partner without touching her, moving his hat in rhythmic imitation of fanning. The woman's *pollera* costume is arguably the most beautiful in Latin America and her handling of the voluminous skirt is an important element of the dance. The *tamborito* is considered to be Panama's national dance and is accompanied by three tall drums. The *cumbia*, which has a common origin with the better-known Colombian dance of the same name, has a fast variant called the *atravesado*, while the *punto* is slower and more stately. The name *mejorana* is shared by a small native guitar, a dance, a song form and a specific tune. The commonest instruments to be found today are the tall drums that provide the basic beat, the violin, the guitar and the accordion, with the last-named rapidly becoming predominant. The *tuna* is a highly rhythmic musical procession with a women's chorus and massed hand-clapping.

Turning to song, there are two traditional forms, both of Spanish origin: the *copla*, sung by women and accompanying the *tamborito*, and the *mejorana*, which is a male solo preserve, with the lyrics in the form of *décimas*, a verse form used by the great Spanish poets of the Golden Age. It is accompanied by the ukulele-like guitar of the same name. Quite unique to Panama are the *salomas* and *gritos*, the latter between two or more men. The yodelling and falsetto of the *salomas* are in fact carried over into the singing style and it is this element, more than any other, that gives Panamanian folk song its unique and instantly recognizable sound. There are other traditional masked street dances of a carnavalesque nature, such as the very African *Congos*, the *Diablicos Sucios* (dirty little devils) and the *Grandiablos* (big devils). In the area of the Canal there is a significant English-speaking black population, similar to those in Nicaragua and Costa Rica, who also sing calypso, while the Guaymí people (Ngöbe-Buglé) in the west and the Kuna and Chocó (Emberá-Wunan) of the San Blas islands and Darién isthmus possess their own song, rituals and very attractive flute music. When travelling in rural areas during working hours, listen for the distinctive yodelling call of Panamanian farm workers, who greet each other in the fields over long distances with the *saloma*, a cry that slides from a rumble in the throat to a falsetto and back into a rumble, usually rendered in Spanish as ¡Ajuuúa! Folk tradition says it was adopted from an indigenous custom, and certainly some of its most expert and frequent practitioners are indigenous. Psychologists say letting fly with such a yelp releases the fatigue and heat-induced tension built up by long hours swinging a machete to eliminate weeds from pastures, or to prepare fields for planting. Complex *saloma*-based calls have heavily influenced Panamanian traditional song and the chanting that accompanies much dance. The ¡Ajuuúa! can also be heard as an expression of approval at baseball games, football matches and anywhere high spirits provide the occasion for whoops of delight.

The rise in popularity of Latin music has been evident in Panama, in particular as a result of the multi-talented **Rubén Blades** (currently Minister for Tourism) whose album *Tiempos*, supported by the Costa Rican trio **Editus**, won a Grammy in 2000.

Education
Education is compulsory from the age of six to 15, and 92% of children attend elementary school. English is the compulsory second language in secondary schools, and many Panamanians speak a little of it. There are several universities, including the massive **Nacional**, with 55,000 students; the **Tecnológica**, with 13,000 students; the important Catholic **Santa María La Antigua**, with 5000 students; and eight small private ones.

Religion
Panama's Constitution makes Roman Catholicism the official religion of the country, but guarantees freedom of practice to all others. As with neighbouring countries, evangelical churches have been active in recent years. Mosques have been built in Panama City and David, the third city of the Republic.

Land and environment
Panama is most easily visualized as a slightly stretched, horizontal 'S', with the 767 km Caribbean coastline to the north and the 1234 km Pacific coast to the south, and lying between 7° and 10° north of the Equator. The Canal, which runs southeast to northwest, bisects the country; the mountains running along the isthmus divide the country from north to south. About one-third of the population lives in Panama City, on the east side of the Canal at its southern terminus. Most of the rural population live in the quarter of the country south of the mountains and west of the Canal. At the border with Costa Rica there are several inactive volcanic cones, the boldest of which is the Volcán Barú, 3475 m high

and the highest point in the country. The sharp-sided Cordillera de Talamanca continues southeast at a general altitude of about 900 m, but subsides suddenly southwest of Panama City. The next range, the San Blas, rises east of Colón (the city at the north end of the Canal) running parallel to the Caribbean coastline, into Colombia. Its highest peak Tacarcuna, at 1875 m, is in the heart of the Darién. A third range rises from the Pacific littoral in the southeast, running along the Pacific coast of Colombia as the Serranía de Baudó. Nature decreed a gap between the Talamanca and San Blas ranges in which the divide is no more than 87 m high. The ranges are so placed that the gap, through which the Canal runs, follows a line from northwest to southeast. To reach the Pacific from the Atlantic you must travel eastwards, so when travelling through the canal, as in much of the country, the sun rises over the Pacific and sets over the Atlantic.

The rate of deforestation in Panama accelerated rapidly in the 1980s and early 1990s, but has fallen considerably. Seventy percent of the country is classified as primary forest, more than any other Central American republic except Belize. The loss of forest in 1990 was estimated at 89,000 ha, against felling of up to 62,300 ha acres per year between 1985 and 1989. The government reported a slowing of deforestation during 1993-1995, but in early 1996 estimated it was continuing at 100 ha a year. Reports record a considerable decrease in deforestation between 2000 and 2005.

Wildlife

Costa Rica, Nicaragua and Panama have a remarkable variety of plant and animal life. This amazing biodiversity is partly due to their geographical situation in the centre of the two huge continental masses, partly because they're a barrier between two oceans and also because of the wide variety of landscapes, including mountains, valleys, coastal plains and prairies.

Spotting wildlife

Use local, experienced guides as these people will know what species are around and where to look for them, and will often recognize bird calls and use these as an aid to spotting them. You should take binoculars; get a pair with a reasonable magnification and good light-gathering configurations (eg 10x40 or 8x40) for use in the dim light of the rainforests. They will also need to be reasonably waterproof. Another enormous aid to wildlife watching is a strong torch or, better still, a powerful headlamp. The latter not only leaves your hands free but it also helps when trying to spot eye shine of nocturnal mammals, the light reflected back from their eyes direct to yours. Some places, such as Monteverde Cloud Forest Reserve in Costa Rica, offer excellent night walks with guides, but with care you can equally well arrange your own. Another strategy to use is to select a likely looking spot – such as a fruiting fig or a watering hole (in dry country) – and wait for the animals to come to you.

Mammals

In Central America mammals tend to be secretive, indeed the majority are nocturnal; hence the need for night walks if you are serious about finding them, though, even then, good views are comparatively rare. That said, you will certainly see some delightful creatures, with views of primates being more or less guaranteed. The rainforests throughout the region contain spider monkeys, howler monkeys and/or capuchin monkeys. The howlers are probably the most noticeable because, as their name suggests, they are inclined to make a huge row at times, especially early in the mornings and in the late afternoons. You have a good chance of seeing them in on the Omotepe Islands in Nicaragua and the rainforests of Costa Rica. The spider monkey is a much more agile, slender primate, swinging around high in the canopy, using its prehensile tail as a fifth limb and again found throughout the region. The smaller, white-throated capuchins are also commonly seen, moving around quite noisily in groups, searching for fruit and insects in the trees and even coming down to the ground to find food. Smaller again, and restricted to Panama and Costa Rica, is the red-backed squirrel monkey. The most likely places to see them are Parques Nacionales Corcovado and Manuel Antonio in Costa Rica. Finally, for the daytime species, you may see a tamarin, both Geoffroy's and the cotton-top tamarin are present, but only in Panama (try Darién or Natural Metropolitano National Parks). Unlike Africa and Asia this area only has one group (10 species) of nocturnal primates and this, appropriately enough, is the night monkey. Panama is the only country in the region to contain night monkeys. Another mammal you are very likely to see in the southern countries of the region are sloths, good places to look are Reserva Monteverde and the forests of Tortuguero and Manuel Antonio in Costa Rica. As they tend to stay in one area for days at a time, local guides are excellent at pointing them out. The most easily seen of the carnivores is not, sadly, the longed for jaguar, but the ubiquitous white-nosed coati, a member of the racoon family. The females and their offspring go around in groups and are unmistakable with their long, ringed tails, frequently held in the air, and their long snouts sniffing around for insects and fruit in trees and on the ground. At many tourist sites, they hang around waiting to be fed by the visitors, particularly in the popular lowland National Parks of Costa Rica. Members of the cat family are rarely seen, those in the area include the jaguar, puma, ocelot and margay. All are more likely to be seen at night, or, possibly, at dawn and dusk. Corcovado and Tortuguero National Parks in Costa Rica, and Reserva Biológica Indio Maíz in Nicaragua are possibilities for jaguar and the other small cats. The largest land mammal in Central America is Baird's tapir, weighing up to 300 kg. It is a forest species and very secretive, particularly so in areas where it is hunted. Corcovado and Santa Rosa National Parks in Costa Rica are places it might be seen, at least there is a reasonable chance of seeing its hoof prints. It might be seen at waterholes or be spotted swimming in rivers. More likely to be seen are peccaries, especially the collared peccary, medium sized pig-like animals that are active both day and night. The collared peccary can be found in both dry and rain forests throughout the region, while the white-lipped peccary is more common in wetter, evergreen forests. Both live in herds, of up to 100 individuals in the case of the white-lipped species. Found throughout the area, in drier, woodland patches, the white-tailed deer can easily be spotted, especially at dawn or dusk, or their bright eyeshine can be seen at night if you are out in a car or on foot with a torch. Also found is the smaller red brocket, this, though, is a rainforest species and is more elusive. Rodent species you might see include the agouti, which looks rather like a long-legged guinea pig, it can be seen moving around on the forest floor. Considerably larger and stockier is the nocturnal paca, another forest species found throughout the region, often near water where they hide when chased by predators. The world's largest rodent, the capybara, is also found near water, but in this region can be seen only in Panama, in Darién, for instance. Bats will usually be a quick fly past at night, impossible to identify but for the jagged flight path which is clearly not that of a bird.

Whales and dolphins occur along both the Pacific and Atlantic coasts and can be watched at a number of sites as far south as Isla Iguana Wildlife Reserve in Panama.

Birds

It is true, the early bird does catch the worm and the earlier you get up, the more species you'll see! All countries have very high numbers of birds on their lists but Panama is the haven for birdwatchers in this area; though relatively tiny, it boasts almost as many (922) bird species as Mexico. One of the best places to go in Panama is the **Pipeline Road** (Sendero Oleoducto) in **Parque Nacional Soberanía**. In this lowland rainforest area, brilliantly coloured species such as the violaceous and slaty-tailed **trogans** or the blue-crowned **motmot** can be seen, along with **parrots, tangers, hummingbirds, antbirds** and many others during the day. It is also a good place to see the spectacular keel-billed **toucan**. At night, eight species of owl, including the crested, can be found, along with potoos and a variety of nightjars. Also, for serious birders, not to be missed in Panama is **Parque Nacional Darién** with mangroves, lowland and montane rainforest where numerous raptors can be seen, including king and black **vultures**, crested **eagles** and, if you're really lucky, the huge, monkey-eating **harpy eagle** with its 2-m wing span. **Macaws, parrots** and **parakeets** are common, along with toucans, hummingbirds, aracaris and tanagers, to mention just a few. At higher altitudes in this park (Cerro Pirre), the golden-headed quetzal can be seen at higher altitudes in Parque Nacional Darién (around Pirre Camp) and nowhere else in Central America. Many of these birds can be seen outside Panama.

Another popular sighting is the scarlet macaw easily spotted near **Puerto Juárez, Costa Rica**. Hummingbirds too are a common sight throughout the region, frequently drawn to sugar-feeders. The harpy eagle is extremely rare with sightings on the **Osa Peninsula, Costa Rica** a possibility.

To find the **resplendent quetzal**, a brilliant emerald green bird, with males having a bright scarlet breast and belly, and ostentatious long green streamers extending as much as 50 cm beyond the end of its tail, **Monteverde Cloud Forest Reserve** or the less atmospheric **Eddie Serrano Mirador** in **Costa Rica** are a couple of the best places to go.

In addition to the quetzal, Costa Rica has around 850 bird species, following close on the heels of Panama as being a good country to visit for bird watchers. **Monteverde** is one of the hotspots and species seen there include black **guans**, emerald **toucanets**, violet **sabrewings**, **long-tailed manakins**, three **wattled bellbirds** and the threatened **bare-necked umbrellabird**. Mixed flocks of small birds such as **warblers, tanagers, woodcreepers** and **wood-wrens** can also be seen in the area. **La Selva Biological Station**, an area of lowland rainforest in Costa Rica, is another area rich in rainforest species such as the **chestnut-billed toucan, mealy parrot** and **squirrel cuckoo**. A very different habitat, with, consequently, different birds, is found in the large wetland area of **Parque Nacional Palo Verde** in Costa Rica. Here one can see **jabirus, black-necked stilts, spotted rails, bare-throated tiger heron, purple gallinule** and many other water birds. In the dry season, **ducks**, including the **black-bellied whistling duck, blue-billed teal, ring-necked duck** and **northern pintail**, congregate in this area in their thousands. More rarely seen here is the **white-faced whistling duck**. Of course, all along the coasts are masses of different seabirds, including **pelicans, boobies** and the **magnificent frigate bird**.

Reptiles

This group covers **snakes, lizards, crocodilians** and **turtles**. Throughout the whole region you are not particularly likely to see snakes in the wild; for those wishing to do so, a snake farm or zoo is the best place to go. You might, though, be lucky on one of your walks and see a **boa constrictor** curled up digesting its latest meal, or, again, a guide might know where one is resting. In contrast, **lizards** are everywhere, from small geckos walking up walls in your hotel room, catching insects attracted to the lights, to the large **iguanas** sunbathing in the tree tops. The **American crocodile** and **spectacled caiman** are both found throughout the area, with the latter being seen quite frequently. Several species of both freshwater and sea **turtles** are present in the region. **Parque Nacional Tortuguero in Costa Rica** is a good place to see freshwater and four species of marine turtles, while at **Ostional Beach** in Santa Rosa National Park you can watch masses of olive Ridley turtles coming in to lay their eggs, particularly in September and October. You'll also be able to see nesting turtles along the Pacific coastal beaches of Nicaragua.

Amphibians

You'll certainly hear frogs and toads, even if you do not see them. However, the brightly coloured **poison-dart frogs** and some of the tree frogs are well worth searching out. Look for them in damp places, under logs and moist leaf litter, in rock crevices and by ponds and streams, many will be more active at night. **Monteverde** and **La Selva Reserves** are both rich in amphibians, and a visit to **Bocas del Toro** will also reveal colourful amphibians on appropriately named Red Frog Beach.

Invertebrates

There are uncounted different species of invertebrates in the area. Probably, most desirable for ecotourists are the **butterflies**, though some of the **beetles**, such as the jewel **scarabs**, are also pretty spectacular. If you are fascinated by spiders, you can always go hunting for nocturnal **tarantulas**. There are **butterfly farms** in Nicaragua (Los Guatusos Wildlife Reserve) and Costa Rica (eg el Jardín de Mariposas in Monteverde) that will give you a close up view of many different species. Watching **leaf-cutter ants** marching in long columns from a bush they are systematically destroying and taking the pieces of leaf to their nest, huge mounds on the forest floor, can be a absorbing sight, while marching columns of army ants, catching and killing all small beasts in their path, are best avoided.

Books and films

www.lab.org.uk (Latin American Bureau) An excellent specialist online guide and bookstore, with country specific titles and international delivery.

Dunkerley, James *Power in the Isthmus: A Political History of Modern Central America* (1989. a good history of the smaller republics.

Emmon, Louise *Neotropical Rainforest Mammals: A Field Guide.* Will help with identifying wildlife.

Reid, F *Field Guide to the Mammals of Central America and Southeast Mexico.* Worth finding.

Ridgely, RS and Gwynn, JA *A Guide to the Birds of Panama: With Costa Rica, Nicaragua, and Honduras* (PrincetonUniversity Press, 1992). The definitive guide for

ornithologists it is richly illustrated and describes 929 species.

Wilson, Jason *Traveller's Literary Companion, South and Central America* (Brighton, UK: in Print, 1993). A general guide to the literature of the region with extracts from works by Latin American writers and by non-Latin Americans about the various countries; it also has very useful bibliographies.

Costa Rica

Costa Rica: A Guide to the People, Politics and Culture (1998), In Focus series, Latin America Bureau. A distilled analysis of the country.

Asociación Ecologista de Vida Silvestre *Areas de conservación y sus parques nacionales* (1998), T/F223-0851.

Beletsky, Les *Costa Rica: The Ecotravellers' Wildlife Guide* (1998). Great nature book.

Boza, Mario A *The National Parks of Costa Rica* (1986), an illustrated book which gives a good impression of the different parks.

Stiles, G, Skutch, A and Gardner, D *A Field Guide to the Birds of Costa Rica.*

Stiles, G and Skutch, A *Guide to the Birds of Costa Rica*, Cornell University Press (1989). The definitive field guide for birdwatchers.

Film

While Costa Rica has been in more nature documentaries than you can count, its presence on the screen is lacking. Its prime role is as a film set for other locations.

Nicaragua

Cabezas, Omar *Fire from the Mountain: The Making of a Sandinista.* Descriptions of León's fight against the Somoza régime.

Cardinal, Ernesto *El Evangelio de Solentiname* (The Gospel of Solentiname).

Darío, Rubén *Cuentos Completos.* The collected stories of this great Nicaraguan poet, the quintessential Latin American author.

Marriott, Edward *Savage Shore: Life and Death with Nicaragua's Last Shark Hunters.* Looks at the life of the shark hunters of Lake Nicaragua.

Rushdie, Salman *The Jaguar Smile,* (1998). A detailed and entertaining account of the writer's visit to Nicaragua during the volatile Sandinista years. Seems to romanticize the revolution.

Films

Loach, Ken *Carla's Song* (Scotland, 1996). An insightful, if feverishly pro-Sandinista portrayal of Nicaragua post-Revolution.

Meiselas, S, Roberts, R and Guzetti, A *Pictures from a Revolution – A Memoir of the Nicaraguan Conflict* (USA, 1991). Susan Meiselas returns to Nicaragua 10 years after covering the revolution to find out what happended to her photo subjects.

Spottiswoode, Roger *Under Fire* (USA, 1983), a film which mixes a lot of fact with some fiction. While the setting may be Nicaragua, it was filmed in Mexico.

Panama

Banks, Iain *Canal Dreams.*

Dinges, John *Our Man in Panama.* For the era of military rule.

Greene, Graham *The Captain and the Enemy.* Greene's last novel.

Greene, Graham *Getting to Know the General* (Torrijos). Subjective and, as such, not historically reliable, but is worth reading.

Le Carré, John *The Tailor of Panama.* A cynical but entertaining view of Panama City society, adapted for the big screen in 2001.

McCullough's, David *The Path Between the Seas.* The history of the Canal.

Noriega, Manuel *America's Prisoner: The Memoirs of Manuel Noriega* (Random House).

Ridgeley, R and Gwynne, J *Field Guide to the Birds of Panama.*

Theroux, Paul *The Old Patagonian Express .* The section on Panama and the Canal Zone is particularly interesting.

Films

Boorman, John *The Tailor of Panama* (USA, 2001). An adaptation of Le Carré's book.

Wiseman, Frederick *Canal Zone* (USA, 1977). A triology documentary series looking at life in the Canal Zone.

Contents

Footnotes

Basic Spanish for travellers

Learning Spanish is a useful part of the preparation for a trip to Latin America and no volumes of dictionaries, phrase books or word lists will provide the same enjoyment as being able to communicate directly with the people of the country you are visiting. It is a good idea to make an effort to grasp the basics before you go. As you travel you will pick up more of the language and the more you know, the more you will benefit from your stay.

General pronunciation

Whether you have been taught the 'Castilian' pronunciation (*z* and *c* followed by *i* or *e* are pronounced as the *th* in think) or the 'American' pronunciation (they are pronounced as *s*), you will encounter little difficulty in understanding either. Regional accents and usages vary, but the basic language is essentially the same everywhere.

Vowels

a	as in English *cat*
e	as in English *best*
i	as the *ee* in English *feet*
o	as in English *shop*
u	as the *oo* in English *food*
ai	as the *i* in English *ride*
ei	as *ey* in English *they*
oi	as *oy* in English *toy*

Consonants

Most consonants can be pronounced more or less as they are in English. The exceptions are:

g	before *e* or *i* is the same as *j*
h	is always silent (except in *ch* as in *chair*)
j	as the *ch* in Scottish *loch*
ll	as the *y* in *yellow*
ñ	as the *ni* in English *onion*
rr	trilled much more than in English
x	depending on its location, pronounced *x, s, sh* or *j*

Spanish words and phrases

Greetings, courtesies

hello	*hola*	thank you (very much)	*(muchas) gracias*
good morning	*buenos días*	I speak Spanish	*hablo español*
good afternoon/		I don't speak Spanish	*no hablo español*
evening/night	*buenas*	do you speak English?	*¿habla inglés?*
	tardes/noches	I don't understand	*no entiendo/*
goodbye	*adiós/chao*		*no comprendo*
pleased to meet you	*mucho gusto*	please speak slowly	*hable despacio por*
see you later	*hasta luego*		*favor*
how are you?	*¿cómo está?*	I am very sorry	*lo siento mucho/*
	¿cómo estás?		*disculpe*
I'm fine, thanks	*estoy muy bien, gracias*	what do you want?	*¿qué quiere?*
I'm called...	*me llamo...*		*¿qué quieres?*
what is your name?	*¿cómo se llama?*	I want	*quiero*
	¿cómo te llamas?	I don't want it	*no lo quiero*
yes/no	*sí/no*	leave me alone	*déjeme en paz/*
please	*por favor*		*no me moleste*
		good/bad	*bueno/malo*

Questions and requests

Have you got a room for two people?
¿Tiene una habitación para dos personas?
How do I get to_?
¿Cómo llego a_?
How much does it cost?
¿Cuánto cuesta? ¿cuánto es?
I'd like to make a long-distance phone call
Quisiera hacer una llamada de larga distancia
Is service included?
¿Está incluido el servicio?

Is tax included?
¿Están incluidos los impuestos?
When does the bus leave (arrive)?
¿A qué hora sale (llega) el autobús?
When? *¿cuándo?*
Where is_? *¿dónde está_?*
Where can I buy tickets?
¿Dónde puedo comprar boletos?
Where is the nearest petrol station?
¿Dónde está la gasolinera más cercana?
Why? *¿por qué?*

Basics

bank	*el banco*	market	*el mercado*
bathroom/toilet	*el baño*	note/coin	*le billete/la moneda*
bill	*la factura/la cuenta*	police (policeman)	*la policía (el policía)*
cash	*el efectivo*	post office	*el correo*
cheap	*barato/a*	public telephone	*el teléfono público*
credit card	*la tarjeta de crédito*	supermarket	*el supermercado*
exchange house	*la casa de cambio*	ticket office	*la taquilla*
exchange rate	*el tipo de cambio*	traveller's cheques	*los cheques de viajero/*
expensive	*caro/a*		*los travelers*

Getting around

aeroplane	*el avión*	insured person	*el/la asegurado/a*
airport	*el aeropuerto*	to insure yourself against	*asegurarse contra*
arrival/departure	*la llegada/salida*	luggage	*el equipaje*
avenue	*la avenida*	motorway, freeway	*el autopista/la*
block	*la cuadra*		*carretera*
border	*la frontera*	north, south, west, east	*norte, sur, oeste*
bus station	*la terminal de*		*(occidente), este*
	autobuses/camiones		*(oriente)*
bus	*el bus/el autobús/*	Oil	*el aceite*
	el camión	to park	*estacionarse*
collective/		passport	*el pasaporte*
fixed-route taxi	*el colectivo*	petrol/gasoline	*la gasolina*
corner	*la esquina*	puncture	*el pinchazo/*
customs	*la aduana*		*la ponchadura*
first/second class	*primera/segunda clase*	street	*la calle*
left/right	*izquierda/derecha*	that way	*por allí/por allá*
ticket	*el boleto*	this way	*por aquí/por acá*
empty/full	*vacío/lleno*	tourist card/visa	*la tarjeta de turista*
highway, main road	*la carretera*	tyre	*la llanta*
immigration	*la inmigración*	unleaded	*sin plomo*
insurance	*el seguro*	to walk	*caminar/andar*

Accommodation

air conditioning	*el aire acondicionado*	power cut	*el apagón/corte*
all-inclusive	*todo incluido*	restaurant	*el restaurante*
bathroom, private	*el baño privado*	room/bedroom	*el cuarto/la habitación*
bed, double/single	*la cama matrimonial/*	sheets	*las sábanas*
	sencilla	shower	*la ducha/regadera*
blankets	*las cobijas/mantas*	soap	*el jabón*
to clean	*limpiar*	toilet	*el sanitario/excusado*
dining room	*el comedor*	toilet paper	*el papel higiénico*
guesthouse	*la casa de huéspedes*	towels, clean/dirty	*las toallas limpias/*
hotel	*el hotel*		*sucias*
noisy	*ruidoso*	water, hot/cold	*el agua caliente/fría*
pillows	*las almohadas*		

Health

aspirin	*la aspirina*	diarrhoea	*la diarrea*
blood	*la sangre*	doctor	*el médico*
chemist	*la farmacia*	fever/sweat	*la fiebre/el sudor*
condoms	*los preservativos,*	pain	*el dolor*
	los condones	head	*la cabeza*
contact lenses	*los lentes de contacto*	period/sanitary towels	*la regla/*
contraceptives	*los anticonceptivos*		*las toallas femeninas*
contraceptive pill	*la píldora anti-*	stomach	*el estómago*
	conceptiva	altitude sickness	*el soroche*

Family

family	*la familia*	boyfriend/girlfriend	*el novio/la novia*
brother/sister	*el hermano/la hermana*	friend	*el amigo/la amiga*
daughter/son	*la hija/el hijo*	married	*casado/a*
father/mother	*el padre/la madre*	single/unmarried	*soltero/a*
husband/wife	*el esposo (marido)/*		
	la esposa		

Months, days and time

January	*enero*	Monday	*lunes*
February	*febrero*	Tuesday	*martes*
March	*marzo*	Wednesday	*miércoles*
April	*abril*	Thursday	*jueves*
May	*mayo*	Friday	*viernes*
June	*junio*	Saturday	*sábado*
July	*julio*	Sunday	*domingo*
August	*agosto*		
September	*septiembre*	at one o'clock	*a la una*
October	*octubre*	at half past two	*a las dos y media*
November	*noviembre*	at a quarter to three	*a cuarto para las tres/*
December	*diciembre*		*a las tres menos quince*
		it's one o'clock	*es la una*

it's seven o'clock	*son las siete*	in ten minutes	*en diez minutos*
it's six twenty	*son las seis y veinte*	five hours	*cinco horas*
it's five to nine	*son las nueve menos*	does it take long?	*¿tarda mucho?*
	cinco		

Numbers

one	*uno/una*	sixteen	*dieciséis*
two	*dos*	seventeen	*diecisiete*
three	*tres*	eighteen	*dieciocho*
four	*cuatro*	nineteen	*diecinueve*
five	*cinco*	twenty	*veinte*
six	*seis*	twenty-one	*veintiuno*
seven	*siete*	thirty	*treinta*
eight	*ocho*	forty	*cuarenta*
nine	*nueve*	fifty	*cincuenta*
ten	*diez*	sixty	*sesenta*
eleven	*once*	seventy	*setenta*
twelve	*doce*	eighty	*ochenta*
thirteen	*trece*	ninety	*noventa*
fourteen	*catorce*	hundred	*cien/ciento*
fifteen	*quince*	thousand	*mil*

Food

avocado	*el aguacate*	goat	*el chivo*
baked	*al horno*	grapefruit	*la toronja/el pomelo*
bakery	*la panadería*	grill	*la parrilla*
banana	*el plátano*	grilled/griddled	*a la plancha*
beans	*los frijoles/*	guava	*la guayaba*
	las habichuelas	ham	*el jamón*
beef	*la carne de res*	hamburger	*la hamburguesa*
beef steak or pork fillet	*el bistec*	hot, spicy	*picante*
boiled rice	*el arroz blanco*	ice cream	*el helado*
bread	*el pan*	jam	*la mermelada*
breakfast	*el desayuno*	knife	*el cuchillo*
butter	*la mantequilla*	lime	*el limón*
cake	*el pastel*	lobster	*la langosta*
chewing gum	*el chicle*	lunch	*el almuerzo/la comida*
chicken	*el pollo*	meal	*la comida*
chilli or green pepper	*el ají/pimiento*	meat	*la carne*
clear soup, stock	*el caldo*	minced meat	*el picadillo*
cooked	*cocido*	onion	*la cebolla*
dining room	*el comedor*	orange	*la naranja*
egg	*el huevo*	pepper	*el pimiento*
fish	*el pescado*	pasty, turnover	*la empanada/*
fork	*el tenedor*		*el pastelito*
fried	*frito*	pork	*el cerdo*
garlic	*el ajo*	potato	*la papa*

prawns	*los camarones*	spoon	*la cuchara*
raw	*crudo*	squash	*la calabaza*
restaurant	*el restaurante*	squid	*los calamares*
salad	*la ensalada*	supper	*la cena*
salt	*la sal*	sweet	*dulce*
sandwich	*el bocadillo*	to eat	*comer*
sauce	*la salsa*	toasted	*tostado*
sausage	*la longaniza/el chorizo*	turkey	*el pavo*
scrambled eggs	*los huevos revueltos*	vegetables	*los legumbres/vegetales*
seafood	*los mariscos*	without meat	*sin carne*
soup	*la sopa*	yam	*el camote*

Drink

beer	*la cerveza*	ice/without ice	*el hielo/sin hielo*
boiled	*hervido/a*	juice	*el jugo*
bottled	*en botella*	lemonade	*la limonada*
camomile tea	*la manzanilla*	milk	*la leche*
canned	*en lata*	mint	*la menta*
coffee	*el café*	rum	*el ron*
coffee, white	*el café con leche*	soft drink	*el refresco*
cold	*frío*	sugar	*el azúcar*
cup	*la taza*	tea	*el té*
drink	*la bebida*	to drink	*beber/tomar*
drunk	*borracho/a*	water	*el agua*
firewater	*el aguardiente*	water, carbonated	*el agua mineral con gas*
fruit milkshake	*el batido/licuado*	water, still mineral	*el agua mineral sin gas*
glass	*el vaso*	wine, red	*el vino tinto*
hot	*caliente*	wine, white	*el vino blanco*

Key verbs

to go	**ir**
I go	*voy*
you go (familiar)	*vas*
he, she, it goes,	
you (formal) go	*va*
we go	*vamos*
they, you (plural) go	*van*

to have (possess)	**tener**
I have	*tengo*
you (familiar) have	*tienes*
he, she, it,	
you (formal) have	*tiene*
we have	*tenemos*
they, you (plural) have	*tienen*
there is/are	*hay*

there isn't/aren't   *no hay*

to be	**ser** (permanent state) **estar**

(positional or temporary state)

I am	soy	estoy
you are	eres	estás
he, she, it is,		
you (formal) are	es	está
we are	somos	estamos
they, you (plural) are	son	están

This section has been assembled on the basis of glossaries compiled by André de Mendonça and David Gilmour of South American Experience, London, and the Latin American Travel Advisor, No 9, March 1996

Index → *Entries in bold refer to maps*

Credits

Footprint credits

Editor: Stephanie Rebello
Map editor: Sarah Sorensen
Colour section: Kassia Gawronski

Managing Director: Andy Riddle
Publisher: Patrick Dawson
Editorial: Felicity Laughton, Nicola Gibbs,
Sara Chare, Ria Gane, Jen Haddington,
Alice Jell, Alan Murphy
Cartography: Robert Lunn, Kevin Feeney,
Emma Bryers
Cover design: Robert Lunn
Design: Mytton Williams
Sales and marketing: Liz Harper,
Zoë Jackson, Hannah Bonnell
Advertising sales manager: Renu Sibal
Finance and administration: Elizabeth
Taylor

Photography credits

Front cover:
Bill Bachmann/Alamy
(painted cartwheel)
Back cover: Danita Delimont/Alamy
(frog on leaf)

Manufactured in Italy by LegoPrint
Pulp from sustainable forests

Footprint feedback

We try as hard as we can to make each
Footprint guide as up to date as possible
but, of course, things always change. If you
want to let us know about your experiences –
good, bad or ugly – then don't delay, go to
www.footprintbooks.com and send in
your comments.

Publishing information

Footprint Costa Rica, Nicaragua and Panama
1st edition
© Footprint Handbooks Ltd
January 2009

ISBN: 978 1 906098 49 0
CIP DATA: A catalogue record for this book
is available from the British Library

® Footprint Handbooks and the Footprint
mark are a registered trademark of Footprint
Handbooks Ltd

Published by Footprint
6 Riverside Court
Lower Bristol Road
Bath BA2 3DZ, UK
T +44 (0)1225 469141
F +44 (0)1225 469461
www.footprintbooks.com

Distributed in the USA by Globe Pequot Press,
Guilford, Connecticut

All rights reserved. No part of this publication
may be reproduced, stored in a retrieval
system, or transmitted, in any form or by
any means, electronic, mechanical,
photocopying, recording, or otherwise
without the prior permission of
Footprint Handbooks Ltd.
Every effort has been made to ensure that
the facts in this guidebook are accurate.
However, travellers should still obtain
advice from consulates, airlines etc about
travel and visa requirements before travelling.
The authors and publishers cannot accept
responsibility for any loss, injury or
inconvenience however caused.

Acknowledgements

Richard Arghiris

In Nicaragua, a sincere thanks to the many pe
useful information or otherwise took the time
country and the rapid changes taking place. W
kindness, conversation and help, none of it wo
any sense. In particular, thanks to Richard Leon
Footprint Nicaragua Handbook, who provided
in getting to grips with it. In Panama, likewise,
kind persons who took the time to talk, particu
Footprint, thanks to Alan Murphy for his contin
Laughton and Stephanie Lambe for their patie
co-author Peter Hutchison for his on-going wis
all the other Footprint staff, and to Patrick Daw
At home, thanks to Terri Wright, Alan Peacock-,
Kennedy, Jo Arghiris, Dan Roberts, Charlie Robe
McCallen, Tom Clay, Sym Gharial, Elk Kovaricek,
Frankie for their continued love and support. Cl

Peter Hutchison

After eight years of working on the Mexico and
Handbook it's great to see the growth in visitor:
and Panama that make a multi-country book via
fortunate to travel through Nicaragua, Costa Ric
November 2007 and see how much sense a boo
    In addition to my research in Costa Rica, sect
country were researched by Jane Koutnik and I
Crowther, with a snippet of information from C
(Footprint, Surfing the World).
    It was a great and wonderfully straightforwar
co-author Richard Arghiris, who has thoroughly
Nicaragua and Panama sections of this book.
    Finally after all the research, tapping, head-sc
writing, all the text and maps are checked in the
thanks to the patient crew down in Bath.